THE HERITAGE OF

NALANDA

THE HERITAGE OF
NALANDA

Edited by
C. MANI

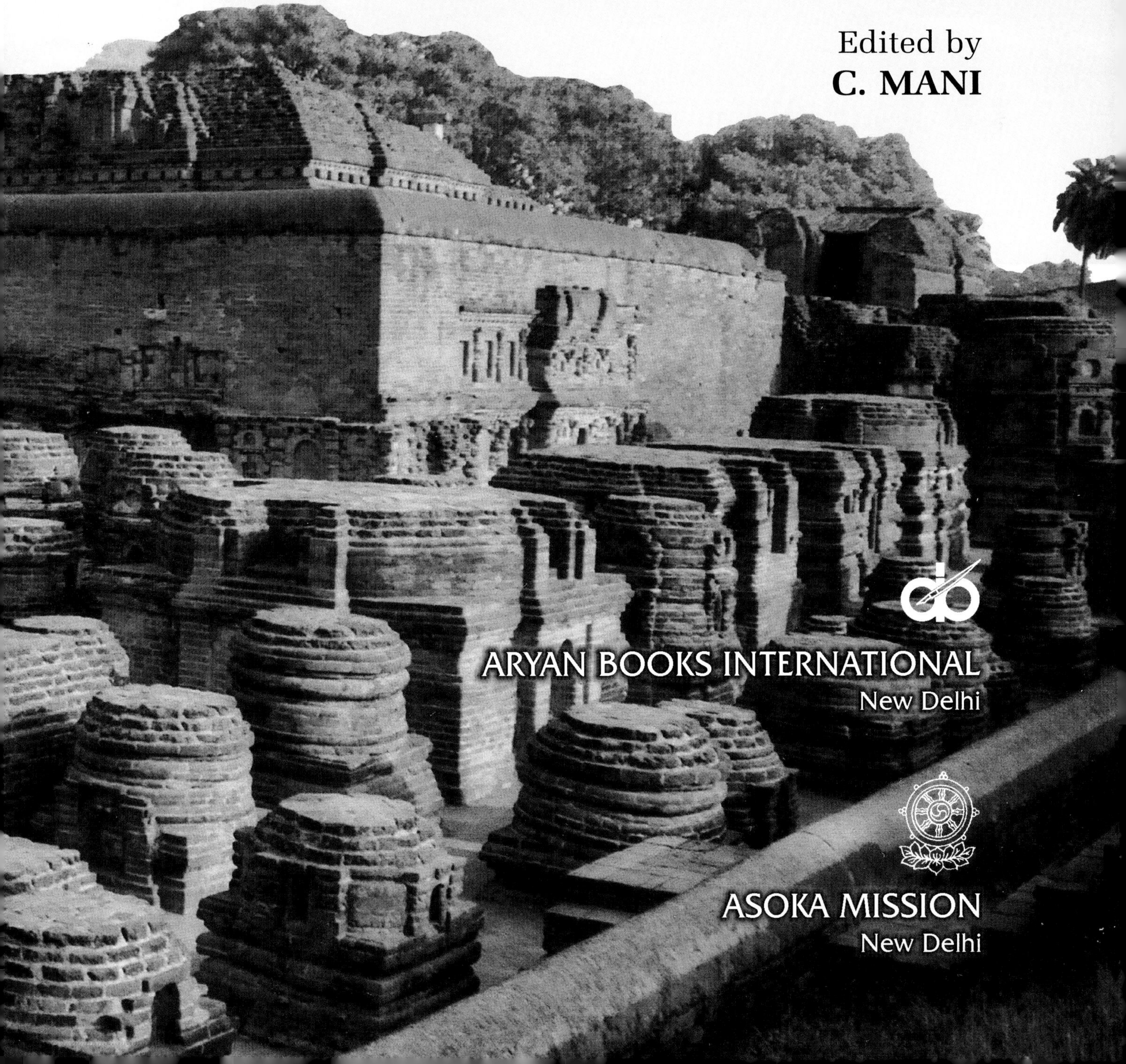

ARYAN BOOKS INTERNATIONAL
New Delhi

ASOKA MISSION
New Delhi

THE HERITAGE OF NALANDA

ISBN-10: 81-7305-330-8
ISBN-13: 978-81-7305-330-6

Published in **2008** by
ARYAN BOOKS INTERNATIONAL
Pooja Apartments, 4B, Ansari Road, Darya Ganj, New Delhi-110 002 (India)
Tel.: 23287589, 23255799; Fax: 91-11-23270385; E-mail: aryanbooks@vsnl.com

and

ASOKA MISSION
Mehrauli, New Delhi-110 030 (India)
www.asokamission.com

Computer Typeset and Printed in India at
ABI Prints & Publishing Co., New Delhi.

FOREWORD

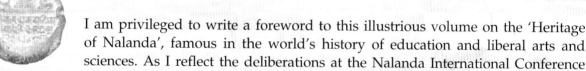

I am privileged to write a foreword to this illustrious volume on the 'Heritage of Nalanda', famous in the world's history of education and liberal arts and sciences. As I reflect the deliberations at the Nalanda International Conference held on 12-14 February 2006, which was blessed by His Holiness the Dalai Lama, and to which I have been closely associated, I am glad to see the Conference material with few additional papers of substantive merit published in the form of a treatise.

The Buddhist literature, both in the northern and southern schools, speaks eulogisingly of the high academic standards and rigorous discipline of the great *vihāra* which were transmitted to other countries as found in accentuated form in the Chinese classics, particularly the Chinese Buddhist *Tripitaka*, compiled by Samuel Beal and Bunjiu Nanjio.

Starting with the *Mūlasarvāstivāda* and *Sarvāstivāda Vinaya*, a large number of works of the four orders, more generally belonging to the *Mādhyamika* and *Yogācāra* philosophies, the *Prajñā Pāramitā Śāstra* of Nāgārjuna, the *Mahāyāna Sūtrālaṅkāra* of Śīlabhadra with its Chinese translation and a new work on *Satyasidhi Śāstra* by Śīlabhadra's Chinese disciple Xuanzang are some of the great works of the Nalanda school that were once preserved in its Library, in its three blocks of lofty pavilion and flying buttresses. Esoterism played a dominant part during the rule of the Pāla kings, who encouraged the scholars, sculptors and painters to produce some of the best replicas of the Nalanda school.

Turning to the Tantric texts of a superior order we draw on the works of the *Mahāsiddhas*, the *Guhyasamāja*, the *Advayavajra-Saṅgraha*, the *Sādhanamālā* texts, the *Tattva Saṅgraha*, the *Hevajra Tantras*, the *Kālacakra Tantra*, *et al*. These works being essential accessories to realisation of the deity by meditational practices are supportive of all sciences, which established religious and commercial links in the subcontinent.

Besides aforementioned works there are various recensions of *Prajñāpāramitā*, *Karaṇḍavyūha*, *Bodhicāryāvatāra* and *Pañcarakṣā* manuscripts illustrated with miniature paintings on them. They are most essential parts of iconographic studies. Severally studied are the Buddhist images, stucco figures, bronzes and other metallic icons. The Nalanda School of Art is reckoned to be among the best of the artistic creations coeval with the art of Gandhāra, Mathurā and Ajantā. Attempts are being made to bring the shadow of this school to art sequences in further India, as far east as Java in Indonesia and Cambodia.

In so far as I know, there is no such other scholarly book on the subject which is capable of taking the Nalanda experience round the world. It is a classic, to be treasured and disseminated.

I congratulate my esteemed friend Venerable Lama Lobzang to have envisioned the work and publish it with the editorial expertise of Professor C. Mani. I have deep appreciation for the perceptive essays of the scholars.

With obeisance to the Three Gems and the Dalai Lama's blessing, I wish happiness to all living beings.

Dharamsala,
13 March 2007

Samdhong Rinpoche
KALON TRIPA

PREFACE

As early as 1862-63 Sir Alexander Cunningham carried out archaeological investigations which were published in 1871 in the first volume of his *Four Reports Made During the Years 1862-65* on Nalanda. The remains at the site consisted of conspicuous rows of massive conical-shaped mounds, which were presumed by him to be lofty temples in alignment with the Nalanda Mahāvihāra. This is how he describes the monastery:

> It can be readily traced by the square patches of cultivation amongst a long mass of brick ruins 1,600 feet by 400 feet. These open spaces show the positions of the courtyards of the six smaller monasteries which are described by Huien Tsang (Xuanzang) as being situated within one enclosure forming altogether eight courts. Five of the six monasteries were built by five consecutive princes of the same family and the sixth by their successor, who is called King of Central India. No dates are given; but from the total silence of Fa-Hian (Faxian) regarding any of the magnificent buildings at Nalanda which are so minutely described by Huien Tsang, I infer that they must have been built after AD 410. Fa-Hian simply states that he came to the hamlet of Nalo, "where Sāriputra was born," and this is all that he says of Nalanda. But surely if the lofty temple of King Bālāditya, which was 300 feet in height, had then existed, it seems scarcely possible that he should not have noticed it. I would, therefore, assign the probable date of the temples and monasteries of Nalanda to the two centuries between the visits of Fa-Hian and Huien Tsang, or from AD 425 to 625. This date is further borne out by the fact recorded by Huien Tsang that the great temple of Bālāditya was similar to that near the sacred peepal tree at Buddha-Gaya. Now, a similarity of style may generally be taken as denoting proximity of date. The erection of Bālāditya's temple at Nalanda may, with great probability, be assigned to the same century in which the Buddha-Gaya temple was built. As I have already shown this to be about AD 500, the date of the Nalanda temple will lie between AD 450 and 550.

The report of the excavation of the site by A.M. Broadlay appeared in 1872. Reports by James Fergusson, Markham Kitto, H. Sastri and John Hubert Marshall *et al.* successfully highlighted Nalanda in international world. The Annual Progress Report of the Eastern Circle of the Archaeological Survey of India for 1915-16 describes the work of D.B. Spooner, whose work was carried over by J.A. Page, till 1932, when it fell on H.N. Sastri to rectify the defects in descriptions of seals, stone epigraphs and copper plates which were found in abundance at the sites. Dr. Sastri's epigraphical work is contained in *Nalanda: Its Epigraphic Material* (MASI, No. 66, published in 1942, revised in 1999).

A recent excavation at Sarai Tila in 1974-82 near the main monastery has yielded a dilapidated temple with a colossal stucco statue of Buddha. The murals found inside the temple are wearing out due to acid and temperature. Some figures of divine dancers are seen as decorative motifs.

Like Buddhagaya, where crude masonry and soap stone images are found in abundance with customary worship of votive *stūpa*s which may be ascribed to the medieval age, Nalanda recalls similar monuments and chapels. The Arakanese had built a temple in Buddhagaya in the 14th century CE to which was offered a votive *stūpa* by the Burmese inscribed in CE 1823.

Nalanda as a monastic institution in the time of Buddha emerged into the greatest academic and spiritual centre of Asia in early medieval times. This alludes to successive stages of development in Buddhism from naïve realism of the early monastic order to developed metaphysic of the Prajñāpāramitā and Yogācāra philosophy which revolutionized the capacity of thinking of men.

The Chinese pilgrims Xuanzang and Yi'jing affirm the most remarkable grandeur and height of the *Mahāvihāra* which at all time had the number of 10,000 along with the works of eighteen principal sects of Buddhism and such other works as the Veda and miraculous spells and eugenic devices of the *Atharva Veda.* They also investigated secular subjects, arts and sciences. Master Śīlabhadra by his great virtue and age was alone capable of revealing the truth contained in the doctrine. In the precincts of the temple everyday about 1000 daises for preaching were arranged for scholars coming to the discourses.

The Tibetan and Chinese histories aver five sciences taught at the *Mahāvihāra* as had been prescribed by Asaṅga. These have been enumerated as (i) *Śabda-vidyā* (grammar, lexicography); (ii) *Śilpasthāna-vidyā* (arts); (iii) *Cikitsā-vidyā* (medical science), (iv) *Hetu-vidyā* (logic, metaphysics); and *Adhyātma-vidyā* (the cosmic science, philosophy).

A mass of secret teaching and modes of worship are contained in Tantric texts, some of which are the *Abhidhānottara Tantra, Kriyāsamuccaya, Vajrāvalī-nāma-maṇḍalopāyikā*, the *Hevajra Tantra*s and the *Kālacakra Tantra* with its commentaries. The *Niṣpannayogāvalī* is such a text with visualisations of Buddhist deities. It has 26 *maṇḍala*s divided into 26 chapters. The *maṇḍala*s mainly belong to the esoteric cult. The work supersedes *Sādhanamālā*. The former is more precise and prolific. The *Niṣpannayogāvalī* is a sort of manual to manifested deities discovered in the forbidden city of Peiping in Manchuria. The same are now preserved in Beijing. In 1926 Stäel Holstein, the Russian archaeologist got permission to enter into the temples of Peiping. In the upper gallery of the temple there were found 787 icons. They were critically examined along with Chinese manuscripts by Professor Walter Eugene Clark to unmask their character and subject matter. Eugene's researches on Buddhist deities were published in 1937 in a monograph from Harvard Yenching Institute. These descriptions are found in three oriental languages, Sanskrit, Tibetan and Chinese. The second volume of Eugene's works contains illustrations of the deities.

In iconography, a new school of authors with critical discernment, as Nebesky Wojkowitz, Walter Eugene Clark and Beyer Stephan with his newly published *Encyclopaedia of Buddhist Deities, Demigods, Godlings, Saints and Demons* (in two volumes) has emerged. In addition to them, Lokesh Chandra has furnished his work *The Buddhist Iconography* in its revised recension (1987) which contains much useful material from four pantheons as:

1. Bla-ma-yi-dam-mchog-gum-bkah-sdod-daṅ-beas-pahi-tshogs-zhin-gl-sku-brñan-gsum-brgyaḥi-graṅs-tshan-ba, of Lcaṅ-śkya Qutuytu Rol-paḥi-rdo-rje Lalitavajra (300 icons)
2. Chu-Fo P'u-sa shêng Hsiang Tsan, also of Lcan-skya Qutuyu (360 icons)

3. Phun-sum-tshogs-paḥi-gtsug-lag-khaṅ pantheon, in its Chinese appellation Pao-Hsiang Lou (780 icons)
4. Rin-ḥbyun Snar-thaṅ-brgya rtsa Rdor-hphren-bcas-nas-gsuṅs-paḥi-bris-sku-mthaṅ-ba-don-Idan (500 gods of Narthang)

It is acceded that Indian art in the earliest stage was based in six centres as Gandhara, Mathura, Sanchi, Sarnath, Ajanta and Amaravati. If the Gandhara school has analogies with the antique Etruscan intermixed with the Graeco-Roman, from which the art of Italy flashed in Christian art and similarly other centres flourished with composite features, the Nalanda school like the other five schools, being purely Indian in conception, traces its roots into the sculptures of Sarnath and Mathura. It has its own ethos and historical development. In early phases the entire art found a firm base in canonical representation of Buddhist and Brāhmaṇical deities. In many cases we find a combination of the West Asiatic features, such as *krobylos* in hair style, Hellenistic drapery, some stereotypes which may not be Indian, namely, a *nimubus* (the *prabhāmaṇḍala*). I have discussed a sharp affinity between the arts of Gandhara, Amaravati and Central Asian mazdeistic art in a research article on the Hārītī image from Afrasiab, Tashkent, in Uzbekistan.

Although Buddhist iconography has been a widely studied subject in the east and west, still exceptions there are, as in a manuscript copy, in 108 folios of the Tibetan bKa-gyur, "the translated word of the Buddha" in the royal library at Berlin, to which attention of the scholars had been drawn by Albert Grünwedel in 1893. The manuscript is illumined with figures of Tibetan gods, executed in gold and bright colours; the gods are all named. A scholar can undertake this work with a view of identifying the figures.

The placement of Brāhmaṇical deities in Buddha's *parimaṇḍala* shows a process of absorption of Brāhmaṇical godheads in Buddhism. It suggests 'empowerment' of Buddhas and *Bodhisattva*s over Brāhmaṇical gods and goddesses. For over half a century Lokeśvara in Sarnath Museum had been known as Śiva. With the figure of Amitābha in the forehead it was identified by the Fourteenth Dalai Lama as Lokeśvara.

The mother conception of Tārā evolving in the yogācāra system of Asaṅga (c. 4th century AC) became more transparent in the 7th century wherein the Chinese pilgrim Xuanzang claims to have seen a large number of Tārā's images in India. Found rarely in the Theravāda, whence a temple was dedicated to her in Java in 779 AC, her worship spread far and wide. In Tibet she came to be known as Sgrol-ma; in China Tuolus, in Mangolia Dara eke and in Japan Tarani Bosatsu. Her emanation from a blue light coming from one of the eyes of Avalokiteśvara which trickled down on his face sorrowing for the miserable world is known all over the world. According to a belief Tārā reincarnates in all virtuous ladies.

Tārā has a unique place in the pictorial art of Asia. Its depiction in a Nepalese MS. dated 1136, preserved in the Boston Museum of Fine Arts confirms its Pāla inscription. The banner of Avalokiteśvara from Dun huong caves in British Museum, London and of White Tārā from Tibet in Cambridge MSs. reproduced by Benjamin Rowland in his *Art and Architecture of India* (Penguin Books) completely bear out the sacred in art and its *rococo* splendour. There has been no deviation in this art except a rare late eighteenth century Nepalese bronze of Tārā figure.

There are reasons to believe that Tārā worship had its beginnings in Nalanda where and in whose environs many Tārā shrines lie with traditional images of the goddesses. Some of those images are substantially reported in Archaeological Survey of India's published documents. They state "In no. I-1051 the goddess is seated on a high lotus throne with the right hand in

Vitarka-mudrā and the left in *Varada*. The hair is tied with a band and hangs down on the back." Another images, no. I-A-304, shows the goddess seated on a lion throne, in *lalitāsana*. The inscription on the back reads: *Om Tāre tuttāre ture svāhā. Om Padmāvatī. Om Kurukulle svāhā. Ye dharmā* (incomplete). A miniature of Tārā bearing the name of a lay-worshipper Kajjalakī reminds one of a great number of Tārā images and miniatures found in the museums and art galleries of the world.

The particular Mahattarī Tārā of Nalanda traces out the integration of Mahāyāna with its transitivity into Vajrayāna-tantricism which subsequently grew into Nepal, Tibet, China and as far as Japan in the east. It accords well with the *stuti* of Tārā in the *Mahattarī Tārā-sādhana* (*Sādhanamālā*, no. 90), as follows:

नमस्तारायै। प्रथमं स्वहृदीन्दुमध्यस्थितां बीजविनिर्गतरश्मिनिर्ष्पन्नान् गुरु बुद्ध बोधिसत्वान् ध्यायात्। तांश्च वाह्याध्यात्म्य-पूजाभिः सम्पूज्य तदग्रे सप्तविधानुत्तरपूजां कुर्यात् ततः शून्यतां विभाव्य ॐ स्वभावशुद्धाः सर्वधर्माःस्वभावशुद्धोऽहमित्युच्चारयेत्। ततश्चन्द्रे तां सम्भूतां सितोत्पलस्य ताँ कारोद्भूतां तारां श्यामां द्विभुजां दक्षिणे वरदां वामे सलिलेन्दीवरधरां सर्वाभरणभूषिता पद्मचन्द्रासने पर्यङ्कनिषण्णां चिन्तयेत्। समयमुद्रां बन्धयेत्। हस्तद्वयेन सम्पुटाञ्जलिं कृत्वा तर्जनीद्वयेन मध्यमे पिधायाङ्गुष्ठाग्रलग्ने विकचोत्पलमुद्रा। ततः ॐ तारे तुत्तारे तुरे स्वाहा इति मन्त्रं जपेत्। इति।

The image of Vajraśāradā was found in a shrine which was once a seat of *Vajrayānic sādhanā*. A manifestation of the goddess of wisdom and arts, she is visualised in *Sādhanāmālā* as resting on a pure lotus (*padma*) with a crescent ornament in her headdress. She is three-eyed and has two hands holding a book in the left hand and lotus in the right. Verse 2 of the *dhyāna* reads:

शुभ्राम्बुजोऽपरि लसत्तनुमादधानां
नेत्रत्रयं मुकुटसंस्थितमर्द्धचक्रम्।

वामेन पुस्तकधराम्बुजमन्यहस्ते
पञ्चात् स्वदेह समतामनयत् प्रयत्नात्॥

A Nepalese counterpart of this image is accompanied by four attendant *Śakti*s including *Prajña* (wisdom). She sits in *bhadrāsana.* The mutilated hands of the *torso* preclude full identification, but as one image carries lotus (*utpala*) and the book in the right and left hands, identification is made specific. The image from Nalanda often described as Koṭiśrī, Vajrasarasvatī and Vāgīśvarī is none of these. Each of these belongs to a different order. Vajrasarasvatī with three faces and six arms, her hair being brown and upbraided stands in the *pratyālīḍha* style on red lotus. Her complexion is red. In her three right hands she holds the lotus on which there are *Prajñāpāramitā* treatise, the sword and the *kartrī,* while in her three left hands are the skulls, the jewel and the *cakra*. On no account is Vajraśāradā to be mistaken for any other forms of Sarasvatī. Ārya Sarasvatī with lotus in the stalk, Vajrasarsavatī with three faces and six-armed with a *khadga* (*asi*) in her upper hand and Mahāsarasvatī sitting on a lotus.

A coroplastic roundel of the Buddhist deity Hārītī remained undiscovered in the Tashkent Museum till restored by me in 1984. It had been labelled as Isis. Recovered from Afrasiab in Uzkbekistan it had been classed with other female figures found in the Serawschan and Tarim basins as Praxitiles, Demeter in Egypt and Catago Isis in Vienna, probably a product of Rhodes.

Similarly, a statuette discovered at Sirkap was taken by H. Hargreeves to represent Hārītī for which John Marshall showed his inability to accept it as such. Marshall claimed it to be Tych with her marks as 'a horn of plenty' or 'the horn of Amalthea' as in Greek and 'a low polos

on the head'. Prototypes, but not identical ones, of this figure in association with the grotesque Pañchika are portrayed on two stele among the Gandhara sculptures in Lucknow Museum of Archaeology (Nos. 47.105; 49.44). These also are representations of Tych and not Hārītī. There are, thus, many local deities in the Hellenistic world with similar emblems, which are known as Aphrodite, Atargatis, Bona Dea and Selene Tych.

Iconographical scanning calls for a movement for the recovery of a large number of sculptures and reliefs installed in temples and art galleries of the world. As a great part of the ancient treasure lies misinterpreted for false identifications, a revision of all these or at least some of the most important ones is desired before they lose their identity.

Tantra is divisible in four types of practice: (a) *Kriyā*, (b) *Caryā*, (c) *Yoga* and (d) *Anuttara-Yoga*. *Kriyā* and *Caryā tantra*s are practised by persons of lesser wisdom and the latter two types by men of superior accomplishments. These practices are reflected by the phenomenalists, the text-masters, the adherents of the 'Mind only' school and the relativists. Women practise the *Mātṛi-tantra* (also called *yoginī tantra*). For men is the *Pitṛ-tantra*. The *Advaya-tantra* is recommended for both the categories of *sādhaka*s. Advayavajra classified the Mahāyāna *tantra*s into 'Pāramitānaya' and 'Mantranaya'. Pāramitā school is the ethical school of Tantra, while the Mantra school is wholly given to chanting and contemplation on the 'Mind' as consciousness with its constituents: memory, desire, cognition and idea. Individual mind is *citta*, which is both gross and subtle. The subtle mind is cosmic consciousness. It is the vital force for pulsating matter, the all existing things.

The philosophy of tantra does not consider anything as absolute pure or impure, clean or unclean. Magnificent images are formed of the materials harnessed to some kind of special purpose. This truth sustains all creation of art, painting, sculpture, murals, tapestry and the like.

Critics imputing unqualified words to esoteric practices are blunt in their appraisal of its normal behaviour. The motifs in tantra are neither obscene, nor vulgar. Esoterism in its accomplishment is a process of stern principles of power transmission in the solar system. Millions of ice-balls, rock and frozen gases are investigated in astronomical laboratories. During the process, several anomalies are observed that, not without stint, remain unaccused and dispel mysteries. That is what the tantra is worth. It is valued in invocation for relief from poisoning, epidemics, removal of poverty, installation of images and bringing prosperity. The traditional vocabulary of tantric practices and the emotivity contained in those practices reveal the universal mystery to a much greater limit than what the scientist or inventor does to master creativity. By comprehending the truth that the whole belongs to the atom the esoterist knows the ultimate destiny of creativity.

It is true that many people do not give credence to self-generated deities, but keeping pace with the fast moving world, it would be dishonesty remaining in weird conditions which image our reprehensible character. We do not generally understand that the physical form which we are constituted of its various limbs is not all; there is a subtle conscious form that transforms us qualitatively. It is a radial energy which unconsumed causes physical imperfections in beings. So, it is desirable to acquire qualities missing in us for completeness and wisdom to be made perfect.

Tantra has dalliance with things of material enjoyment in the same way and spirit as do the scientist of the new age offer us powerful tools for his invention. The tantric approach is radical. Material desires distance it from the divine. It placates desired energy from unwholesome situation to be transmuted to another by cutting through every unpromoted object and reaching its goal.

It is after hard persuasion that people have come to discriminate between the true and false in Tantra. For centuries did Tantra remain tainted by unscrupulous men who took it as a subterfuge for the gratification of their cupidity and performance of loathsome action.

Buddhism faced a serious blow from a savage tribe of the Huns living in the north of China between the rivers Irtush and Amur, in the Steppes. The Hun General Mihirakula is credited in the *Rājataraṅgiṅī* to have founded the temple of Mihireśwara and the city of Mihirapur in Kashmir, but at the same time demolished a number of Buddhist monasteries and plundered their wealth. His strategy in the middle country during the reign of the Gupta emperors, Kumaragupta and Skandagupta, was defeated by the latter with difficulty.

The Muslim chronicler Minhaj narrates the carnage of Nalanda by Muhammad Bakhtiyar Khalji at the close of the 12th century CE (*Tabquāt-i-Nāsiri*, tr. H.G. Raverty, Calcutta, 1881, p. 532).

Tārānātha, the Tibetan historian, testifies the ravages of Nalanda so that many monks fled the place to find refuge abroad (F.A. Schiefner, Tārānātha: *Geschichte des Buddhism in Indien*).

The myth of Nalanda's decay in the 7th and extinction of Buddhism in the 12th century CE, as people generally believe, should not be entertained for the following facts: 1. The seventh and eighth centuries were the palmiest days of Nalanda whence great philosophers, such as Dharmapala, Candrakīrti, Śāntideva, Dharmakīrti, Śīlabhadra, Xuanzang and Yi'jing, two great Chinese masters, flourished and wrote their treatises. It is a wrong view that Buddhism had been rooted out on account of the expansion of Śankara's *Vedānta*. 2. The general assumption that the Nalanda University was destroyed by Turk invasion is only partially correct, as there are references in Chinese annals, of Emperor Yuanting of Yuan dynasty (CE 1324-27) which refers to a monk named Vinayabhadra from Nalanda, who preached in China. It shows that in certain part of the old buildings education was imparted along with the teaching practices and tantric activities of Vikramaśilā to which Tibetan scholiasts refer approvingly. 3. It is stated in Tibetan history that in Ratnodadhi which was nine-storeyed, there were the holy scripts called *Prajñāpāramitā Sūtra*, and tantric works like *Samājaguhya et al.*, which suffered much at the hands of the Turuṣka invaders who caused great destruction to Nalanda. Its library and *caityas* were afterwards repaired by a sage named Muditabhadra. In subsequent days Kukkuṭasiddha, minister of the king of Magadha, erected a temple at Nalanda. This shows that the usual worship and temple ritual were not wholly obliterated and had permeated in the form of cult worship. The faith prevailed in the foothills of the Himalayas and in the hinterland of the Western Ghat rock-cut caves, as much as in the Coromandal coast and Nagapattanam. It is a fact that some Pallava kings deified the Buddha and made sojourns in places of Buddha's worship as confirmed in Telugu inscriptions of later times.

A monastery known as Nalanda sprang up in the 15th century CE north of Lhasa. It had 2500 resident lamas.

A similar temple is known as Nalanda shrine in Ceylon [Plate I, fig. a, see MASI, No. 66].

There are tantras giving instructions in inculcating clear light for assuming non-duality. The idea took root in art consciousness by taking the imagery of space which is streamlined by the blue colour of the sky and the blue ocean. This colour became a favourite colour of Tantra artists. The emblematic tantric art contains powerful images of unity and completeness. The image of male and female deities in sexual embrace, as in *yab-yum*, or *ardhanārīśvara* symbolisms, mistaken for lewd art, are a symbolic portrayal of the inner unification of our physical energies.

Apart from blue, other colours have also been used by the painter to paint the image of the deities, *ḍāka*s and *ḍākinī*s. They appear peaceful or wrathful and loathsome, in different postures and colours.

While reviewing the sculptures and paintings in two apparently similar but epistemologically different pantheons, Brāhmaṇical and Buddhist, I have found similar features in them, though sometimes, redolent and in irreconcilable form.

Connected with Nalanda have been many illustrious Chinese monk-scholars, Master Faxian, Master Zhiyan, Master Xuanzang and Master Yi'jing, whose discipleship of the Nalanda Ācaryas, particularly of Dharmapāla and Śīlabhadra, belonging to the Yogācāra system of Asaṅga and Vasubandhu, became the motivation for continuation of the teachings of this system. In addition to these, Master Yi'jing described Nalanda in detail. The most distinguished among Chinese scholars was Xuanzang, who after a sojourn for seventeen years in India returned to China and translated many Mahāyāna texts, as: the *Mahāprajñāpāramitāsūtra* (Da ban re jing, 大般若經) in 600 fascicles, the *Yogācārabhūmi-śāstra* (Yu qie shi di lun, 瑜珈師地論), the *Mahāvibhāṣa-śāstra* (Da pi po sa lun, 大毗婆沙論, T.1545), the *Vijñaptimātratāsiddhi-śāstra* (Chen we shi lun, 成唯識論, T.1585), the *Abhidharmakoṣa-śāstra* (u she lun, 俱舍論, T.1558) and other voluminous ones, over seventy texts in 1,300 fascicles.

It is complementary to the aforementioned that the works of Master Faxian's *A Record of Buddhist Kingdoms* (Fo guo ji, 佛國記, T. 2058), *Buddhist Records of the Western World* (Datang Xiyu ji, 大唐西域記, T. 2087), Master Yi'jing's *A Record of the Inner Law Sent Home from the Southern Seas* (Nan hai ji gui ne fa zhuang, 南海寄歸內法傳, T. 2125) are basics to the study of the history of Buddhism.

Some strong Buddhist associations and cultural organizations functioning under multi-national goodwill have moderated the Chinese biases against reformed temple institutions. Their portals are open for masses and scholars. A Chinese temple with its three components, the shrine, monastery and school is replica of calm and perfect order with its name inscribed over the gate, in its premise are the drum-tower and the gong-tower on either side and further is the smiling image of Maitreya Buddha (Milei Fu) and the four protectors of the four quarters; on the main altar is a triad of Buddha, Amitābha (Qmito Fu) and the healing Buddha (Yao-Shih Fu).

The term Xuanzangology of Chinese academics may appear new to western scholars, but it has been in long practice in China as a legacy for the study of higher learning, specially the Buddhist philosophy, Chinese history and literature as interpreted in Chinese circles by Xuanzang. Translations and glossaries of scriptures prepared by him are taught in the Hsuan Chuang University in Taiwan with Wei-Shih texts. Cognate disciplines of Pāramitāyāna and Mantrayāna are in vogue in Japan.

We are elated to see the legacy of Nalanda being enlivened through national and international organisations. In India, the foundation of Nava Nalanda Mahavihara was laid by His Excellency Dr. Rajendra Prasad, the first President of India on November 20, 1951.

Nalanda Buddhist Centre of Brazil is a cultural and religious organisation. It came into existence in 1989 motivated by Theravāda Dharma and as a tribute to the ideals of the Nalanda University. It was created soon after the erection of the Ceylonese temple (in 1967). The Brazilian Centre of Buddhism imparts traditional Buddhist teachings with meditational opportunities, bridging the Buddhist outlook and Brazilian life in our time.

As I conclude my preface on the subject of Nalanda experience, it is sincerely desired that the experience will grow from much to more. Let this prayer be granted by the Compassionate Buddha. I offer my reverence to His Holiness the Dalai Lama whose blessings are enclosed in the book. I am indebted to Venerable Prof. Samdhong Rinpoche and Venerable Lama Lobzang for their endorsement of my editorship and facilitating me to complete this work on time.

I revere the memory of my dear parents and the loving care of my small family that sustains me in all my work. My son Dr. B.R. Mani deserves every credit for procuring and processing whole of the illustrations in the book. I appreciate the cooperation of the employees of Asoka Mission and Shri M.K. Shaji for his secretarial assistance.

I am glad to say that Shri Vikas Arya of Aryan Books International has always been cooperative with us and I thank him for his innovative performance in printing.

New Delhi
1 May 2007

C. Mani

ACKNOWLEDGEMENTS

We are glad to launch this profusely illustrated and well-documented volume on the heritage of Nalanda. The idea of bringing out such a desirable work in congruence with the outburst of literature of renascent Buddhism has its inception in the prescient realization of heightening different disciplines of ancient Indian educational system that met with the admiration and willingness of many other institutions, particularly in the monastic orders, as for example in Tibet, Mongolia, China, Japan and as far as Brazil and the United States of America on the other side of the globe that are adopting the Nalanda experience in their teaching skill and monastic discipline.

The idea synchronized with a discussion about holding a conference on Nalanda in a meeting of our organising committee convened on 8 November 2002 in Karnataka Bhawan, New Delhi under the Presidentship of His Excellency Shri T.N. Chaturvedi, Governor of Karnataka. The Committee had ratified the proposal to hold the Conference on Nalanda on 28 to 30 April 2003 to be inaugurated by His Holiness the Dalai Lama at New Delhi. We had entered into a series of correspondence with scholars, religious heads and high dignitaries of India and overseas. We had made all preparatory arrangements for the conference, such as circulation of a printed brochure among a large number of persons interested in joining the conference. We had received positive replies from them and relevant documents had started being finalized for the participants with financial support received from venerables Jamyang Khentse Rinpoche and Thomtok Rinpoche. A great number of renowned scholars had shown their willingness to read papers at the conference. But a little before the proposed schedule a fell disease called Severe Acute Respiratory Syndrome (SARS) spreading over a greater part of the Pacific east obstructed our plans over which we had spent a good deal of money and precious time. On receiving information from many reputed scholars of the area where the disease had been rampant, such as Taiwan, Singapore, Malaysia, Hongkong *et al.*, that they felt inability to join on account of the severity of the syndrome, we were left with no alternative but to reschedule our planning for the conference.

We immediately started negotiating with the headquarters of His Holiness the Dalai Lama to give us fresh dates for the above purpose. Ultimately, we obtained the consent of His Holiness for holding the conference from 12 to 14 February 2006. In consonance with it the Conference was inaugurated by His Holiness the Dalai Lama with whose blessings the Conference had a series of discussions on various subjects connected with the history, art, religion, philosophy and other aspects of early medieval scholasticism, touching upon esotericism of the Vajrayāna order, which has been both eulogized for its potential and condemned for the weird practices of its degenerate inadepts.

In reference to the conference, I am specially beholden to the following dignitaries and heads of various Ministries of the Union Government and State Government of Bihar and certain other organisations whom I have found very much supportive in our conference on Nalanda. I would like to express my gratitude to His Excellency, Sardar Buta Singh, Governor, Bihar; Smt. Renuka Chaudhary, Hon'ble Minister for Tourism and Culture; Shri Nitish Kumar, Hon'ble Chief Minister of Bihar; Shri P.K. Thungon, Former Chief Minister, Arunachal Pradesh; Shri A.K. Mishra, Secretary, Ministry of Tourism; Shri J.P. Batra, Chairman, Railway Board; Shri I. Majumdar, General Manager, ITDC (Ashok Travel and Tours); Shri C. Babu Rajeev, Director General of the Archaeological Survey of India; Shri L. Rynjah, Joint Secretary, Ministry of Culture, Govt. of India; Dr. Urmila Sant and Dr. P.K. Mishra, Superintending Archaeologists, Mid-Eastern Circle, ASI, Patna; Shri R.S. Tiwari, Tourism Secretary, Govt. of Bihar; Shri A.N. Prasad, General Manager, Ordnance Factory, Rajgir, Nalanda; Shri Amit Singh, Administrative Officer, Ordnance Factory, Rajgir, Nalanda; Col. R.S. Nehra, Principal, Sainik School, Nalanda and Col. Pramod Sharma of the Defence Research Development Organisation (DRDO); Dr. Ravindra Panth, Director, Nava Nalanda Mahavihara; and Shri A. Sai Giridhar, Principal of Institute of Hotel Management, Hajipur, Bihar.

I wish to record my deep appreciation of the valuable role played by Shri C.B. Tripathi, coordinator of the conference, in entirely handling the academic aspect of the conference as well as working for months together in regard to all other management logistics of the conference. The success of the conference goes in a large measure to the devoted and untiring work performed by Shri Tripathi. He received able secretarial assistance from Sarvashri Pradip Kumar, S.K. Gupta and Mukesh Kumar.

Based on the papers discussed in the conference and a few research articles which were not discussed in the conference, this comprehensive book has come out, comprising subjects from canonical transmission to history of lineages and arts; stratigraphic study of temple sites, the mysterious goddesses of Nalanda, stupa architecture and monastic education that has established international links for a Nalanda movement across the continents. The trend is important in our time to bring the people of the world closer by mutual interaction. Readers will find in the book landmarks of inestimable value, specially in philosophy and religious developments with stylistics in art of the time of the Gupta and Pala sovereigns some of which greatly influenced the art of the Khmers of Cambodia and the Javanese art of Indonesia.

With blessings from His Holiness the Dalai Lama, I owe my grateful acknowledgement to Ven. Professor Samdhong Rinpoche, Prime Minister in his Kashag, obliging us with his foreword to the book.

I express my sincere gratitude to all of my colleagues in the Mission, who have been promoting its cause, especially its Chairperson Dr. Nirmala Deshpande, the Gandhian social worker and Member of Parliament, whose selfless service and deep interest in the Mission's work have been great hallmarks in our endeavour. At the same time, I would express my sincerest thanks to Prof. Pema Gyalpo of Toin University of Yokohama, Japan and the Vice-Chairman of the Organising Committee of the Conference who took keen interest in the publicity of the Nalanda Conference in Japan.

For the well-documented and critically edited volume with sumptuous illustrations and clearly arranged layout, I am very much obliged to Professor C. Mani, the Editor; Dr. B.R. Mani, Director, Archaeological Survey of India for his technical advice and documentation of pictorial material got from Nalanda; and Shri Vikas Arya of Aryan Books International for quality printing and production.

New Delhi
9 April 2007

Lama Lobzang
President, Asoka Mission
Mehrauli, New Delhi-110 030

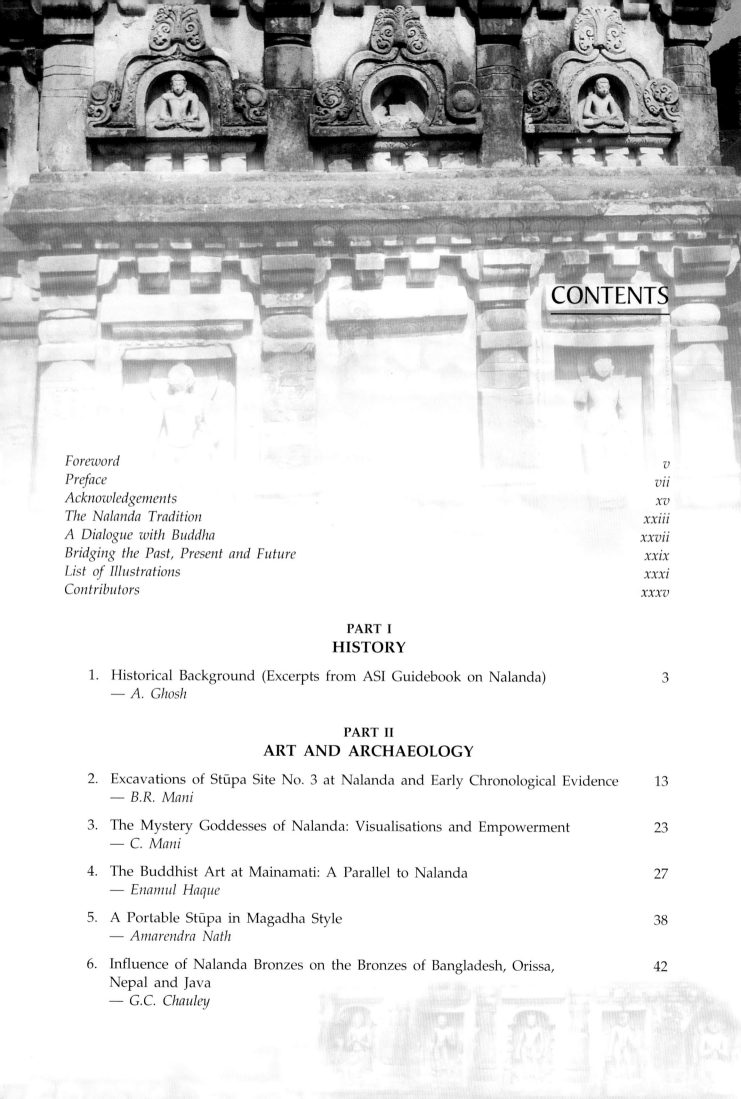

CONTENTS

PART III
EARLY MEDIEVAL SCHOLASTICISM: LOGIC, PHILOSOPHY AND ESOTERISM

PART VI
NALANDA EXPERIENCE

BLESSINGS

His Holiness the 14th
Dalai Lama Tenzin Gyatso

THE NALANDA TRADITION

I have always been a student of the great Nalanda masters, particularly Nāgārjuna, Āryadeva, Ārya Asaṅga and so on; one of whom Śāntarakṣita went to Tibet. I think the main responsibility to establish and proliferate the *Buddha Dharma* in the snow land belongs to him. His main disciple Kamalaśīla also came to Tibet and carried further the standard of the *Dharma* in Tibet. His disciples let flourish the *Dharma* all round. I feel happy that many of them had gone from the institution of Nalanda. This makes Tibetans so very closeted to Nalanda.

Let me recall the event leading to the construction of the building in which we meet here. It is assumed that the construction of this building owed to a donation from the Government of China. In fact, in 1956 while Prime Minister Chou En Lai and Vice Prime Minister Wo Lung came to Delhi, Prime Minister Chou En Lai is said to have come to this place and handed over a cheque of donation from the Chinese Government to Pandit Nehru personally. The fact is that Chou En Lai asked me to represent the Republic of China. So, on behalf of the Chinese Government I handed over the cheque, here, in Nalanda, to Pandit Nehru. I can still recall those past memories. By then, I had not yet become a refugee. I was actually in a high position. Now, I can only wish some Chinese delegation to participate in this conference; but I do not think that there is a delegation from the mainland China. Perhaps, my presence made it difficult. I just want to extend my warm welcome to any delegation from China.

As far as Nalanda is concerned, my knowledge is very limited. I know, first among human civilizations was the Chinese civilization, succeeded by Egyptian civilization and then civilization in this area in India. But, in doctrinal studies Indian civilization may have been the most advanced, most sophisticated. For the last two to three thousand years there has been a lot of intellectual thinking in theistic and non-theistic religions, both types having simultaneous growth. Within the known theistic religions, the concept of deliverance (*mokṣa*) created Buddhist concept if there is liberation or not. Similarly, the theory which was much talked about was that whether there is next life or not. All these different theories developed in this country. A greater number of philosophical enquiries ensued. There has been significant contribution of philosophical understanding in Indian civilization. For the matter of that, in all different traditions, different concepts were encountered by the Buddha who created another system of law on the basis of existing traditions and personal experience. Certain new ideas cropped up in his mind from his own experiences. This has given incentive to several important concepts and traditions. One unique thing about the *Buddha Dharma* might be the concept of interdependence. That is the basic concept of non-violence, compassion and Buddhahood. Interdependence involves the concept of the law of cause and effect. Concepts vary. One type of development succeeds other types. Developments and discussions occur more frequently. So, during Buddha's time and after him new concepts brought about different traditions in the country. The religion of Buddha had conceptual change among men. Thus, through centuries brilliant Indian farsighted scholars discussed their theories. Nalanda happened to possess a great many prominent Buddhist masters and scholars. One of them was Nāgārjuna. I do not know the period of time when Nalanda developed its monastic institution and when Nāgārjuna joined this institution and I think he studied there. In his time and as the Nalanda institution grew in learning, at one occasion the number of students in this academic organisation was nearly 10,000. I just wonder how Nalanda grew into a great academic centre from a modest monastery. I can imagine that some lay people had also joined the alumni and not only the Buddha *Dharma*, Buddhist philosophy, also logic, poetry and many different subjects, may be medicine also, began to be taught. Nāgārjuna himself wrote some Āyurvedic medicinal literature. This continued for several generations since the Buddhist masters engaged themselves in disseminating the Buddha's message from the time of Nāgārjuna and onwards. Nāgārjuna put great efforts in discussing the reality of the four noble truths, not of course simply the Buddhist way of prostration, but the value of these truths based on logical reasoning. This made clear the middle path, the truth of cessation and association: a lot of intellectual work. These are obviously signs of further development in the realm of thought.

If you look in the historical event of evolution of the signs of Mahāyāna Buddhism or the thematic theism of Buddhism the subject was further interpreted in seven different ways and still further developed by Śāntarakṣita in his commentarial work. In perpetuating the Sanskrit tradition of Buddhism, I think Nalanda masters were superb. The way of their exposition of the texts were accepted by scholars of the other countries, firstly China and finally Sri Lanka, Burma, Thailand and so on. The Sanskrit tradition flourished, mainly in China and then to other countries, through Tibet and Mongolia. When I describe Mongolia I say Mongolia not only as the independent Mongolia, but also those parts of Russia, Kalmuk, Buriat and Tuva, belonging to the ancient Mongols, kins of the Tibetans. Tibetans and Mongols are twin brothers and sisters. Perhaps, before the Buddha's religion spread we all must have been mere warriors, killers, and fighting men. With the coming of Buddhism our old society became pacified, more peaceful and more compassionate. So, today, among those Buddhist countries, from Sri Lanka to Mongolia and Tibet, there is a thrust for studying from Pāli to the esoterics. When I speak of Pāli, it carries over the essence of the Pāli traditions along with Pāli literature and language. The Sanskrit tradition which has been adhered to by Tibetans as a great mass of intuitive treatises is based on texts like the *Prajñāpāramitā*, the *Saddharmapuṇḍarīka*, the *Vajracchedikā* and others. So many Tibetans tried to learn by heart these texts – of course not in my case. When I studied these things I found myself to be a lazy student. These texts are most difficult. They are the products of the Nalanda school of scholasticism. Tibetan Buddhism is purely a tradition of Nalanda.

Some western scholars are usually in the habit of describing Tibetan Buddhism as the lamaist. I think that is not correct. The correct description of Tibetan Buddhism is the study of such texts which were written by Nalanda masters.

However, as for now, past is past. Some say history will repeat, but I do not believe in this theory. History is now a reality. Once those concepts which have been handed down to posterity by the Nalanda masters are grasped it is the best thing for us to take as history's actuality.

If you don't find relevance in it, then Okay, just music. If those concepts have any relevance in today's world, then we have to think how to preserve those concepts for enlightenment. In general tone, as we are in the 21st century in which material development is immense which has brought to humanity a lot of comfort, amenities, we need so much. But meanwhile material prosperity does not solve all human problems and we cannot find full satisfaction. To me, it is plain that money or material comfort cannot bring inner peace. As such, we can only say that satisfaction and pain both persist in our body (at sensational level common with every kind of model). Material comfort is no exception. Because human beings have special intelligence, they have a preponderance of expectations, large suspicions, doubts which produce unnecessary jealousy, unnecessary anger, unnecessary attachment, unnecessary hatred. These make us very unhappy. Unhappiness sometimes brings great constraints to us. This kind of problem cannot be solved by money or material amenities. The problem which is mainly of our own intelligence can be solved as laid down in the Buddha's law of universal human intelligence. After visualizing reality our approach must be more realistic. Through that way, try to solve some of the problems which pester you. I think that is the Buddhist way of approach, not through faith of course but, as I said before, mainly through work. You try transformation through work, not through blessing. That is, I think, the basic Buddhist philosophical approach.

The essence of all Buddhist literature is that all faults (vices) are rooted in ignorance (*avidyā*). So, Buddha blamed all insinuating problems on ignorance. In order to overcome all problems we have to remove the ignorance. How to remove it, through injection, through medicine or through operation? May be in some future, I jokingly tell, some scientists may find ways and means to remove the part of our brain which creates the assemblage of attachments or anger, or hatred, then it would be the best remedy. Then we may no longer need meditation or hard work, just let the scientists do the job. But, I think it may not be an easy task. In order to remove ignorance, Buddha emphasized inculcation of wisdom, which is the medicine to remove ignorance. And, what is wisdom? It is understanding of the ultimate reality as freedom from the chain of cause and effect. This concept ingressed in the doctrine of dependent origination of things as elaborated by Nāgārjuna and Āryadeva and such other philosophers may help us. It may arouse in us a deep concern for others, which is the call of compassion. Compassion teaches non-injury (*ahiṁsā*), a panacea for all ills and sorrows in the world.

It is good that in the 21st century medical scientists have grown to realize the implication of health and also cure of diseases. For mitigating emotional stresses there is need of training the mind for which meditation is the only exercise. If one goes through the treatises of old masters, as of Nalanda, one may be fairly inclined towards adopting the various systems of applied medicine, meditation for one-pointed concentration of mind, protuberance of economy/ global economy, we can see human reality more holistically. To my mind if politicians of today acted with a holistic view, their politics will be more acceptable and successful. Let this resound among all religious circles, intellectual circles as well as the secular ethos.

[From the Inaugural Speech of **His Holiness the 14th Dalai Lama Tenzin Gyatso**]

A DIALOGUE WITH BUDDHA

I would, at the outset, like to apologise to you for having come to Nalanda surrounded by a battery of officers, wearing uniforms and bearing guns. I greatly regret this, not because they (the officers) are doing something wrong – they are not – but because our times are such that guns have become necessary. You taught us *ahiṁsā*, but the chief guest (that is me) has come to this function marking the 2550th anniversary of your passing surrounded by guns!

What has happened to us in India, Śākyamuni, and what has happened to us everywhere in the world? Śākyamuni, we are living in violent times. You were not living in times like this. You had other distresses. You spoke from your heart and mind, from a combination of your heart and mind. You were not too simple for scholars; you were not too scholarly for simple people. You spoke directly to people. It is easier to listen to a conversation than to a speech. Śākyamuni, you spoke, you did not theorize. You taught, you did not preach.

Xuanzang, a great scholar, came here, spent ten years here, more than that, and was able to carry back with him from here, manuscripts, which were translated into Chinese. So you linked great civilizations, Śākyamuni, the Indian civilization and the Chinese civilization. They need linking together again, today. You linked them then; you are linking them now.

I do not know about life after death.

I do not know about God and non-God and do not claim to know whether you, Śākyamuni, are there, somewhere, listening to me. You did not speak on the blessing of God, Śākyamuni. You left it to us to figure it out.

I am yet to figure it out. I am confused. It is better to speak the truth, is it not Śākyamuni, than to say that I believe or do not believe? I am confused, Śākyamuni, for though I would like to believe there is a Divine Eye watching over us, when I see the *duhkha* in our midst, I get confused. I am honest, I have to be honest with you. You are our teacher. We have to be honest to our teachers.

Today we have persons here marking the anniversary of your passing away. There are so many mythologies about how you were born. Some say that Mahāmāyā dreamt of an elephant, some say you were born immaculately. What is the reality? We are great about creating controversies, Śākyamuni. Some say you died after you ate pork, some say you died after you ate mushrooms. Even in your death, we have surrounded you with controversies, Śākyamuni.

It does not matter how you came. It does not matter how you went. What matters is that you were with us, that you were part of us.

Are we losing you, Śākyamuni?

Today, when we mark your anniversary of death, are we comfortable with you Śākyamuni? If you were to walk into this room just now, we would, of course, like to touch your feet. But I think you would disturb us in our different smugnesses, in our preconceived positions, in our habits, in our routine. But it is necessary that you should disturb us. It is important that you should wake us from our complacencies. There are so many of us, like me who are confused and who are complacent.

They say the person who gave you your last meal was a smith; that he belonged to a 'low caste'. How do we treat our castes today? Are we different from when you were with us? How do we treat our plants and our trees? You spoke under a *Bodhi* tree; that tree was a witness of your enlightenment. Do we treat our trees well? Do we treat our animals well? We are cruel to our animals. I am not saying vegetarians are necessarily kind. I am a vegetarian. But, look at my shoes. They are made of leather. The medicines I take, Śākyamuni, have animal parts in them. We are all compromisers, Śākyamuni.

Please show us the light: show us the path of truthfulness. You will tell us to be honest, to be sincere, and you will tell us: If you have done something wrong, say so.

Above all, Śākyamuni, on the commemoration of your passing, we should ask ourselves, are you living with us or are you dead for us? We, your legatees, your descendents, are we alive to your living truth or are we dead to it? Is it comforting to see you in meditation and to light a lamp and place our flowers before you and go away as exactly as we are? Or, Śākyamuni, are we wanting to be shaken by you to a new life of compassion, active compassion?

You just heard a scholar from the West, who was using your methodology to help people in psychological distresses. There are people here from different parts of the world, the chairperson is from China, there are people from Japan, Taiwan, Tibetans, and there are Lankans ....

If on this occasion, Śākyamuni, you help us to listen – which is different from hearing – if you help us to take notice – which is different from seeing – your anniversary of 2550 would not have gone in vain.

[From the Speech of **His Excellency**
Shri G.K. Gandhi, Governor of Bihar]

BRIDGING THE PAST, PRESENT AND FUTURE

'Nalanda' is a word that has thrilled millions of people, century after century, across country after country, in the past and also in the present, only widening the reach from continent to continent to create vibrations of mellifluous kind, in future as well, because it was the first international university attracting scholars from all parts of Asia, the then known world in an era, when no easy modes of transport were available. One had only to walk or ride a horse, crossing long deserts or snow-clad mountains, to reach Nalanda. As the Chinese saying goes, when Huien Tsang asked for the route to India to reach Nalanda, he was told 'go to the western desert and follow the heaps of bones on the way,' as it was believed that when hundred pilgrims started for India – the western heaven according to the Chinese – only one could reach while the rest died on the way, along with their horses, if they had any. And still the pilgrimage of year after year continued for centuries, seekers of truth and knowledge with destination to Nalanda.

The most well known amongst them was Huien Tsang (spelt as Xuanzang by present Chinese experts), set off from China in CE 627 and returned in CE 645, travelling 10,000 miles after eighteen years. He studied Mahāyāna texts of Buddhism in Nalanda, and also became a professor there. His life and works continue to be of great interest to scholars all over the world. It is his books that helped to find Buddhist temples, and *vihāra*s in India, lost in the debris for centuries, which ushered the revival of Buddhism. India can never repay his debt. He was, is and shall continue to be the best bridge between India and China. As the story goes, the great master of Nalanda, Śīlabhadra, was in his nineties and very ill; he was about to die. But he had a dream in which he saw three divinities of Avalokiteśvara, Vairocana and Maitreya asking him to wait for a monk from the North, whom he had to teach. The old scholar literally waited and waited; he had nothing but tears of joy to offer when the Chinese monk Huien Tsang actually reached Nalanda. He left the world only after imparting the knowledge to the Chinese monk. This Chinese monk has left us a legacy of wisdom and understanding to create a world of unity and peace amidst the people of the world.

The impressive monument created at Nalanda, near the Nava Nalanda Mahāvihāra was conceived during the era of the first Prime Minister of independent India Pandit Jawaharlal Nehru, with the financial contribution of the then Prime Minister of China Chou-en-lai, gifted through His Holiness the Dalai Lama, then a young monk.

Nalanda traces its origin to the hallowed presence of Buddha himself, who gave his early teachings in Rājagṛha (modern Rajgir), the capital of the then Magadha empire, which is just 11 km from Nalanda. The emperor Aśoka, 'the only moon in the firmament of the stars of kings and emperors of the world', as H.G. Wells, the great historian, would have him, also visited Nalanda and erected a temple there. It was Aśoka alone, who conquered the world not by weapons, but by love and compassion. Aśoka proved the efficacy of Buddha's teachings by sending ambassadors of compassion and non-violence to far off countries and thus conquering the hearts of people – a unique example indeed in world's history.

The foremost Buddhist philosopher Nāgārjuna, coming from the south, presided over Nalanda University in second century CE. Other Buddhist great masters like Āryadeva, Asaṅga, Vasubandhu, Śīlabhadra, Diṅgnāga, Dharmapāla, Dharmakīrti, Śāntarakṣita, Padmasambhava, Naropā and the famous scientist Āryabhaṭa, have all been part of the glory of Nalanda where knowledge was the main deity and all these scholars the high priests. Historians say that Sanskrit was the main language of learning but Pāli also was used. Jain masters also lived there. Vedas and Āyurveda were also parts of the syllabus. Beside Buddhist texts, secular subjects were taught. For centuries Nalanda used to attract scholars and pilgrims like the honey of flowers attracts the bees.

Future beckons Nalanda again. To be in tune with the modern age, the international university at Nalanda needs to be planned on the pattern of Nalanda Mahāvihāra with scientific innovations. Mahatma Gandhi, the apostle of non-violence of the present age, can be our guiding spirit.

Ācārya Vinoba Bhave, the spiritual heir of Mahatma Gandhi, has said 'where science and spirituality meet, you find Mahatma Gandhi, standing'. It is this synthesis of science and spirituality that is the need of the hour. Spirituality is the essence of all religions. Every religion can be divided into two parts, the sectarian part and the spiritual part; the former changes according to time, place and circumstance, while the latter is unchanging. Spiritual values like truth, love, compassion, non-violence *et al.* remain constant in every era, every country and in all circumstances. Sectarianism divides while spirituality unites people. Spirituality can be termed as universal faith.

In this age of space travel, our common home, this planet earth, brings the whole humanity together. As the saying in the ancient Vedas goes – 'This earth is like a small abode, where people belonging to different faiths, speaking different languages, live like members of one family.' This earth not only needs to be made a happy home for all human beings but also needs to be protected from the human greed, which results in all kinds of pollution. To make this earth free from hatred, violence and wars and build a peaceful better tomorrow, the teachings of Buddha are as relevant today as they were when Nalanda was at the height of its glory.

Nalanda again beckons, not only Indians but also all right-minded people. Let the search for truth make us adopt compassion as a way of life and take the path of love.

[Nirmala Deshpande, M.P.,
Chairperson, Organising Committee]

LIST OF ILLUSTRATIONS

FIGURES

PLATES

CONTRIBUTORS

Dr. B.R. Mani
Director, Archaeological Survey of India, B 82, Pandara Road, New Delhi-110003.

Prof. C. Mani
Senior Fellow, Indian Council of Historical Research (New Delhi), SA-14/96 A-7, Sarnath-221007, Varanasi.

Prof. Enamul Haque
Chairman & Academic Director, The International Centre for Study of Bengal Art, 32-E, Road 17-A, Banani, Dhaka-1213, Bangladesh.

Dr. Amarendra Nath
Director, ASI, Janpath, New Delhi-110011.

Dr. G.C. Chauley
Ex-Director, ASI, House No. 2269/7, Dakra Bhivisan Lane, Linga Raj Road, Old Town, Bhubaneswar-751002, Orissa.

Dr. Gautam Kumar Lama
Lecturer, Dept. of Ancient Indian History, Culture & Archaeology, BHU, Varanasi-221005.

Prof. S.K. Pathak
Akash-Deep, Abanpalli, Santiniketan-731235, West Bengal.

Dr. Adelheid Herrmann-Pfandt
Europabadstr.1, D-35041 Marburg/Lahn, Germany.

Dr. Naina Pandeya
D 44/201, Ramapura, Varanasi-221010.

Dr. Archana Sharma
L-5, Birla, Warden Flat, Jodhpur Colony, Banaras Hindu University, Varanasi-221005.

Dr. Arpita Chatterjee
D-32/127, Simon Chouhatta, Varanasi-221001.

Dr. (Mrs.) Anandamayee Ghosh
'Bhavani Bhavana', Surashripalli, P.O. Bolpur, District Birbhum-731204, West Bengal.

Dr. Lobzang Tsewang
Reader, Central Institute of Buddhist Studies, Choglamsar, Leh-194101, Ladakh.

Prof. Kimiaki Tanaka
3-14-4 Minamiyukigaya Ota-ku, Tokyo-145-0066, Japan.

Prof. Marie-Louise Friquegnon
Professor, William Peterson University, 277 Ave. C # 7 E New York, NY-10009, USA.

Dr. Bimalendra Kumar
Senior Lecturer, Dept. of Pali & Buddhist Studies, Faculty of Arts, BHU, Varanasi-221005.

Shri Manotosh Mandal
Purva Palli Vidya-Bhawan Hostel, Block No. A/6, Visva-Bharati, Santiniketan-731235, Dist. Birbhum, W.B.

Ven. Damba Ayasheev (Hambo Lama)
Supreme Head, Buddhist Traditional Sangha of Russia, Datsan Khambin Khure, Ulan-Ude Buryatia, Russia.

Dr. Wang Bangwei
President, Academy of Oriental Studies, Wai Wen Lon, Peking University, Beijing-100034, China.

Dr. Linnart Mäll
University of Tartu, Ulikooli/18, Tartu-51014, Estonia.

Ven. Lozang Jamspal
Center for Buddhist Studies, Department of Religion, 623 Kent Hall, Columbia University, New York-10027, USA.

Prof. Tashi Paljor
Director, Central Institute of Buddhist Studies, Choglamsar, Leh-194101, Ladakh.

Dr. Nawang Tsering
Principal, Central Institute of Buddhist Studies, Choglamsar, Leh-194101, Ladakh.

Prof. Michael Willis
Dept. of Oriental Antiquities, The British Museum, Great Russell Street, London WC183DG United Kingdom.

Prof. Ramesh Chandra Tiwari
B-315, Sector B, Mahanagar, Lucknow-226006.

Dr. Charles Willemen
Belgian Royal Academy of Sciences, P.B. 656, 8400 Oostende, Belgium.

Shri C.D. Tripathi
A2/77, Safdarjang Enclave, New Delhi-110029.

Dr. (Mrs.) Kalpakam Sankarnarayan
Director, K.J. Somaiya Centre for Buddhist Studies, Management Building (Floor II), Somaiya Vidya Vihar Campus, Vidyanagar, Vidyavihar, Mumbai-400077.

Dr. Hsiu-O-Chien
Assistant Professor, Ling Tung University, Taichung, Taiwan.

Dr. Shih-Ching Shiu
Associate Professor, Hsiuping Institute of Technology, Dali City, Taichung County, Taiwan.

Dr. B.B. Kumar
12/604, East End Apartment, Mayur Vihar, Phase-I Extension, Delhi-110096.

Rev. Heng Sure
Institute for World Religions, Berkeley Buddhist Monastery, 2304 McKinley Avenue, Berkeley, CA 94703, USA.

Ms. Yayoi Tachibana
5-24-3, Kugahara Ota-ku, Tokyo-146-0085, Japan.

Prof. Angraj Chaudhary
Vipassana Research Institute, Dhammagiri, Igatpuri-422403, Dist. Nasik, Maharashtra.

Prof. J. Sitaramamma
Centre for Mahayana Buddhist Studies, Acharya Nagarjuna University, Nagarjunanagar-522610, Andhra Pradesh.

Dr. Cheng Wei-Yi
Assistant Professor, Dept. of Religious Studies, Hsuan Chuang University, Taiwan.

Dr. Satya Dev Kaushik
Professor of Pali, Dept. of Sanskrit, Aligarh Muslim University, Aligarh-202002.

Ven. Dhammadipa
c/o Petr Gilbert, Maly Semerink 1030, Janov nad Nisou 48711, Czech Republic.

Ven. Dr. Fa Quing and Ven Wei Wu
Than Siang Temple, 132 Jalan Sultan Azlan Shah-11900, Penang, Malaysia.

Dr. Joseph Loizzo
Nalanda Institute for Meditation and Healing, 16 East, 65th Street, 4th Floor, 417 Riverside Drive 9A, New York-10025, USA.

Ven. Bhikshuni Chuehmen
Chief Executive, International Buddhist Progress Society, Fo Guang Shan Monastery, Ta Shu, Kaosiung-84010, Taiwan, ROC.

Mr. Ricardo Sasaki (Dhanapala)
Director, Nalanda Buddhist Center, R. Albita 606/101, 30310-160, Belo Horizonte, MG-Brazil.

Lee Ki Woon
Dongguk University, c/o Ven. Bo-ryun, 242-48 Gui 1 Dong, Kwangjin-gu, Seoul, South Korea.

Mr. Sulak Sivaraksa
Santi Pracha Dhamma Institute, 666, Charoen Nakorn Road, Klongsan, Bangkok-10600, Thailand.

Part I

HISTORY

1

HISTORICAL BACKGROUND

(EXCERPTS FROM ASI GUIDEBOOK ON NALANDA)

A. Ghosh

EARLY REFERENCES

Nalanda[1] has a very ancient history dating back to the days of Mahāvīra and Buddha in the sixth and fifth centuries BC. According to Jaina texts it was a suburb (*bāhiriyā*), situated to the north-west of the famous city of Rājgṛha. Indeed, so important was the place that Mahāvīra spent as many as fourteen rainy seasons there. The Pāli Buddhist literature as well contains many references to Nalanda. It is said that in the course of his journeys Buddha often halted at the place, which is mentioned as prosperous, swelling, teeming with population and containing a mango-grove called Pāvārika. The distance from Rājgṛha to Nalanda is given as a *yojana*.[2]

Another place near Rājgṛha was Nāla, which is mentioned in the *Mahāsudassana-Jātaka* as the birthplace of the Elder Śāriputra, a chief disciple of Buddha. In other texts the same place, under the name of Nālaka or Nālakagrāma, appears as a centre of Śāriputra's activities.[3] But the *Mahāvastu*, a Sanskrit Buddhist text, gives Nalanda-grāmaka, half a *yojana* distant from Rājgṛha, as the place of birth of Śāriputra and finds support in some Tibetan texts, including Tārānātha's *History of Buddhism*, a seventeenth-century Tibetan work.[4] It is therefore reasonable to hold that Nāla, Nālaka, Nālakagrāma and Nalanda are all the variants of the same place name.

ORIGIN OF THE NAME

Hiuen Tsang, the renowned Chinese traveller of the seventh century, says that according to tradition the place owed its name to a Nāga of the same name who resided in a local tank. But he thinks it more probable that Buddha, in one of his previous births as *Bodhisattva*, became a king with his capital at this place, and that his liberality won for him and his capital the name Nalanda or charity without intermission.[5]

EARLY HISTORY BY TĀRĀNĀTHA

According to Tārānātha, Aśoka, the great Mauryan emperor of the third century BC, gave offerings to the *chaitya* of Śāriputra that existed at Nalanda and erected a temple here; Aśoka must therefore be regarded as the founder of the Nalanda Vihāra.[6] The same authority adds that Nāgārjuna, the famous Mahāyāna philosopher and alchemist of about the second century AD, began his studies at Nalanda and later on became the high priest here. It is also added that

Suviṣṇu, a Brāhmaṇa contemporary of Nāgārjuna, built one hundred and eight temples at Nalanda to prevent the decline of both the Hīnayāna and Mahāyāna schools of Buddhism.[7] Tārānātha also connects Āryadeva, a philosopher of the *Mādhyamika* school of Buddhism of the early fourth century, with Nalanda.[8] Further, Asaṅga, a Buddhist philosopher of the *Yogācāra* school, belonging to the fifth century,[9] is said to have spent here twelve years of his later life and to have been succeeded by his still more famous brother, Vasubandhu, as the high priest of Nalanda.[10]

UNDER THE GUPTAS

These statements of Tārānātha would lead one to believe that Nalanda was a famous centre of Buddhism already at the time of Nāgārjuna and continued to be so in the following centuries. But it may be emphasized that the excavations have not revealed anything which suggests the occupation of the site before the Guptas, the earliest datable finds being a (forged) copper-plate of Samudragupta and a coin of Kumāragupta. This is fully confirmed by the statement of Hiuen Tsang that "a former king of the country named Śakrāditya selected by augury a lucky spot" and built here a monastery and that his successors, Buddhagupta, Tathāgatagupta, Bālāditya and Vajra built some monasteries nearby.[11] As some of these names were borne by the Gupta emperors, it has been held that all of them refer to the imperial Guptas of the fifth and sixth centuries.

The assumption that the monasteries of Nalanda were the creation of the Gupta emperors beginning with Kumāragupta-I receives confirmation from the fact that Fā-hien, the Chinese pilgrim of the early fifth century, does not mention the monastic establishments of Nalanda. He speaks of the village of Nālo, the place of birth and death of Śāriputra, and of a *stūpa* existing here.[12] As has been suggested above, this place may be identical with Nalanda, but the absence of any other monument except a *stūpa* at the time of Fā-hien is significant.

UNDER HARṢA

Hiuen Tsang saw here a 24.4 m-high copper image of Buddha raised by Pūrṇavarman, 'the last of the race of Aśoka-rāja,'[13] belonging to the early sixth century. And the illustrious Harṣavardhana of Kanauj (606-647) no doubt greatly helped the institution by his munificence: he built a monastery of brass, which was under construction when Hiuen Tsang says that Harṣa remitted "the revenues of about a hundred villages as an endowment of the convent and two hundred householders in these villages contributed the required amount of rice, butter and milk." "Hence," he adds, "the students here, being so abundantly supplied, do not require to ask for the four requisites. This is the source of the perfection of their studies, to which they have arrived." This statement makes it clear that the students did not have to beg for their daily food.

Harṣa highly revered the Nalanda monks and called himself their servant.[14] About a thousand monks of Nalanda were present at the royal congregation at Kanauj. Royal patronage was, therefore, the key-note of the prosperity and efficiency of Nalanda. As Hiuen Tsang says, "A long succession of kings continued the work of building, using all the skill of the sculptor, till the whole is truly marvellous to behold."[15]

HIUEN TSANG

Hiuen Tsang also recounts a few of the monasteries and temples that he saw here, giving their directions in most cases. Thus, the monastery built by Budhagupta was to the south of the one built by his father Śakrāditya; to the east of Budhagupta's monastery was the one of Tathāgatagupta; the one built by Bālāditya was to the north-east of the last; while Vajra's monastery was to the west. After this an unnamed king of mid-India is said to have built a great monastery to the north and erected a high wall with one gate round these edifices. Hiuen Tsang also gives a long list of the other monasteries and *stūpa*s that he found. Modern attempts to identify them with the existing ruins have met with scanty success, as the six centuries that separated Hieun Tsang and the final desertion of the site must have produced many new buildings and modified the existing ones.

Hiuen Tsang was very warmly received at Nalanda and resided here for a long time. The courses of study, says Hiuen Tsang, included the scriptures of the Mahāyāna and Hīnayāna schools, *Hetu-vidyā* (logic), *Śabda-vidyā* (grammar), and *Cikitsā-vidyā* (medicine), as well as such purely Brāhmaṇical texts as the Vedas including the *Atharvaveda*. From the accounts of the pilgrim it is clear that Nalanda was bustling with literary activities:

> The priest to the number of several thousands are men of the highest ability and talent. Their distinction is very great at the present time, and there are many hundreds whose fame has rapidly spread through distant regions. Their conduct is pure and unblamable. They follow in sincerity the precepts of the moral law. The rules of the convent are severe, and all the priests are bound to observe them. The countries of India respect them and follow them. The day is not sufficient for asking and answering profound questions. From morning till night they engage in discussion; the old and the young mutually help one another. Those who cannot discuss questions out of the *Tripiṭaka* are little esteemed and are obliged to hide themselves for shame. Learned men from different cities, on this account, who desire to acquire quickly a renown in discussion, come here in multitudes to settle their doubts, and then the streams (of their wisdom) spread far and wide. For this reason some persons usurp the name (of Nalanda students), and in going to and fro receive honour in consequence. If men of other quarters desire to enter and take part in the discussions, the keeper of the gate proposes some hard questions; many are unable to answer, and retire. One must have studied deeply both old and new (books) before getting admission. Those students, therefore, who come here as strangers, have to show their ability by hard discussion; those who fail compared with those who succeed are seven or eight to ten.

Hiuen Tsang received here the Indian name 'Mokṣadeva' and was remembered by the inmates of the Nalanda monastery long after he had left the place. Several years after his return to China, Prajñādeva, a monk of Nalanda, sent him a pair of clothes, saying that the worshippers everyday went on offering to Hiuen Tsang their bows and salutations.

Nalanda had by now acquired a celebrity spread all over the east as a centre of Buddhist theology and educational activities. This is evident from the fact that within a short period of thirty years following Hiuen Tsang's departure, no less than eleven Chinese and Korean travellers are known to have visited Nalanda.[16]

I-TSING

Next in importance to Hiuen Tsang stands I-Tsing, who reached India in 673 and studied at Nalanda for a considerable time. His work records very minute details about the life led by the Nalanda monks, which he regarded as the ideal to be followed by Buddhists all over the world. He says that the number of monks of the Nalanda monastery exceeded three thousand in number, maintained by more than two hundred villages bestowed by previous kings.[17] He also gives details of the curriculum, which, besides the Buddhist scriptures, included logic, metaphysics and a very extensive study of Sanskrit grammar.[18] He further testifies to the strict rules of discipline that the monks observed, their daily life being regulated by a water-clock.[19]

UNDER THE PĀLAS

The Pāla emperors held East India from the eighth to the twelfth century AD and were noted for their patronage of Mahāyāna Buddhism. At the same time they established other monasteries at Vikramaśilā, Somapura, Odantapurī and Jāgaddala,[20] which must have created a diversion in the activities of Buddhist scholars. It is even stated by Tārānātha that the head of the Vikramaśilā monastery had control over Nalanda.[21] Still, there are ample epigraphic and literary evidences to show that the Pālas continued to be liberal in their munificence to Nalanda.

RENOWNED SCHOLARS

Mention may be made here of some famous scholars who, by their deep learning and excellence of conduct, created and maintained the dignity which Nalanda enjoyed. It has been already stated above that the early Mahāyāna philosophers, Nāgārjuna, Āryadeva, Asaṅga and Vasubandhu, were all, according to Tārānātha, the high priests (*paṇḍita*) of Nalanda. Next in point of chronology comes Diṅnāga, the founder of the medieval school of logic; he was a Southerner who was invited to Nalanda to defeat in disputation a Brāhmaṇist scholar and received the title *Tarka-pungave*.[22] The next famous *paṇḍita* was Dharmapāla, who had retired just before Hiuen Tsang arrived. At the time of the pilgrim's stay the head of the monastery was Śīlabhadra, under whom the pilgrim studied and whose scholarship and personal qualities he describes eloquently. Śīlabhadra was probably succeeded by Dharmakīrti, who is credited by Tārānātha to have defeated a Brāhmaṇical philosopher, Kumārila.[23]

The next important figure was Śāntarakṣita, who was invited by King Khri-sron-deu-tsan to Tibet, where he lived for many years till his death in 762. About the same time Tibet was also visited by Padmasambhava, who acquired great fame as the founder of the institution of Lamaism in Tibet. It was no mean honour for Nalanda that one of its scholars gave to the Tibetan religion a form that is continuing to the present day.

Thus, Nalanda succeeded in attracting the best Buddhist scholars whose fame spread to distant countries and persisted through ages. Rightly has it been said that 'a detailed history of Nalanda would be a history of Mahāyānist Buddhism.'[24]

EPIGRAPHIC AND LITERARY REFERENCES

The following epigraphic and literary evidences help in the reconstruction of the history of Nalanda:

1. Inscription on an image found at Shahpur (near Bihar-Sharif) of the *Harṣa* year 66 (AD 672-673), belonging to the reign of Ādityasena and recording the erection of the image at Nalanda-*mahāgrahāra*.[25]
2. Copper-plate of Devapāla (*c.* 810-850) issued from Mudgagiri (Monghyr). It records that being requested by the Mahārāja Bālaputradeva of Suvarṇadvīpa (Sumatra) through a messenger, Devapāla granted five villages in the district of Rajagṛha in the Śrīnagara (Patna) division for the upkeep and maintenance of monks and copying of manuscripts in the monastery built by the Sumatran king, on the twenty-first day of *Kārttika* in the thirty-ninth regnal year. It was found in Monastery Site 1 and is now in the Indian Museum.[26]

3. Inscription on a Tārā image found at Hilsa (Patna District) of the thirty-fifth year of Devapāla. It mentions Mañjuśrīdeva, a monk of Nalanda.[27]
4. Inscription found at Ghosrawan (Patna District) belonging to the rule of Devapāla and recording the activities of a monk named Vīradeva, who was appointed by Devapāla to look after Nalanda.[28]
5. Pillar inscription in a Jaina temple in the Bargaon village (Nalanda) of the twenty-fourth year of Rājyapāla (*c.* 908-935).[29]
6. Vāgīśvarī image inscription found at Nalanda by Cunningham in 1862. It records the erection of the image in the first year of Gopāla-II (accession c. 935).[30]
7. Nepal manuscript of the *Aṣṭasāhasrikā-prajñā-pāramitā*, copied at Nalanda in the sixth year of Mahīpāla-I (*c.* 988-1038).[31]
8. Nalanda stone inscription, found in 1863, of the eleventh year of Mahīpāla-I. It refers to the destruction of Nalanda by fire and its subsequent restoration.[32]
9. Bodleian Library manuscript of the *Aṣṭasāhasrikā-prajñā-pāramitā*, copied at Nalanda in the reign of Rāmpāla (1077-1120).[33]
10. The Royal Asiatic Society manuscript of the same text, copied in the reign of Govindapāla in the latter half of the twelfth century.[34]

It is evident from the account of Hiuen Tsang that Buddhism was slowly decaying when he visited India. Important centres of early Buddhism were deserted, though some new centres, such as Nalanda in the east, Valabhī in the west, and Kāñchī in the south, had sprung up. After some time Buddhism lost its hold in other provinces and flourished only in Bihar and Bengal, where royal patronage succeeded in keeping alive a dying cause. But it is clear that Buddhism was no longer popular and centred round a few monasteries. The Buddhism that was practised at these places was no longer of the simple Hīnayāna type, nor even had much in common with the Mahāyāna of the earlier days, but was strongly imbued with ideas of Tantricism, inculcating belief in the efficacy of charms and spells and involving secret practices and rituals.

The crusades of the Brāhmaṇical philosophers and preachers such as Kumārila and Śaṅkarācārya in the eighth century must have been another potent factor in rendering Buddhism unpopular. The final blow was delivered by the Muslim invaders, who according to their own accounts, drove away the monks and destroyed their cloisters. Cut off from and divorced of the support of a laity which had been its greatest strength in early days, Buddhism virtually disappeared from India with this onslaught.

The Muslim historian Minhāj describes how Muhammad Bakhtiyār Khalji (end of twelfth century) fell upon and destroyed a city in western Bihar, which they called Bihār (Sanskrit *vihāra*) and which was found to be a place of study.[35] It is not unlikely that Nalanda is being referred to here. Tārānātha says that "the Turks conquered the whole of Magadha and destroyed many monasteries; at Nalanda they did much damage and the monks fled abroad".[36]

The summer of 1235 saw another attack on Nalanda, at that time with only two surviving monasteries inhabited by some seventy monks, including a Tibetan Dharmasvāmin, who has left an eye-witness account of the incident.[37]

Another Tibetan text, the *Pag-sam jon-Zang*, however, adds that after the raid of the Turks the temples and *chaityas* were repaired by a sage, Muditabhadra.

> Soon after this, Kukuṭasiddha, minister of the king of Magadha, erected a temple at Nalanda, and while a religious sermon was being delivered there, two very indignant Tīrthika (Brāhmaṇical) mendicants appeared. Some naughty young novice-monks in disdain threw washing water on

> them. This made them very angry. After propitiating the sun for twelve years, they performed a *yajña*, fire-sacrifice, and threw living embers and ashes from the sacrificial pit into the Buddhist temples, etc. This produced a great conflagration which consumed Ratnodadhi,[38]

one of the libraries of Nalanda.

The first European account of the village Bargaon containing the ruins of Nalanda was given by Buchanon-Hamilton, who visited the place in the first quarter of the nineteenth century and found here some Brāhmaṇical and Buddhist images.[39] But it was only in the sixties of that century that Alexander Cunningham identified the place with the ancient Nalanda on the basis of the distances and directions given by the Chinese pilgrims and of some image inscriptions that he found here.

In fact, it was he who drew the attention of the archaeological world to the importance of this site.[40] After a few years A.M. Broadley carried out some unsystematic excavation in Chaitya Site 12 and published a monograph on the place.[41]

For about twenty years beginning with 1915-16, the Archaeological Survey of India excavated the site. The activities of the survey in the direction of excavation, preservation of the remains from further ruin, and collection of antiquities have resulted in making Nalanda a place which no archaeological pilgrim should leave unseen.

NOTES AND REFERENCES

1. In ancient literature both the forms Nālanda and Nālandā occur indiscriminately.
2. For references, see Hirananda Sastri in *Proceedings of the Fifth Oriental Conference*, I, Lahore, 1930.
3. See B.C. Law, *Geography of Early Buddhism*, London, 1932, p. 31.
4. F.A. Schiefner, *Tāranātha's Geschichte des Buddhismus in Indien*, p. 65. See also N.L. Dey, *Geographical Dictionary of Ancient and Mediaeval India*, London, 1927, *s.v.* Nālandā.
5. S. Beal, *Buddhist Records of the Western World*, London, 1906, II, p. 167. The derivation *na-alam-dā* has been proposed, but it does not satisfactorily convey the sense that it is intended to.
6. Schiefner, *op. cit.*, pp. 65ff.
7. *Ibid.*, pp. 69ff.
8. *Ibid.*, p. 83.
9. Some scholars are in favour of a date earlier by a century.
10. Schiefner, *op. cit.*, p. 122.
11. For Hiuen Tsang's description of Nalanda, see Beal, *op. cit.*, pp. 167ff. His biographer Hwui Li adds some interesting details: S. Beal, *Life of Hiuen Tsang* (London, 1911), pp. 109ff.
12. Legge, *Travels of Fā-hien*, Oxford, 1886, p. 81.
13. Beal, *Records*, II, p. 118.
14. Beal, *Life*, p. 160.
15. *Ibid.*, p. 177.
16. For a list, see Beal, *Life*, pp. xxviiiff.
17. J. Takakusu, *A Record of the Buddhist Religion*, Oxford, 1896, pp. 65 and 154.
18. Takakusu, *op. cit.*, pp. 167ff. It appears from his account that all the existing grammatical texts of the Pāṇinian school, including the *Aṣṭādhyāyi* itself, were taught to the students. It is strange that in spite of this many Buddhist texts in Sanskrit are written in incorrect language.
19. *Ibid.*, p. 145.
20. Vikramaśilā was founded by Dharamapāla (Schiefner, *op. cit.*, p. 217) and is generally identified with Patharghata in Bhagalpur District, Bihar. The Somapura monastery was, according to Tārānātha (*ibid.*, p. 209), founded by Dharmapāla's successor Devapāla and has been identified with Paharpur in Rajshahi District, East Bengal. According to inscriptions found there the monastery was named after Dharmapāla. Odantapurī or Uddaṇḍapura was erected near Nalanda by either Gopāla or Devapāla

(*ibid.*, pp. 204 and 206), and may be identified with modern Bihar in Patna District. Jagaddala was founded by Rāmapāla, one of the last kings of the dynasty, somewhere in North Bengal.

21. Schiefner, *op. cit.*, p. 218.
22. *Ibid.*, pp. 131ff.
23. The identification with the famous Brāhmaṇa *mīmāṃsaka* Kumārila is at once suggested but does not seem to be very likely, as Kumārila probably lived somewhat later.
24. *Encyclopaedia of Religion and Ethics*, IX, Edinburgh, 1917, *s.v.* Nālandā.
25. J.F. Fleet, *Gupta Inscriptions*, Corpus Inscriptionum Indicarum, Calcutta, 1888, p. 208. The image is now lost. It is probable that the word was *mahāvihāra*.
26. *Epigraphica Indica*, XVII (1923-24), pp. 310ff.
27. *Jour. Bihar and Orissa Res. Soc.*, X (1924), pp. 31ff.
28. A.K. Maitra, *Gauḍalekhamālā*, Rajshahi, 1913, pp. 45ff.
29. *Indian Antiquary*, XLVII (1918), pp. 110ff.
30. Maitra, *op. cit.*, pp. 86ff.
31. *Proc. Asiatic Soc. Bengal*, 1899, pp. 69ff.
32. Maitra, *op. cit.*, pp. 101ff.
33. *Catalogue of Sanskrit MSS in the Bodleian Library*, II, Oxford, 1905, p. 250.
34. *Jour. Roy, Asiatic Soc.*, N.S., 1876, p. 3.
35. *Tabaqāt-i-Nāṣiri*, tr. H.G. Raverty, Calcutta, 1881, p. 552.
36. Schiefner, *op. cit.*, p. 94.
37. *Biography of Dharamasvāmin* (eds.), G. Roerick and A.S. Altekar, Patna, 1959, pp. xixff.
38. S.C. Vidyabhusana, *History of Indian Logic*, Calcutta, 1921, p. 516.
39. Martin, *Eastern India*, I, London, 1838, pp. 94ff.
40. *Archaeological Survey of India*, I, Simla, 1871, pp. 28ff.
41. *Ruins of the Nālandā Monasteries at Burgaon*, Calcutta, 1872.

Pl. 1. Nalanda: General view of excavated remains.

Pl. 2. Nalanda: Monastery site 1 and 1A.

Pl. 3. Nalanda: General view of *Stūpa* site no. 3.

Pl. 4. Nalanda: *Stūpa* site no. 3.

Pl. 6. Nalanda: *Stūpa* site no. 3, corner tower.

Pl. 5. Nalanda: Stucco panels on *Stūpa* site no. 3.

Pl. 7. Nalanda: *Stūpa* site no. 3, corner tower.

Pl. 8. Nalanda: South-east corner tower of *Stūpa* site no. 3, showing stucco figures of Buddha.

Pl. 10. Nalanda: Stucco figure of standing Buddha within a niche of *Stūpa* site no. 3.

Pl. 11. Nalanda: *Stūpa* site no. 3, stucco figure of Bodhisattva.

Pl. 12. Nalanda: *Stūpa* site no. 3, stucco figure of Bodhisattva.

Pl. 9. Nalanda: *Stūpa* site no. 3, stucco figures.

Pl. 13. Nalanda: *Stūpa* site no. 3, votive *stūpa*s.

Part II

ART AND ARCHAEOLOGY

2

EXCAVATIONS OF STŪPA SITE NO. 3 AT NALANDA AND EARLY CHRONOLOGICAL EVIDENCE

B.R. Mani

Taxila, Nalanda and Vikramaśilā have been recognized as the greatest organized centres for learning in ancient India besides many other seats of scholarship in Kashmir, Kasi, Kanchi, Valabhi and other scattered centres throughout the country which attracted students from far-off places including foreign countries, traditionally to earn knowledge and wisdom for generations together. These centres witnessed various ups and downs during different phases of history. The centres for organized studies were 'live' universities imparting rigorous training in the fields of art, culture, sciences, theological studies, literature and grammar. With the downfall of Taxila, generally attributed to the Hūṇas around the fifth century CE, the focus shifted to Nalanda and later to Vikramaśilā as well, although individual houses of scholars and smaller centres including temples, *gurukulas*, *maṭhas* and *vihāras* in different parts continued to impart initial and higher studies.

Nalanda definitely gained the status of an advanced centre for learning during the times of the Guptas around fifth century CE and developed into a large university in the following years, particularly during the rule of the Pālas and continued its status till the end of the twelfth century as reflected from archaeological evidence. But the process of development at the site seems to have had a much earlier beginning suggested by traditional and literary evidences which should be given equal importance in understanding the process of development of the place into a university. Though there are archaeological indications of earlier antiquity, further substantial probing into archaeological data is required for attesting the traditional beliefs.

In this context, it is suggested that structural phases noticed during excavations of monasteries and shrines in Nalanda indicate on one hand the continuity of traditional religious and academic activities in these buildings and on the other, repeated constructions over earlier existing structures. Extensive ruins of a great Buddhist establishment near village Bargaon, about 11 km north of Rajgir, were identified by Alexander Cunningham with Nalanda, suggesting the antiquity of temples and monuments within the span of about 200 years from c. 425 CE to 625 CE or the period after Faxian and before Xuanzang.[1] When Xuanzang visited Nalanda, it had more than 1500 teachers to guide 10,000 students. Faxian had visited Nalanda and called it Nālo, the birthplace of Śāriputra, the chief disciple of Lord Buddha, which can also be equated with Nāla, Nālaka-grāma or Nālikā repeatedly mentioned in *Aṅguttara Nikāya, Majjhima Nikāya, Saṁyutta Nikāya*

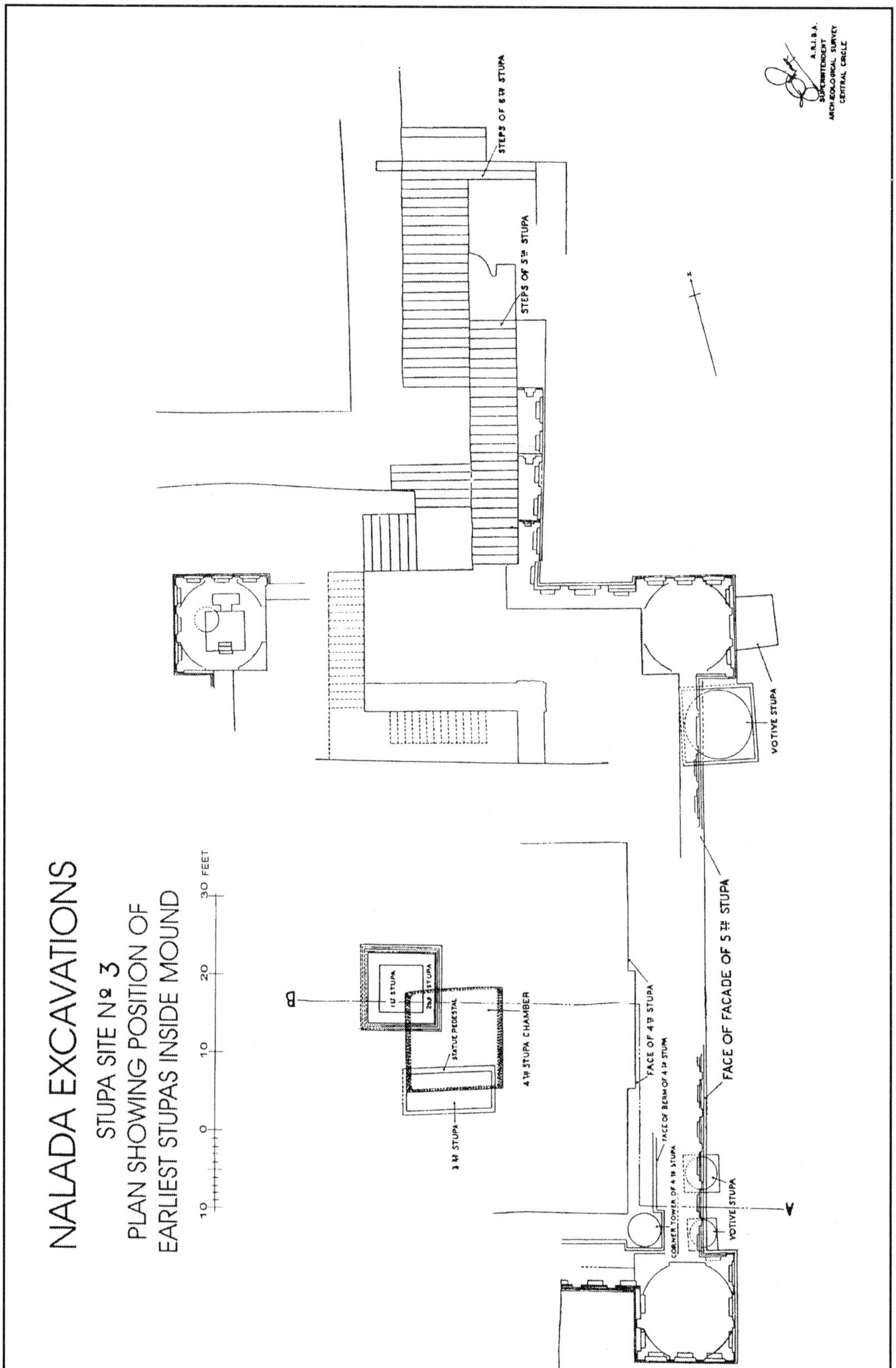

Fig. 2.1. Nalanda: *Stūpa* site no. 3. Plan showing position of earliest *stūpas* inside mound.

or in *Dhammapadaṭṭa Kathā*[2] in connection with the birth and death of Śāriputra in the same room of the house there or in connection with Buddha's preaching various *suttas* in the Pāvārikāmbavana at Nalanda. The present village Sarichak towards east from the ruins of Nalanda seems to be the name of the village of the mother of Śāriputra where he was born. Mahāvīra is also supposed[3] to have spent three rainy seasons at Nalanda.

Thus, one thing is apparent that the archaeological evidence available so far is either insufficient or does not confirm the tradition of early antiquity of the site. There is no point in not believing the tradition which takes back Nalanda to the Buddha's times around sixth century BCE. The Tibetan tradition, as contained in the work of Lāmā Tārānātha, records activities in chronological span beginning from the time of Buddha mentioning Śāriputra and Mahāmoggalāna through Aśoka's construction, Nāgārjuna's association with the site in the Kuṣāṇa period and the famous Buddhist *ācāryas* of the Gupta and later periods.

Writing on the extensive spread of Mahāyāna, Tārānātha[4] opines that Nalendra was the birthplace as well as place of *nirvāṇa* of Śāriputra. There was a *chaitya* of Śāriputra there. Aśoka built a large temple of Buddha at the site. The two *ācāryas* – the Brāhmaṇa brothers – built eight temples (at Nalanda) and placed there all the scriptures of the Mahāyāna. Aśoka was the founder of the first *vihāra* at Nalendra. Five hundred *ācāryas* along with Udbhaṭa and his brother enlarged the centre. Rāhulabhadra spread the Doctrine (of Mahāyāna) still further and Nāgārjuna made it most extensive. With the help of the art of secret science, he (Nāgārjuna) maintained for many years five hundred teachers of the Mahāyāna doctrine at Śrī Nalendra and at that time a Brāhmaṇa of Magadha built one hundred and eight temples at Śrī Nalendra. He made these the centres of the *mātṛkādharas* so that the *Abhidharma* of both Mahāyāna and Hīnayāna were not lost. Ārya Nāgārjuna has been mentioned as *upādhyāya* of Nalendra. Nāgārjuna's disciples Āryadeva and Nāgāhvaya also stayed at Nalendra. Ācāryas Asaṅga and his brother Vasubandhu stayed at Śrī Nalendra, the former for twelve years and the latter was ordained there and studied the three *Śrāvaka-piṭakas* and became *upādhyāya* of Śrī Nalendra after passing away of Ārya Asaṅga. Later Brāhmaṇas and *śramaṇas* were engaged in debates and Ācārya Diṅgnāga defeated the former thrice.

Although it is quite clear that the archaeological evidence of early antiquity of Nalanda is still insufficient and is more explicit from Gupta period (c. fifth century CE) onwards, there are certain indications which definitely push back the history and antiquity of Nalanda to many centuries. Such evidences were exposed at *Stūpa* Site No. 3 but not studied in details or rather not taken into account seriously. Regular excavations at Nalanda were carried out by the Archaeological Survey of India from 1915-16 to 1935-36 under John Marshall and D.B. Spooner by Hirananda Sastri and J.A. Page. During this period a large area was excavated and many monasteries, *stūpas*, shrines and temples were exposed but in the absence of new scientific techniques involving the study of stratigraphy, classification of ceramics and minor antiquities, organic samples for absolute scientific dating and in view of still more areas remaining to be excavated, we may hope that future excavations would definitely confirm the early antiquity of the site. We may discuss here the excavation of *Stūpa* Site No. 3 which no doubt indicates the evidence of antiquity of the site several centuries earlier than what is normally mentioned.

The *Stūpa* Site No. 3 was initially called a *vihāra* in 1916-17[5] and later as *Stūpa* Site No. 3. Presently, some scholars prefer calling it Temple 3 as the existence of a Buddha shrine at the top of each of at least fifth, sixth and seventh stages of the edifice indicates it to be a temple.[6] It is sometimes also identified with Śāriputra-*chaitya* or *stūpa*.

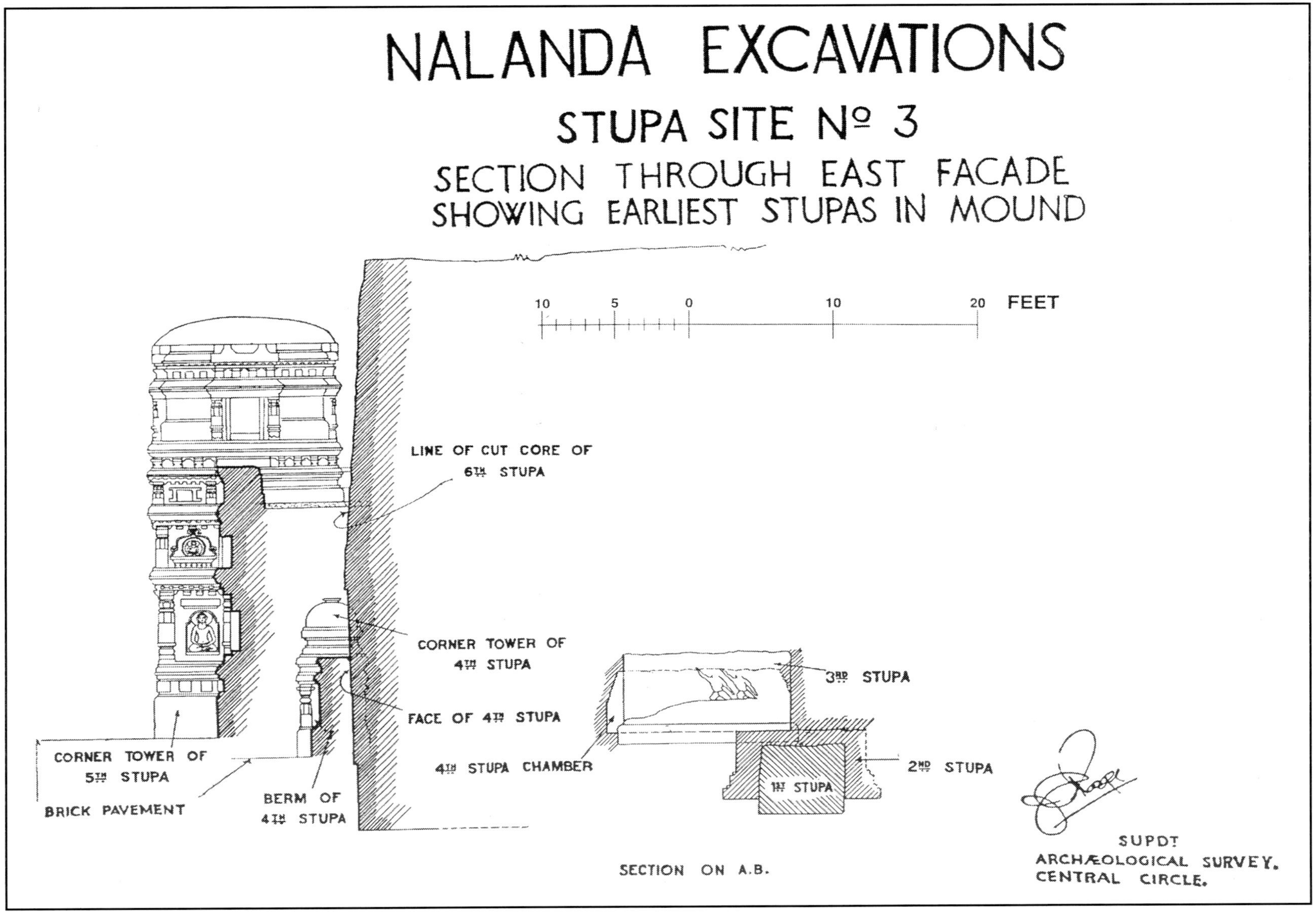

Fig. 2.2. Nalanda: *Stūpa* site no. 3. Section through east facade showing earliest *stūpa*s in mound.

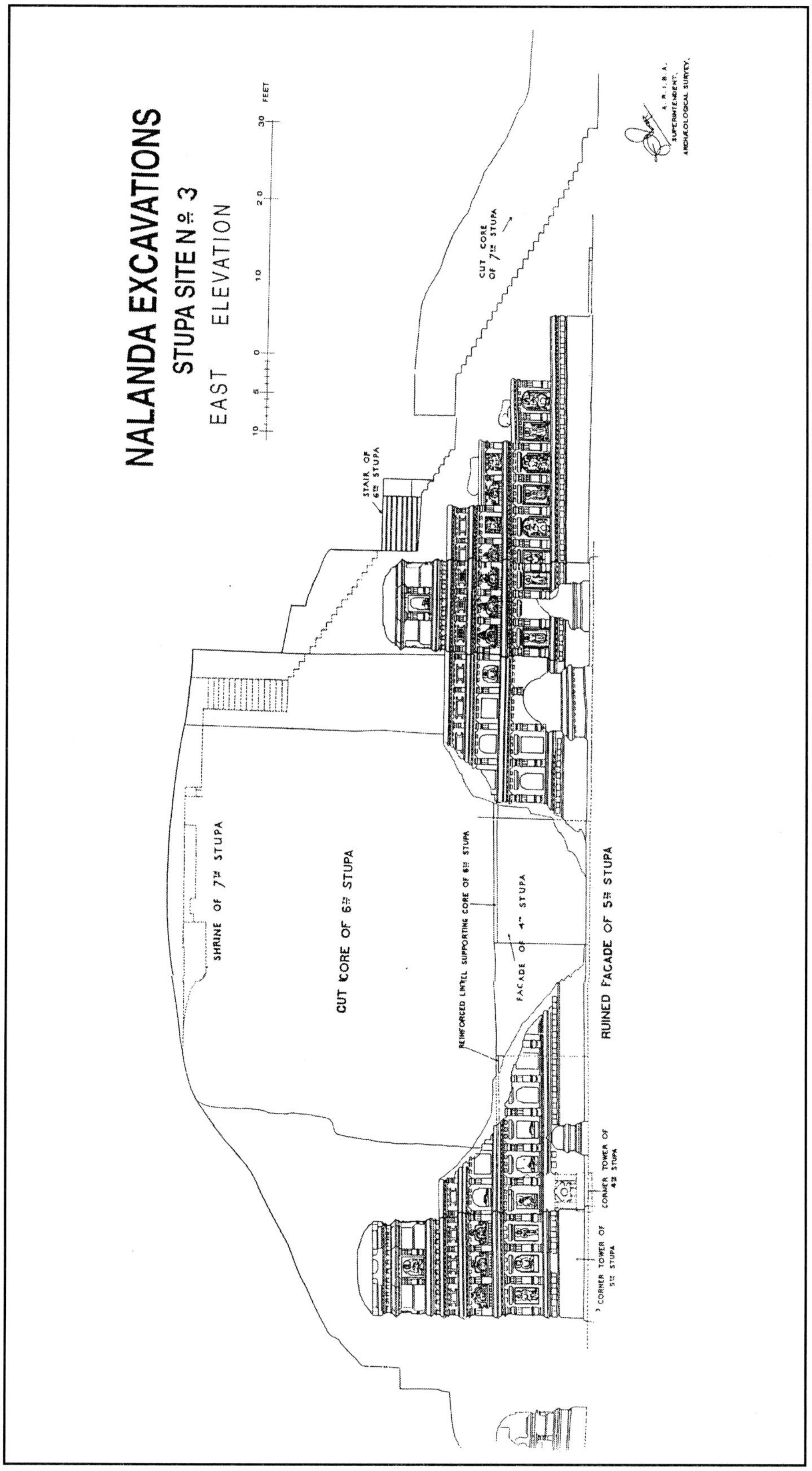

Fig. 2.3. Nalanda: *Stūpa* site no. 3. East elevation.

After Cunningham's identification of the site in 1861, Broadley carried out some unsystematic excavation at Site 3 and Site 12.[7] Site 3, the tallest of the edifices of Nalanda,

> represents the result of seven accumulations, the earliest three of modest dimensions being buried deep under the later ones. The temple of the fifth stage, with four corner towers, had its façade ornamented with stucco figures of Buddha and *Bodhisattvas* in Gupta tradition, which were encased within the extension of the sixth stage. The level of the shrine at the top rose with each reconstruction with a resultant higher flight of steps at each stage. The ruins of the shrine of the last stage with a pedestal for the installed Buddha image are seen at the top. Each stage had its own votive *stūpas* all around, often engulfed in the latter's extensions. One of such *stūpas*, of the fifth stage contained in its core a clay tablet inscribed with sacred text *Pratītya-Samutpādasūtra* and dated CE 516-17. Another manifestation of devotion is the enshrinement within votive *stūpas* of clay lumps or miniature clay *stūpas*, each having in its core two clay tablets impressed with the Buddhist creed. The temple of the seventh stage externally measures 130 x 80 ft.[8]

> To locate the earliest structures of the edifice a deep vertical trench was cut from the outermost eastern face of the *stūpa* right through to the centre. The bottom-most foundations of the earliest phase are about 60 ft. deep from the top of the mound. No relic casket could be located during cutting through a huge mass of solid laid-brick. "Right at the very bottom of the foundations, based on the virgin clay and crossing the narrow pit from north to south, was at least disclosed the smooth face of a low brick structure, corbelled out with two offsets in the form of footings, to which fragments of surface-plaster still adhered.[9]

Its external corner suggested that it was the outer face of the wall. Its distance from the north-east external corner was found to be 9 feet. Later the inner face of the wall was also noticed which enclosed the chamber. The remains of the innermost structure, though did not yield any relic casket, was found to be square in plan with 5 feet 8 inches a side and no higher than 4 feet 6 inches, apparently the base of a little square *stūpa*. The size of bricks used in this earliest structure is mentioned to be 18 inches x 13 inches x 4 inches which could be bricks of Maurya period and not later than it on the analogous ground of evidence from other Mauryan sites, such as Paṭaliputra (18 x 11 1/2 x 2), Bhiṭa (20 x 13 1/2 x 3), Kuṣinagar (18 to 19 x 12 x 3), Sārnāth (15 to 20 x 10 to 14 x 3 to 3 1/2), Śrāvasti (17 to 21 1/2 x 9 to 14 1/2 x 3 to 3 1/2), Vaiśalī (18 to 19 x 10 to 13 x 3), Rājghāṭ (18 3/4 x 11 x 2), and Kauśambi (18 x 12 x 2 1/2).[10] Though the Maurya tradition continued during Śuṅga period, the size of bricks was gradually reduced which became quite apparent during the Kuṣāṇa period when its size was normally 36 x 24 x 6 cm or around 14 1/2 x 10 1/2 x 2 1/2 inches.

The 2 feet-high outer wall with its plastered surface encasing the lower earliest structure represents the base of a second *stūpa* that had been built over and around the first. A little above these lowermost structures, but located slightly to the south-east of them, the low remains of a later chamber, measuring about 9 feet north-south and 12 feet east-west (revised in the year 1926-27 as 11 feet 6 inches east-west and 5 feet 6 inches north-south) filled with earth and debris attached to a low platform with a rounded concrete top were found. This was the third stage of enlargement of the structure. The torsos of two mutilated small plaster images in relief were noticed besides a very small fragment of a 'black glazed pot' from the earth filling which seems to be either a sherd of Northern Black Polished Ware or Black-Slipped Ware as these pottery types were not popularly known to the excavators in 1925-26 as their nomenclature was fixed during 1940s.

Excavation work at the *Stūpa* Site No. 3 reached a logical conclusion in the year 1926-27 when more parts of the edifice were exposed through a solid mass of brick work, 40 feet high

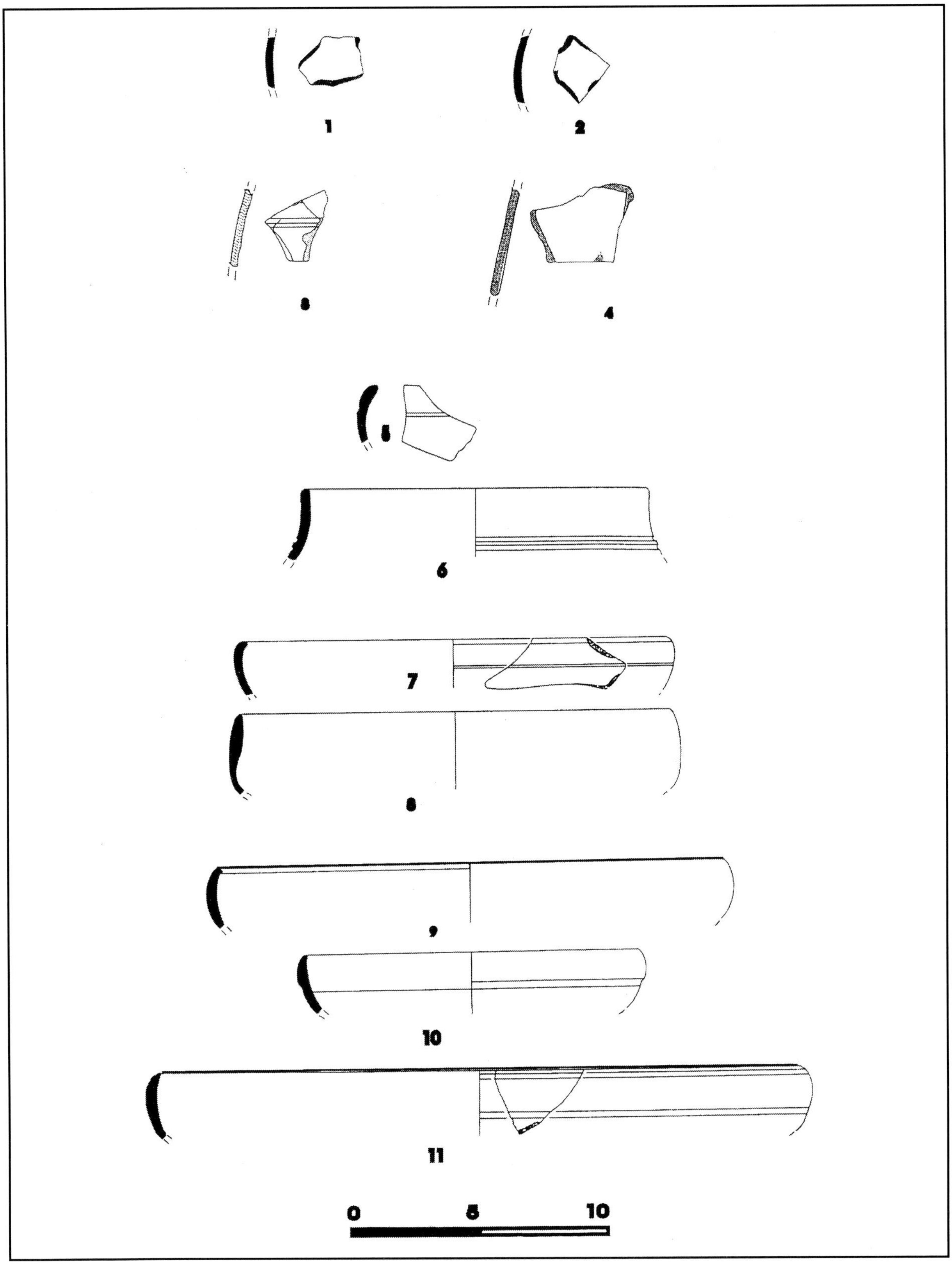

Fig. 2.4. Nalanda: Jaffaridih (5, 10); Black Slipped Ware (1, 6-8, 11); NBPW (2-4, 9).

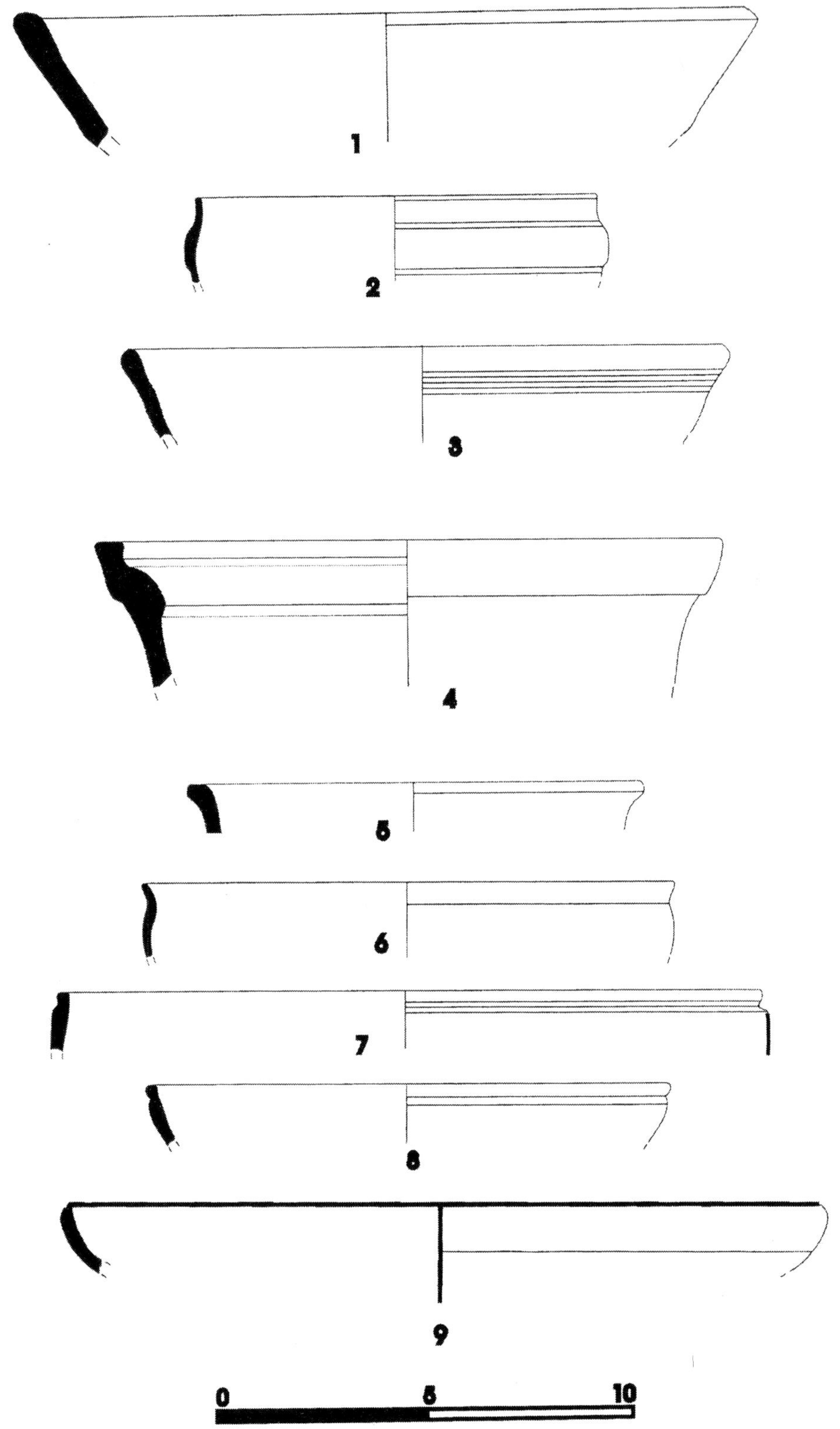

Fig. 2.5. Nalanda-Garh: Red Ware (1, 3-5); Black Slipped Ware (2, 6-8); Black-and-Red Ware (9).

with dismantling and removal of over a lakh and a quarter cubic feet of laid brickwork in front of it. The excavations proved that instead of three there were four earliest constructions at the site. Besides the earlier mentioned three stages, it was found that in the fourth stage there was a low hollow chamber about 12 feet 6 inches square with rough overhanging corbelling around the sides, which was filled with earth and its floor was 1 feet above the third structure. The chamber was perhaps made to accommodate relics which were not found there. For proper preservation these earliest structures were filled up after excavations.

The two larger *stūpa*s at fifth and sixth stages with top shrine of the seventh stage were most probably constructions belonging to the 6th century onwards as reflected from their artistic embellishments and the evidence of inscribed clay tablet mentioned earlier. The corner towers with sculpted figures of Buddha and *Bodhisattva*s in stucco, terraced structure of the *stūpa*, the flight of steps and circumambulatory pathways are representative of late and post-Gupta art and architecture. In the course of clearing the passage between stucco-covered facade and the earlier *stūpa* inside it, the remains of the little corner tower of the *stūpa* were exposed which give a picturesque idea of *stūpa* below the *stūpa* even at the later stage of the construction. Thus the evidence of four earlier stages of construction of edifices prior to the sixth century CE indirectly suggests earlier antiquity of the site which may well go back to the Maurya period for the earliest construction at the site.

In this connection the author explored three archaeological mounds in the vicinity of Nalanda monastic complex to its south-west around Jagdishpur village, within 2 km distance in the second week of February 2006 and noticed the evidence of Northern Black Polished Ware, Black-Slipped Ware, Black-and-Red Ware, and Red Ware (Fig. 2.4) from Jaffaridih. The mound has a diameter of about 50.0 m and a height of nearly 10.0 to 12.0 m from the surrounding ground level and may represent a *stūpa* with stone figures of seated Buddha and other fragments located on the north-eastern side. A water-body is located towards the south-east of the mound. About 500 m to its west is a mound called Garh or Garhpar which seems to be another early historical monastic establishment with ceramics including Black-Slipped Ware, Black-and-Red Ware, Red Ware and other associated types and shapes (Fig. 2.5). The site measures around 150 m in north-south and about 80 m in east-west direction with a height of about 4 to 5 m. A carnelian bead was also found there. About 1 km to its south-east is the mound called Rukmiṇī-sthāna which has a huge statue of seated Buddha in Pāla style within a recently constructed temple and the ceramics of the site include shapes and types of Red Ware and Black Ware of c. 9th-10th century CE. The mound is around 200 m in north-south and about 100 m in east-west direction. A broken terracotta votive *stūpa* was found from the surface in the exploration. The cultural assemblage of the first two sites definitely suggests a very early antiquity which may find a parallel if further excavations are carried out at these sites and also in the main complex at Nalanda.

Finally, in view of the firm tradition of early antiquity of the site as contained in the Buddhist texts, the evidence of *Stūpa* Site No. 3 requires further detailed study besides archaeological investigations afresh at the site to confirm the beginning of the settlement in and around the extensive area of the monastic complex of Nalanda University. The evidence of brick size of the earlier stage of *Stūpa* Site No. 3 and that of 'black glazed pot' being possibly a sherd of NBPW, together with the seven stages of relative chronological succession together with the evidence of early archaeological material available in the neighbourhood sites, indicate the possibility of dating the earliest stage of structure to the Maurya period, if not earlier. A thorough exploratory survey around the area followed by fresh and planned problem-oriented excavation at the site may reveal astonishing facts on the likelihood of the presence of hitherto unknown earlier stratigraphic sequence.

NOTES AND REFERENCES

1. A. Cunningham, *Archaeological Survey of India: Four Reports Made During the Year 1862-63-64-65* (Reprinted), Vol. I, New Delhi, 2000, p. 30.
2. R. Panth (ed.), *Nalanda and Buddhism*, Nalanda, 2002, pp. 46-55.
3. *Ibid.*
4. Lama Chimpa and Alaka Chattopadhyaya (tr.), *Tārānātha's History of Buddhism in India*, Simla, 1970, pp. 101, 106, 109, 111, 125-27, 171 and 182.
5. John Marshall (ed.), *Archaeological Survey of India – Annual Report 1916-17*, Part I (Reprinted), New Delhi, 2002, p. 15.
6. A. Ghosh (ed.), *An Encyclopaedia of Indian Archaeology*, Vol. 2, New Delhi, 1989, p. 305.
7. *Ibid.*, p. 314.
8. *Ibid.*, p. 305.
9. J.F. Blakiston (ed.), *Archaeological Survey of India – Annual Report 1925-26* (Reprinted), New Delhi, 2002, p. 101.
10. T.N. Mishra, *Prachina Bharatiya Inton ka Adhyayana* (in Hindi), Varanasi, 1989, pp. 161-82.

3

THE MYSTERY GODDESSES OF NALANDA

VISUALISATIONS AND EMPOWERMENT

C. Mani

THE FIVE SPELL DEITIES

The particular goddesses retrieved by me in the labyrinth of Nalanda sculptures belong to a class of spell deities known as *Pañcarakṣā,* variously found in scripts. Like the *Prajñāpāramitā* text restored by Nāgārjuna from the underworld and deificated in icons as the bronze statuette of *Prajñāpāramitā* of Nalanda *Pañcarakṣā* images are also deificatory. They are known in all northern Buddhism. The text[1] by this name is compulsorily found in every house in Nepal.

The order in which the deities are placed is:

1. Mahāpratisarā
2. Mahāsāhaśra-Pramardinī
3. Mahāmantrānusāriṇī
4. Mahāśītavatī
5. Mahāmāyurī

The *Sādhanasamuccaya,* a Sanskrit work rendered into Tibetan as *Sgrub-Thabs-Kur-las-btus-pa,* contains the following *sādhanas* for their visualisation:

1. Mahāpratisarā-Sādhana
2. Pratisarā-Sādhana
3. Ārya Mahāmāyūrī-Sādhana
4. Ārya Mahāsāhaśra pramardinī-Sādhana
5. Ārya Mahāmantrānusāriṇī-Sādhana
6. Mahāśītavati-Sādhana

The Five Buddhas,[2] canonically known as 'Pañca Tathāgata', are affiliated with these *mantra*-administering goddesses. The affiliation occurs thus:

Vairocana	:	Mahāsāhaśra-Pramardinī
Akṣobhya	:	Mahāśītavatī
Amitābha	:	Mahāmāyūrī
Ratnasambhava	:	Mahāpratisarā
Amoghasiddhi	:	Mahāmantrānusāriṇī

Fig. 3.1. Goddess with serpent hoods (Stone, Early Medieval), Nalanda.

The Five Buddhas (Rgal-ba rigs. lṇa) dominate over the jealous, the lusty, the envious and the infatuous activities of the beings of the world of the series of the spell goddesses. I have identified Mahāmantrānusāriṇī and Mahāmāyurī. The other three are badly mutilated. Mahāmantrānusāriṇī[3] is a four-armed goddess, of black colour, with one face; she holds the sword in the right and the battle-axe and noose in left hands; she is depicted in the *varada mudrā* by her second right hand.

Images of the deity are found in Tibet, China and India. Meditational practices lead to visualisation of the deity in other forms as 12-armed (Pañcarakṣāmaṇḍalaṁ, Niṣpanna-yogāvalī) and the goddess as of white colour, in *ālīḍha mudrā* (Sādhana No. 206, SM).

Fredrick W. Bunce[4] offers four images of the deity in his *Iconographic Encyclopedia*, containing emerging perceptions of Buddhist divinities, e.g., Five Hundred Gods of Narthang (c. 1810); the Pao Hsiang Lous temple of the Forbidden City, Beijing (786 deities), the Chu Fo Sheng Hsiang' Tsan (360 deities); and the three hundred icons (Tib. Sku-brnan-brgya-phrag-gsum, 756 deities *et al.*).

The description of the goddess emanating from Tathāgata Akṣobhya, the imperturbable one, has the same status as the four other spell deities of the *Akṣobhya maṇḍala*, in which one among them alternately takes the middle place, when called up to perform a certain deed. This goddess is in blue colour and has four arms, in *varada mudrā*.

The Nalanda image of Mahāmantrānusāriṇī does not conform any *dhyāna* given in the earlier tāntric works known to the *Niṣpanna-yogāvalī*;[5] but she is literally described in a later text, the *Sādhanamālā*[6] (Sādhana 199). This prescribes the four-armed deity as:

> Mahāmantrānusāriṇī, caturbhujaikamukhī Kṛṣṇā dakṣinabhujadvaya-vajravaradavatī Vāmabhujadvaya paraśupāśavatī Hūṁkārabīja Akṣobhya kirīṭinī Sūryāsanaprabhā ceti.

I translate it as under:

> Mahāmantrānusāriṇī is a four-armed and one-faced goddess of dark-blue complexion. She holds in her two right hands the *vajra* and the *varada mudrā*, and in her two left hands she has the *paraśu* and *pāśa*. She has emanated from the bījākṣara "Hūṁ" and bears the image of Akṣobhya in the crown; she sits on the orb of the sun and shines forth like the sun.

In another text (Sādhana No. 201, SM) the description is a little different which tallies with our figure, with *asi* (sword) and the *varada mudrā* in her right hands.

Mahāmāyūrī,[7] the great peacock goddess, known as 'Vidyārājñī' is deity of the same class, being deified from a text of that name. The work is greatly popular in Nepal, since its first codification in the tenth century CE in the time of Govindacandra, a vassal of Mahīpāladeva (c. 975-1016 CE). Several recensions of the text are available with fine calligraphy and miniatures of the goddess placated for curbing the effect of snake-poison and granting desires.

In Nalanda she is a four-armed deity with a peacock at the left edge of the pedestal. The figure recalls the Mahāmāyūrī image painted on wall in a cave at Ellora, which for a hundred years had been known as Sarasvatī. The correct identification was made by J. Banerjee.[8] A miniature of the goddess of the time of King Rāmapāla (c. 1057-1102 CE) is preserved in the Bharat Kala Bhavana of Banaras Hindu University. It differs from the usual description of the goddess in painting in blue colour.

Mahāpratisarā is a popular goddess in Tāntric Buddhism. She is worshipped either singly, or in *maṇḍala* rites along with the four other goddesses of the Pañcarakṣā group. In single-form of worship she is depicted as a deity with four faces and eight arms, her colour being yellow. She assumes the white colour in a *maṇḍala* and is a four-faced, eight-armed deity. She is also depicted with three faces and ten arms, or three faces and eight arms. As depicted with three faces she bears the image of Ratnasambhava on the crown.

The *Sādhanamālā* paints her in yellow and as three-faced, each face with three eyes and ten arms; her right and left faces are painted blue and white. In her five right hands she carries the sword, the *vajra*, the *cakra* and is in *varada mudrā*. Her five left hands carry the bow, the banner, the jewel, the battle-axe and the noose. On her crown is the image of Ratnasambhava. The deity wears a blue jacket and a red scarf and is profusely bejewelled. She sits in the half-reclining posture.

The goddess is popular in Tibet and China. A miniature of the goddess is kept in Cambridge University.

Mahāsāhaśra Pramardinī is a goddess meditated upon in the *Niṣpanna-yogāvalī* as four-faced, ten-armed and white complexioned. She sits on the orb of the moon set on double lotus. Her emblems of five right hands are a wheel with eight spokes on lotus, the goad, the arrow, the sword and the *varada mudrā*. In her five left hands, she holds the *vajra*, the raised index finger, the bow and the noose.

A different form is described in the *Sādhanamālā*, with eight arms. Her images are found in Nepal, Tibet and China. A miniature is preserved in the collection of Dr. Evans Wentz.

Mahāśītavatī is the third goddess of the *Pañcarakṣā* group of images. Being a protectress of the western direction she is described in the *Niṣpanna-yogāvalī* as three-faced, eight-armed and installed on a double lotus on the orb of the Sun. Her faces are red, blue and white. She is to be cognized by her protective *mudrā*s with the four right hands holding lotus, arrow, thunderbolt and sword. In the four left hands she has noose in the first finger, bow, jewel banner (*ratnadhvaja*) and manuscript against the chest. She is well preserved in the Chinese collection at Peiping. A miniature of the deity is found in the collection of Evans Wentz. N.K. Bhattasali has illustrated her figure in his *Iconography of Brahmanical and Buddhist Sculptures* (Pl. XXIV).[9]

As these images belong to the order of *Vajrayāna* the traditional vocabulary of tāntric practices and the emotivity contained in those practices reveal the universal mystery to a much greater limit than what the scientist or inventor does to master creativity. By comprehending the truth that the whole belongs to the atom the esoterist knows the ultimate destiny of creation.

A comparable study of the manifestation of deities conjures images of perfection and accumulated virtues underlying superior vigour, unabated compassion and deep love calling for justification of natural law and value.

Since we possess limited understanding of ourselves and the things round us we underestimate ourselves and our energies that do not let us rise above the level of misconceptions and superstitions. A complete absorption in the inevitable deity stimulates our mind to imbibe his or her qualities whom we cherish as our 'awakener'.

There are esoteric rites for compulsive results. The way lies through creating images from the practices of *maṇḍala, mantra, yantra* and a cumulative contemplative mind off these *maṇḍala* is a mystic diagram suggestive of great possibilities from the contemplated object levelled into the higher, the lower and the middle substrata. It may be a tapestry, icon or a mystic syllable in which the mind visualizes the deity granting favour.

NOTES AND REFERENCES

1. The first codification of the text started in the time of the Pāla King Govindacandra, a contemporary of Mahīpāladeva (c. 975-1066). Several recensions of the work are found specially in Nepal and Tibet. There is a copy in the University of Cambridge (in 12 folios and 36 figures). Another manuscript containing twenty figures carved in wooden block written in the time of King Ramapāladeva (1057-1102 CE) is in Banaras University Library. Similar maps are preserved in the Indian Museum Calcutta with 6 folios and 12 wood blocks and in Los Angeles County Museum, which has two folios and six figures.
2. For the Five Buddhas, see *Guhyesamāja Tantra* (ed. Benoytosh Bhattacharya, No 53 GOS, Baroda); see also the initial verses in *Piṇḍīkramoktākṣobhya-maṇḍalaṁ* in *Niṣpanna-yogāvalī*, Gos No. 109, Baroda, 1949.
   Glossarial inventories of 'Dhyānī Buddha', the non-canonical term concocted by Brian Houghton Hodgson, the British regent at Kathmandu and first used by him in 1888 for 'Tathāgata' (B. Hodgson, *Essays on the Languages, Literatures and Religion of Nepal and Tibet*) has no ground for its further use. For Tathāgata, q.v. Pāli *Sumangala-vilāsini* text. The scriptures are prone to use 'Pañca Tathāgata' as in the *Sarva Tathāgata tattva-sangraha*, a work illustrated on a scroll by Śubhākara Siṁha (CE 635-735) and translated into Chinese in CE 723 by Vajrabodhi.
3. *The Museum Catalogue Nalanda*, ASI 2006. Fig. 9-201, Plate VIII B.
4. Fredrick W. Bunce, *A Dictionary of Buddhist and Hindu Iconography*, 1997.
5. Benoytosh Bhattacharya (ed.), *Niṣpanna-yogāvalī*, Gos No. 109, Baroda, 1949.
6. *Sādhanamālā*, 2 volumes, Gos, Nos. 20, 41, Gos, Baroda, 1925-1928.
7. *The Museum Catalogue Nalands*, ASI, 2006; Fig. 1A-305.
8. For evolution of Hindu iconography see his *Development of Hindu Iconography*, Calcutta, 1941.
9. N.K. Bhattasali, *Iconography of Buddhist and Brāhmaṇical Sculptures in the Dacca Museum*, Dacca, 1929.

Pl. 14. Nalanda: Votive *stūpa*s and miniature shrines in the complex of *Stūpa* site no. 3.

Pl. 15. Nalanda: *Stūpa* site no. 3, apsidal shrine.

Pl. 16. Nalanda: Close-up view of the spoked wheel of a miniature shrine in the complex of *Stūpa* site no. 3.

Pl. 17. Nalanda: Votive *stūpas*.

Pl. 18. Nalanda: General view of the monastery no. 6.

Pl. 19. Nalanda: Close-up view of monastery no. 6.

Pl. 20. Nalanda: General view of temple no. 12.

Pl. 21. Nalanda: Temple no. 13.

Pl. 22. Nalanda: Exterior wall of temple no. 14.

Pl. 23. Nalanda: Mouldings on southern wall of temple no. 14.

Pl. 24. Nalanda: Front portion of Sarai Mound.

Pl. 25. Nalanda: Front wall of Sarai Mound.

Pl. 26. Nalanda: Floral design on front wall of Sarai Mound.

Pl. 27. Nalanda: Close-up view of decoration on front wall of Sarai Mound.

Pl. 28. Nalanda: Buddha.

Pl. 29. Nalanda: Bronze statue showing Buddha in *Abhaya mudrā*.

4

THE BUDDHIST ART AT MAINAMATI
A PARALLEL TO NALANDA

Enamul Haque

In the present paper an exploratory attempt will be made, perhaps for the first time, to see aspects of Buddhist art and architecture as have been revealed at Nalanda and Mainamati, the last named site being situated in Bangladesh. The aim is not to make a comparative study of the two celebrated monastic sites, which though originated at different times, witnessed their general decline almost at about the same time. Apart from being the birthplace of venerable Śāriputra and one of the unique places where the Buddha carried on his religious propaganda, there is hardly much reliable information about Nalanda till the visit of Xuanzang in about CE 637, when it was already a great centre of learning and culture. As of this moment, based on the archaeological evidence, the patronage of Nalanda by Gupta and post-Gupta dynasties are well corroborated by the finds of coins, seals and inscriptions discovered on the sites.

Briefly referring to the Nalanda buildings, the most imposing structure is the Main Temple, or as has been called the Main Temple Site 3, standing at the southern extremity of the row of temples. East of this Main Temple, are situated Monasteries 1B and 1A, in rather an irregular alignment. Then the Monasteries no. 1, 4, 6, 7, 8, 9, 10 and 11 are in a row, all facing towards west with single entrances from the same side. Temple sites 12, 13 and 14 are also in a row placed on the west of the monasteries. An exceptional location is for Temple Site 2, behind the monasteries 7 and 8, entered from the east. A passage between monasteries 1 and 4 leads a visitor towards the Main Temple and entrances of other monasteries.

The monasteries are very similar in layout and general appearance. In each of them the central cell just facing the entrance beyond courtyard contained a shrine with an image. There is evidence that each monastery was deserted and reoccupied.

The temples no. 12, 13 and 14 on the western row also more or less conform to the general layout, having similar dimensions and features. However, Temple Site 2, situated behind monasteries no. 7 and 8, is specially interesting. There are 211 sculptured stone panels over the moulded plinth. These are symmetrically arranged. There is a large variety of scenes depicted on them – Religious, secular and natural themes, as well as compositions with Buddhist and Brāhmaṇical identities. These are dated to c. 6th-7th century CE, probably belonging to an earlier temple, and thereafter reused as have been done at Paharpur. A circumambulatory path skirts the temple chamber. A very rich collection of bronzes was found in the Monastery Site 1, which was established by Bālaputradeva, a king of Śailendra dynasty of Suvarṇadvīpa and Yavadvīpa/

Java-Sumatra, during the reign of King Devapāla. The latter donated, on request from the founder, five villages to defray the expenses of the monastery. However, this monastery does not appear to be an exclusive one for Buddhist education; it admitted of Brāhmaṇical studies and practices as well of Vedic rituals. The participation of a sovereign of a distant country in the development of Nalanda is unique and speaks volume of the fame of the site.

Besides being the premier centre for Buddhist learning, Nalanda made great contribution in the sculptural art. Obviously, it was not a place of pilgrimage associated with one of the great events in the life of the Master. Being in the heartland of Gupta empire, Nalanda carried on, rather for too long, idioms and norms of the Gupta art of Sārnāth traditions. Though the pre-eminence of Nalanda originated primarily from its being a centre of Buddhist learning par excellence, an intellectual fermentation, philosophical speculations and doctrinal innovations were the hallmark of Nalanda Vihāra. The environment was just conducive for the development of art which had already taken a firm root in the early Gupta period. After a modest beginning, the Nalanda artists developed a vigour for creativity in the post-Gupta period.

> The vitality of the pre-Pāla art of Nalanda was largely due to the successful blend of Magadhan idiom with Gupta classicism, inherited directly from Sārnāth (Debjani Paul 1995: 107).

The Pāla period saw further development of these achievements with more pronounced depth of carving and adding more intricate details.

There were some superb bronze images cast in Nalanda during the early Pāla period. They were gilded, and also profusely embellished with precious or semi-precious stones. The advent of 10th century witnessed the involvement of the Nalanda artists more and more with Tantric divinities. Iconography overtook the artists in favour of esoteric complexities.

Nalanda enjoyed unrivalled royal patronage till the establishment of the *vihāras* of Vikramaśilā, Somapuri and Udantapuri. These were single-*vihāra* complex of huge dimensions and became renowned in their own rights. However, Nalanda could retain its fame as usual.

The prosperity of Nalanda was disturbed even when the royal patronage was continuing. Tragic events took place as early as the end of 5th or the beginning of 6th centuries CE. Centuries later, destructions took place in about 10th century CE when a Vangala army burnt down the house of ascetic Karuṇāśrīmitra at Somapuri Vihāra, presumably affecting the monastery as the same was repaired by Vipulaśrīmitra, another ascetic, the builder of Nalanda Monastery no. 7 in the c. 11th century.

Finally, fate overtook the establishment towards the end of the 12th century when Bakhtiyar Khalji invaded, and again in 1234-35, when the Turko-Afghans repeated the onslaught, as witnessed by Tibetan monk Dharmasvāmin. However, the end of Nalanda could not be attributed to these calamities alone. In the face of the increased Brāhmaṇical power, Buddhism as a religion or as a culture, had already lost "its vitality and dynamism" that sustained this great centre for nearly a thousand years.

Having recapitulated briefly the achievements of Nalanda, it is now time to introduce the art of Mainamati, as flourished on the low-height hill range in Comilla District of Bangladesh. Situated at the south-east corner of the subcontinent, on the crests and slopes of the Mainamati Hills, an astonishing number of Buddhist monasteries and shrines were built, over a period of six to seven hundred years, almost contemporaneously to the great monasteries and shrines of Nalanda.

More than sixty years ago (1943), the writers of the *History of Bengal*, Vol. I, published by the Dhaka University, knew of only one excavated ruins of the Somapuri Vihāra at Paharpur and did not have the slightest idea of the existence of such a grandiose complex at Mainamati.

In the wake of the military contractors of the Second World War collecting bricks from 'natural mines' for the Advanced Base of the Allied Force, they were ruthlessly destroying the archaeological monuments, till then unknown and unprotected. At the intervention of the then Archaeological Survey of India, this spoliation was stopped in 1946. Subsequently, 49 specific mounds were identified with cultural remains; of them so far 23 are protected. Archaeological excavations were started in 1955, and during the last half of a century, 9 sites have been investigated. Although no proper excavation reports have been published, introductory small-scale publications are available.

The excavated remains of the Buddhist architecture at Mainamati present us with varieties of *stūpas*, *vihāras* and temples established by royalties and nobles, mostly related to Buddhist dynasties of Khadga, Deva, and Chandra, but occasionally by non-Buddhist donors also. I shall very briefly refer to certain salient features of a few of these monuments only aiming to point out the general and special types of architecture at Mainamati as far as related to Buddhism.

We already knew about the donation to a Buddhist monastery in the region of south-east Bangladesh from a copper-plate of Mahārāja Vainyagupta of CE 507 found at Gunaighar, in Comilla District. That on the Mainamati hills flourished in the early medieval times an active centre of Buddhist faith and culture has been well established from the excavated ruins.

The most outstanding of the monastic architecture exposed at Mainamati is the Salban Vihāra by the side of the Archaeological Museum. The complex represents a plan (Fig. 4.1) of four ranges of living cells, a total of 115, round a central courtyard. The quadrangle is a perfect square with 167.68 m each side externally. There is a cruciform temple situated in the centre of the courtyard. The only entrance on the north side is approached by a brick-paved 53.08 m-long and 0.91 m-wide road. The entrance hall is flanked by guard-rooms. All the rooms are fronted by a continuous verandah. The outer walls of the cells are 5.03 m in thickness. Excavations have revealed four periods. A few subsidiary buildings, probably shrines, have been found within the quadrangle.

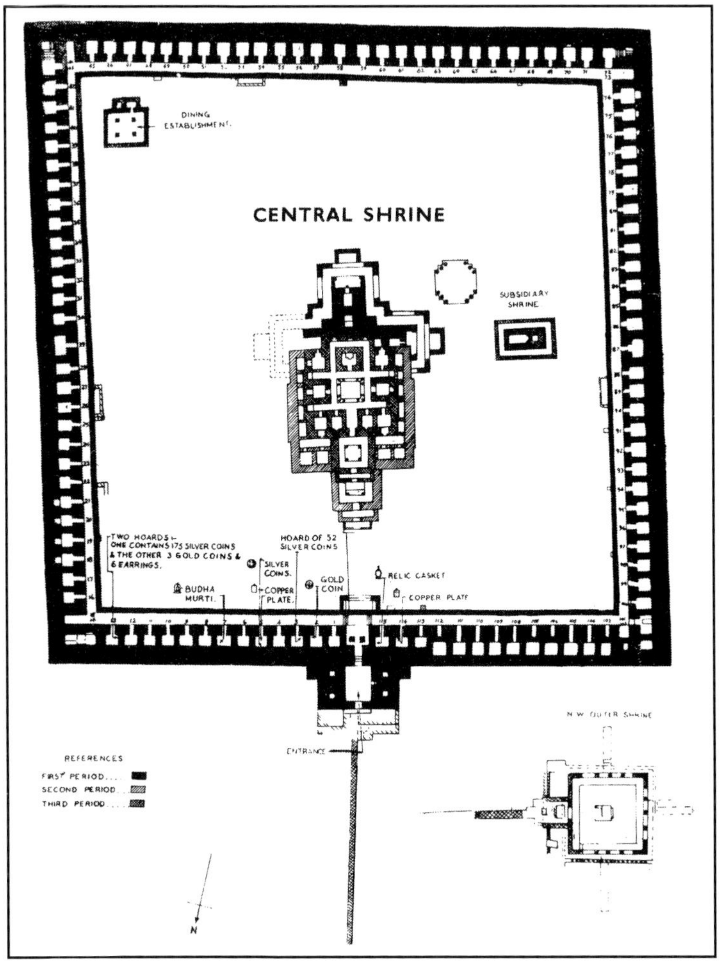

Fig. 4.1. Mainamati: Plan.

The central temple of the Salban Vihāra, as has been found today, is an accumulation of the remains of four temples built at successive stages beginning with the huge cruciform temple at the bottom. Subsequently, the temple took a rectangular shape. The first shrine was built in the form of a Greek Cross measuring 51.82 m from arm to arm "with additional chapels built in the projecting arms facing the cardinal points". The basement walls were decorated with a string course of terracotta plaques. The frieze looked wonderful when excavated. Later, some plaques were stolen and the rest removed to the museum. The exposed structure shows a broad staircase on the north side leading to an entrance hall, with a pillared pavilion in the centre. It was connected with the *caitya* or the inner hall by a covered passage. The roof of the *caitya* rested on 12 brick pillars. The sanctum cella with a tiered pedestal for the image is at the southern end of the hall, surrounded by a 1.52 m wide *pradakshiṇā-patha*. The Salban Vihāra quadrangle and the central cruciform temple appear to have been founded around c. 750 CE.

Outside the monastery walls, on the north-west corner, is a ruined temple of a type unknown in Mainamati or elsewhere. It is neither cruciform nor oblong. The temple faces east with columned terrace in the front. The enclosed cella of oblong shape in the centre has a 2 m-wide ambulatory walk all around, decorated with colonnade of circular pillars in the south, west and northern sides.

A large number of antiquities, some of which are of immense importance, have been found from the excavations. Eight copper-plate inscriptions – one of a Gupta king, three of the Khadga kings, and four of the Deva kings – have been found. Nearly three hundred and fifty coins, of gold and silver, have been recovered. A small terracotta sealing with a 3-line inscription, *Śrī Bhavadeva Mahāvihāra Ārya Bhikṣu Saṅghasya* (of the order of noble monks of the monastic establishment of Śrī Bhavadeva), has been discovered. This indicates the greatness of the *vihāra* with its founder Bhavadeva, the Deva king. The Bhavadeva portion of the copper-plate of Ānandadeva found at Salban Vihāra refers to land gifts to a *vihārika* (small monastery) dedicated to *Ratnatraya* (Buddha, *Dharma* and *Saṅgha*). Another copper-plate, found at the same place, belonging to Rājaputra Balabhaṭa of the Khadga dynasty, describes the world famous (*bhuvanavismayāni*) *Mahābhogāśrama*, eight *vihāra*s adorned with large number of white coloured *caitya*s."

Larger than the Salban Vihāra, and the largest in Mainamati, is the Ananda Vihāra, probably founded by King Ānandadeva, father of King Bhavadeva. Extensively damaged, very little of the structure remains. Excavations have revealed the remnants of the gateway complex on the northern side, patches of wall on the southern side and portions of the central cruciform temple. Each arm of this square monastery measures 190.5 m (Salban Vihāra 167.68 m). The monastic cells were arranged in rows in four wings around the courtyard. A frieze of terracotta plaques *in situ* have been found on the basement wall of the western projection of the shrine.

The Itakhola Mura Vihāra, 39.63 m square, is a typical one with 20 living cells but its entrance is from the east. Instead of a temple in the centre of the quadrangle, a rather detached and complex shrine is situated outside, on the south of the *vihāra*. Interestingly, the temple is of earlier construction than the *vihāra*, the latter being established during the third of the five periods of building and rebuilding of the temple. The oblong temple with east-west axis has a square and solid shrine measuring 13 m x 13 m situated at the western end. During the fourth period, three *stūpa*s were erected right in front of the main entrance to the rectangular enclosure (80.49 x 56.10 m). At the same time, a cruciform shrine was added on the west of the solid platform with separate walled enclosure. Previously, during the third period, was installed a huge image of Tathāgata Akṣobhya made of stucco, a rare medium of sculpture in Bangladesh. The Akṣobhya was found damaged and headless and sealed with brick cover. Itakhola Vihāra temple can be dated to about the third quarter of the 7th century, and the *vihāra* itself, another 30-50 years later.

The Rupban Mura Vihāra (Figs. 2 & 3) and the attached temple together present a unique Buddhist establishment at Mainamati. Built over three phases, the monastery was of oblong shape (35 m E-W and 26 m N-S) with the entrance from the northern side. To the 15 cells of the first phase, later on were added another 9 cells, making the monastery nearly square (35 m x 38 m). This arrangement of a monastery in two parts with separate courtyards is the only known example of its kind. About 30 m west-northwest of the monastery is the temple, also built in three phases. The first phase temple is a square and solid shrine with a projected cella for images in each of the cardinal direction. In the next phase, on the top of the square shrine, was erected a cruciform temple (28.19 m x 28.19 m). Flanking the main gateway, inside the enclosure, are foundations of two votive *stūpa*s: the one on the north is square and the other on the south is octagonal. A significant aspect of the Rupban Mura Vihāra is that a small portion of corbelled roof of an image chamber in the western side was found intact by the excavators. This is so far the only extant roof of an ancient building in Bangladesh. However, it still remains difficult to conjecture the superstructure of the temple. The most important of the antiquities found at Rupban Mura is the colossal sandstone image of a standing (2.44 m) Buddha (Fig. 4.4) of c. 7th century betraying lingering Gupta idioms.

The Bhoja Vihāra at Mainamati is a site where the central temple, a few cells and the gateway complex of the monastery have been excavated so far. The square monastery quadrangle has a cruciform temple in the centre of the courtyard, each arm measuring 46.44 m. On each of the four faces of the central solid shaft is a sanctum and a *maṇḍapa*, the whole being surrounded

Fig. 4.2. Mainamati: Rupban Mura Vihāra.

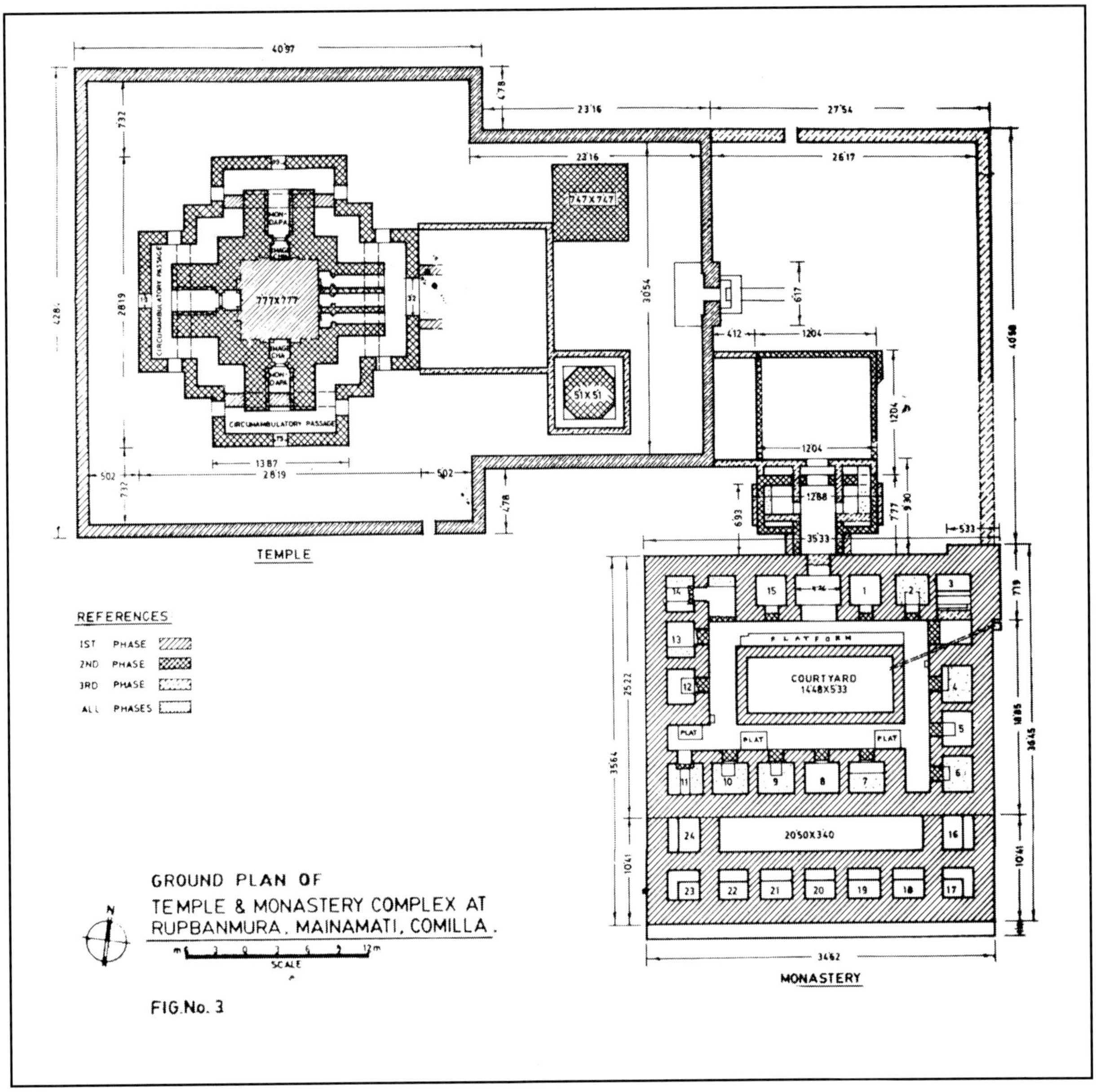

Fig. 4.3. Ground plan of temple and monastery complex at Rupban Mura, Mainamati, Comilla.

by a circumambulatory path. Among the antiquities, the most remarkable is the c. 9-10th century magnificent bronze image of seated Vajrasattva (Fig. 4.5), found inside the northern *maṇḍapa*. A large number of terracotta plaques were recovered from the temple basement. On the grounds of large scale similarities with the Ananda and Salban Vihāras, the Bhoja Vihāra appears to have been established during the Deva period.

Xuanzang visited a large number of Buddhist establishments all over Bengal in 7th century, but left behind specific names and descriptions of only two monasteries: Lo-ta-mo-chih in Karnasuvarna, in Murshidabad district, West Bengal, and Po-shi-po in Pundravardhana, Bangladesh. Po-shi-po has been identified by Alexander Cunningham with the village Bhasu Bihar, 3-4 miles north-west of Mahasthangarh in Bogra District.

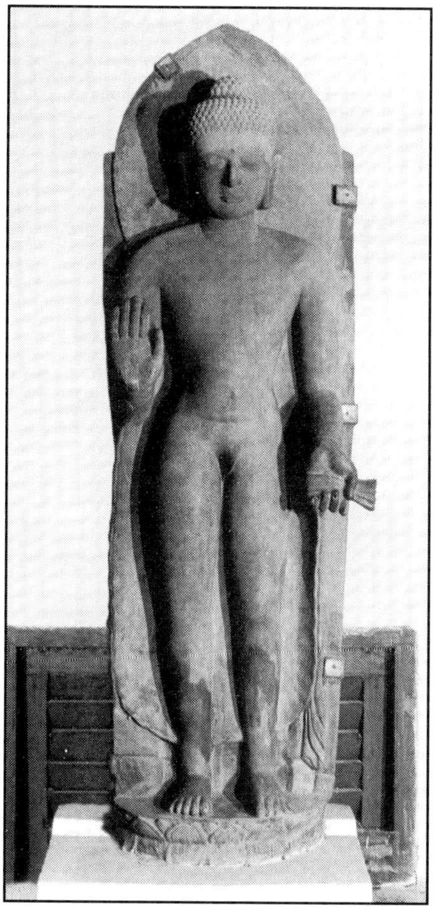

Fig. 4.4. Colossal image of standing Buddha at Rupban Mura, Mainamati.

Fig. 4.5. Bronze image of seated Vajrasattva, Mainamati.

So far, it was held that the Paharpur temple could have greatly influenced the architectural activities of South-East Asia, particularly of Myanmar and Indonesia.

> There is little doubt that the architectural activity in Pagan received some inspiration and ideas from the exclusively Buddhist types of monuments in Bengal and eastern India. The shape and elevation of the Paharpur temple must have afforded some possible scope for imitation by the Burmese builders.

Further, "In Indonesia, the Tjandi Sewu (Buddhist) and the Tjandi Loro Jonggrang (Brāhmaṇical) in Central Java offer the nearest approximation to the plan and elevation of the Paharpur temple." Subsequent discoveries at Mainamati, which are earlier in date of Paharpur by one hundred to fifty years, would require to re-examine the above conclusions. A perusal of the Buddhist architecture at Mainamati is highly assuring. This, indeed, adds a new dimension to the Buddhist architecture of Bengal. Numerous monasteries were established of square or rectangular sizes, sometimes with a temple inside, sometimes a temple outside, and sometimes with no separate temple for them, with only a few monastic cells converted as places of worship.

Three *stūpa*s in a row have come to light at Kotila Mura (Figs. 4.6 & 4.7) in Mainamati. In each case, a drum in cylindrical shape supports the hemispherical dome. The basement is ornately designed. The method of the construction of the central *stūpa* is somewhat unusual.

Fig. 4.6. Three *stūpa*s in a row, Kotila Mura.

Instead of being solid, it is hollow inside, the radiating eight partition walls meeting the circular wall. The cells thus created are filled with stone and clay sculptures and numerous miniature *stūpa*s of unbaked clay, produced from moulds. The chambers also contained minute round sealings impressed with the Buddhist creed. Behind the three main *stūpa*s are nine votive *stūpa*s of different sizes. The three main *stūpa*s at Kotila Mura have been called *Tri-ratna* or Three Jewels of Buddhism, representing the Buddha, the *Dharma* and the *Saṅgha*. A number of copper-plate inscriptions have been found in the region with references to the shrine of Ratnatraya.

Several bronze votive *stūpa*s have been discovered in Bangladesh. A remarkable piece of bronze votive *stūpa* has been found during excavation at Salban Vihāra at Mainamati with four female deities, each seated under a shrine, placed against the drum of the *stūpa*.

The Mainamati sculptures in general depict a style of certain elongation of the figure of the main deity. The treatment of their bodies bear marked influence of Gupta norm and ideal. The same treatment and facial expression can be seen with the colossal stone Buddha from Rupban Mura, already mentioned (2.15 m tall and 66 cm broad). It provides another landmark in the evolution of sculptural art of south-east Bengal. Another remarkable piece of sculpture, though fragmentary, made of stucco, has been discovered. Stucco is a rare medium for Bangladesh. The Itakhola Mura Tathāgata Akṣobhya *in situ* proves the existence of another kind of sculpture, that is, of stucco medium, which was widely prevalent in Nalanda.

Mainamati has yielded a large number of bronze images, both of small and big sizes. The most outstanding of the Mainamati sculptures is the bronze Vajrasattva, also mentioned earlier,

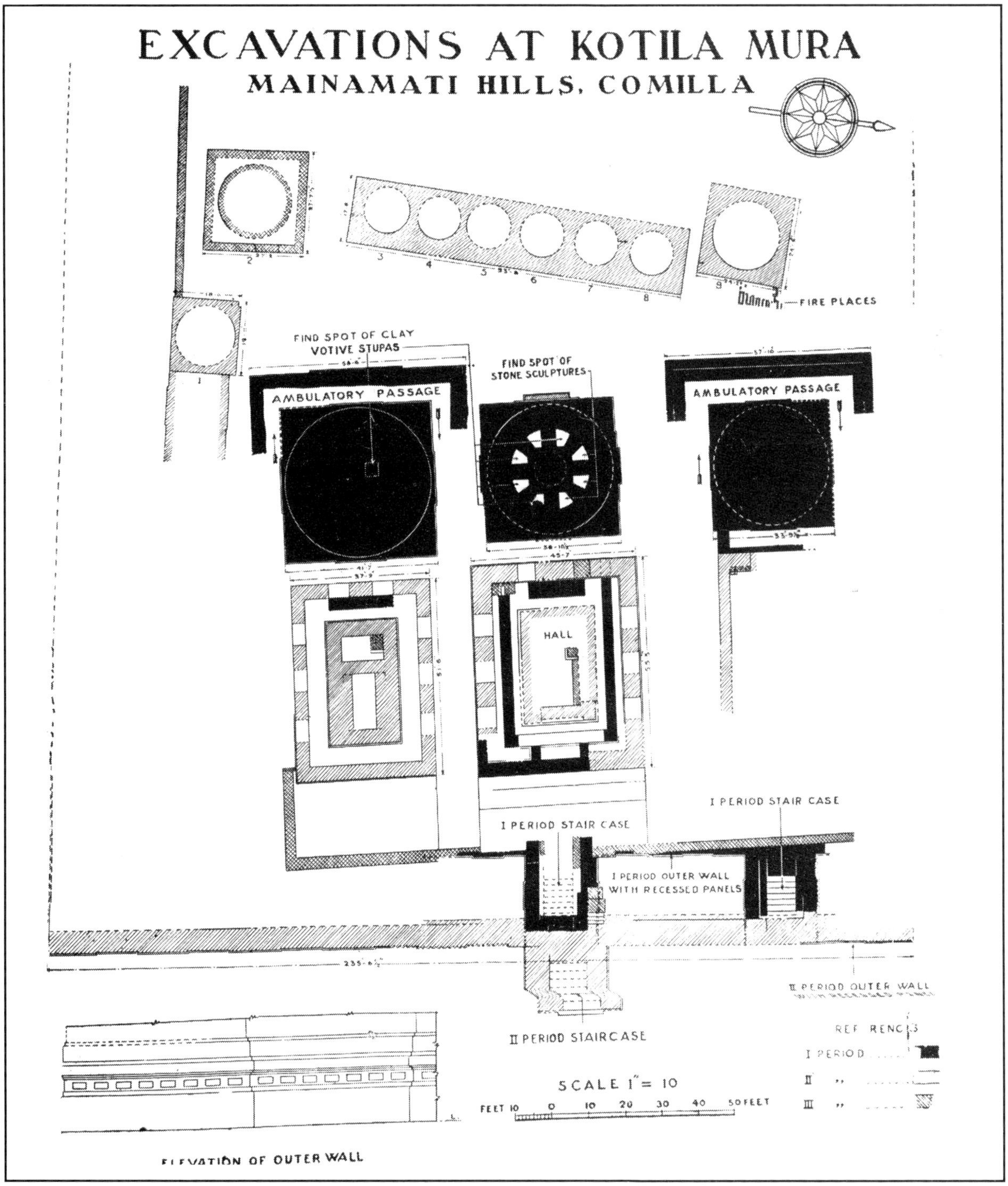

Fig. 4.7. Excavations at Kotila Mura, Mainamati Hills, Comilla.

from Bhoj Vihāra discovered in 1995, 1.5 m high when seated. This image is a "wonder of bronze casting and technical and artistic perfection". This piece has been dated to c. 9th-10th century CE. A solid life-size head of a bronze *Bodhisattva* Avalokiteśvara (30.1 cm long x 15.2 cm wide) was collected from the vicinity of Bairagir Mura. Stylistically it can be dated to the same as the Vajrasattva from Bhoj Vihāra. Another mutilated image of a seated colossal Avalokiteśvara, more than life size, has been found from Ananda Vihāra.

The height of technical expertise in metal casting can be confirmed once again from the large bronze bell, about half a ton in weight, which is indeed a rare find. It has been recovered in almost unharmed condition. The bell is of 1 m height and 2.2 m circumference. The natural shape of the bell resembles a *stūpa*. It has a substantial ring for hanging and two couchant lions decorate the sides of the ring. This bell also has been dated to early 10th century CE.

A major part of the sculptural treasures of Mainamati are the numerous terracotta plaques often of immense historic importance depicting the contemporary society, and representing the free expressions of the artists. These were mostly used for surface ornamentation of the basement walls of the temples. The subject matter of these plaques could be both religious and secular. The themes of the secular subjects were drawn on the everyday experience of the artists. The flora and fauna were also depicted in plenty. A few geometric and scroll designs were also employed. In matters of religious subjects, whereas at Paharpur many Brāhmaṇical deities are included in the decoration, in Mainamati, no such plaques have been used at all. The most distinctive characteristics of the plaques are their naturalism. The sculptural art developed at Mainamati over the centuries, whether in stone, bronze or terracotta, for their individuality as well as excellence, without doubt have created a new school of art.

Having presented the parallel development of art at Nalanda and Mainamati, it is very difficult to refrain from putting up a comparison between the two. In my opinion, there is no necessity to indulge in such an exercise. Nalanda is already great. Mainamati is a new claimant to greatness. There were Xungzang, Yi'jing and many other eminent scholars visiting Nalanda. Mainamati had Xungzang and Sheng-Chi, but strangely, both the visitors forgot to name the capital of the country or the city they visited. In Nalanda, the total number of monastic rooms comes to nearly 300. But in Mainamati, with excavations carried out in 9 of the 49 mounds, the number of such cells is in the range of 450. If the colossal bronze and stone images discovered so far represent the skill and ability of the artists or their patrons, then the position of Mainamati, as far as artistic activities are concerned, would hardly be inferior to Nalanda.

A scholar devoted to Buddhist religion and culture may look for in vain for any reference of Mainamati in any Tibetan sources. It is indeed a mystery as why no Tibetan monk appeared at Mainamati between 6th and 13th centuries in spite of so many and so large Buddhist monasteries and temples, devoted to the Mahāyāna, and subsequent Tantric development of the Vajrayāna, Kālacakrayāna or Sahajayāna Buddhism.

The quantity and variety of the archaeological finds from Mainamati, apart from the monastic temple and *stūpa* architecture, are incomparable in historical importance in Eastern India. The numerous spectacular stone and bronze images, from tiny to colossal sizes, the 23 copper-plate inscriptions found *in situ* and the immediate neighbourhood belonging to six or more dynasties ruling from early 6th to 13th centuries, the vast number of terracotta plaques, the numerous coins of gold and silver, and the amazing range of pottery and household antiquities, cannot be ignored any more.

The archaeological evidence that we have met with at Mainamati so far have unravelled a story of extraordinarily intense Buddhist religious activities in this corner of the subcontinent and perhaps unequalled in Eastern India, Nalanda included. We must not forget the fact that these are results of investigations made in nine out of forty-nine identified mounds only, all situated on the Mainamati hills. The *vihāras* and temples, now famous and reflective of the genius of the builders, were before excavations in recent decades, nothing but mounds, heaps of ruins and debris clad with nearly inaccessible jungles. The temples, valuable coins, priceless inscriptions and significant artefacts, together substantially add new chapters to history. Who knows what and how much is hidden in the adjacent untouched mounds, nearly 40 in number. Historians have to watch these mounds with justifiable hopes.

5

A PORTABLE STŪPA IN MAGADHA STYLE

Amarendra Nath

In the repository of Rajendra Krittishala at Agartala can be seen an outstanding portable bronze *stūpa* bearing registration No. Wdt. TP. 47(b). It was bought from a shopkeeper dealing in metalware at Subrum, a sub-divisional headquarters of South Tripura District. Thanks to Shri Jahar Acharjee, the founder head of the Krittishala, with an ardent interest in collecting curios, a masterpiece in bronze was saved from going into oblivion. Stylistically alien to the region, this object of veneration remained unpublished till now. Here an attempt is made to evaluate its art and iconography eventually leading to the determination of its chronology and provenance.

Save for the portion above the drum, the *stūpa* is preserved in a fairly good condition. Hollow from within, the four-footed squarish pedestal has two bevelled mouldings with a faceted recess in between. Above the pedestal, the cylindrical *medhi* supports two rows of lotus petals arranged in *viśva padma* order, over which originally existed a hemispherical dome (*aṇḍa*) supporting a *harmikā* (Fig. 5A). Facing each of the four cardinals of the *medhi* are four Buddhas of the 'Four Quarters' seated in their respective *deva koṣṭhaka*s. Embellished with moulded pilaster, the *deva koṣṭhaka*s have rhythmically divided the cylindrical *medhi* into bays. Each of the proportionately slender pilasters endowed with a *pūrṇa ghaṭa*-shaped base, is surmounted by an inverted bell-capital moulding. The abacus over it supports an entablature which forms a ring band around the drum.

Fig. 5A. Bronze *stūpa*, portion above *medhi* conjectured.

The four Buddhas, but for their hand poses, are apparently identical. Akṣobhya in the *bhūmisparśa mudrā* (Fig. 5.1.a), Vairocana in *dharmacakrapravartana mudrā* (Fig. 5.1.b), Amoghasiddhi in *abhaya mudrā* (Fig. 5.1.c), and Amitābha in *dhyāna mudrā* (Fig. 5.1.d) are seated over the pericarp of the *viśva padma* in the *vajraparyaṅkāsana* attitude, with soles visible. These Buddhas are alternately draped in *upavīti* (right shoulder bare) and 'covering' (both shoulders covered) modes. The *saṅghāṭī* in each case is transparent, 'wet type', adhering to the body contours without any exaggeration. In case of the 'covering' mode the crescent-like treatment of the upper hemline simulates the fall of the *saṅghāṭī* whereas in the 'opening' mode

Fig. 5.1.a Bronze *stūpa* showing Buddha Akṣobhya in *Bhūmisparśa mudrā.*

Fig. 5.1.b Bronze *stūpa* showing Buddha Vairocana in *Dharmacakrapravartana mudrā.*

the hem-line runs in an orthodox manner, left to right across the chest. In both the modes a frilled portion of the diaphanous *antarvāsa* is spread realistically in a semi-circular fashion over their respective seats. The gentle and well-defined swell along the waist line, formed due to the tying of the *antarvāsa,* reflects the artist's perception of supple human forms and their delineation. Though their facial features are worn out due to constant handling yet vestiges of transcendental contemplation can be recognized. As usual, their hair is rendered in tiny curls terminating in a more flattish rather than conical or spiral *uṣṇīṣa*. Other auspicious renderings, though worn out, are noticed in the treatment of elongated earlobes, consecutive lines on the neck, and plain nimbus represented by two concentric lines.

The order in which the four Buddhas of the 'Four Quarters' are housed in the niches belies the tenets of Buddhism. To illustrate this point, it is seen that Akṣobhya (Fig. 5.1.a), the Buddha of east, has been placed diametrically opposite to Amoghasiddhi (Fig. 5.1.c), the Buddha of north. Likewise Amitābha, the Buddha of west has been set opposite to Vairocana, the Buddha of the inner shrine of the *stūpa*. Why this departure from the accepted canons cannot be explained at present. However, such deviations are not rare. Example of deviation in the representation of the Buddhas of the 'Four Quarters' on the cardinals of *stūpa*s have been noticed not only in India but also in Pan-Asian Buddhist centres. A Chinese relic portrays Akṣobhya and Amitābha along with Maitreya and the Śākyamuni obviously forming a particular group of Buddhas of the 'Four Quarters'. Soper rightly observes that in such departures from the norms, the Buddhist institution was becoming flexible enough to permit Maitreya and Śākyamuni to assume a relationship of convenience with the other two directions.

Fig. 5.1.c Bronze *stūpa* showing Dhyānī Buddha Amoghsiddhi in *Abhaya mudrā.*

Fig. 5.1.d Bronze *stūpa* showing Dhyānī Buddha Amitābha in *Dhyāna mudrā.*

What was the precise reason for overlooking Buddhist tenets is a moot point; but one thing which strikes us conspicuously is the representation in art forms, almost simultaneously, of the concepts of *Caturmukha sūrya, Caturmukha liṅga* and *Sarvatobhadra* of the Brāhmaṇical religion during the Gupta period. Incidently, scholars have tried to draw similarities between the architectural schemes of the *stūpa* and the Śiva-*liṅga.* It is believed that the *stūpa* followed the familiar tripartite division of the *liṅga,* usually consisting of a square base representing the Mother Earth, an octagonal shaft signifying the atmosphere, and a circular top symbolizing the vault of sky. However, one should be wary in accepting the analogy because of the basic difference in the concepts of these two religions.

Reverting to the issue of chronology and provenance, the *stūpa*, though found far away from its place of origin, exhibits certain elements which would help us in this regard. For example, the profile view of the *cakra* set on a pedestal with the hub projecting on either side; the cylindrical pilasters with mouldings of *pūrṇa ghaṭa* at the base; the inverted bell-like capital; and the disposal of the hands and fingers, specially in displaying the gesture of *dharmacakrapravartana*, are some of the characteristic elements suggesting it to be a product of the Gupta period. Even the pedestal of the *stūpa* having a faceted recess in between, compares well with that of its precursor at Chausa, where *Candraprabha* is shown seated on it. Besides, the diaphanous *saṅghāṭī*, the weightless physiognomical proportions, and the effortlessly seated postures of the Buddhas seemingly recall their stylistic affiliation with the classical tradition of Magadha. These images demonstrate an amalgamated imprint of a style which flourished at centres like Nalanda, Rajgir and Bodhgaya. A formal and stylistic comparison of the seated Buddha images from Tetrawan (ancient

Tendaligrāma) and Telhara (both in Patna District) with the present example points in the transparent treatment of the *saṅghāṭī* and the semi-circular spread of the *antarvāsa* over the lotus seat. Incidentally, the narrative element of the 'First Sermon' relegated to the base in the Telhara image is quite similar to the one noticed in the *stūpa* below the seat of Vairocana (Fig. 5.1.b). The lingering of such sensuous body proportions can be noticed in images of later centuries at Nalanda. The Buddha statues, installed in the *deva koṣṭhaka*s at the *gavākṣa*s of a *stūpa* built in the locality of Site No. 3 at Nalanda, are some of the reminiscences of classical Gupta style.

Of all the known Magadha centres of art, Nalanda was the one where the art of casting metal images was patronized most; hence in all likelihood the present *stūpa* could be an out-mould of the Nalanda atelier. The above discussion brings to light not only the earliest but one of the finest portable *stūpa*s in bronze which travelled from a Magadha centre of art to some contemporary monastic destination situated on the eastern frontiers of India.

NOTES AND REFERENCES

1. The author is thankful to Shri Jahar Acharjee for his kind permission to photograph and publish this important find.
2. The earliest epigraphical evidence of the Kuṣana period, engraved on the front side of a pedestal, refers to the installation of the image of Amitābha. It is the first reference of its kind in the Indian context so far known. See S.P. Tiwari, 'Two Kushana Inscriptions from Govindnagar', Year 12 and 25, *Epigraphica Indica*, Vol. XL, Pt. V, pp. 197-200.
3. The excavations at Lalitagiri, District Cuttack, Orissa have brought to light interesting evidence from the circular base of a *stūpa* where a voluminous head of the Buddha was found laid in the centre, perhaps consecrated before filling the core. This could be the first ever reported evidence of its kind which may be considered as one of the archaeological corroborations of the ritualistic installation of the Buddha *Vairocana* inside the *stūpa* (personal observation).
4. Benoytosh Bhattacharya, *The Indian Buddhist Iconography* (Second edition), Calcutta, 1958, p. 48. Even female divinities have been installed in the four cardinal directions of the *stūpa*. See Debala Mitra, *Bronzes from Achutrajpur, Orissa*, Delhi, 1978, Pl. 124, p. 132.
5. Alexander C. Soper, *Literary Evidence for Early Buddhist Art in China*, Ascona, 1959, p. 131.
6. C. Sivaramamurti, 'An Interesting Gupta Chaturmukha of Sūrya', *Bulletin (of the) National Museum*, New Delhi, No. 3., 1972, pls. I to IV, pp. 1-7.
7. T.A. Gopinatha Rao, *Elements of Hindu Iconography* (Second edition), Delhi, 1968, pp. 97-102.
8. P. Pal, *Light of Asia: Buddha Sakyamuni in Asian Art*, Los Angeles Country Museum of Art, 1984, p. 137. However, Jitendra Nath Banerjee prefers to call these three segments as *Brahmabhāga, Viṣṇubhāga* and *Rudrabhāga*. Refer his *The Development of Hindu Iconography*, University of Calcutta, 1956, p. 458.
9. Nihar Ranjan Ray, Khandalavala and Gorakshkar, *Eastern Indian Bronzes*, pt. I, Lalit Kala Akademi, New Delhi, 1986, Pls. 3-4.
10. Fredrick M. Asher, *The Art of Eastern India*, 300-800, Delhi, 1980, Pls. 78 and 79; also refer Susan L. Huntington, The *'Pala Sena' Schools of Sculpture*, Leiden, 1984, Figs. 14 and 15.
11. Archaeological Survey of India, *Annual Report*, 1925-26, Pl. XLIX, Figs. a and b, pp. 103-04.

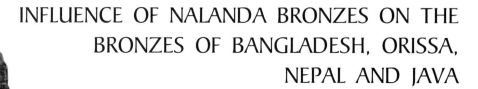

6

INFLUENCE OF NALANDA BRONZES ON THE BRONZES OF BANGLADESH, ORISSA, NEPAL AND JAVA

G.C. Chauley

Bronze is technically known in Indian *Śilpaśāstra* as *Aṣṭadhātu* (an alloy of eight metals), for which N.K. Bhattasali had coined the term octo-alloy. In this compound there are copper, tin, lead, antimony, zinc, iron, gold and silver in varying proportions. Copper was evidently the chief ingredient and the proportions of the last two, gold and silver, are either nil or quite insignificant. Metal images became increasingly popular from about 8th century CE onwards.

The eastern school of the Pālas produced, simultaneously with stone sculptures, remarkable series of bronze images of which the principal centres were Nalanda and Kurkihar. As bronze is a more handy and pliable medium than stone and susceptible to more minute execution and precise definition, it was easy to transport from one place to another by the devotees and pilgrims. Elegance in form and richness in spirtitual expression characterized the bronzes of the Pāla period.

The metal images were cast by the *cire-perdue* or lost wax process, so-called as the subject was first modelled in wax and the model coated with clay, after the wax melted out, the liquid metal was poured into the mould. This was the technique employed in making all images of bronze or brass. The process as described by Shri Bhikhuraj, the owner of an image factory in Nepal, is worth mentioning here. The first stage of the casting is the preparation of the wax model (*Madhūcciṣṭa-Vidhānaṁ*). The object to be cast is first modelled in wax, which is wrapped in a thick coating of soft clay mixed with cowdung applied in two or three layers. When sufficiently dry, a few more coatings of clay mixed with husk are applied over it. When dry again, the wax model is melted by the application of heat, which leaves a vacuum into which the molten amalgam is poured. After the amalgam has set and cooled the clay mould is removed and the figure is chiselled in rough outline. The finishing touch is given later on. This very process is also referred to in the *Viṣṇu Saṁhitā* as quoted by Gopainath Rao. This process would very nicely suit the making of image in solid casting as prevalent in South India and Sri Lanka.

In Nalanda however as appears from the inner core of the damaged image, a sort of non-metallic substance of clay mixed with husk, cowdung in charred form existing in the majority of the images, images were cast in hollow, the inner core being stuffed with non-metallic substances. The colossal copper Buddha from Sultanganj exhibits similar inner stuffing. It appears that the wax model was worked over and around a stump of husk and other combination. For a close parallel in the present-day, mention may be made of the straw core of the clay icons of modern times in Bengal, Orissa and Bihar. The stuff remains within the mould even when the wax is melted. The molten amalgam drips in the crevices between the mould and the stump encasing the latter. The non-metallic substances, like husk in the stump, assumes a charred character, blackish or reddish complexion and sufficient hardness in the process of casting due to high temperature. This technique is known as *cire-perdue* hollow casting.

The Nalanda school seems to have specialized in producing smaller pieces giving scope for detailed work and finish of execution in bronzes. This particular art depends for its success upon metallurgical process and metal casting. The best of the Nalanda bronzes are of the time of Dharmapāla and Devapāla (CE 780 to 892). The lines and soft curves of the figures are pleasing and their expression has an appeal, which justifies the modern enthusiasm for Pāla bronzes.

Images wholly cast in brass or silver are also known from Bengal, though in the later period the bronzes were plated over with a thin coating of gold gilting and inlayed with silver. Nalanda produced a few gold-gilted images of which the image of Buddha and of Avalokiteśvara (Acc. Nos. 00156, 00153) are worth mention.

The bronzes of Kurkihar have also yielded evidence of both inlay and gilt work. The setting of precious stones in the different parts of the images as described in the *Mānasāra*, is exemplified in the bronzes of Nalanda. The existence of sockets in the crowns of some of the images indicates that once jewels or precious stones were set in them. The remains of a broken crown with several empty sockets were found during the excavations. Possibly this crown was set in with jewels or precious stones which are now lost. One bronze image of a seated Buddha reflects two red gems still visible on both sides of halo above the shoulder level. In this way the amount of wealth or labour was spared to make the images rich and beautiful with a view to increase the religious merit of the elegant concerned donor.

Evidences of metal casting are found in the series of ovens on the courtyard in some of the monasteries as a place of casting bronzes.

As already stated above, majority of the bronze images found at Nalanda are of Buddhist divinities, i.e., Buddha, *Bodhisattva*, Tārā, Jambhala, Prajñāpāramitā, Trailokya-vijaya, etc. but Brāhmaṇical deities were not altogether absent. The images of Sūrya, Gaṇeśa, Caṇḍī (Pārvatī), Viṣṇu, Goddess Gaṅgā, Umā Maheśvara are some of the best specimens.

The pedestal and halo of the bronze images of Nalanda are of special interest. They are round, oblong, square, rectangular or of the *Ratha* types. The earliest bronzes are those having the background or *Prabhāvalī* made of thin sheets of wire of metal with floral or vegetal decoration or images cast in complete round without a *prabhāmaṇḍala*. Some of the representative examples belonging to these groups are figures of Avalokiteśvara, Maitreya, Vajrapāṇi, and *Bodhisattvas* in *varada* pose. They belong to the early Pāla workmanship as demonstrated by some of its features like round fleshy face with sharp nose, absence of armlets, plain *ekāvalī* or necklace of beads, proportionate body, etc. The diaphanous drapery or *uttarīya* and *antaravāsaka* have been represented in a stylistic way forming two edges in the shape of a fan which is a copy of the style exhibited on Sultanganj Buddha and also noticed in those existing images of *Bodhisattva* Sāmantabhadra of black stone. They are but the continuation of Gupta style of Sārnāth and Mathurā Buddha.

The diaphanous drapery is shown in the same stylistic way hanging downwards in folds above the ankles and part of it held by the left hand. The stylistic incised parallel lines indicate the folds of drapery, a good synthesis of both the Sārnāth and Mathurā styles.

The discovery of bronze images in Orissa (Achutrajpur hoard), the bronzes of Chittagong and Mainamati and other parts of Bangladesh if studied carefully, one may be confused to term them of Nalanda or Kurkihar bronze but in reality the bronzes found in Bangladesh and Orissa are the products of the region but got influenced by Pāla metal-art skill and tradition of eastern India.

The contributions of Nalanda towards nourishment of contemporary schools of ancient Bengal, Orissa and Java are immense and it may not be ruled out that Nalanda products are used as models for products reported from Sirpur (M.P.), Achutrajpur (Orissa), Pillak in Tripura, and Jewary in Chittagong and other parts of Bangladesh. Nepal and Java images bear close resemblances with those of Nalanda and Kurkihar. This fact demonstrates the existence of a vigorous and independent school having a definite style of its own, which was able to influence the bronze ateliers in greater India and beyond its borders. Some of the bronzes were brought from Java as offering by the pilgrims which are recovered from excavations at Nalanda.

7

FUSION OF NALANDA SCHOOL OF ART IN INDONESIAN SCULPTURES

G.K. Lama

During the lifetime of the Buddha, Nalanda was a prominent centre of religious activity. But it became a famous centre of intellectual discipline from the period of the Imperial Guptas. It was one of the great seats of Buddhist education for nearly seven hundred years between the 5th and 12th centuries CE.

Nalanda has, perhaps, received the highest amount of scholastic attention till date, than any other archaeological sites in India. Scholars like Alexander Cunningham, D. Spooner, John Marshall, H.N. Sastri, B.C. Law, Samuel Beal, R.C. Majumdar, A.S. Altekar, H.D. Sankalia, D.C. Sircar, Amlanand Ghosh and many others have contributed in their own way to reconstruct the history and culture of Nalanda.

What is interesting to note here is that along with its religious and theological activities, Nalanda also developed into a great centre of Buddhist art. This is admitted in an inscription of the time of Yaśovarmadeva. At the present state of our knowledge it is difficult to say if the famous artist Dhīmāna or his illustrious son, Bitpāla were ever associated with Nalanda. There is, however, no doubt that there was definitely a workshop of art at Nalanda where images of gods and goddesses were made and moulded on the advice of expert architects and sculptors. It may even be concluded that the training in visual art was included in regular curriculum of the *Mahāvihāra*. However, I agree with A. Ghosh where in his book *Nalanda* he has written that the Pāla school of art is seen at its best in Nalanda. In fact, the so-called 'Pāla Art' may be called 'Nalanda Art', for its origin was due to a system of religion which flourished at Nalanda. Here I would like to quote Havell's remarks that the university of Nalanda was school of art and crafts. Nalanda has yielded some hundreds of sculptures in stone and bronze. It is almost impossible to have so many sculptures without a regular school of arts and crafts.

In the history of Buddhist art in India, Nalanda occupies a special place. Such was the fame of the school that its influence can be seen in Pan-Asian Buddhist art.[1] The Nalanda school of art emerged as a full-fledged school with the establishment of Pāla rule in Magadha and most of the creative workmanship in stone and bronze falls within the Pāla Age along with remarkable iconographic development. Nalanda during its glorious days extending over four centuries had intimate cultural links with the neighbouring countries like Indonesia. Scholars from this country flocked to the great ancient Nalanda Mahāvihāra to receive instructions at the feet of its great *ācāryas*.

Scholars from Nalanda also went to Indonesia on cultural and religious mission. It might be assumed that along with them the Nalanda school of art travelled to this country and inspired the artistic efforts of this region.[2]

Indonesian art would at once remind us of their ancestry and their closeness with Nalanda school of art. But the point is, one has to trace beyond any doubt, the routes through which the artistic idioms went to Indonesia from Nalanda. The migration of art, to a certain extent, was made possible by the visiting religious teachers specialized in the architecture and sculpture of India. Dharmapāla, a teacher of Nalanda, stayed for a while in Indonesia. Kumāraghoṣa, Vajrabodhi and his disciple Amoghvajra on their way to China halted for some time at Śrīvijaya. It appears that they were mainly responsible for preaching the various aspects of Buddhism there.[3] Scholars believe that ancient Śrīvijaya possibly served as the media through which Buddhist traditions of India penetrated Indonesia.

A. Ghosh thinks that Nalanda played a significant role in transmitting Indian religion and religious art to Indonesia.[4] Yi'jing, the Chinese traveller, was in Śrīvijaya in the second half of the seventh century. He recorded that thousands of monks, scholars and pilgrims were studying Sanskrit texts which were translated into other local languages. In this connection it may be stated that the ports of Tamralipti in Bengal, Palur in Orissa and Bhrigukaccha in Gujrat served as the gateways through which Gupta and Pāla artistic traditions flowed down to Indonesia.

It appears that the artistic trends from Indian mainland were introduced to Indonesia through small-sized bronze and terracotta images, and with the help of portable seals and sealings inscribed with religious creed and images *Mahāyāna-Tantrayāna* iconography and art spread in Indonesia. In this connection mention must be made of a large copper-plate grant of Śrīdevapāladeva[5] in which King Devapāla granted five villages and apparently, built a monastery in Nalanda at the instance of Śailendra king Bālaputradeva for the students hailing from Suvarṇadvīpa. The above references are sufficient to prove how early Indian religions and art spread in Indonesia.

In the paragraph below an attempt is being made to analyze some bronze and stone images of Indonesia and their close association with Nalanda. Standing postures of the Buddha images which are found to be carved on stone in Borobudur are, curiously enough, met with certain standing images of the Buddha in Nalanda. The image of the Buddha in the Leiden Museum, Holland (Acc. No. 1403-2844), also needs a detailed analysis in order to estimate its iconographic and stylistic indebtedness to Indian Buddha on an artistically conceived throne. A circular halo encircles his head. The halo is plain in the middle and its edges all along moulded and decorated with scalloped designs. At the bottom of this halo and almost behind the neck, a few flames still survive which state that the halo was originally surrounded with flames. The enthroned image of the Buddha is placed on a *tri-ratha* pedestal. In front of a central projection at the base there appears a four-spoked wheel which is flanked on either side by the profiles of two deers. On the other side of the throne on which the Buddha is shown seated, a decorative motif has been very carefully and artistically adjusted. The motif includes at its bottom a couchant elephant in profile, a dwarfish *Siṁha-Vyāla*. A knobbed crossbar from the back-rest of the throne projecting to the left has suffered mutilation. From the right-side knobbed projection hangs a narrow and designed strip which is found to be divided into three registers inscribed with a common motif which, however, is difficult to identify.

These elements in their decorative details betray strong Indian affiliation. The wheel between the two deers is a well known Indian symbol and the parallel is taken from the clay seals of the Pāla period.[6] The knobbed crossbar projected on either side of the throne is very commonly found designed on Pāla bronzes at Nalanda (cf. Buddha image in Patna Museum, Acc. No. 4859 and Hārīti image in National Museum, New Delhi, Acc. No. 681712). The *Siṁha-Vyāla* or *Siṁha* standing on a couchant elephant is also noticed in Nalanda bronzes.[7] The flames that encircle the halo of the bronze Buddha were noticed in many Pāla bronzes (cf. Nalanda Buddha in the Patna Museum, Acc. No. 8459).

The impact of the Sārnāth school crossed boundaries of India and was felt in Sumatra and Java. However, this migration of Sārnāth idiom could be made possible through Nalanda in Bihar. When the Sārnāth idiom passed through Nalanda, the idiom received certain Nalanda orientations. As a result of this, certain characteristics of Nalanda sculptures went to Indonesia.

Nalanda, a pre-eminently Buddhist site, played a very vital role as a centre of Pāla sculptures and it not only dispatched religious ambassadors to south-east and far-east but also had spread the divine message of the Buddha through its stone, metal, terracotta and stucco images. Considering the facts noted above, it can be concluded without any doubt that Nalanda played a very important role in the evolution of Indian sculpture in Indonesia.

NOTES AND REFERENCES

1. Debjani Paul, *The Art of Nalanda*, Introduction, p. XVII.
2. G.C. Chauley, *Art and Architecture of Nalanda*, 2002, p. 38.
3. *Ibid.*, *Hindu Civilization in South East Asia*, p. 644, vide Ghosh, 'Indonesia: Past and Present', *Amrit Bazar Patrika*, Puja Annual, p. 231.
4. Vide D.P. Ghosh, *Coomaraswamy and South East Asian Art*, Paper read in Coomaraswamy centenary seminar organized by the Centre of Advance Study, Deptt. of Ancient Indian History and Culture, Calcutta University.
5. *ASOI, AR*, 1920-21, Ed. Sir John Marshall, Calcutta, 1923, p. 27.
6. A.J. Bernett Kempers, 'Hindu Javenese Bronzes', lecture delivered in Indian Society, Jan. 24, 1934.
7. 'I found among the remains of Nalanda something that may be recognized as the immediate models of Central Javanese Art.' Stutter heim; Vide Rama Legenden and Rama reliefs in Indonesia (Munche, 1925) 1, 215. Relation of Nalanda and Śhailendra dynasty in Java has been clearly disclosed by the *Nalanda Charter* of King Devapāla. Bālaputradeva asked for a grant of five villages for the upkeep of an Indonesian monastery to accommodate greater number of Indonesian pilgrims. Vide *MASI*, No. 66, pp. 96ff and see also Hussain, Shahanara, *Everyday Life in the Pala Empire*, Dacca, 1968, p. 68 and see *EI*, XVII, pp. 325-26.

8

NALANDA METAL ICONS SPEAK WHAT NALANDA MAHĀVIHĀRA WAS

S.K. Pathak

INTRODUCTION OF ICONS IN BUDDHISM

Skepticism prevails regarding the introduction of innumerable icons of deities in different manifestations in Buddhism. The first teaching of the Buddha was more ethical with spirit of social altruism. His followers in subsequent days interpreted the Buddha's saying in multiple significance. As a result the unitary structure of the Buddhist organization, *Saṅgha,* faced schism. No less than eighteen groups and subgroups in India came in existence within half a millennium after his demise.

According to records of the Chinese travellers like Xuanzang, several important *nikāyas* (factional groups) had prevailed. The inmates of Nalanda Mahāvihāra were both Hīnayānists and Mahāyānists. Separate enclaves within the extensive campus were established in which each group could maintain its doctrinal specialities from the others along with specified rituals. The *Sthavira nikāya* had been bifurcated as *Vibhajyavādin sthavira* (Theravāda in Pāli), and *Mahāyāna sthavira* to which Xuanzang belonged. Also, *Mahāsaṅghikas*, who invited schism in the Vaiśalī council held in 4th century BCE, had been strong in South India though they were divided in subgroups like *Pūrva Śaila* and *Aparaśaila*. Among the *Sarvāstivadin sthaviras*, who were mentioned as Hināyānists, both *Mūlasarvāstivāda* and *Sarvāstivāda* factions prevailed. The *Mahāsammatīya,* generally named *Sammītīya,* were mentioned with their separate disciplinary code. Above that, the Indian Buddhists followed what the Buddha had allowed to preserve his teachings in one's own speech. As such the vast Buddhist scriptures and subsequent literature were composed in various languages: Prākṛts, Apabhraṁśas, and Sanskrit in its mixed form with Prākṛts and Apabhraṁśas, or in pure Sanskrit according to the Pāṇinian grammar.

However, the recluse adherents to different Buddhist *nikāyas* lead a coporate life with a spirit of integrated co-existence of fourfold discipline. Those aspects were material, academic, spiritual and esoteric expediences. The trade of icon-making could coordinate every aspect of the monastery to disseminate what Nalanda Mahāvihāra was.

The icon, being a sacred image of the introvert mind, used to be the 'means' (*upāya*) for *bhāvanā* towards the withdrawal of the extrovert mind from multi-diversions. The extrovert mind generally wavers from one item to another like a jumping monkey from branch to branch. For concentration of the mind, every recluse was instructed to ponder over quietly in a lonely place, or in a vacant room. Despite that, the functional mind runs here and there to discriminate the phenomenal characteristics. For spiritual awakening and esoteric visualization, icon-making and icon worship had been regarded important means.

Śākyaputra Gautama could forego the birth-based caste divisions but he admitted the psychic stratification under three heads: persons with low intelligence, mediocre quotient and those with sharp intellect. In analogy, the world of the sentient beings is like a water-place to which lotuses belong. Many of the lotuses have blossoms, some are at the water level, yet blossom and the remaining are in the mud in buds. That refers to the process of advancement towards fully blossomed status of the perfect mind.

A painter or sculptor endeavours to represent vision with form and colour. In the case of an esoteric in-vision it manifests within with effulgence in the introvert mind under deep meditation. That becomes sanctified by rituals as the sacred deity for the person concerned to experience bliss. That is the superior state of the introvert mind but not the sublime. Thereafter, the said in-vision manifestation is represented in paintings, drawings and icons. These are made of some material objects like paper, linen, silk for painting, and clay, stone, wood and metal for sacred icons. An icon of a deity is creative and concentrative in manifestation of an in-vision within the introvert mind. In another way the image that effulges within, tends to be the unification of the formlessness with phenomenal forms and colours, as visualized by the concerned person.

DHĀTU-ŚILPA: METAL ICON ART

Among materials used for iconic manifestations of the in-vision experienced by a deep meditation practitioner, metals are precious. Metallurgic technology has a long history that may be traced in India, China, Japan, West Asia and Europe. Metallurgy has been enriched by more than one faculty of scientific knowledge, mathematics with adequate knowledge of measurement, knowledge in use of inorganic chemical materials and the mechanical know-how of metals.

The improvised technology of metal in India may be traced in Kauṭilya's *Arthaśāstra* (c. 321-296 BCE) with ores of gold, silver, copper lead, tin and iron in smelting, refining, alloying with artisan workmanship. The practice of alloying metals may be traced since the use of bronze came in vogue. Copper and tin being composed together bronze was prepared and that was discovered long back in human history. The proportion of the alloy in preparing icons had been followed and that was mentioned most sacred by the use of eight metals (*Aṣṭadhātu mūrti*) like gold, silver, copper, lead, tin, iron, zinc, and brass. Six metalled icons were also composed.

The metal icon-casting in bronze and other metals or materials is to be modelled in moist clay, wax and plaster. Again, clean and smooth moist clay in consistent texture is generally preferred. Clay models sprinkled with water and covered by moist cloth while casting are wrapped between the sessions of the artisan work. Piece mould process may be applied if necessary for decoration of an icon.

The composite multi-metalled elements in an icon is believed to represent various powers and forces attributed to the deity. For instance, *bhagavān* holds six forces and *īshvara* is possessed with eight attributive powers. Besides the composite base metals, the technique of gilding and enamelling of the cast form generally exuberate the quality of the metal product. The Nalanda icon-gilt technique is said to have excelled that of other metal-producing centres as Kanchipuram and Mathurā, etc. The Bangala and the Magadhan metal artisan workmanship had been famous in those days.

ĀKĀRAVIDHI: ICONIC STRUCTURE

Next course of the in-visioned person prompts to perpetuate that which had been visualized as a spark of light within. The *Mañjuśrī mūlakalpa tantra* (chapters 3-5) deal with the scroll-painting procedures of deities. The image becomes translated in form *ākāra*, posture *āsana*, gait and gesticulation *mudrā*. In some cases an efficient practitioner may have the experience in visualizing the spark in multi colours and light vibrations in a *maṇḍala* visualization. That would appear with reference to the *mantra* syllables muttered internally.

Among metal-icons unearthed so far, a few structures are chosen for a brief discussion.

Vajra-paryaṅka-āsana Buddha (19 x 14.1 x 8.9 cm)
Indian Museum, No. 9426/A 24292, Kolkata.

The icon shows the Buddha in seated posture avowed with admantine determination for being the Buddha. That might refer to the account mentioned in the *Lalitavistara Sūtra*. He is said to have touched the Earth with his fingers (*bhūmisparśa mudrā*). His eyes half-opened to overview the spheres, the sphere of desire or *kāmāvacara-loka*, the sphere of form or *rūpāvacara-loka* and above, that of no-form, *arūpāvacara*. The icon represents the Buddha in the robe *cīvara* of mendicant with a compassionate look. The facial expression of the icon represents serenity with compassion.

His lips are firm and eyebrows elongated. The pedestal stands decorated with a blossomed lotus, the symbol of sacredness.

Attention may be invited to the metal-icon (1M no. 9440/A24784 of Kolkata Museum) (size 23.8 x 12.2 x 8.9 cm). The seated image of the Buddha encircled by the sparks of light with beaded borders shows a typical design of Mahāyāna deities produced from Nalanda foundry.

1. The icon is placed on a high pedestal having a blossomed lotus-base as wide as the icon requires.
2. The Buddha in *padmāsana* cross-legged physical posture represents the display of teaching gesticulation *deśanā-mudrā* for turning the wheel of the Truth (*dharmacakra*). That is regarded as the core of the Buddha's Middle Path Doctrine *(Madhyamā pratipadā)*.
3. The icon with a design of radiant sparks around shows the excellence of the supra mundane being, image Fully Awakened (*samyaksambuddha)*.

Comparatively, the image of Kanaka-varṇā Prajñāpāramitā (1M. 9430/A24285 Pāla Gallery c. 10th cent.) may be referred (size 13.4 x 7.8 x 5.9 cm). The oval circumference of the spark of radiance identifies the Mahāyāna deity.

Prajñāpāramitā practice in Mahāyāna is the highest excellence amongst *pāramitā* vows. Obviously, the deity Prajñāpāramitā is regarded as the sublime manifestation of being. The deity is seated in *candrāsana* having a red double-petalled lotus pedestal.

The deity has four hands with (1) rosary *mālā*, (2) *abhayamudrā* for safeguard from hindrance, (3) *Prajñāpāramitā Sūtra*, and (4) blue lotus (*Sādhanamālā* no. 156). She appears in *Brahmavihāra* with a compassionate look by casting the effulgence of *śūnyatā*.

In *Mahāyānic Mantranaya* manifestations the female image of Tārā with two hands (1M no. 9422/A24286 Pāla Gallery c. 9th cent. AD) may be referred (size 18.8 x 7.4 x 4.7 cm). The metal icon stands on a pedestal having a design of a blossomed lotus in the bestowing gesticulation *varadamudrā* of right hand and a lotus with stalk in the left hand. It manifests the pleasant look of the saviour female deity, as the name Tārā suggests. The well proportioned body structured by unique aesthetic excellence speaks about Nalanda's iconic art motifs. The back slab decorated with flowers and sparks of light protects the open space in the structural balance.

Similar tendency may be traced in the Mahāyāna *tantra* image of *tribhaṅga-āsana siddhaikavīra Mañjuśrī* (1M no. 9439/A24294, Pāla Gallery, c. 8th/9th cent. AD) belonging to the Nalanda metal-icon model (size 21.5 x 8.4 x 6.7 x cm). Its aureola flamed with sparking radiance in a bead pattern (typical designs of Nalanda metal-icons).

1.) The image stands on a pedestal covered by blossomed lotus.
2.) The matted hair of the Siddhaikavīra being locked falls on the shoulder despite a high crown on the head. The ornamentation of Mañjuśrī being engaged in strenuous austeries is symbolized by tiger-nail necklace.

MAṆḌALA-VIDHĀNA: MEASURES OF SPHERIC-UNIVERSE AROUND

The external descriptions of the images hold no efficacy in understanding their symbolic significance. *Mahāyāna-mantranaya* is a culmination of spiritual esoterism in which the individual becomes a part of the whole and the whole inculcates within the part. That means a capable invisioner experiences the radiance of the universal effulgence within spheres to which the image affiliates. A new world sphere appears in the vision of the contemplative mind in which the specific rays are visualized. In this respect the radiance of colours refers to the Five Tathāgatas.

Precisely speaking, Mañjuśrī, Tārā, Prajñāpāramitā manifested out of the in-vision of the esoteric practitioners of high capabilities do not belong to the same spheric universe *(maṇḍala)*. The *maṇḍala* is significant in respect to a practitioner with reference to the family of the deity concerned. For instance, the *Garbhadhātu maṇḍala*, the *Vajradhātu maṇḍala*, and the *Guhyasamāja maṇḍala* have separate spherical jurisdictions. These deities hold different *mantra* and *mudrā* applications as relevant to their respective *maṇḍala*s.

The universe is conditional for being a-formed or non-formed. A form may be either physical or *caitasika* because matter and mind in this solar globe is always generated by cause and effect. That refers to the Law of Dependent Origination (*Pratītyasamutpāda*) in respect to each *Dharma* (phenomenon). In other words, the sphere of desire (*kāmāvacara*), that of form (*rūpāvacara*) and the sphere of no-form (*arūpāvacara*) are conditioned by the spiritual purification and respective effectuation. The spherical realm *maṇḍala* may be conditional and beyond (*lokottara*). The latter is experienciable through higher contemplation. That is the status of the *anuttarayoga* in which the relativeness and non-relativeness undergo no distinction. That is otherwise named unification (*Yuganaddha*). In visual art total unification of the psyche with the physical universe is explicit in *Kālacakra maṇḍala*. That is the *Mahāmudrā sādhana* which is also undertaken in the *Guhyasamāja maṇḍala*, the spherical diagram for the *Yogatantra* practice with different emanations.

MULTIPURPOSE SOCIAL ENTERPRISE

The metal-icons of Nalanda foundry had once high demand for its art-value and spiritual negotiations among the Buddhists in India and abroad. Some of them reached South China through the bamboo-road of the Eastern Himalayas and by sea-route as well. Moreover, those metal-icons had interface reference in developing the Buddhist images in South-East Asia. A wider out-turned exchange in the spread of the Indian Buddhist metal-icons in China, Central Asia and in South-East Asia may be traced and that requires further searches on the metal technology what Nalanda had developed since the 4th century CE.

9

MAṆḌALA ELEMENTS IN TANTRIC BUDDHIST ARCHITECTURE IN INDIA, TIBET AND INDONESIA

Adelheid Herrmann-Pfandt

Before it fell to ruins, the medieval monastery of Paharpur in Bangaladesh must have been one of the most spectacular examples of Indian Buddhist temple architecture. The size and symmetry of the enormous cruciform structure, rising in receding terraces to a central temple, and the huge courtyard enclosed by a line of monastic cells without doubt made a deep impression on visitors and pilgrims.

For a long time scholars did not know anything about the architectural affiliation or the ideological context of this temple. The archaeologist K.N. Dikshit stated in his Paharpur book of 1928[1]:

> The type of plan on which the main temple of Paharpur was erected is so far unknown to Indian archaeology nor is its further development on Indian soil traceable. Its cruciform shape with angles of projection between the arms, its 3 raised terraces and complicated scheme of decoration of walls developed styles of temple architecture in India; nor can it be supposed to have evolved from the ancient Buddhist Stūpa as its symmetrical arms constitute an entirely novel development.

In the last decades, the architectural singularity of Paharpur has been relativized. Some more Paharpur type *Mahāvihāras* with cruciform temples were discovered and excavated since the 1960s in India (Antichak) and Bangladesh (Mainamati).[2] Moreover, historians of architecture recognized the cruciform temple as a "consequent result of an architectural evolution",[3] be it in terms of its association with the well-known Hindu-Buddhist *sarvatobhadra* temple type[4] or as part of the development of terrace temples in India.[5]

What actually suggests itself in view of this kind of building even more than the question of its architectural affiliation is its obvious religious symbolism, the idea that such symmetrical and centralized architecture must carry a deep symbolical significance – a significance that was so important for its creators that they had to convert it into the most powerful monumental architecture. My impression when I first encountered the ground plan of Paharpur many years ago was that this structure must have been conceived as a three-dimensional *maṇḍala*, although these temples obviously belong to the same religious movement within Buddhism that also developed the *maṇḍala* in particular. Recently, a few other scholars, among them Adalbert Gail[6] and Geoffrey Samuel,[7] introduced similar thoughts on the meaning of the Paharpur temple-cum-monastery complex as a *maṇḍala* structure.

I shall start with a short description of three extant examples of this architecture (section 1), followed by some considerations about architectural elements in *maṇḍala* symbolism (2) and a tentative interpretation of the Paharpur-type temples as three-dimensional *maṇḍala* (3). By comparing these with some well-known *maṇḍala* temples in Tibet and Indonesia (4), I will try to answer the question which *maṇḍala* in particular might be represented by the Paharpur-type monasteries (5).

Since the enclosing wall with the monks' cells will play an important part in my argument, I am confining myself to three Paharpur-type temple complexes that possess this feature, i.e., Paharpur, Antichak and Salban Vihāra in Mainamati. Three more monasteries in Mainamati, viz., Ananda Vihāra, Bhoja Vihāra, and Rānir Bungalow, are mentioned. This importance of the monks' cells is also the reason why I use the term 'monastery' instead of just 'temple', for those building complexes.

1. Description of Paharpur-type Monasteries

Paharpur (Somapura): Local inscriptions tell us that the monastery ruins of Paharpur are those of ancient Somapura,[8] one of the major monastic universities of medieval Indian Buddhism. According to different traditions, it was founded around CE 800 by the Pāla king Dharmapāla (ca. 770-810) or else by his son Devapāla (ca. 810-850,[9] destroyed around 1200 and excavated in 1923-34.[10] Famous tantric Buddhist teachers worked here. According to a Tibetan source, it was on the cemetery of Somapura that the *mahāsiddha* Tilopā (late 10th/early 11th century CE) had his famous encounter with a Śākina in the form of an ugly old woman who initiated him into the *maṇḍala* of Cakreśvara.[11] According to *mahāsiddha* legends, Somapura was the home monastery of the *mahāsiddhas* Kaṇhapā and Virūpā.[12] The latter was thrown out of Somapura because, having become a tantric, he started eating meat.

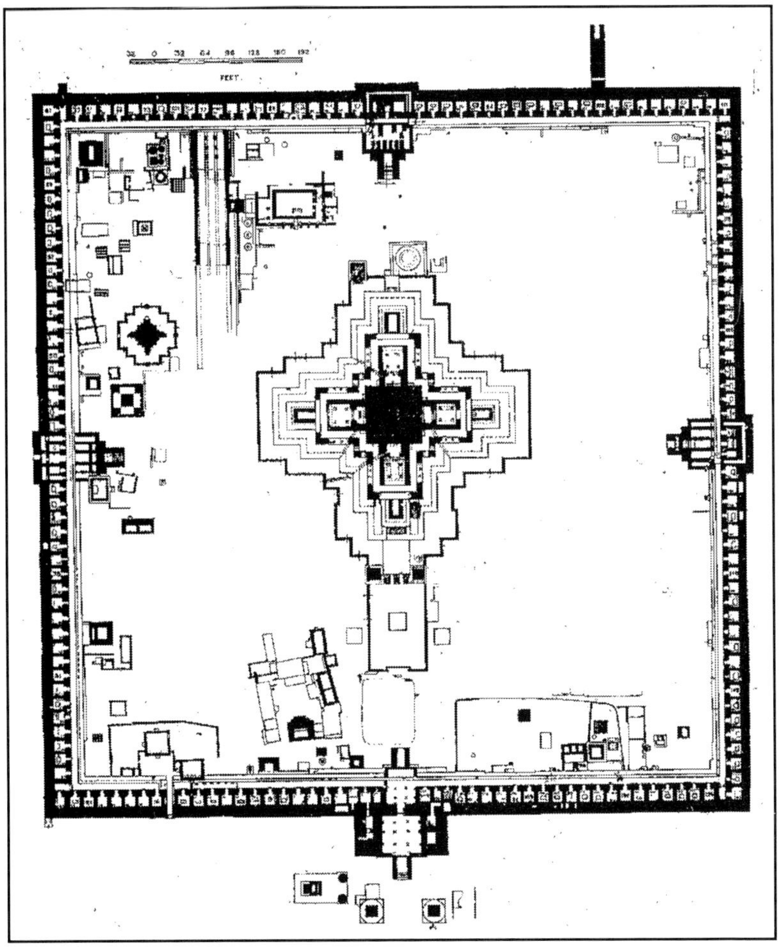

Fig. 9.1. Paharpur, Somapura Mahāvihāra (from Dikshit, Excavations, Plate 1).

The Paharpur monastic complex[13] consists of three main elements (Fig. 9.1):

1. An enormous *cruciform structure* of 111. 5 m N-S by 96 m E-W erected in the centre[14] of

2. A huge *courtyard* 281 m by 280 m, enclosed by
3. A massive *rectangular wall* with a row of 177 monks' cells opening to a verandah.

The cruciform temple was raised on two receding terraces with circumambulatory paths. The arms of the cross were formed by four large shrine chambers at the level of the second terrace with large ante-chambers, opening to the four cardinal directions. Buddha statues were housed in the shrine chambers. The top of the hollow but inaccessible central structure was probably crowned by a central temple chamber.[15]

> There are clear traces of a verandah, 11 ft. broad, at a height of 28 ft. from the level of the ante-chambers to which access was provided by the stairway in the southem ante-chamber. The main place of worship or cella must have been at the top as we find in some of the Burmese Pagodas. The great height at which the main sanctuary stood must have made this monument a prominent landmark in the country around, and spread its fame far and wide, but in the days of its decline its prominent situation must have also made the shrine the main target for the enemy and the vandal.

On the basement wall of the cruciform temple, 63 stone bas-reliefs are distributed (most on the southern and rather few on the northern walls) and above these there are two rows of terracotta plaques. Another two rows of plaques decorate the inner wall of the circumambulatory path on the first terrace; although many plaques are lost, 2800 have survived, including those scattered around somewhere in the area. Surprisingly, of all the bas-reliefs and terracotta plaques only one (a *Padamapāṇi* stone relief on the southem wall) has a definitely Buddhist subject; all others display Hindu motives or mundane scenes, animals and so on.

The main entrance to the courtyard is in the middle of the northern wall. According to Dikshit,[16] as many as 92 of the 177 monks, cells round the courtyard,

> contain ornamental pedestals occupying the central position as one would enter the cells from the verandah. The presence of such a large number of pedestals in rooms, which must have undoubtedly something to do with worship or ceremonials, is certainly not in accord with their character as living accomodation for the monks attached to this *Vihāra*, such elaborate niches and pedestals do not occur in the monasteries of Nalanda and Sārnāth and the purpose of constructing so many places of worship instead of a few private chapels remains obscure.

It is possible that the pedestals have been installed later, changing dwelling-places of monks into shrine-rooms.

The most remarkable peculiarity of this form of *vihāra* architecture is the fact that the cells obviously form an integral part of the holy space occupied by the whole complex of temple, courtyard and wall. This means that the *vihāra*, and maybe the monks themselves as well, must have been part of the symbolism that formed the basis of the whole complex – they were part of the *maṇḍala*.

Antichak (Vikramaśilā): The nearly contemporaneous temple and monastery of Antichak[17] is most probably identical with the famous medieval Tantric centre Vikramaśīlā. It was built by King Dharmapāla around CE 800,[18] destroyed 400 years later, and excavated in the years 1960-1969 and 1972-82.[19] Many well-known scholars taught here, among them Nāropā, Abhayākaragupta and Vairocanarakṣita. Atīśa (Dīpaṅkaraśrījñāna), one of the main actors in the late propagation of Buddhism in Tibet, was dwelling as a teacher in Vikramaśilā when Tibetan messengers came in 1040 to invite him to Tibet[20] (Fig. 9.2).

The cruciform temple in the middle of the courtyad is 90 by 90 m,[21] there are two receding terraces with circumambulatory paths, and on the level of the second terrace one reaches the four cult chambers with ante-chambers. The cult chambers seem to have housed colossal Buddha images.[22] Like in Paharpur, the central shaft of the temple is not accessible, but has probably carried a fifth cult chamber on its top.

The courtyard is surrounded by a square wall of 330 by 330 m with 208 monks' cells opening to a verandah, 42 on each wall. From every fifth cell, another cell is projecting in the outside direction through the outer enclosure wall. The projecting cells are partly circular and partly rectangular, and their function is not clear. Additionally some undergound cells have been discovered. The main entrance to the courtyard is, again, in the middle of the northern wall.

Salban Vihāra, Mainamati: The monastery Salban Vihāra[23] or, after its founder's name, Bhavadeva Mahāvihāra, belongs to an extensive group of Buddhist buildings near Mainamati (Chittagong division, Bangladesh) hitherto only partly excavated. It was built under King Bhavadeva between CE 770 and 790[24] and excavated from 1955 onwards (Fig. 9.3).

Salban Vihāra is about half the size of Paharpur and Antichak. The wall with the monastery is 167. 64 m square, containing 115 cells, and the cruciform temple itself may have been 51-52 m square, part of it being destroyed when it was built over several times by oblong buildings. However, it seems to be established that the cruciform temple belongs to the same archaeological layer as the square monastery.[25]

Rows of terracotta plaques were found at the basement walls like in Paharpur and Antichak, but whether the temple had receding terraces and circumambulatory paths can only be guessed

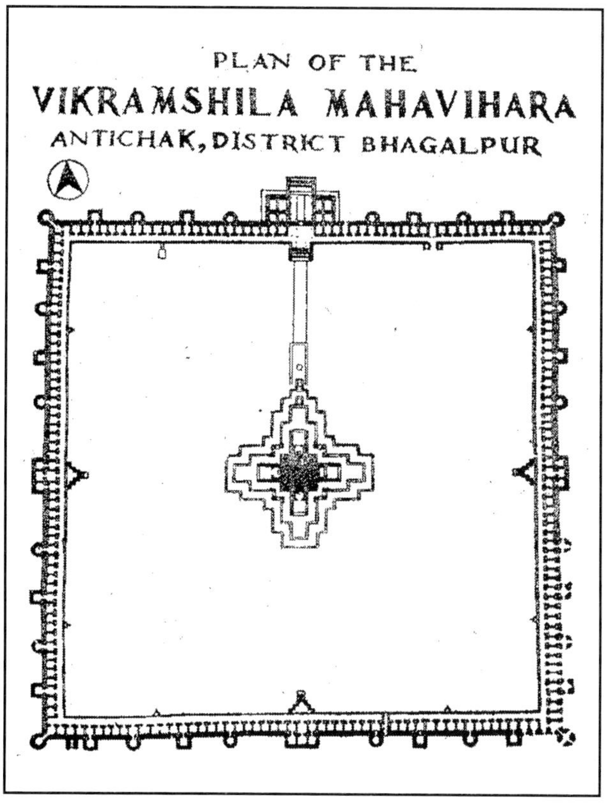

Fig. 9.2. Antichak, Vikramaśilā Mahāvihāra (from Saran, Vikramaśilā University, Pl. 1).

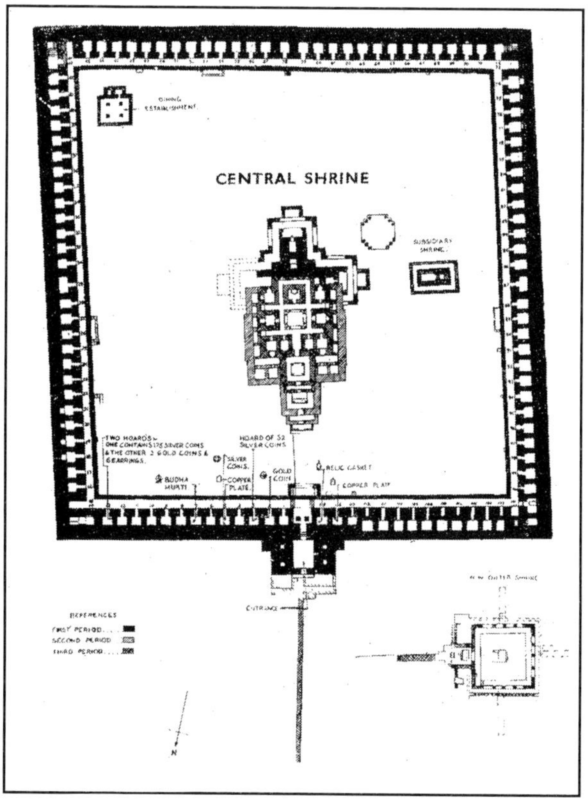

Fig. 9.3. Mainamati, Salban Vihāra Bhavadeva Mahāvihāra (from Imam, Mainamati, Plate 2.1).

looking at the damages the building has suffered.[26] Cult chambers can be identified in the southern and western arms of the cross only. The main entrance is, again, in the middle of the north wall.

So far Mainamati is the only place known in the whole of Bengal that possesses more than just one Paharpur-type monastery: three more of them displaying the same structure have been found at Ananda Vihāra,[27] Bhoja Vihāra,[28] and Mainamati Rānir Bungalow.[29] There seems to be another type of cruciform temples built without the quadrangle of monastic cells, e.g., Rupban Mura.[30]

This overview of some Paharpur-type monasteries shows their very uniform structure, the most important common elements being the fourfold symmetry of the whole ensemble, the cruciform temple with four, maybe five, cult chambers, the monastic quadrangle, the terracotta plaques with non-Buddhist motives, and the courtyard entrance in the north.

2. Architectural Elements in the *Maṇḍala*

Undeniably *maṇḍala*s are of central importance in Tantric Buddhism. *Maṇḍala* meditation means to visualize not only one deity, but to create a whole world – the diamond world of an enlightened being. The *maṇḍala* represents symbolically the outer cosmos seen as sacred outer space and the inner cosmos of the human mind and body seen as sacred inner space. It stands for the mystical identity of macrocosm and microcosm which it makes accessible to the practitioner in meditation. In all, the *maṇḍala* is a highly spiritual symbol. However, the iconographical frame it takes when it is painted or sculptured even though in an idealized form – extremely common or even trivial – it is simply a fourfold symmetrical building in a courtyard, fenced in by a symmetrical (quadrangular or circular) enclosure. And it is in this way the *maṇḍala* is to be visualized by the meditator.

Architectural elements of the *maṇḍala*: Enclosure and Palace. The outer enclosure of the *maṇḍala* is normally formed as a circle or square forming the border of the sacred space within the *maṇḍala* (Fig. 9.4). Therefore, it contains some elements emphasizing its border quality, e.g., a circle of flames and sometimes also a circle of eight cemeteries in which the adept has to overcome fear and death in order to be admitted to the centre.

In the centre of the *maṇḍala* courtyard there is a pure place that is fourfold symmetrical and endowed with four entrances in the four directions. The palace represents the whole cosmos, and its centre is regarded to be the axis of the world. Therefore the *maṇḍala* palace is the place where the deities manifest, the main deity of the *maṇḍala* residing at the centre like a king or a queen, the accompanying deities surrounding the main deity. The most simple ensemble of *maṇḍala* deities consists of five: the main deity or main Buddha dwells in the centre, the other four in the four cardinal points.

Two-dimensional representations of the *maṇḍala*: The most common way of creating visible *maṇḍala* reproductions is by painting. However, every *maṇḍala* painting must remain inadequate in a way, since it has to represent a three-dimensional object in but two dimensions. Nepalese and Tibetan *maṇḍala* painters do not solve this problem by using the central perspective like Western painters; instead, they show certain elements as seen from above, others from the side. Thus, the layout of the painted *maṇḍala*[31] as a whole is, as Martin Brauen has observed, designed as a mixture of elements shown in the ground plan perspective (*Grundriss-sicht*, i.e., from above) and other elements designed in the elevation perspective (*Aufriss-sicht*, i.e., from the side). The perspective chosen for each part of the *maṇḍala* depends on how the respective object is best discernible. For recognizing a *maṇḍala* painting as the image of a building, we have to 'read' it properly.

The main feature from which to derive the architectural character of the *maṇḍala* is the use of the elevation perspective for the portals, showing them as architectural elements (Fig. 9.4). Otherwise, one would see only a rooftop from above, without knowing whether a portal or any other building is to be imagined under the roof (Fig. 9.5). Because of this the deities of the *maṇḍala* paintings are done in the elevation perspective, too. They are always shown from the front.

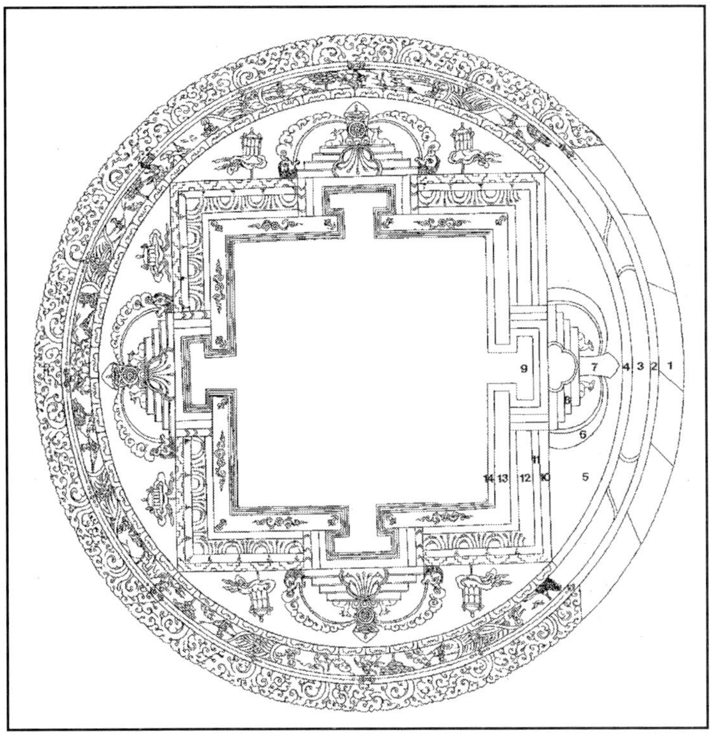

Fig. 9.4. Architectural structure of a *maṇḍala*. Ground plan perspective: 1. Circle of flames, 2. *Vajra* tent, 3. Eight cemeteries, 4. Circle of lotus flower leaves, 5. Outer court with standards, 6. Spokes of the double *vajra* forming the basis of the palace. Elevation perspective, 7. Entrance with *Dharma* wheel, 8. Four canopies on columns, 9. Palace entrance with guardian deity, 10. Ornament roof, 11. Brick palace wall, 12. Garlands ornamenting the wall, 13. Gallery, 14. Palace wall, shining in rainbow colours. The innermost part of the palace with the deity (missing) to emphasize the architectural parts of the *maṇḍala*.

In any case, 'reading' the two-dimensional *maṇḍala* painting as a mixture of ground plan and elevation perspectives makes it possible to reconstruct a three-dimensional palace from any two-dimensional *maṇḍala* painting.[32]

Three-dimensional *maṇḍalas*: Three-dimensional representations of *maṇḍalas*, much smaller than real buildings, are also quite common, e.g., in Nepal,[33] Ladakh,[34] Tibet,[35] or China,[36] any three-dimensional reproduction, be it a model or a real building, is of course nearer to the visualized reality of the *maṇḍala*.

It would be more than plausible to expect that tantrics who created immaterial *maṇḍala* architecture for meditation should create real *maṇḍala* architecture as well.

3. The Paharpur-type Monastery as an Architectural *Maṇḍala*

A comparison shows that the indispensable features of a *maṇḍala* are present in any Paharpur-type temple complex as well: the fourfold symmetrical palace in the middle, the courtyard and the enclosure. The fact that the enclosure is rectangular in the Paharpur-type monastery and circular in most *maṇḍalas* is one of the obvious differences.

The central building of Paharpur-type monasteries seems to fit the requirements of a *maṇḍala* palace with four cult chambers in the four cardinal directions. Probably four deities or Buddhas stayed there as part of a group of five with the main deity residing on top of the central shaft of the building in an elevated position.[37]

4. Some Well-known Architectural *Maṇḍalas* in Buddhism

1. Odantapuri. The oldest known *maṇḍala* building of India is no longer extant, but we find it described in Tibetan literature.[38] It is the famous early Pāla monastery Odantapuri created shortly after CE 750.[39] From the sources we know that Odantapuri was a three-dimensional representation of the *maṇḍala*-like Buddhist world model described in the *Abhidharmakoṣa* (4th century CE). Odantapuri was completely destroyed during the Turk invasion of India around CE 1200,[40] but since the Tibetan moastery bSam-yas is said to have been modelled after it, bSam-yas can give us an idea of how Odantapuri looked like before its destruction. Whether Odantapuri's enclosure wall was circular like the one of bSam-yas, cannot be verified at present.

Fig. 9.5. Mongolian monastery model as seen from above. The buildings are concealed under the roofs (from Brauex, *Maṇḍala*, 49 Abb. 26).

2. bSam-yas: Known as the Tibetan replica of Odantapuri,[41] bSam-yas (south-west of Lhasa)[42] is the first Tibetan monastery consecrated in CE 775.[43] The quadrangular main temple in the centre representing Mount Meru[44] is surrounded by four side temples in the four main directions standing for the four side continents.[45] The most striking feature is the circular enclosure of the whole temple complex that can be seen best from the air.

3. Chaõçi Sewu: The Chaõçi Sewu (Temple of the Thousand[46]) in Central Java, built at the end of the 8th century CE, was identified by F.D.K. Bosch[47] as a *vajradhātu-maṇḍala* (*maṇḍala* of the *vajra* world)[48] drawn from the *Sarvatathāgata-tattvasaṅgraha-sūtra* (ca. 700 CE), the root text of the *yogatantra* class of esoteric Buddhism (Fig. 9.6).

The centre of the *vajradhātu-maṇḍala* is formed by the five Buddhas, Vairocana, Akṣobhya, Ratnasambhava, Amitābha and Amoghasiddhi, Vairocana having four accompanying goddesses, the other four Buddhas and four *Bodhisattvas* each. Bronze statues of these deities together with other accompanying deities according to the STTS had, before being removed by robbers, their places in the five cult chambers of the Chaõçi Sewu. Another 960 deities representing the 1000 Buddhas[49] of the *vajradhātu-maṇḍala* were once dwelling in groups of four in 240 side chapels which are situated in four rows round the central temple.[50]

4. Chaõçi Borobudur: Another three-dimensional *vajradhātu-maṇḍala* is included in the famous Borobudur, erected before CE 824 in Central Java.[51] Here the *maṇḍala* elements are integrated in a multifunctional building that includes aspects of Hīnāyana (relief sculptures of the life story of Buddha Śākyamuni) and Mahāyāna (life story of Prince Sudhāna from the *Gaṇḍavyūha sūtra*) as well.[52] The five Buddhas of the *maṇḍala* are present in Borobudur just as the thousand Buddhas.[53]

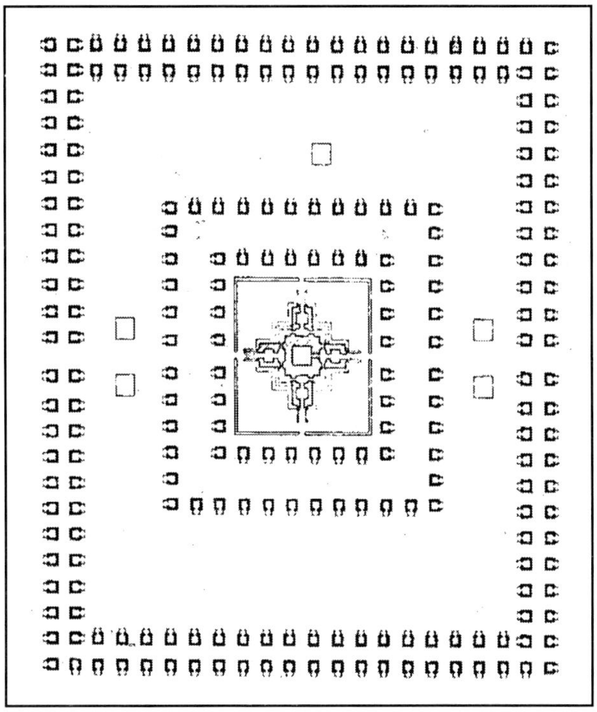

Fig. 9.6. Chaõçi Sewu, Central Java, ground plan (from Soekmono).

5. Chaõçi Mendut: Chaõçi Mendut, erected between CE 782 and 812, was identified by Lokesh Chandra[54] as a three-dimensional *garbhadhātu-maṇḍala* (*maṇḍala* of the Womb World) drawn from the *Mahāvairocana-sūtra*, the main text of the *caryātantra* class of esoteric Buddhism.

The author succeeded in identifying the deity images or dwelling places inside the cella and outside on the temple walls with the main deities of the *garbhadhātu-maṇḍala*. In particular, Vairocana's threefold role as central deity of the triad with Avalokiteśvara and Vajrapāṇi, as the main Buddha of the five Buddhas and as the head of a group of eight *Bodhisattva*s is typical for the *garbhadhātu-maṇḍala* and can be identified with the deity in the Chaõçi Mendut.[55] Moreover Lokesh Chandra has observed a historial connection between the Chaõçi Mendut as a *garbhadhātu-maṇḍala* and the Chaõçi Borobudur, situated less than 3000 m apart[56] as a *vajradhātu-maṇḍala*. Both have been erected at the same time (before 824 CE) with the aim to keep away some imminent danger from the declining Javanese Śailendra monarchy.[57]

6. Tholing: Temple of Yeśes 'od. One of the most impressive *maṇḍala* temples of Tibet was – until its destruction by the Chinese occupation forces in the 20th century[58] – the Temple of Yeśes 'od in Tholing, West Tibet, founded by Rin chen bzaṅ po (ca. 985-989 CE[59]). According to Giuseppe Tucci's notes of his visit in 1933,[60] it was a three-dimensional *vajradhātu-maṇḍala* with the five Buddhas in a cruciform structure of five cult chambers in the middle, surrounded by 20 side-chapels that must have housed the accompanying *Bodhisattva*s and other deities.

7. Tabo: A very different way of representing the *vajradhātu-maṇḍala* can be seen in the Tibetan Buddhist Tabo monastery[61] in Spiti/North India (also founded by Rin chen bzaṅ po in CE 996[62]). The *maṇḍala* design is easily discernible in the non-symmetrical ground plan, but is present in sculptures of each of the deities of the *vajradhātu-maṇḍala* positioned in the *gtsug lag khaṅ*, the building at the exact centre of the whole ensemble.[63] Astonishing is the fact that in Tabo, the *vajradhātu-maṇḍala* is combined with the same Hīnayāna and Mahāyāna motives as in Borobudur: the life of the Buddha and the Sudhāna story from the *Gaṇḍavyūha-sūtra*.[64]

8. Gyantse: More *maṇḍala*-like and bearing some similarities to the equally multifunctional Borobudur is the *stūpa* of Gyantse[65] in southern Central Tibet (founded CE 1418) that in many cult chambers on eight levels represents the whole pantheon of Tibetan Buddhism of the time. It also contains a *vajradhātu-maṇḍala*, albeit in a concealed and subordiate form: On the third floor, there are chambers with the four Buddhas of the four cardinal directions with their accompanying *Bodhisattva*s according to the STTS.[66] Two storeyes higher, on the fifth floor, we find a chamber with Vairocana, the fifth and central Buddha, together with some frescoes of the whole *vajradhātu-maṇḍala*. [67] There is no doubt that these five deities together with their attendants represent an architectural *maṇḍala* pattern in the *maṇḍala*. The residence of Vairocana, the main deity of the

vajradhātu-maṇḍala, on the fifth floor is not the most prominent place of the *stūpa*. There are three higher storeyes containing *anuttarayoga-tantra* deities, culminating in the *ādibuddha* of the *Kālacakra-tantra* on top of the building.[68]

Historical context: From these examples we can draw some information useful for recognizing the historical context of our Paharpur-type monasteries. Apart from Odantapuri and its Tibetan replica bSam-yas, both are based on the non-Tantric *Abhidharmakoṣa*. The buildings mentioned above are conceived as Tantric *maṇḍala*, viz., either the *garbhadhātu-* (one case) or the *vajradhātu-maṇḍala* (five cases).

The *maṇḍala* of the *garbhadhātu* and *vajradhātu* came into being before or around CE 700 and flourished in India between the 8th and 10th centuries, the *garbhadhātu-maṇḍala* representing a slightly earlier stage of development and being by far the less prominent of the two in India. Their textual sources, i.e., the *Mahāvairocana-sūtra* and the *Sarvatathāgata-tattvasṅgraha-sūtra (STTS)*, were exported to China via Java[69] by Vajrabodhi and Amoghavajra in 717 and subsequently translated.

It was probably in China that two important changes happened: Firstly, the Indian *vajradhātu-maṇḍala* was, perhaps under Taoist influence,[70] transformed into a rather complex ninefold *maṇḍala* in the central part of which the original Indian *vajradhātu-maṇḍala* survives. Secondly, this ninefold *vajradhātu-maṇḍala* was connected with the *garbhadhātu-maṇḍala* to form a pair, the "*maṇḍalas* of the two worlds", that from now on dominated East Asian esoteric Buddhism[71] and extended their influence as far as Indonesia.

For in Borobudur and Chaõçi Mendut in Indonesia were built together as pair of *vajradhātu-* and *garbhadhātu-maṇḍala*, the probability is very high that the inspiration for erecting these did not or not only came from India[72] but from China, either with Indian teachers like Amoghavajra who after having taught in China for several years travelled back to India via Java (714-9)[73] or with Javanese disciples of Chinese teachers bringing Chinese esoteric Buddhism to their country.[74]

In India and Tibet, on the other hand, quite a different development took place. *Caryātantra* and *Yogatantra* were gradually superceded by the *Anuttarayoga-tantra* class from the 9th century onwards. At the end of the 10th century, when the Tholing and Tabo monasteries were built by Rin chen bzaṅ po before the advent of Atīśa, this development had not yet been victorious everywhere in the Indo-Tibetan area. Therefore, Tabo and the Ye Śes'od temple of Tholing are still dominated by *vajradhātu-maṇḍala* deities, although, as can be seen on the frescoes, e.g., in Tholing,[75] *Anuttarayoga-tantra* deities had already begun to take over. But in the 15th century, when Gyantse was built, the *Anuttarayoga tantra* deities kept the dominating position in the divine hierarchy, and the *vajradhātu-maṇḍala* was reduced to the second place in the Gyantse pantheon. The *garbhadhātu-maṇḍala* is absent from the Gyantse pantheon[76] as it is obviously also from other Tibetan pre-*Anuttarayoga-tantra* sites.

These short notes show that the Paharpur-type monasteries in North-East India and Bangladesh were built in a time that preceded the *Anuttarayoga-tantras* and that was dominated in India and Tibet by the *vajradhātu-maṇḍala* alone, while in China, Japan and Indonesia it was in combination with the *garbhadhātu-maṇḍala* that the *vajradhātu-maṇḍala* was most influential.

5. Which *Maṇḍala*?

With which *maṇḍala* can we identify the Paharpur-type monasteries? In view of the chronological information given above, the *vajradhātu-maṇḍala* is definitely the most probable candidate. In the following passage, the particular elements of the *vajradhātu-maṇḍala* are compared to the corresponding elements of the Paharpur-type monastery.

Fig. 9.7. Central *maṇḍala* of the ninefold *vajradhātu-maṇḍala* (http: durgaegroupwarelogin.phpfrom Snodgrass, *Maṇḍalas*, 577, Fig. 299).

1. The five Buddhas and their retinue: Firstly, the cruciform central group of the *vajradhātu-maṇḍala* coincides with the cruciform ground plan of Paharpur-type temples. The four cult chambers (plus a possible additional central chamber) are ideal places for the five Buddhas of the inner circle of the *vajradhātu-maṇḍala*, and we can presume that Vairocana had his four companion goddesses and the other four Buddhas with their companion *Bodhisattvas*.

2. The twelve goddesses: For the twelve attendant goddesses of the *vajradhātu-maṇḍala* there were certainly lots of places where they could have been positioned in the temple, e.g., outside in the corners between the four arms of the cross. If the layout of the *maṇḍala* in the monastery was, perhaps, similar to Fig. 9.7, this could have meant that four of the twelve goddesses were placed in the outside corners of the cruciform temple and the remaining eight between the 1000 Buddhas. This means that (for example) in Paharpur they would have been in the corners and the middle parts of the four walls between the monks' cells. But it is equally possible that all twelve goddesses were placed in or at the cruciform temple.

3. The 1000 Buddhas: The five *maṇḍala* Buddhas and their retinue are fenced in by an assembly of the 1000 Buddhas[77] of the *bhadrakalpa*. The tradition of the 1000 Buddhas originated in the first part of the *Sarvatathāgata-tattvasaṅgraha-sūtra*.[78] They are displayed regularly in the Japanese *vajradhātu-maṇḍala* paintings, but also in the *maṇḍala* temple of Central Java, especially the Chaōçi Sewu (Fig. 9.5) that is even named after the 1000 Buddhas.[79] Tibetan *vajradhātu-maṇḍala* does occasionally display the 1000 Buddhas,[80] thereby showing that this tradition is not a peculiarity of East Asia, but was present in India.

If we compare the ground plans of Chaōçi Sewu and Paharpur with a Japanese *vajradhātu-maṇḍala* drawing (Fig. 9.8), we recognize that in Paharpur the monks' cells are at the same place where Chaōçi Sewu and *vajradhātu-maṇḍala* drawing display their 1000 Buddhas.

I am convinced that the monks' cells in the outer walls of Paharpur-type monasteries are a symbolic equivalent to the thousand Buddhas of the *vajradhātu-maṇḍala*, more so as the monks' cabins were at least partly used as shrine rooms.

This inclusion of the monks' cells in the architectural plan of a Buddhist *maṇḍala* temple seems to me the only possibility to intergrate all *maṇḍala*-like elements of the Paharpur-type monastery ground plans into the interpretation of these temple complexes as *maṇḍala*. Without this, the holy circle of the *maṇḍala* would be, so to say, not cast sufficiently, because the border between the sacred and the profane, the inner and outer spheres, would not be drawn.

However, this interpretation of the role of monks seems to have been realized only in the Indian *maṇḍala* temples like Paharpur, Antichak and Mainamati. It was not even transferred to

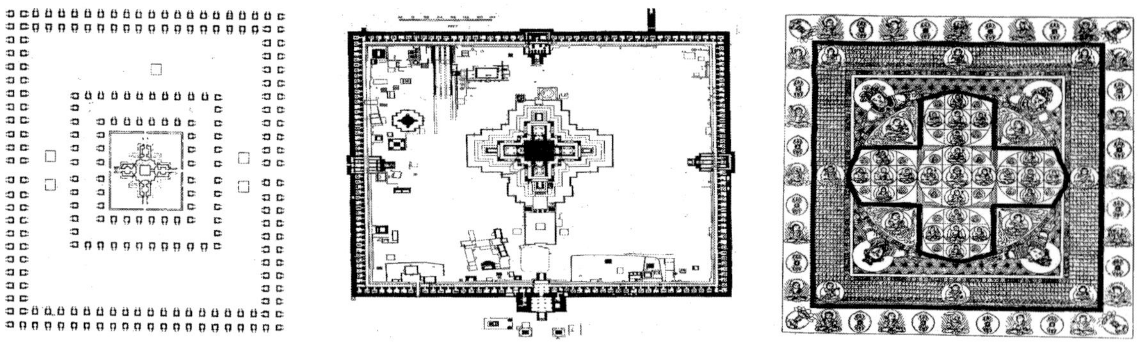

Fig. 9.8. Comparing Chaõçi Sewu, Paharpur and *vajradhātu-maṇḍala*.

the Chaõçi Sewu which is the only temple outside of India with that degree of similarity to Paharpur.[81]

4. The deities of the 'section outside the *vajras*': Another detail to be explained is the fact that the outer walls of the cruciform structures are decorated with deities and everyday motives which are, with the exception of Padmampāṇi in Paharpur, more Hindu or secular than Buddhist. This has led several scholars to believe that temples with so much non-Buddhist decoration could not be really Buddhist.

The first scholar to have analyzed and disproved this argument with regard to Paharpur monastery was Adalbert Gail. Taking some examples of the *dharmadhātu-maṇḍala* prevalent in the Kathmandu valley and the temple no. 2 of Nalanda, Gail has shown that the use of Hindu iconography at the outside of temples or *maṇḍalas* is a more or less 'normal' feature of Buddhist *maṇḍalas* and *maṇḍalaic* temples.[82] The use of Hindu deities and secular scenes for the outer area of the *maṇḍala* can therefore "plausibly be interpreted in terms of a *maṇḍalaic* structure where Hindu deities form part of the outermost ring".[83]

There is, however, no need to leave the sphere of the *vajradhātu-maṇḍala* for an explanation of the non-Buddhist images, because we find here a smaller but very similar outer section as well.[84] The so-called 'section outside the *vajras*', the outermost layer of the central *maṇḍala* just beyond the 1000 Buddhas, is the abode of 20 Hindu deities, among them Nārāyaṇa, Kumāra, Brahmā, Śakra, Agni, Yama and four elephant-headed form of Gaṇeśa. According to Amoghavajra these are protectors of Buddhism having been defeated and converted by the *Bodhisattva* Vajrapāṇi.[85]

One difference between the temple complex and the *maṇḍala*, however, must be noted. To be at the same place as in the Japanese *maṇḍala*, the sculptures and terracotta plaques in Paharpur, Antichak and Mainamati should have been placed on the outside of the enclosure wall, and not, as it really was the case, on the wall of the cruciform structure, i.e., within the ring of the 1000 Buddhas. But in view of the many correspondences between the *vajradhātu-maṇḍala* and the Paharpur-type monastery, this seems to be a minor deviation from the *maṇḍala* layout.

The Paharpur Padmapāṇi: Of all deity images on the outer walls of Paharpur temple it is the one and only Buddhist deity that poses a problem, because it cannot be explained by relating it to the *vajradhātu-maṇḍala*: the *Bodhisattva* Padmapāṇi residing on the outer wall in the south. According to the research by Geri Malandra, there is one *maṇḍala* in Ellora in which Avalokiteśvara, being one of the eight *Bodhisattvas* accompanying the Buddha, is associated with the south of the *maṇḍala*. The text apparently used for this *maṇḍala* is the *Āryamahābodhisattva-maṇḍala-sūtra*.[86] As far as I can see, this is the only contemporary source which associates Avalokiteśvara with the south. It is uncertain whether it had an influence on Paharpur.

5. The quadrangular form of the monasteries: There is a last argument in favour of the identification of Paharpur monasteries as *vajradhātu-maṇḍala*: their quadrangular form. As can be drawn from Fig. 9.7, the *vajradhātu-maṇḍala* is always quadrangular. The circular enclosure shown on most Tibetan *vajradhātu-maṇḍala* images, e.g., on Alchi murals, was definitely a later addition in order to assimilate the quadrangular *maṇḍala* to the structure of other Tibetan *maṇḍalas*.

NOTES AND REFERENCES

1. K.N. Dikshit, *Excavations at Paharpur*.
2. See below.
3. Reitz, 'The cruciform temple type.'
4. Reitz, 'Cruciform temple.' The connection of the Paharpur temple with the *sarvatobhadra* temple was already suggested in 1943. See Chakrabarti, *Ancient Bangladesh*, p. 115, quoted after Samuel, 'Technologies', p. 41.
5. Franz, *Von Gandhara bis Pagan*, p. 91.
6. Gail, '*Maṇḍalaic* Structure'.
7. Geoffrey Samuel, 'Technologies'.
8. Dikshit, *op. cit.*, p. 3 *et passim* (see inde); Dutt, *Buddhist Monks*, 374; Bhattacharaya, *Essays*, p. 434, quoted after Samuel, 'Technologies', p. 40.
9. Dutt, *Buddhist Monks*, pp. 354; 374ff; Dikshit, *op. cit.*, p. 3ff. If Somapura did serve as a model for the Chaoçi Sewu in Central Java (see below, section 4), its erection date after CE 800 should be late.
10. Dikshit, *op. cit.*, p. 2ff.
11. According to the *Padma dkar po*, cf. Hoffmann, *Religionen*, p. 138.
12. Cf. Abhayakara, *Caturavimśatisiddha-pravṛtti*, trans. Robinson, *Buddha's Lions*, pp. 27ff and 81ff.
13. For the following description see Dikshit, *op. cit.*, pp. 7-17 and 18-36.
14. Actually, there is a slight shift of the temple to the south of the courtyard, because of the buildings erected north of the northern arm of the cross.
15. Dikshit, *op. cit.*, p. 14.
16. *Ibid.*, p. 20.
17. Satish Chandra Saran, 'Vikramasila University'.
18. Dutt, *op. cit.*, p. 359.
19. Anon., *Vikramsila Museum*, p. 3.
20. Dutt, *op. cit.*, pp. 360-63.
21. An exact number was not accessible.
22. Jamuar, *Ancient Temples*, p. 87, here quoted after Samuel, 'Ritual Technologies,' p. 43, writes that 'attached with the central shrine have been found four sufficiently spacious chambers facing the four cardinal points in which colossal images (three in clay and one in stone) of the Buddha and the *Bodhisattvas* were installed.'
23. Imam, *Mainamati*, pp. 25-45.
24. *Ibid.*, p. 45.
25. *Ibid.*, p. 36.
26. *Ibid.*, p. 34.

27. *Ibid.*, pp. 79-90. The size of the monastery is 190 m square, and the cruciform shrine is ca. 55 m square; the entrance is in the north.
28. *Ibid.*, pp. 99-103. The monastery is 137.2 m square, the cruciform shrine 34 m. square. The entrance is in the north. Outside the western chapel, a colossal bronze *Vajrasattva* and two smaller plaques showing Amitābha and Amoghasiddhi have been found.
29. *Ibid.*, pp. 103-105. The sizes of the monastery and temple are not known.
30. *Ibid.*, pp. 67-78.
31. *Ibid.*, p. 66.
32. Brauen, *Maṇḍala*, p. 72, fig. 45.
33. *Ibid.*, p. 73, figs. 46-47.
34. Visiting Ridzong monastery in Ladakh in 1983, I was shown a three-dimensional *Cakreśvara maṇḍala* model of about 3 to 5 m in diameter.
35. Brauen, *op. cit.*, p. 73, figs. 21-23.
36. *Ibid.*, p. 25, figs. 14-15; 74, fig. 48; Rhie/Thurman, *Wisdom*, p. 382, fig. 159.
37. Considering the 'possibility that there was a shrine-chamber *on top* of the central shaft', Geoffrey Samuel ('Technologies', 53 n. 7) notes that 'no evidence seems to have been found of such a structure.' Dikshit, though, was very certain about the former existence of the central chamber. This is a problem that has to be taken into account in further research, an argument that stands in favour of the existence of the elevated shrine chamber is the *stūpa* of Gyantse where Vairocana as central deity of the *vajradhātu-maṇḍala* is positioned two storeyes higher than the four accompanying Buddhas. Imam, *op. cit.*, see section 4, no. 8 below.
38. Cf. e.g. Bla ma bTsan po sMin grol me loo śes bya ba (ed. and tr. W. 431).
39. See R.C. Majumdar, 'The Pālas' A 115: 1.
40. Today the city Bihar-Sharif.
41. See No. I above.
42. Chan, *Tibet Handbook*, pp. 295-313.
43. Date according to G. Tuccl.
44. Geoffrey Samuel has called attention to *Vihāra* near Mahasthan (Bogra distt.).
45. For reconstructions of the bSam-yas.
46. Cf. Lokesh Chandra, 'Comparative.'
47. Bosch, 'Buddhist Data', pp. 111-133.
48. Lokesh Chandra, 'Indonesian Sanct.'
49. See below, para. 5, no. 3.
50. Soekmono, 'Architektur', 226; Lokesh Chandra, Borobudur, pp. 31f; 53.
51. Lokesh Chandra, 'Borobudur', pp. 53-60.
52. Soekmono, 'Architektur', p. 218, Abb. 177.
53. Lokesh Chandra, *op. cit.*, p. 53-60.
54. *Ibid.*, pp. 43-48.
55. *Ibid.*, p. 44f.
56. *Ibid.*, p. 68.
57. *Ibid.*, p. 67.
58. Hein/Boelmann, *Tholing*, p. 82.
59. *Ibid.*, p. 82.
60. *Ibid.*, p. 90. The material on Tholing collected by Tucci to be published in a fifth volume of his *Indo-Tibetica*, including a photographic documentation of this lost temple, has never appeared.
61. Handa, *Tabo Monastery*, pp. 102-108.
62. *Ibid.*, pp. 10-90.
63. *Ibid.*, p. 95, fig. 22.
64. *Ibid.*, p. 107; cf. Steinkellner, *Sudhāna's Miraculous Journey*, 3 note 10.
65. For Gyantse, see Ricca/Lo Bue, *Gyantse*.

66. Ricca/Lo Bue, *Gyantse*, p. 263 (overview of third floor), 264f (temple room 3 South, 270f (3 West, 276f (3 North); 282f (2 East).
67. *Ibid.*, p. 305 (temple room 5 East).
68. *Ibid.*, pp. 306-313.
69. Miksic, *Borobudur*, 21.
70. Taoism knows a magical quadrangle consisting of nine small quadrangles; cf. Orzech. 'Seeing Chen-yen Buddhism', pp. 111-113.
71. Snodgrass, *Maṇḍalas*.
72. There are, however, some researchers who want to find the origins of both the ninefold *vajradhātu-maṇḍala* and the pairing of *vajradhātu-* and *garbhadhātu-maṇḍala* in India. As 'Ten Grotenhuis', *Japanese Maṇḍalas*, mentions, Malandra, unfolding a *Maṇḍala*, has recently discovered that the twelve Buddhist cave temples of Ellora stand for the development of early Buddhism between CE 600 and 730. The final cave no. 12 contains, according to Malandra, 'five nine-square *maṇḍala*-like configurations carved in low relief on the walls of cave 12' (quoted from 'Ten Grotenhuis', *Maṇḍalas*, 49). These carvings provide the same structure as the *vajradhātu-maṇḍala*, but since the identification of the nine figures in Ellora shows that it is not nine Buddhas, but one Buddha and eight accompanying *Bodhisattvas*, this arrangement could be the germ of the *garbhadhātu-maṇḍala* stemming from the *Mahāvairacana-sūtra* as well (*loc. cit.*). A third textual source might be the *Āryamahābodhisattva-maṇḍala-sūtra* ('Ten Grotenhuis', *Maṇḍalas*, 49). These and other findings made by Yoritomi Motohiro in Orissa 'may offer evidence of a mingling of Diamond World and Womb World lineages in India, prefiguring the association of the lineages in China' ('Ten Grotenhuis', *Maṇḍala*, 51). As long as it is possible, to identify eight of the nine figures with *Bodhisattvas*, the *vajradhātu-maṇḍala* (51) is not necessary for the interpretation of the Ellora figures group. Apart from that, as evidence for the Indian prefiguration of the East Asian *maṇḍala* pair or of the ninefold *vajradhātu-maṇḍala*, one single Indian finding is not enough.
73. Miksic, *op. cit.*, p. 38.
74. Lokesh Chandra, *Borobudur*, p. 38.
75. Hein/Boelmann, Tholing, p. 90: Tucci describes *Anuttarayoga-tantra* paintings on the walls of the side-chapels of the Yes' od temple. It seems to be possible, though these were added later.
76. This can be drawn from Ricca/Lo Bue, *Gyantse*, *passim.*
77. Snodgrass, *Maṇḍalas*, pp. 634-6, identifies them as the 'thousand Buddhas of the present aeon of virtue' (Skt. *bhadrakalpa*) who symbolize all Buddhas of the three times.
78. Lokesh Chandra, 'Comparative Study', 193.
79. See paragraph 4, no. 4 above.
80. For a representation of the '1037 deity *vajradhātu-maṇḍala* of the Tathāgata family as enunciated in the first part of the 'Tattva-sangraha' in the Tibetan *maṇḍala* collection *Tantra-samuccaya*, see Raghu Vira/Lokesh Chandra, *Pantheon*, pt. 13, no. 13.22; cf. Lokesh Chandra, 'Comparative Study', p. 193. For an example of a 'thangka' painting see Tanaka/Burton, *Tibetan Legacy*, p. 23 pl. 7.
81. This similarity was already noted by Dikshit, *op. cit.*, 7.
82. Gail, *Maṇḍalaic Structure*, pp. 133; 139.
83. *Ibid.*, p. 139.
84. Snodgrass, *Maṇḍalas*, II, 637-643. Cf. Samuel, 'Technologies', p. 13, who has first made this observation with regard to Paharpur-type temples, a rich variety of Hindu deities is to be found in the so-called 'quarter outside the *vajras*' (Kinokuni *et al.*, *Maṇḍala*, nos. 207-408; Snodgrass, *Maṇḍalas*, II, 454-554). This outermost part of the *maṇḍala* fences it in as its least holy area, its sphere of transition to the secular world. In this courtyard only lowly and non-Buddhist deities are dwelling.
85. *Ibid.*, p. 637, quoting Amoghavajra.
86. Malandra, *Unfolding*, quoted after 'Ten Grotenhuis', *Maṇḍalas*, p. 49.

BIBLIOGRAPHY

Caturaviṁśatisiddhapravṛtti, Abhayākaradatta, translated into Tibetan as *Grub thob brgay cu risa bzhi'i lo rgyus* (ed. and trans.) into English by James B. Robinson: *Buddha's Lions: The Lives of the Eighty-Four Siddhas*, Berkeley, California: Dharma Publishing, 1979.

Anon., *Vikramasila Museum Antichak* (ed.) Archaeological Survey of India, Patna Circle, 2004.

Bhattacharya, Gouriswar, *Essays on Buddhist Hindu Jain Iconography and Epigraphy* (ed.) Enamul Haque, Dhaka: International Centre for the Study of Bengal Art, 2000.

Bal ma bTsan po sMin grol on mo han, *Dzam glio chen po'i rgyas bad snod bcud kun gsal me lo zes bya ba* (ed. and trans.), Turrel V. Wylie, *The Geography of Tibet* according to the 'Dzam-gling-rgyas-bshad. Text and English translation, Roma: Istituto Italiano per il medio ed estremo oriente, 1962.

Bosch, F.D.K., 'Buddhist Data from Balinese Texts, and Their Contribution to Archaeological Research in Java', in: idem, *Selected Studies in Indonesian Archaeology*, The Hague: Martinus Nijhoff, 1961 (original publication: 1929), 111-133.

Brauen, Martin, *Das Maṇḍala: Der Heilige Kreis im tatrischen Buddhismus*, Köln: duMont Buchverlag, 1992.

Chakrabarti, Dilip K., *Ancient Bangladesh: A Study of the Archaeological Sources with an Update on Bangladesh Archaeology*, 1990-2000, Dhaka: The University Press, 2001.

Chan, Victor, *Tibet Handbook: A Pilgrimage Guide*, Chico, California: Moon Publications, 1994.

Dikshit, Rao Bahadur K.N., *Excavations at Paharpur*, Bengal, New Delhi: Archaeological Survey of India, 1938, reprint 1999 (Memoires of the Archaeological Survey of India, 55).

Dutt, Sukumar, *Buddhist Monks and Monasteries of India: Their History and their Contribution to Indian Culture*, Delhi: Motilal Banarsidass, 1962, repr. 1988.

Franz, Heinrich Gerhard, *Von Gandhara bis Pagan: Kultbauten des Buddhismus und Hinduismus in Süd-und Zentralasien*, Graz: Akademische Druck-und Verlagsanstalt, 1979.

Gail, a[dalbert] J., 'On the *Maṇḍalaic* Structure of the Paharpur Temple', *Journal of Bengal Art*, 4 (1999), 131-139.

Grotenhuis, Elizabeth, *Japanese Maṇḍalas: Representations of Sacred Geography*, Honolulu: University of Hawai'i Press, 1999.

Handa, O.C., *Tabo Monastery and Buddhism in the Trans-Himalaya: Thousand Years of Existence of the Tabo Chos-Khor*, New Delhi: Indus Publishing Company, 1994.

Hein, Ewald/Gunther Boelmann, *Tilbet – Der Wei Be Tempel von Tholing*, Ratingen: Melina-Verlage, 1994.

Imam, Abu, *Excavations at Mainamati: An Exploratory Study* (ed.), Enamul Haque, Dhaka, Bangladesh: The International Centre for Study of Bengal Art, 2000 (Studies in Bengal Art Series, 2).

Jamuar, B.K., *The Ancient Temples of Bihar*, Ramanand Vidya Bhawan, 1985.

Kinokuni, Kenichi *et al.*, *Eros + Cosmos in Maṇḍala: The Maṇḍalas of the two words at the Kyōō Gokoku-ji*, Tokyo: The Seibu Museum of Art, 1978.

Lokesh Chandra, *Borobudur as a Monument of Esoteric Buddhism*, *Journal of the Asiatic Society*, Calcutta, 27.4 (1927), 22-77.

——, *A Comparative Study of the Tibetan, Japanese, Indonesian and Khotanese Maṇḍala of the Tattva-Saṅgraha, Amalā Prajñā: Aspects of Buddhist Studies. Professor P[urushotam] V[ishvanath] Bapat Felicitation Volume* (ed.) N[arayan] H [emandas] Samtan/H.S. Prasad, Delhi: Sri Satguru Publications, 1989, 187-200.

Lokesh Chandra, 'The Indonesian Sanctuary of Chaoçi Sewu as a Stereomorphic Vajradhātu Maṇḍala', *Indologica Taurinensia*, 7 (1969), 159-169, reprint in: Lokesh Chandra, 'Borobudur', 22-23.

Majumdar, R.C., 'The Pālas', in *The History of Bengal*, Vol. I: Hindu Period, ed. idem, Lohanipur Patna: N.V. Publications, 1943, 93-190.

Malandra, Geri H., *Unfolding a Maṇḍala: The Buddhist Cave Temples at Ellora*, Delhi: Sri Satguru Publications, 1997.

Miksic, John, *Borobudur: Das Pantheon Indonesiens*, München: Prestel, 1991 (Eng.) original edition Berkeley, 1990.

Orzech, Charles D., 'Seeing Chen-Yen Buddhism: Traditional Scholarship and the Vajrayāna in China', in *History of Religions*, 29 (1989-90), 87-114.

Raghu Vira and Lokesh Chandra, *A Neo Tibeto-Mongol Pantheon*, pt. 13., New Delhi: International Academy of Indian Culture, 1967.

Reitz, Falk, 'The Cruciform Temple-type of the Buddhists in Comparison with that of the Hindus', paper abstract to the Biennial Conference of the European Association of South Asian Archaeologists, Clare Centre at the British Museum, July 4-8, 2005, Panel: 'The Temple in South Asia'.

Rhie, Marylin M. Robert A.F. Thurman, *Wisdom and Compassion: The Sacred Art of Tibet*, New York: Harry N. Abrams, 1991.

Ricca, Franco and Erberto Lo Bue, *The Great Stūpa of Gyatse: A Complete Tibetan Pantheon of the Fifteenth Century*, London: Serindia Publicatios, 1993.

Samuel, Geoffrey, 'Ritual Technologies and the State: The Maṇḍala-form Buddhist Temples of Bangladesh', *Journal of Bengal Art*, 7 (2002), 39-56.

Saran, Satish Chandra, *Vikramaśilā University – A Centre of Tantricism*, K.P. Jayaswal Commemoration Volume (ed.), J.S. Jha, Patna: K.P. Jayaswal Research Institute, 1981.

Snellgrove, David Lewellyn, *Indo-Tibetan Buddhism: Indian Buddhists and Their Tibetan Successors*, London: Serindia Publications.

Snodgrass, Adrian, *The Matrix and Diamond World Maṇḍalas in Shingon Buddhism*, Vol. I-II, New Delhi: Aditya Prakashan, 1988, Śata-Pitaka Series, 354. 355.

Soekmono, R., 'Die Architektur der klassischen Zeit', Versunkene Königreiche Indonesiens (ed.) Arne und Eva Eggebercht, Mainz: Verlag Philipp von Zabern, 1995, 205-248.

Steinkellner, Ernst, *Sudhāna's Miraculous Journey in the Temple of Ta pho.* The inscriptional text of the Tibetan 'Gaṇḍavyūha Sūtra', ed. with introductory remarks. Roma: Instituto Italiano per il medio ed. Estremo Oriente, 1995 (Series Orientale Roma, 76).

Tanaka, Kimiaki and Richard Blurton, *Tibetan Legacy: Paintings from the Hahn Kwang-ho Collection* (Exhibition British Museum, London, 203), Seoul: The Hahn Cultural Foundation, 2003.

Tucci, Giuseppe, *Minor Buddhist Texts*, Part II: *First Bhāvanākrama of Kamala Śīla*. Sanskrit and Tibetan Texts with Introduction and English Summary, Roma: Is.M.E.O., 1958 (Series Orientale Roma, IX, 2).

10

THE NALANDA STONE INSCRIPTION OF YAŚOVARMADEVA

Naina Pandey

The Nalanda stone inscription of Yaśovarmadeva[1] (c. 725 CE) provides some noteworthy information about the features of Buddhism during that period. This inscription presents a benedictory donation and temple record. It begins with the eulogy of Gautama Buddha:

संसारस्थिरव (ब)न्धनात्कृतमतिर्मोक्षाय यो देहिनां।
कारुण्यात्प्रसभं शरीरमपि यो दत्वा तुतोषार्थिने[1]
सेन्द्रैर्यः स्वशिरः किरीटमकरी घृंष्टांहि पद्मः सुरै
स्तस्मै सर्व्वपदार्थतत्त्वविदुषे वु (बु) द्धाय नित्यं नमः।।

> Continual salutation to the Buddha who made up his mind to emancipate living beings from the strong tangles of the world to attain salvation, who felt true bliss even after giving his body to the supplicants, and whose foot-lotus is worshipped by gods including Indra, with the fish (engraved) in the crown on their head. We pray to the Buddha who has the true knowledge of the real nature of all the categoric elements of the world.

The text further describes that King Bālāditya constructed an enormous temple and a victory tower and consecrated a statue of Śāstā at Nalanda. Mālāda, the son of a minister of King Yaśovarmadeva, gave donations to the temple. The description of things provided for the temple includes *naivedya*, milk, butter, curd, pure and fragrant water, used for daily rituals (*Pūjā*) at the temple. In the same context, there is also reference to provide *Akṣyaneevi*. Though the amount of *Akṣyaneevi* is not mentioned, it is clear that its interest was meant for the regular worship of Buddha at the temple. Mālāda also took care of the monks. He made arrangements for the Buddhist monks to provide them with sufficient amount of food, butter, curd, milk and aromatic water.[2]

The *Maṅgalācaraṇa* reflects the Buddhist belief in existence during that time. 'सर्व्व पदार्थ तत्वविदुषे वु (बु) द्धाय नित्यं नमः' and implicates the four *Ārya Satya* (the four noble truths) and *Pratītyasamutpāda,* the two allied principles of Buddhism. The inscription tells that Buddha made up his mind to emancipate living beings from the strong tangles of world. This can be better understood by the description given in the *Mahāvagga*. In the *Mahāvagga*[3] it is said that after enlightenment, Buddha was peaceful and self-contented. He realized that the awareness of truth was so deep, subtle, hard to comprehend and beyond the scope of conjecture that it was to be experienced by the wise only. Buddha realized that if he was to teach the *Dhamma* and if others would not understand, that would be tiresome for them, troublesome for him. Having known of this line of thinking in Buddha's awareness, Brahmā himself appeared in front of the Buddha and asked him to teach the *Dhamma* for salvation of people. The phrase 'देहिनां मोक्षाय' in the inscription (*Maṅgalācaraṇa*) echoes this. There are a number of examples in Pāli literature to indicate that gods such as Indra had appeared and bowed down to Buddha.[4] The inscription almost repeats it. The inscription emphasizes Buddha's acts of self-sacrifice for the benefit of others in his former births. *Jātakas*[5] such as *Maitrībala, Śibi, Hasti* and *Vyāghrī* relate that Buddha, out of compassion for people had even given up parts of his body or even laid down his life. In *Maitrībala Jātaka, Bodhisattva* was able to arouse compassion and benevolence in cruel Yakṣas, who fed on human flesh and blood, by giving his own flesh and blood and ending his life. Similarly, the *Śibi Jātaka* describes how *Bodhisattva* donated both his eyes. In the *Hasti Jātaka*, the compassionate *Bodhisattva* let him fall from a hill so that starving people wandering in the desert could feed on his body. In the *Vyāghrī Jātaka*, when a starving tigress was about to eat her newly born cubs, *Bodhisattva* gave his own body to save the life of cubs. It is to be noted here that the first two *Jātaka*s are available in both Sanskrit and Pāli tradition but the *Hasti Jātaka* and *Vyāgrhī Jātaka* are not available in Pāli collection. These two *Jātakas* have been described in detail in *Jātaka-Mālā* by Āryaśūra. It can therefore be assumed that the work of Āryaśūra served as the source of the present Nalanda inscription. Yi'jing (CE 673) confirms the popularity of *Jātaka-Mālā*.[6]

According to the Nalanda inscription it had a huge Buddha temple constructed by King Bālāditya. The Buddha statue consecrated in temple was worshipped with milk, butter, curd and lamps in the traditional way like other gods. *Akṣyaneevi* was provided to meet the expenditure of daily worship. Probably this *Akṣyaneevi* was managed by the temple council. There was also a monastery associated with the temple, which was managed by donation of resourceful people such as Mālāda. There is also evidence that there was a shop corner (*saṅghaṅṭikā*) for purchasing things required for worship at the temple as Mālāda had bought milk, curd, and fragrant water from there to donate them to the temple. There is a description of Mālāda buying a monk-robe for himself.

In Mahāyāna several Buddhas other than Śākyamuni such as Amitābha, Maitreya, and Vairocana have been given importance. The concept of eternal Buddha (*Dharmakāya*) makes Śākyamuni a manifestation. However, this inscription brings Śākyamuni to the forefront. It is important to mention the Mahāyana text *Karuṇāpuṇḍarīka* in this context.[7] In this text, Śākyamuni emerges as the focal point whereas Amitābha and Askṣobhya play only assisting role. In the third chapter of the work Śāntimati *Bodhisattva* questions Śākyamuni, why did you take birth and desired for enlightenment and preached *Dhamma* in the world full of sorrow and suffering? Why you did not choose a world with less sorrow and suffering? Buddha replied that out of his own determination *Bodhisattvas* choose a place for their activity. I, too, did accordingly. Thus, according to the *Karuṇāpuṇḍarīka*, Śākyamuni chose on his own accord a world full of sorrow and suffering so that he could bring salvation to all.

Thus, in summary, the Nalanda inscription indicates that it is related to a branch of Mahāyāna of which the *Karuṇāpuṇḍarīka* was the most revered text. Since this text was translated into Chinese in the fourth century, it must have been an important book at the time of the Nalanda inscription.

NOTES AND REFERENCES

1. Rajbali Pandey, *Historical and Literary Inscriptions*, Varanasi, 1978, pp. 155-58.
2. Hiranand Sastri, *Nalanda and its Epigraphic Material*, Delhi, Sri Sataguru Publications, 1986, pp. 78-82; *Epigraphica Indica*, Vol. XX (1929-30) 1983, New Delhi, pp. 78-82.
3. Rahul Sankrityayan, *Vinaya-Piṭaka*, Varanasi, 1994, p. 64; N.N. Dutta and K.D. Vajpeyee, *Uttar Pradesh Main Bauddha Dharma Ka Vikas*, Lucknow, 1950, p. 20.
4. *Gradual Sayings – Aṅguttara Nikāya*, E.M. Hare (tr.), Vol. IV, London, Pali Text Society, 1995, p. 54; J. Legge, *A Record of the Buddhistic Kingdoms*, Delhi, Munshiram Manohar Lal, 1991, pp. 47-53; Rahul Sankrityayan, *Buddhacharya*, Varanasi, 1980, p. 88.
5. *Jātakamālā*, S.N. Chaudhari (tr.), Delhi, Motilal Banarasidas, 1991, pp. 68-86, 10-25, 332-45, 3-10.
6. I-tsing. *The Record of the Buddhist Religion at Practice in India and Malay, Archipelago (671-695)*, J. Takakusu (tr.), Delhi, 1966, pp. 162-63.
7. Yamada Isshi, *Karuṇāpuṇḍarīka*, Vol. 1, 2, London, School of Oriental and African Studies, Vol. 1, pp. 77-78, Vol. 2, 1968, pp. 51ff.

11

THE NALANDA COPPER-PLATE OF DEVAPĀLADEVA

Archana Sharma

This record was published by Hiranand Sastri in *Epigraphica Indica*, Vol. 17 under the title 'The Nalanda Copper-plate of Devapāladeva'.[1]

The plate bears forty-two lines on the obverse and twenty-four on the reverse. The inscription is written in early Devanagari script and its language is Sanskrit. The formal part of the grant is in prose and the rest in verse, except the word *Svasti* and *tathā cadharmānuślokaḥ*, written at the commencement of the first and the second side, respectively.[2] A structural analysis of this record shows that it is not simply a land-grant but a combination of *Bhumidāna* and *Pratiṣṭhā-śāsana*. It is easily divided into two parts: part one goes up to line 51 where ends the land-grant. From line 52 begins *Pratiṣṭhā-śāsana*. Generally in the land-grants the description of the grant of land/village is followed by the praise of *dāna* and benedictory and imprecatory verses.[3] At the end the name of Balavarman who acted as the *dūtaka* in this 'meritorious undertaking' and whom it describes as the 'overlord of *Vyāghra maṇḍala*'[4] signifies that he was the official of the king of Magadha entrusted with all arrangements to be made in connection with the grant.[5] It is thus clear that the land-grant ends with line 52. The donor of five villages is Devapāla; this part belongs to Pāla ruler. From line 52 starts the description of Bālaputradeva who constructed a *vihāra* at Nalanda. Inscriptions describing the construction of religious centers/temples, etc. end with the laudatory formula expressing desire that the monument and the fame attached to its construction should remain for eternity. The *vihāra* was constructed by Bālaputradeva; this part (*Pratiṣṭhā-śāsana*) belongs to him. A reading of the entire record shows that it was Bālaputradeva the Śailendra ruler who constructed a Buddhist monastery at Nalanda.[6] It was therefore his responsibility to make proper arrangement for the livelihood of its monks, their education and religious activities, monastery's upkeep and maintenance. But instead of doing himself he made request through his ambassador to Devapāla to donate land for the purpose[7] and Devapāla happily donated five villages to the monastery, four of which lay in the Rajagṛha (Rajgir) and one in the Gaya Viṣaya (district) of Śrī Nagar *bhukti* in the Rajagṛha. The four villages of the former were Nadīvanaka, Maṇivāṭaka Nītika and Hastigrāma and the one in Gaya Viṣaya was called Palamak.[8] From the first part of the inscription it is clear that Devapāla was the donor. In the second part it has been mentioned that Bālaputradeva constructed the *vihāra* and having duly informed Devapāla through his envoy,[9] he donated five villages to the monastery suggesting that Bālaputradeva was the donor. When both the parts of the record are considered together it becomes obvious that Devapāla donated five villages on behalf of Bālaputradeva. Devapāla was indeed donor in the legal sense, whereas Bālaputradeva was a donor only in the religious sense, so that he may get the complete merit of the construction and maintenance of the monastery. What did Devapāla get from Bālaputradeva as compensation of the revenue loss of five villages has not been told in this record. He might have economic interest in maritime trade activity with the south-eastern countries.[10] It is well known that the merchants from Bengal were doing trade with the islands of Malaya Archipelago. A record from Province Wellesly shows the presence of a *Mahānāvika* from Rakta mṛittikā (Murshidabad district of Bengal). It is possible that Devapāla strengthened bond of relations with the Śailendra king. We learn from this inscription that Bālaputradeva was the son of Tārā, the daughter of King Dharmasetu[11] of the lunar family. Does this name stand for Dharmapāla? If so, was Dharmapāla of lunar family (*Somakula*), which links with Somapura Vihāra[12] which Dharmapāla had constructed? These are the questions which require further investigation. However, it can be noted that religious activity had been the part of diplomacy in ancient India. The *Besnagar Pillar Inscription* stands testimony to the construction of a Garuḍa Pillar by Heliodorus, the envoy of Indo-Greek king Antialkidas.[13] Similarly, Meghavarṇa of Ceylon founded a *vihāra* at Bodhgaya during the Gupta epoch to shelter his own people as well as others.[14] The Śailendra kings constructed Chūḍāmaṇi Vihāra at Nagapattanam and made arrangements for its upkeep through Choḷa rulers.[15]

This inscription is distinct from many others as it combines two records on land-grant of Devapāla and the *Pratiṣṭhā-śāsana* of Bālaputradeva. This record is a kind of joint statement of the heads of two states or their representatives sealing the friendship bond of their countries.

NOTES AND REFERENCES

1. *Epigraphica Indica*, Vol. XVII, p. 318ff. This copper-plate was unearthed by H.N. Shastri at Nalanda during the course of his archaeological explorations of the well known Buddhist site there in 1921. Archaeological Survey of India, *Annual Report*, Central Circle 1920-21.
2. *Ibid.*, p. 310.
3. *Ibid.*, p. 311.
4. *Ibid.*, p. 311.
5. *Ibid.*, p. 311.
6. *Ibid.*, p. 313. Buddhist Monuments, Debala Mitra, p. 86.
7. 'Viharas in Central and Eastern India' (*Viharas in Ancient India*), D.K. Barua, p. 146, *Epigraphica Indica*, Vol. XVII, p. 313.
8. *Epigraphica Indica*, Vol. XVII, p. 311.
9. *Ibid.*, p. 325.
10. *Ibid.*, p. 314. 'Cultural Relation between India and Southeast Asian Countries', G.B. Sarkar, p. 247.
11. *Epigraphica Indica*, Vol. XVII, p. 311, 324.
    राज्ञः सोमकुलान्वयस्य महतः श्रीधार्मसेतोः सुता तस्या भूदवनौ भुजोऽग्रमहिषी तारेः ताराहया माया.
12. Archaeological Survey of India, *Annual Report*, 1927-28, p. 138, Buddhist Monuments, Debala Mitra, p. 240. The establishment of Somapura Monastery was due to munificence of Dharmapāla (CE 770-810), the second ruler of the dynasty, as is evident from the discovery of a sealing with the legend Śrī Somapura Śrī Dharmapāladeva-mahāviharīy-ārya-bhikṣu-saṅghasya.
13. D.C. Sarkar, *Select Inscriptions*, Vol. 1, pp. 90-91 (देवदेवस्य वासुदेवस्य गरुडध्वजः, अयं कारितः इह हेलियोदोरेण भागवतेन......।, Archaeological Survey of India, *Annual Report*, 1908-9, p. 126.
14. *Epigraphica Indica*, Vol. XVII, p. 313.

15. *Ibid.*, pp. 312-13.

Buddhist Monuments, Debala Mitra, pp. 194-96. From the Tamil portion of the larger Leiden plates it is gathered that Choḷa king Rājarāja I in the twenty-first year of his reign (CE 1006) granted the revenues of the village of Anaimangalam to the Pāli (temple) in the Chuḷāmaṇivarma Vihāra which was erected by King Chuḷāmaṇivarman at Nagapattanam.

12

MANAGEMENT OF NALANDA MAHĀVIHĀRA FROM EPIGRAPHICAL MATERIAL

Arpita Chatterjee

The inscriptions and travel accounts of the Chinese pilgrims tell us that Nalanda Mahāvihāra was donated with many land-grants for its maintenance by several rulers. Zuanzang[1] informs that Nalanda Mahāvihāra possessed 100 villages. According to Yi'jing[2] the number of such villages granted to the institution was not less than 200. It can be conceded that Nalanda Mahāvihāra had ownership of a large number of villages. Although the identification of these villages is not possible now, yet it is probable that maximum number of villages were in the neighbourhood.

It is a well known fact that granted villages were disconnected from the main administrative units in ancient time. For example, we can refer to the description of *Banskhera Inscription*.[3] In such situation the administration of granted villages became the responsibility of the grantees. Naturally, Nalanda Mahāvihāra was also responsible for the administration of its subordinate villages. Now the question arises were those villages really ruled by the Nalanda Mahāvihāra? Or did the Nalanda Mahāvihāra play the role of a real administrative unit? We have a few examples by which it has been seen that some neighbouring villages remained connected with the main administrative units and only their revenues were to be transferred to the Mahāvihāra. The seal of village names Purika found here was connected to Rājgṛha Viṣaya.[4] Another seal which has a legend in two lines is also found here. It reads: 'Jakkurakā-(sthāna)-Sujā-grā)-(ma)-janapadasya'.[5] It proved that the village Sujā was under the (police) station of Jakkurakā. Similar may be the situation with the villages situated in far-flung areas.

But the same cannot be said about all the villages. However, examples are not wanting of villages which were donated to the monastery with full powers. The Nalanda copper-plate of Devapāladeva[6] tells us that the Pāla ruler had granted full ownership of five villages to Nalanda Mahāvihāra. He granted villages along with their lands as undivided plots, with their pasture lands, grounds, spaces, mango and *Madhūka* trees, with their waters and dry lands, *uparikara*, *daśāparādha* and *caurodharaṇa* and with all taxes due to the king. Such villages were Nandivanāka, Maṇivātaka and Hastigrāma, etc. Thirteen seals discovered from here are significant for assuming their organisation. There are the seals of different village assemblies or *Grāma Janapada*s. Among these villages two were connected to Nalanda. The inscribed legends on the seals are as follows:

Srī - Nālandā-pratibaddha-Āṅgāmi-grāma-Vihāra-stha-jānapadasya.[7]
Śrī - Nālandā - pratibaddha Māṁnayik grāma-jānapadasya.[8]

Besides these, the seals of villages refer to Varakīya, Brāhmaṇī, Udradvāra sthāna, Navakā, Ghanāñjana, Kālīgrāma, Danthā Chand (ēKaya), Māṁnāvika, etc.

These seals prove that the mentioned villages were ruled by their village assemblies. They were more or less sources of income for the *Mahāvihāra*. It is thus clear that Nalanda Mahāvihāra was not concerned with the day to day administration of these villages. This arrangement really suited the monks of the *Mahāvihāra* because in this condition they enjoyed the benefits of the land-grant without bearing the administrative responsibilities. But how the revenue of these villages was collected by the *Mahāvihāra* is a question to be further investigated.

In this connection the statement of Zuanzang is worth noting. He says, "Two hundred householders of 100 villages, day by day, contribute several hundred piculs of ordinary rice and several hundred cattles in weight of butter and milk."[9] It seems that two hundred householders were charged with the collection of the revenue of the villages. Probably they were the members of *Grāma Janapada*s or they could be middlemen securing the interest of Nalanda Mahāvihāra in lieu of some profit. The entire responsibility of timely collection of revenue was theirs. This arrangement was beneficial for both the parties, the *Mahāvihāra* and the middlemen. The *Mahāvihāra* regularly got the articles of daily need and the middlemen earned the profit through the entire collection. During excavation some fire-places were found here.[10]

It appears at least some villages of the neighbourhood were probably looked after by the *Mahāvihāra*. According to Yi'jing there were many monasteries in India where the cultivation was done under the supervision of monks themselves.[11] This might also have been a case with Nalanda Mahāvihāra.

INTERNAL MANAGEMENT OF THE *MAHĀVIHĀRA*

Nature of internal management depends on the structure of the *Mahāvihāra*. Nalanda Mahāvihāra was a conglomeration of many monasteries. According to Zuanzang there were six monasteries built by six religious kings and all the buildings were surrounded by a brick wall.[12] Ruins of 11 monasteries are found in the excavated site.[13] Definitely each of these monasteries had its own management committee which dealt with all internal matters.

It appears from the available records that there was an apex committee of the *Mahāvihāra* to look after the entire campus and the *Bhikṣu Saṅgha* of different monasteries served under its supervision. Many seals have been discovered here with the legend –

Srī Nālandā-Mahāvihāra-ārya-bhikṣu-Saṅghasya.[14]

These appear to be the seals of the apex committee. Seals of other monasteries have also been discovered with such legends –

1. Srī-Kara (jña-)-mahāvi (hā)-rē bhikṣusaṅghasya.[15]
2. ... (ndā)yām Śrī-Śakrādiya-Kārita-hāre Cāturddiśīy-ārya-mā(ma)hā bhikṣusaṅghasya.[16]
3. Śrī-Harivarmma-Mahāvihārīy-āryabhikṣusaṅghasya.[17]

The existence of many quarters of *Bhikṣus* is also proved by the description of Nalanda Stone Inscription of Yaśōvarmadeva.[18] We learn from this inscription that Mālāda had made gift of food along with *ghrit, dadhi* and different *Vyañjana*s to *Bhikṣu*s of all quarters.

Discovered seals prove the existence of several departments which served different affairs.

For example:

Śrī-Nālandā–Mūlanava-Karmmavārika-bhikṣūṇāṁ.[19]

Nava Karmik Bhikṣus are also mentioned in *Vinaya Piṭaka.*[20] They were in-charge of constructing and repairing of buildings on the campus.

Śrī-Nalandā-Cīvarakā (jya)-(pān-ā)rya-bhikṣusaṅghasya.[21]

They were in-charge of provisions such as clothes and grains. We can compare them with the *Bhaṇḍāgārika* of *Vinaya Piṭaka.*

The Nalanda Stone Inscription of Yaśōvarmadeva informs us that Mālāda, the son of a minister, gave to the temple of Bālāditya various articles of worship such as *ghee*, curds, lamp and also an *akṣyanīvikā* for facilitating the regular worship.[22] *Akṣayanīvikā* is a fixed deposit. The interest accrued to it was used to meet approved expenditure. The *Bhikṣu Saṅgha* was expected to manage the *akṣayanīvikā*. The *Bhikṣus* indulged in some financial activities with this amount, mainly to increase it or to earn interest out of it. Thus the *vihāras* of Nalanda were also engaged in some kind of banking activities.

Seals prove the existence of classification among the monastic staff, e.g.

1. Śrī - Nālandā - Ca (or va) Krā-rē Vārika-bhikṣūṇāṁ.[23]
2. Śrī - Nālandā-Satraka Samavārika - bhikṣūṇāṁ.[24]
3. Śrī - Nālandā-Cātu- (rddiśika-Samavāri) Ka- bhikṣusaṅghasya.[25]

The word *Vārika* means the Head of the Department. Therefore, it appears that the *Samavārika Bhikṣus* were working under their supervision.

While talking about the internal management of this institution it is necessary to evaluate the role of its Chairman as he enjoyed the highest position among the members of the *Mahāvihāra*. His decision was the ultimate decision on each and every matter. In brief he was the supreme authority of this institution. So the outstanding persons were needed to fill this post. The appointment of eminent scholars like Śīlabhadra[26] and Vīradeva[27] are a testimony to this fact. From the Ghosrawan Inscription[28] we can say that one had been selected for the post by the decision of the members of the *Saṅgha.*

Many maids and servants were associated with internal management. The travel account of Yi'jing refer to engagement of servants here.

Nalanda Mahāvihāra was a centre of religious and educational activities with departments of banking, stores, and kitchen. The apex committee coordinated with the committees of other monasteries and temples on the campus. This committee also looked after the welfare and necessities of the pilgrims. The pilgrims could purchase various items of worship from the stalls run by the *Bhikṣu Saṅgha*. Nalanda Stone Inscription of Yaśōvarmadeva informs us that in Nalanda the donor purchased various items from such stalls (*Saṅghaṇṭikā*) for giving gifts to *Bhikṣus*.[29]

NOTES AND REFERENCES

1. Samuel Beal (trans.), *The Life of Hiuen Tsang*, Delhi, 1911, p. 112.
2. J. Takakusu (trans.), *A Record of the Buddhist Religion as Practiced in India and the Malay Archipelago*, by I-tsing, Delhi, 1966, p. 65.
3. D.C. Sircar, *Select Inscriptions Bringing on Indian History and Civilization (from the sixth to the eighteenth cent. CE)*, Vol. II, Delhi, 1983, pp. 221-23.

4. Hirananda Sastri, *Nalanda and Its Epigraphic Material,* Delhi, 1942, p. 33.
5. *Ibid.,* p. 48.
6. *Epigraphica Indica,* Vol. XVII, pp. 310-27.
7. Hirananda Sastri, *op. cit.,* p. 32.
8. *Ibid.,* p. 32.
9. Samuel Beal, *op. cit.,* pp. 110-111.
10. A. Ghose, *op. cit.*, New Delhi, 1986, pp. 25, 27.
11. J. Takakusu, *op. cit.,* p. 61.
12. Samuel Beal, *op. cit.,* pp. 110-111.
13. A. Ghose, *op. cit.,* pp. 20-28.
14. Hirananda Sastri, *op. cit.,* pp. 36, 39, 40, 41.
15. *Ibid.,* p. 37.
16. *Ibid.,* p. 38.
17. *Ibid.,* p. 40.
18. D.C. Sircar, *op. cit.,* Vol. II, pp. 229-32. *Epigraphica Indica,* Vol. XX, pp. 37-45.
19. Hirananda Sastri, *op. cit.,* p. 37.
20. Rahul Sankrityayan (trans.), *Vinaya Pitaka* (First Edition), Varanasi, 1994, p. 462.
21. Hirananda Sastri, *op. cit.,* p. 40.
22. D.C. Sircar, *op. cit.,* Vol. II, pp. 229-32. *Epigraphica Indica,* Vol. XX, p. 37.
23. Hirananda Sastri, *op. cit.,* p. 37.
24. *Ibid.,* p. 39.
25. *Ibid.,* p. 39.
26. Samuel Beal, *op. cit.,* p. 105.
27. Hirananda Sastri, *op. cit.,* pp. 89-91.
28. *Ibid.,* pp. 89-91.
29. D.C. Sircar, *op. cit.,* Vol. II, pp. 229-31. *Epigraphica Indica,* Vol. XX, pp. 37-45.

13

NALANDA FROM THE CHINESE AND TIBETAN SOURCES

Anandamayee Ghosh

NALANDA IN THE CHINESE SOURCES

According to the Chinese tradition, Gautama Buddha is said to have been in vicinity of Nalanda in course of his penance prior to his *Bodhi* (Enlightenment). During his asceticism, Indra came to encourage his austerity. Soothil refers to the account in the following lines,

> The mountain of small isolated peaks located near Nalanda where on this south crag of the west peak is a rock cave, broad but not high, which Śākyamuni frequently visited. Indra is said to have written forty-two questions on stone to which the Buddha replied.

E.J. Eitel in his handbook of the *Student of Chinese Buddhism, London,* 1897 mentioned that Nalanda had been a small village in olden days.

Later on the village was called Baragong, probably a dialectical change in transformation from *vihāragrāma* with reference to the *Mahāvihāra* demolished in CE 1200. The causes of the decline of Nalanda might be more than one, but its importance was of singular kind as ancient academic centre of India. Its fame spread.

As regards the naming of the Great Centre several legends are afloat. In Chinese Nalanda suggests 'unwearying benefactor' which may not agree with the Sanskrit Nalanda. That may be expounded 'no-alanda' (no more to bestow). Suggestively such enormous donation had been forwarded by the benevolence, as it sufficed. Probably that might be one of the causes of this fall of *saṅghārāma* on account of profuse wealth and splendour from 10th century downwards.

In Indian history the Pālas were the great benefactors of Nalanda. An inscribed copper-plate from Nalanda of King Bālaputradeva of Śailendra dynasty of Java mentions that a *vihāra* complex was donated and five villages were purchased for the maintenance of the recluses of the said premises. Besides those instances of profuse donations Nalanda metal foundry could produce metal products, particularly the icons of different size having excellent gild and bright enamelling.

The Chinese record referred to a king named Śakrāditya said to be the founder of Nalanda monastery. Xuanzang narrated the distance from Rāhula Tope from Nalanda monastery about 30 *li.* The epithet of Nalanda is insatiable in giving account of the benevolence showered upon it. Śakrāditya built the first monastery and his son Budhagupta installed another portion to the south of that built by his father. And Tathāgatagupta built the third complex to the east of that of Budhagupta. Again Bālāditya built the fourth one to the south-east. Bālāditya's son and successor Vajra built the western complex of the monastery. Another complex was built by a South Indian ruler. According to the pilgrim the monastery built by Śakrāditya could accommodate forty brethren who were provided with food out of the donated land for them. In the whole complex as Xuanzang mentioned, there had been thousands of inmates in the *Mahāvihāra*.

Also a Nāga king bestowed huge wealth to establish the *Mahāvihāra* in olden days. Śakrāditya was a Magadha ruler contemporaneous of Gautama Buddha, a devotee like Bimbisāra and Prasenajit. Śakrāditya might be junior to Bimbisāra of Magadha. Śakrāditya is said to have installed a *stūpa* in memory of the Buddha after his *parinirvāṇa*.

The *Fang chih* referred to one hundred sacred vestiges. To the west was a temple. Buddha observed the *vassāvasa* for three months to preach human beings and the divinities. Hundred paces to the south of this vestige remained a Toe. To the south of the Toe, there was a standing image of Kuan tzu tsai pu sa and it was this centre of performing *pradakṣiṇā* of the temple. South-east from it there had been a big tree along the wall. To the east of the tree a large temple above two thousand feet high was built. Buddha is said to have preached at that place.

The Pāli sources (*Cullavagga, Mahāvaṁsa*) mention that after the Śākyaputra Gautama his relics were carried by many devotees who established votive-*stūpa*s. Regarding the Nāga-legend in construction of the *Mahāvihāra* in Chinese the following may be jotted down:

i) Nalanda is said to be established in the vicinity of a big water-place in which a great Nāga used to reside.
ii) In the development of Buddhism the association of the Nāga or Nāgarāja may be significant. In Chinese the benevolence of (*mahā*) mu. ci. lin. da, Nāga Rāja of Nalanda and that of the daughter Sāgara-rāja (*Saddharmapuṇḍarīka, Lotus-sūtra*) deserve mention.

In Indian culture Nāga is a term referring to an elephant and serpent as well. In Chinese dragon is an auspicious symbol. Occasional mention of Nāga in Buddhist literature may signify Buddha's association with underground universe. In Indian history the Nāga was a dynastic name who might have the serpent as a community emblem. Among the Dravidians serpent-worship cult still prevails.

Buddhist monks used to visit China since the 4th century BCE. Among the Madhyadeśa scholars Dharmakṣema entered China through land-route. Yi'jing is said to have spent ten years for study in Nalanda. He copied several Buddhist texts from Nalanda Library. He is said to have carried a voluminous collection of four hundred Sanskrit manuscripts while he returned in 695. Nanjio in his *Catalogue* mentions fifty-six titles of Buddhist texts translated by Yi'jing. Out of them thirteen on *Mūlasarvāstivāda Vinaya* (MSV) were translated by him. Yi'jing promoted *Mūlasarvāstivāda Vinaya* in China.

Chinese Buddhist pilgrims visited India as Indian Buddhist savants visited China either by land-route or by sea voyage particularly during the T'ang period (618-907). Among them the Nalanda scholar Dharmadeva, Chinese, Fatien visited Chang Ngan and spent the rest of his life in China by devoting himself in translation of Sanskrit texts into Chinese in collaboration with Chinese emeritus. The *Nanjio Catalogue* enumerates forty-six texts belonging to Tantra, *Dhāraṇī* and Mahāyāna *sūtras*.

Another Indian teacher of Nalanda Vajra-*Bodhi* had gone to China with his disciple Amoghavajra through sea-route and reached China in 719 and reached the then capital Canton in 720. He expired at Loyang in 732 at the age of 71. He and his disciple introduced Indian Tantra in China.

An alumni of Nalanda named Śubhaṅkarasiṁha went to Chang Nan in 716 with a large collection of Sanskrit manuscripts along with the party of Bodhiruchi; he died in China in 735. He contributed a large number of Indian texts to be translated in Chinese.

NALANDA IN TIBETAN SOURCES

In the Tibetan accounts Nalanda has been referred again and again. Tibetan historians like Buston. rin. chen. grub (12th cent.), Gzhon. nu. dpal (14th cent.), Kung. dga. snying. po (15th cent.) otherwise named Tārānātha, and ye. shes. dpal. byor (17th cent.) or popularly known as Sun. pa. mkhen. po occasionally mention Nalanda. Moreover many Tibetans in quest of learning visited Nalanda. Among them chos. kyi. gon. po. Dharmaswāmī witnessed the last days of Nalanda.

Tibetan Buddhist historians usually speak highly of Nalanda and the eminent teachers of Nalanda for two reasons:

i) Srong. bsan. gam. po accepted Buddhism on the request of two Buddhist queens from Nepal and China. Whereas Khri srong lde tsan had faced both internal and external disputes regarding Buddhism, Bonpas were strong enough against Buddhism since the time of Srong bsan gum po. They were anti-Buddhist. The Chinese queen favoured the Chinese Mahāyāna monks for leadership. The Nepali faction also claimed their prominence. As such Śāntarakṣita from Nalanda was invited and Padmasambhava followed him to spread Buddhism in Tibet.

ii) After disaster in Nalanda Māhavihāra in the 12th century, a large number of eminent teachers flocked to Tibet for refuge under the patronage of important Buddhist monasteries in Tibet and Nepal. Mahapandit Rahul Sankrityayana had occasion to witness a great store-house of Indian Buddhist Sanskrit texts in Ngor monastery as he elaborated in his diary published in different issues of the *Journal of Bihar Research Society*, Patna.

Mar. pa also occasionally mentioned his experience in Nalanda with reference to Nāropā and Metipā (Maitreya pāda).

a) One-fifth of the *Mahāvihāra* is said to be excavated so far out of the area identified by Alexander Cunninghum by the sixties of the 19th century. The structural plan as far as available, refers to eighty-four bases inside. The scriptural basement was named *Dharmagañja* in which three major buildings were enclaved, namely, (i) Ratnasāgara, (ii) Ratnodadhi (said to be) nine-storeyed building, and (iii) Ratnakaraṇḍa.

   These buildings consisted of Buddhist texts either *Tripiṭaka* or *śāstra*. According to Rga. gar. chos. byung ascribed to Tārānātha, Aśoka is said to have built Nalanda Saṅghārāma by the 3rd century BCE. Presumably the Nalanda complex consisted of multi-blocks. The records of Tārānātha mention that Mahīpāla contributed wealth for building some centres at Nalanda. Among them probably the *Kālacakra* centre was prior to him. Gopāla took initiative in *Mahāvihāra* campus extention.

(b) Among the Buddhists a donation for a noble cause is always praised. Donations are of two kinds, either voluntary or obligatory. For instance, a merchant contributes for the cause of monastic institution for the maintenance of a monk or a nun with all requirements. It may be regarded as a voluntary contribution while a donation for personal cause or a family cause like ailment, etc. may be regarded as obligatory in which case monastic service and rituals used to be undertaken.

According to the Buddhist monastic rules, monks and nuns who used to leave their homes had no scope to possess or inherit wealth.

(c) For stable economy of a big *saṅghārāma* having thousands of inmates like the Nalanda Mahāvihāra authorities innovated several projects of self economy. Among them icon-making, *paṭa*-painting (scroll), etc. deserve mention. Tibetan records are not vivid in this respect in face of academic programmes of five major sciences (*pañca mahāvidyā-sthāna*) of learning and eight auxiliary subjects.

(d) Tārānātha referred to many eminent teachers who rendered their services for promoting education of the *Mahāvihāra*. On the other hand, vast *Āgama* literature of the *Sarvāstivādin* developd in North-West India and Gandhāra. Chinese records show that these *Āgāma* texts like *Saṁyuktāgama, Ekottarāgama, Madhyamāgama, Dīrghāgama,* were rendered into Chinese.

Nalanda teachers did not confine themselves to experimental studies. They were inclined to narrate their experiences in developing Tantra, divided in three *Yānas*, namely, *Vajrayāna, Sahajayāna* and *Kālacakrayāna*. Tārānātha mentioned the growth of three *Yānas*.

(e) About the teachers who promulgated the academic activities at Nalanda Māhavihāra vast collections of the Tibetan version of *Tripiṭaka* may focus specific contributions. Buddha's teachings in due course underwent multi-interpretations that amounted to the division of *nikāya* among Buddhists.

(f) Tibetan sources, however, provide further information about the models of scriptural dialogue *Śāstrārtha* as an important academic activity. *Śāstrārtha* had prevailed in the Indian academic centres since long. Dpag. bsam. lZong. bZong of Sumpa mkhen po narrated the instance of Nalanda academic dialogue. Tārānātha also provides similar information. The programme of debating had been in practice twice or thrice a week other than the festive days. *Pravāraṇā, Dharmacakra pravartana,* the full moon days and the eighth day of a lunar fortnight were usually suspended for normal work. Above that occasional ceremonies like *Kālacakra maṇḍala* worship and *Vajradhātu maṇḍala* worship were arranged usually after mid-day meal and these continued for hours till evening in the lunar fortnight.

Two types of debating presumably used to be held:

i) Inter-disciplinary debate, and
ii) Intra-disciplinary debate.

As a result of this, Nalanda innovated a new approach to Buddhism.

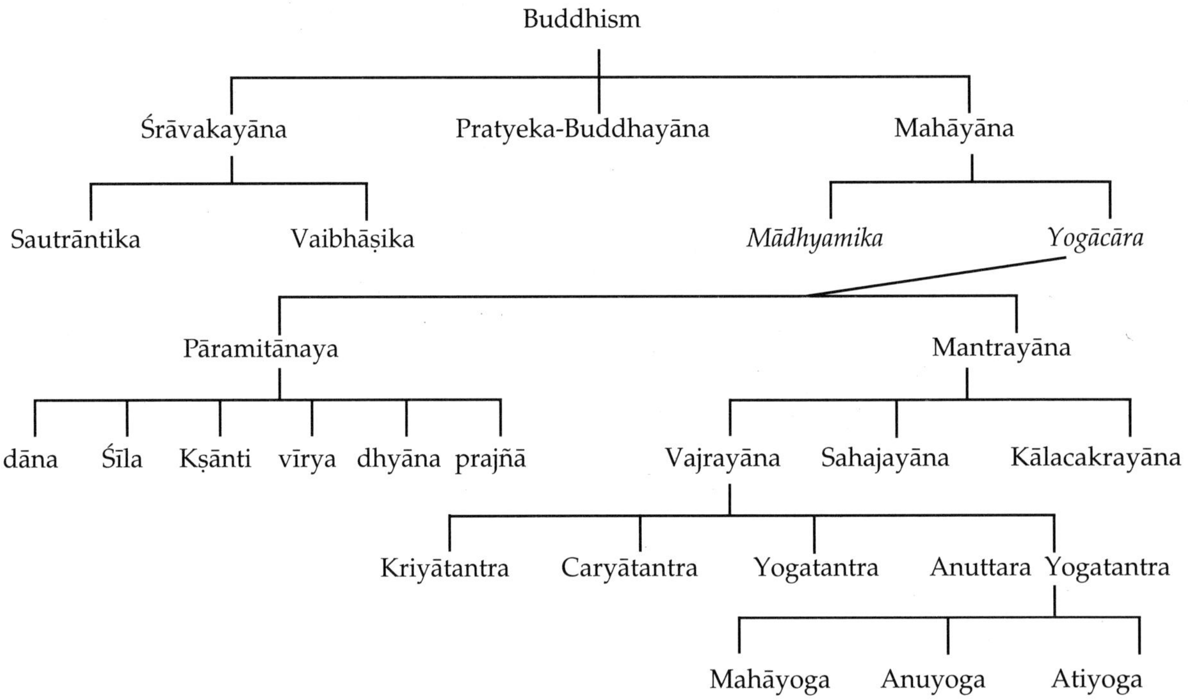

It is mentioned by Tibetan historians that intra-diciplinary debates used to be held outside the campus adjacent to a gate. In those debates eminent scholars other than the Buddhists were invited and inquisitive listeners of adjacent areas are said to be present as audiences and spectators. On one occasion Chandragomī was present when Chandrakīrti had been in the *Śāstrartha* Programme, outside the complex.

g) Contribution in spirituality by the Nalanda teachers and their disciples through generations may require an evaluation in the parameter of the then Indian society. Spirituality cannot be defined but it enriches the human value. The Buddhist way of life laid emphasis upon the ethical aspects in enunciating the eightfold proper path.
Eventually, the spiritual traits of Buddhist life may be divided into two categories:

   i) The renunciated yellow-robed recluse, and
   ii) The laity observing five *śilā*. Both were interdependent in the prospective growth of spirituality. In that respect the inmates of Nalanda and the Buddhist community around the *Mahāvihāra* succeeded until hostilities were thrust upon them on occasions.

Tārānātha in his account referred to three occasions of hostility by external influx of the Muslims since the 12th century. Gauḍavardhana who is said to be the ruler of eastern Bengal took measures to revive the damage caused by Muslim attack at the first instance. In the second instance Nalanda was heavily damaged when the Turk army led expedition in Magadha. A large number of monks were massacred and properties were looted. Losses were recovered when King Buddhapakṣa of Aparanta succeeded in driving out the Turk hoard. But it did not last long when the third hostility was organized by the beginning of the 13th century as Dharmaswamī witnessed and recorded in his biography.

Pl. 30. Nalanda: Buddha.

Pl. 31. Nalanda: Buddha.

Pl. 32. Nalanda: Buddha in *Bhūmisparśa mudrā*.

Pl. 33. Nalanda: Buddha.

Pl. 34. Nalanda: Miracle of Buddha.

Pl. 35. Nalanda: Stucco head of Buddha.

Pl. 36. Nalanda: *Mahāparinirvāṇa* of Buddha.

Pl. 37. Nalanda: Miniature temple.

Pl. 38. Nalanda: Miniature temple.

Pl. 39. Nalanda: Buddha.

Pl. 40. Nalanda: Buddha.

Pl. 41. Nalanda: Bust of Buddha.

Pl. 42. Nalanda: Stone sculpture of Nāgarāja.

Pl. 43. Nalanda: Jambhala.

Pl. 44. Nalanda: Tārā.

Part III

EARLY MEDIEVAL SCHOLASTICISM: LOGIC, PHILOSOPHY AND ESOTERISM

14

THE DOCTRINE OF APOHA WITH REFERENCE TO DHARMAKĪRTI

Lobzang Tsewang

INTRODUCTION

All Buddhist philosophical schools and religious sects unanimously accept the four great seals, viz., all composite things are impermanent, all contaminated things are suffering, all the phenomena are empty and selflessness, alone, is liberation and perfect peace as propounded by Buddha. These great seals are the central theme of Buddha's teachings, which consist of bulky volumes. Out of them selflessness, the negation of the self, is to be regarded as a major point because the sentient beings have been revolving in the *saṁsāra* since beginningless time being ignorant of the real nature of the self. All beings illusively experience that the so-called "I" or self exists substantially. This illusive concept of the self is considered as the root cause of irremovable sufferings. Without developing the cognition of the not-self or *Apoha* of substantial nature of the self, this nescience cannot be eliminated.

This situation entails to delineate the nature of negation or *Apoha*; what exactly it is, which was at the outset Buddha himself propounded, just as in *The Essence of Wisdom Sūtra*, "form is empty; emptiness is form, emptiness is not other than form; form also is not other than emptiness".[1] Later, this doctrine of *Apoha* or negation was developed and preserved by successive *ācārya*s in India and Tibet. Moreover, Master Diṅgnāga purposely and extensively exposited this doctrine, and made clear what the *Apoha* or negation and its importance is. Ācārya Dharmakīrti makes this doctrine more comprehensive and irrevocable by removing all criticisms made against this doctrine by the Hindu realists.

This doctrine of *Apoha* actually related to the ontological and epistemological problem, because Diṅgnāga and Dharmakīrti admit that the real referent object of the words and concepts must be *Apoha* or negation, because words and concepts cannot directly touch the unique particular. In contrast, the Hindu realist assumes that the referent object of the words and concepts are universal or qualified with universal. The whole controversy falls around the import of words and concepts which is very complex and knotted. It needs elaborate discussion.

ORIGIN OF THE DOCTRINE OF *APOHA*

It is considered that the doctrine of *Apoha* is a unique contribution of Ācārya Diṅgnāga who was a brilliant star in Nalanda in the 6th century CE. He revolutionized Buddhist logic by introducing several new concepts. In order to elaborate them, he composed many treatises, e.g., *Pramāṇasamuccaya*, *Nyāyapraveśa*, *Ālaṁbanaparīkṣā* and so on. He was an eminent dialectician at that time in India whose whole life passed in giving intellectual blows and receiving counter-blows. No dialectician can compare him in intellectual wrestling. Hence, Stcherbatsky, the eminent Russian logician, says,

> Just as an universal monarch brings under his sway all India, so is the successful winner of disputations the propagator of his creed over the whole of the continent of India.[2]

Diṅgnāga discovered the unique logical techniques which were applied to prove Buddha's teaching as to be stainless and purified, fully free from faults. On the basis of that he established that Buddha is an incomparable teacher in the world who possesses four kinds of perfect characteristics, viz., great compassion, the wisdom of selflessness, the complete cessation, and perfect saviourhood. Hence, Ācārya Diṅgnāga pays homage to Buddha in *Pramāṇasamuccaya*.

> I prostrate to incontrovert person who is beneficial to all.
> Possesses wisdom, cessation, being perfect saviour.[3]

Dharmakīrti from South India, who sought admission in Nalanda and deeply studied Diṅgnāga's logic, followed Diṅgnāga's tradition and used to indulge in intellectual combat, against adversary realists. He intended to save this logical and epistemological technique of Diṅgnāga. S.C. Vidhyabhusana says in *A History of Indian Logic*,

> It seems that in 635 Dharmakīrti was very young as Xuanzang does not mention him. On the other hand Yi'jing, who travelled over India during 671-695 declares eloquently how Dharmakīrti made further improvement in logic after Diṅgnāga. The Brāhmaṇic logician Uddyotakara is attacked by him.[4]

He composed seven treatises on logic as the commentaries of Diṅgnāga's *Pramāṇasamuccaya*, viz., *Pramāṇavārtika*, *Pramāṇa Viniścaya*, and *Nyāya Bindu*. He tried to explicate all the complexities and twisted points, which are found in *Pramāṇasamuccaya*. He extensively illustrated the system of perception, inference and syllogism which is the central theme of *Pramāṇasamuccaya* and what enriched the logical system of Diṅgnāga. After that, numerous commentaries and sub-commentaries have subsequently been written by the logicians who appeared from time to time in Nalanda and Vikramaśilā in India. This celebrated logical method was transferred to Tibet in 8th century when Śāntarakṣita was introducing Buddhism in Tibet. In the course of time, the chief works of Diṅgnāga and Dharmakīrti, and other commentaries on logic, were mostly translated into Tibetan language. Moreover, the indigenous works on logic developed by Tibetan monks, continued the Indian tradition. The original Tibetan works on logic began to develop in the 11th century CE and the first author Chāpa composed an independent work on logic. He discovered a special Tibetan logical debating style, which continued in all learning centres in Tibet. In later 11th century Saskya Paṇḍita wrote a short treatise in mnemonic verses and its auto-commentary. In 13th century Tsongkhapā and his pupils composed treatises on every work of Diṅgnāga and Dharmakīrti. The literary composition in this field has never stopped. Therefore, Stcherbatsky says,

> Every remarkable work on Indian Buddhism was immediately translated into Tibetan. When the Buddhism in India proper had become extinct, an indigenous independent production on logic by Tibetan monks gradually developed and continued the Indian tradition.[5]

Later on, this tradition traversed to Mongolia and flourished till the Russian invasion in Mongolia.

THE PROBLEM

Hindu Realist and Buddhist Nominalist have controversy about the problem of the nature of universal and the import of word and concept whether subjective or objective. They also have different views concerning the conceptual cognition and its relation to external reality. The *Nyāya-Vaiśeṣika* postulates that the so-called universal exists of its own right. As an objective reality it is also the import of the word and concept, otherwise there would be no basis to synthesize among the multiple particulars. This contention is supported by the successive eminent philosophers, viz., Uddyotakara, Jayanta, Śrīdhara and Vācaspatimiśra. Ācārya Diṅgnāga severely rejected this opinion by introducing the doctrine of *Apoha* or negation, which developed by Dharmakīrti, was strengthened by successive philosophers, Śāntarakṣita, Kamalaśīla and Ratnakīrti.

The Realist assumes that the universal subsists in diverse particulars, which has separate entity apart from them. The Nominalist advocates, in contrast, that no universal has independent existence as an external reality. However, it is a mere subjective construction. In the Realist's term, the perception of 'Jar' takes such a form that 'This is a jar'. In this sentence 'this' is a subject which refers to a particular object and it has 'a jarness' as its predicate. In this way, all perceptual judgements express the relation of the subject with its predicate. In every determinate perception, the object appears qualified by its universal. The comprehension of the qualified object is impossible, unless developing the previous cognition of qualification. Hence, the Realist says that the determinate perception is necessarily preceded by the indeterminate perceptions or sensation. It means, in the indeterminate perception of 'jar' we have comprehension of both 'jar' and 'jarness' but the 'jar' which is qualified by the 'jarness' is not comprehended, because the relation of the 'jar' with its 'jarness' is ignored.

In the determinate perception, the Nominalist admits that every object is comprehended in its generalized form which is not an external reality, but it is mere subjective construction. The particular alone is real which is mere momentary and point instants. The determinate perception which contains an unreal factor, i.e., generalized form, is neither real nor true perception. According to the Nominalist, the indeterminate perception contains mere particular or *svalakṣaṇa* as its object. So, it is alone true perception, whereas the determinate perception is not true. In fact, we are oblivious of indeterminate perception in terms of thought, but it is prerequisite of determinate perception.

The Realist intends to establish the validity of determinate perception, which is the background of controversy with the Nominalist. The validity of determinate perception depends on the objective reality of universal. In contrast, the Nominalist declares that the determinate perception contains the word element in object.

Through the above discussion the theory of universal is intrinsically associated with the theory of determinate perception. This theory of universal is the conflict point between the two schools with regard to the universal as ontological and epistemological aspects.[6]

UNIVERSAL

The Realist assumes that the universal, which is a natural and eternal class essence, e.g., redness, cowness and potness and so on, is permanent characteristic of the particulars. The things which are absolutely discrete and desperate and which have no bond of unity, in case, no comprehension of same class is impossible. The multiple particulars can be reduced into types or class. The common feature, which is found among the discrete particulars, is innate essence that is neither imported from the outside world nor from inner mind. In fact, the things possess a common

attribute, and on the basis of that we classify them and give a common designation. The universal which exists in the external world unites the divergent particulars in various classes. Although the universals reside in particulars, they have a distinct nature apart from the particulars. It is discerned by the Realist that both of them are equally true and real. Hence, M. Hiriyanna says,

> The manifold entities, so far alluded to are reducible to types. There is order in them which is due to objective features and is not imported into them by perceiving mind.[7]

Dharmakīrti contends that if the universal subsists in its individuals, then it will be absurd. The universal cannot move to reside where its particular is newly born, because it is motionless. It was already not present there because its particular is yet to come. The universal cannot be regarded as born when its particular is born, because it is permanent.

The Hindu Realist postulates that among composite things, we find different nature which depends on different causal efficiency. The universal is the determinant of the casual potency, so that the homogenous effect can be generated. The rice, for example, can exclusively produce rice and never barley. In the opposite case, a rice shoot would be produced by the barley seed or any kind of seeds. In fact, this condition is untenable. So, the entity of universal cannot be rejected. Hence, the cause-effect relation is determined without exception by the class nature of the cause and effect. The different causes cannot produce the same effect, and the different effects do not follow from the same kind of cause.

Dharmakīrti eliminates the above conception of the Realist that the different causes may produce the same effect. For example, different medicinal plant, fruit, root and matter may cure the same disease. In converse, the same cause produces different effect. For example, a rice seed may produce fruit, stem, leaves and a straw.

> Thus, the myrobalan, the *amalaki* fruit and other substances seem to cure diseases of the same sort. Now these substances are admittedly different from one another and yet they are found in experience to possess a common efficiency. It cannot be supposed that these different medicinal herbs, fruits possess a common nature.[8]

The Realist maintains that the universal is different from the particular, because its cognition is distinct from the particulars. Moreover, it is opposed to its particulars with respect to the essential characteristics, because it has the quality of eternality, commonness and inherence, whereas the particulars are absent of these qualities. The particulars are generated, abide and finally perish, whereas the universal is permanent and eternal, which is bereft of such qualities. The distinction between the universal and particulars is more radical rather than the difference which is found among the particulars, because they possess an identical class essence.

Against this theory may be raised objection that if the universal is distinct from its particulars, then why is the universal independently not apprehended apart from the particulars. In fact, the cognition of the universal depends on the particulars. Moreover, if the universal is distinct from its particulars, how can any relation be established between them? The relation must be casual relation, but not identical, because both of them are different from one another. It may not be the causal relation too, because both of them are not cause and effect.[9] This conception seems very obscure and absurd, which has no clear illustration what accords with experience.

The Realist maintains that the *samavāya* or intimate relation makes link between the universal and its particulars, cause and effect, and parts and whole and the like. Hence, the universal is associated with its particulars by the *samavāya*, and at the time it reserves the distinction between the universal and particulars. This point will also be clear that the 'cowness' is perceived in the 'cow' because of getting an intimate relation between them. So, the central function of the *samavāya* is to establish relation among different things.

These statements cannot solve the above-mentioned problem, because the so-called *samavāya* is a mere speculation of the Realist which has no existence, in case it cannot operate function to make link between the universal and its particulars.

> If, however, the universal is supposed to exist in the particular mediums by the relation of co-inherence (*Samavāya*), it does not make any improvement on the situation; on the contrary, it further complicates the issue. The universal is a bold assumption in itself and to justify this you are making another assumption which is equally absurd.[10]

Ācārya Dharmakīrti does not maintain that there is an objective universal over and above the particulars. It is mere thought construction or intellectual fiction. If we analyze this construction of thought, we will find nothing beyond particulars. Thus, we first experience the particular, and then it is assimilated to other particulars. As a result, a generic image is formed and then a symbolic expression, i.e., a name is attached which is used as a medium to communicate our ideas to others. It is a state of mere exclusion of its opposites. It still has pragmatic value, because it is remotely related to objective facts.[11]

IMPORT OF THE WORD

The problem of the import of word is stern and a disputed point, because the Hindu Realist postulates that the import of word is the universal which exists in the external world. In the contradictory way, the Buddhist Nominalist holds that the import of word is subjective construction, i.e., the generic image.

The Realist maintains that the direct import of word is external reality, because the word directly relates to the universal. In the proposition, the subject and predicate must be accorded with the real facts. The proposition may be either positive or negative, the terms really connote the factual relation which subsists in the objective facts. Such kinds of linguistic usages are warranted by practical experiences. In the same way, there would be correspondence between words and facts. This agreement would be unaccountable, unless depending on the supposition of objective basis.

> The realist of the Nyāya-Vaiśeṣika School and the Mīmāṁsaka maintain that words have direct reference to objective realities and as words relate to universals in the first instance. These universals should be looked upon as stern realities existing in their own right and not subjective construction, as Buddhists would have it.[12]

Some Realists conceive that the import of word is a particular, not the universal. The word simply refers to the individual alone, because the individual can be the subject of qualification. The universal uniformly resides in all individuals, so it cannot be the substantive of qualifications. For example, 'A cow grazes' or 'Bring a cow'. These sentences express action and command which can be applied to the individual, because in fact, the individual is capable to act and obey the command.

The Buddhist Nominalist rejects that if the word refers to a particular 'cow' in case, it cannot denote another cow. Hence, this expression does not serve the main purpose of the language, for which it is used. In such a condition, we cannot comprehend this conventional relation with regard to all individual cows, which are present, had been in the past and will be in the future. Therefore, this theory of particular is not satisfactory.

> So, the word 'cow' would mean only a particular cow and not any other. But these will not serve any purpose. And it is humanly impossible that a man should apprehend these conventional relations with regard to all the individual cows that are and had been and will be in existence.[13]

The *Mīmāṁsaka* Realist postulates that the direct import of the word is universal, because at first, we hear the word 'cow' and occurs comprehension of the universal 'cowness'; at that time, we do not have any idea of individual cow. The cognition of individual is preceded by the comprehension of the universal. For example, the universal 'cowness' must be the first thing which is cognized, when the word cow is heard, otherwise the word 'cow' may denote any kind of individual, which may be tree, house and so on.

The word 'cow' gives rise to a uniform conception of 'cowness' irrespective of individual cows which possess many divergent features with respect to colour, horn, and size. When a person is instructed to bring a cow, in case, he may choose and bring any sort of cow because he has the conception of 'cowness'. The *Mīmāṁsaka's* theory of universal is criticized by *Nyāya-Vaiśeṣika* that the universal alone cannot be the import of word, because its manifestation depends on the individuals. No word ever generated the cognition of the universal without apprehension of the particulars, because both of them are as if fused together, like a fire and iron in the red hot piece of iron ball. The verbal expression refers to the motion, e.g., 'bring a cow' and the like. It cannot be said that it refers to the universal, because the universal is incorporeal, so it is incapable to act or move at all.[14]

THE GRAMMARIAN'S VIEW

Bhartṛhari assumes that the word has neither beginning nor end, which is the cause of phoneme. There would be no cognition in the absence of word. All cognitions are intertwined with words. The determinate perception arises only when the word seed is germinated, and then it manifests in the form of expressive words, and demonstrates a specific meaning. And it leads to cause cognition of object. Thus, all experience and thought come into existence only through words. Bhartṛhari, therefore, maintains that both word and meaning are eternal. In the same way, the relation of the word and meaning is also eternal. Hence, the word is considered to be ultimate reality.[15]

Bhartṛhari maintains that it is legitimate to accept the universal alone as the import of word. The object should be the import of word which is comprehended when the word is uttered. In such case, the universal alone would be the denotation of the word. For example, the word 'pot' does not denote such specific characteristics which distinguish it from other pots, whereas it denotes only the universal or general feature, which makes it 'pot'.

The universal is a direct import of the word as assumed by the Realist and Grammarian, which is criticized by the Nominalist who contends that the so-called universal is mere speculation which has no real entity because this supposition is unwarranted either by practical experience or valid reasoning.

Dharmakīrti argues that if a word 'cow', 'horse' and so forth refers to individuals, then they would be proper names. In case innumerable words would be required to refer to numerous individuals. In such a situation, no one can make common discourse about the individuals.[16]

Generic image is an import of word as regarded by the Nominalist. The conceptual image or *Apoha* is an import of word. For example, a word 'cow' directly denotes the concept of cow, and it also implies its meaning which excludes its opposite meanings, what is called *Apoha*. There is indirect causal relation between the reality and concept, which is denoted by the word.

The language is not a separate source of cognition, and names are not direct expression of reality. The names correspond with the images or concept, which express only the universal. In the matter of fact, language does not differ from the inference, which is regarded as an indirect mode of cognition. It is one way to reach to the reality, which exists outside of the mind. Therefore,

> the speaker and the hearer are both labouring under a common delusion like two ophthalmic patients who see two moons and communicate their experience to each other.[17]

Whatever knowledge is conceptual must be considered to be inferential because it is directly linked with unique particular. We find here agreement between the import of word what is conceptual construction and objective reality.

In short, the doctrine of *Apoha* can be elucidated through three points:

1. The main import of words and concepts are mere image of external reality.
2. The words and concepts are indirectly connected with outside object.
3. The conceptual cognition is illusive, but touches reality.[18]

CONCLUSION

Diṅgnāga intends to define the exact nature of negation or *Apoha* through the long discussion which was held with Hindu Realists. The selflessness of a person is the negation, particularly non-affirming negation. The wisdom of a selfless person is regarded a direct antidote of the misconception of the self. Without realizing this fact, no one can eliminate the root cause of suffering and will not attain liberation. Therefore, Dharmakīrti identifies that the misconception of the self is an ultimate root cause of *saṁsāra*, wherein all sentient beings have been suffering since immemorial period of time. He says:

> If there is self, conceives as other.
> Attachment, hatred arise towards self and other
> By relating these misconceptions
> All the faults will be sprung.
>
> Hence, so far, one attaches to the self
> Till that *saṁsāra* will be sustained.
>
> The nescience is the root of the faults.
> It is nothing rather than conception of I.[19]

NOTES AND REFERENCES

1. Buddha, *The Essence of Wisdom Sūtra.*
2. Theodore Stcherbatsky, *Buddhist Logic*, Vol. I, Dover Pub. Inc., 1962, p. 34.
3. Diṅgnāga, *Pramāṇasamuccaya.*
4. S.C. Vidhyabhusana, *History of Indian Logic*, Motilal Banarasidass, 1978, p. 306.
5. Theodore Stcherbatsky, *op. cit.*, p. 55.
6. Cf. D.N. Shastri, *The Philosophy of Nyāya-Vaiśeṣika and its Conflict with Buddhist Digñaga School*, Bharatiya Vidya Prakashan, 1976, pp. 307-08.
7. M. Hiriyanna, *Outlines of Indian Philosophy*, London, George Alllen and Unwin Ltd., 1973, p. 233.
8. *Ibid.*, p. 91.
9. R.R. Dravid, *The Problem of Universal in Indian Philosophy*, New Delhi, Motilal Banarasidass, 1972, p. 179.

10. S. Mookerjee, *Buddhist Philosophy of Universal Flux*, New Delhi, Motilal Banarasidass, 1975, p. 102.
11. Cf. Śāntarakṣita, *Tattvasuṁgraha*.
12. S. Mookerjee, *op. cit.*, p. 107.
13. *Ibid.*, p. 108.
14. Cf. R.R. Dravid, *op. cit.*, p. 192.
15. Cf. *Ibid.*, p. 209.
16. Dharmakīrti, *Pramāṇavārtika*.
17. S. Mookerjee, *op. cit.*, p. 116.
18. Steherbatskyth., *op. cit.*, p. 457.
19. Dharmakīrti, *op. cit.*, Chap. II.

15

NALANDA AS A CENTRE OF ESOTERIC BUDDHISM

Kimiaki Tanaka

Nalanda, founded in the 5th century CE, is famous as an ancient seat of learning. However, Nalanda has mainly been associated with the esoteric phase of Buddhism, particularly with *Mādhyamika* and Vijñaptimātra philosophy, the two main currents of Mahāyāna Buddhism. For example, Xuanzang (602-664) stayed here in the 7th century and studied Vijñaptimatra philosophy, which he then transmitted to China.

On the other hand, esoteric Buddhism has been associated with three great monasteries established by the Pāla dynasty, namely, Odantapurī, Vikramaśilā and Somapurī. These three monasteries were established after the second-half of the 8th century. According to a Tibetan Buddhist source, the first *Vajrācārya* of Vikramaśilā was Buddhajñānapāda, the founder of the *Jñānapāda* school of interpretation of the *Guhyasamājatantra*, and I have been able to confirm the existence of a deep-rooted tradition of the *Jñānapada* school in Vikramaśilā. The three monasteries were, from the very beginning, associated with late Tantric Buddhism.

Where, then, did esoteric Buddhism preceding late Tantric Buddhism beginning with the *Guhyasamājatantra* come into existence? And where did it develop and where and how was it studied and transmitted?

In this paper, I shall consider the importance of Nalanda in the history of esoteric Buddhism, mainly in its early and middle phases, through an analysis of documentary sources and excavated items.

Śubhākarasiṁha (637-735), known as Shanwu-wei in China, the Indian monk who first introduced esoteric Buddhism to China, was born in Uḍra, present-day Orissa, as a son of King Buddhakara, probably one of the kings of the Bhaumakara dynasty. Due to a struggle for succession with his elder brother, he abdicated the throne and entered the Buddhist order. He studied esoteric Buddhism under Dharmagupta at Nalanda Monastery. In 716 he went to China and was welcomed by Emperor Xuanzang of the Tang dynasty. There he translated a number of esoteric scriptures, including the *Mahāvairocanasūtra* and the *Susiddhikarasūtra,* representative scriptures of the early and middle phases of esoteric Buddhism. We cannot confirm Dharmagupta's activities at Nalanda in other historical records and inscriptions excavated here.

Meanwhile, Vajrabodhi (671-741), known as Jingangzhi in China, who first introduced to China the *Sarvatathāgatatattvasaṁgraha* and its cycle, the so-called *Vajraśekhara*, is also said to have visited Nalanda and ordained as a monk here. Vajrabodhi's biography says that he received the *Vajraśekhara* cycle from Nāgabodhi in South India.

In Sino-Japanese esoteric Buddhism, Śubhākarasiṁha and Vajrabodhi have been regarded as experts on the *Mahāvairocanasūtra* and the *Sarvatathāgatatattvasaṁgraha*, respectively. On the basis of the *Gobu shinkan*, a collection of iconographical line drawings in hand-scroll form depicting the deities of the Vajradhātumaṇḍala which was attributed to Śubhākarasiṁha and brought to Japan from China by Enchin (814-891), we can confirm that Śubhākarasiṁha also had extensive knowledge of the *Sarvatathāgatatattvasaṁgrahatantra* and the *Vajraśekhara* cycle.

Recently, Japanese scholars have identified several statues of Vairocanābhisambodhi, the main deity of the *Mahāvairocanāsūtra*, from three important Buddhist sites in Orissa, the birthplace of Śubhākarasiṁha. Moreover, a statue of Vajradhātuvairocana, the main deity of the *Sarvatathāgatatattvasaṁgraha*, was also discovered at the Udayagiri site in Orissa. The estimated date of the single statue of Vajradhātuvairocana from Orissa is 9th century, and it is to be surmised that in the 7th century, when Śubhākarasiṁha was born, the *Sarvatathāgatatattvasaṁgraha* had not yet become popular in Orissa.

From the Nalanda site, on the other hand, several statues belonging to the middle phase of esoteric Buddhism have been unearthed and are now kept in the Nalanda Archaeological Museum and other museums in India. Among these, a statue of Vairocanābhisambodhi (identified by Indian scholars as *Vāk*, a form of Mañjusrī, and now kept in Nalanda Archaeological Museum) and three statues of Vajradhātuvairocana (two kept in Nalanda Archaeological Museum and one kept in the National Museum in New Delhi, wrongly identified as Vajrasattva) are quite remarkable. Vajrasattva with four consorts (namely, Lāsyā, Mālā, Gītā and Nṛtyā) and two Trailokyavijaya statues (one with only the lower part surviving) are also typical examples of the iconography of the *Sarvatathāgatatattvasaṁgrahatantra* and the *Vajrāśekhara* cycle.

Among these, the Trailokyavijaya statue (1-224) bears an inscription on the back which reads as follows:

> *ākāśalakṣaṇaṁ sarvvākāśaṁ cāpy alakṣaṇaṁ /*
> *ākāśasaṁatāyogāt sarvvāgrasamatā sphuṭāḥ //*
> (A. Ghosh 1986, p. 45)

This verse is frequently quoted in ritual manuals of late Tantric Buddhism. But the source of this verse is the *Paramādyatantra* and the *Sarvabuddhasamayogatantra*, and according to Sino-Japanese esoteric Buddhism, both of these scriptures were included in the 18 Tantras of the *Vajraśekhara* cycle. Trailokyavijaya is the main deity of the second chapter of the *Sarvatathāgatatattvasaṁgraha*, and the inscription also shows familiarity with the *Vajraśekhara* cycle.

Our attention is also drawn to the fact that Xuanzang and Yi'jing (635-713), who both visited Nalanda, translated early versions of the *Prajñāpāramitānayasūtra* after it had developed into the *Paramādyatantra*, and the *Paramādya* in turn developed into the *Sarvabuddhasamayoga*.

According to Tibetan sources, on the other hand, Śantarakṣita (725-784) was invited from Nalanda to Tibet. If the *Tattvasiddhi*, the sole work on esoteric Buddhism attributed to Śantarakṣita, is to be relied on, it is very interesting since it also quotes several times the *Paramādyatantra* and the *Sarvabuddhasamayogatantra* (as *Saṁvara*), including the verse mentioned above.

Stylistically, some statues of the middle phase of esoteric iconography from Nalanda came into existence after the appearance of late Tantric Buddhism. At any rate, we can confirm that in Nalanda there existed a deep-rooted tradition of the middle phase of esoteric Buddhism, particularly the *Sarvatathāgatatattvasaṁgrahatantra* and its cycle, known as the *yogatantra* by Tibetan Buddhists.

When Śubhakārasiṁha visited Nalanda, he already possessed some knowledge of the *Mahāvairocanasūtra* and its cycle since Vairocanābhisambodhi statues are abundant in Orissa and some of them were created in the 8th century. But the *Sarvatathāgatatattvasaṁgraha* and *yogatantra*s were not so popular in 7th-century Orissa. I surmise that Śubhākarasiṁha gained his knowledge of the *Sarvatathāgatatattvasaṁgraha* at Nalanda from Dharmagupta, which had probably just been introduced here from South India, the cradle of the *Vajraśekhara* cycle.

In this paper, I have discussed esoteric Buddhism and have considered the role that Nalanda University played in the history of esoteric Buddhism, particularly in its early and middle phases.

The *Mahāvairocanasūtra,* which once flourished on Indian soil, fell into decline after the 9th century. The *Sarvatathāgatatattvasaṁgraha,* on the other hand, continued to be regarded as one of the basic Buddhist Tantras after the appearance of late Tantric Buddhism even though it was thought inferior to the so-called highest *yogatantra*s.

After the construction of the three major monasteries initiated by Pāla kings, the status of Nalanda as a Buddhist seat of learning may have declined to a certain extent, and the centre of esoteric Buddhism also shifted from Nalanda to the newly constructed Vikramaśilā. Now, many Buddhist scholars associate esoteric Buddhism with Vikramaśilā and underestimate the importance of Nalanda.

The importance of Nalanda in the history of esoteric Buddhism, particularly before the construction of three major monasteries by Pāla kings, should not be overlooked.

After Yi'jing's return to China (695), we have no detailed information on Nalanda written by foreign monks, and contemporary records by Tibetans are available from only after the second-half of the 8th century. This coincides with the establishment of the Pāla dynasty and the inauguration of Odantapurī, the first of the three great monasteries. Hence, for Tibetans, historic Nalanda seemed to be less important than newly constructed Vikramaśilā. Therefore, when and how esoteric Buddhism was introduced to Nalanda is not clear. I believe that the historical records and excavated items taken up for consideration here throw some light on the state of Nalanda from the 7th to 8th centuries and its role in the history of esoteric Buddhism.

16

ŚĀNTARAKṢITA AND MODERN PHILOSOPHY

Marie-Louise Friquegnon

The philosopher Śāntarakṣita was born in Bengal, the son of the king, in the same family as Atisa. Renouncing worldly honours, he became a monk. Eagerly pursuing knowledge, he became one of the greatest Buddhist philosophers of all time. Professor of philosophy and abbot at the famous university – monastery of Nalanda in North India – he analyzed and refuted many tenets of Buddhist and non-Buddhist schools.

SUMMARY

Śāntarakṣita asserted nothing to be true on the absolute level. But on the relative level he claimed that all of reality was nothing other than mind. He arrived at his philosophical position in the following way: There are two possible candidates for the nature of reality – material and mind only. If reality is material, it must be made of parts. The smallest of these are said to be atoms. But if they are the smallest, they must be indivisible. However, if they are indivisible, they can have no extension. (For the only number which is indivisible is zero.) Nor can they have sides to attach to one another, for if they had sides, they would be divisible into those sides. So they cannot combine to make up larger objects.

So it would seem that the only alternative is that reality is mind only. It is, after all, impossible to deny awareness without utilizing awareness. But there are problems with the concept of mind and its relation to an object. Mind is either one or many, a unity or a plurality, one with its object or different. If mind is one with its object, that is, the same as its object, there is no way one mind could become aware of a changing world. If it is distinct from its object, the following problems arise: 1) If it is one and unified, how could a single state perceive an entire flowered cup while catching the diversity of its differently coloured flowers? 2) But if mind is compounded, other problems arise. How could a diversified mind perceive diversity in a single instant and recognize the different aspects of the cup to be the same? 3) And if the perceptions occur sequentially and very rapidly, as with a torch whirled around forming a circle of light, then one perceives what is not really there. Further, if mind is claimed to be real, we must ask how we know it. To know one's mind, we would need a mind to know it, and a mind to know that mind, etc. generating an infinite regress.

In spite of this, Śāntarakṣita was not a nihilist. He believed that through non-conceptual meditation, one could have direct awareness of reality. This experience resulted in great spiritual bliss. It was enlightenment itself.

Śāntarakṣita was also a great tantric master. He believed that certain practices on the relative level, with wisdom, compassion and mantra could lead to enlightenment. He is revered by Tibetan Buddhists as an emanation of Buddha Varjrāpaṇi.

Śāntarakṣita is famed for having held the reins of the two chariots of the *Mādhyamika* philosophy mainly associated with Nāgārjuna, and the Chittamātra (*Yogācāra*) school often associated with Asaṅga. The *Mādhyamika* school held that everything is emptiness. The Chittamātra school had many divisions, but all maintained the ontological primacy of mind.

My goal in this paper is twofold, first to show how Śāntarakṣita anticipated many of the ideas in Western philosophy from Descartes onward, and to show how modern philosophy can elucidate important points in his philosophy which were ahead of his time and perhaps were not fully understood by his contemporaries.

Like Descartes, Śāntarakṣita makes self-awareness[1] central to knowledge. He differs from Descartes, in that he will not consider the self to be a thinking thing. Self-awareness is not an instance of xRy, that is as a relation between a subject and an object. Bertrand Russell in his *History of Western Philosophy*,[2] quotes L. Wittgenstein approvingly as saying that Descartes only had the right to conclude from his 'cogito' argument, that there are thoughts, not that there is a thinker. Śāntarakṣita would agree.

Śāntarakṣita was under attack from those philosophers who feared that in accepting self-awareness, he would commit himself to the existence of a separate self. In defence, Śāntarakṣita makes a move that could be associated with Wittgenstein, who said that a picture could have us in its thrall.[3] The picture here is of a subject looking at an object which happens to be itself, like a person looking in a mirror. The same insight was at work in Gilbert Ryle's critique of Cartesian dualism as captivated by the picture of a ghost in the machine.[4]

Śāntarakṣita claims that the standard picture or model of knowledge, the knower (subject), the known (object), and knowing (activity) fails to apply in the case of self awareness.[5] The Wittgensteinian philosopher G.E.M. Anscombe makes a similar point. 'I' is not a word that refers. Is Śāntarakṣita saying the same? I'm not sure, but certainly he wants to break the hold of the standard model of subject, object and activity, when we consider self-awareness.

Śāntarakṣita has often been compared to Kant because his distinction between the absolute level of reality and the relative level looks very much like Kant's distinction between phenomena and noumena. Gudnursen's fine book on Wittgenstein and Buddhism rightly warns the reader not to identify these two distinctions because the absolute level, namely, emptiness, unlike Kant's noumenon, is not to be understood as an entity, but only as a negation of the relative level.[6] But Gudnursen is not entirely fair to Kant who at times insists that we must interpret noumena in a rather negative way. Nevertheless, Kant does not always heed his own warnings. For example, he claims there are three such noumena: God, the cosmos and the self.

Like the early empiricists, Locke, Berkeley and Hume, Śāntarakṣita tends to reduce all objects to combinations of sensory data. And like Hume, he denies that causality is a necessary connection between events. In fact following Nāgārjuna he goes further and denies the possibility of a causal relation altogether, considering it as only a useful illusion.

Śāntarakṣita's philosophical position is often characterized as idealist on the relative level and *Mādhyamika* on the absolute level. But his 'holding the reins of the two chariots' seems to me to be more complex than just joining two views. Śāntarakṣita does use Vasubandhu's[7] arguments against materialism, but he then uses Sautrāntika arguments against the Cittamātras.

Although I am really going out on a limb here, it seems to me that rather than accepting a straightforward idealist position on the relative level, Śāntarakṣita is defending self-awareness, but understands that cognitive processes cannot arise from physical processes. In other words, he is against reducing them to physical processes.

On the relative level, real entities can be said to be composed of atoms, but only in the sense that the mind is able to divide things into smaller and smaller parts. The smallest, which is not divisible, is the atom. This atom is not the same as the empirically understood atom of modern physics, which is divisible. It is an *a priori* notion. And upon analysis, one discovers its paradoxical nature. If it is really indivisible, it must have an extension of zero, because zero is the only number that cannot be divided. And since zero plus zero is zero, atoms could not combine to add up to anything. Also, they could not combine, because they could have no sides. If they contacted another atom, therefore, they would take up the same space. (This is Vasubandhu's argument. Neither Śāntarakṣita nor Vasubandhu puts the argument in terms of the number zero, but I suppose that is what they had in mind, for Indian mathematicians had invented the zero.)

One might argue that modern theories of the smallest particle are just as much a matter of logic as those of Śāntarakṣita. The latest theory, that of vibrating strings existing in eleven dimensions, can only be understood in mathematical terms. And mathematical entities, many people believe, are conceptual constructs.

Śāntarakṣita also argues that the atom cannot be either one or many. If it is a single indivisible particle, the above problems arise. If it is compound, it is not really an atom. I was surprised to learn that this dichotomy is an issue for modern physics. In *Scientific American*, January 1996,[8] one prominent scientist was reported as saying that it may not be possible any longer to identify fundamental particles as single or compound. (Perhaps these notions have to be understood contextually or relatively.)

The compatibility of Śāntarakṣita's view with recent philosophical interpretations of quantum mechanics has been argued in a letter to me, by Michel Bitbol, the French philosopher of science:[9]

> ... The major argument of Śāntarakṣita is that whereas atoms are supposed, by their very definition, to be partless, their being embedded within a spatial continuum is enough to define parts. In the text, the parts are (so to speak) 'facets': fractions facing different directions, and different atoms in the same directions. If the conclusion that atoms have parts is to be avoided, then the only option is to accept that they are one and the same, since this would entail there is nothing external the unique atom can be related to. Some similar problems of compatibility between the spatial status and the definition of atoms arose in classical western atomism. In all these examples, one sees the intermingling of metaphysical and geometrical arguments. The geometrical properties of atoms are often seen to be hardly consistent with their ascribed metaphysical properties. I think Śānkarakṣita's argument is of this type.
>
> 2) How are these problems overcome in modern atomism? Few people usually raise this question. But I think interesting answers are available. The answers are quite simple to state: (a) The 'properties' of elementary particles, including their spatial properties such as position or size, are not intrinsic but contextual (or relational); (b) The very "existence" of these elementary particles is not intrinsic but contextual (or relational).
>
> Point (a) was soon made clear by Bohr and Heisenberg. Heisenberg thus said that in modern physics a Lockean distinction between non-spatial 'secondary' qualities and spatial 'primary' qualities had become pointless. In fact, all the 'qualities' of microphysics are 'secondary', where secondary means relational.

> Point (b) arises from a straightforward reflection about Quantum Field Theory (see P. Teller, *An Interpretive introduction to Quantum Field Theory*). Indeed, in QFT, the number of particles is an 'observable', namely a value which arises with probability P when an interactive relation between the environment and an apparatus occurs. The number of particles is thus not inherently defined. P. Teller says that this means particles are not the sort of things that either exist or do not exist in the absolute.
>
> It is then very clear that the modern answer to the conundrums of classical atomism is exactly what Śāntarakṣita had in mind in *sloka*s 14 and 15: partless atoms are ascribed no intrinsic nature, no intrinsic existence. They are only correlates of a certain activity of investigations, whose byproduct is ordered by quantum theories. No intrinsic partlessness but rather partlessness relative to a certain range of method of partitioning; no intrinsic directions, or geometrical properties, but rather spatial properties relative to certain modes of geometrical measurements; no intrinsic existence but rather existence relative to one another and to certain methods of detection. The difference between the two cases is that Śāntarakṣita formulated this idea as part of the *Mādhyamika* systematic deconstruction of any 'essence', or assertion of inherent being, showing that it provided a rational dissolution to the problem of classical Indian atomism. Whereas modern physics was so to speak forced to this solution by the very limits of operativity of the old schemes of classical physics in the microscopic domain. But there is still reluctance against this solution nowadays: many physicists think this is a renunciation of the ideal of their science, and desperately look for 'realist' interpretations of quantum theories (where they mean interpretation that ascribes inherent properties and inherent existence to their entities).

Because of these problems with the notion of the atom, Śāntarakṣita rejects materialism, even on the relative level, except for practical purposes (e.g., how much lumber do we need to build our house?) He does not, however, reject awareness.

And just as there is a problem today in physics of making sense of fundamental particles, there is a similar problem in making sense of mind. Because when Śāntarakṣita turns to both the Sautrāntika and Cittamātra views on how the mind perceives, he finds none of them to be coherent.

In addition to his critique of causality, a further proof that the relative level is not the ultimate level is provided by his critique of perception. It was generally assumed that the object of perception must be present since the past no longer exists and the future does not yet exist. But the object of perception cannot be present because the present is instantaneous and the object of perception endures over time. Sautrāntikas and Cittamātrins alike see the mind as an entity that can be thought of as one or many, and the perceptual object as one or many, and the inability to match up the mind with its object in an instantaneous present. For it is given in all these systems that perception is only of what is in the present.

Through these considerations, Śāntarakṣita is led to the conclusion that the mind cannot contact reality through perception. But if perceptions are not the cause of knowledge, what is? The mind cannot produce all its objects out of whole cloth. What is making us know successively, and not all at once? Śāntarakṣita answers that the mind is not its own master. It is dependent on causes other than itself. In modern terms, it is in a matrix, and we are clueless about the causes that govern the mind.

Śāntarakṣita's final step is to appeal to Nāgārjuna's critique of causality. If mind is dependent on cause and effect, and we cannot make sense of cause and effect, then the final word is emptiness. Reality is, on the absolute level, beyond conception.

So what we have now is what has often been pointed out, a parallel between Śāntarakṣita and Kant. Kant's noumenon, which is beyond conception, resembles Śāntarakṣita's absolute level. His phenomena resemble Śāntarakṣita's relative level.[10] I'm not sure how far I can push this similarity. For Kant, phenomena are objectively real – objects of scientific knowledge. Yet we know them through categories, and in terms of transcendental modes of apperception of space and time. Ultimately their reality is noumenal, that is, the way in which the cosmos manifests itself to consciousness. Also Kant believes in relative permanence through space and time, a view which I doubt Śāntarakṣita would accept even on the relative level.

Śāntarakṣita is again more consistent than Kant, because Kant thinks of the noumenal as including self, world and God. But since number is on the phenomenal level, how can Kant maintain that the noumenal is three? In fact, there is one place in the critique where Kant says that all three forms of the noumenal are really God.[11] This obviously creates problems in trying to identify God with that which is beyond categories. Śāntarakṣita, wisely, is silent on the nature of emptiness.

But if emptiness is ultimate reality, Śāntarakṣita is faced with the problem of how it can be of religious concern. If all is emptiness, so what? Why pay homage or endeavour to experience it as wisdom, compassion and bliss? What saves the Buddhist from pure scepticism or nihilism?

The answer to these questions is to be found in the *Tattvasiddhi.* Here Śāntarakṣita argues that the way to reality (*tattva*, or suchness), involves a perspectival shift. Śāntarakṣita argues that there is a hierarchy of perspectives that one can take, beginning with the common sense view of reality in terms of physical objects.

The next step in the hierarchy is yogic perception. This results from familiarization with non-conceptual meditation which is non-dualistic, i.e., devoid of subject and object. The result of yogic practice, which is not of the ascetic sort, but relies on bliss, is to produce in the meditator a non-dualistic state of happiness. All of experience is coloured by this special form of bliss, which cannot be understood exactly in terms of ordinary bliss, but bears some similarity to it.

How are we as modern philosophers to understand this? Virgil Aldrich in his insightful *Philosophy of Art*[12] has given us a clue. Wittgenstein in his *Philosophical Investigations*, placed great weight on the duck-rabbit figure, a figure which could be viewed either as a duck or a rabbit. Aldrich applies this perspectival notion to works of art (with the qualification that, while it is unimportant if one sees the duck-rabbit figure as either a duck or a rabbit, someone who is incapable of taking the aesthetic perspective is aspect blind). There is the material thing, which can be viewed as either a physical object or an aesthetic object. A Jackson Pollack drip painting may be viewed by someone incapable of appreciating modern art as just oil paint dripping on canvas, i.e., as a physical object. The lover of modern art will see it as brilliant, intriguing, vibrating with colour, etc., i.e., as aesthetic object. How could one prove to the one who saw it only as a physical object that there was more to be seen? Perhaps going to art school might bring about a change. But how would one put this perspectival shift into words? Perhaps one could not. Similarly, Wittgenstein says in his *Notes on Religion*, that if one were to ask someone who had become religious, what had changed, the person may be unable to say.

In *Tattvasiddhi*, Śāntarakṣita admits that there is no proof that the yogic perspective can be had. But he does say that given a special set of causal conditions or circumstances, it is not illogical to admit the possibility of this special result. And this is true not only of the meditation on bliss. In an extraordinary passage, Śāntarakṣita links logical analysis with yogic perception, as a cause of a perspectival shift.

Tattvasiddhi Folio 74

> One explains everything through realization of the particularity of the cause and the particularity of the effect. Nevertheless, after examining names and categories, grasping and excluding [inference], there may be complete agreement or clarity [about concepts] such as the nature of the compounded [impermanence], nevertheless the appearance of subject and object are not clear and manifest. Renowned Ācārya Dharmakīrti also taught that in *saṁsāra*, whatever knowledge which arises appearing clearly, following from the careful distinctions of subject and object is due to logical analysis. Therefore names and categories are distinguished and are clearly apparent. Different from worldly knowledge, the direct perception of enlightened beings is nondualistic and does not rely on conventional characteristics, etc. Ācārya Dharmakīrti taught that one must thoroughly analyze subject and object, through analyzing names and categories, relying on the perfect knowledge of subject and object, which arises from experience of objects. Then if one confirms this with categories of establishing and reversing, becoming accustomed to this type of experience [through meditation], then one must agree this will not block clear perception of reality.

If one analyzes this phenomena carefully, discovering them to be unsubstantial and empty, then meditates on the emptiness one has discovered, familiarity with this meditation will lead to yogic perception.

But if yogic perception is so different from ordinary perception, how is it possible to speak of it as a mode of perception? Śāntarakṣita says it is possible because yogic perception has some similarity to our ordinary mode of perception. What can he mean by that? Let us return again to the analogy with art. A painting by Magritte may be said to have a quality of lightness. Objects may float in space. If someone inured to aesthetic qualities were to seize a Magritte painting, and throw it into a pond where it sinks, and deny this floating quality, we might say that such a person had missed the point. The words light, or float have an aesthetic meaning here, not a physical meaning. Yet the aesthetic meaning of the words bears some resemblance to the physical meaning, just as balance in a work of art bears some resemblance to physical balance but is not identical with it. Similarly, words such as bliss from the *yogi*'s or *yogini*'s perspective have quite a different meaning from ordinary bliss, but bear some similarity to it.

The final step in the hierarchy of awareness is Buddhahood, or enlightenment. Not only is awareness non-dual, awareness of subject and object having been transcended, but awareness has 'melted into' reality or suchness.

This suchness is beyond conception. Yet in view of Śāntarakṣita's Dzogchen associations, noted by George Dreyfus[13] (and his close association with Guru Padmasambhava), one may speculate that his notion of Buddhahood in the *Tattvasiddhi*, may be the same as that of primordial wisdom (an important Dzogchen concept). Although primordial wisdom is beyond conception, it could perhaps be appealed to as that which holds things together, rather than the *ālaya*.

That all reality is illusory is only true for Śāntarakṣita in an epistemological sense, not an ontological one. There is a reality, but we cannot put it in words, or know it discursively. Reality is emptiness. We cannot describe it. We can only melt into it through non-conceptual meditation. Then we experience (as a result) wisdom, compassion and bliss.

NOTES AND REFERENCES

1. *Madhyamakālaṅkāra Śloka* 16.
   Consciousness arises
   As the opposite of insentient matter.

Its own nature is not material,
But rather self-awareness.

2. B. Russell, *History of Western Philosophy.*
3. L. Wittgenstein, *Philosophical Investigations.*
4. G. Ryle, *The Concept of Mind,* New York, Barnes and Noble, 1949, p. 15.
5. *Madhyamakālaṅkāra Śloka, 17.*
   Because its nature is single and partless
   It is impossible for it to have a threefold nature.
   Therefore self-awareness is neither subject, object nor result.
6. Chris Gudmunsen, *Wittgenstein and Buddhism,* London, Macmillan, 1977, pp. 50-51.
7. *Madhyamakālaṅkāra Ślokas,* 10-15.
8. M. Mukerjee, 'Explaining Everything', in *Scientific American,* January, 1996.
9. De : 'Friquegnon, Marie' <FriquegnonM@wpunj.edu>
   >À : 'BITBOL' <Michel.BITBOL@wanadoo.fr>
   >Objet : RE: Re : book on Sāntarakṣita
   >Date : Mar 10 fév 2004 19:02
10. *Madhyamakālaṅkāra Śloka,* 78.
    As for myself, I never disputed
    The relative reality of the nature of appearances.
    Having established this view of things,
    One will not be confused about the relation of premise and conclusion.
11. If I think of a being as existing which corresponds to a mere idea, and a transcendental one, I ought not to admit the existence of such a being by itself, because no concepts through which I can conceive any object definitely, can reach it, and the conditions of the objective validity of my concepts are excluded by the idea itself. The concepts of reality, of substance, even of causality, and those of necessity in existence, have no meaning that could determine any object, unless they are used to make the empirical knowledge of an object possible. They may be used, therefore, to explain the possibility of things in the world of sense, but not to explain the possibility of a *universe itself,* because such a hypothesis is outside the world and could never be an object of possible experience. I can, however, admit perfectly well such an inconceivable Being, being an object of a mere idea, relative to the world of sense, though not as existing by itself.
12. V. Aldrich, *Philosophy of Art,* Englewood Cliffs, Prentice Hall, 1963.
13. G. Dreyfus, 'Would the True Prāsangika Please Stand? The Case and View of "Ju. Mi. pham"' in the *Svātantrika-Prāsangika Distinction* (eds.), G. Dreyfus and S. McClintock, Somerville, MA, Wisdom, 2003, pp. 330, 333 and 339.

17

CONTRIBUTION OF ĀCĀRYA DHARMAPĀLA OF NALANDA

Bimalendra Kumar

There are two Dharmapālas – one Vijñānavādin Dharmapāla, who was the teacher of Śīlabhadra, and the other, the Dharmapāla of Suvarṇadvīpa. From the informations of *Sun pa mu khan po* and Tārānātha and from the descriptions in the colophones of the Tibetan *Tripiṭaka,* it can be concluded that Dharmapāla was a Mahāyāna teacher who wrote several commentaries on *śāstras* of Mahāyāna such as the *Abhisamayālaṁkāra* (ascribed to Maitreya) and Śāntideva's *Bodhicaryāvatāra.* N. Aiyaswami Sastri has discussed at length all the points relating to the persons and dates of these two Dharmapālas.[1] He has discussed the date of Dharmapāla in his *Ālambanaparīkṣā* and *Vṛtti* by Diṅgnāga with the *Commentary of Dharmapāla.*[2] Tom J.F. Tillemans regards Dharmapāla of Suvarṇadvīpa as a Vijñānavādin, calling him "a Vijñānavādin Dharmapāla of Suvarṇadvīpa, who was guru of Atīśa Dīpankara-śrījñāna".[3] However, there is anotherr Dharmapāla of the Theravāda school, who has composed commentaries on the texts such as Buddhaghoṣa's *Viśuddhimagga Paramatthadīpanī* and some of the texts of *Khuddakanikāya.*

Ācārya Dharmapāla was a native of Kāñchipuram in South India and was the son of a minister. A royal feast was arranged in his honour by the king and queen and there arose in him distaste for the worldly life and he left home without attending the feast. Travelling for some time, he reached Nalanda and became a monk. He completed his study there and eventually became the *ācārya* of the monastery. Under his supervision, Śīlabhadra learnt all the teachings of Buddhism and attained his efficiency in explaining the subtleties of the Buddhist texts. His fame as a great Buddhist scholar spread to foreign countries. At that time a Brāhmaṇa from South India who was proud of his learning, came to Magadha and challenged Dharmapāla for a religious discourse. Dharmapāla engaged Śīlabhadra who was then thirty years old, for initiating discussion with the Brāhmaṇa. Śīlabhadra thoroughly outwitted his opponent and succeeded in proving the soundness of his Faith. Ācārya Dharmapāla was succeeded by his illustrious disciple Śīlabhadra under whom Xuanzang studied at Nalanda. He went to Suvarṇadvīpa at a ripe age.

A brief account of the life of Dharmapāla as given by Tārānātha, differs in a few more points in biographical details from the one given by Vidyabhushan and other scholars based on the Chinese travellers. According to Tārānātha, Dharmapāla, born in South India, became famous for his proficiency in the Buddhist as well as non-Buddhist *śāstras* even as a young *Upāsaka*. After having been ordained by and receiving instructions in *Vinaya* from Ācārya Dharmadāsa he became a great scholar and came to Madhyadeśa. He became supreme among scholars after getting instructions in *Tripiṭaka* from Diṅgnāga. He propitiated *Bodhisattva* Ākāśagarbha at Vajrāsana (in Bodhgaya) and received his vision atop the *Bodhi* tree. He taught the doctrine at Vajrāsana for over thirty years and succeeded Chandrakīrti as the *Upādhyaya* of Śri Nālendra (Nalanda). Instead of begging from any other donor, he obtained his and his *saṅgha*'s maintenance from Ārya Ākāśagarbha's treasury and silenced his *tīrthika* opponents by the power of *Krodhāgnidaṇḍa*. While at Vajrāsana, he composed a commentary on the *Madhyamaka-Catuḥ-Śataka*.[4] He is respected in the Tibetan tradition in being counted along with Āryaśūra, Rāhula nad Guṇaprabha as one of 'the Great Four'.

Ācārya Dharmapāla was famous for his scholarship throughout the Buddhist world. Indians in that age did not suffer from the complex of having a monopoly of great learning. In fact, one of the eighty-four *Siddhas*, Ratnākaraśānti, who had earned the title of *Kalikālasarvajña*, omniscient of the Kali Age, was a disciple of Ācārya Dharmapāla. Jñānaśrīmitra, the great exponent of dialectics and Ratnakīrti had also sat at the feet of Ācārya Dharmapāla. Atiśa Dīpaṅkara Śrījñāna had met these scholars at Vikramaśilā and had probably learnt a good deal from the disciples of Dharmapāla.[5] The prince Lha-lama Yeshe-hod of Tibet invited Pandit Dharmapāla, Guṇapāla and Prajñāpāla, from the eastern quarter of India. From these, Gyal-wai-Se-srab of Shang Shung took the vows of monkhood and afterwards went to Palpa in Nepal to learn *Vinaya* and philosophy from the Hīnayāna sage named *Pretaka*.[6] With the assistance of these, Yeshe-hod encouraged the teaching of religion, arts and especially *Vinaya*.

Among the works of Dharmapāla the commentaries on *Vijñaptimātratāsiddhi* and *Catuḥśataka* are famous. Dharmapāla's commentary, *Guang-bai-lun-shi-lun* or 'Commentary on the Extensive Hundred Treatises' has equal importance in comparison with Candrakirti's *Bodhisattvayogācāracatuḥśataka-ṭīkā* in terms of the philosophy of Āryadeva. The theory of perception (*pratyakṣa*) has been advocated by Dharmapāla and Candrakīrti. Candrakīrti denies perception in its capacity of an immediate, non-deceptive form of knowledge. In his opinion, an object of perception is interpreted as real only by those who have not realized voidness (*śūnyatā*). Quite in contrast to Candrakīrti, Dharmapāla adopts classical *Yogācāra* position, constructing Āryadeva's text as a refutation of *parikalpitasvabhāva* but not *paratantrasvabhāva*, despite the fact that he is an 'idealist' not only in the sense that he accepts mind dependence of all existence, but also in the fact that he recognizes the reality of mind *qua paratantra* and thus gives to mind a preferred ontological status.[7]

Dharmapāla has also written a commentary on *Ālambanaparīkṣā* of Diṅgnāga, who belonged to the school of Vasubandhu. He also wrote a small text, namely, *Mahāyānaśata-dharmavidyādvāraśāstra*, which is available in both Chinese and Tibetan versions.[8] The Chinese version of this text maintains that the author of this text is Vasubandhu, but according to local belief in Tibet, the author of this text is Śrīmad Dharmapāla.

Thus, from above discussions, it can be said that Ācārya Dharmapāla was famous for his scholarship throughout the Buddhist world, and his texts attracted the attention of the scholars of modern time to carry out the investigations. Unlike other eminent *ācāryas* of Nalanda, his purpose was to study more about Buddhism. According to Xunzang, he gave fragrance to the Buddha's teachings.

NOTES AND REFERENCES

1. 'On Dharmapāla', *Journal of Śrī Venkateśvara Oriental Institute*, Vol. 2, Part II, Tirupati, p. 347ff.
2. N. Aiyaswami Sastri (ed.), *Ālambanaparīkṣā and Vṛtti by Diṅnāga with the Commentary of Dharmapāla*, The Adyar Library, 1942, pp. xix-xxii.
3. Tom J.F. Tillemans, *Materials for the Study of Āryadeva, Dharmapāla and Candrakīrti*, Vol. I, Weiner Studien Zür Tibetologie und Buddhisumskunde, Heft-24, 1-2, Arbeitskreis for Tibetische und Buddhistsche Studien, Universitat Wien, Wien, 1990, p. 11, n. 26, referred to in the *Book Review of Acta Orientalia*, 53, (1992) by Akira Saito of University of Miye, Japan.
4. Kewal Krishan Mittal (ed.), *A Tibetan Eye-view of Indian Philosophy*, Munshiram Manoharlal Publishers Pvt. Ltd., New Delhi, 1990, p. 197.
5. P.V. Bapat (ed.), *2500 years of Buddhism*, Publication Division, New Delhi, 1987, p. 202.
6. Alaka Chattopadhyaya (ed.), *Tibetan Studies: Sarat Cahndra Das,* K.P. Bagchi *et al.*, Calcutta, p. 83.
7. Cf. *Acta Orientalia,* 53 (1992), p. 201.
8. 'An Analytical Study Mahāyānaśata-dharma-vidyā dvāraśāstra', *Tibetan Journal*, Vol. XXIV, No. 3, Autumn, Library of Tibetan Works and Archives, Dharmasala, pp. 10-31.

18

NALANDA AND ŚĀNTARAKṢITA: HIS *MADHYAMAKĀLANKĀRA ŚĀSTRA* IN TIBETAN VERSION

Manotosh Mandal

NALANDA AND THE MĀDHYAMIKA THOUGHT

Nalanda was not a unitary *śaṅghārāma*. Different factions of the Buddhists had their separate units inside the Nalanda campus. An inscription of South-East Asian ruler mentions that he purchased five villages and those were donated to a *vihāra* inside Nalanda. Xuanzang mentioned that different factions of Buddhist *Nikāyas* had separate abodes within the *Mahāvihāra*. Xuanzang came in the 7th century CE. By that time eighteen schools of Indian Buddhism flourished. It was a glorious period of Nalanda Mahāviharā.

Śāntarakṣita was a teacher of Nalanda in the 8th century CE. His life account of royal birth is available in Tibetan. By the 8th century Buddhist doctrine got a new dimension in exposition of *śūnyatā*. It became the central focus of the Mahāyānist adherent to the method of *Pāramitā* or that of *mantra*.

Tibetan historian, Tāranātha records that there were eighteen branches of Indian Buddhists.

From the philosophical point of view, the Buddhist thought may be divided into four strata such as *Sautrāntrika, Vaibhāṣika, Yogācāra* or *Vijñānavāda* and *Mādhyamika*. In that case, the question may arise, like, who promoted the *Mādhyamika* thought, especially the doctrine of *śūnyatā* – the essencelessness of phenomena.

Nāgārjuna is said to have brought from the *Nāgaloka* the *Prajñāpāramitā sūtra* in which the doctrine of *śūnyatā* had been laid. *Prajñāpāramitā sūtra* is regarded as a *Vaipulya sūtra*. He expounded the *śūnyatā* doctrine in his own way in his *Mūlamadhyamaka kārikā*, otherwise named *Prajñā*.

According to *Chos. 'byung. zin. bris. nor. bu 'phreng ba* (English translation: 'Jewel Garland of Buddhist History'), Nāgārjuna had been at Nalanda and he developed the teaching procedure of higher training in threefold manners, namely, discipline, meditation and wisdom. The said information may suggest that Nalanda had been an academic centre by the second century CE when Nāgārjuna had been present there as an abbot. It was a debating centre in which two critical expositions of the *Mādhyamika* doctrine continued for centuries.

DEVELOPMENT OF THE MĀDHYAMIKA OUTLOOK

In due course *Mādhyamika* thought developed in two dimensions.

1. Bhavya or Bhāvaviveka (500-570) followed the interpretation by Saṅgharakṣita (5th century) and composed *Prajñāpradīpa*. He claimed that Nāgārjuna's *Prajñā* with independent middle term *svātantrikā hetu* would be more understandable.
2. Whereas Candrakīrti in the line of Buddhapālita (400-450) related the middle term *prasaṅga hetu* critically by the argument of the *reductio ad absurdum.*

These two separate lineages are called *prāsaṅgika* and *svātantrika*. Their main difference lies in that *prāsaṅgika* gives emphasis on *prasaṅgānumāna* in which refutation of other person's statement is the goal for the refutation of a contradictory implication of a *prasaṅgānumāna*. Chandrakīrti belongs to the group of *prāsaṅgika* whereas Bhāvaviveka is *svātantrikā*. S.K. Mukherjee rightly observed that:

> A divergence of opinion regarding the necessity of the contradictory position being accepted, which is the third condition of *prasaṅgānumāna*, seems to have been responsible for the two main divisions of Nāgārjuna's followers into the *prāsaṅgika* and *svātantrika* schools, the latter insisting on the necessity of independent arguments for the refutation of the contradictory implication of a *prasaṅgānumāna* (The Buddhist Philosophy of Universal Flux, Chapter XXV, p. 404).

To clarify the nature of both *prasaṅgānumāna* and *svātantrika* we can discuss some points here a bit more. *Prasaṅgānumāna* is regarded as *tarka* by Vācaspati Miśra. *Tarka* is regarded as a helping instrument of knowledge. It is *apramā* according to Nyāya philosophy. *Prasaṅgānumāna* is therefore an indirect proof of some statement. Actually it is a hypothetical negative argument to point out logical defects in the position of the adversary. *Prasaṅgānumāna* shows that the opposite decision of an inferential conclusion is not tenable. It can also refute a decision by showing that if the decision is taken then we are compelled to accept some undesirable or unreasonable judgement. On the other hand, *svatantranumāna* is direct proof of some decisions, on basic universal concomitant *vyāti* from the knowledge of *hetu* to the knowledge of *sādhya*. It is a direct way to reach the conclusion as shown in the inference, "hill is fiery for being smokey". But in the case of *prasangānumāna* if we suppose that there is no fire in the mountain then we have to accept that there is no smoke also, but it is purely hypothetical because existence of smoke is proved by perception. So we should not deny it. Hence we should not deny the existence of fire also. One can strengthen his inferential decision. But in this way Nāgārjuna's main tendency is to deny the statement of opponent party by showing that if the statement is accepted then we would be compelled to accept some undesirable decision also.

The analysis of *śūnyatā* in dialectic method by Nāgārjuna was not an innovation. The Theravāda texts mention *śūnyatā* occasionally. In that case *śūnyatā* suggests a state of evacuation, for the sake of meditation as if in a vacant room having no objects.

By the process of meditation the phenomenal objects of craving are to be withdrawn. That leads to a process of evacuating tension, strains and stresses.

ŚĀNTARAKṢITA'S VIEWPOINT

Śāntarakṣita promoted the *svātāntrika* interpretation of the self-naturelessness of phenomenon *Dharma-nis-svabhāvatā*. His *Madhyamakālaṅkāra-kārikā* and *Madhyamikālaṅkāraṭīkā* go in support of the *Svātantrika-Mādhyamika* school which flourished at Nalanda as Kamalaśīla followed. On scrutiny of those commentaries the possibilities of divergent interpretation may be traced prior to the advent of Śāntarakṣita.

a. Nāgārjuna wrote a commentary of the *Prajñāpāramitā sūtra*. Buddhapālita composed a commentary of *Mūlamadhyamaka vṛitti* (Toho No. 3842). On the commentary by Bhāvya or Bhāvaviveka on Nāgārjuna's *Madhyamaka kārikā*, it was studied by Vimuktasena of Maghadha.

b. Bhāvya of Malabara Coast in South India probably belonged to the Apara Śaila school. He interpreted the *Mūlamādhyamika kārikā* with reference to the independent middle term *svātantra hetu*.

c. Chandrakīrti, a subsequent scholar of South India, probably interpreted the related middle term *prasaṅga hetu*. By the sixth century, the Buddhist logical and epistemological structure developed with distinct model in Diṅgnāga's Buddhist thought and Dharmakīrti succeeded him. Chandrakīrti followed Buddhapālita's views and Bhāvaviveka's stand of the independent middle term in examination of Nāgārjuna's *Prajñā, Madhyamaka kārikā*. In due course separate interpretations of Nāgārjuna's doctrine of *śūñyatā* developed namely, *svātantrika mādhyamika, prāsaṅgika mādhyamika*, and *mādhyamika vijñānavāda*.

MADHYAMAKĀLANKĀRA TEXT

Madhyamakālankāra-śāstra is not available in original Sanskrit. It is available in Tibetan translation (*Bstan 'ghur*, Toh No. 3864). It was translated by Ye shes sde (8th century) with the collaboration of Surendrabodhi. An auto-commentary of this text ascribed to Śāntarakṣita is also preserved in *Bstan 'ghur* (Toh No. 3885). It was translated by Ye she sde of Zhu Chen and Śailendrabodhi of Kashmir. There are ninety-six verses in this *kārikā*.

ŚĀNTARAKṢITA'S INTERPRETATION

The excellence of *Madhyamakālankāra* is that it refutes the analysis of *Mādhyamika* doctrines in the logical process of *reductio ad absurdum*, that is, *prasajya-pratiṣedha*. In this regard Śāntarakṣita's *Tattvasaṁgraha* defines *prasaṅga sādhanaṁ*, the application of reduction by stating that the invalidity is carried over to refute in itself. [*Apramādapyanayā nityā svata eva prasajyate (Tattva saṁgraha-230).*] It goes against Nāgārjuna. As a result of that Chandrakīrti's interpretation of *Mādhyamika* by the method of *reductio ad absurdum* had been interpreted as a kind of nihilism by some modern academicians like Harsha Narain (*Mādhyamika Mind*).

Śāntarakṣita, therefore, followed the line of Bhāvaviveka to interpret *Mādhyamika* dotrine by holding independent cause having no depdendable condition. In *Tattvasaṁgraha pañjikā* of Kamalaśīla, it is explained that *prasaṅga hetu* may be the cause of negation of the relationship of barren child (*bandhyā putra*). That may be applicable, in the case of jar which is not animate.

> *Bandhyāsunivṛttau tadasambandhanāmapi prāgadināmnivṛttiṁ prāpnoti ghaṭādi vad iti kenacit prasaṅgāmpadaṁ kriyamāṇokāntikaṁ bhavati* (Tattvasaṁgraha pañjikā, 198)

Reductio ad absurdum or argument as absurdum may suggest the evacuating of the cyclic elements by negation of negation. Because that holds no propositional stand like *pratītya samutpāda*.

Epistemologically, the relationship of *pakṣa* is debarred to go into relationship between the major term and the postulate because of absurdity. Nāgārjuna reads thus his standpoint of opposition.

> *Śūnyatāyāṁ adhilayaṁ yaṁ punaḥ kurute bhāvanā.*
> *Saprasaṅgo nāsmākaṁ sa śūnye nopapadyate.*

(*Mūlamadhyama kārikā*, Chapter 24, Verse 13)

You have repeatedly refuted *sūnyatā* but we do not fall into any error. The refutation does not apply to *śūnyatā*. That is not appropriate in the context of void.

Chandrakīrti in commenting the benedictory verse clearly explained his position by *reductio ad absurdum*. Despite that Śāntarakṣita followed here, the *svātantrika* method represented by Bhāvavivekâ by admitting a positive thesis in support of his dialectic in order to refute his opponent's views in *Madhyamakālaṅkāra-kārikā-śāstra* and its auto-commentary *svavṛtti*.

That may be jotted down below in brief.

1. The objective of his work is to justify his own stand by negating the scope of an existent when the ideation of the mind only cognizes the existent of the phenomenon. The non-Buddhists including the Jainas and the Vedists, could not follow what the Buddha said. (*śloka* No. 1 to 12).

བསྒོམས་ལས་འདུས་བྱུང་བའི་ཤེས་པ་ཡིས།།ཤེས་བྱ་འདུས་མ་བྱས་སྨྲ་བའི།།

ལུགས་ལ་འཐད་གཅིག་མིན་དེ་དག་ནི།།རིམ་ཅན་ཤེས་དང་འབྲེལ་ཕྱིར་རོ།།3

Those who claim that the unconstituted phenomena are knowable by the knowledge arising out of thought process may require probing how the knowledge arising in progressive order would coordinate the causality of that which are not in cause and condition.

2. The forms of a phenomenon arise by the thought construction in an average person under the veils of the knowledges (*jñeya-āvaraṇa*). The measure of refuting them by the method of *reductio ad absurdum* would be fruitless (*śloka* 14 to 40).

རྣམ་ཤེས་བེམ་པོའི་རང་བཞིན་ལས།།བཟློག་པ་རབ་ཏུ་སྐྱེ་བ་སྟེ།།

བེམ་མིན་རང་བཞིན་གང་ཡིན་པ།།དེ་འདི་བདག་ཉིད་ཤེས་པ་ཡིན།། 16

The self nature of consciousness of inanimate is the negation of consciousness because self nature of the conscious is not inanimate by which knowledge of awareness arises.

3. Śāntarakṣita placed his own stand by claiming that *Mādhyamika* doctrine might be easy to appreciate by positive understanding. The epistemological significance of the Buddha's teachings on the law of dependent origination (*pratītya samutapāda*) becomes an instrument to understand *śūnyata* in *Mādhyamika* thought. The rest of the *śloka* is mentioned here.

སེམས་ཙམ་ལ་ནི་བརྟེན་ནས་སུ།།ཕྱི་རོལ་དངོས་མེད་ཤེས་པར་བྱ།།

ཚུལ་འདིར་བརྟེན་ནས་དེ་ལ་ཡང་།།ཤིན་ཏུ་བདག་མེད་ཤེས་པར་བྱ།།92

On accepting the postulate of the mind only or the consciousness only the knowledge of the external phenomena would be incompetent because depending on the method, the knowledge of unreality of the extent would be determined.

In this regard Śāntarakṣita justified his stand in the light of that Nāgārjuna had focused in his *Mādhyamika kārikā*. It may be cited here: *Yaḥ pratītyasamutpādaḥ Śūnyatāṁ tāṁ pracakṣmahe*

Sā prajñaptir upādāya pratipat saiva madhyamā (*Mūlamadhyamaka kārikā*, 24:18). We state that whatever is dependent arising, that is void that is dependent upon convention that itself is the Middle Path.

BIBLIOGRAPHY

Chimpa, Lama and Alaka Chattopadhyaya, *Tārānāth's History of Buddhism in India,* Delhi: Motilal Banarsidass Publisher, 1997.

Harsha, Narain, *Mādhyamika Mind*, Delhi: Motilal Banarsidass Publisher, 1997.

Kalupahana, David, *Mūlamadhyamaka kārika of Nāgārjuna*, Delhi: Motilal Banarsidass Publisher, 1999.

Losang, Norbu, *Indian Buddhist Pandits*, Delhi: Library of Tibetan Works and Archives, 1985.

Negi, J.S. (ed.), *Tibetan Sanskrit Dictionary*, Vol. 1 to 12, Sarnath: Central Institute of Higher Tibetan Studies, 2003.

Pathak, Suniti Kumar, *Tibbat*, (Bengali), Santiniketan, W.B.: Gita Pathak, 1960.

——, *An Analytical View of Buddhist Logic*, Calcutta: 2003.

Shaw, J.L., *Causality and its Application Samkhya, Buddha & Nyaya*, Calcutta: Punhi Pustak, 2005.

The Buddhist Philosophy of Universal Flux, Delhi: Motilal Banarsidass Publisher, 1993.

Vidyabhushana, Satish Chandra, *A History of Indian Logic*, Delhi: Motilal Banarsidass Publisher, 2002.

19

NĀGĀRDZHUNA AND PARTITION OF MĀDHYAMIKA TECHNOLOGY

Damba Ayasheev

We would try to make a brief commentary of Nāgārdzhuna's *Partition of Mādhyamika's Teaching* which consists of 27 parts.

The first part of the present work explains the main notions of *Mādhyamika* on four conditions.

The first condition – causality.
The second condition – striving.
The third condition – newly born in consciousness.
The fourth condition – arising of the own ego.

The first and the third conditions depend on external factors, the second and the fourth conditions are our inner state. In this correspondence *nirvāṇa* is one pacifying the fire.

The second part is devoted to the notion of movement. One step is not yet moving itself, and the second step is not already moving since it is just a repetition.

All of us are deep in the ocean of suffering. If only we would learn to move, we would already have stepped away of these sufferings.

In the third part ability of right viewing has been developed, which itself cannot but should have negation. Only negation of the four causes gives the knowledge of true viewing.

The fourth part opens the common essence of the five *skandhas* which are equal. These five elements have no true existence.

The sixth part explains the notion of passion and wish. Both these notions have no common thing.

One once appeared separately has unified striving, and one once appeared together had different strivings.

All phenomena are similar to our wishes.

The seventh part states that the unique state of body is birth, abiding and destruction. Nāgārdzhuna makes a sample of the butter flame, which destroys darkness. If there is no darkness, the butter flame is not needed. What relation has the butter flame to the unique state of body?

Also it is mentioned that the present development of *karma* is possible, if the birth is similar to the viewing of the butter flame.

Hereon, I would like to mention as an example our Great Teacher, Dasha Dorzhi Itigilov who had kept his body in an imperishable state.

September 10th, 2002 we had lifted up the sarcophagus with the body of Pandita Khambo Lama D. Itigelov in accordance with his will and found his body uncorruptible during 75 years after he passed away.

XII Pandita Khambo Lama D. Itigelov was recognized as reincarnation of the first Pandita Khambo Lama Damba Darzha Zayaev, the founder of Buddhism in Russia.

D. Itigelov was born in 1852 and from the age of seven began his study on Buddhism in the Anninsky datsan in Buryatia. He achieved perfection in Budddhist sciences and received the highest Buddhist degrees. Furtheron D. Itigelov wrote more than 50 scientific works.

In 1911 D. Itigelov was elected as XIIth Pandita Khambo Lama of the Eastern Siberian Buddhists of Russian Empire among the ten candidates. At this highest position he held wide social and enlightening activity.

Dasha Dorzho Itigelov was not only a scholar but also practised Buddhism at the highest level.

On the basis of the teachings by Nāgārdzhuna, Chandrakīrti, Atīsha, Tzonkhapa Lama and other teachers Pandita Khambo Lama Itigelov had achieved the realization of *Samādhi*, void of all phenomena, before his passing away. He passed away on June 15th, 1927 before destruction of Buddhism in Russia and left his will to check the state of his body after 30 years.

In the years of totalitarian regime the *lamas* twice secretly had lifted up the sarcophagus with his body and made sure it did not perish.

At the present day, the uncorrupted body of Pandita Khambo Lama Itigelov has become an object of worship and adoration of all holy relic.

In the 27th part of Nāgārdzhuna's teaching there is comparison of movement of the five *skandhas* and the butter flame. Anybody after its appearance and abiding had to be destroyed.

What had happened with the body of Khambo Lama Itigelov?

Today for us worship of the imperishable body of XII Pandita Khambo Lama is like an eternal butter flame. A sample of imperishable body and the only truth of burning butter flame is to destroy darkness.

The eighth part mentions the doer and his actions. About what the human being has taken with into his future life and what fruits he has left, we learn only after he has gone away from the present life.

All seen before is not true but from the viewed the phenomena arise in different way and in different time.

The tenth part explains the interrelation between fire and wood. Only the fire element is burned out in wood, the water element vapors out, the earth element remains in ash and embers, and smoke is an element of air.

In the sixteenth part of the text it is said that liberation from the own ego is a possibility of achieving liberation, and achievement of liberation is achieving of true 'I'.

The seventeenth part explains the law of virtuous actions and *karma*. Virtuous actions are customs and traditions which are being established only after 12 years.

Imperishable *karma* is similar to the universal duty which is necessary to return back.

We are paying back our duty to the Great Teacher, Dasha Dorzhi Itigelov whose five reincarnations had taken place in India.

Thus, in accordance with the Teachings 'Adorance of the perfect line of the highest reincarnations of the Teacher' and 'With the words gifted to the virtuous donators of Khambo Lama, on behalf of the teacher – Great Wise reincarnation' Pandita Khambo Lama Dasha Dorzho Itigelov in his previous reincarnations was famous as five perfect Indian sages.

He was recognized as reincarnation of 'The Gone through the Highest Testings', the 'Lion-like *Lotsva*', the 'Holder of *Vinaya Geleg Bal Sambu*', the 'Wise *Khambo lama*', the 'Scholar *Gunga Odchen*'.

We consider that in his previous reincarnations Pandita Khambo Lama Itigelov could be one of Nalanda's scholars.

The nineteenth part explains the notions of three times. The present time unifies the left of the past time and the part of the future time.

In the twenty-fourth part of the text it is written that without relative notions it is impossible to understand an absolute truth. Without understanding of an absolute truth one cannot be liberated from *kleśa*s.

The twenty-fifth part explains that all the phenomena came out from the void.

We are getting rid of *kleśa*s in the northern side, worshipping to the southern side. That's why in our *datsan*s and temples an altar is situated in the northern part and the temple doors are faced south.

In the twenty-seventh part, where Buddha's teaching is explained, it is said that adorance to the destructive *skandha* limits the universe. And worshipping the non-destructive *skandha* we achieve unlimited liberation.

20

NALANDA AND THE MŪLASARVĀSTIVĀDINS

YI'JING'S ACCOUNTS WITH FURTHER CONSIDERATION

Wang Bangwei

As one of the most important centres of Buddhism in ancient India, Nalanda has drawn much attention from the people in and out of India. Since the discovery of this place scholars started to undertake research on it in various perspectives. One of the main achievements is the successful archaeological excavation at the site of Nalanda which provides us a lot of information on this sacred place. Meanwhile, scholars tried to trace its history and relations to the development of Buddhism through other materials. The efforts have gained many results as it can be seen today in publications related to Nalanda. In this process the accounts left by Chinese pilgrim monks, Xuanzang, Yi'jing and the others, played an important role. Together with the archaeological discoveries, these accounts let scholars be able to retrieve a clearer picture of life in the Buddhist community of Nalanda of those days.

Nearly fifteen years ago, in a paper which was presented by me at the 10th Conference of International Association of Buddhist Studies held in Paris in 1991, I suggested as a hypothesis for further consideration that during Yi'jing's time, and before him also, at Nalanda the prevailing *Vinaya* was the *Vinaya* of the *Mūlasarvāstivādin*s. The community of Nalanda, on the whole, belonged to this *nikāya*.[1] I discuss the issue in detail.

The direct reference of *Mūlasarvāstivāda*, so far as I know, is by the Chinese Buddhist pilgrim monk Yi'jing. In his book *Datang xiyu qiufa gaoseng zhuan*, Yi'jing says that in 665, a *Vinaya* text of the *Mūlasarvāstivādins* arrived at Luoyang. It was brought to China by another Chinese Buddhist pilgrim, likely from Nalanda.[2] The text was translated by Yi'jing later in 700.

In his excellent book *Datang xiyu ji (A record of the western regions during the great Tang)* Xuanzang indicated in many places the *yāna* and the *nikāya* affiliation of Buddhist community when he visited each province of India. As for Nalanda, though he gave a whole paragraph to describe its origin and the related stories, he did not mention the status of disciplinary practice and the *nikāya* affiliation of community at the place.[3] Xuanzang visited India from 627 (or 629) to 645.

Yi'jing arrived in India about forty years later than Xuanzang. He started off from Guangzhou in South China in 671, and came back to China in 694. Yi'jing spent more than ten years to study Buddhism at Nalanda. He wrote two important books at Sumatra, Indonesia in 691, on his way back to China. One is the above-mentioned *Datang xiyu qiufa gaoseng zhuan*. Another is *Nanhai*

jigui neifa zhuan (Accounts of the inner law sent home from the South Sea).[4] In the latter Yi'jing provides a complete picture of the Buddhist disciplinary life in India, South-East Asia and China. Based on his own observation he described in his book every detail related to life in Buddhist monasteries. To start with, he said he discussed all matters according to the rules of the *Mūlasarvāstivādin*s and one should not mix or confuse them with the rules of other *nikāyas*.[5] In his discussion he frequently mentioned Nalanda, fourteen times altogether, saying the monastic life at Nalanda was a standard way which other Buddhists should follow. To judge what is right or wrong, Yi'jing made the way of disciplinary life at Nalanda as a model. This, together with other relevant accounts, may show a certain special connection with Nalanda.

And in his *Datang xiyu qiufa gaoseng zhuan*, the name of Nalanda comes twenty-nine times. During his time Nalanda was a place every Chinese pilgrim monk had to visit and pay their homage. At the end of the first fascicle of the book Yi'jing describes many details of the place. He said that the rules and rituals of the monks of Nalanda were showed in two books, the first being *Zhongfang lu (A record of Madhyadeśa)* and the second *Nanhai jigui neifa zhuan.*[6]

There are some other evidences to support this conclusion. We know that when Xuanzang and Yi'jing visited and studied at Nalanda, it was a centre of the *Yogācārabhūmi* scholars, or the *Vijñānavādin*s. Xuanzang's teacher in Nalanda, Śīlabhadra, was a Master of the *Yogācārabhūmi* and what led Xuanzang to go to India and to study at Nalanda was to learn this text.[7] L. Schmithausen has shown that there might exist some special relationship between the text *Yogācārabhūmi* and the *Mūlasarvāstivādins*.[8]

As for Yi'jing himself, he started to translate the *Vinaya* text of the *Mūlasarvāstivādin*s while he was staying at Nalanda.[9] When he left India he took with him a great number of *Vinaya* texts, being exclusively of the *Mūlasarvāstivādin*s, which he had obtained from Nalanda, back to China. He afterwards translated a complete set of the *Vinaya* texts of this *nikāya*, though only part of them is extant today.[10]

Among the texts Yi'jing translated, there is one entitled *Genbensapoduobu lü she*, the *Mūlasarvāstivādavinayagāthā*[11] which was compiled by an Indian Buddhist scholar called Viśvāmitra,[12] probably in the late 6th or early 7th century.[13] The text was rendered into Chinese in 700.[14] From other sources we know Viśvāmitra was one of the ten prominent Yogācārabhūmi Masters of that time in India. And from the *Datang xiyu qiufa gaoseng zhuan*, we know that before Yi'jing, in 665,[15] the same text had arrived at Luoyang, probably having been brought to China by another Chinese Buddhist pilgrim Xuanzhao.[16] Xuanzhao had been to India twice. He also spent a few years at Nalanda, learning *Yogācārabhūmi* from an Indian Master Ratnasiṁha.[17] After he came back to China, he was encouraged by other monks to render it into Chinese, but was prevented from doing so because of another imperial mission. This is, so far as we know, the earliest direct reference of the *Mūlasarvāstivādin*s in Chinese literature.

The name of *Mūlasarvāstivādin* appeared quite late, in fact as the latest of the *nikāya*s in Chinese Buddhist literature. Of course, it does not mean that the *Mūlasarvāstivāda nikāya* arose so late, but it may indicate that the title of *Mūlasarvāstivāda* came into usage in a wide range at a comparatively late stage. Before Yi'jing Chinese Buddhists mentioned only the *Sarvāstivādin*. However, for the Chinese Buddhists in ancient times, when they referred the *Mūlasarvāstivādin*s, sometimes they omitted the first part of the title, *Mūla*, rather preferring its simplified form, *Sarvāstivāda*. Probably the same holds true for those foreign monks who arrived in China from India and Central Asia. Thus, there exists the possibility that some texts traditionally attributed to the *Sarvāstivādin*s in ancient China might actually belong to the *Mūlasarvāstivāda*, particularly those comparatively late translated texts. Xuanzang consistently used the term *Sarvāstivādin*. Yi'jing, in most cases, used the term *Mūlasarvāstivādin*, but he also used the term *Sarvāstivādin* occasionally, though by this he sometimes clearly meant the *Mūlasarvāstivādin*s, sometimes both. We are not sure whether, when Xuanzang referred the *Sarvāstivādin*, he was also including the *Mūlasarvāstivādin* under this title. From a comparison of his *Record* with Yi'jing's Account we might be able to say this is possible. In any case, for another example, two great texts, the *Mahāvibhāṣā* and the *Abhidharmakoṣabhāṣya*, both being translated by Xuanzang, in ancient China were said to be the texts of the *Sarvāstivādin*s on the one hand, while of the *Mūlasarvāstivādin*s on the other. The result of the studies achieved recently by some scholars may support the latter assertion.

To sum up, though we do not have direct evidence to show the status of Buddhist disciplinary practice at Nalanda of Yi'jing's time, through above analyses we may get a conclusion that the *Vinaya* of *Mūlasarvāstivādin*s was the main text guiding the disciplinary life of the Nalanda community in the time of Yi'jing. This conclusion, if being accepted, will help us in understanding more the history of this great Buddhist centre of ancient India.

NOTES AND REFERENCES

1. The paper afterwards was published at Göttingen, Germany. See 'Buddhist Nikāyas through Ancient Chinese Eyes, with Three Appendices', in *Untersuchungen zür buddhistischen Literatur* (ed.), von F. Bandurski, B. Pāsādika, M. Schmidt, B. Wang, Vandenhoeck and Ruprecht in Göttingen, 1994, pp. 165-203.
2. See Wang Bangwei, *Datang Xiyu Qiufa Gaosengzhuan Jiaozhu (Biographies of the prominent monks who went in search of the law in the western regions during the Great Tang: A newly collated and annotated text)*, with an introduction and three appendices, 大唐西域求法高僧传校注, Beijing: Zhonghua Book Company, 1988, reprinted 2000, p. 11. The book thereafter will be mentioned as Wang's version of *Qiufa*. Of course, we believe that the title of *Mūlasarvāstivāda* appeared before Yi'jing's arrival in India. The Sanskrit manuscripts of the *Vinaya* texts of this *nikāya* discovered in Gilgit in the thirties of last century show that title for the first time from Indian side. The manuscripts are generally dated to the 7th century, the same time of Yi'jing.
3. See Ji Xianlin *et al.*, *Datang xiyu ji jiaozhu*, 大唐西域记校注, Beijing: Zhonghua Book Company, 1985, reprinted 1990, 1995, 2000, pp. 747-58.
4. See Wang Bangwei, *Nanhai jigui neifa zhuan jiaozhu (Accounts of the inner law sent home from the South Sea: A study with a newly collated and annotated text)*, 南海寄归内法传校注, Beijing: Zhonghua Book Company, 1995, reprinted 2000. The book thereafter will be mentioned as Wang's version of *Nanhai*.
5. All that I have discussed here is in accordance to the *Mūlasarvāstivādanikāya*. The contents of the *Vinaya* of other *nikāya*s cannot be mixed with it.' 凡此所論，皆依根本說一切有部，不可將餘部事見糅於斯. Wang's version of *Naihai*, p. 28.
6. See Wang's version of *Qiufa*, pp. 112-16 and Appendix II of this paper. 其間僧徒綱軌出納之儀，具如《中方錄》及《寄歸傳》.
7. Among the relevant publications available in the western languages, see K. Shōshin: 'How Xuanzang learned about Nalanda', in *Tang China and Beyond: Studies on East Asia from the Seventh to the Tenth Century* (ed.), A. Forte, Kyoto, 1988 (Italian School of East Asian Studies, Essays, 1), pp. 1-33.
8. See L. Schmithausen: 'Zu den Rezension des Udānavarga', *Wiener Zeitschrift für die Kunde Südasien*, 14 (1970), 47-124, particularly, 94-97; and 'Beiträge zür Schulzugehörigkeit und Textgeschichte kanonischer und postkanonischer buddhistischer Materialien', *Zür Schulzugehörigkeit von Werken der Hīnayàna-Literatur* (Abhandlungen der Akademie der Wissenschaften in Göttingen, Nr.154), Zweiter Teil, ed. by H. Bechert, Göttingen, 1987, 304-404.

9. That is the *Genbenshuoyiqieyoubu pinaiye song*, the *Mūlasarvāstivādavinayagāthā* 根本说一切有部毗奈耶颂, Tsisho 24, No. 1459), compiled by a Buddhist scholar called Viśākha, Pishequ 毘舍佉 in Chinese. Cf. A. Yuyama: *Vinaya-Texte* (*Systematische Übersicht über die Buddhistische Sanskrit Literatur, Erster Teil*), Wiesbaden, 1979, 1.25.C.1.k.1. Why did Yi'jing choose it as his first sample of *Vinaya* translation project? A possible answer, I think, is that it presumably was a manual of the disciplinary life for the Nalanda community when Yi'jing was at Nalanda.
10. According to a memorial *stūpa* inscription written by Lu Can 卢灿 in 713 (the 2nd year of Xiantian 先天) just after Yi'jing died, the latter had translated 107 texts, totally in 428 *juan*s. But today we find only about 60 texts which belong to Yi'jing's translation. See my introduction to the *Datang xiyu qiufa gaoseng zhuan jiaozhu*, Beijing, Zhonghua shuju, 1988, pp. 12-14.
11. *Gengben saposuobu lü she* 根本萨婆多部律摄, Taisho 24, No. 1458.
12. Shengyou 胜友 in Chinese.
13. Cf. A.Yuyama: *Vinaya-Texte*, 1.21.C.1.k.14. Yuyama gave a reconstructed name Jinamitra, but according to Guiji's *Cheng weishi suji*, Taisho 43, No. 1830, 232a and to Xuanzang's *Record*, it should be Viśvāmitra.
14. The 1st year of Jiushi 久视元年.
15. The 2nd year of Linde 麟德二年.
16. 玄照 in Chinese.
17. Baoshizi 宝师子 in Chinese.

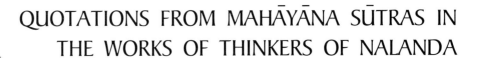

21

QUOTATIONS FROM MAHĀYĀNA SŪTRAS IN THE WORKS OF THINKERS OF NALANDA

Linnart Mäll

The history of Nalanda is exceptionally rich in general, but particularly because of its extraordinary scholars. I have translated Śāntideva's *Bodhicaryāvatāra* into Estonian language and currently I am translating Kamalaśīla's *Bhāvanākrama.*

There can be no doubt that in Nalanda there was high regard for both the Mahāyāna *sūtra*s as well as for the scriptures of these schools, which were called Hīnayāna by the Mahāyāna supporters of that time. Testimony for this is provided by Śāntideva's *Bodhicaryāvatāra.* Already in the first verse of Chapter 1 he announces that he proceeds from the *āgama*, meaning the Mahāyāna *sūtra*s. There is an excellent passage in Chapter 9, in Verses 41 to 44, where he claims, on the one hand, that he cognises the *Hīnayāna āgama*, and, on the other hand, he calls upon the supporters of Hīnayāna to also recognise the Mahāyāna *āgama* (i.e., the Mahāyāna *sūtra*s).

In *Bodhicaryāvatāra*, Śāntideva considers it important to emphasise that in order to study the words of Buddha we need to learn from the *sūtra*s. I quote from Chapter 5, Verse 103 and 104.

> *śrīsambhavavimokṣācca śikṣedyadguruvartanaṁ/*
> *etaccānyacca buddhoktaṁ jñeyaṁ sūtrāntavācanāt//*
> *aśikṣāḥ sūtreṣu dṛśyante tasmātsūtrāṇi vācayet/*
> *ākāśagarbhasūtre ca mūlāpattirnirūpayet//*

In *Bodhicaryāyatāra*, Śāntideva also refers to some *sūtra*s. These are *śrīsaṁbhavavimokṣa* and *Ākāśagarbhasūtra.* The first is actually a part of the *Gaṇḍavyūhasūtra.*

At the same time, however, Śāntideva exhorts that his second text *Śikṣāsamuccaya*, which is just as famous, needs to be read repeatedly and thoroughly:

> *śikṣāsamuccayo 'vaśyaṁ draṣṭavyastu punaḥ punaḥ/*
> *vistareṇa sadācāro yasmāttatra pradarśitaḥ//*

Indeed, let us now look at this second work of Śāntideva, the *Śikṣāsamucchaya*, which could be seen as an anthology of random quotes taken from the *sūtra*s, if it weren't for the fact that the purposeful organisation of the work is immediately obvious, i.e., Śāntideva had indeed selected the quotes to illustrate his thoughts. There are over one hundred *sūtra*s, to which there are references. There are especially many quotes, however, that have been taken from the following *sūtra*s:

Akṣaymatisūtra, Adhyāśayasaṁcodana, Ugraparipṛcchā, Upāyakauśalyasūtra, Kṣitigarbhasūtra, Gaganagañjasūtra, Gaṇḍavyūhasūtra, Candrapradīpasūtra, Daśbhūmikasūtra, Dharmasaṁgītisūtra, Bodhisattvapratimokṣa, Ratnakūṭasūtra, Ratnameghasūtra, Ratnarāśisūtra, Vajradhvajasūtra, Vimalakīrtinirdeśa and Sāgarmatiparipṛcchā.

Aṣṭasāhasrikā Prajñāpāramitā is mentioned directly only once. There are, however, more quotes from this work but it is referred to simply by using one of its epithets, *Bhagavatī*. References are also made to the *Prajñāpāramitā* in general.

Since *Prajñāpāramitā*, and above all, *Aṣṭasāhasrikā Prajñāpāramitā* are my favourite texts, let us next look at which topics from the *Prajñāpāramitā* texts Śāntideva considers it necessary to quote in his work. To summarise: *kalyāṇamitra, mārakarma, saṁprajanya, dānapāramitā, kṣānitpāramitā, dhyānapāramita, buddhakāya, śrāvakayānika pudgala, bodhisattva mahāsattva* and *puṇya*.

Some brief examples in Sanskrit are given below:

1. *kalyāṇamitra*:
   kalyaṇamitreṣu ca tvayā kulaputra tīvraṃ gauravamutpādayitavyaṁ.
2. *saṁprajanya*:
   saṁprajanyaṁ tu prajñāpāramitāyāmuktaṁ, caraṁścarāmīti prajānāti, sthitaḥ sthito 'smiti prajānāti, śayanaḥ śayāmīti prajānāti, nihaṇṇo niṣaṇṇo 'smīti prajānāti.
3. *bodhisattva mahāsattva*:
   Punaraparaṁ śāriputra vyālakāntāramadhyagatena bodhisattvena mahāsattvena notrasitavyaṁ, na saṁtrāsamāpattavyaṁ, tatkasmāddhetoḥ, tathā hi tena sarvaṁ parityaktaṁ sarvasattvānāmarthāya.

Let us now look at Kamalaśīla's *Bhāvanākrama*. Here also references are made to many *sūtras*. Many quotes have been taken from the following: *Akṣayamatinirdeśa, dharmasaṁgītinirdeśa, Sandhinirmocana* and *Samādhirāja*.

Only three references to the *Prajñāpāramitā* have been made, and these are only in the first Bhāvanākrama. The topics are *śūnyatā, śamatha*, and *nirmāṇa*.

1. *śūnyatā*:
   rūpaṁ subhūte rūpasvabhāvena śūnyaṁ yāvad vijñānaṁ vijñānaṁvijñānasvabhāvena śūnyamiti svalakṣaṇaśūnyatām upādāya.
2. *śamatha*:
   ayaṁ ca śamathamārgo bhagavatā āryaprajñāpāramitādau nirdiṣṭaḥ, yadāha, tatra cittaṁ sthāpayati, saṁsthāpayati, avasthāpayati, upasthāpayati, damayati, śamayati, vyupaśamayati, ekotīkaroti, samādadhāti iti navapadaiḥ.
3. *nirmāṇa*:
   kaścit śrāvakanirmitaḥ, kaścit pratyekabuddhanirmitaḥ, kaścid bodhisattvanirmitaḥ, kaścit tathāgatanirmitaḥ, kaścit kleśanirmitaḥ, kaścit karmanirmitaḥ, anena subhūte paryāyeṇa sarvadharmā nirmitotpannaḥ.

In conclusion, it could be said that the references have been recorded correctly by both authors, and the purpose of their use is basically to provide weight to the authors' claims; the authors' claims, however, are themselves based on Mahāyāna *sūtras*, and the considerable number of references to *sūtras* demonstrates their spiritual education based on the *sūtras*.

22

NALANDA: STRONGHOLD OF ANCIENT SCHOLARLY DEBATES

Lozang Jamspal

EARLY HISTORY OF NALANDA

The glory of Nalanda as the greatest Buddhist centre in Magadha kingdom is very much related to the Venerable Śāriputra.[1] Nalanda is the place of the birth and death of this learned venerable *śrāvaka*.[2] Among his disciples, Buddha had recognized Śāriputra and Mahā Maudgalyāyana as endowed with the most excellent wisdom and performance of miracles, respectively (*agrayuga*).[3] Nalanda was a learning and debating centre of Brahmaṇa elite before becoming a Buddhist learning and debating centre, according to *Sarvastivādin Vinaya*.[4] The story is summarized according to the *Vinayavastu* as follows:

> A brahmin boy, wishing to find the secret words of the Vedas, travelled to the South. He went to a brahmin who was learned in Vedas and *Vedāṅgas* and was accepted to study. The learned brahmin had many brahmin students who had come from many different places. During the recess from studies, students had conversations about their native places. The Magadha boy told his classmates wonderful stories of his native country. 'Are there learned men like our teacher?' They asked. 'O boys, in Magadha there are brilliant teachers; our teacher cannot bear to see their bright faces,' he said. After hearing these astonishing tales of Magadha, the students wanted to see that region and requested permission from their teacher to go there. The teacher replied, 'Boys, did I say that I am the only teacher and that there are no other excellent teachers? Although we hear about many other places, we need not go to all of them. The earth is full of many good people and many good things.'
>
> However, preparing sacrificial necessities, the students insisted that the teacher and they all go together to Magadha to defeat others in debate and serve other brilliant brahmins. The brahmin teacher did not have many affairs to look after besides taking care of his students, and so he accepted their request. On the way, the teacher defeated many other debaters. He and his students were received respectfully and provided with chariots, umbrellas, and other things, while many became his followers.
>
> Passing through villages, towns and cities, they arrived at Rājgṛha. The brahmin thought, 'As all the learned debaters and important people are close to the king, I should go and approach the king.' He went to King Bimbisāra and greeted him, 'May you be victorious and live long!' Then, he sat to the side and addressed the king, 'O Divine One, I have studied some literature

with my teacher. Therefore, I seek to debate with a learned debater in the presence of the Divine One.' The king asked his ministers, 'Gentlemen, do we know if there are any debater in my kingdom who can engage in scholarly debate with this brahmin?' They replied, 'Divine One, there is a brahmin named Vasalaputra, learned in the Vedas and *Vedāṅgas*, who lives in the village of Nalanda. With his sharp fiery intellect, he will be able to engage in scholarly debate with this brahmin.'

Vasalaputra was invited to debate with him. Brahmin Vasalaputra went to the king, paid veneration to the king, and sat to the side. The king said to Vasalaputra, "Can you debate with this learned brahmin from the South?" Vasalaputra said to the king, 'I will do my best, Your Majesty.'

The king ordered the ministers to make a *maṇḍala* and a stage for the debate. When everything was ready, they said, 'The Southern brahmin is our guest, therefore, he should be the first debater.' Then the Southern brahmin recited the Five Hundred *Sambaddhatantra*s (*Tib. rgyud chagsṅa brgya*). Then brahmin Vasalaputra recited it back to the Southern brahmin and said, 'Your recitation of this is farce. It is contradictory, and not correct.' Thereby, he refuted the Southern brahmin's recitation. The Southern brahmin became silent. Among states of defeat, to become silent is the worst. The king asked the ministers, 'Who won?' The ministers replied, 'Divine sir, Vasalaputra has won.'

The king was pleased and said, 'That such a learned debater lives in my country is my great gain.' Highly praising the brahmin Vasalaputra, the king said, 'Take Nalanda village as your victory reward.' Then, Vasalaputra, pleased and happy, and surrounded by many learned people, went to his village Nalanda.

Since worldly people like the wealthy and dislike the poor, many brahmin families asked him to marry their daughters. He married a woman from a family equal in status to his own. His wife gave birth to a boy, whom they named Dīrghordhvakāya (*Tib. stod rings*). As the boy grew up, he was well-educated in the brahmin sciences of the four Vedas. He became a capable person, able to clarify his own views and refute the erroneous doctrines of others.

Then, after sometime, they had a daughter. All their relatives and friends gathered together in celebration of her birth. The daughter's eyes were like those of the *Sārikā* bird, and so they named her Sārikā. She also received a good education in literature. One time, when the brother and sister had a scholarly debate, Dīrghordhvakāya was defeated by Sārikā. Then, his father said to him, 'O, son, you are a man, but you are defeated by a woman. After my death, how will you be able to keep this land of sustenance through debate? Another learned debater will take it.'

After sometime, a brahmin named Tiṣya, learned in the Vedas and *Vedāṅgas* and a specialist of *Lokāyata*, who was surrounded by his retinue, came to the King Bimbisāra and said, 'May you be victorious and live long Your Majesty!' He continued, 'Your Majesty, I studied some literature with my *guru* and wish to debate with another learned one in your presence.' Calling upon the brahmin Vasalaputra from Nalanda, they started to debate. The ministers asked the king to recommend the first to start the debate. The king said, 'Since the Brahmin Tiṣya is our guest, he should be the first to start the debate.' But Tiṣya said, 'Divine One, Brahmin Vasalaputra is older than I, therefore, he should be first to start the debate.' Vasalaputra thought, 'It is clear that Brahmin Tiṣya is upholding a new doctrine, and I cannot compete with this young man. I should debate him by reciting texts.' He then recited the Five Hundred verses from *Sambaddhatantra*, but the Brahmin Tiṣya recited it back to him and said, 'Your recitation is not logical. It is contradictory and incorrect.' Brahmin Vasalaputra then became speechless, and Brahmin Tiṣya won in this debate.

The King said to the ministers, 'Now we must bestow a prize to the winner, Brahmin Tiṣya.' The ministers said to the king, 'Divine One, we cannot grant a new reward to every winner. We must take back Nalanda village from Vasalaputra and give it to Brahmin Tiṣya, who was the winner. We should make Nalanda village the winning banner [the prize]. Then, if another learned one comes and wins the debate, we would give Nalanda to the winner. Otherwise, we would lose all the lands of Magadha and Aṅga, by giving them to the winners in scholarly debates.' The king agreed with them.

The government of Magadha then took back the village of Nalanda and gave it to Brahmin Tiṣya. The old Brahmin Vasalaputra was sad, and prepared to go into exile. He said, 'I helped this King Bimbisāra so many times, and this is how he is now helping me!' His relatives told him, 'Please do not go away. You can stay with us at our home.' However, Vasalaputra repeated a verse:

For a man to live in another country is better
Than to live in his own country where he is despised.
Man lives where there is no contempt
That is his own country and there are his relatives.

The young Brahmin Tiṣya also did not want Vasalaputra and his family to go into exile, and he said to Vasalaputra, 'I am just a visitor here for a short while. When I am gone, you can take back all the land. Even now you and I can each have half.' Vasalaputra thought, 'This young Brahmin is very generous. I must give him my daughter, Sārikā in marriage.' He told his thought to his wife, and they asked their son Dīrghordhvakāya about it, but their son did not agree to it and said, 'You are giving everything to your opponent. In the end the opponent will destroy every one of us.' The parents did not listen to the son and gave their daughter, Sārikā to Tiṣya. The couple married. Dīrghordhvakāya thought, 'I was humiliated because I don't have enough education. Since Tiṣya knows the *Lokāyata*, I must also study it.' Thereupon, he went to the South to study *Lokāyata* philosophy.

Sārikā gave birth to a boy. The grandfather named the boy Upatiṣya. Tiṣya thought, 'My son has been named after me, but he should be named after his mother.' So he named the boy Śāriputra.

Under his father, Upatiṣya studied all the brahmin sciences and became an expert in the four Vedas and *Vedāṅga*s. His father Tiṣya taught Upatiṣya the *Indravyākaraṇa*, and at the age of the pair of eights (16), he defeated all his opponents in scholarly debate. This event is also recorded in the *Karmaśatakasūtra*.

Once when reading a Vedic text, Upatiṣya asked his father, 'Father, what is the meaning of these words of this Vedic text?' the father replied, 'Son, even I also do not know the meaning of the words of this Vedic text. The ancient sages wrote, read and praised these secret words of the Vedas, but now we brahmins just read and praise these secret words of the Vedas.' Then, Upatiṣya explained the meaning of the secret words of the Vedas and his father was delighted by Upatiṣya's explanation. His father then thought, 'The duty of a son is to insure and carry on his father's occupation. My son is able to do all these things. My son knows more than I do.' Thinking like that with great joy and delight, the father Tiṣya handed all his five hundred brahmin students to Upatiṣya. When Upatiṣya was teaching the secret words of the Vedas, he changed the words of the Vedas: he lengthened those short verses lacking explanation, and shortened those with excessive words. He changed the meaning and etymology of words, making fewer words and letters.

Maudgalyāyana was also known as Kolita (*Tib. Pang nas skyes*). Kolita and Upatiṣya were both famous teachers of the Vedas. Upatiṣya and Kolita became friends and both went searching for the *Dharma*. First they encountered the six *Tīrthika* teachers, but were dissatisfied with their teachings. They went to a teacher named Sañjaya and became monks under Sañjaya's guidance. Sañjaya told Upatiṣya and Kolita, 'I did not attain the state of *Amritatva* (*nirvāṇa*) but I heard that the Śākya Prince is searching for *Amritatva* through divine words. You should go to him and become his disciples.' He then passed away. Upatiṣya and Kolita discussed whether their teacher, Sañjaya, attained the state of *Amritatva* but did not share it with them. Kolita thought, 'Upatiṣya is intelligent and it would be possible that he could attain the state of *Amritatva* and not tell me.' Kolita convinced Upatiṣya to promise that whoever first attained the state of *Amritatva* must inform the other.

Then, sometime later, Upatiṣya heard the following verse from Aṣvajit, one of the Buddha's first five disciples:

All things have arisen from causes
The Tathāgata explains their causes and their cessation,
The great Ascetic explains it that way.

Upon hearing this verse Upatiṣya opened the stainless eye of *Dharma*, and he went to tell Kolita. Kolita asked Upatiṣya again to recite it and upon Kolita's hearing this verse recited, he also attained the stainless eye of *Dharma*, and they became the disciples of the Buddha.

Then, after sometime, all of Śāriputra's grandparents and parents had passed away. His uncle, Dīghordhvakāya, known now as Dīrghanakha, returned from the South and he also became a disciple of the Buddha.

Dharmakīrti's Debates with Kumarālila and Śankarācārya

Ācārya Dharmakīrti was born in the South and in Jinendracūḍāmaṇi Vihāra. In his late teens, he became interested in Buddhism and went to Nalanda. He received ordination from Ācārya Dharmapāla and became learned in all of the *Tripiṭaka*s. He especially became expert in Buddhist logic and composed the seven treatises of logic. Dharmakīrti defeated three Śankarācārayas. There was a famous Vedic master named Kumāralila. Dharmakīrti studied all the key points of his theories disguised as one of his assistants. He then defeated many of his followers. He had a debate with Dharmakīrti, who defeated him.

Kumāralila accepted Buddhism and his five hundred followers became Buddhists. The Buddhists got back many lands that had been formerly lost to the Vedics. Dharmakīrti then went into retreat, spending all his time in meditation.

At that time in Bengal there was a learned Vedic master named Śankarācārya. He defeated many arrogant Buddhists and took their lands and converted Buddhist *upāsaka*s into Vedic followers. In Orissa he had a disciple named Bhaṭṭācārya who debated and defeated Buddhist logicians. As a result, many lands went to the Vedics and many *vihāra*s (temples) were ruined. Then Śankarācārya sent a message to Nalanda inviting the monks there to debate. Nalanda's logicians were not arrogant, and they could not defeat Śankarācārya in debate. By making various excuses, they delayed the debate until Dharmakīrti could arrive from the South. Then, in Varanasi, Raja Prakāśa called together the debaters. In the assembly of the witnesses and the king, Śankarācārya said, "If I win the debate, you have to choose whether you will become a Vedic follower or submerge into the Ganges. If you win, I will submerge into the Ganges." Dharmakīrti won. He made efforts to save his life, nevertheless, Śankarācārya, telling his disciple Bhaṭṭācārya that he should debate and win against this bald-pated one, he announced, 'I will be reborn as your son.' Submerging himself into the Ganges he sacrificed his life for his doctrine.

Then Bhaṭṭācārya, after spending six years preparing for the debate, challenged Dharmakīrti who defeated him, too. He also submerged into the Ganges just as his teacher, Śankarācārya. Śankarācārya's elder son, who was called the second Bhaṭṭācārya, and his yonger son, who was considered Śankarācārya's reincarnation, quietly went away.

But, after some time the next Śankarācārya reincarnation at fifteen or sixteen years of age, again, challenged Dharmakīrti to debate. He had even sharper intellect than the previous one. Dharmakīrti came from the South. Five thousand brahmins, the king and many others assembled. This Śankarācārya was also defeated, and, like before, although entreated not to, he sacrificed his life as his predecessors did. Observing their doctrine was refuted, many Vedic followers became monks and many became *upāsaka*s.

At the end of Dharmakīrti's life, again Śankarācārya's reincarnation, son of the second Bhaṭṭācārya, having even more powerful wisdom than the former ones, at age twelve again challenged Dharmakīrti to debate. Some elder brahmins advised him, 'First you should debate with some others and win those debates.' But he did not listen to them. 'If I will not win in debate with Dharmakīrti, winning a debate with others will be no victory.' Saying this he went to the South and challenged Dharmakīrti. Dharmakīrti again won the debate. This third Śankarācārya reincarnation converted and became a Buddhist *upāsaka*.

Although the fourth Śankarācārya is well known as the uprooter of Buddhism in India, there is not a word about him in Tārānātha's book. However, I believe that there have been four Śankarācāryas debating against the Buddhist logicians. Plausibly the present four Ahankaracharyas, as abbots of the four monasteries of the Vedanta sect represent the four Shankaracharyas who debated against the Buddhist logicians. Whether the three former Shankaracharyas are known or not in Vedic tradition, I do not know. But, it would seem that respective historians do not like to mention the losses on their own side.

Here are cited some contemporary scholars' views on Śankarācārya:

> Many biographies of Śankarācārya were written in Sanskrit, such as the *Śankara-digvijaya*, *Śankara-vijaya-vilasa*, *Śankara-jaya*, etc. It is regarded as almost certain that he was born between CE 700 and 800 in the Mālābar country in the Deccan. Many miracles are related to Śankara, and he is believed to have been the incarnation of Śiva. He turned ascetic in his eighth year and became the disciple of Govinda, a renowned sage then residing in a mountain cell on the banks of the Narbuda. It is said that he wrote his illustrious *bhāṣya* on the *Brahma-sūtra* in his twelfth year. He then travelled to various places, and defeating his opponents everywhere he established his *Vedānta* philosophy, which from that time forth acquired a dominant influence in moulding the religious life of India (Dasgupta).

> Śankara was an orthodox brāhmaṇ, for whom all the Vedic literature was sacred and unquestionably true. To harmonize its many paradoxes he had recourse to an expedient already known in Buddhism, that of a double standard of truth.... Śankara's *Brahman* is different from the 'Void' or *nirvāṇa* of Mahāyāna Buddhism, a fact well recognized by his opponents, who called him a crypto-Buddhist (Basham).[5]

> In the ninth century the great Hindu monist philosopher Śankarācārya hastened the doctrinal debate defeat of Buddhism everywhere. But in one region of India, the Northeast, including parts of Orissa, Buddhism flourished greatly under the patronage of the Pāla Dynasty (c. 750-1150) and took on a new fascinating lease of artistic life, partly in direct response to the Hindu challenge (Rawson).[6]

Although the fourth Śankarācārya was a brilliant debater, he was unable to conquer the Buddhist debaters of Nalanda and of its vicinities, such as Vikramaśilā, Odantapurī and parts of Orissa.

Although the debate practice of Nalanda protected Buddhism long and well from being dismantled through the debate of its opponents, they could not escape the Turk invasion in CE 1205. There are three reasons that are usually given for the disappearance of Buddhism in the land of its birth:

1. Śankarācārya's excellence in dialectical debate,
2. The Turk invasion, and
3. The widespread practice of Tantra in Buddhism, e.g. the *vajrayāna*.

The first reason is suitable to apply to those places where the Buddhists emphasized meditation and de-emphasized logic and debate. We can understand this by taking as an example the debate between Hvashang Mahāyāna and Kamalaśīla at bSam yas monastery in Tibet.[7] The second reason is, of course, most suitable to explain the disappearance of Buddhism in Magadha and Orissa. The third reason does not indicate direct cause, but rather indirect cause.[8] The tantric monks were involved in many sophisticated rituals and meditations. They simply did not have sufficient time to practice logic that was very necessary to protect their beliefs, their monasetry lands and their patrons in India. When outside debaters challenged them, they were unable to respond to their challengers; they lost in debate, resulting in losing everything. Because of the loss of the tantric monk debaters to Śankarācārya, the practice of Tantra became the scapegoat as the cause of the decline of Buddhism in India.

APPENDIX

The Tentative Founders

Aśoka visited Nalanda, worshipped the Śāriputra *stūpa*, and erected a Buddhist temple.[9] Sometime after this, five hundred Mahāyāna *Ācārya*s decided to teach the Mahāyānist doctrine at Nalanda. King Lakṣasva promoted the copying of hundreds of thousands of Mahāyāna scriptures, probably in Saurașțra. All of these copies eventually came to Nalanda. Later, somewhere between the first century BC and AD Udbhatasiddhasvāmin and Śaṅkarasvāmin, two brothers who were learned brahmins and had studied both Vedic and Buddhist scriptures, took the Buddhist *upāsaka* vow. They composed treatises praising the Buddha, exalting him above other deities,[10] built eight libraries for the Mahāyāna books, and sustained five hundred Mahāyānists at Nalanda and five hundred Theravādins at Vajrāsana (Bodhgaya). In that way King Aśoka was Nalanda's temple builder, and the five hundred teachers and the Svāmin brothers were its founders as a great learning centre.

Developers

The first developer was the great Ācārya Brahmin Rāhulabhadra, although its greatest developer was Ācārya Nāgārjuna. Rāhulabhadra was contemporary to the four great *ācāryas* of Vaibhāṣika.[11] He studied Mahāyāna doctrine with Ācārya Avikalpa and propagated Madhyamaka doctrine. In his time there were about eight *ācārya*s who taught the Madhyamaka doctrine. After him Ācārya Nāgārjuna became the preacher for the Buddha's teaching. He successfully propagated the Madhyamaka doctrine, while also materially helping the Sthaviravādins. At Nalanda he supported five hundred Mahāyānist monks. Nāgārjuna obtained the Perfection of Wisdom in One Hundred Thousand Lines[12] from the realm of the Nāga spirits. The Sthaviravādins accused him of making it up himself.

At this time, under Nāgārjuna's influence, a brahmin named Viṣṇu erected 108 temples and established a different land for each to derive income from in order to preserve the teachings of the greater and lesser vehicles for a long time. In that way Nāgārjuna was beneficial to all the Buddhists by his teaching, writing, defeating of opponents through debate, and by being a patron not only of Nalanda but also of the South.

A powerful brahimin debater named Mātriceta, came to Nalanda to challenge the Buddhists to debate. Āryadeva defeated this famous scholar. Afterwards, Mātriceta composed many treatise praising the Buddha.[13] Ācārya Rāhulabhadra II was born in a lower caste but he was handsome and rich. He became monk at Nalanda and studied under Āryadeva and mastered the *Three Baskets* (*Tripiṭaka*). He became a patron of many communities of monks.

In his old age, Ācārya Asaṅga spent twelve years at Nalanda. Everyday in the winter a different non-Buddhist debater used to come to him. He debated all of them and everyone took teachings from him. There were around a thousand of these. After Asaṅga passed away, his younger Bother Vasubandhu became the abbot of Nalanda. He was very learned and was known as a second Buddha. Ācārya Vasubandhu had four disciples who were more learned than himself in some specific subjects, such as Guṇaprabha in *Vinaya*, Sthiramati in *abhidharma*, Diṅgnāga in *pramāṇa* (logic), and Āryavimuktisena in *Prajñāpāramitā*. Ācārya Diṅgnāga defeated the brahmin debater Sudurjaya at Nalanda as well as many other non-Buddhists. Buddhists got back most of the land previously lost in debate. He converted many non-Buddhists to Buddhism.

Ācārya Buddhapālita and Bhāvaviveka were both born in the South and they might have studied at Nalanda. King Harṣa made Ācārya Gaṇaprabha his *Rājaguru*, and King Śila, son of King Harṣa, reigned in the last part of Ācārya Gaṇaprabha's life. He was affluent and served the whole spiritual community of monks in all four directions with good foods. This king as well as Candragomin, Śāntideva, and Virupā were all near contemporaries.

Candrakīrti was born in a place named Samanta in the South, and studied Madhyamaka philosophy with Kamalabuddhi, a disciple of Buddhapālita, as well as with many disciples of Bhāvaviveka. He became the abbot of Nalanda, and defeated many non-Buddhists. In the later part of his life Candrakīrti went back to the South and defeated many non-Buddhists and converted them to Buddhism in the province of Koṅkaṇa.

Ācārya Candragomin was born in the eastern province of Vārendra. He went to Nalanda. Once while the abbot Candrakīrti was teaching outside the wall, there was a man standing and listening. Those who wish to debate act that way; otherwise one would sit and listen respectfully to the teaching, or none would pay any attention to it. Candrakīrti, thinking that he was a challenger, asked him, 'Where do you come from?' Candragomin replied, 'I come from the South.' Candrakīrti: 'What do you know?' Candragomin: 'I know the Pāṇini Grammer, the One Hundred and Fifty Verse of Praise, and the Chanting of the Names of Mañjuśrī.' Candrakīrti thought that in his humbleness he had indicated that he knew all of Sanskrit grammar and the *sūtra* and tantra systems. Candrakīrti respectfully received Candragomin. There was a debate between Candrakīrti and Candragomin that lasted for seven years, the former holding the doctrine of intrinsic naturelessness and the latter the doctrine of Mind Only. Many people always gathered to watch this debate. Even small boys and girls knew some part of it. They sang this song:

> O! The Doctrine of Ārya Nāgārjuna
> Is medicine for some, but poison for others;
> The Doctrine of Ajita and Āryasaṅga
> Is ambrosia for all.

Ācārya Dharmapāla, who was born in the South, became an abbot of Nalanda. Ācārya Śāntideva and the adept Virupā were his disciples. Śāntideva was born as a prince in Saurāṣtra. He went to Nalanda and took ordination from the abbot, Jinadeva. He appeared to be neither engaged in studying, pondering, nor meditating. Yet he composed several monumental books,[14] of which many have been popular up until the present.

Ācārya Haribhadra was a *Rājaguru* of King Dharmapāla (c. 770-810). This king reigned for 64 years and supported the development and spread of the techings of the *Pāramitā* literature. He also supported the establishment of the Vikramaśilā Mahāvihāra.

NOTES AND REFERENCES

1. J. Nehru, *The Discovery of India*, rept. 1983. 'Between Pataliputra and Gaya lie the impressive remains of Nalanda University, which became famous in later days. It is not clear when this began functioning and there are no records of it in Ashoka's time.' p. 134. A.L. Basham, *The Wonder That Was India*. 'The most famous of these was the Buddhist monastery of Nalanda, which founded in Gupta times, remained the most famous teaching centre of medieval Buddhism until it was pillaged by the invading Muslims,' p. 164.
   Lalmani Joshi, *Studies in the Buddhist Culture of India*, 'The greatest centre of Buddhist learning in Asia, was founded by Kumara-Gupta Mahendraditya,' p. 10.
   C.S. Upasak, *Nalanda: Past and Present*, p. 7, 'Hiranada Sastri etymologically derives the name as "Nalam dadati—giver of lotus stalks".' This etymology of Nalanda is supported by its Tibetan translaton, 'dam bu sbyin', in the story of Shariputra in Karmashataka, Tog bKa'gyur, volume 'a', folio 3.
2. Upasak, *Nalanda: Past and Present*, p. 35, and Tārānātha, *History of Buddhism in India*, Tib. p. 72, Hindi tr. by Rigzin Lundup Lama, *Bharata mein Bauddhadharma ka Itihasa*, p. 39.
3. Asvaghoṣa, *Buddhacarita*, chapter 17th, v. 20.
4. *Sarvastivādhin Vinaya* is preserved only in Tibetan translation.
5. A.L. Basham, *The Wonder That Was India*, p. 328.
6. P.S. Rawson, *A Cultural History of India*, p. 202.
7. Dr. E. Obermiller, Buston, English tr., *History of Buddhism*, pp. 193-96.
8. Bhikṣu Saṅgharakshita, *A Cultural History of India*, 1975. 'The reason for the decline and alleged disappearance of Buddhism in the land of its birth ... lies in the relation of the religion to ... Hinduism ... neither hesitated to borrow from the other what was required for its own development .... The result was that if Buddhism appropriated the forms of Hinduism, Hinduism assimilated something of the spirit of Buddhism .... The suggestion that the disappearance of Buddhism was somehow connected with the introduction of Tantrism (i.e., the *Vajrayāna*) not only involves the grossest misunderstanding of this form of Buddhism, but also fails to explain why Hinduism, which had also developed a tantric aspect, failed to disappear too,' pp. 98-99.
9. Tārānātha, p. 73, Hindi tr., p. 39.
10. Udbhaṭṭasiddhasvāmi, Viśeṣastava and Sarvajñāmaheśvarastava, and Śankaraswāmi, Devātiśayastuti. See Losang Norbu Shastri's edition of the original Sanskrit and Tibetan translation, Tibetan Institute, Sārnāth, Varanasi, 221007 (U.P.) India.
11. Bhadanta Dharmatrata, Ghosaka, Vasudeva, and Buddhadeva. See the foreword of the *Tattva-Saṁgraha of Śāntaraksita*, Oriental Institute, Baroda edition, pp. XXXIX-Xli.
12. *Śatasasrikaprajñāparamitā.*
13. Adhyardharadhaśatakaṁ, in *Baudhastotra-saṁgraha*, compiled by Janardan Shastri Pandey, Motilal Banarsidass, pp. 10-23.
14. *Śikṣāsamuccaya*, *Sūtrasamuccaya* and *Bodhicarayāvatāra*.

23

DEBATE BETWEEN ĀCĀRYA CANDRAKĪRTI AND CANDRAGOMĪ OVER VIJÑĀNAVĀDA AND MĀDHYAMIKA PHILOSOPHY

Tashi Paljor

NALANDA MAHĀVIHĀRA

In ancient age Nalanda was considered as the best centre of learning. This centre produced a great number of scholars, *Sādhaka*s, and authors, whose great contribution made it famous. Ārya Śāriputra was born in Nalanda village. In the memory of Ārya Śāriputra the kings of India and four directions (*antas*) built the Nalanda Mahāvihāra. On behalf of those kings a proper arrangement was made for the residence and livelihood of monks. Besides, an orphanage was also built there. Due to building of many *vihāra*s it became famous in the world.

On arrival of the Chinese monk Thangjan Chang at Nalanda, there were ten thousand monks residing therein. Great scholars like Nāgārjuna, Āryadeva Śāntarakṣita, Ācārya Candrakīrti, etc. had studied there. Candrakīrti was a great scholar of *Prāsaṅgika-mādhyamika*. He has many works to his credit. Among them *Prasannapadā*, a *ṭīkā* on *Mūlamādhyamakaśāstra*, and *Pradīpodyotana*, a *ṭīkā* on *Tantrarāja Guhyasamāja mūlatantra* are much famous. It is said about these texts that the two texts are established on the earth just as the sun and moon in the sky. *Mādhyamākāvatāra*, written by Candrakīrti is very useful. In the monasteries of Tibet the *Mādhyamikaśāstra*s are studied and debated continuously for two years. In Tibetan Buddhist tradition the original text and commentaries on the *Mādhyamika* philosophy are studied, debated, memorized and contemplated.

In *Mādhyamakaśāstra*, there are ten *Cittotpāda* (chapters). The base of this text is *Daśabhūmikasūtra*. The subject of its sixth chapter is *prajñā* (wisdom). It presents the description of *Dharmanairātmya* from the standpoint of knowledge. The rise of the four extremes of the *Dharmanairātmya* has been negated skilfully. The *Pudgalanairātmya* has been described with a simile of five chariots. Ācārya Nāgārjuna in his *Mādhyamakaśāstra* has negated *Pudgalanairātmya* only through the simile of five chariots. Ācārya Candrakīrti has enumerated it by those similes, adding to it two more similes, the size (*ākāra*) and group (*samūha*).

Ācārya Śāntideva has described *Pudgalanairātmya* from cultivation point of view in the ninth chapter of his text *Bodhicaryāvatāra*. Just as there is no tooth, hair, nail, etc., similarly *Pudgalanairātmya* has been described. Through the four mindfulness, the *Dharmanairātmya* has been described.

This has been done from contemplation point of view. Our body is full of thirty-six abominable things. No substance/thing of the body is pure. While examining the body, self characteristics and general characteristics have been used. Ācārya Nāgārjuna did not describe *Mahākaruṇā* and *Mahāsāmañna* as synonymous words.

MEANS TO KNOW MĀDHYAMIKA PHILOSOPHY

Rev. Negi Lama has stated that the principle of *Mādhyamika* philosophy is deep and extensive. The knowledge of *śabda vidyā* is essential for its right understanding. Thereupon the texts of *Mādhyamika* philosophy should be learnt from authentic teachers. The attainment of the knowledge of deep subjects is not possible also because of the immoral deeds of the previous births. Therefore, the purification of immoral deeds/vices and the earning of merits are essential. Besides, the *Iṣṭadeva* and *Vajrācārya* should be prayed. Only then *Mādhyamika* view could be understood. *Prāsaṅgika-mādhyamika* view is also essential for the practice of *Vajrayāna*.

DEBATE BETWEEN CANDRAKĪRTI AND CANDRAGOMĪ

Ācārya Candrakīrti belonged to the 7th century. He was born in a Brāhmiṇ family in South India. Ordained in Buddhism, he studied *Mādhyamika* texts of Nāgārjuna. Candrakīrti became *ācārya* of Nalanda monastery. He composed several commentaries on *Mādhyamika* philosophy such as *Prasannapadā* and *Madhyamakāvatāra*, etc. He enunciated *Prāsaṅgika-mādhyamika* philosophy by keeping intact the tradition of Buddhapālita and Śāntideva.

Once Candrakīrti was preaching in Nalanda. At that time Candragomī, a Buddhist scholar of Nepal reached there. He did not salute him and remained standing there. Candrakīrti thought that he might have come to debate with him. Thinking so, he went to Candragomī and asked him as to which place he had come from. Candragomī replied that he had come from Nepal. Candrakīrti asked him what religion he knew. Candragomī told him that he knew Pāṇini Vyākaraṇa, Pāramitānaya, Śatapañcāśata ṭīkā and Mañjuśrīnāmasaṅgīti. Candrakīrti thought that Candragomī knew the basics of Vyākaraṇa, Pāramītā, and Mantrayāna, and he was further a scholar of both Āgama and Yukti and also talked politely. Candrakīrti asked him, "Are you Ācārya Candragomī?" he replied that he was known so in the world. Candrakīrti thought that Candragomī was a great scholar of Buddhism, and knew aforesaid subjects, in which entire learning of Buddhism lay.

Ācārya Candrakīrti told him that it did not look good that a great scholar like him come in the *Mahāvihāra* that way. He should have to come in the *Mahāvihāra* with great honour and requested him to go out of the *Mahāvihāra* for a while. Candrakīrti, then, postponed his programme of preaching and ringing the bell collected the resident monks of the *vihāra* and told them that Candragomī, a great scholar of Nepal, had reached there. It was necessary to welcome him according to the tradition of the *Mahāvihāra*. Candragomī told Candrakīrti that he was a lay-person and it was against the *Vinaya* rule that monks should welcome him. Replying to this Candrakīrti told him that he had a device to it. He would keep a statue of Mañjuśrī on the chariot before him (Candragomī) and he would sit behind the statue. In this way, he would be properly welcomed. Thereupon, Candrakīrti ordered to prepare two chariots for the purpose.

Ācārya Candragomī was a poet also. While entering Nalanda, he composed hymns praising the merits of Mañjuśrī. Being pleased with him, Ārya Mañjuśrī turned his head towards Candragomī and asked him if he really possessed such qualities. This bent-necked statue of

Mañjuśrī was considered as one of the most important statues of Nalanda. Candrakīrti asked him several questions related to Buddhism. He replied all the questions. These two *ācārya*s continued to debate on Vijñānavāda and *Mādhyamika* philosophy for seven years at Nalanda. Candrakīrti was the follower of *Mādhyamika*, while Candragomī was that of Vijñānavāda. But Candrakīrti was always defeated in the debate while Candragomī won.

Ācārya Candrakīrti thought that there was certainly someone who was supporting Candragomī in the debate. Thinking so, he once went to the residence of Candragomī. At the time Avalokiteśvara was answering the questions of Candragomī. Candrakīrti saw this. When Candrakīrti asked, "Ārya! why do you do partiality," the finger of Avalokiteśvara remained straight.

Again Candrakīrti went to the statue of Avalokiteśvara and prayed him to appear before him (Candrakīrti) as he appeared before Candragomī. One day Avalokiteśvara appeared in his dream and told him that he was established as scholar for five hundred births by Ārya Mañjuśrī, and he required no help of him. Thereupon Candrakīrti woke up. He again prayed him for his audience. Then, Avalokiteśvara gave him complete audience. The debate between the two scholars continued for seven years. Even the people of Nalanda heard and understood it. Villagers said that Buddhahood could be attained even in one life by understanding properly the *Śūnyatā* (voidness) of Ācārya Nāgārjuna; and in case of not understanding it properly people would fall in the path of *Ucchedavāda dṛṣṭi* (annihilistic view) due to which beings fall in the miserable state and experience unbearable suffering.

Ācārya Nāgārjuna's philosophy is useful for some like nectar and harmful for some like poison. Ārya Asaṅga's view of Vijñānavāda is helpful for all, just like nectar. It is said that once a conference of 500 scholars was held on Vijñānavāda and *Mādhyamika* philosophy for detailed discussion. In this conference the view of Vijñānavāda was considered as beneficial, for it does not harm anyone.

Ācārya Nāgārjuna was the founder of *Mādhyamika* philosophy. He did not regard *Svātantrika* and *Prāsaṅgika-mādhyamika* as different. His *Madhyamakaśāstra* has 27 chapters and 429 verses. Ācārya Buddhapālita composed *vṛtti* while explaining *Madhyamakaśāstra* from *Prāsaṅgika* angle. Bhāvaviveka has contradicted Buddhapālita while explaining it from *Svātantrika-mādhyamika* point of view. Ācārya Buddhapālita could have contradicted Bhāvaviveka but he did not think it proper to contradict him as Bhāvaviveka belonged to a royal family.

VIJÑĀNAVĀDA AND MĀDHYAMIKA VIEWS

Vijñānavāda does not acccept/believe in the existence of outer world/phenomena. It accepts only the existence of *Vijñāna* (consciousness). Vijñānavāda believes in *Trikāya*, *Svasaṁvedana*, *Ālayavijñāna*, etc. Vijñānavāda accepts five *mārga*, ten *bhūmi*, etc. just as *Mādhyamika*. The principle of *Prāsaṅgika-mādhyamika* does not accept self-proved thing but practically accepts subject and verb, etc. Therefore, the *Mādhyamika*'s views are superior to Vijñānavāda. According to *Prāsaṅgika-mādhyamika*, *citta* has no existence just as there is no existence of outer phenomena. While rejecting the existence of consciousness, the *Prāsaṅgika Mādhyamika* says that the future of *citta* has not arisen as yet. The *citta* of past has elapsed after arising and the *citta* of the present is constantly changing. Considering so, there is no existence of *citta*. The same thing has been mentioned by Buddha in the text *Vajracchedikā*. In *Madhyamakāvatāra*, Ācārya Candrakīrti has told the *Vijñānavādin*s, in short, that as they do not accept the existence of knowable things, in the same way there is no existence of consciousness.

Pl. 45. Nalanda: Vasudhārā.

Pl. 46. Nalanda: Aparājitā.

Pl. 47. Nalanda: Vajratārā.

Pl. 48. Nalanda: Yamāntaka.

Pl. 49. Nalanda: Mārīci.

Pl. 50. Nalanda: Stone image of Khasarpaṇa-Avalokiteśvara.

Pl. 51. Nalanda: Avalokiteśvara.

Pl. 52. Nalanda: Stone image of Avalokiteśvara.

Pl. 53. Nalanda: Avalokiteśvara.

Pl. 54. Nalanda: Bodhisattva Padmapāṇi.

Pl. 55. Nalanda: Bodhisattva Vajrapāṇi.

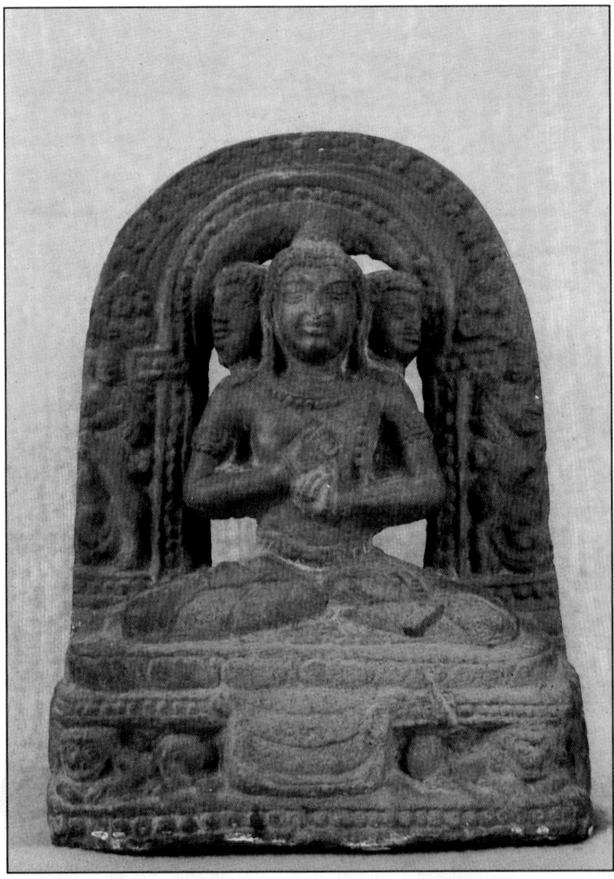

Pl. 56. Nalanda: Bodhisattva Vajrapāṇi.

Pl. 57. Nalanda: Votive *stūpa*.

Pl. 58. Nalanda: Bronze figure of Viṣṇu.

Pl. 59. Nalanda: Stone sculpture showing a donkey playing flute within a niche in temple no. 2.

Pl. 60. Nalanda: Stone sculpture showing a lady playing *veena* within a niche in temple no. 2.

Pl. 61. Nalanda: Stone sculpture showing a drummer within a niche in temple no. 2.

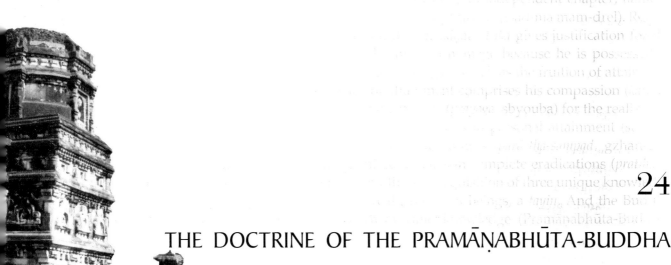

24

THE DOCTRINE OF THE PRAMĀṆABHŪTA-BUDDHA

Nawang Tsering

The idea of the Pramāṇabhūta-Buddha represents the climax of Buddhological doctrine. The notion of Buddhahood as the ultimate ontological principle has excercised the minds of earlier Buddhist philosophers. The human Buddha or Śākyamuni has been viewed as a phenomenal manifestation of the Absolute Truth. The human Buddha has been honoured as the revealer of the Absolute Truth as well as the teacher of the way leading to the realization of the Absolute Truth. His religious and spiritual authority is derived from his transcendental perfection. The virtue of great compassion (*mahākaruṇā*) serves as the functional link between the Buddha and the being in *saṁsāra*. Thus, while in the early Buddhist text the Buddha is called *dharmabhūta* (embodiment of absolute truth), *jñānabhūta* (embodiment of wisdom), and *mahākaruṇika* (embodiment of great compassion) in the standard treatises of the Buddhist philosophers of the critical school, we have a new epithet of the Buddha, that is, *pramāṇabhūta* (embodiment of right knowledge).

Ācārya Diṅgnāga (6th-7th cent. CE) is the first among the Buddhist philosophers of the critical school, who in the opening verse of the *Pramāṇasamuccaya*[1] pays homage to the Buddha by attributing to him the five epithets, viz., embodiment of valid knowledge (*pramāṇabhūta*, tsad-mar gyur-pa), great compassion (*jagaddhitaiṣin*, gro-ia phan bzhed-pa), teacher (*śāstā*, ston-ba), all round perfect (*sugata*, bde-gshegs), and saviour (*tayin*, skyob-ba).

Dharmakīrti (7th cent. CE) who belongs to the celebrated logical school of Diṅgnāga deals with these attributions to the Buddha *in extenso* by allocating an independent chapter, namely, *pramāṇasiddhiparicched*a (tsad-ma grub-pa' ile'u) in his *Pramāṇavārttika* (tsad-ma mam-drel). RGyal-tsab rJe (14th-15th cent. CE) in his commentary on the *Pramāṇavārttika* gives justification for the attribution to the Buddha. The Buddha is worthy of such homage because he is possessed of both the means of attainment (*hetu-sampad*, rgyu phun-tsogs) as well as the fruition of attainment (*phala-sampad*, bras-bu phun-tsogs). The means of attainment comprises his compassion (*karuṇā*, bsamba), and his undertaking of incessant spritual practices (*prayoga*, sbyouba) for the realization of Truth for others, whereas the fruition of attainment results in personal attainment (*svārtha-sampad*, rang-don phun-tsogs), as well as attainment for others (*parārtha-sampad*, gzhan-don phun-tsogs). While his personal accomplishment culminates in complete eradications (*pratihāra-sugattva*, spang-pa bde-gshegs), his attainment for others in acquisition of three unique knowledge (*pratijñāsugattva*, rtogs-pa bde-gshegs) – he is a real saviour of beings, a *tayin*. And the Buddha is an embodiment of valid knowledge or born of valid knowledge (Pramāṇabhūta-Buddha) through the accomplishment in two *hetus* and its two *phalas*. It is an accepted principle that valid knowledge (*pramāṇa*) consists of an invariable relation between *hetus* and *phalas*. When the Buddha is possessed of *hetus* and *phalas*, then by implication we must accept that the Buddha is embodiment of valid knowledge (*pramāṇabhūta*). This is a novel concept introduced by Ācārya Diṅgnāga, which also helps in making distinction between the Buddhist way of interpreting valid knowledge and that of the non-Buddhist.[2] The significance of the term *pramāṇabhūta* in innovatory verse of the *Pramāṇasamuccaya* of Ācārya Diṅgnāga is that the suffix *bhūta* is added in order to exclude eternality (*abhūta*). Eternal *pramāṇa* does not exist. Validity always consists of dependent of productive factors (*sādhana*).[3] The productive factors of validity of the following explanation illustrates how the Buddha is being born as Pramāṇabhūta-Buddha.

Pramāṇabhūta-Buddha

- *hetu sampad*
  - *āśaya-sampad*
    - *Jagaddhitaiṣitva*
  - *prayoga-sampad*
    - *śāstitva*
- *phala-sampad*
  - *Svārtha-sampad*
    - *sugatattva*
  - *parārtha-sampad*
    - *tāyitva*

The Buddha is possessed of both the means of attainment *hetu-sampad* as well as the fruition of attainment, or *phala-sampad*. The means of attainment comprises his compassion (*karuṇā, āśaya*) and his spiritual practice (*prayoga*), whereas the fruition of attainment results in personal attainment (*svārtha-sampad*), as well as attainment for others (*parārtha-sampad*). His compassion (*karuṇā, āśaya*) gives rise to attainment for others (*parārtha-sampad*) which justifies the epithets, *jagaddhitaiṣin* and *tayin*, while his spiritual practice (*prayoga-sampad*) gives rise to personal attainment which justifies the epithets, *śāstā* and *sugata*. In order to remove the doubts raised by opponents regarding the comprehension of Pramāṇabhūta-Buddha and transcendental knowledge acquired by the Buddha, Gyal-tsab rje (15th cent. CE) refers to the twofold method of arrangement, viz., *anuloma* (*lugs-byung*, regular sequence) and *pratiloma* (*lugs-ldog*, reverse sequence). Opponents may raise the following doubts:

(*a*) What is the cause of the emergence of the Buddha as embodiment of valid knowledge (*utpatti-hetu*, skied-byed kyi rgyu).

(*b*) Even if it is the cause of the emergence of the Buddha as embodiment of knowledge, there is no means of conveying (*jñāpaka-hetu*, shes-byed kyi rgyu), the transcendental knowledge (*sarvajñāna*) acquired by him. Buddhism does not believe in an uncaused effect, so there should be some cause of the Pramāṇabhūta-Buddha. And the answer to the above-mentioned first question is that Pramāṇabhūta-Buddha is not an uncaused effect, but is an effect caused by *jagaddhitaiṣin, śāstātva, sugatatva*, and *tāyitva*, which are essentially the *utpatti-hetu* cause of origination of Pramāṇabhūta-Buddha. Again, *jagaddhitaiṣitva śāstātva, sugatatva*, and *tāyitva* are not different from each other, but are themselves causally connected in succeeding causal sequence as *jagaddhitaiṣitva* is the cause of *śāstātva*, is the cause of *sugatatva*, is the cause of *tāyitva*.

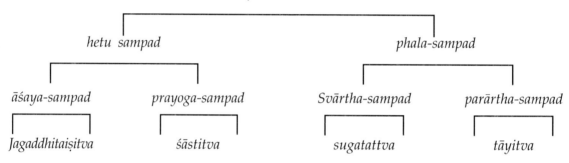

The second doubt is removed when we take into account the doctrinal preaching of the Omniscient Buddha. His doctrinal preachings are essentially the means of conveying to others (*jñāpaka-hetus*) the transcendental knowledge he has himself acquired (*sarvajñāna*). The Buddha is *tayin*, because he preaches others the fourfold truth which he has himself perfected. Through the ascertainment of a nature of a *tayin*, we can infer *sugata*, *śāstā* and *jagaddhitaiṣin* in preceding sequence, as from *tayitva*, there comes *sugatatva*, *śāstātva* and *jagaddhitaiṣitva*. And the Omniscient Buddha is established as a Pramāṇabhūta-Buddha in the order of reverse sequence. Of the two methodologies adopted by Ācārya Dharmakīrti to explain the doctrine of the Pramāṇabhūta-Buddha, we will see in brief how the Buddha is established as *pramāṇabhūta* in *anuloma* way. The great compassion is the prime cause for establishment of the Buddha as embodiment of valid knowledge. The desire to remove the miseries of beings along with the causes of misery is the meaning of compassion. The Buddha realizes that the cultivation of compassionate mind for the sake of others' well-being is inevitable for him, as the immediate task before him is to liberate all beings from *saṁsāra*. In order to carry out his mission for others successfully, he undertakes incessant practices and trainings in compassion so that he may well be equipped with all necessary means, i.e., wisdom, etc. to remove the sufferings of all beings. Further, the compassion does not arise in absence of cause or that of affiliated cause, but it is caused by incessant practice and training in compassion in its homogeneous series of previous consciousness in several lives.[5] Though love, wisdom, etc. which could be seen in all beings as their seeds are present in consciousness due to their own previous homogeneous causes yet they are devoid of uninterrupted love, wisdom, etc. as they have not undergone incessant practices. Incessant practices cause the spontaneous rise of its own nature. For instance, passionate mind of a commonfolk breeds passionate love, but in the *Bodhisattva* there arises only dispassionate love for which the *Bodhisattva* has to undergo incessant practices which involve serveral lives. The *Bodhisattva* attains the great compassionate mind directed towards others' well-being (*jagadddhitaiṣitva*) through practices. Through incessant practices arise homogeneity of compassion in consciousness, and finally, the *Bodhisattva* attains the stage when the great conscious mind rises spontaneously without any exertion.[6] And the Buddha is a valid knowledge because he has undertaken incessant practices and training in the great compassion. Having thus cultivated great compassion for others, the *Bodhisattva* resorts himself to realize the true-wisdom (*nairātmya-darśana*), the means of redeeming the suffering for oneself as well as for others, which justifies the Buddha in being called *Śāstātva*. The would-be-Buddha undertakes incessant spiritual practices and meditation by adopting infinite means in several lives for several aeons to realize non-egoity (*nairātmya-darśana*) for the eradication of misery, not for himself alone but for the welfare of others. Such *Bodhisattva* finally attains the stage of *samyag-sambuddha*. The Śākyamuni Buddha is the *samyag-sambuddha*, because he has incontrovertibly realized the knowledge what is desirable (*guṇa-vipāka of dukha-hetu-nairātmya-darśana*). He has uprooted, by the very root, the subconscious impulses. He is the perfect one. The *samyag-sambuddha* is *sugata*, because he is endowed with the three unique qualities, gained after completely eradicating the cause of misery. The three qualities are: *praśastatā* (legs-par spang-pa), *apurnavavṛtti* (slar mi-idog-pa) and *wiśeṣatā* (ma-lus-pa). His efforts to eradicate misery is commendable (*praśastatā*) because he has realized non-existence of egoity after spiritual practices and meditation. Eradication of repeated recurrence of the defilements is possible only when the notion of ego-clinging, the root of all ills, is destroyed. The realization of non-egoity which is the antidote to ego-clinging causes the eradication of the repeated recurrence of defilements. The Buddha has eradicated them by practicing non-egoity, and hence there is no question of repeated recurrence of defilements for him. And the Buddha has eradicated all *kleśāvaraṇa*, without leaving any residue. For him, there is nothing left to be eradicated. What is eradicable has been eradicated without leaving any residuum (*niḥśeṣa*). He is thus the *sugatatva*.[7] The Buddha is *tayin*, because he preaches others the path of eradicating the cause of misery which he himself perfected. He has trod the path from the very start of his journey step by step like a learner (*śaikṣya*, slob-lam), and has to undertake various means of incessant spiritual practices and meditation for the realization of impermanence, non-egoity, etc. with an intention to benefit others with his achievement. His entire achievements for attaining the highest stage of spiritual perfection is for the sake of others. He is thus a saviour of others.

In the above sections the doctrine of the Pramāṇabhūta-Buddha has been discussed following the *anuloma*-way of establishing the Buddha as the *pramāṇabhūta*. Hereunder, the establishment of the *pramāṇabhūta*-Buddha in the *pratiloma* way is dealt with. In the *pratiloma* way, *tayitva* is considered first and then *sugatatva śāstātva* and *jagaddhitaiṣitva* in the following manner.

TĀYITVA

The Buddha is a *tāyitva* or saviour of those suffering beings who seek emancipation. The Buddha teaches the suffering beings the truth of emancipation and the way to emancipation, which he has himself first realized. His teaching of the Four Noble Truths is aimed at redeeming the suffering beings from the misery of *saṁsāra*.

SUGATATVA

On the basis of *tāyitva* about the intentions in the proclamation of the Four Noble Truths, it is established that the Buddha is attributed with three unique knowledge (*viśeṣa-jñāna*, stogs-pa lhag-pa) and hence is the *sugata*: (i) The Buddha is attributed with the knowledge of reality (*tattva-jñāna*, de kho-na nyid mkhyen-pa), because he has realized the wisdom of non-egoity directly and incontrovertibly. (ii) He is also the embodiment of stable knowledge (*sthira-jñāna*, mikhyen-pa brtan-pa), because his teaching, revealing the truth of impermanence, non-egoity, are without any contradiction with the reality either directly or indirectly. (iii) His knowledge is also a complete knowledge (*asasa-jñāna*, ma-lus pa mkhyen-pa), because he has directly realized both spiritual perfection (abhyudaya, mngon-tho) and summum bonum (*niḥśreya*, nges-legs) which he also teaches others. *Sugatatva* as explained in the *anuloma* refers to the eradication that the Buddha has himself done (*pratihāra*, spang-pa bde-grhegs), the *pratilojma sugatatva* means the three unique knowledge what the Buddha has acquired (*pratīti*, stogs-pa bde-gshegs).

ŚĀSTATVA

Śaśtatva is established in the fact that knowledge acquiesced by the Buddha is unique (*viśeṣa*). This unique acquisition of the Buddha involves incessant practices of spiritual discipline.

Jagaddhitaiṣitva (great compassion) is established on the ground that the Buddha has undertaken incessant practices of spiritual discipline which inspired and benefitted others. His entire spiritual achievements are for the sake of others and for redressing others from the miseries of *saṁsāra*, because he practices compassion in the course of his spiritual discipline, and hence he is *jagaddhitaiṣin*. In the absence of the great compassion his wisdom would have remained ineffective and less meaningful. The Buddha is, thus, the *pramāṇabhūta*, embodiment of right knowledge, because whatever he teaches is for the benefit of others and this is due to the fact that the Buddha is possessed of great compassion.

NOTES AND REFERENCES

1. *Cf. Pramāṇabhūtāya jagaddhitaiṣiṇe Paramya,*
   Śāstesugataya tayine
   Pramāṇasidhyai svamata samuccayaḥ
   Kariṣyate viprastadiaikataḥ
   Pramāṇasamuccaya-I

   Tsad-mar gyur-pa 'gyur-la phan-par bzhed-pa
   Ston-pa bde-gshegs skyob-la phyag 'tsal-nas
   Tsad-ma sgrub-phyir rang-gi gzhung kun-las
   Btus-te sna-tsogs, thor-rnams 'dir-geig bya
   Tsad-ma kun-btus-I
2. *Mchod-brjod kyis ston-pa Ia rgyu phun-tsogs dang/'bras-bu phun-tsogs gnyis kyis bstod-do/. Rgyu phun-tsogs Ia gnyis-te/bsam-ba dang sbyor-ba phun-tsogs bsam-ba ni/'gro-ba la mtha' goig-tu phan-bzhed-pa 'I thugs-rje chen-po yin-la/sbyor-ba ni/bdag-med rtogs-pa 'I shes-rab gzhan-gyi don-du gorns-par byed-pa'I ston-ba'o/ 'gras-bu la-yang/ rang-don dang gzhan-don phun-tsogs gnyis-te/de-la rang-don no/spang-pa dang rtogs-pa'I bdag,;nyid kyi bde-bar gshegs-pa-kyad-par gyi chos-gsum dang Idan-pa dang/gzhan-don ni rang-nyid kyis gzigs-pa'I lam gzhan-la bstan-pa'I sgo-nas ' gro-ya skyab-pa'I mtsan-nyid an-no/de-ltar rgyu phun-gsum tsogs-pa las 'gras-bu don-gnyis phun-sum tsogs-pa'I dbag-nyid can gyi tsad-mar 'khrungs-par gyur-pa'I sang-rgyas bcom-ldan 'das de-ni tsad-ma yang-dag ces-bya 'o/*
   rNam-'grel that-lam gsal-byed, p. 226-27
3. *tadvat pramāṇaṁ bhagavān abhūtavinivṛttāya/*
   bhūtoktiḥ sakhanapekṣā tato yukta pramāṇasta/
   Pramāṇavārttika 9

   de-ldan bcom-ldan tsad-ma nyid, ma-skyes-pa ni blzog don-du/
   gyur-pa nyid-gsungs de-yi phyir, sgrub-byed la Itos tsad-yin rigs//
   rNm-rtza,
4. *de la tsigs. Bcad kyi go-rims dangmthun-par bshad-pa lugs-'byung dang/de las ldog-ste bshad-pa lugs-Idog gyi 'chad-tsul gnyis so\der gyur-ba'I kum- mkhyen yod-de/ de'I bras-bu'm rang-bzhin 'di-'dra mthong-ba'I phir/zhes-pa Ita-bu' I kun-khyen shes-byed kyi rgru-yang med-do/zhes rgol-by dag gi log-par rtog-pa dang-po dgag-pa'I ched-du lugs- 'byung gi bshad-pa mdzad-la/gnyis-pa dgag-pa'I ched du lugs-ldog gi bshad-pa mdzad do/*
5. *sādhanaṁ karuṇābhyāsāt sā-pramāṇavārttika, L 36 and its vṛtti Sgrub-byed thugs. Rjes goms las de-33 rNm-rtza.*
6. *Ibid.*, PV., I. 132 and their *vṛttis*, and rNam-thar, pp. 292-93.
7. PV, I. 141-45 and their *vṛttis* and Rnam-thar, pp. 297-300.

25

RELICS OF THE BUDDHA

BODY, ESSENCE, TEXT

Michael Willis

The *Khuddakapāṭha*, an early Buddhist text preserved in Sri Lanka, opens with

> *buddhaṁ saraṇaṁ gacchāmi*
> *dhammaṁ saraṇaṁ gacchāmi*
> *saṅghaṁ saraṇaṁ gacchāmi*
> I go for refuge to the Buddha!
> I go for refuge to the *Dharma*!
> I go for refuge to the *Saṅgha*!

These lines are known throughout the Buddhist world and their recitation represents a profession of belief in the essential elements of Buddhism: the enlightened master – the Buddha, his religious teachings – the *Dharma*, and his monastic followers – the *Saṅgha*. Known as the 'Triple Gem' or *triratna*, the Buddha, *Dharma* and *Saṅgha* constitute the essence and historical foundation of Buddhism.

The Triple Gem's parts are closely related. The Buddha and *Dharma* are interlocked because the teachings of the Buddha focus on the state of enlightenment which he had himself realized. To lead others towards this state, the Buddha developed the 'Middle Way', a balanced system of ascetic practice and monastic life. This involved the creation of the *Saṅgha*, the third element of the *triratna*. The close relationship of the *Dharma* and *Saṅgha* is shown by the fact that they were launched simultaneously at Sārnāth when the Buddha gave his first sermon. There he won five converts who formed the first community of Buddhist monks.

Although the Buddha gained many followers over his long career as a teacher, he refused to appoint a successor. He stipulated rather that the *Dharma* should guide the monks and nuns after his death. This prompted an institutionalization of the Triple Gem: the teachings were gathered together and passed on to the next generation by recitation and eventually by copying; the *Saṅgha* was organized according to the monastic rule or *Vinaya*; and the presence of the Buddha was perpetuated by images and relics.

The particulars of the *Dharma* and *Saṅgha* vary from place to place and have complex histories as one would expect in a religious organization established more than two thousand years ago. For all that, the *Dharma* has remained the Buddha's teachings – preserved and transmitted in canonical literatures with supplementary texts and commentaries. And the *Saṅgha* has remained the living community of Buddhist monks and nuns – organized according to the relevant monastic rules.

Early texts indicate how the Buddha's presence was represented before the advent of image-making. A particularly striking indication is given in the *Milindapañho*, a work of the early centuries BCE. At one point in this text, King Milinda asks the sage Nāgasena to define the Buddha's general shape. To this question the king receives the following reply[1]:

> The Lord's general shape, O King, is the nine-limbed speech of Buddha, the shrines for his bodily relics and the things he used as the jewel of the *Saṅgha*.

Nāgasena's words are of interest for the way they provide a commentary on the *triratna*, the central concept of Buddhism with which we opened this essay. Nāgasena's 'speech of the Buddha' is the teaching or *Dharma*, while his 'jewel of the *Saṅgha*' is, more obviously, the monastic community. Nāgasena's 'shrines for relics and the things he used' completes the triad. This shows that the Buddha's bodily remains and the things he used in his lifetime – such as his begging bowl – represented the Buddha within the *triratna* frame. To put the matter other way, Nāgasena's statement shows that in the early days of Buddhism, before the making of images became widespread, the Buddha was understood to be a shrine containing relics. The word used by Nāgasena for these shrines is *cetiya*, a synonym of *stūpa*, the dominical mound built to house relics. The containers made to hold relics frequently repeat the *stūpa*-shape in miniature.

That the Buddha within the *triratna* was indeed a relic is shown by an episode in the *Mahāvaṁsa* which recounts the early days of Buddhism in Sri Lanka. At the end of his first rainy season on the island, Mahinda – the famous Buddhist elder who introduced Buddhism there in the third century BCE – was impatient to return to India. This troubled King Devānaṁpiyatissa who wished him to stay. Mahinda told the king:

> O great king it has been a long time since we have seen Our Teacher, the Fully-enlightened One; we have dwelt without a refuge; there is nothing here for us to worship (*Mahāvaṁsa* 17: 2-4).

The king, confused by this remark, replied: 'But did you not tell me, sir, that the Fully-enlightened One has passed away?' Mahinda's reply succinctly sums up the efficacy and importance of relics: 'When the relics are seen, the Buddha is seen.'[2] This story clearly shows that the spread of the Buddhist dispensation in the early historic period went hand-in-hand with the movement of relics. Moreover this shows that the establishment of the *triratna* – the full complement of Buddhism – involved not only the transmission of the teachings and the settlement of monks, but the movement of holy relics.

Of course, things like hair and nail-clippings were saved during the Buddha's lifetime, and have their own sacred narratives. But the most important relics were the burnt remains collected immediately after the Buddha's cremation. According to the well known account in the *Mahāparinibbānasutta*, the ashes of the Buddha were divided into eight parts, one for each of the kings in whose territory the Buddha lived and taught.[3] The kings deposited the remains in eight *stūpas*. Seven of these were subsequently opened so the relics could be divided and carried to all parts of India. This dispersal of relics – and concomitant spread of Buddhism – took place under the patronage of King Aśoka in the third century BCE.[4] Although part of a pan-Indian programme of empire-building, Aśoka's concerted support for Buddhism is celebrated throughout the Buddhist world. He has long been remembered as *dharmarāja* or 'king of *Dharma*' and his example marked the beginning of Buddhism's long association with political power.

In the perpetuation and spread of Buddhism, authenticity was a central and natural concern. To preserve the *Dharma*, texts were carefully memorized and meticulously copied; to preserve the *Saṅgha*, ordination lineages with strict rules of initiation and transmission were developed.

For relics, great care was taken to preserve and guard important remains in a monastic setting. That the most important relics were placed in monasteries is confirmed textually by the Buddha's stipulation that the relics of Śāriputra, one of his leading disciples, should be held by monks rather than lay-followers.[5] The genre of *vaṁsa*-literature was also developed in Sri Lanka to establish the authenticity of relics and the transmission of the *Dharma*. The purpose of this literature was to trace the Buddha's relics and his teachings back to their authentic source, i.e., the Buddha himself. For relics this involved detailed narratives charting the movement of the Buddha's remains. Episodes in these narratives leave little doubt that the history of Buddhism's spread is the story of old *stūpa*s being opened so relics could accompany and sanctify the ever-widening horizon of the Buddhist dispensation. Archaeological finds corroborate that *stūpa*s were opened repeatedly from early times.[6]

The terminology for relics reveals much about how these objects were understood and classified. The most important were corporeal relics or *śārīrika dhātu*. These relics were not just tokens or reminders of the Buddha, but powerful objects in and of themselves. Simply put, the presence of a Buddha relic equalled the presence of the Buddha himself. This meant that the activity of building a *stūpa* and placing a genuine relic in it had the power to create a new place of living religious significance.

Early inscriptions show that this was not regarded as a strictly symbolic matter. On the Shinkot reliquary, for example, the contents of the container are described as follows: '[this is] the body, endowed with life, of the Blessed Buddha'.[7] In textual accounts there are analogous descriptions of relics having a force which resembles life itself (*jīvitasannibha*).[8] It is this 'living presence' which allows relics, like the Buddha, to fly through the air, give off marvellous rays and assume the physical appearance of a great being (*mahāpuruṣa*).[9]

The Buddha's relics have living energy because they contain his elemental essence or *dhātu*. This term is used consistently to describe relics in Buddhism. Although we speak of 'relics' for the sake of linguistic convenience, the words *śārīrika dhātu* actually mean 'the essence of the Buddha's body'. The idea is that the cremation pyre functioned something like a furnace which refined the Buddha's corporeal remains in their essential elements. Thus, the pyre did not yield charred bones, as one might expect, but small spherical objects like pearls. In those places where relics have been recovered and identified as belonging to the Buddha – as at Qingshan in China – the relics are small pearl-like spheres or crystallized grains.[10] Even today there is a custom of sifting through the funeral pyres of especially holy monks in search of small spherical objects which are understood to be the monks' *dhātu* or spiritual essence.

When the Buddha relics were divided into eight parts after his death, the pot in which they had been temporarily stored was taken away and placed in a *stūpa* of its own.[11] This introduces the second class of relic, namely, things which are worthy of veneration because they have been sanctified by the Buddha's use or presence. These are called *pāribhogika dhātu*, objects which embody the Buddha by virtue of the fact that he used or enjoyed them. This kind of relic, already encountered in the *Milindapañho*, was well known in the fifth century as shown by commentaries on the *Jātaka* stories and *Khuddakapāṭha*.[12] Relics of use included the Buddha's begging bowl, robe, etc. but the most pre-eminent was and is the *bodhi* tree at Bodhgaya.

The *bodhi* tree is classified as a 'relic of use' because the Buddha sat beneath it in meditation and because this meditation resulted in the Buddha's attainment of *bodhi* or supreme knowledge, the tree is intimately tied to the Buddha's identity and spiritual achievement. The *bodhi* tree has been venerated, and the area around it regarded as sacred ground, from at least the third century BCE. This is shown by King Aśoka's ritual illustration of the tree and his placement of an elaborately-carved stone slab at the spot where the Buddha sat in meditation. Since the slab's rediscovery in the nineteenth century, it has been reactivated as a focal point of worship. This is the diamond throne or *vajrāsana*, the place where, in the elaborate cosmology of later Buddhism, all Buddhas of the past meditated and the place where all future Buddhas will come to find the same imperishable truth.

The most remarkable thing about the *bodhi* tree is that it is an actual living link to the Buddha and his times. This makes the tree analogous to the Buddha's corporeal remains which are understood as being imbued with the Buddha's living presence. This is why *bodhi* trees, like corporeal relics, were transported to other parts of South Asia when Buddhism began to spread beyond its original homeland in North India. The most notable instance of this is the *bodhi* tree sapling carried to Sri Lanka and planted at Anuradhapura, the first capital of old Ceylon. This took place in the third century BCE. As Buddhism was disseminated throughtout the island, *bodhi* trees were planted at newly established monasteries. Each tree was placed in an enclosure known as a *bodhighara* or 'house for the *bodhi* tree'.

In addition to a *bodhighara*, new monasteries also had a *stūpa* for relics and residential buildings for monks or nuns. Another feature of Sri Lankan monasteries of the mature type is the *paṭimāghara* – a hall for images.[13] This brings us back to the question of Buddha's figural representation. Historically speaking, the making of images did not emerge as a significant religious and artistic practice until the second century CE. Before that time, symbols were used to indicate the Buddha. Thus the *bodhi* tree, already in circulation as a living relic, was frequently used in sculptures to indicate the Buddha's moment of enlightement at Bodhgaya. Similarly, a wheel was used to represent the inauguration of the Buddha's career as a spiritual teacher at Sārnāth, an event described canonically as the 'turning of the wheel of *Dharma*.' The closing chapter of the Buddha's life and his final passing at Kuśinārā were represented by the *stūpa*. More immediate and visually compelling are *Buddhapada*, representations of the Buddha's footprints. The point of these, of course, is that the Buddha entered *nirvāṇa* so his footprints indicate the 'mark' he made on the world before passing completely beyond its limitations. That the Buddha's feet were a subject of veneration in their own right from early times is demonstrated by early stone plaques and seals.

Symbols like the tree, wheel, *stūpa* and footprints were used widely from the inception of Buddhist art in the second century BCE. These symbols are neither bodily relics nor relics of use – thus neither *sārīrika dhātu* nor *pāribhogika dhātu*. Symbols nonetheless indicated the presence of the Buddha and so mark the beginning of what came to be termed *uddesika dhātu*, 'relics of indication'. The development of *uddesika dhātu* as a formal category appears to have been prompted by the emergence of figural representations of the Buddha in the second century CE. That images were an innovation which call for explanation is shown by the *Dhātuvaṁsa*, a fourteenth-century historical work. In this text there is an account of the deposition of the Buddha's forehead bone and hair-relic in the Mahāmaṅgala *stūpa* in Sri Lanka. A golden image of the Buddha, we are told, had been placed in the *stūpa*'s inner chamber. As the relics were enshrined there, they displayed a number of miracles, the culmination coming when the forehead bone of the Buddha established itself on the forehead of the golden image and the hair relic, again through its own power, fixed itself on the sculpture's head.[14] In detailing these marvellous events which are assigned anachronistically to the reign of Kākavaṇṇatissa in second century BCE, the *Dhātuvaṁsa* is authenticating the sancity of images by showing that bodily relics attached themselves to the Buddha image of their own accord. The relics had the power to do this beacuse they were imbued with the Buddha's living presence. The homology of Buddha and relic thus show that it was the Buddha himself who sanctioned figural representations.

The Buddha has been a constant focus of meditation and philosophical speculation because the faithful seek refuge in him and have the Buddha's inner nature as their ultimate spiritual goal. The ubiquity of these concerns is shown by *Buddhānusmṛti*, 'the remembrance of the Buddha', not an esoteric practice, but one of the basic themes of Buddhist meditation.[15] In *Buddhānusmṛti* one is supposed to reflect on the Buddha and his virtues with trusting faith so that one may come to see and understand him. This 'seeing' can be ephemeral or substantial, as we learn from Xuanzang's personal account of seeing the Buddha's shadow in a meditation cave in Gandhāra during his visit from China in the seventh century. The central assumption is that if one is able to see the Buddha, one will come to know him also. The equation of seeing and knowing was given canonical expression in the *Saṁyutta Nikāya* (3: 120) where the Buddha states: 'He who sees the *Dharma* sees me; he who sees me sees the *dharma*'.

The practice of remembering and seeing prompted reflection on the nature of the Buddha's body or form. When the faithful take refuge in the Buddha and remember him, they are not, rather obviously, taking refuge in his frame, but in the sublime qualities he perfected over many lifetimes and embodied by superlative example in his final incarnation. This is why a relic is not a commonplace piece of bone, but a *dhātu* or elemental essence. A conundrum was nonetheless created by combining sublime essence with mundane corporeality. This problem was resolved by ascribing several bodies to Buddha. The most important for understanding the cult of relics are the *rūpakāya* – the mundane physical body – and the *dharmakāya* – the sublime Dharma-body.[16] The *Dharma*-body represents both the Buddha's teachings and his sublime qualities. This double-meaning was possible because the word *Dharma* designates both: the point is that Buddhism aims to use the *Dharma* – the Buddha's teaching – to replicate the *Dharma* – the Buddha's good qualities.[17]

By the early centuries CE, the *Dharma*-body – the teachings of the Buddha and his essential qualities as a Buddha – were located in the philosophy of causal genesis or dependent origination. Termed *pratīyasamutpāda*, this philosopy became a key feature of mature Buddhist speculation.[18] Although highly nuanced and the basis of a whole system of thought, its core tenets were summarised in a single verse or *gāthā*.[19]

> *ye dharmā hetuprabhavā hetuṁ teṣām tathāgato hy*
> *avadat teṣāṁ ca yo nirodho evaṁvādī mahāśramaṇaḥ*
>
> The Buddha alone has explained the conditions that arise from causes, and the great mendicant has also proclaimed their confinement.

Just as relics were a distillation of the Buddha's manifold qualities into an elemental *dhātu*, so the whole philosophy of causation was condensed into a single religious statement. This verse – the 'Hymn of dependent origination' – was seen as having talismanic properties and became a source of speculation in its own right. Especially important were the parallels made between the verse and the Buddha, the *Dharma* and the *Dharma*-body. Extending earlier equations between seeing, knowing and the Buddha, the *Majjhima Nikāya* (1: 190-91) states:

> He who sees the *pratīyasamutpāda* sees the *Dharma*, and he who sees the *Dharma* sees the *pratīyasamutpāda*.

The implication of this understanding for the construction of *stūpas* is explained in the *Sūtra on the Merit of Building a Stūpa*, an Indian work surviving in Tibetan and Chinese translation. After discoursing on the merit of building a *stūpa*, the Buddha comments on the 'Hymn of dependent origination'[20]:

> Noble son, this verse signifies the Dharma-body of the Buddha. You should write this verse and place it in a *stūpa*. If a living being understood the import of causes you should know that this person would then see the Buddha.

Because the 'Hymn of dependent origination' is the *Dharma*-body, it embodies the Buddha and is a valid *dhātu* in every respect. Small votive *stūpas* show how these ideas were carried into everyday practice. This *stūpa* does not contain any kind of relic, only the 'Hymn of dependent origination stamped' into the clay. The verse was also inscribed on stone statues with great regularity after the fifth century. As a '*Dharma*-deposit', the verse added further validation to the object which was already a 'relic of indication' or *uddesika dhātu*. A text entitled the *Noble Treatise of the Great Vehicle on Dependent Origination* further develops the long-standing equation between seeing and knowing:

> This *pratīyasamutpāda* is the *Dharma*-body of the Buddha. He who sees the *Pratīyasamutpāda* sees the Buddha.[21]

NOTES AND REFERENCES

1. *Milindapañho* (ed.), V. Trenckner (London, 1928), 341: *sabbāpaṇaṁ kho mahārāja bhagavato navaṅgaṁ buddhavacanaṁ śārīrikāni pāribhogikāni cetiyāni saṅgharatanā ca*; to be read with translation of B. Horner, *Milinda's Questions*, 2 vols. (London, 1963).
2. *Mahāvaṁsa* (ed.), W. Geiger (London, 1908); trans. Geiger (London, 1912), 17: 3: *dhātusu diṭṭhesu diṭṭho hoti jino*. The Buddha is here referred to as Jina, 'the Conqueror', a common epithet. The most important study of the relic cult is Kevin Trainor, *Relics, Ritual and Representation in Buddhism* (Cambridge, 1997) upon which we have partially drawn for this essay. The *triratna* and its relation to the architectural configuration of monasteries was first explored in S. Bandaranayake, *Sinhalese Monastic Architecture* (Leiden, 1974): 27.
3. *Mahāparinibbānasutta* (Skt. *Mahāparinirvāṇasūtra*); Pāli version in *Dīgha Nikāya*, 16: 6: 23-28.
4. The question of Aśoka's role is dealt with in J. Strong, *Legend of King Aśoka* (Princeton, 1983).
5. G. Roth, 'Symbolism of the Buddhist Stūpa', in *The Stūpa: Its Religious and Historical Significance* (ed.) A. Dallapiccola (Wiesbaden, 1980): 183-85.
6. For an account of relics in central India known from nineteenth century excavations, see my 'Buddhist Saints from Ancient Vidisa', *Journal of the Royal Asiatic Society*, 11 (2001): 219-29.
7. D.C. Sircar, *Select Inscriptions Bearing on Indian History and Civilization*, 2 vols. (Calcutta and Delhi, 1965-83), 1: 104; *praṇasameda śarīrabhagavato śakamumisa*. The key word *praṇasameda* = Skt. *prāṇasametaḥ*, i.e., endowed with or possessed of life. Further discussion in G. Schopen, *Bones, Stones and Buddhist Monks* (Honolulu, 1997): 117-18.
8. Trainor, *Relics, Ritual and Representation*, p. 99, note 8 citing the *Mahāvaṁsa*.
9. Instances are given in *Ibid.*, pp. 168, 187. The Buddha's presence in Theravāda seems to have been figurative rather than actual: the resolution (*adhiṭṭhāna*) of the Buddha and the Arhats explains the marvels (*Prātihārya*) that may occur at relic monuments. See *Milindapañho*, pp. 309-10. Compare the Mīmāṁsaka view about the actual sentience of dieties in *Śabarabhāṣya* (*Devatādhikaraṇa*, 9: 1: 5: 6-9).
10. Illustrated in Michaelson, *Gilded Dragons* (London, 1999): 146.
11. *Mahāparinirvāṇasūtra*, 51: 1-17; *Dīgha Nikāya*, 16: 6: 25.

12. *Jātakas* (ed.), V. Fausboll, 5 vols. (London, 1877-91), number 479; *Khuddakapāṭha*, pp. 221-22.
13. Bandaranayake, *Sinhalese Monastic Architecture.*
14. The text is summarised in Trainor, *Relics, Ritual and Representation*, p. 170.
15. Edward Conze, *Buddhist Meditation* (London, 1956), 14-15.
16. The number of bodies was elaborated over time to meet philosophical and theological needs. See Strong, *Legend of King Aśoka*, pp. 105-19; F.E. Reynolds, 'The Several Bodies of Buddha: Reflections on a neglected aspect of Theravāda Tradition', *History of Religions*, 16 (1976-77), 374-89. More recently, P. Harrison, 'Is the Dharmakāya the Real Phantom Body of the Buddha?' *Journal of the International Association of Buddhist Studies*, 15 (1992) 44-93, with response in J. Makransky, *Buddhahood Embodied: Sources of Controversy in India and Tibet* (Albany, 1997).
17. There are seven basic meanings of the term *Dharma* in Buddhism. See Conze, *Buddhist Thought in India* (Delhi, 1996), 92-106.
18. R.C. Jamieson, *Nāgārjuna's Verses on the Great Vehicle and the Heart of Dependent Originatiion* (Delhi, 2000).
19. D. Boucher, 'The *Pratītyasamutpādagāthā* and its Role in the Medieval Cult of Relics', *Journal of the International Association of Buddhist Studies* 14 (1991), 1-27. Also G. Schopen, 'The Phrase *sā pṛthvīpradeśaś caityabhūto bhavet* in the *Vajracchedikā*: Notes on the Cult of the Book in Mahāyāna', *Indo-Iran Journal*, 17 (1975), 147-81; Y. Bentor, *Consecration of Images and Stūpas in Indo-Tibetan Tāntric Buddhism* (Leiden, 1996).
20. Divākara's translation into Chinese given in Boucher, pp. 8-10.
21. *Āryapratītyasamutpādanāmamahāyānasūtra*, translation from Tibetan *Ibid.*, p. 11.

26

YOGIC TRADITION OF NĀROPĀ AND ITS UNINTERRUPTED CONTINUITY IN TIBET, LADAKH AND HIMACHAL PRADESH

Ramesh Chandra Tewari

It is well known that with the emergence of tantra, that combined various practices related to ritualistic symbolism with advanced yogic exercises, Buddhism reached the third and final stage of its development in India. This stage is known as Vajrayāna. Its philosophical foundations were deeply rooted in the *Mādhyamika* and *Yogācāra* metaphysics. Vajrayāna is also known by its earlier name *Mantrayāna.* Contemporary traditional scholars hold that Mantrayāna is the connecting link berween Mahāyāna and Vajrayāna.[1] Most of the modern Buddhist scholars today are of the opinion that Vajrayāna is the right word to identify the last stage of the development of Buddhism.[2] There can be no two opinions about the fact that the origins of Vajrayāna are located in the philosophies (*Mādhyamika* and *Yogācāra*) and practices (perfecting six *pārmitās*) of Mahāyāna. It is also incontestable that the specific goal of Vajrayāna is to attain direct experience of enlightenment or Buddhahood as *Mahāsukha* or Great Bliss, is a *vajra*-like state of mind and a yogin who attains it is said to have entered the sphere of *Vajrasattva.*[3]

The great yogins who attain the indescribable experience of *Mahāsukha* are known as *Mahāsiddhas*, i.e., 'great perfected ones' or 'great adepts'. Traditionally, *eighty-four mahāsiddhas* are the most famous among great adepts. The legendary accounts of their lives are recorded in the hagiographical Sanskrit work by the Indian Ācarya Abhayadattaśrī. Its Tibetan translation is available in the Kanjur collection. Some of the *Mahāsiddhas* had earlier been famous *ācāryas* and abbots of *Mahāvihāras* or great monasteries and had authored important philosophical tracts or commentaries. Many among them flouted all social norms of caste or class and led unconventional lives.

As indicated above, some of the *Mahāsiddhas* had held high academic positions in most famous *Mahāvihāras* or monastic universities that flourished in Bihar and Eastern India initially during the Gupta period and later during Pāla period. The most famous *Mahāvihāra,* which became a model for other *Mahāvihāras* that were to follow, was that of Nalanda which existed for nearly eight centuries, i.e., from 5th to 13th century CE. Apart from being great centres of monastic and spiritual learning the *Mahāvihāras* also grew up as seats of liberal learning. Among other great monastic universities of the Pāla period, Odantpura, Vikramaśilā, Somapura and Jagaddala are better known.

Among the *Mahāsiddhas* associated with Nalanda, the most prominent were Sarahapā, Nāgārjuna and Nāropā. Nāgārjuna was given ordination by Rāhula, the grand abbot of Nalanda. The extraordinary genius of Nāgārjuna flowered in Nalanda where he not only earned name and fame as a scholar but also as a great *siddha* and a master *rasajña*.[4] Nāropā was yet another great *Mahāsiddha* associated with Nalanda Mahāvihāra where he spent eight years of his life.

Like many other *Mahāsiddhas*, Nāropā's life history is a heroic saga of spiritual quest.[5] He was born in a royal family in Bengal. At the age of eleven he went to Kashmir for study and within three years mastered all the *pañca mahāvidyās*, the five branches of Buddhist learning. After returning to his home in Bengal while he was continuing his higher studies his parents forced him to marry. His wife was herself an accomplished scholar. Perhaps she very well appreciated her husband Nāropā's strong urge to lead a spiritual life. Ultimately, the marriage was dissolved after eight years. Thereafter, Nāropā went to Kashmir where he stayed for three years. Later, he went to Phulahari, a place which was sanctified by his presence. After spending six years in Phulahari he went to Nalanda and joined the famous *Mahāvihāra*. When the great Ācārya Jetāri, who was the *Dvārapāla* of the northern gate, died the pandits of the *Mahāvihāra* requested Nāropā to take his place. He accepted their request and took over as the *Dvārapāla*. It is noteworthy that according to some Tibetan sources Nāropā was the *Dwārapāla* of northern gate of Vikramaśilā Mahāvihāra located near Nalanda. Padma Karpo, the renowned Tibetan Kargyudpa scholar, is of the opinion that Nāropā was associated with Nalanda and Vikramaśilā Mahāvihāras both.[6] After accepting the post according to the academic convention of *Mahāvihāras* he had to prove his superiority as a scholar by winning a prestigious philosophical debate with both the Buddhist and Hindu scholars separately. Consequently, after establishing his intellectual superiority he became the abbot of Nalanda Mahāvihāra and came to be known as Abhayakīrti and held this highly honoured position for eight years. It was in CE 1057 that while he was deeply immersed in his studies he had the vision of an extremely ugly old and decrepit woman who derisively told him that acquisition of objective knowledge is a waste of time and energy, and that he should seek out a guru who would reveal the real sense behind the words. Thereafter, he resigned from his coveted position in Nalanda and headed eastwards. While he wandered in search of his would-be guru he continuously repeated the *mantra* of the tantric deity Cakrasaṁvara. Ultimately, the deity appeared before him and told that one Tilopā who lives somewhere in the East will be his guru. Nāropā set out in search of Tilopā.

Nāropā's guru Tilopā was an unusual figure. In the beginning of his extraordinary career he was a monk at Somapura where he meditated for twelve years. Later Tilopā deserted the *Saṅgha* and engaged himself in meditation for another twelve years. Outwardly he led a very ordinary life. He was called Tilopā because during the day he pounded *til* (sesame) seeds to earn his living. He had no human root guru. His root guru was none other than Vajradhara Buddha himself. He also received secret instructions from four masters, belonging to four different lineages.[7]

Facing immense obstacles Nāropā continued his search for Tilopā. At one point he lost all hope of finding his future guru. Then Tilopā appeared before him and accepted him as his disciple. Thereafter, Nāropā constantly served his guru for twelve years. During all these years of apprenticeship he had to undergo various physical tests and receive punishments and abuses at the hands of Tilopā. Ultimately, when Tilopā was fully convinced that Nāropā had all the qualities of a perfect disciple who could obtain higher tantric teachings and practices, he empowered Nāropā to receive and practice *guhya* or secret tantras. After prolonged *sādhanā*

Nāropā realized the highest twelfth spiritual level and became a fully accomplished *Mahāsiddha*. Thereafter, his guru Tilopā exhorted him to go out and act for the benefit of others and specifically told him that when a Tibetan named Mārpā comes to him in future he should accept him as his disciple. He told Nāropā that Mārpā would spread the highest teachings of Vajrayāna in his homeland Tibet. Following the exhortation of his guru Nāropā spent rest of his life in initiating and training numerous disciples in secret tantras. The number of his Buddhist and non-Buddhist disciples ran into hundreds. Among his famous seven disciples were *siddhas* like Maitrīpā, Dombīpā, Śāntipā, Śrī-Śāntibhadra, Prajñāsiṁha and Akṣarsiddhi from Kashmir. Among his disciples there were one hundred accomplished *yoginīs* also. However, his most important disciple was Mārpā from Tibet. Nāropā was a prolific scholar also who authored or translated twenty-five tantric works which are preserved in Tibetan Tanjur collection. When Nāropā attained the age of eighty-five and had completed his mission he felt that it was time for him to go. He passed away in his excellent lamasery at Phulahari in CE 1100. His relics are preserved in the Kanika monastery situated in the Janskar area of Ladakh.

Mahāsiddha Nāropā occupies a unique place in the history of Buddhism in Tibet, Bhutan, India and Nepal. He is particularly known for his two major contributions. Firstly, he is known for reordering and developing the four special transmissions, which he received from his guru Tilopā, into his 'six yoga system' known as *Na-ro chos drug*. Secondly, he is known for transmitting the most developed Indian tantric lineage to Mārpā, the founder of the Kargyudpā school of Tibetan Buddhism which gives primacy to tantric meditation. Mārpā had many Tibetan disciples among whom Milarepā was the most outstanding. Milarepā is known as the greatest *Mahāsiddha* and mystic poet of Tibet. Milarepā's chief disciple Gampopā introduced monasticism in the Kargyudpā tradition. The Kargyudpā school spread not only in Tibet but became deeply entrenched in Bhutan. It also acquired firm foothold in Nepal and in the Himalayan areas of India like Ladakh, Lahoul and Kinnaur.

*****

The most significant contribution of Nāropā in the development of Vajrayāna is his six-yoga system of tantric *sādhanā*. This yogic system was a sort of improvement in the methods of practising the tantric transmissions which he had received from his guru Tilopā. Nāropā systematised the four special transmissions received from Tilopā and developed them into the system of six yogas for the benefit of future tantric practitioners. Tilopā himself had received the four transmissions from four main teachers belonging to different *Āgama* lineages originating from tantric gurus, viz., Nāgārjuna, Caryāpā, PuKa siddhi and Luiapā.[8] Thus, Nāropā's main contribution was to unify the yogic teachings of all the aforesaid lineages into a well ordered system of six yogic practices. These practices are basically meant for determined and qualified persons who possess all the conditions necessary for tantric practitioners. At the initial stages these practices must be carried out under the strict guidance of a competent *Vajraguru*, who gives spiritual empowerments through various highly symbolic rituals of consecration.

The six tantric yoga practices developed by Nāropā are as follows: 1. *Cāṇḍālī* yoga (Mystic Heat yoga); 2. *Māyākāya* yoga (Illusory heat or Apparition yoga); 3. *Svapna* yoga (Dream yoga): 4. *Prabhāsvara* yoga (Clear or Radiant Light yoga); 5. *Antarābhava* yoga (Intermediate State yoga); and 6. *Sankramaṇa* yoga (Transference of Consciousness yoga). These yogic practices are extremely difficult and it is not easy for everyone to undertake them. Only those who have renunciated everything and who are intensely driven by the highest motivation of achieving Buddhahood in this life are considered suitable for undertaking these yogas.

The first or the *Cāṇḍālī* yoga is a highly complex yoga and is the most difficult yogic technique to arouse 'inner heat' by internal visualizations and through *prāṇāyāma* or breathing exercises. These visualizations and exercises are aimed to control and direct the three subtle *nāḍī*s (channels) and energy current (wind) called *prāṇa*. Among these three *nāḍī*s the central *nāḍī* plays a crucial role. It is through this channel that the yoga practitioner causes the flow of *bodhicitta* energy current rise upwards through a series of *Cakra*s or levels.[9] With the rising of energy current one feels the sensation of increasing heat in the body. This state is known as the heat generated by *Cāṇḍālī.* That is why the practitioners of *Cāṇḍālī* yoga remain naked or half naked. Sometimes even in winters they wrap themselves in wet sheets or, in extreme cases, they sit on ice or snow mounds. After further practices the channels are fully opened and the energy current flows freely. When the *sādhaka* or the yoga practitioner reaches this stage one meditates on the nature of mind by visualizing it as the subtle 'drop' rising through the central channel. The resulting experience makes the mind free of false conceptions. Thus by successfully controlling energy channels, subtle winds and drops, the yoga practitioner completes the *Cāṇḍālī* yoga practice and becomes eligible to move ahead to complete the rest of the five yogas.

The second or the *Māyākāya* yoga or the illusory body yoga is aimed to make the yogic practitioner aware that everything in this world, all objects and all subjective states, are bereft of any self nature. They are *māyic* or illusory like a rainbow or a mirage. In this yogic practice the practitioner uses his mind and the subtle energies for the formation of a tantric deity. Although this deity appears to be real it is in fact also an illusory body. This illusory body is formed by various yogic exercises involving subtle channels, vital energies and visualisations.[10] Through the creation of illusory body one not only comes to realize the illusory dream-like nature of all existence but also develops compassion for all sentient beings and visualizes their ultimate liberation.

The *Svapna* yoga or the dream yoga is the third yoga of Nāropā's six-yoga system. Through this yoga the principle of *māyāvāda,* which formed the basis of yogic experience related to the preceding *Māyākāya* yoga, is expanded. The dream yoga makes the practitioner aware of the fact that whatever experience one acquires in the state of dreaming are as illusory as that experienced in the waking state. Through this yoga one learns to control dreams and vital energies through the manipulation of *nāḍī*s or channels. A successful practitioner learns to manipulate the forms and contents of dreams about Buddha, *Bodhisattva*s, Buddha verses, etc. The aim of dream yoga is to free the yoga practitioner from the *māyic* or illusory sleep-like state so that he or she is liberated like Buddha from the iron grip of *māyā* which has enmeshed her/him in the endless cycle of life and death.

Through the practice of the fourth yoga, i.e., the *Prabhāsvara* yoga or the clear light yoga the yogi becomes aware of the absolutely unblemished radiant nature of mind. This radiance is nothing else than *śūnyatā* or emptiness. It is the experience of *parmārtha satya* or absolute truth, as different from conventional truth. Through this practice the *sādhaka* successively visualizes all the four forms of emptiness. The fourth or the highest form of emptiness, i.e., *sarvaśūnyatā* is perceived as spontaneous radiant light. This perception of emptiness is experienced by the yogin as the highest state of *Ānanda* or bliss called *Sahajānanda.*

The *Antarābhava* yoga ('Bardo' in Tibetan) or the Intermediate state yoga is the fifth yoga. *Antarābhava* is the intermediate state between death and birth. The theory of this yoga is explained in detail in the relevant Tibetan literature of which *Bardo Thodol* or the *Tibetan Book of the Dead* is the most known. The Tibetan Kargyudpa school of Buddhism, the inheritor of Nāropā's yogic lineage distinguishes six *bardos*. These six stages or types of *bardo* are experienced by all human beings. According to tantra tradition if the prescribed practices and visualisations are followed, these *bardos* relating to death offer great opportunities for liberation, i.e., for attaining Buddhahood. At the time of death one's consciousness reaches a state which does not exist in normal lifetime. An advanced meditator can actualize such a state of mind much before death through yogic exercises. All the subtle states of consciousness which arise at the time of death are experienced by the *sādhaka* or meditator very much prior to the actual event of death. One who has successfully completed *Antarābhava* yoga gets liberated from the cyclic bondage of birth and rebirth.

The last stage of Nāropā's six yoga system is *Sankramaṇa* yoga or the Transference yoga. This is the heart or the core of the six yogas. It enables the yogin to actualize either the consciousness of pure Buddhattva or the consciousness of the highest level of future birth. This yoga is practiced at different levels. The practice of transference has been given very high importance by common people belonging to the extensive Tibetan cultural area. At the common level it is practiced in the form of receiving empowerments from a qualified lama. Any person who has received relevant teachings and empowerments can recall the teachings at the time of her/his death. It is believed that if the dying person recalls the teachings properly she/he enters the pure Buddhattva after death. The yogins practise this yoga at the highest level in which practitioner's mind is trained in such a way that at the time of death her/his consciousness escapes through a subtle aperture known as *Brahmarandhra* or Brahma fountain situated at the crown of the head.[11] This highly developed practice involves *Avadhūti nāḍī,* eight tantric root letters and *prāṇic* winds. During the course of this practice the *sādhaka* undergoes certain specific experience. This yogic practice ends when the *sādhaka* experiences that a liquid yellow light is flowing out of the crown of the head. A yogin is supposed to undertake the transference practice from time to time during his life.

Nāropā's six yogas are meant only for those who have firm determination to achieve Buddhahood in their lifetime, can endure hardships, and are free of wordly worries. That is why these yogas are best suited for monks or those who have renounced the world like the great *Mahāsiddhas*. The practice of these yogas enables a *sādhaka* to actualize Buddha's *Trikāya* or 'Triple body', namely, *Dharmakāya, Sambhogakāya,* and *Nirmāṇakāya*. At the time of death the *sādhaka* attains the *Dharmakāya,* the highest Buddha body.

Mahāsiddha Nāropā's another important contribution was the transmission of the *Vajrayanist siddha* lineage to his Tibetan disciple, Mārpā. This transmission proved to be the turning point in the historical development of the *siddha* tradition. Thence the current of the Buddhist tantric tradition turned northwards, i.e., towards Tibet. It was in Tibet that the great tradition found a fertile ground where it proliferated.

Mārpā (1012-1097) was the founder of the famous Kargyudpa School of Tibetan Buddhism. It is one of the most widely known schools of Buddhism and its vibrancy is reflected in the religious and spiritual activities of its monasteries and meditation centres. In Tibetan religious history Mahāsiddha Mārpā is better known as Mārpā Lochawa or Mārpā, the translator. His life story is as extraordinary as that of any Indian *Mahāsiddha*. After receiving his early education his father sent him far away from his birthplace to receive religious education. Very soon he proved his credentials as a translator. Later, the strong urge for receiving higher and authentic religious training made him to undertake arduous journeys to India. Before leaving for India

Mārpā underwent hardships to collect gold for his journeys and stay in India. On the way to India he stayed in Nepal for three years. In Nepal he met and received teachings from Che-ther-wa and Pen-ta-wa, two renowned Nepalese disciples of Mahāsiddha Nāropā. They asked him to go to India to receive higher tantric teachings from the Mahāsiddha Nāropā and dispatched him to Nalanda. When Mārpā reached Nalanda, Nāropā was not available. Later Mārpā met him at his Phulahari lamasery. Nāropā welcomed Mārpā and recalled that his guru Tilopā had predicted about the arrival of his future disciple from Tibet. Mārpā received teachings and initiations of Hevajra from him. Nāropā sent him to tantric *ācārya*s like Maitrīpā, Jñānagarbha and Śāntabhadra from whom he received the teachings of *Guhyasamaja Tantra, Mahāmāyā Tantra,* etc. Later, Nāropā transmitted his six-yoga system to Mārpā. Mārpā returned to Tibet after spending twelve years in India and Nepal. Afterwards, he visited India twice and received advanced tantric teachings and empowerments from Nāropā. During his second and third visits he also visited Nepal and South India to meet his other old teachers like Chi-ther-wa and Maitrīpā and Kukkuripā. After completion of his third sojourn, when he was departing for his homeland, Nāropā delivered the farewell speech at the *Gaṇa Cakra Pūja,* a special tantric gathering, in which he declared Mārpā as his successor and entrusted him to carry the task of spreading the pristine secret tantric teachings in Tibet. In this way Mārpā's third and last visit ended and he came back to Tibet to continue the legacy of Nāropā. During his three visits Mārpā had spent a total of sixteen years seven months at the feet of his guru Nāropā.

Milarepā (1040-1123), the greatest *siddha*-poet of Tibet, was the chief disciple of Mārpā. When he was very young his father died. Consequently, he was cheated of his property by his cruel uncle and aunt. As a young boy he was left helpless along with his mother and young sister. They had to face hunger, disease and ignominy. Felt humiliated and cheated by his own kin he decided to take revenge. For this purpose Milarepā learnt the black art of *abhicāra*. By using it he caused death not only of his uncle and aunt but of thirty-five others and destroyed their crops by causing hailstorm. After committing such a crime a strong feeling of remorse led him to lead a life of total renunciation and piety. His guru advised him to go to Mahāsiddha Mārpā and become his disciple. Mārpā already knew that one day his future successor, Milarepā would come to him as predicted by his guru Nāropā. Before accepting Milarepā as a disciple, Mārpā asked him to purify his evil *karma* by undertaking extremely difficult and time-consuming physical tasks. When Mārpā was satisfied that after undergoing long and severe hardship and suffering Milarepā had purified his *karma* the guru gave him the pristine tantric teachings of Nāropā's six yogas. Mārpā asked Milarepā to engage himself in meditation at solitary places. After meditating for a number of years in caves and other solitary places Milarepā perfected *Cāṇḍālī* and all the other five yogas and became enlightened. Then he started imparting the teachings to his disciples among whom Gampopā and Rechung Dorji Drakpa were the most prominent ones. Of the two it was Gampopā who became the chief inheritor of the Kargyudpa tradition. He is credited to have introduced monasticism in the Kargyudpa order.

Since the founding of the Kargyudpa School of Tibetan Buddhism in the eleventh century by Mārpā Lochawa, the tantric lineage of Nāropā has been preserved by the followers of this school till today. As has been noted, this lineage started with Tilopā who was not a disciple of any human guru but was the direct disciple of Vajradhara, the supreme Buddha of tantric tradition. Thus, Kargyudpa lineage follows the line of Vajradhara – Tilopā – Nāropā – Mārpā – Milarepā – Gampopā. After Gampopā this school branched off into 'the great four and eight lesser schools'. The Karmā Kargyud school founded by Gampopā's disciple Tusum Khyenpo in the 12th century is the only 'great' school that survives till this day. Among the 'lesser' schools the three that survive are the Drukpa Kargyud, Drikung Kargyud, and Taklung Kargyud sub-schools. The Karmā Kargyud school had a strong base in Eastern Tibet. After the Chinese occupation of Tibet the supreme head of this school, Karmāpā took refuge in India and established the world famous Karmā Kargyud monastery at Rumtek in Sikkim. Among the 'lesser' schools of Kargyudpa the most prominent is the Drukpā school. It was founded by Siddha Ling-Chen-Raspa. It is the dominant school in Bhutan where Buddhism is the state religion. Kargyudpa school has a strong presence in Nepal and various Himalayan regions of India, viz., Ladakh, Lahoul, Spiti, Kinnour, Sikkim, Darjeeling-Kalingpong and other areas.

It is believed that in Ladakh the six-yoga system was introduced by none other than Nāropā himself. The site of Lamayuru, the oldest monastery of Ladakh, was selected by him.[12] According to oral tradition Mahāsiddha Nāropā and his Tibetan disciple Mārpā both meditated and preached in the Janskar area of Ladakh. The Tongde monastery located in the same area was founded by Mārpā, the founder of the Kargyudpa school. He stayed in the cave shrine situated near the monastery. Similarly, it is said that his teacher Nāropā meditated in a cave near Dzongkhul monastery. Nāropā's mortal remains are preserved in the Kanika monastery in Janskar.[13]

When the Drukpa Kargyud branch of Kargyudpa school extended westwards from Ralung monastery near Lhasa, one of the early missionaries of this branch reached Ladakh. He was known as Gotsangpa. After reaching Ladakh he transmitted the teachings of Nāropā, Mārpā and other *siddhas* of the Kargyudpa sect to many Ladakhi disciples. He himself meditated in the 'Vulture's Nest' cave near Hemis (Gonpa sometimes in the fourth quarter of sixteenth century). Later, the Kargyudpa school gained ascendance during the reign of the most renowned king of Ladakh, Senge Namgyal. The king was the patron of the renowned Drukpa lama Tagtsang Raspa. The great lama also visited the remote Janskar area of Ladakh which had already been sanctified by the visit and stay of Mahāsiddha Nāropā and Mārpā. He later went to Lahoul and other adjacent areas in Himachal Pradesh. It was because of Lama Tagtsang Raspa and King Senge Namgyal that Hemis monastery later devdoped into a renowned centre of Drukpa Kargyud school. This monastery still occupies a prominent position in the Himalayan areas and attracts people from all over the world. Stakna monastery is yet another important centre of this school in Ladakh. This monastery controls all the Drukpa monastries in the Janskar area.

The Drikungpa sect – which like the Drukpa sect is a branch of the main Kargyudpa school founded by Mārpā – is yet another sect which spread in Ladakh region as early as 13th century. The first main centre of the Drikungpa in this region was the Lamayuru monastery. However, it was in the last quarter of the 18th century that this branch of the Kargyudpa school became firmly established in Ladakh. It was mainly due to the presence of the sixth Togdan Rinpoche of Tibet that Drikungpa school rose to eminence in this region.[14] Apart from the old Lamayuru monastery a new monastery known as the Phiyang monastery became the centre of activity of this school. Like the Drukpa sect the Drikungpa sect also follows the tantric tradition of Tilopā, Nāropā, Mārpā, Milarepā and Gampopā. In recent years it has extended its activities in Ladakh, Himachal Pradesh and Uttaranchal. Renowned Drikungpā lamas from Ladakh visit centres like Dehradun and Almora where they have their establishments and lamaseries and guide practitioners of Nāropā's six-yoga system.

Since the time of Nāropā and Mārpā the Janskar area of Ladakh has been attracting and producing successive generations of scholars, monks and *yogins*. Being situated in a terrain surrounded by high rising Himalayan ranges this area has always remained far away from the main trade route and has been less affected by various social, economic and political changes in Ladakh. This explains why it is sometimes called as 'The hidden kingdom'. Its seclusion has made it best suited for meditation, pious living and serious scholarly pursuits. Down the centuries, great *siddhas*, saints and erudite monk scholars have lived, worked and meditated at various monasteries, hermitages and secluded caves situated in this area. In the eighteenth century the Dzongkhul monastery situated near the hallowed cave of Nāropā, was a renowned centre of meditation where accomplished *siddhas* used to live and meditate. Drubchcn Nawang Tsering was the greatest among these *siddhas*. He was an accomplished *siddha*, saint and a great exponent of the *tantric* teachings. His teachings, instructions on meditation and mystic compositions in poetic form are preserved in the Dzongkhul monastery.[15]

The yogic lineage of Nāropā is continuing mainly in the Janskar and the Indus Valley areas of Ladakh. Small groups of *yogins* are being trained at Gotsang Gonpa near Hemis monastery in the Indus Valley. A few *yogins* can be found practicing in isolated spots like Lamayuru, Shila and Urgyen Dzong.[16] They continue the tradition of Nāropā's six-yoga practices which have been received through the famous meditators from Kham of Tibet in the nineteenth century. Among these meditators Śākyaśrī was most prominent. He took great interest in the revival of Buddhism in Himalayan areas.[17] A Ladakhi monk named Nawang Padma Chogyal who went to Tibet became one of his chief disciples. He was given the title of 'Tipun' – 'Master of Questions'. He became the chief religious successor of Śākyaśrī in Tibet and other Himalayan areas.[18] Among Tipun's disciples was Awo Rinpoche who had many disciples in Janskar and Indus valley area in Ladakh.

NOTES AND REFERENCES

1. Vraj Ballabh Dwivedi and Thinley Ram Shashni, *Bauddha Tantra Kosh*, Sarnath, Varanasi, C.I.H.T.S. Publication, 1990, p. 13.
2. For example see, D.L. Snellgrove, *Indo-Tibetan Buddhism*, Vol. I. Sambhala, Boston, 1987, pp. 129-34.
3. *Vajra*, from which the name *Vajrayāna* is derived, is the most significant symbol of Buddhist tantra. It stands for the highest goal of tantric practice, i.e., the goal of reaching the state of mind in which an indivisible and indestructible union of wisdom (*prajñā*) and means (*upāya*) is attained after rigorous practices.
4. Buston, *History of Buddhism*, translated by Eugene Obermiller (Heidelberg, 1931), pp. 112-30. See also S. Dutta, *Buddhist Monks and Monasteries of India* (George Allen and Unwin, London, 1962), pp. 278-79.
5. The very brief account of Nāropā's life given here is mostly based on the information given in *The Life and Teachings of Nāropā*, translated from Tibetan by Herbert V. Guenther (Oxford University Press, Oxford, 1963).
6. *Tibetan Chronicle of Padma Karpo*, Lokesh Chandra (ed.) referred by Thakursain Negi, in his *Vajrayāna Anuttarayoga*, CIHTS, Sārnāth, 1999, p. 491.
7. See Thakursain Negi, *op. cit.*, pp. 489-90. See also, *The Life of Mārpā: The Translator*, English translation from Tibetan by Nalanda Translation Committee, Shambhala, Boston, 1982, pp. *XXXI-XXXII*.
8. Gampopā, *The Guru Ornament of Liberation*, Translated from Tibetan by H.V. Guenther, Rider and Co., London, 970 (2nd Edition), p. XIII, Note 1. See also, Chogyam Trungpa's Nalanda Translation Committee, *The Life of Marpā the Translator* (English Translation), *op. cit.*, p. *XXXII*, note 2.
9. John Powers, *Tibetan Buddhism* (Snow Lion Publications, Ithaca, N.Y., 1995), p. 353.
10. *Ibid.*, p. 355.
11. *Ibid.*, p. 361.

12. Luciano Petech, *The Kingdom of Ladakh,* Institute Italiano II Medio Ed Estremo Oriente, Rome, 1977, p. 165.
13. Herbert V. Guenther, *op. cit.,* Introduction, p. ii.
14. Luciano Perech, *op. cit.,* pp. 166-67.
15. Nawang Tsering, *Buddhism in Ladakh,* New Delhi, Sterling, 1979.
16. John H. Crook and Henry A. Osmaston, *Himalayan Buddhist Villages,* New Delhi, Motilal Banarsidass, 2001, p. 692.
17. James Crook and Osmaston, *op. cit.,* p. 672.
18. James Crook and James Low, *The Yogins of Ladakh,* New Delhi, Motilal Banarsidass, 1997, p. 23.

Part IV

LITERATURE

27

THE CHINESE *BUDDHACARITA*

Charles Willemen

The complete Chinese version of Aśvaghoṣa's *Buddhacarita* is found in the Japanese Taishō edition, Volume 4, no. 192. This *Fo* (Buddha) *suoxing* (carita) *zan* (kāvya) counts 54 pages, 28 chapters. The Chinese colophon says:

> Composed by *Bodhisattva* Aśvaghoṣa.
> Translated by the Indian Tripiṭaka Tan Wuchen, during the Northern Liang.

A note added to the title says: 'Also called *Fo Benxing Jing*.' The colophon informs us that the Indian Tan Wuchen brought out the text during the Northern Liang (397-439), probably in the capital Guzang, also known as Liangzhou, presently in the district of Wuwei in Gansu Province. The information probably comes from the *Kaiyuan Lu*, i.e., Zhisheng's catalogue of 730, Taishō ed. 2154. This catalogue uses Fei Changfang's catalogue *Lidai Sanbao Ji* of 597, Taishō ed. 2034. Fei Changfang's work is notoriously faulty. One might even say that he succeeded in obscuring most which had been clear so far. Sengyou (445-518) and his catalogue *Chu Sanzang Jiji*, Taishō ed. 2145, of 510-518, is definitely more reliable. So, it is necessary to look at the historical facts again.

AŚVAGHOṢA (EARLY SECOND CENTURY)

Aśvaghoṣa has been considered the most prominent poet of classical Sanskrit before Kālidāsa (4th-5th century). His poetic discourse, *kāvya*, is at the beginning of *kāvya* literature. He was a Brāhmiṇ from Sāketa (Ayodhya, Oudh), who was converted to *sarvāstivāda* Buddhism. He was deeply influenced by *Mahāsāṅghika* ideas, much in the same way as the other converted Brāhmiṇ from Sāketa, Harivarman, circa 300 CE. Harivarman was the author of the *Chengshi Lun*, Taisho ed. 1646, i.e., *Jñānakāya-prodbhūtopadeśa*, or just *Prodbhūtopadeśa*. Harivarman was a non-*vaibhāṣika sarvāstivādin*, who later took to the local *Mahāsāṅghika* ideas about emptiness.

Aśvaghoṣa was a contemporary of King Kaniṣka, of early second century. He precedes the recension of seven *abhidharma* texts and the *Mahāvibhāṣā* in Kashmir (end of second century). So, he is a non-*vaibhāṣika sarvāstivādin*, of which there were many kinds. One reserves the term *sautrāntika* for the north-western, the Gandhāran non-*vaibhāṣika sarvāstivādins*. Their *mūlācārya*, master, was Kumāralāta, a somewhat younger contemporary of Aśvaghoṣa. This Kumāralāta was the author of the *Kalpanāmaṇḍitikā*, Taishō ed. 201, for a long time wrongly called Aśvaghoṣa's

Sūtrālaṁkāra. Because Aśvaghoṣa precedes the *vaibhāṣika* 'orthodoxy', precedes the *Mahāvibhāṣā* and the term *sautrāntika*, he cannot – strictly speaking – be called *sautrāntika*, but just *sarvāstivādin*. As an excellent teacher, propagator of the law, he could be called *bodhisattva*. Excellent teachers were called *bodhisattvas* in China, a habit which may have had its origin in Dharmaguptaka circles.

Aśvaghoṣa is famous for his *Buddhacarita*, but also for his *Saundarananda*, about the conversion of Buddha's half-brother, Nanda, and also for his nine-act play called *Śāriputraprakaraṇa*, about the conversion of Śāriputra and Maudgalyāyana. The *Buddhacarita* also reads like a play, a scenario. It is very lyrical and graphic in its descriptions of palaces, women, etc. The work belongs to world literature.

BAOYUN (376-449)

Ōminami Ryūshō, the author of the latest Japanese translation and study of the Chinese *Buddhacarita* in 2002, in *Shin Kokuyaku Daizōkyō, Hon'en-bu* 1, makes use of all existing studies about the *Buddhacarita*. He investigates the Chinese catalogues again. The conclusion is that Sengyou's information is sound, and that the author of the Chinese *Buddhacarita* is the Chinese monk Baoyun and not the Indian Tan Wuchen. Baoyun was from Liangzhou. He travelled to Central Asia, to Khotan and to India in circa 397. There he met Fazian and other Chinese pilgrims. In India he studied the languages, and then he returned to Chang'an and followed Buddhabhadra there. Buddhabhadra (359-429) was in Chang'an in 406-408. Baoyun then followed Buddhabhadra south to Mount Lu, and ultimately to Jiankang (Nanjing). His good friend Huiguan was there all the way. All of them stayed in the Daochang temple in Jiankang.

Baoyun then moved to the Liuheshan temple, outside Jiankang. In these last two temples he made his translations. He held the Indian text in his hands and translated it orally. In this way the *Buddhacarita* was rendered in 421, i.e., *Yongchu* 2 of the *Liu Song*, in the Liuheshan temple. Some alternative Chinese titles are: *Maming Pusa Zan*, *Bodhisattva Aśvaghoṣa's Kāvya*, and *Fo* (*Buddha*) *Benzing* (*carita*) *Zan* (*kāvya*). Sengyou mentions a *Fo Benzing Jing*, *sūtra*. Hikata Ryūshō thinks that this text was written shortly after Zhi Qian (third century), before Kumārajīva (344-413). Fei Changfang mistook this *sūtra* for the *kāvya*, and this mistake has found its way into the colophon of the Taisho edition.

TAN WUCHEN (385-433)

Tan Wuchen belonged to Central India. The phonetic rendering of his Indian name, Tan Wuchen, looks like a real Chinese name, translation of which is '*Dharma* abundance'. This ġives 'Dharmarddhin' (Dharmavṛddhin). Tan Wuchen is phonetically quite possible in either case. A variant phonetic rendering is 'Tanmoluochen', where *luo* renders an *r*. Tan Wuchen's biography informs us that he was versed in incantations, in magic, and that he had a nickname Da Zhoushi, Great Spell-Master. This information points to the name Dharmarddhin.

He arrived in Guzang in 412, where he did his translating between 414 and 421. There in 421, he brought out his famous translation of the *Mahāparinirvāṇasūtra*, Taishō ed. 375, known as the northern version. That same year Baoyun brought out his *Buddhacarita* near Jiankang. Tan Wuchen's text was revised in Jiankang during the Yuanjia era (424-453), i.e., Taishō ed. 374. The text is known as the southern version. It was brought out later than the Chinese *Buddhacarita*.

Baoyun's good friend Faxian had also brought out a version of the *Nirvāṇasūtra* in Jiankang in 418, with the help of Buddhabhadra (Taishō ed. 376). The fifth of the five volumes of the

Chinese *Buddhacarita* corresponds with the contents of the *Nirvāṇasūtra*. It seems that Tan Wuchen's name was added to the *Buddhacarita* for a number of reasons. For instance, both texts are from 421. The northern *Nirvāṇasūtra* was being studied in Jiankang and another version had just been brought out there. An important part, the last, of the *Buddhacarita* agrees with the *Nirvāṇasūtra*; Baoyun was from Liangzhou (Guzang).

THE CHINESE TEXT

As the result of Baoyun's oral 'translation', the text shows us his understanding and his explanation of the original Sanskrit. The explanation of early *sāṁkhya* in Chapter 12, stanzas 14-33, is a good example. One must be careful not to draw any hasty conclusions for the original Sanskrit on the basis of the Chinese text. Baoyun's Sanskrit text was probably different from the Nepalese texts we have now, but the differences are so numerous that one can say that Baoyun gave his own oral version of the contents, at the same time making the contents clear to his Chinese audience.

The text has many technical stock phrases. Its pentasyllabic verse is split up in 2/3 or 3/2. This requirement explains many compounds and redundant terms, such as *jin* (now), *ji* (immediately, then), *youruo* (as if), *ze* (then), etc. The text has many Chinese grammatical particles and pronouns, etc. unusual in poetry but usual in colloquial language. Sometimes the grammatical elements are used to render Sanskrit morphology. For instance, instrumental case, locative case, etc. Compounds are the norm.

The language of the thirteen Confucian Classics is quite different. Baoyun leaves out much of the descriptive parts, which make the Sanskrit text so suave and alive. Hindu mythology is simplified to make it understandable to Chinese public. The circumstances of Buddha's birth (conception, child-birth) are not as mythological, but much more realistic. The role of women is explained, but abbreviated, and in modest terms. The characteristics of Baoyun's text can be explained at length, but the conclusion is that the Chinese is not as poetic and lyrical but rather explanatory in a vernacular style. Of course, Baoyun had to use some terms and transcriptions of names, which were well known at the time. This established terminology was probably based on a Prākrit language, but Baoyun's text was Sanskrit.

Some instances where Baoyun uses his knowledge of Chinese mythology and history:

– Chapter 10, stanza 18:

> His robe of the Law helped morning freshness arise, just as when the sun is shining from the mulberry tree.

Chinese mythology believes that the sun comes up far to the east, underneath a giant mulberry tree, which has one root, but two mutually supporting trunks. This tree, the *rodhra* tree, has yellow flowers, like the colour of the robe of the Law.

– Chapter 11, stanza 31:

> An execution underneath a banner in the eastern marketplace.

During the Han the eastern market in Chang'an was a place for executions.

Furthermore, Mount Tai is often mentioned.

Chapter 24, stanza 26 mentions 'the one vehicle', *ekayāna*. This definitely gives the impression that Baoyun shared the ideas of Huiguan in Jiankiang. This 'one vehicle' comes from the *Lotus Sūtra*, and was propagated by **Huiguan**. This is one more reason to say that Baoyun is the author of the Chinese *Buddhacarita*. A complete English translation of the whole Chinese *Buddhacarita* will be published shortly by the Numata Foundation in Berkeley.

28

BEGINNINGS OF THE APABHRAṀŚA POETRY

THE CONTRIBUTION OF NALANDA

Chandra Dhar Tripathi

Yā sā saṁsāracakraṁ viracayati manaḥ sanniyogātmahetoḥ
Yā dhīryasya prasādāddiśati nijabhuvaṁ swāmino niṣprapañcaḥ /
Tacca pratyātmavedyaṁ samudayati sukhaṁ kalpanājālamuktaṁ
Kuryāt tasyāṅghriyugmaṁ śirasi savinayaṁ sadguroḥ sarvakālaṁ //

That is Śrī Sarahapāda invoking the *Sadguru*. Who was his *Sadguru* we do not know; may be he was addressing the Sammāsambuddha himself unless it was his teacher at Nalanda, Haribadhra or his teacher's teacher, Śāntarakṣita. As for me, I bow down to Saraha who was the first to compose mystic songs in Apabhraṁśa, a language that was precursor of the modern languages of northern India.

Dazzled by the brilliance of the great logicians of Nalanda like Diṅgnāga, Dharmakīrti, Śāntarakṣita and Kamalaśīla and Nalanda's other contributions to the philosophical thought and the art heritage, we tend to overlook another very significant contribution of Nalanda, namely, that in laying down the foundations of the Apabhraṁśa poetry.

First, a semantic clarification. We come across the word Apabhraṁśa as early as in the second century BCE in the *Mahābhāṣya* of Patañjali where it signifies a language distinct from the Vedic *Chānda*s as well as the *laukika* Sanskrit and Pāli. It was a synthetic language belonging to the generic Prākṛt group. However, the Apabhraṁśa we are talking about was an analytic language that had its origin in the synthetic Sanskrit-Pāli-Prākṛt family but being analytic it was of a new kind. It was placed at a distance from those three languages and, in the words of Rahul Sankrityayana,

> it was not only the mother or grandmother of Hindi and other modern languages of the north but of the same nature as theirs.

We have references indicating that by the seventh century it had become a language of poetry although no actual specimens of such poetry have survived. Not only did a new kind of analytic language take birth around this period but so did many new metrical forms like *dohā, caupāi, paddharī* and so on. We find these for the first time in the works of Sarahapā and they continue to prevail till date particularly in Hindi.

The age of the Apabhraṁśa poetry runs from the eighth to the thirteenth century. During these six centuries poetry in this language was written by the Vajrayāna saints, Jain *muni*s and court poets. But the major portion of this literature was produced by the Vajrayāna saints belonging to the set of eighty-four *Siddhas*. Rahul Sankrityayana published a monumental book titled *Hindi Kavyadhārā* in 1945 containing a selection of the surviving Apabhraṁśa poetry. He has included the works of forty-seven poets, of whom the names of four are not traceable. Of the remaining forty-three poets, as many as eighteen are Vajrayāna *Siddhas* from Sarahapā of the eighth century to Śantipā of c. 1000 CE.

Now, who were these *Siddhas*, what were their affiliations and what were they writing? Until about a century ago the songs composed by these *Siddhas* were virtually unknown except to a few learned lamas well-versed in the Tan-jyur and a few *Vajrācāryas* in Nepal. Even to those lamas the songs of the *Siddhas* were known primarily in their Sanskrit or Tibetan translations. Even the names of the eighty-four *Siddhas* were not fully known. The first ever collection of these poems was published by the great scholar Har Prasad Shastri in 1916 in a book titled *Hājār Bacharer Purāno Bāṅglā Bhāṣāya, Bauddha Gāna O Dohā* (known in short as *Bauddha Gāna O Dohā*). These poems were discovered by him in 1907 in manuscripts preserved in the Nepal Durbar Library. Since then these songs have been known either as *Caryāpadas* or *Caryāgītis*, the latter name being used in some of the Tibetan collections as well as by the *Siddhas* themselves in the titles of some of their works. However, a number of the works of the *Siddhas* are titled *Dohā kośa* being compendiums of their *Dohās*. Later, Prabodh Chandra Bagchi and Rahul Sankrityayana discovered many more songs in Tibet and Nepal and published them.

After Har Prasad Shastri's work the first major work was that of Md. Shahidullah in French titled *Les Chants Mystiques de Kanha et de Saraha* published in 1928 in which he gave French translations of the *Caryāpadas* of Kāṇhapā and Sarahapā. Then appeared two works of P.C. Bagchi in 1934 and 1938 containing new material to determine the correct texts. In the 1940s Sukumar Sen and Shashi Bhushan Dasgupta brought out analytical works based on the texts as determined by Shastri and Bagchi. But the most significant work to appear in the 1940s was Rahul Sankrityayana's *Hindi Kāvyadhārā* that dealt with the Apabhraṁśa poetry from the eighth to the thirteenth century including that of the *Siddhas*. Earlier, in 1928, in his *Purātatva Nibandhāvalī* he had published, for the first time, a complete list of the eighty-four *Siddhas* obtained from the Sā-skya monastery in Tibet along with the names of the books authored by them, their places of origin, study or *Sādhanā* and probable dates. Since the researches of Rahul we now have a detailed, though hagiographic account of the eighty-four *Siddhas* which was originally compiled in Tibetan by Ācarya Abhayākaradattaśrī and has now been translated into Hindi by Sempa Dorje. In the 1950s and 1960s, a number of works throwing light on the poetry of the *Siddhas*, the development of related traditions and sects came out including Hajari Prasad Dwivedi's *Nātha Sampradāya* and Parashuram Chaturvedi's *Uttar Bhārat kī Sant Paramparā*. A comprehensive analytical work is Dharam Vir Bharati's *Siddha Sahitya* (1955) and Tarapada Mukherji's *The Old Bengali Language and Texts*. Then there was Prabodh Chandra Bagchi and Shantibhikshu Shastri's *Caryāgīti-Koṣa of Buddhist Siddhas* and new English edition of Md. Shahidullah's *Buddhist Mystic Songs*. Perhaps the most important publication of this period was Sarahapā's *Dohā Kośa*, edited and translated by Rahul Sankrityayana with long introductory chapters. One of the most recent works is *An Anthology of Buddhist Tantric Songs: A Study of the Caryāgīti* by Per Kvaerne published by the Universitetforlaget, Oslo in 1977. The tradition of Bengali scholarship on *Caryāpadas* is being kept up in Bangladesh and the latest works on the subject have come out from Dhaka in 1984 and 1986 and these are *Caryāgīti (Bauddha Gāna O Dohā)* by Syed Ali Ahsan and *Caryāgīti Prasaṅga* by the same author.

With this short sketch of the bibliography on the subject, we turn to the list and chronology of the eighty-four *Siddhas*. While the roots of tantra are very ancient – the Hindu tantras tracing them to the Vedas and the Buddhist ones to the *Buddha-vacana* – the tantrik systems as such developed in the post-Gupta period only. Every tantrik system had its own deities and methods of *Sādhanā* and those who attained perfection by the *Sādhanā* were designated as *Siddhas*. Every system developed its own list of *Siddhas* and their number was taken to be a mystical eighty-four. Thus the different systems had – and have – different lists of the eighty-four *Siddhas*. Some names are, however, common to two or more lists. Here, I am concerned only with the eighty-four Buddhist *Vajrayāna Siddhas*. There is a considerable controversy regarding the chronology of the eighty-four *Vajrayāna Siddhas* but Sarahapā is universally regarded as the earliest *Siddha* even though the Sā-skya Vihāra list enumerates Luipā as number one. Luipā was actually a disciple of Śabarapā who was a disciple of Sarahapā and thus he was the third *Siddha*. The reason for giving Luipā primacy was undoubtedly based on sectarian traditions. As regards the date of Saraha Shahidullah and K.L. Barua take him to be a contemporary of the King Ratnapāla of Kamarupa who flourished in the tenth century. But Rahul Sankrityayana, basing his chronology on *guru-śiṣya paramparā* from the Tibetan and other sources, places him in the middle of the eighth century and takes the date of his death as c. 780 CE. The age of Saraha is the period when Nalanda was at the zenith of its glory.

In the account of Abhayākaradattaśrī the places of origin of the eighty-four *Siddhas* have been recorded and these were located in all corners of India – north, west, south, and east. A number of these have not been satisfactorily identified, but it is noteworthy that at least sixty-four out of the eighty-four hailed from eastern India by which term the country of Magadh or further east is indicated. As many as fifteen are specifically stated to hail from Magadha, Nalanda or Vikramaśilā. Significantly, most of the *Vajrapīṭhas*, the places where *Sādhanā* would be most efficacious, were also located in the east.

It is easy to see that if not all the *Siddhas*, at least those hailing from eastern India flocked for enlightenment to Nalanda, the most prominent seat of learning, or to the teachers schooled at Nalanda. In fact, we learn, Sarahapā, his desciple Nāgārjuna, Maitrīgupta, Bhusukupā, Virupā, Tilopā and Nāropā were *ācaryas* at Nalanda. In the late eighth century, King Dharmapāla established the great university at Vikramaśilā which became the greatest-ever centre of tantra; needless to say, that Nalanda was the nursery that supplied great teachers to the new university. Majority of the later *Siddhas* were connected with Vikramaśilā.

The age of Sarahapā was one of great political and religious ferment. In the sphere of religion and philosophy, the great Śankara was propagating his *Advaita Vedānta* and its influence was widely felt throughout India. In Buddhism itself, the new system of Vajrayāna was founded in which the unique *Śūnya* of Buddhism became *Vajra*, and *Nirvāṇa* was replaced by *Mahāsukha*. New gods and goddesses, new forms of worship, invocation and *Sādhanā* were continuously evolving; the *Vedantic Advaita* was facing the Buddhist *Advaya*. In the midst of this philosophical ferment, Saraha felt the need of a system free from the ritual on the one hand and abstruse scholasticism on the other. He and his followers started pleading for living a simple, natural life – the *Sahaja* way. It is ironic that the *Sahaja* was soon overtaken by the supernatural elements in tantra and gross physical and carnal interpretations of the subtle and allegorical tenets of Vajrayāna and Sahajayāna too failed to save Buddhism in India though they gave impetus to its acceptance and spread in Tibet.

For Sarahapā and his followers it was imperative that they spread their message in a language commonly understood and spoken by the masses. So, they chose to compose their songs in the Apabhraṁśa though they continued to write in Sanskrit for intellectuals and the elite.

It is noteworthy that Har Prasad Shastri treated the language of *Caryāpadas* as Old Bengali. Rahul Sankrityayana was inclined to declare it as Old Hindi. Protagonists of Assamese (Banikant Kakati), Oriya (Arta Ballabh Mohanty), Maithili (Jayakant Mishra) saw the beginnings of their respective languages in the *Caryāpadas*. Rahul Sankrityayana, while declaring this Apabhraṁśa as Old Hindi, hastened to add that the language of these poems was such as could not be claimed exclusively to be Hindi or Bengali; in fact, it was the common literary language of the age and contained elements that subsequently became characteristic features of Assamese, Bengali, Oriya, Maithili, Bhojpuri, Avadhi, Hindi, Punjabi, Marathi and Gujarati. This was so because this language – commonly described as Apabhraṁśa, that is degenerate and also as *Desī* or simply *Bhāṣā* as opposed to Sanskrit – had evolved from the mixed forms of Prākṛit prevailing in North India, essentially the Maharāshtrī, Śaurasenī and Māgadhī or Ardhamāgadhī.

The *Siddhas* composed their songs in the tongues of the places of their origin. They were, however, a highly peripatetic lot and not bound to any particular place or region. As a matter of fact, Abhayākaradattaśrī gives vivid descriptions of their wanderings in course of which they met their preceptors and would-be followers. They travelled from Śrīparvata in the south, the seat of Nāgārjuna, the great *Mādhyamika* philosopher of the first-second century, to Jalandhar in the north and from Maharashtra in the west to Kamarupa-Kamakhya, Oddiyāna and Śrīhaṭṭa in the east. Saraha's own example is typical. He hailed from a place named Rājñi in eastern India that is identified with modern Rani in the Kamrup district of Assam. He studied and later became *ācārya* at Nalanda and attained *Siddhi* in Maharashtra. Similarly, Śabarapā hailed either from Bhangala or Mantravikrama Parvata – both in eastern India – but studied from Nāgārjuna and attained *Siddhi* at Śrīparvata. Luipā is said to have hailed from Siṁhaladvīpa, received instruction from a Ḍākinī at Bodhgaya and attained *Siddhi* on the banks of Ganga near Pāṭaliputra. Such wanderings of the *Siddhas* naturally influenced their language which assimilated elements from different regions and the result is reflected in their songs.

Let me begin with a *Dohā* of Śarahapā:

Jāva ṇa āpa jaṇijjai tāva ṇa sissa karei /
Andhā andha Kaḍhāva tima veṇṇavi Kūva paḍei //

I draw attention to the word *veṇṇavi,* meaning the 'two both' which in modern Hindi will be spoken as *donoṅ hī* or *donoṅ bhī.* The word 've', meaning two, is used in Gujarati while *vi* or *vī* is used in Punjabi for the Hindi *bhī* or *hī.* Incidentally, *ve* instead of *do* from the Sanskrit *dvi* seems to be a favourite of the *Siddhas* and so is the word *vi.* Thus Luipā says in a *caupāī*:

Kā'ā taruvara pañcaviḍāla / Cañcala cīe paiṭṭhā Kāla //

Here, *pañcavi,* means 'the five'.

Here are a few examples of verb forms (past tense) of Bhojpuri:

Saraha says: *'Saraha bhaṇai bapa ! ujubaṭa bhailā'/*

Virūpā says: *'āila garāhaka apane bahiā.'*

Similarly, here is a line of Kukkuripā: *'Rāti bhaile Kāmarū jā'a'* and another example from Luipā: *'āja Bhusuku baṅgālī bhailī / nija gharanī caṇḍālī lelī. //'*

The verb forms used in the *Caryāpadas* are most faithfully preserved in Bhojpuri, Maithili and Avadhi. That is not to say that they are not to be found in other languages. Here is an example from Gorakhanātha:

Habaki na bolibā ṭhabaki na calibā dhīrai dhokhā pāṅva /
Garaba na Karibā sahajai rahibā bhaṇata Gorakharāva //

The forms *bolibā, calibā, Karibā, Rahibā* are used exactly as such in modern Assamese.

Some verbs used by the *Siddhas* are typical Assamese and Bengali today. For example, Saraha says, *'Nauvahi naukā ṭāna'a guṇe / nirmali sahaje nāu ṇa āṇe //*
The word *ṭāna,* meaning to pull, is used as such today.

In his *Hindi Kāvyadhārā,* Rahul Sankrityayana has appended a list of typical rural words used in the *Caryāpadas* that are used in the various modern languages. I am just adding to the list.

Guṇḍarīpā says: *'Tiaḍḍā cāpi joini de añkavālī.'*

The word *añkavālī*, meaning embrace, is preserved as *ankavāra* in Bhojpuri and Assamese.

A line of Saraha goes like this: *'Kā'a nāvaḍi khānṭi maṇa Keḍuāla.'*

The word *Khānṭī*, meaning pure, is used as such in both Assamese and Bengali.

A *caupāī* of Bhusukupa goes like this:

Tiṇa ṇa chūpai pibai ṇa pāṇī /
hariṇā hariṇīra ṇilāṇa jāṇī //

Use of the word *Pāṇī* is surprising. Bhusuku has rejected the Sanskrit word *Jala* in favour of *Pāṇī* whose origin is unknown. What is equally surprising is that this word was not accepted in Bengali but is the common word for water in all dialects of Hindi and western languages like Punjabi, Marathi and Gujarati as well as Assamese. *Pāṇī* is also a favourite of the *Siddhas* who always prefer it to *Jala.* Thus Ḍombipā says, *'Gaṇa'a dukhīleṅ siñcahū pāṇī na paisa'i sāñdhī.'*

A few more words to continue with the examples:

Śafarapā says: *'Safara bhujañga nairāmaṇi dārī pekkha rāti pohāilī'*

In just one line we have usages from two or three modern languages. The word 'dārī' in the sense of a prostitute is used in Oriya and Oriya only and this line is often cited to support the view that Śafarapā hailed from Orissa and possibly belonged to the Śafaratribe.

The word *rāti* for night is used in Assamese and Oriya but in Bengali and Hindi it becomes *rāta.* The *lī*-ending *pohāilī* sounds like Bhojpuri (which it is) but the word *pohā* or *povā* is Assamese meaning dawn or end of night and is used only as a verb like *povāise.* Speaking of Oriya recalls two lines of Saraha:

Amia acchante bisa gīlesi re ci'a para rasa appā /
ghareñ pareñ kā bujjhīle māri kha'iba mai duha Kañḍavañ //

Here *Acchante* is clearly Oriya while *mai* for me or is Assamese. Further, *gīlesi* is clearly Avadhi while *bujjhile* is Assamese. Another line of Saraha that I recall is:

Saraha bhaṇai ghara sūna goñhālī Ko mo dūṭha balandeñ.

Here *mo* for me or I is Oriya and *gohalī* for cowshed is used in Assamese as well as Oriya.

These are just a few stray examples of the words – nouns, verbs, adjectives – used by the *Siddhas* that are found in the modern languages of North India and show how the Apabhraṁśa of the *Siddhas* is the precursor of these languages. Since most of the *Siddhas* hailed from the east the elements of the eastern tongues are predominant in their language. The examples cited by me that, in a way, supplement the list given by Rahul Sankrityayana, are by no means exhaustive but they do indicate the connection between the Apabhraṁśa of the *Siddhas* and modern languages.

A century after Sarahapā, from the time of Luipā, we find a mixture or synthesis of the Buddhist and *Śaiva tantras* and evolution of *Nava Nāthas* (Nine *Nāthas*). Luipā is said to be identical with Matsyendranātha, possibly the second *Nātha.* His desciple, Gorakṣanātha became the most famous of the *Nava Nāthas* whose influence and sect continues to flourish in different parts of India and Nepal even to this day. In the Buddhist list of the eighty-four *Siddha*s he is known as Gorakṣapā, disciple of Machhendrapā, who was a disciple of Jālandharapā, disciple of Ghanṭāpā who was in the third generation from Luipā or fifth from Saraha. Gorakhanātha himself describes his relation with the other *Nātha*s and *Siddha*s in these words:

Gudaḍī meñ atīta Kā vāsā / bhaṇanta Gorakha Machyandra Kā dāsā //

and again,

Pyaṇḍa brahmaṇḍa nirantara vāsa / bhaṇanta Gorakha Machyandra Kā dāsa /

and more elaborately:

Mana Machindranātha pavana Īsvaranātha Cetanā Cauraṅgīnātha /
Gyāna Śrī Gorakhanātha //

and further,

Nau nātha nai caurāsī sidhā, āsaṇadhārī hūva. or, Anahada sabada bājata rahai /
Sidha-Saṅketa Śrī Gorakha Kahai //

and again:

Ādinātha nātī Machindranātha pūtā / vyanda tolai rākhīle Gorakha Avadhūtā //

Ādinātha is generally identified with Jālandharnātha or Jālandharapā.

The eighty-four *Siddha*s had been expounding the tenets of the Buddhist tantra in their songs which abound in words like *Suṇṇa, nibbāṇa, Mahāsu'a* (or *Mahāsukha) Ci'a* (that is *Citta*), *Kamala-Kuliśa, Sadguru*. The synthesis with the Śaiva tantra brought new vocabulary to them like *Anahada, Alakha, Nirañjana, Nāda, Bindu, Avadhū*. Their adherents and the saint poets influenced by them continued to employ this vocabulary down to the fourteenth and fifteenth century. The most prominent example of such poets is that of Kabir. Not only does he use the *Siddha* vocabulary but often adopts the ideas of *Siddha*s – sometimes *verbatim*. For example, take this *Dohā* of Kabir:

Jākā guru bhī andhalā celā kharā nirandha /
andhai andhā ṭheliyā dūnyuñ Kūpa paḍanta //

This is clearly the same as the *Dohā* of Saraha that I cited in the beginning.

There were conventions introduced by the *Siddha*s that were carried on by the later poets and have survived till the present day. One of these is the mention of one's own name in a poem – what came to be termed as *Bhaṇitā*. Saraha was the first to use his name in his songs like:

Saraha bhaṇai khavvāṇa mokkha mahu Kimpi na bhāva'i /
tatta-rahi'a kā'ā ṇa tāva para Kevala Sāha'i //

Or,

Sa'a-saṁvittī tattaphalu Sarahapā'a bhaṇanti

The practice was adopted by all the *Siddha*s. Thus, we have,

Diḍha Kari'a mahāsuha parimāṇa / Luī bhaṇai guru pucchiya jāṇa //

A peculiar term that we come across in Kabir is *Avadhū* – *Avadhū bhajana bheda hai nyārā*. This *Avadhū* was also invented by the *Siddha*s – perhaps by Gorakhanātha who says:

Baiṭhā Avadhū laukī khūṅṭī, Calatā Avadhū pavana Kī mūṭhī /
Sovatā Avadhū Jīvatā mūvā, Bolatā Avadhū pyañjarai sūvā //

Or,

Avadhū sahaja hansa Kā khela bhaṇījai, Suni hansa Kā vāsa.

and *Avadhū ravi amāvasa candasu paḍivā / Aragha mahārasa ūradha lai caḍhivā /*

Kabir is famous for his *Ulaṭabañsīs* or verses containing *virodhābhāsa.* I would like to call them 'contrarian verses'. This device was also introduced by the *Siddhas*; as a matter of fact, by Sarahapā himself. Here are some examples:

Baddho dhāvahi dasa disahi, mukko niccala ṭṭhā'a /
Ema'i Karahā pekkha sahi, vivara'a mahu paḍihā'a //

and,

Āgge āccha'a bāhire āccha'a / pa'i dekkha'a paḍavesī puccha'a //

An *ulatbansi* of Tentaṇapā is even more startling:

Balada biā'ala gavi'ā bāñhje / piṭahu duhi'ā'i e tino sāñjhe' //

The idea of a bull giving birth to a calf and the cow remaining barren has been used by Kabir in one of his *ulaṭabāñsis.*

Then here is Gorakhanātha:

Gagana manḍala maiñ gāya biā'ī, Kāgada dahī jamayā /
Chāchi chāñḍi piñutā pāṇī sidhā bhākhaṇa khāyā //

and,

Nātha bole amṛta vāṇī, varikhaigī Kambala bhījaigā pāṇī

Also,

Kau'ākī ḍālī pīpala bāsai, mūsā Kai sabada bilāi'ā nāsai.

or,

Ḍhūkile Kūkura bhūki lai cora, Kāḍhai ghaṇī pukārai ḍhora.

We may recall that Kabir also says:

Barasai Kambala bhījai pānī.

Then the term *Sadguru* that became so common in later traditions is met for the first time in Saraha. In my invocation I have cited Saraha's invocation of *Sadguru* in Sanskrit. In his *Bhāṣā* poems he says, *Kā'a nāvaḍi khānṭi maṇa keḍuāla, Sadguru ba'aṇe dhara patavāla.*

And Bhusukupā says,

Mā'ājāla pasārī bāñdheli mā'ā hariṇī /
Sadguru boheñ būjhi re Kāsu (Kāhiṇī) //

A century later, Bhādepā says:

Etakāla hā'ñu ācchila svamoheñ, eveñ ma'i būjhila Sadguru boheñ.

Apart from the philosophical words there are some usages that caught the fancy of later-day poets. We have heard the famous line of Amir Khusro of the thirteenth century: *'Cala Khusro ghar āpane rain bhaī cahuñdes'.* The idea of *cahuñdes* instead of *cahuñ o'r* seems to have come from Bhusukupā's *caupāī*: *'Kāheri gheṇi meli acchahū kīsa, baiṭhila hāka paḍau caudīsa.'*

Tulasidasa in the sixteenth century, familiar with the poetry of the *Siddhas*, uses the term *Mahāsukha* in the *Hanumāna Chālisā* (Forty Verses in Praise of Hanumāna). This term is not found anywhere in the Vaiṣṇava literature. Clearly, Tulasidasa acquired it from the poetry of the *Siddhas*.

Part V

MONASTIC EDUCATION: IDEALS OF NALANDA MAHĀVIHĀRA

29

THE VIHĀRA IN BUDDHIST TRADITION AND NALANDA

K. Sankarnarayan

I want to explore the concept of *vihāra* in Buddhist tradition, especially the *vihāra*s at Nalanda. Is *vihāra* and monastery one and the same? Is it an abode for the peaceful place of meditation? Or is it a residential educational centre with academic activities? In Sanskrit the term *vihāra* (*vi* + *hṛ*) means to take away, a pleasure garden, park, etc. In Pāli as it is referred *'vi + harati = vihāra'*, meaning – spending one's time or walking about, staying in one place of living, abode in forest (*aranna*) or a hut; lodging for a *bhikṣu*, etc.[1] Gustav Roth[2] discusses at length all the three terms *ārāma*, *vihāra* and *Mahāvihāra* quoting from the original Pāli scripture besides giving parallel quotes from the Sanskrit epics like *Rāmāyaṇa*[3] and *Mahābhārata*.[4] It is interesting to note that there is no reference to *ārāma* in the sense of garden or abode in *Ṛgveda*.[5] Gustav Roth opines that the reference to *ārāma* in Pāli scripture must be one of the earliest references in the whole of Indian tradition in general.[6] He remarks, "It contains a kernel of the Buddhist Order's residential history."

Buddhism being the religion of meditation,[7] sound was considered to be thorn.[8] Therefore silent atmosphere, in *vihāra*s and other places where monks and laymen assembled, was insisted upon and behaviour pattern and culture which maintained quiet and used the minimum of verbal sound was inculcated and developed. In the *Dīghanikāya* in the *Ambaṭṭha Sutta* is mentioned how the Buddha is to be visited.[9] In the same *nikāya*, there is a vivid description of the visit of King Ajātaśatru to the Buddha.[10]

The assemblies of monks with Buddha at the head presented a picture of perfect silence. This, indeed, was the sobering influence of Buddha's constant instructions to monks to maintain silence when they got together. The same example can be seen in *Poṭṭhapāda Sutta* of *Dīghanikāya*.[11]

The above examples speak of the reputation of the Buddha as one who rejoiced in silence and quietude and instructed others also to follow the same. Thus, Buddhist *vihāra*s were surcharged with calm suitable for practising meditation.

REFERENCES IN PĀLI SCRIPTURES

The Bimbisāra samāgama kathā[12] refers to the bamboo grove offered by King Bimbisāra to Buddha as a wooden enclosure of peace.[13]

> *Etahaṁ bhante veḷuvanaṁ uyyānaṁ Buddha-ppamukhassa bhikkhusaṁghassa dammi ti / patiggahesi Bhagavā ārāmaṁ /*

Here the term *ārāma* which originally means in Sanskrit, 'a place of joy' (*a+ram* = to enjoy) and its association with *uyyānaṁ*, meaning garden/grove is explained as a place suitable for meditation in *Cullavagga*[14] – "a place neither too far from the village nor too near, suitable for coming and going, accessible for people whoever are desirous, not crowded by day, having little noise at night, quiet, fit to lie undisturbed by men, suitable for meditation in solitude" –

> *atha kho Anāthapiṇḍako gahapati Sāvatthaṁ gantvā katha nu kho Bhagavā vihareyya? Yaṁ assa gāmato neva atidūre na accasanne gamanāgamana sampannaṁ Divā appakiṇṇaṁ, rattiṁ appasaddaṁ, vijana vasaṁ paṭṭisallana sarūpaṁ' ti.* -

This reference shows that initially the place *ārāma* or *uyyāna* as mentioned by Buddha himself is meant for "a calm place for meditation" and not in the sense of a pleasure garden. Gutsav points out here that Bimbisāra's ritual presentation of pouring the (holy) water from the golden jar while offering the bamboo grove – the royal garden to the order of monks, as the symbol of purity turned the *uyyāna* – a pleasure garden into an *ārāma*. To support this point,[15] further how existed different dwelling places in size '....*khuddake vihāre ekaṁ antaṁ mahallake majjhe ti*...'-here *khuddakavihāra* and *mahallaka vihāra* are distinguished, as pointed out by Gustav[16] – a small dwelling place and a large dwelling place.

However, in *Mahāvagga*[17] the Buddha insists that 'going forth is depending on lodging at the root of a tree' – *rukkha mūla senāsanaṁ nissaya pabbajjā, tattha te yāvajīvaṁ ussaho karaṇīyo; atireka lābho, addha-yogo, pasādo, hammiyaṁ guhā.* (In this respect effort is to be made by monks for life only by resorting under a tree for shade a place of resting.) Whereas the aquisition of a dwelling place, a half-finish lodging, a terraced building, a mansion, a cave, are instructed to be avoided. It is rightly mentioned in *Mahāvastu*.[18]

But later[19] a merchant of Rājgṛha seeing monks in the morning going out from place to place, from forest to forest (even during the rainy seasons) suggested that he would like to arrange dwelling places (*vihārā*) for them. The monks, however, insisted that they first have to seek the opinion and consent of the *Mahāśramaṇa*. Accordingly, the injunction was issued –

> *anujanāmi, bhikkhave, pañca senasanāni: viharaṁ, addha-yogaṁ, pāsādaṁ, hammiyaṁ guhāṁ.*

The Buddha authorized the following five abodes – a dwelling place, a half-finished lodging, a terraced building, a house or a cave. This consent provided sixty *vihāra*s. While thanking the merchant the Buddha points out the requisites of the dwelling place as: *sītaṁ unhaṁ patihanti tato vala –migāni ca / Sarisape ca makase sisire cāpi vutthiyo//* – (The sixty *vihāra*s ward off cold and heat, and serpents, mosquitoes, sticky heat and rainfall[20]). Further, it is pointed out by the Buddha that the gift of a dwelling place to the Order is considered as the highest merit.

Once the acceptance of a *vihāra* is made by the Buddha, he gave the detailed descriptions of how a *vihāra* should be, how the inside chamber should be, and how the door is to be made of, etc.[21] When Anāthapinḍika came to know of his brother-in-law's donation of dwelling places (*vihāra*s) for monks in the service of the *Dhamma*, he approached the Blessed One to accept him as a lay disciple and later requested him to spend the rainy season at Sāvatthī[22] to which he replied:[23]

> They indeed, who accordingly have arrived (at the path of salvation) enjoy solitude –

(*Suññāgāre, kho, gahapati, Tathāgatābhirami ti*). Anāthapinḍika who got so excited of this acceptance informed the people about Tathāgatā visiting Sāvatthī along with the order of monks.[24] Anāthapinḍika found the park of Prince Jeta (*jetassa kumārassa uyyānaṁ*) to be suitable for the Blessed One – *gāmato neva atidure .... patisallāna saruppaṁ*, not too far from a village, a suitable place for solitude.

However, Jeta was not willing to part with it but agreed to sell the ground by a prize fixed by himself. Anāthapiṇḍika covered the ground with gold as the cost for the land from Jeta, but was left with no gold to cover one portion of the ground. Jeta came forward to cover the open ground with gold as a gift.

– '*Jeto kumāro tasmim okase koṭṭakaṁ māpesi.*[25]'

DIFFERENT KINDS OF DWELLING PROVIDED FOR A *SAṄGHA*

Thus we have seen how and when the different kinds of *vihāra*s were provided and gifted for the monks. An *upāsaka* offering a quantity of wood cut in the forest for a *vihāra* in ruins. Udena (Udayana), a Kosalan devotee, having a *vihāra* built for the *Saṅgha*, sent a messenger to the Buddha and his monks, then spending the rains at the Jetavana at Sāvatthī.[26] Thus the dwellings covered a wide range both as regards their building and structure. From the mere hut made of sticks or grass collected in the forest or gifted by an *upāsaka*, and the solitary cell or cave, the development to higher and higher forms of building in the *vihāra*s either as detached houses or as complex wholes, *Prāsāda*s, storeyed houses and *vihāra*s equipped with all kinds of dwelling – assembly halls, dining halls, council chambers with diverse kinds of satisfying the requirements for good health and life securing a fair level of comforts.

India was specially noted for its four chief centres or cities at each of which the *Saṅgha* owned a number of monasteries serving initially as the place of peaceful solitude and later as the seats of Buddhist learning. Thus we read of Yaṣṭivana, Veṇuvana, and Sītavana at Rajgṛha;[27] Jetavana and Purvārāma at Śrāvastī; Mahāvana at Kuṭāgāra hall, and Mango Grove at Vaiśalī; Nyagrodhārāma at Kapilavastu; and Ghoṣitārāma at Kauśambī.

THE TRANSITION OF *ĀRĀMA* TO *VIHĀRA* AND INTO *MAHĀVIHĀRA* AS CENTRE OF LEARNING

When was the mere *uyyāna ārāma* – a mere residential place of peaceful meditation – turned into a centre of learning? Did it happen during the lifetime of the Buddha or after his *Mahāparinirvāṇa*? It was clear that gift/donation of any kind to build or as a built *vihāra* to the *Saṅgha* was already in vogue at the time of the Buddha and that was considered as the highest merit. There are references as *Dhammārāma*[28] and the *ārāma* represent two different connotations: 1. *ārāma* and *udyāna*, and 2. *ārāma* and *vihāra* indicating (a) park and pleasure garden; and (b) groves of peaceful seclusion and residential quarters for recluses.[29]

R.K. Mukherji[30] calls it 'residential school' and further describes:

> the unit of the Buddhist educational system was thus this group of young *bhikkhu*s or monks living under the guardianship of a common teacher, the *Upājjhāya* or *Ācārya*, who was individually responsible for their health and studies, manners, morals, and their spiritual progress.

It is to be noted that the impulse to the construction of *vihāra*s for monks came from the words of the Buddha himself, such as:

> To give *vihāra*s to the *Saṅgha* where in safety and in peace, to meditate and think at ease, the Buddha calls the best of gifts. Let then the able man, regarding his own weal, have pleasant monasteries built and lodge there learned men.[31]

Incidentally, we may again note that this growth of collective life and organization in education is a fundamental point of distinction between the Buddhist and the Brāhmaṇical system, which depended more upon the solitude of hermitages in the woods as an aid to spiritual life than the social atmosphere of a *Saṅgha* humming with the activities of several thousands of monks in residence in the neighbourhood of busy haunts of men where they could go for alms.

MONASTERY AS THE ABODE OF LEARNING

History of the Buddhist system of education is practically that of the Buddhist Order or *Saṅgha*. Buddhist education and learning centred round monasteries. The Buddhist world did not offer any educational opportunities apart from or independently of its monasteries. All education, sacred as well as secular, was in the hands of the monks. They had the privilege of learning as well of the leisure to impart it.

Mukherji[32] discusses in detail the qualification of a teacher (*upājjhāya*), application to *upājjhāya* by a *bhikkhu* for his studies, daily duties of a *upājjhāya* and a *bhikkhu*, number of *bhikkhus* in the *vihāra* and framing the rules governing the establishment as a whole and binding upon all members, the teachers and the taught alike. As much the rules governing the number of *bhikkhus* to be under a *upājjhāya*, how the sick monk to be taken care of by another, a strict governing rule was prescribed by the Buddha. Thus the *Saṅgha* – the collective life of monks federated into a larger unit called the *vihāra* / monastery – as parts of the larger organization and in their relations to its general, collective life developed its own code of discipline and regulations binding upon all. This was very important to maintain the harmony of relations between different groups as students as well the teachers from different communities from various parts of the country speaking different languages and with different background irrespective of caste and creed in the pursuit of common culture. This helped to maintain to avoid the intrigues of the teachers of the *vihāra* with disciples and preserve a proper standard of academic etiquette and decorum governing the delicate relations among the staff/monks.

All these ideals as following the 'middle path' between the extremes of self-indulgence and self-suppression is systematically and consistently worked out in all details of Buddhist monastic life and discipline which took care of the three primary requisites of human existence, viz., food, clothing and shelter. As much as there is the code of conduct, there is the code of wealth. As much as the food and clothing are gifted to the monks, there was the gift of shelter. When the number of monks increased to stay together, the place of shelter slowly turned into a place of learning with a large space and with more chambers. This led to the commitment of taking care of the welfare of the teacher and the taught with due respect. As all could not be put on the same pedestal with reference to their learning capacity, some who took longer time had been given a kind of work to take care of the maintenance of the *vihāra/Saṅgha* as well as to take care of the fruit gardens, corn-field, etc. of the *Saṅgha* from which also the finance for the expenditure of the *vihāra* was taken care of.

INSCRIPTIONAL REFERENCE OF GIFTS TO THE *SAṄGHA/VIHĀRA*[33]

In this context, I would like to acknowledge the extensive work done by Ajita Jha on "Vihāras as sponsored donation by kings."[34]

As much as reference to donation and gifts to monks and to the *Saṅgha* in commentaries of Buddhaghoṣa[35] the earliest inscriptional references to *ārāma* are found in Mathurā inscription.[36] The passages found[37] in Buddhaghoṣa, show that the Asoka *ārāma* has grown into the Aśoka-*mahāvihāra*. Moreover, it is clear that according to the tradition represented by

Buddhaghoṣa,[38] *ārāma*, *vihāra*, and *mahāvihāra* are well attested monastic institutions.[39] The account given by Fa-xsien in the early years of the fifth century CE applies almost the same to the 7th and 8th centuries.[40] The development of the Nalanda Mahāvihāra gives clear picture of the transition.

According to Xuanzang, the ground of the monastic establishment was originally a Mango-grove belonging to a *Śreṣṭhin* or merchant-prince whose name was Amara.[41] It is noted that it was purchased for ten lacs (or *koṭis*) of gold pieces by a group of merchants who gifted it to the Buddhist *Saṅgha*. Later, King Śakrāditya (identified with Mahendrāditya Kumāragupta, AD 415-455) built a monastery here. The bounty of King Śakrāditya was enjoyed by monks in the monastery. The Nalanda monastery had a farmhouse where Xuanzang was given a refreshment before entering the *mahāvihāra*.[42]

HERITAGE OF NALANDA MAHĀVIHĀRA

It is understood from the accounts of Xuanzang that during his visit Nalanda had already been established as *mahāvihāra* with foreign Buddhist scholars being associated with it.

Among the royal patronage[43] of Nalanda Mahāvihāra, mention should be made of Emperor Harṣavardhana, King Pūrṇavarman of Magadha, Kumāra Bhāskaravarman of Kamarupa and perhaps King Aṁśuvarman of Nepal in the 7th century CE. Among the royal patrons belonging to 8th century CE, Gopāla and Dharmapāla, the first two kings of the Pāla dynasty, were specifically mentioned. It is noted that even the Tibetan king Khri-sron-lde-btsan (CE 755-797) was one of the patrons of this monastery.

During the time of Yi'jing in India, the endowments bestowed on Nalanda had doubled. There were more than 200 villages recorded as possessions of Nalanda by then. The kings who made endowments and land grants for the convents of Buddhist monks also took care of their upkeep. The fund was pooled out not only by gifts but also by the produce of the farms and gardens. Besides the land/villages, even animals like horse, sheep, and elephants were gifted to the monastery by kings and rich lay followers of Buddhism of that time.

A Vasgiri image inscription found at Nalanda refers to King Gopāla.[44] A very comprehensive and interesting information relating to the benefactions of a rich layman at Nalanda, viz., Malada, son of Tegina, minister of Emperor Yaśovarman, is a stone inscription found at Nalanda[45] belonging to the reign of King Yaśovarmadeva, identified with Emperor Yaśovarman of Kanauj. His bountiful charity to Nalanda Mahāvihāra was recorded. It is also noted by H. Sastri that Malada, not being satisfied with his charity to the Buddhist monks, purchased everything of Nalanda and gave it back to the *bhikṣus* of Nalanda. Though initially such monasteries were guided and administered by the traditional laws of the *Saṅgha*, slowly the royal control on the monasteries could be noted. The *sthavira* or *kulapati*, the head monk of the *vihāra*/*mahāvihāra* was highly respected and his orders obeyed in all important activities.

It is noted that slowly the patron had the privilege to appoint or recommend the *sthavira*/*kulapati* of the *mahāvihāra*.[46] Nalanda stone inscription of Malada refers to the authority and management of the order of the monks.[47]

NOTES AND REFERENCES

1. *Vin*. II., 207; *D*.II.7; *A* III.51, 299-'*yathāviharan*'.
2. For details see Gustav Roth, *Ārāma, Vihāra, and Mahāvihāra*, Bauddha Sanskriti Kendra, Patna, 1997.
3. *Ibid*., p. 8.
4. *Ibid*., p. 9.

5. *Vedic Concordance*, Hoshiarpur, 1953-65.
6. Gustav Roth, *op. cit.*, p. 6.
7. George Grimm, *The Doctrine of the Buddha: Religion of Reason and Meditation*, Delhi, 1982.
8. V. Aṅguttaranikāya, p. 135; See also Viśuddhimagga, VIII.155 (Kosambi Edition).
9. *Dīghanikāya*, I, p. 89.
10. *Ibid.*, I, p. 50; see also *Dialogues of the Buddha*, tr. Rhys Davids, London, 1973, Pt I, p. 67.
11. *Ibid.*, I, p. 179.
12. *Vinayapiṭaka*, Nalanda Devanagari Pāli.Series, 1956, pp. 45-50.
13. *Ibid.*, cf. *Cullavagga*. VI.2.14; cf. *Milindapañho* IV.11.27.
14. *Cullavagga*, VI.2.14, pp. 252, 24-26.
15. *Ibid.*, VI.1.7.
16. Gustav Roth, *op. cit.*, p. 30.
17. *Mahavagga*, I.30.4.
18. *Mahavastu*, III.i.
19. *Cullavagga*, VI.1., Nalanda ed., p. 239.19.
20. *Ibid.*, VI.2.
21. *Ibid.*, V.8.18; VI. 1.17, VI.2, VIII.8.2, V.14.3; *Mahavagga*, I.25.12.
22. *Ibid.*, VI.2.13.
23. Pācittiya, 8, pp. 41, 27-28.
24. *Cullavagga*, VI.2.14.
25. Radha Kumud Mookerji, *Ancient Indian Education*, Reprint, 1998, pp. 442-43.
26. *Bhikkhu-gatika*, V.1-5 cf. Radha Kumud Mookerji, *op. cit.*, p. 436.
27. *Mahāparinibbānasutta*, III.57.
28. *Dhammapada*, 364 –*dhammārāmo dhammarato*.
29. cf. *Rāmāyaṇa*, 2.45.21a, 2.80.21a; *Mahābhārata*, 'Udyoga parvan', V.22.33.
30. *Ibid.*, p. 406.
31. *Cullavagga*, VI. I.5.
32. Radha Kumud Mookerji, *op. cit.*, pp. 402-07.
33. Buddhaghoṣa's Commentary on the *Vinaya-Samanatapāsādika* I.42.2 ref. to *Saṅghārāma* of King Asoka – *puna rājā asokāramaṁ nāma mahāvihāraṁ kārāpetvā satthi – sahassānaṁ bhikkūnāṁ nicca – bhattaṁ paṭṭhapesi* - ('the King Aśoka after he got established a great monastery by the name of a retreat of peaceful joy in seclusion, he arranged permanent food supply for sixty thousand monks') *Cf.* Gutsav Roth, *op. cit.*
34. Ajita Jha, *Vihāra Sponsored Donations by Kings*, New Delhi, 1999.
35. *Ibid.*, *Sayaṁ ca Asokārāme asoka mahāvihārattha kammaṁ paṭṭhapesi* – (Aśoka himself, started in Aśoka's retreat the construction work for the great monastery of Aśoka).
36. See K.L. Janert (ed.), *Mathura Inscriptions*, 1st-2nd cent. AD.
37. Buddhaghoṣa's Commentary on the *Vinaya-Samanatapāsadika*, p. I.42.2, 42.14.
38. Buddhaghoṣa, 5th cent. AD.
39. However there is no reference to an *ārāma*, *saṁghārāma*, or to *mahāvihāra* in the inscriptions of Aśoka, cf. Hutzsch, Intr. XXXVI, D.C. Sircar, *Aśokan Studies*, Indian Museum, Calcutta, 1979.
40. Lalmani Joshi, *Buddhist Culture of India*, Motilal Banarsidass, New Delhi, 1987, pp. 65-90.
41. *Yuan Chwang*, tr. Samuel Beal, London, 1914, II.165.
42. *Ibid.*, pp. 164-65.
43. H. Heras, *The Royal Patrons of the University of Nalanda*, cf. Lalmani Joshi, *op. cit.*, p. 66.
44. H. Sastri, *Memoirs of the Archaeological Survey of India*, (*MASI*), no.66., p. 75.
45. *Epigraphica Indica*, XX, pp. 43ff; H. Sastri, *Nalanda and its Epigraphic Material*, *MASI*, *ibid.*
46. *Mṛcchakaṭika*, Act X.
47. *MASI*, no. 66, *op. cit.*, pp. 36, 87ff; *Nalanda mahāvihāra – āryabhikṣu-saṅghasya.*

30

THE INFLUENCE OF MASTER ŚĪLABHADRA ON MASTER XUANZANG'S THOUGHT

Hsiu-O Chien and S-C Shiu

The great Master Xuanzang (602-664) was an eminent monk and outstanding translator during the Tang dynasty. He introduced the *Vijñānamātra* (Consciousness-Only) theory of Dharmapāla and propagated it in China. He was the right expediter of the cultural exchange of India and China, and he was a great traveller both in China and abroad.

Having studied various Buddhist treatises of erudite monks in China, Master Xuanzang scrutinized their teachings and found that each of them specialized in some particular sect. When compared with the sacred scriptures, they showed differences either vaguely or manifestly, so that he was at a loss to decide which of the theories he should follow. Thus he resolved to travel to the West in order to seek the *Dharma*. In the third year (629) of Zhenguan 貞觀 period, Master Xuanzang started on his journey, went through all conceivable hardships, came to Qinzhou 秦州, Liangzhou 涼州, the kingdom of Gaochang 高昌 and other places, and finally arrived at the borderland of India. In other words, he reached the north of Xianjiang 新疆 province, the west of Turkistan and Afghanistan through which he got to the border of India.

In the fifth year (631) of Zhenguan period, Master Xuanzang reached the Nalanda monastery, studied there for five years and became the disciple of Master Śīlabhadra. When Xuanzang arrived in India, at that time, Master Śīlabhadra was 106 years old and was on the first place among the senior monks. Thus Master Śīlabhadra was respected and was named "the Right *Dharmapiṭaka*." There was a very particular and unusual lot and luck between the teacher and disciple – Master Śīlabhadra and Master Xuanzang.

I. THE MOTIVATION OF MASTER XUANZANG TRAVELLING WEST

A. Asking Questions and Dispelling Doubts

The main motivation of Master Xuanzang travelling to India according to the *Biography of the Tripiṭaka Dharma Master of the Great Ci'en Monastery of the Great Tang Dynasty* (Datang daci'en shi sanzang fashi zhuang, 大唐大慈恩寺三藏法師傳 T.2053), is narrated as follows:

> I resolved to travel to India in order to clear doubts and bring back the *Saptadaśabhūmiśāstra* (十七地論) to resolve the doubts of all.[1]

The doubts according to the *Biography of the Tripiṭaka Dharma Master of the Great Ci'en Monastery of the Great Tang Dynasty* (Datang daci'en shi sanzang fashi zhuang, 大唐大慈恩寺三藏法師傳, T.2053), are narrated as follows:

> The translators came from distant lands, their interpretations differed, and the time of the Buddha has gone far, his doctrines have been misinterpreted. Thus the unique teaching that the Buddha left at the twin *sala* trees has been divided into the two views of non-substantial ego and substantial *Dharma*, and the unequalled doctrine of the Mahāyāna has been split into the Southern and Northern Schools. Dissensions and disputes have lasted for several hundred years, and doubts have prevailed in the whole country with nobody to provide a solution.[2]

B. Follow the Step of Saints and Sages

Master Xuanzang took Master Faxian 法顯 and Zhiyan 智嚴, who went to India for the sake of seeking the *Dharma* and propagated it for the benefit of all sentient beings, as models, so he hoped that he would be able to equal and emulate them. According to the *Biography of the Tripiṭaka Dharma Master of the Great Ci'en Monastery of the Great Tang Dynasty* (Datang daci'en shi sanzang fashi zhuang, 大唐大慈恩寺三藏法師傳, T.2053), it follows:

> Since Master Faxian and Master Zhiyan, prominent figures of former times, could travel to India to seek the *Dharma* for the benefit of all living beings, why should there be nobody to follow their footsteps, so that the line of noble tasks should be discontinued? A real man should have the ambition to carry forward their tradition.[3]

C. The Inspiration of Auspicious Dream

In August of the third year (629) of Zhenguan period, before Master Xuanzang's starting on his journey, he prayed for the auspicious omen. According to the *Biography of the Tripiṭaka Dharma Master of the Great Ci'en Monastery of the Great Tang Dynasty*, (Datang daci'en shi sanzang fashi zhuang, 大唐大慈恩寺三藏法師傳, T.2053), it recounted as follows:

> In August of the third year (629) of Zhenguan (貞觀) period, when Master Xuanzang was about to start on his journey, he prayed again for a good omen. In the night he dreamed that he saw Mount Sumeru made of the four precious jewels, standing in the middle of the great sea. He desired to climb up the mountain, but the billows were turbulent and there was neither boat nor raft in sight. He was not daunted at all but decided to go into the sea. Suddenly he saw stone lotus flowers emerging out of the waves below his feet. When he turned back to look at the flowers, they disappeared as soon as he lifted his feet. In a moment he reached the foot of the mountain, which was so precipitous that it was impossible for him to climb. While he was trying to ascend the mountain by leaping, a strong whirlwind came and carried him up to the top of the mountain. He looked around and saw that everything was clear in sight without any hindrance. Then he awoke from the dream elated with joy. After that he started on his journey, when he was twenty-six years of age.[4]

Since Master Xuanzang had an auspicious omen, he became more determined to go to India for the sake of seeking the *Dharma*, and he started at once. When Master Xuanzang was born, his mother had dreamed that he went to India to seek the *Dharma*.[5] According to these signs, Master Xuanzang's travelling to India seems destiny and he probably was a Great *Bodhisattva* coming into the *sahā* world again to complete his duty.

II. THE RELATIONSHIP BETWEEN MASTER ŚĪLABHADRA AND MASTER XUANZANG

A. Nalanda Monastery

According to the first fascicle of the *Buddhist Records of the Western World* (Datang Xiyu ji, 大唐西域記, T. 2087) by Master Xuanzang, it follows:

> When Master Xuanzang arrived at Nalanda Saṅghārāma, he heard from senior people: There was a pool within the mango grove in the south of *Saṅghārāma*, in which there was a dragon named Nalanda. The *Saṅghārāma* was established near it, so it was named after the dragon's name – Nalanda. People said: When the Buddha was a king in his previous life practising the Path of *Bodhisattva*, the king constructed his capital here, having compassion for all sentient beings, being fond of almsgiving. People at that time praised his virtue and named him "almsgiving without tiredness". Thus the *Saṅghārāma* was also named after him – Almsgiving without tiredness. This place was originaly mango grove. Five hundred businessmen bought it and offered to the Buddha. The Buddha discoursed the *Dharma* here for three months and many merchants attained the sainthood. After Buddha had entered his *nirvāṇa*, the late king of this kingdom named Śakrāditya who esteemed *Ekayāna* (One Vehicle) and respected the Triple Gem (the Buddha, *Dharma*, and *Saṅgha*), practised divination for a good place to build the *Saṅghārāma*. When he began the monastery, the dragon's body was injured. At that time, there was a heretic, who was the follower of Nirgranthajñātiputra, skilled in divination who remarked: if a *Saṅghārāma* is built here it must be prosperous, and be the model of all monasteries in the five parts of India. One thousand years later, this monastery will be more prosperous. However, although the young students will easily achieve in studying, they will suffer the disease of blood vomit (haemotemesis), because the dragon has been injured.[6]

According to the ninth fascicle of the *Buddhist Records of the Western World*, it was the king Śakrāditya 帝日 who started to build the Nalanda monastery; after him, there were five kings who continued to construct it. They were King Budhagupta 覺護, King Tathāgatagupta 如來, King Bālāditya 幻日, King Vajra 金剛. The King Śīlāditya 戒日 was the sixth one building the Nalanda monastery.[7]

Furthermore, according to the third fascicle of the *Biography of the Tripiṭaka Dharma Master of the Great Ci'en Monastery of the Great Tang Dynasty:*

During the time of Master Śīlabhadra, the situation of Nalanda monastery was as follows:

> Ten thousand monks always lived there, both natives and foreigners. They studied Mahāyāna teachings and the doctrines of eighteen schools, as well as worldly books such as the Vedas. They also learned works on Veda, logic (*hetu vidyā*), grammar and composition (*śabda*), medicine (*cikitsā*), arts and mathematics (*śilpakarmasthāna*) too. Those who could understand twenty scriptures and *Abhidharma*s amounted to over a thousand persons. More than five hundred persons mastered thirty works, while ten persons, including Master Xuanzang, were experts of fifty works. Master Śīlabhadra was the only person who had thoroughly mastered all the texts; and being at an advanced age and unusual virtue, he was a great teacher of all the monks. Lectures were given at more than one hundred places in the monastery every day, and students

studied diligently without wasting a moment. As all the monks who lived there were men of virtue, the atmosphere in the monastery was naturally solemn and dignified. For more than seven hundred years since its establishment, none of the monks had committed any offence. Owing respect for them, the king gave more than one hundred villages' tax for their sustenance. Each village had two hundred families, who daily provided seven hundred *dan* 石 of polished non-glutinous rice, butter, and milk. Thus the learners could enjoy sufficient supplies of the four provisions (clothing, victuals, bedding, medicine) without the trouble of going to beg for them. It was because of this effort of their supporters that the scholars could gain achievements in learning.[8]

B. *Dharma* Lineage of Master Śīlabhadra

Master Śīlabhadra (529-645 or 528-651) was an *Abhidhārmika* of *Yogācāra* of Mahāyāna Buddhism, being the highest priest of Nalanda monastery of Magadha Kingdom, and he was from the noble race of Samataṭa kingdom, belonging to the Brahmin caste. Master Śīlabhadra took tonsure under Master Dharmapāla of Nalanda monastery of Magadha kingdom, researching into *Yogācāryabhūmi-śāstra* (瑜珈師地論, T. 1579) deeply, and mastered logic and grammar. Thus he got great prestige at that time. People said, Master Śīlabhadra had written ten works. However, at present, only the *Explanation on the Shengfodi jing* (聖佛地經) survives which had been translated into Tibetan.[9]

According to the eighth fascicle of the *Buddhist Records of the Western World*:

> Master Śīlabhadra arrived at the Nalanda monastery to meet Dharmapāla *Bodhisattva*. After listening to the *Dharma*, he was awakened and enlightened. Thus he asked to become a monk wearing the dyed robe. Among the disciples of the Master Dharmapāla, Master Śīlabhadra was the best. At that time, Master Śīlabhadra was only thirty years old. Śīlabhadra was so young that monks looked down on him, thinking he was unable to complete the duty alone. Master Dharmapāla had known their mind and explained to them: 'The most important is one's virtue and wisdom, it doesn't matter to discuss his age.'[10]

Thus we know that when Master Śīlabhadra studied at Nalanda monastery, at that time, Master Dharmapāla was the abbot of the monastery. At that time, Master Śīlabhadra was only thirty years old, and he was the best among Dharmapāla's disciples.

According to Yin Shun's research:

> Master Śīlabhadra was born in AD 531, and Dharmapāla passed away in AD 560. Master Xuanzang met Master Śīlabhadra in CE 636.[11]

C. The Guidance of Mañjuśrī *Bodhisattva*

When Master Xuanzang reached Nalanda monastery, Master Śīlabhadra was 106 years old. People did not dare to call his name but gave him an honorific title – "Right Dharmapiṭaka." When Master Śīlabhadra got fatal sickness, he had no desire to live any longer in the world. However, he had dreamed that Mañjuśrī *Bodhisattva* gave him direction, demanding him to try his best to teach the Chinese monk who was to come to Nalanda monastery. It was proved that the Chinese monk was Master Xuanzang.

According to the third fascicle of the *Biography of the Tripiṭaka Dharma Master of the Great Ci'en Monastery of the Great Tang Dynasty*:

After they had taken their seats, Master Śīlabhadra asked Master Xuanzang where he had come from. In reply, Master Xuanzang said, "I came from China with the wish to study *Yogācārabhūmiśāstra* under the instruction of the teacher." Upon hearing these words, the teacher shed tears and called for his disciple Buddhabhadra, who was the Dharmapiṭaka's nephew, over seventy years old, well versed in the scriptures and *Abhidharma* and eloquent in discussion. The Dharmapiṭaka said to him, 'You may tell the monks here how I suffered from illness three years ago.' On hearing this, Buddhabhadra wept and wiped his tears, while narrating the events that had happened before, saying: The teacher used to suffer from gout. Each time he had an attack of it, his hands and feet were convulsed as painfully as if they were burned by fire or pricked by a knife. His illness was sometimes better and sometimes worse for more than twenty years. Three years ago the pain was aggravated to such an extent that he became disgusted with his body and wished to put an end to his life by starvation. One night he saw three celestial beings in a dream. One was golden yellow, another one purplish blue, and the third one silvery white in colour. All of them had regular features and were dressed in light and brilliant garments. They came and asked the teacher, 'Do you intend to get rid of this body of yours? It is said in the scriptures that the corporeal body is a cause of suffering, but it is said that one should discard one's body with a feeling of abhorrence. You were once a king in a past life and caused much trouble to the people; so you incurred your present retribution. It befits you to contemplate on your past misdeeds and repent with sincerity. Bear the pain with patience, preach the scriptures and *Abhidharma* diligently, and then it will disappear by itself. Even if you do away with your body, you can never terminate your suffering.' Having heard this admonition, the teacher worshipped the divine beings. The golden one, pointing at the blue one, said to the teacher, 'Do you recognize him? He is Avalokiteśvara *Bodhisattva*.' He also pointed at the silvery one and said, 'This is Maitreya *Bodhisattva*.' The teacher immediately worshipped Maitreya *Bodhisattva* and asked him, 'Master Śīlabhadra has always wished to be reborn in your pure land, but I do not know whether I can realize my wish.' In reply, the *Bodhisattva* said, 'If you widely spread the Right *Dharma*, you will be able to be reborn there.' Then the golden figure introduced himself, saying, 'I am Mañjuśrī *Bodhisattva*. As we saw that you intended to relinquish your body without any beneficial result, we have come to advise you not to do so. You should act according to my words to propagate the Right *Dharma* and preach the *Yogācārabhūmiśāstra* (瑜珈師地論, T. 1579) and other texts to all those who have not yet heard about them. Your body will then gradually regain peace and health, and you need not worry about it. A Chinese monk who takes delight in understanding the Great *Dharma* will come to study under you. You may wait for his arrival and teach him.' After having heard these words, the Master Śīlabhadra worshipped the *Bodhisattvas* and promised them, 'I shall act according to your instruction.' When he had said so, the *Bodhisattvas* vanished. Since then the teacher has been cured of his painful disease.' All the monks heard about this remark with praise and said that it was an unusual event. Having personally heard this account, Master Xuanzang could not refrain from feeling both excited and being happy. He again worshipped the teacher with gratitude, saying, 'If it is just as you have said, I shall study with the utmost effort. May the teacher be compassionate and accept me as his pupil to receive his instructions.' The Dharmapiṭaka asked again, 'How many years have you spent on the way?' 'Three years,' was the reply. Since the time coincided with the dream, the teacher gave Master Xuanzang various advice and counsels, expressing the fraternity of a tutor with a pupil, to his delight.[12]

From this time on, Master Xuanzang studied the Buddha-*dharma* at Nalanda monastery under the instruction of Master Śīlabhadra.

III. THE INSTRUCTIONS OF MASTER ŚĪLABHADRA

Master Śīlabhadra was the abbot of Nalanda monastery. He propagated the doctrine of the Consciousness-Only on the basis of the *Sandhi-nirmocana-sūtra* (Jie sheng mi jing, 解深密經), the *Yogācārabhūmi-śāstra* (Yu qie shi di lun, 瑜珈師地論) and other texts.

He divided the doctrine of the Buddha into three parts – the reality of phenomena, the unreality of ego and things, and *Madhyama* – the mind or spirit is real, while things are unreal. Master Śīlabhadra considered that the doctrine of Dharmalakṣana revealed the whole truth and advocated the theory of five germ-natures.[13]

Master Śīlabhadra was the follower of the Dharmalakṣana's sect of Vasubandhu. Since he was very old, he did not teach by himself. However, when Master Xuanzang arrived at Nalanda monastery, Master Śīlabhadra discoursed the *Yogācārabhūmiśāstra* for him in particular. He lectured it for three times which took nine months. Furthermore, he also discoursed upon other texts. Therefore, we know that Master Śīlabhadra had a great influence on Master Xuanzang's thoughts.[14]

At Nalanda monastery, Master Xuanzang studied under the instruction of Master Śīlabhadra. The content of his studying is very wide. According to the third fascicle of the *Biography of the Tripiṭaka Dharma Master of the Great Ci'en Monastery of the Great Tang Dynasty*:

> All these sacred sites Master Xuanzang visited and worshipped all around. It was not until returning to Nalanda monastery Master Xuanzang asked Master Śīlabhadra to expound the *Yogācārabhūmi-śāstra.* Several thousand monks attended the lectures together with him. In this monastery Master Xuanzang listened to the exposition of the *Yogācārabhūmiśāstra* three times: to that of *Nyāyānusāra-śāstra* (Shun zhen li lun, 順正理論), the *Prakaraṇāryavācāśāstra* (Xian yang sheng jiao lun, 顯揚聖教論), the *Abhidharmasamudaya Prakaraṇa* (Duei fa, 對法), one time each; to that of the *Hetuvidyāśāstra* (Yin ming, 因明), the *Śabdavidyā -śāstra* (Sheng ming, 聲明), the *Samuccayapramāṇaśāstra* (Ji liang, 集量論) etc; two times each; as well as to that of the *Mādhyamika-śāstra* (Zhong lun, 中論), and the *śata-śāstra* (Bai lun, 百論), three times each. As regards the *Abhidharmakoṣa-śāstra* (Ju she lun, 俱舍論), the *Vibhaṣā -śāstra* (婆沙論), the *Jñānaprasthānaśatpadābhidharma* (六足阿毗曇), etc.; which he had already studied in Kashmir and other countries, he merely read through them and clarified dubious points he had found in them. He also studied some Brahmaṇic books at the same time.[15]

Thus we know Master Śīlabhadra had a great impact on Master Xuanzang's Buddhist learning and thoughts.

IV. MASTER XUANZANG RECEIVING THE INSTRUCTION FROM MASTER ŚĪLABHADRA

In addition to receiving the instruction under Master Śīlabhadra, Master Xuanzang had another two teachers who were a senior Brāhmaṇa from the kingdom of Ṭakka, the other was Jayasena.

With regard to the teachings of the Brāhmaṇas, according to the second fascicle of the *Biography of the Tripiṭaka Dharma Master of the Great Ci'en Monastery of the Great Tang Dynasty*:

> Master Xuanzang reached the eastern part of the country of Ṭakka and arrived in a big city. At a large mango grove to the west of the city and by the northern side of the road, there lived a Brāhmaṇa seven hundred years old, who looked like a man about the age of thirty, with a

> stalwart built and a clear mind of deep discernment. He was well versed in the *Mādhyamika-śāstra* (Zhong lun, 中論), the *śata-śāstra* (Bai lun, 百論), and other treatises, as well as in the Vedas and other books. He had two attendants, both of whom were over one hundred years old. When he saw Master Xuanzang, he received him with great pleasure. The Master stayed there for one month to study the *Sūtraśata-śāstra* (Bai lun, 百論), and the *śataśāstravaipulya* (Guang bai lun, 廣百論), with him. This person was a disciple of Nāgārjuna and had received his teacher's tradition personally, of which his expositions were clear and lucid.[16]

Master Xuanzang studied the doctrine of the Contemplation on the Mean (Zhong guang, 中觀) under the instruction of the aged Brāhmaṇa, which was very useful for him to debate with scholars of Contemplation on the Mean. Since Master Xuanzang knew the doctrine of both sides, he was able to win when debating with the opposite side. Although Master Xuanzang is learned, he is versed in the thought of the Consciousness-Only.

Concerning the lineage of Jayasena's thought and learning, according to the fourth fascicle of the *Biography of the Tripiṭaka Dharma Master of the Great Ci'en Monastery of the Great Tang Dynasty*, it is described as follows:

> Jayasena 勝軍 was a native of *Surașțra* 蘇剌侘 country and *Kṣatriya* 剎帝利 by birth. Since his youth he loved learning, and at first he studied *hetu-vidyā* with the Śāstrin Bhadraruci 賢愛. Then he learned *śabda-vidyā* 聲明 and the treatises of both Mahāyāna and *Hīnayāna* schools from Sthiramati 安慧 *Bodhisattva*. He also learned *Yogācārabhūmi-śāstra* from Master Śīlabhadra. As regards various non-Buddhist books, such as the *Four Vedas*, astronomy, geography, medicine, and the art of divination, he thoroughly mastered all their fundamental sources as well as the subjects that branched from them, since his learning included both Buddhist and non-Buddhist lore and his virtue was esteemed by the people of the time.[17]

The Master Jayasena determined to get rid of all kinds of defilements and suffering declined the king's invitation and donation, and lived at Stickwood Hill, training and teaching his pupils. According to the fourth fascicle of the *Biography of the Tripiṭaka Dharma Master of the Great Ci'en Monastery of the Great Tang Dynasty*:

> Since then he often stayed at Stickwood Hill, training and educating his disciples, and he always lectured on Buddhist scriptures. The number of monks and laymen who came to study under him always exceeded several hundred. Master Xuanzang stayed with him for two years to learn the *Vijñānamātraparikalpanā-śāstra* (唯識抉擇論), the *Mānasābhidheyatā-śāstra* (成無畏論), *Abhayasiddhi-śāstra*, (意義理論), the *Asaṅgamanirvāṇa-śāstra* (不住涅槃論), the *Dvadaśāṅgapratītyasamutpāda-śāstra* (十二因緣論), and the *Sūtrālaṁkāra-śāstra* (莊嚴經論). Master Xuanzang also resolved some dubious points in the *Yogācārabhūmi-śāstra*, the *Hetuvidyā-śāstra* and some other works.[18]

After Master Xuanzang had studied scriptures and treatises of *Yogācāra* sect and returned to Nalanda monastery, Master Śīlabhadra asked him to lecture on the *Mahāyānasaṁparigraha-śāstra* (She da cheng lun, 攝大乘論), and the *Vijñānamātraparikalpanā-śāstra* for the monks.[19]

V. MASTER XUANZANG'S PROPAGATION AND TEACHING OF THE *DHARMA*

In the middle of the seventh century, Master Xuanzang returned to China. After having come back to China, he translated a series of texts of *Yogācāra* from the nineteenth year (645) of Zhengoan 貞觀 period to the first year (661) of Longsuo 龍朔 period. Among his translations, the *Vijñaptimātratāsiddhi-śāstra* in ten fascicles is the essential of Master Xuanzang's thought. Thus people named his teachings as *Yogācāra* or *Dharmalakṣaṇa* sect.

Yin Shun 印順 pointed out:

> The *Vijñaptimātratāsiddhi-śāstra* is the mixture of ten commentaries on the *Triṁśikavijñaptikārikā*, and it took the point of view of Dharmapāla which represented the orthodox doctrine of *Yogācāra* developing in India.[20]

Sheng Yan 聖嚴 considered:

> Since Master Xuanzang studied under Master Śīlabhadra who was the follower of Aśvaghoṣa 無著 and Vasubandhu 世親, he taught the teachings of the Consciousness-Only and the *Abhidharmakoṣa-śāstra* (Ju she lun, 俱舍論) which laid the foundation for the sect of *Dharmalakṣaṇa* 法相, and *Abhidharmakoṣa* 俱舍.[21]

Master Xuanzang's teachings can be divided into two parts – Consciousness-Only and the *Abhidharmakoṣa-śāstra* propagated by different disciples. Pu'guang 普光, Fa'bao 法寶, and Sheng'tai 神泰 wrote commentaries for the *Abhidharmakoṣa-śāstra* translated by Master Xuanzang, explaining its profound meaning. They formed the sect of *Abhidharmakoṣa*.

Before the sect of *Abhidharmakoṣa* had been founded, the *Abhidharmakoṣa-śāstra* had been translated by Paramārtha 真諦. However, the *Abhidharmakoṣa-śāstra* did not prevail at that time until Master Xuanzang translated it again. Pu'guang 普光 wrote commentaries for Master Xuanzang's new translation, and Fa'bao 法寶 and Sheng'tai 神泰 also wrote commentaries for it. At that time, the *Abhidharmakoṣa-śāstra* had been propagated widely.[22]

WORKS CITED

Primary Sources

Datang daci'en shi sanzang fashi zhuang, 大唐大慈恩寺三藏法師傳 (*Biography of the Tripiṭaka Dharma Master of the Great Ci'en Monastery of the Great Tang Dynasty*), T.2053, V.50.

Datang Xiyu ji, 大唐西域記 (*Buddhist Records of the Western World*) by Xuanzang, T.2087, V.51.

Datang xiyu qiufa gaosanzang, 大唐西域求法高僧傳 (*Biographies of Eminent Monks Seeking the Dharma in the West During the Great Tang Dynasty*), T. 2066, V.51.

Nanhai jigui neifa zhuan, 南海寄歸內法傳 (*A Record of the Inner Law Sent Home from the Southern Seas*) by Yi'jing 義淨, T.2125, V.54.

Secondary Sources

Lu Cheng 呂澂 in his work *The Five Sciences of Buddhism Propagated by Xuanzang and Yi'jing* (奘淨兩師所傳的五科佛學).

Lu Cheng, 呂澂 points out in his work *Discussion on Practicing Concentration in Six Subjects* (六門教授習定論).

Sheng Yan, 聖嚴,中國佛教史概說 (*An Essential Expatiation on Chinese Buddhism*), Taipei: Fagu Chubanshe, 1999.

Sheng Yan, 聖嚴, 比較宗教學 (*A Comparative Study on Religions*), Taipei: Fagu Chubanshe, 法鼓出版社, 1999.

Yin Shun, 印順, *The History of Buddhist Thought in India*, (印度佛教思想史), Taipei: Zhen wen chu ban she, 正聞出版社, 1992.

Yin shun, 印順, 華雨集·大樹緊那羅王所問經偈頌講記 (*The Lectures on the Verses of Drumakinnararājapariprccha*), Volume 1, Taipei: Zhen wen chu ban she, 正聞出版社, 1993.

Yin Shun, 印順, 佛教史地考論 (*A Critical Study of the Buddhist History and Geography*), Taipei: Zhenwen chubanshe, 正聞出版社, 1993.

Yin Shun, 印順, 如來藏之研究 (*A Study on Tathāgatagarbha*), Taipei: Zhenwen chubanshe, 正聞出版社, 1993.

Foguang Shan, 佛光大辭典 (*Foguang Buddhist Dictionary*), supervised by Master Shing-Yun, 1989.

Zhong hui fojiao baike qiansh, 中華佛教百科全書 (*The Encyclopedia of Chinese Buddhism*), supervised by Master Kai'zhen, 開證, 1994.

NOTES AND REFERENCES

1. See T. 2053, V. 50, P. 222c. All references of Chinese canonical texts are those of the Taisho edition. Through this work the abbreviation 'T,' is used to indicate the Taishō *shinshū daizōkyō* 大正新修大藏經, edited by Takakusu Junjiro 高楠順次郎 and Watanabe Kaigyoku 渡邊海旭 (Tokyo: Taishō Issaikyō Kankai, 1924-1932).
2. See T. 2053, V. 50, p. 225c.
3. See T. 2053, V. 50, p. 225c.
4. See T. 2053, V. 50, p. 222c.
5. See T. 2053, V. 50, p. 222c.
6. T. 2087, V. 51, p. 923b.
7. T. 2087, V. 51, p. 923b-c.
8. T. 2053, V. 50, p. 237b-c.
9. See *The Encyclopedia of Chinese Buddhism*, p. 2565a-b, and *Foguang Buddhist Dictionary*, p. 2916b-c.
10. T. 2087, V. 51, p. 914c.
11. Yin Shun 印順, Fo jiao shi di kao lun, 佛教史地考論 (*A Critical Study of the Buddhist History and Geography*), Taipei: Zhenwen chubanshe, 正聞出版社 1991, p. 341.
12. T. 2053, V. 50, pp. 236c-237a.
13. See *The Encyclopedia of Chinese Buddhism*, p. 2565a-b, and *Foguang Buddhist Dictionary*, p. 2916b-c.
14. See *The Encyclopedia of Chinese Buddhism*, p. 2565a-b, and *Foguang Buddhist Dictionary*, p. 2916b-c.
15. T. 2053, V. 50, pp. 238c-239a.

16. T. 2053, V. 50, pp. 238c-239a.
17. T. 2053, V. 50, p. 244a.
18. T. 2053, V. 50, p. 244a.
19. T. 2053, V. 50, p. 244b
20. Yin Shun, 如來藏之研究 (*A Study on Tathāgatagarbha*), p. 187.
21. Sheng Yan, 中國佛教史概說 (*An Essential Expatiation on Chinese Buddhism*), pp. 118-19.
22. Sheng Yan, 中國佛教史概說 (*An Essential Expatiation on Chinese Buddhism*), p. 122.

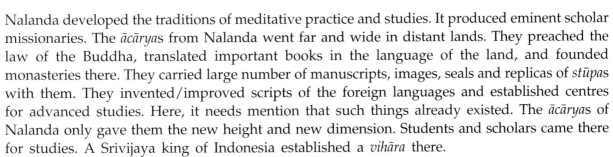

31

NALANDA: ITS SIGNIFICANCE

B.B. Kumar

Nalanda developed the traditions of meditative practice and studies. It produced eminent scholar missionaries. The *ācārya*s from Nalanda went far and wide in distant lands. They preached the law of the Buddha, translated important books in the language of the land, and founded monasteries there. They carried large number of manuscripts, images, seals and replicas of *stūpa*s with them. They invented/improved scripts of the foreign languages and established centres for advanced studies. Here, it needs mention that such things already existed. The *ācārya*s of Nalanda only gave them the new height and new dimension. Students and scholars came there for studies. A Srivijaya king of Indonesia established a *vihāra* there.

Buddha wanted his teachings to be conveyed to people through their own languages. Buddhist texts were translated in languages of different countries to facilitate the same. The missionaries from different countries, and from different parts of India, went out to propagate the tenets of the *Dhamma* and translated the texts. This started before the establishment of Nalanda. A Parthian prince abdicated his throne, went to China and translated numerous Sanskrit books into Chinese language. Dharmarakṣa and Kaśyapa Mātaṅga translated Buddhist texts into Chinese in the first century BCE. The texts reached China quite early, perhaps in the second century BCE. A large number of Buddhist scholars went to China between the 3rd and 6th centuries.[1]

Among those who went to China, Gautama Saṅgha, Puṇyatrāta, Dharmayaśas, Yaśa, Kumāravijaya, Vimalākṣa, Buddhajīva and Dharmakṣema were from Madhyadeśa; Upaśūnya and Paramārtha from Ujjain; Jñānabhadra, Jinayaśas and Yaśogupta from Bengal and Kamarūpa (Assam); Buddhabhadra and Vimokṣasena from Swat; Guṇavarman from Kashmir; Jīvagupta from Gandhāra; Dharmagupta from Lāṭa; and others like Prabhākarmitra, Bodhiruci, Sudhākarasiṁha, Vajrabodhi, Amoghavajra Bodhidharma and Dharmadeva from various other places.

A large number of *ācārya*s who went to China, Tibet, Japan, Korea, and other countries were from Nalanda. Viṣṇugupta, on the request of the Chinese Emperor Wu, selected Paramārtha to work in China. He reached China by sea route in CE 546, carried a large number of Buddhist manuscripts with him and translated more than seventy works into Chinese. He died there in CE 569.[2] Dharmtrāta-Yaśas (CE 481) and Guṇavṛddhi (5th century CE) translated several works into Chinese.[3] Jñānayaś as, along with his disciples, Yaśagupta and Jñānagupta, between 564 and 572, translated six works into Chinese.[4] Some important scholars of Nalanda who went to China were Prabhākaramitra, Vajrabodhi, his disciple Amoghavajra, Muniśrī, Buddhakīrti, and Dharmadeva. Prabhākaramitra studied Asaṅga's *Yogācārabhūmi/Saptadaśa-bhūmi-śāstra* under Śīlabhadra. He was a scholar of Hīnayāna; he taught *Abhidharma* at Nalanda. He left Nalanda, reached the kingdom of Western Turk-Kagan in Tokharistan and Eastern Iran, where he, along with his ten monks and lay disciples, was warmly welcomed by the Kagans. He reached the Chinese capital on an invitation from the T'ang Emperor Tai-tsung in 626 and stayed in Hingtsien monastery. He translated *Mahāyāna-Sútrālaṅkāra* of Asaṅga and two other books in Chinese. He died in China in 633 at the age of 69 and his disciples erected a *stūpa* over his ashes.[5]

Amoghavajra carried 500 texts with him to China and translated 77 of them into Chinese between 746 and 771. He went to China via Ceylon at the age of 21 with his teacher Vajrabodhi and died there in CE 774.[6] Vajrabodhi, the son of King Īśānavarman, was born in 661[7] and died in China in 731.[8] He translated eleven tantric works,[9] including *Vajraśekhara*[10] in Chinese; he propagated and deepened the roots of the Guhya cult, *Tantrayāna*, there.[11] In 25 years, Vajrabodhi and Amoghavajra translated 500 scriptures into 130 volumes. Vajrabodhi, when only of 20, studied Vinaya and *Mādhyamika* doctrines with Śāntabodhi in Nalanda for six years. He also studied Hīnayāna for 11 years there. Śubhākarasiṁha, once the king of Orissa and the contemporary of I-zing, studied in Nalanda under the abbot Dharmagupta. He went to China in 716 at the age of eighty, established a Tantric school there, translated Buddhist texts in Chinese and died there in 735.[12] Dharmadeva was the last and the greatest translator of Sanskrit works in China. He translated 46 books up to 981[13] and further 72 works,[14] including *Sukhāvatīvyūha*,[15] up to 1001. He went to China in 971 and died there in 1001. Emperor Chin-Tsong posthumously awarded him the title of 'Xsuan Chiao Chan Shih' or the 'Dhyāna Teacher of Profound Learning'. Muniśrī was Chinese, who taught *Śīla* and *Dharma* in Nalanda. He translated a Japanese work into Chinese in collaboration with Hanyā (Sanskrit, *Prajñā*). After the destruction of Nalanda, Shiku went to China and then to Korea and taught Buddhist law there.

There was an Imperial Bureau of Translators of Buddhist scriptures in Chinese, and at least three Indians headed it and they translated some two hundred volumes between 982 and 1011.[16] Proper arrangements were always made to facilitate the translation work in China. When Chinese emperor asked Prabhākaramitra to take up translation work, nineteen monk-scholars, including two Indians, Saṁha and Gupta, were appointed to assist him. One of the two Indians acted as interpreter.[17] Among the scholar-monks, some translated words, some verified the translation, and some others wrote it. Others copied it. High officials, as ordered by the emperor, examined and supervised the work.[18]

The prominent *ācārya*s of Nalanda who went to Tibet were Śāntarakṣita, Padmasambhava, Kamalaśīla, Mātṛigupta, Dīpaṅkara Śrijñāna (Atiśa), Somanātha, Śākyaśrībhadra, and Śrījaganmitra. Śāntarakṣita (also known as *Bodhisattva* in Tibet) was invited by the Tibetan King Khri-srong-Iden-btsan to consecrate the Sam-yās monastery, when he was seventy-five.[19] He became the head of that monastery and died there at the age of hundred.[20] He wrote several books/commentaries and translated many Sanskrit texts into Tibetan. Śāntarakṣita, for the first time, introduced Buddhist monasticism in Tibet.[21] Padmasambhava, the founder of Sam-yās, the first Buddhist monastery in Tibet,[22] and a contemporary of Śāntarakṣita,[23] the son of King Indrabhūti of Uḍyāna or Udyāna (Swat in Afghanistan),[24] and a native of Ghazni, belonged to the Tantric *Yogācāra* School of Nalanda.[25] He was the chief tantric teacher there and taught yoga and occult sciences.[26] It is said that he introduced Vajrayāna Buddhism in Tibet.[27] He translated, in collaboration with the Tibetan scholar Dpal-gyi-senge (Vairocana), the tantric text *Vajramantrābhisandhi-mūla Tantra* into Tibetan.[28] Dīpaṁkara Śrījñāna studied at Vikramaśilā and Nalanda. He wrote about 200 books in Sanskrit and Tibetan. His eighty-three tantric books are recorded in ITBU.[29] He was the abbot of Vikramaśilā Mahāvihāra and was taken from there to Tibet where he stayed for thirteen years.[30] He died in Tibet at the age of 73 in 1053.[31] He was called 'rovo Je' by the Tibetans, which means 'Prabhu'.[32] He was even deified and called 'Atiśā'.

Nalanda attracted a large number of scholars and students from almost every part of Asia. There was great rush for study there. Some of the scholars who came to Nalanda, such as Thon-mi-sam-bhoṭa from Tibet and I-zing and Xuanzang from China, were very famous.

*Ācārya*s of Nalanda did not only go to Central, Eastern and Northern Asia, but also to South-East Asia to propagate and teach, also to learn. Dharmapāla was a great scholar and the abbot of Nalanda.[33] He wrote voluminously in Sanskrit[34] and translated books in Tibetan.[35] Xuanzang said that Dharmapāla 'gave fragrance to Buddha's teachings'.[36] Dharmapāla left for Suvarṇadvīpa after more than thirty years of meritorious career, for studies.[37] Dīpaṁkara Śrījñāna also went to Suvarṇadvīpa (Indonesia) via Bengal, Burma and Malaya, to learn tantra.[38] He visited Tāmradvīpa (Ceylon) also during his return journey.[39]

Nalanda functioned as the centre of excellence due to many reasons. The *Samrāṭ*/the State remained facilitator and protector throughout. The massive complex of *stūpa*s, *caitya*s and *vihāra*s were extensively built and rebuilt by different dynasties. The highest standards were maintained as merit was the only criteria for admission and the academic standards of teaching and learning were rigorously maintained. It imparted education in secular and religious fields. Nalanda remained at the height of glory even on the day of its destruction by Bakhtiar Khalji. It was ruined due to the reversal of the role of the State. Bakhtiyar Khalji represented the 'Destroyer State'. But it was not the first experience of its kind for the Indians. Indians had already experienced the menace of Mahmood two centuries earlier and that of the intolerant Islam. Al-Beruni has mentioned the ruinous effects of his raids on the prosperity of the country. Mahmood looted immense wealth and ruined the sacred heritage. The Indians 'became like atoms of dust and their sciences retired far away from the conquered areas to distant Kashmir and Benares and other places.' Not even Bengal was distant at the time of the Second Holocaust. India's great institutions of learning – Nalanda, Vikramaśilā – were attacked and destroyed; the libraries were burnt. This time our sciences, our knowledge sources retired to Nepal and Tibet. India became a knowledge-starved country.

Entire Asia and parts of Europe formed an India-centric culture continuum zone; Islamic invasion brought a break in the same. Islamic invasion caused the rout of Buddhism and Hinduism in many parts of Central, Western and South Asia.

No translation of Sanskrit books was done in South-East Asia as Sanskrit was widely used in that region. Sanskrit and Prākrit were widely used in Central Asia also. Indian scripts or scripts derived from Brāhmī were widely used in Asian countries. Siddhaṁ script (Siddhamātrikā; derived from Brāhmī) was also used in China, especially for writing Sanskrit. It was written vertically, as well as from left to right.[40] This script was also used in Korea.

A great part of the Tibetan canonical texts were translated, revised and block-printed in Mongolian during Chinese Emperor K'ang Hsi's period (1662-1722). Chinese Emperor Chien Lung commissioned scholars to translate the texts of the Bstan-hgyur collection.[41] India lost vast treasure of its literature during the last 800 years because of consequent devastations.

NOTES AND REFERENCES

1. Radha Kumud Mukherjee, *Ancient India*, Allahabad, 1956, p. 478.
2. P.C. Bagchi, *India and China*, Bombay, 1944, pp. 42-44.
3. B.A. Saletore, *India's Diplomatic Relations with the East*, Bombay, 1960, p. 126.
4. *Ibid.*, p. 161.
5. Rahul Sankrityayana, *Bauddha Samskriti*, p. 136.
6. R.C. Majumdar and A.D. Pusalkar (eds.), *The Classical Age*, 1954, p. 610.
7. B.N. Misra, 'Ācāryas of Nalanda', in *India's Contribution to World Thought and Culture*, p. 25.
8. R. Sankrityayana, *op. cit.*, p. 346.
9. *Ibid.*
10. B.N. Misra, *op. cit.*, p. 25.
11. R.C. Majumdar, *op. cit.*, p. 610.
12. B.A. Saletore, *op. cit.*, p. 322.
13. R. Sankrityayana, *op. cit.*, pp. 355-56.
14. *Ibid.*
15. R.K. Mookerjee, *Ancient Indian Education* (Brahmanical and Buddhist), p. 578.
16. Majumdar and Pusalkar, *The Age of Imperial Kanauj*, Bombay, 1955, p. 443.
17. R.C. Majumdar and A.D. Pusalkar (eds.), *op. cit.*, pp. 609-10.
18. R. Sankrityayana, *op. cit.*, p. 336.
19. B.N. Misra, *op. cit.*, p. 28.
20. R. Sankrityayana, *op. cit.*, p. 405.
21. B.N. Misra, *op. cit.*, p. 28.
22. *Ibid.*
23. *Ibid.*
24. *Ibid.*
25. *Ibid.*
26. B.N. Misra, *op. cit.*, quoted from the *Tibetan Book of the Dead: Essentials of Buddhist Philosophy.*
27. *The Cultural Heritage of India*, Vol. V, p. 721.
28. *Ibid.*
29. P.N. Bose, *Indian Teachers of Buddhist Universities*, Madras, 1923, pp. 72-79.
30. *Ibid.*, p. 72.
31. *Ibid.*
32. *Ibid.*, p. 71.
33. B.N. Datta, *Mystic Tales of Lama Tārānāth*, translation, p. 15.
34. B.N. Misra, *op. cit.*, p. 26.
35. *Ibid.*
36. *Ibid.*
37. *Indian Historical Quarterly*, Vol. XXXII, 2 & 3, p. 302.
38. R.P. Aniruddha, *An Introduction to Lamaism*, p. 42.
39. R.C. Majumdar, *The History of Bengal*, Vol. 1, p. 674.
40. *The Cultural Heritage of India*, p. 735.
41. *Ibid.*, p. 727.

32

MASTER XUANZANG BRINGS THE BUDDHA'S WISDOM TO TANG CHINA

Rev. Heng Sure

Master Xuanzang's (CE 602-664) pilgrimage to the West, to Nalanda University and back to China is a saga that has challenged the imaginations and stirred the admiration of Buddhists, scholars, travellers, historians, and pilgrims the world around for millennia. We will first look at the numerous and extraordinary accomplishments of Master Xuanzang. He was first and foremost a Buddhist Dharma Master, an ordained Buddhist *Bhikṣu*, whose precepts led him to teach the methods of the Buddha's *Dharma*-teachings. True to his monastic vows he maintained his vegetarian diet from the start to the finish of his long road and refused the lavish gifts of kings in favour of simple non-meat offerings. During his journey and after returning to China he was honoured by kings and emperors; he was recognized by bandits and barbarians as a religious teacher, a place of spiritual refuge. He sought the truth of the Buddha's experience in the Holy Land of the Buddhists and found spiritual solace. His pilgrimage took him on foot across mountains and deserts that contemporary travellers find challenging in well-equipped, all-terrain vehicles. From the perspective of history his intrepid courage and determination is hard to match. He visited lands that are to this day considered exotic and remote. He was a philosopher who founded a school of Buddhist thought, the 'Consciousness-only School' which revolutionized concepts of the nature of mind and its potential for awakening.

He kept a journal of his adventures, and his meticulous notes served as official histories of the region. He asked about the history of each new place he went and checked sources when he heard old legends, measuring the geographical distances with accuracy that became the standard for reckoning until modern instruments replaced his calculations only recently. As an author Master Xuanzang's *Xuyuji* (*Journal of A Trip to the Western Regions*) has been read and re-read for its exciting adventures, its marvellous stories and its unique historical accounts of the territories he crossed. His biography, written by a monastic disciple, provides a chronology of Xuanzang's life and times.

He enrolled in Nalanda University, the foremost seat of Buddhist and secular learning in India, and studied there for seven years, mastering Sanskrit and the available schools of doctrine and intellectual discourse. He became Nalanda's most illustrious foreign student and a favourite student of Śīlabhadra, the Chancellor of the University. After mastering his studies of the various treatises he became the debate champion of India, defeating all challengers in a nation-wide competition.

As a diplomat he stopped conflicts and pacified bandits. Rulers sought his advice in healing disputes and making peace. Always an ambassador, he served as representative of Tang China in places where Chinese had never been, or rarely visited. He returned home with hundreds of scrolls of *sutras* which he proceeded to translate into Chinese with unprecedented accuracy and rigour. As a translator of Buddhist texts he created Chinese versions of favourite *sutras* that are being used to this day.

From beginning to end he was a monk on a mission, informed by dreams and premonitions, guided by Avalokiteśvara and devoted to Maitreya *Bodhisattva*. Master Xuanzang followed an auspicious dream into the unknown, along a route that defeated nine out of ten who attempted it, and completed his mission to bring back the proper *Dharma* from India to China, so that his countrymen could benefit from the Buddha's teaching.

His legacies include contributions in the fields of archaeology, cultural anthropology, history, literature, textual criticism, translation, philosophy and contributions in Buddhist scholarship to *madhyamaka*, *hetuvidyā*, *abhidharma*, *Vinaya*, and Sanskrit philology. Because of him, the practice of Chinese Mahāyāna *Dharma* inherited the scholarly and liturgical traditions of Nalanda University.

He is best known to posterity for his translations of Buddhist texts which remain in general use to the present. His methods of translation were known for their extensive participation, intellectual breadth and rigourous methodology. He established such benchmarks as 'The Five Terms Left Untranslated'. Xuanzang identified five categories of Sanskrit terms that he left in romanized characters, and to which he did not apply Chinese equivalents: 1) Secret, esoteric terms; 2) Terms with multiple meanings; 3) Terms that were unknown locally; 4) Terms that were traditionally not translated; and 5) Terms which sound goodness. These and other translation conventions brought his works lasting renown.

The primary reason for embarking on his perilous journey was to reform the state of Buddhist teachings in China. Master Xuanzang's mission was to find a higher quality, more accurate source of *Dharma*-teachings and to translate them for the Chinese. *Sutras* in China before the Tang dynasty were incomplete or inaccurate, or else their translations contained inconsistencies and wrong interpretations.

Xuanzang vowed to find and translate the Buddha's words and to standardize their interpretations in China. He had seen inaccurate, fragmented partial texts create contention, increase sectarian rivalry, and lead sincere Buddhists astray in their spiritual cultivation. Other monks had begun similar pilgrimages; very few of them returned alive.

He departed from Chang'an in CE 629, with the stigma of fugitive from justice, having violated Imperial law by crossing the border during a national 'security alert' (the Dynasty had been established only recently and travel across insecure borders was restricted). Master Xuanzang cited his allegiance to a higher law, the *Dharma*, and under cover of darkness, snuck past the border posts, braved the arrows of the patrols and headed into the desert beyond the borders of the Tang Empire. He returned in 645 and received a hero's welcome from the Emperor's envoy.

Master Xuanzang replaced the incomplete and inaccurate *sutras* and *śāstras* with original works he personally carried back from India, and translated the Buddha's words.

Ancient wisdom has much to offer contemporary readers and practitioners; Master Xuanzang's quest renew our understanding of the value of the Buddha's wisdom.

33

THE EDUCATIONAL SYSTEM OF NALANDA FROM CHINESE RECORDS

S-C Shiu and H-O Chien

The Nalanda monastery was constructed during the fifth century. Its scale and achievement in academic field was first-rate at that time in the world. Many students from abroad were attracted to Nalanda monastery by its reputation. The famous and outstanding monks Master Xuanzang and Master Yi'jing during the Tang dynasty were among them.

The ninth fascicle of the *Buddhist Records of the Western World* (Datang Xiyu ji, 大唐西域記, 2087), relates as follows:

> The king Śakrāditya 帝日 started to build the Nalanda monastery; after him, there were five kings who constructed it. They were king Budhagupta 覺護, king Tathāgatagupta 如來, king Bālāditya 幻日, king Vajra 金剛. The king Śilāditya 戒日 was the sixth one constructing the Nalanda monastery.

Arriving at Nalanda monastery, Master Xuanzang found that the monastery was divided into eight parts. The courtyards, towers, gardens, buildings were splendid and brilliant, and its scale was enormous, and it was the largest monastery in India. Nalanda monastery was extremely courteous towards learned and eminent monks. Whatever they needed, including food, cloth, residence, sleeping mat, etc., the monastery offered the best to them in order to make them propagate the *Dharma* wholeheartedly. When Xuanzang studied at Nalanda monastery, its style of study stressed both *Mādhyamika* and *Yogācāra*.

The Nalanda monastery followed the teaching ideals of Buddha, and was the largest university in India. It was one of the topmost universities in the world. The monastery got the best facility, faculty, student, and administration. Besides Buddhist philosophy (*adhyātma*), students learned Veda, logic (*Hetu vidyā*), grammar and composition (*śabda*), medicine (*cikitsā*), arts and mathematics (*śilpakarmasthāna*). About 1300 years ago, more than 30,000 students studied in the university which included students from overseas. The famous and outstanding monks Master Xuanzang and Master Yi'jing during the Tang dynasty studied here.

Nalanda monastery, located north of Rājgṛha of the kingdom of Magadha in Bihar province, was the education and research centre in India from fifth century to twelfth century.

I. THE PROCESS OF ESTABLISHING NALANDA MONASTERY

1. The Original Name of Nalanda Monastery

A. The Dragon's Name Called Nalanda

According to the third fascicle of the *Biography of the Tripiṭaka Dharma Master of the Great Ci'en Monastery of the Great Tang Dynasty* (Datang Daci'en Shi Sanzang Fashi Zhuang, 大唐大慈恩寺三藏法師傳, T.2053):

> Nalanda monastery means the monastery of insatiable almsgiving. It was said by old tradition that there was a pond within a mango grove near the south of the monastery, where lived a dragon named so.[1]

B. The Monastery of Insatiable Almsgiving

According to the third fascicle of the *Biography of the Tripiṭaka Dharma Master of the Great Ci'en Monastery of the Great Tang Dynasty* (Datang Daci'en Shi Sanzang Fashi Zhuang, 大唐大慈恩寺三藏法師傳, T.2053):

> When the Tathāgata was practising *bodhisattva* path in one of his former lives, he was a Great king and founded his capital at this place. As he had pity on the poor and the lonely, he often gave them alms; and in memory of his beneficence people called the place 'Insatiability in Almsgiving'.[2]

2. The Process of Building Nalanda Monastery

According to the ninth fascicle of the *Buddhist Records of the Western World* (Datang Xiyu ji, 大唐西域記, T. 2087) by Xuanzang, it follows:

> This place was originally mango grove which five hundred businessmen bought and donated to the Buddha. Buddha delivered the *Dharma* here for three months and many merchants obtained the sainthood. After Buddha had entered *nirvāṇa*, the late king of this kingdom named Śakrāditya who esteemed *Ekayāna* (One Vehicle) and respected the Triple Gem (the Buddha, *Dharma*, and *Saṅgha*), practiced divination for a good place to build the *Saṅghārāma*. When beginning to build the monastery, the dragon's body was injured. At that time, there was a heretic, who was the follower of Nirgrantha, skilled in divination. He prophesied, "This is a place of nature if a *Saṅghārāma* was built here it must be prosperous, and be the model of all monasteries in the five parts of India. One thousand years later, this monastery will be more prosperous. However, although the young students will easily achieve in studying, they will suffer the disease of blood vomit (haemotemesis), because the dragon has been injured."[3]

According to the ninth fascicle of the *Buddhist Records of the Western World* (Datang Xiyu ji, 大唐西域記, T. 2087), it follows:

> The King Śakrāditya 帝日 started to build the Nalanda monastery; after him, there were five kings who constructed it. They were King Budhagupta 覺護, King Tathāgatagupta 如來, King Bālāditya 幻日, and King Vajra 金剛. King Śilāditya 戒日 was the sixth one constructing the Nalanda monastery.[4]

II. The Architectural Design of Nalanda Monastery

1. The Architecture of Nalanda Monastery

Arriving at Nalanda monastery, Xuanzang found that it was divided into eight parts. The courtyards, towers, gardens, buildings were splendid and brilliant, and their scale were enormous. It was the largest monastery in India.

According to the third fascicle of the *Biography of the Tripiṭaka Dharma Master of the Great Ci'en Monastery of the Great Tang Dynasty* (Datang daci'en shi sanzang fashi zhuang, 大唐大慈恩寺三藏法師傳, T.2053), it follows:

> Thus six kings built as many as monasteries one after another, and an enclosure was made with bricks to merge them all into one monastery with one common entrance. There were separate courtyards divided into eight departments. Precious ranged like stars in the sky and jade stored pavilions, spired like lofty peaks, the temples stood high in the mist, and the shrines hovered over the rosy clouds. Breeze and fog rose from the doors and windows, and the sun and moon shone alternately at the eaves of the buildings. Moreover, brooks of clear water meandered through the compounds, with blue lotuses and water lilies growing in them. The flowers of sandalwood trees glowed inside the enclosure, and outside it there was a dense mango grove. All the monks' chambers in the different departments had four storeys. The ridgepoles were carved with little dragons, the beams were painted all the colours of the rainbow, and green beam-supporters constructed with crimson pillars. The frontal columns and railings had ornamental engravings and hollowed out carvings. The plinths were made of jade, and the tips of the rafters were adorned with drawings. The ridges of the roofs stood high in the sunlight, and the eaves were connected with ropes from which hung coloured silk pendants. In India there were thousands of monasteries, but this was the most magnificent and sublime of them all.[5]

When Yi'jing 義淨 reached India, Nalanda monastery was divided into eight big courtyards. According to the fourth fascicle of *A Record of the Inner Law Sent Home from the Southern Seas* (Nanhai jigui neifa zhuan, 南海寄歸內法傳, T.2125) by Yi'jing 義淨, it follows:

> There were numerous persons at Nalanda monastery. There were over three thousands monks, so many people that it was hard to assemble them. Nalanda monastery was divided into eight big courtyards which included three hundred houses. Monks were able to recite the scriptures at any time in any place within the monastery.[6]

2. The Size of the Monks' Rooms at Nalanda Monastery

According to the biography of Hui'chuan 慧輪 in the *Biographies of Eminent Monks Seeking the Dharma in the West During the Great Tang Dynasty* (Datang xiyu qiufa gaosanzang, 大唐西域求法高僧傳, T.2066), it relates that the monks' rooms were all 3 and 1/3 metres wide, each side, at Nalanda monastery.[7]

According to the second fascicle of *A Record of the Inner Law Sent Home from the Southern Seas* (Nanhai jigui neifa zhuan, 南海寄歸內法傳, T.2125), it follows:

> Before summer was coming, the rooms had been distributed to monks in advance. The senior priests had got the good ones; the other monks occupied the rest rooms in sequence. This law was carried out at present at Nalanda monastery. Buddha set up this law which was very useful and benefic. It could get rid of our attachment and widely protect the monks' chambers.[8]

3. The Big Pool for Bathing

In India, people are used to taking bath in a river or pond. There were over ten big ponds being used as bathing place at Nalanda monastery. The third fascicle of *A Record of the Inner Law Sent Home from the Southern Seas* (Nanhai jigui neifa zhuan, 南海寄歸內法傳, T.2125), states as follows:

> There were eight places which had some pools, and Buddha was used to taking baths there. The water there was pure and clear which were different from others. More than ten big ponds were used as bathing place in Nalanda monastery. Whenever in the morning, after the bell was sounded, hundred or thousand monks took their bathing skirt coming to these pools, taking baths at the same time.[9]

4. The Source of Finance

When Xuanzang was studying at Nalanda monastery he said,

> For more than seven hundred years since its establishment, none of the monks had committed any offence. Out of respect for them, the king gave more than a hundred villages for their sustenance. Each village had two hundred families, who daily provided several hundred *dan* 石 of polished non-glutinous rice, butter, and milk. Thus the students could enjoy sufficient supplies of the four requisites without the trouble of going to beg for them. It was because of this effort of their supporters that the scholars could gain achievements in learning.[10]

According to the second fascicle of *A Record of the Inner Law Sent Home from the Southern Seas* (Nanhai jigui neifa zhuan, 南海寄歸內法傳, T.2125), it follows:

> The law was very strict at Nalanda monastery, which made monks over three thousand and the kings of several generation gave more than two hundred villages for their sustenance. If it was not the strict precepts ... none of the monks had committed any offences which made Nalanda monastery able to prosper for a long period, who could do it?[11]

III. The Courteous Treatment of Talents at Nalanda Monastery

Nalanda monastery was extremely courteous towards learned and eminent monks. Whatever they needed, including food, cloth, residence, sleeping mat, Nalanda monastery offered the best to them in order to make them propagate the *Dharma* wholeheartedly.

When studying at Nalanda monastery, Xuanzang was elected as the tenth 'Dharma Master,' who got exceptional treatment. According to the third fascicle of the *Biography of the Tripiṭaka Dharma Master of the Great Ci'en Monastery of the Great Tang Dynasty* (Datang daci'en shi sanzang fashi zhuang, 大唐大慈恩寺三藏法師傳, T.2053), it follows:

> After the conversation, the Master took his leave. He was lodged on the fourth storey of the house of Buddhabhadra 覺賢 in the courtyard of King Bālāditya 幼日. When the seven days' entertainment was over, he was again lodged in the main chamber to the north of the house of Dharmapāla *Bodhisattva* with an increase in provisions. He was provided daily with one tael of borneol incense, and one *sheng* 升 of Mahasaali rice. A grain of this rice was bigger than a black bean, and when cooked it had a fragrance and delicious taste that no other kind of rice possessed of this quality. This kind of non-glutinous rice was produced only in Magadha and was not found elsewhere. As it was supplied only to kings and learned monks of virtue, it was called 'rice supplied to great persons'. He was also given a monthly supply of three *sheng* 升 of oil; and as regards butter and milk, he could take as much as he needed everyday. Master Xuanzang had a servant and a Brāhmaṇa to serve him and was exempted from monastic duties; and when he went out he had an elephant to carry him. Among the ten thousand native and foreign monks of Nalanda monastery, only ten persons, including Xuanzang, got such provisions. Wherever the Master Xuanzang travelled, he was always treated in such a courteous manner.[12]

Nalanda monastery treated the ten eminent monks, including Xuanzang, extremely courteously. Now analyze how Nalanda monastery treated the talents as follows:

1. The Best Rooms for Them

Nalanda monastery provided first-class rooms for the eminent monks. According to the third fascicle of the *Biography of the Tripiṭaka Dharma Master of the Great Ci'en Monastery of the Great Tang Dynasty* (Datang daci'en shi sanzang fashi zhuang, 大唐大慈恩寺三藏法師傳, T.2053),

> Xuanzang was again lodged in the main chamber to the north of the house of Dharmapāla *Bodhisattva* with an increase in provisions.[13]

2. The Best Food and Drink for the Talents

Nalanda monastery also provided best food and drink for the eminent monks. According to the third fascicle of the *Biography of the Tripiṭaka Dharma Master of the Great Ci'en Monastery of the Great Tang Dynasty* (Datang daci'en shi sanzang fashi zhuang, 大唐大慈恩寺三藏法師傳, T.2053),

> Xuanzang was provided daily with one hundred twenty betel leaves, twenty areca nuts, twenty nutmegs, one tael of borneol incense, and one *sheng* 升 of Mahasaali rice. A grain of this rice was bigger than a black bean, and when it was cooked it had a fragrance and delicious taste that no other kind of rice can compare with. This kind of rice was produced only in Magadha and was not found elsewhere. As it was supplied only to kings and learned monks of virtue, it was called 'rice supplied to great persons'. He was also given a monthly supply of three *sheng* 升 of oil; and as regards butter and milk, he took as much as he needed everyday.[14]

3. The Attendants Looking after Them

Nalanda monastery also provided servants for the learned and eminent monks. According to the third fascicle of the *Biography of the Tripiṭaka Dharma Master of the Great Ci'en Monastery of the Great Tang Dynasty* (Datang daci'en shi sanzang fashi zhuang, 大唐大慈恩寺三藏法師傳, T.2053), 'Xuanzang had a servant and a Brāhmaṇa to serve him'.[15]

4. They were Exempted from Monastic Duties

The eminent and learned monks had no duties at Nalanda monastery. According to the third fascicle of the *Biography of the Tripiṭaka Dharma Master of the Great Ci'en Monastery of the Great Tang Dynasty* (Datang daci'en shi sanzang fashi zhuang, 大唐大慈恩寺三藏法師傳, T.2053), 'Xuanzang was exempted from monastic duties'.[16]

5. Going Out in Sedan Chairs on Elephants

Nalanda monastery provided elephants for talented monks. According to the third fascicle of the *Biography of the Tripiṭaka Dharma Master of the Great Ci'en Monastery of the Great Tang Dynasty* (Datang daci'en shi sanzang fashi zhuang, 大唐大慈恩寺三藏法師傳, T.2053), it states as follow:

> When Xuanzang went out he had an elephant to carry him. Among the ten thousand native and foreign monks of Nalanda monastery, only ten persons, including Xuanzang, enjoyed such provisions. Wherever the Master travelled, he was always treated in such a courteous manner.[17]

The first fascicle of *A Record of the Inner Law Sent Home from the Southern Seas* (Nanhai jigui neifa zhuan, 南海寄歸內法傳, T.2125), describes as follows:

> The virtuous and learned monks at Nalanda monastery were provided sedan chairs on elephant. Nobody rode horse or elephant directly. All their belongings were carried by servants, or a young boy dispatched to hold it. These were the manners to treat eminent monks in India.[18]

IV. The System of Education in Nalanda Monastery

1. Equally Emphasizing the Doctrines of both Mādhyamika and Yogācāra

When Xuanzang studied at Nalanda monastery, its style of study stressed both *Mādhyamika* and *Yogācāra*. He listened to the lectures by Śīlabhadra on the *Yogācāryabhūmi-śāstra* (瑜珈師地論, T.

1579) for three times. At the same time, he also listened the *Mādhyamika-śāstra* (Zhong lun, 中論) and the *Śata-śastra* (Bai lun, 百論) three times each. Thus we can see that there was nothing high or low between them.

Lu Cheng 呂澂 in his work *The Five Sciences of Buddhism Propagated by Xuanzang and Yi'Jing* (奘淨兩師所傳的五科佛學) records that:

> Xuanzang and Yi'jing both had profound research in this two areas because at that time the style of study at Nalanda monastery stressed both *Mādhyamika* and *Yogācāra*, and both of them had studied there before coming back to China. Xuanzang listened the lectures by Śīlabhadra on the *Yogācārabhūmi-śāstra* (瑜珈師地論, T. 1579) for three times. At the same time, he also listened the *Mādhyamika-śāstra* (Zhong lun, 中論), and the *Śata-śāstra* (Bai lun, 百論) three times each.

Thus we can see that Xuanzang did not differentiate between them whether they were high or low. Afterwards, Xuanzang reached the South to study 'Jing bai lun' (經百論) and 'The Śataśāstravaipulya' (Guang bai lun, 廣百論) and probed its profound meaning. As regards Yi'jing, he studied under Bao shi zi (寶師子) at Nalanda monastery, listened the *Yogācārabhūmi-śāstra* (瑜珈師地論, T. 1579), and under Sheng guang (勝光) he also listened the *Mādhyamika-śāstra* (Zhong lun, 中論) and the *Śata-śāstra* (Bai lun, 百論). He also studied under some learned and virtuous monks' instruction; so he understood both the doctrines of *Mādhyamika* and *Yogācāra*.[19]

2. The Five Sciences: Logic, Abhidharma, Disciplines, Mādhyamika and Yogācāra

After the fifth century, since the great masters Cheng'na 陳那, Dharmapāla 護法, Dharmakīrti 法稱, Guṇamati 德慧, Sthiramati 安慧, and Hui'ju 慧護 appeared one after another, the scope of education was broad and profound at Nalanda monastery. The teachings had been divided into several academic subjects.[20]

Under the instruction of Śīlabhadra at Nalanda monastery, the subjects of Xuanzang's study were as follows:

> All these holy sites the Master visited and worshipped all around. It was not until returning to Nalanda that the Master asked the Dharma Master Śilabhadra to expound the *Yogācārabhūmi-śāstra* (Yu qie shi di lun, 瑜珈師地論). Several thousand men attended the lectures together with him.
>
> In this monastery Xuanzang listened to the exposition of the *Yogācārabhūmi-śāstra* (Yu qie shi di lun, 瑜珈師地論) three times; to that of *Ñyāyānusāra-śāstra* (Shun zhen li lun, 順正理論), the *Prakaraṇāryavāca-śāstra* (Xian yang sheng jiao lun, 顯揚聖教論), the *Abhidharmasamudaya Prakaraṇa* (Duei fa, 對法), one time each; to that of the *Hetuvidyā-śāstra* (Yin ming, 因明), the *Śabdaviidyā-śāstra* (Sheng ming, 聲明), the *Samuccayapramāṇa-śāstra* (Duei fa, 對法), etc. two times each; as well as to that of the *Mādhyamika-śāstra* (Zhong lun, 中論), and the *Śata-śāstra* (Bai lun, 百論) three times each. As regards the *Abhidharmakośa-śāstra* (Ju she lun, 俱舍論), the *Vibhāṣā-śāstra* (婆沙論), the *Jñānaprasthānaṣatpadābhidharma* (六足阿毗曇), etc. which he had already studied in Kashmir and other countries, he merely read through them and clarified dubious points he had found previously. He also studied Brāhmaṇic books at the same time.[21]

3. The Subject of Concentration (Adhicitta 定學)

When studying at Nalanda monastery, Yi'jing 義淨 practised concentration (*adhicitta*, 定學) which belonged to *Yogācāra* school. Lu Cheng 呂澂 points out in his work *Discussion on Practicing Concentration in Six Subjects* (六門教授習定論), that:

When Yi'jing 義淨 studied at Nalanda monastery, at that time the teachings of Aśvaghoṣa were flourishing. The works concerning Concentration were Aśvaghoṣa's *Ben lun* 本論 and Vasubandhu's *The Work on Discussion on Praising Śamatha and Vipassanā.*[22]

4. *Kālacakra-tantra* (時輪金剛)

Yin Shun 印順 indicates that:

> Vairocana is the original Buddha. As time went on, it developed to the summit which was the *Kālacakra-tantra*. During the regime of King Mahīpāla (840-899), Virūpā began to propagate the *Kālacakra-tantra.*[23]

Yin Shun 印順 indicated that at that time, there were some words pasted on the entrance of the Nalanda monastery which described as follows:

> Those who do not know the original Buddha also do not understand the doctrine of *Kālacakra-tantra*; those who do not understand the doctrine of *Kālacakra-tantra* also do not realize what are the correct teachings; those who do not realize what are the correct teachings also do not know the *Prajñā-kāya* of Vajradhara; those who do not know the *Prajñā-kāya* of Vajradhara also do not understand the doctrine of *Mantra* school; those who do not understand the doctrine of *Mantra* school are ignorant and kept away from the path of Vajradhara of the Buddha.[24]

Nalanda monastery originally was the centre of *Yogācāra* school. Later it became the centre of esoteric Buddhism.

5. *The Heretical Texts* (外道之學)

Nalanda monastery was the biggest temple in India. There were always over ten thousand monks in it. They studied both Mahāyāna – the Great Vehicle – and Hīnayāna – the Lesser Vehicle, and even heretical texts, for instance Veda, logic (*hetu*), grammar (*śabda*), medicine (*cikitsā*), arts and mathematics (*śilpakarmasthāna*) and so on. They profoundly studied all of them.

According to the third fascicle of the *Biography of the Tripiṭaka Dharma Master of the Great Ci'en Monastery of the Great Tang Dynasty* (Datang daci'en shi sanzang fashi zhuang, 大唐大慈恩寺三藏法師傳, T.2053):

> In India there were thousands of monasteries, but this was the most magnificent and sublime of all. Ten thousand monks always lived there, including hosts and guests. They studied Mahāyāna teachings and the doctrines of eighteen schools, as well as worldly books such as the Vedas. They also learned about works on logic (*hetu*), grammar (*śabda*), medicine (*cikitsā*), arts and mathematics (*śilpakarmasthāna*).[25]

V. The Organizational Operation at Nalanda Monastery

Since there were thousands of monks living together at Nalanda monastery the regulations were necessary. The process of change and development, scope, and the style of study had great influences in the history of Buddhist education. Even if there are only vestiges left at present, we still are able to know its sights by means of the record of some texts.

1. *Lectures on the Buddhist Texts at Nalanda Monastery*

When Xuanzang was studying at Nalanda monastery or after he returned to China, the scriptures of Buddhism were expounded in some big temples everyday – no matter whether they were Mahāyāna or Hīnayāna texts. They gave lectures on how to practice the teachings of Buddhism and disciplines. At that time, Buddhism was in full flourish.[26]

2. Debating

According to the system of Nalanda monastery, it was not all scholars who were able to debate in public but that there were only few learned monks having such qualifications. Both Xuanzang and Yi'jing had studied at Nalanda monastery; they recorded circumstances of Nalanda monastery, for example the big courtyards, lodgings, shrines, *stūpa* and its organization. They mentioned that three thousand monks lived there and it had two hundred farmsteads. Yi'jing drew a sketch attached in the *Biographies of Eminent Monks Seeking the Dharma in the West During the Great Tang Dynasty* (Datang xiyu qiufa gaosanzang, 大唐西域求法高僧傳, T. 2066) which was lost.[27]

3. Evaluating the Scholars

According to the third fascicle of the *Biography of the Tripiṭaka Dharma Master of the Great Ci'en Monastery of the Great Tang Dynasty* (Datang daci'en shi sanzang fashi zhuang, 大唐大慈恩寺三藏法師傳, T.2053), it follows:

> Those who could understand twenty scriptures and commentaries amounted to over a thousand persons. More than five hundred persons had mastered thirty works, while ten persons, including Xuanzang, were experts on fifty works.[28]

Thus we can see that there was a system relating to how to appraise a person's learning and knowledge.

At that time, among thousand monks the outstanding talents were able to enjoy the best offerings and exemption from the monastic duties. The monastery provided a servant to look after them, and they were able to ride an elephant when going out. Their food was better than others. At that period, Xuanzang was one of the ten learned and outstanding monks.

4. The System of Three Administrators

According to the *Biographies of Eminent Monks Seeking the Dharma in the West During the Great Tang Dynasty* (Datang xiyu qiufa gaosanzang, 大唐西域求法高僧傳, T.2066), it relates that:

> Nalanda monastery established the system of having three main administrators who were Sthavira, the abbot and the chief administrator - *Karma-dāna*.[29] They led and gave orders to the priests and maintained regulations at Nalanda monastery. These three professional titles came from India. Setting up these three professional titles was very useful for managing affairs of big monasteries with dozens or hundreds of monks. However, it was not every monastery having these three professional titles. Sthavira was the senior and virtuous *Bhikṣu*; *Vihāra-svāmin* – the abbot – was in charge of constructing and managing the monastery; and the chief administrator – *Karma-dāna* – also translated as *cidi* 次第, *shou'shi* 授事 and *yue'zhong* 悅衆. His duty was to manage affairs of monastery in accordance with its regulations.[30]

Some European scholars investigated Nalanda monastery that was based on Xuanzang's records and Buddha statues as well as inscriptions excavated near Nalanda monastery in 1861. After 1915, the Archaeological Survey of India continued to excavate the cultural and historical relics at the ruins of Nalanda. They found the ruins of Nalanda monastery over one million square metres. The cultural and historical relics unearthed from the ruins of Nalanda monastery included the Buddha statues, seals, shrines and pagoda and so on, the amount of which were plenty. At present they are kept in the museum in the proximity of it. After India's independence, the Archaeological Department of India is devoted to the preservation of the historical remains and the beautification of environment.

The government of Bihar constructed a new Nalanda monastery in the south-east of the ruins that attracts scholars from Asia. They assemble together discussing the extensive teachings of Buddhism.[31]

CHINESE SOURCES

Primary Sources

Datang daci'en shi sanzang fashi zhuang, 大唐大慈恩寺三藏法師傳 (*Biography of the Tripiṭaka Dharma Master of the Great Ci'en Monastery of the Great Tang Dynasty*), T.2053, V.50.

Datang Xiyu ji, 大唐西域記 (*The Buddhist Records of the Western World*) by Xuanzang, , T.2087, V.51.

Datang xiyu qiufa gaosanzang, 大唐西域求法高僧傳 (*The Biographies of Eminent Monks Seeking the Dharma in the West During the Great Tang Dynasty*), T. 2066, V.51.

Nanhai jigui neifa zhuan, 南海寄歸內法傳 (*A Record of the Inner Law Sent Home from the Southern Seas*) by Yi'jing, 義淨, T.2125, V.54.

Secondary Sources

Lu Cheng 呂澂 in his work *The Five Sciences of Buddhism Propagated by Xuanzang and Yi'jing* (奘淨兩師所傳的五科佛學).

Lu Cheng 呂澂 points out in his work *Discussion on Practicing Concentration in Six Subjects* (六門教授習定論).

Yin Shun 印順, *The History of Buddhist Thought in India* (印度佛教思想史), Taipei: Zhen wen chu ban she 正聞出版社, 1992.

Yin shun 印順, *The Lectures on the Verses of Drumajñārarājaparipṛcchā* (華雨集・大樹緊那羅王所問經偈頌講記), Volume 1, Taipei: Zhen wen chu ban she 正聞出版社, 1993.

Zhong hui fojiao baike qiansh, 中華佛教百科全書 *The Encyclopedia of Chinese Buddhism*, supervised by Master Kai'zhen 開證, 1994.

NOTES AND REFERENCES

1. T. 2053, V. 50, p. 237b. All references of Chinese canonical texts are those of the Taisho edition. Through this work the abbreviation 'T', is used to indicate the Taisho *shinshu daizokyo* .大正新修大藏經 edited by Takakusu Junjiro 高楠順次郎 and Watanabe Kaigyoku 渡邊海旭, Tokyo: Taisho Issaikyo Kankai, 1924-1932.
2. T. 2053, V. 50, p. 237b.
3. T. 2087, V. 51, p. 923b.
4. T. 2087, V. 51, p. 923b-c.
5. T. 2053, V. 50, p. 237b.
6. T. 2125, V. 54, p. 227a.
7. Zhong hui fojiao baike qiansh, 中華佛教百科全書 *The Encyclopedia of Chinese Buddhism*, supervised by Master Kai'zhen 開證, 1994, p. 1361b.
8. T. 2125, V. 54, p. 217b.
9. T. 2125, V. 54, p. 220c.
10. The third fascicle of the *Biography of the Tripiṭaka Dharma Master of the Great Ci'en Monastery of the Great Tang Dynasty*, Datang daci'en shi sanzang fashi zhuang, 大唐大慈恩寺三藏法師傳, T. 2053, V. 50, p. 237c., and see Zhong hui fojiao baike qiansh, 中華佛教百科全書 *The Encyclopedia of Chinese Buddhism*, p. 2649b.
11. T. 2053, V. 50, p. 214a.

12. T. 2053, V. 50, p. 237a-b.
13. T. 2053, V. 50, p. 237a-b.
14. T. 2053, V. 50, p. 237a.
15. T. 2053, V. 50, p. 237a.
16. T. 2053, V. 50, p. 237a
17. T. 2053, V. 50, p. 237a.
18. T. 2125, V. 54, p. 208a.
19. Lu Cheng 呂澂 in his work *The Five Sciences of Buddhism Propagated by Xuanzang and Yi'jing* (奘淨兩師所傳的五科佛學), Volume 3, p. 1386-1387.
20. Lu Cheng 呂澂 in his work *The Five Sciences of Buddhism Propagated by Xuanzang and Yi'jing* (奘淨兩師所傳的五科佛學), Volume 3, pp. 1381.
21. T. 2053, V. 50, pp. 238c-239a.
22. Lu Cheng 呂澂 points out in his work *Discussion on Practicing Concentration in Six Subjects*, 六門教授習定論, Volume 2, p. 1068.
23. Yin Shun 印順, *The History of Buddhist Thought in India* (印度佛教思想史), p. 410.
24. Yin Shun 印順 *The History of Buddhist Thought in India* (印度佛教思想史), pp. 410-411.
25. T. 2053, V. 50, p. 237b. *pañca-vidyā*, the five sciences or studies of India: (1) *śabda* 聲明, grammar and composition; (2) *śilpakarmasthāna* 工巧明, the arts and mathematics; (3) *cikitsā* 醫方明, medicine; (4) *hetu* 因明, logic; (5) *adhyātma* 內明, philosophy, which Monier Williams says is the 'knowledge of the supreme spirit, or of *ātman*, the basis of the four Vedas; the Buddhists reckon the *Tripiṭaka* and the 十二部教 as their 內明, i.e., their inner or special philosophy (Tib. *rig gnas che ba lnga*).
26. Yin shun 印順, *The Lectures on the Verses of Drumakijnararajapariprccha* (華雨集・大樹緊那羅王所問經偈頌講記), Volume 1, p. 72-73.
27. Lu Cheng 呂澂 in his work *The Five Sciences of Buddhism Propagated by Xuanzang and Yi'jing* (奘淨兩師所傳的五科佛學), Volume 2, p. 759.
28. T. 2053, V. 50, p. 237b.
29. T. 2066, V. 51, p. 5c-6a.
30. Zhong hui fojiao baike qiansh, 中華佛教百科全書, *The Encyclopedia of Chinese Buddhism*, p. 402.
31. Zhong hui fojiao baike qiansh, 中華佛教百科全書, *The Encyclopedia of Chinese Buddhism*, p. 1603b.

34

GENJO-SANZO E: THE BIOGRAPHICAL STORY OF HSÜAN-CHUANG IN JAPAN

Yayoi Tachibana

I

Genjo-sanzo E (twelve volumes) is a biographical story of Hsüan-chuang. Originally, this scroll was handed down to the Daijo-in monastery of the Kofukuji temple in Nara. It is one of the designated 'important cultural treasures', belonging to the Fujita Art Gallery in Osaka now. In the 16th century the biographical story was recorded as *Genjo-sanzo E*, though since the 18th century it has been called *Hossoshu Hiji Ekotoba*. It is considered more appropriate to call it 'Genjo-sanzo E'. Hsüan-chuang went to India and there he studied the doctrines of Mahāyāna and Hīnāyana. His special stress was on the study of Yuisiki Theory. After going over to China, he began to spread the theory abroad. A sect named 'Hosso-shu' came to be formed by Hsüan-chuang and his pupil Kiki. The Kofukuji temple in Nara has come down as the head cathedral of 'Hosso-shu' introduced by Japanese priests who learned the theory from Kiki in China.

II

The whole scroll is the portrayal of the life of Hsüan-chuang, according to the diary written in 1457 by Bishop Jinson, the principal of the Kofukuji temple. *Genjo-sanzo E* was accomplished at the beginning of the Kamakura era when in the Kofukuji temple, Bishop Shin-en, the brother of Fujiwara Kanezane who then possessed the greatest political and lineal power, was wielding dominating influence. It can be imagined the style of the scroll was similar to that of *Shigisan Engi Emaki*. At the Daijo-in monastery of the Kofukuji temple, *Genjo-sanzo E* was handed down as the secret treasure of Hosso-shu and it is quite evident that they existed there in that era. Then, according to Fujiwara Sanetaka's diary in 1488, another *Genjo-sanzo E* drawn by Takashina Takakane, existed at the same place, i.e., the Daijo-in monastery of the Kofukuji temple. Takakane is the painter of *Kasuga Gongen Genji E* (20 volumes) perfectly kept as one of the royal property. The catalogue belonging to this scroll makes it clear that in 1308, at the end of the Kamakura era, the scroll was dedicated by Saionji Kinhira, an important family of Fujiwara. When we compare this *Kasuga Gongen Gengi E* with *Genjo-sanzo E* of the Fujita Art Gallery, we can see the complete concurrence of style between these two scrolls, and can believe that *Genjo-sanzo E* is the very thing that Sanetaka mentions in his diary. The old text of *Genjo-sanzo E* drawn at the beginning of the Kamakura era does not exist today. The present *Genjo-sanzo E* is undoubtedly based upon the words of the original text and the pictures may have some relation to the original ones; yet, in connection with the style of painting, there is no doubt that it is Takakane's style. In the Kamakura era the reproduced scroll was not a mere copy as the imitation of the original work, but really a free copy. The artist made the copy in the style and technique completely of his own, so that the copy, by itself, looked as if it was the original work. This *Genjo-sanzo E* was not an exception.

Takashina Takakane was *Edokoro Azukari* (the Principal of the Royal Painting Studio). The painters of the studio in obedience to the various demands of court, offered themselves in drawing on screens and fans, and in working up scrolls and various ornamental designs. Their style was academic, minute, refined and graceful. It is remarkable the scroll is typical of the style of Edokoro painters.

III

During that era, people knew not about geography and custom of the nations beyond China. Probably in the painter's mind, the geographical facts and custom formed a single image – 'a strange land'. Therefore, the buildings and dress portrayed in his pictures are of Chinese style, because China was the only foreign country he knew of. Of course, even these images were no more than the images the painter drew in his mind, referring to the imperfect pictures introduced from China. Plants and animals in the scroll were changed, the shape of those in Japan, into more imaginary ones. At first sight we feel as if we were looking at the nature of our own country. As for the portrayal of the landscape for background, he chose pine tree, Japanese cedar, willow, bamboo and such autumn plants as fuji-bakama and pampas grass. All of these were the elemental materials for Japanese landscape.

IV

The active era of the painter of this scroll can be regarded as the era between 1308 (year of the accomplishment of 'Kasuga Gongen Genki Emaki') and 1330 (year of the accomplishment of the copy of certain scroll). It is considered that *Genjo-sanzo E* appeared immediately after the accomplishment of 'Kasuga Gongen Genki Emaki'. The Kasuga Shrine was under the government of the Kofukuji temple and the erection of these two was due to the Fujiwara's faith in Buddhism. Although 'Kasuga Gongen Genki Emaki' is drawn on silk and *Genjo-sanzo E* is on paper, both scrolls are quite common in size and in binding; thus, they can be regarded as 'sister scrolls'.

V

Explanation of Plates (Pl. 6)

Hsüan-chụang listens to Master Śīlabhadra's lecture on the *Yogācārabhūmi-śāstra* at the Nalanda monastery (Section 6 of 6th scroll).

Śīlabhadra was a high priest at the Nalanda monastery and was reportedly one hundred and six years old at the time Hsüan-chụang studied the *Yogācārabhūmi-śāstra* under him. This section illustrates the scene of Śilabhadra's sermon with the addition of the story about the Brāhmaṇa – Śīlabhadra, seated on a chair at the centre with an abbot's rule in his hands, and giving his lecture. On his right sitting on a low seat, Hsüan-chụang is listening to him. Others present there are looking at them. Inside the building are priests, kings and princes seated surrounding Śīlabhadra, while numerous people sit outside. All men and women are portrayed vividly each with different expression and clothing. Even the patterns on their clothing being described in details. Focused on the main subject of the scene, clouds cover the upper and lower borders of the painting. Compositions of this kind, together with precise depiction of detailed parts, are among the characteristics of this painting.

35

THE IDEAL EDUCATIONAL SYSTEM OF ANCIENT NALANDA MAHĀVIHĀRA

Angraj Chaudhary

When we were children we were taught by our elders to observe precepts like not telling a lie, not to steal and not to do other sinful acts. As we grew up we understood more clearly and comprehensively what sinful acts included. We were also told that if we indulged in such immoral acts we would suffer endlessly in hell. What had great impact on us were the visuals over the doors of houses which graphically depicted horrible punishments given to those who committed such acts. We were so much afraid to see such visuals that our hair would stand on their ends and we would make up our minds to shirk from committing such actions.

Times have changed now. Neither do we have such fear-producing visuals over our doors nor do we as easily believe in Yama's messengers giving punishments for sinful acts. We don't have faith in such things. They have become anachronistic. We are now proud to have a rational outlook.

People think why should they believe in such injunctions when they see people around them doing all sorts of immoral actions and living a comfortable life with pelf and power. They have a conflict within. Should they remain honest and poor or should they make money by hook or by crook and live a life of luxury, wearing good clothes, eating sumptuous food and giving good and expensive education to their children? All fear of suffering in the hell is gone. They have become fearless.

It is this crisis of faith that prompts young men and women who make up the top cadres of society such as bureaucrats, doctors, engineers, managers and politicians to amass wealth by any means. They conveniently forget their primary duty to serve society in their different capacities and make people live better. Seeing this tragic phenomenon in human life on a mass scale, Erich Fromm[1] gives a sane advice not to neglect the 'to be' aspect of life and replace it by the 'to have' aspect of it.

The important question is how to develop the 'to be' aspect of life in the present time when there is a crisis of faith. The 'to be' aspect of life can be developed through education.

To educate means 'to bring up (a child) so as to form habits, manners, etc., to train intellectually and morally.' Developing qualities like *metta* (loving kindness), *karuṇā* (compassion), *muditā* (sympathetic joy), and *upekkhā* (equanimity), he must get rid of defilements such as greed, anger, pride and develop qualities such as non-greed, friendliness, humility, compassion, etc.

He must shun selfishness and develop altruism. Mahatma Gandhi rightly said that intellectual development without the simultaneous development of our conscience and heart is very sad and dangerous. Sad because our noble qualities are not developed and dangerous because we may create Frankensteins and take the world near a catastrophe. Einstein knew what a cataclysmic catastrophe the atom bomb was going to cause to humanity. He therefore wrote a letter requesting the American President not to press for making the atom bomb. Learning a lesson from what a great disaster the dropping of an atom bomb could bring to humanity, the scientist who made the hydrogen bomb said very feelingly in the meeting arranged for honouring him as the father of the hydrogen bomb, 'Do not call me the father of the hydrogen bomb. I am the father of two children.'

For developing these qualities a course of systematic instruction to develop character must form part of an educational curriculum. Tagore says that some kind of idealism has to find a place in our educational system. Then only the young men and women trained in this system will not be swayed away by the temptation of material self-seeking and material well-being. They will definitely go in for spiritual well-being. Further he says,

> The time has now come when humanity can only be saved by the awakening of a new faith. For this, the one thing that is needed most of all is to make a place in our education for some great idealism. The principle of material self-seeking which pervades the atmosphere today can never give us new life. It carries with it unchecked passion which, as it burns itself out exhausts vitality and brings its own doom.

What education should do has been brought out by Abraham Lincoln. He wrote to the teacher of his son that the education imparted to him should be such as to make him a citizen of good character. Such qualities should be instilled in him as would enable him to give more importance to the one buck that he earns by honest means than the five bucks he earns by dishonest means. He should also be taught to smile in moments of misery and show his sympathy to the miserable.

The educational system that we have today does not deliver the goods. It produces bureaucrats who have the power to run the government of the country but do not have the heart to show compassion to the people who need it most. Instead of working for the people's welfare they think only of their own welfare and are often involved in scams.

There were many causes why Nalanda Mahāvihāra became a famous centre of quality education which developed the character of its alumni. They were not only intelligent but they were men of character whose hearts were full of loving kindness for all and compassion for the poor and afflicted. It is true that students had to pass through a hard test before they were admitted. The tutorial system and the discussion methods adopted here went a long way to sharpen their intelligence and made them alert and quick-witted to think of new points to take the rival by the horns.

The Buddha has shown the path for character building and purifying oneself. The observation of precepts enables a man to concentrate his mind. When his mind is concentrated he is able to see the real nature of the things of the world and develop wisdom.

The professors of Nalanda Mahāvihāra understood the importance of walking on the 'eight-fold path' in order to drive out the defilements of the mind and purify it – the mind which is the spring of all actions. Walking on the eight-fold path was uppermost in their minds. They themselves walked and taught and inspired their students to walk on this path. They understood it very well that cluttering one's mind with a lot of information and not living a moral and ethical life is like becoming a cowherd who counts the cows of his master but does not and cannot drink their milk.[2] The educational system of Nalanda Mahāvihāra prepared every alumnus to keep cows and drink their milk.

Apart from other secular subjects the main subject of study at Nalanda Mahāvihāra was the Buddha's philosophy. The philosophy that the Buddha propounded was based on his experience. He experienced that suffering is caused by desires. He also directly realized how desires can be extirpated. He discovered the path, walked on it and taught others to walk on it and end their sufferings. Here is a combination of philosophy, ethics and religion.

Such a person, shorn of desires and filled with the four *brahmavihāra*s, will be a good person thinking not only good of others but also doing good to others.

One may say that it was possible for Nalanda Mahāvihāra to impart such an ideal education to the students there because all students were monks. They had:

> no care about food, lodging and clothing which were supplied to them *gratis*. In fact the monks had hardly any secular care and their whole endeavour was given to intellectual and spiritual improvement.

Their primary duty was to walk on the eight-fold path and observe *sīla*, *samādhi* and *paññā*. And even though in later centuries strangers were admitted, they also emulated the monk alumni who far outnumbered them and lived like *brahmacārin*s and cultivated the higher moral values of life.

When we think of Nalanda we feel proud of its heritage in respect of the educational system which gave importance to both *pariyatti* (theory) and *paṭipatti* (practice). It took great care for the development of character of students. This is what we need in modern times. We need our students to develop their character and be good human beings. A man of good character will develop wisdom and know how to make the best use of the wealth he has, but a wealthy man without a good character will waste it. A man of character is sure to make good use of his intelligence so that Frankeinsteins are not produced by him and all his efforts and intelligence will be put to the use of bringing benefits to mankind. He will not be selfish but he will always think of doing good to others. A moral and ethical training is sure to bring about such a change in him.

The syllabus that we follow in modern times does not take care of developing our character. Our moral growth is stunted. Our educational institutions produce students who have agile and brilliant minds but who have not developed the capacity to exercise restraint on their growing greed and power. They have not learned to realize the importance of non-attachment to the things of the world.

It is time now we adopted the syllabus followed at Nalanda between the 5th and 12th centuries. Education imparted in the light of this syllabus produced balanced persons.

One may argue that the syllabus followed at Nalanda will be anachronistic for us in modern times. But this is not true. It was not the monopoly of the monk students of Nalanda to follow that syllabus but we can also follow it to lay the foundation of moral development in our students. Is it necessary only for monks to develop their character? Isn't it equally necessary for us to develop it? The answer is it is more necessary for us to develop it, because we are more exposed to temptations than those monks at Nalanda were. We need to fortify ourselves.

I do not know how practical training was given to the monks at Nalanda to develop their character. But one thing is sure. They followed the teachings of the Buddha and for sure they

walked on the eight-fold path developing *sīla*, *samādhi* and *paññā*. I give here a relevant observation made by Xuanzang.

> In the establishment were some thousands of Brethren, all men of great ability and learning, several hundreds being highly esteemed and famous; the Brethren were very strict in observing the precepts and regulations of their Order; they were looked up to as models by all India; learning and discussing they found the day too short; day and night they admonished each other, juniors and seniors mutually helping to perfection.[3]

What is necessary for building men's character has been pointed out by Socrates. He asks the judges to reprove his sons if they "seem to care about riches, or anything, more than about virtue; or if they pretend to be something when they are really nothing."[4]

We do not know whether the alumni of Nalanda University practised *vipassanā*, but it is on record that they observed precepts strictly and cared more about virtue than about riches.

The teachings of the Buddha have nothing sectarian in them. They are based on universal laws. If you have cravings misery will multiply. But if you see where and how they arise you will be able to root them out.

Today, we are more fortunate and better equipped to lay the moral foundation of our students. If we teach them the technique of *vipassanā* meditation and inspire them to practise it, it is sure to have its salubrious effect on them. It is a technique of meditation to look within.

If this technique of meditation is taught to our students (and its foundation can be laid while they are at school), they will learn to see why they should observe moral precepts. And observing moral precepts is sure to bring about a qualitative change in their life inasmuch as they will develop moral character.

The educational system at Nalanda did not also lose sight of the physical development of students, i.e., did not neglect their health because only healthy persons free from physical ailments can practise *vipassanā*.

This heritage of Nalanda in respect of its educational curriculum can salvage us out of a great crisis of culture that we are passing through.

NOTES AND REFERENCES

1. Erich Fromm, *Psychoanalysis and Zen Buddhism*.
2. *Bahum pi ce sahitaṁ bhāsamāno, na takkaro hoti naro pamatto/*
   Gopova gāvo gaṇayaṁ paresāṁ, na bhagavā samanassa hoti//
   Dhammapada, 19
3. S. Beal (Trans.), *Travel Accounts of Hiuen Tsang*.
4. B. Jowett and S. Beal (trans.), *The Dialogues of Plato*, Vol. I, Random House, New York, 1937, p. 423.

36

NALANDA AS AN INTERNATIONAL CENTRE OF LEARNING

J. Sitaramamma

The scope of education is extensive with the varied interests of human life. In its wider sense education may be described as a creative process of progressive development of individual and social life.

With regard to the ideals of education, there has never been a perfect unanimity among educational thinkers. And this is not to be wondered at, for the educational ideals are correlative to the ideals of life. And so long there is divergence of ideals of life, so long will there be divergence of educational ideals.

Developed educational institutions existed in ancient and medieval times in India. Buddhism had educational institutions which played an important role as centres of learning and training for the monks and dissemination of knowledge among the laity. The system of Buddhist education had some specific characteristics, some of which are of relevance to present times.

This paper highlights some of the unique and contemporary relevant characteristics of Buddhist educational system. They are briefly:

1. Open access of education for men and women of all classes;
2. Emergence of large educational centres of learning;
3. Learning imparted to laity as well as monks; and
4. Teaching in the language used by the people instead of the elite language of Sanskrit.

In today's world there is a hue and cry over cultural value, moral value and the value education of children in schools which is geared to make the younger generation of today a better citizen of tomorrow. All parents and policy-maker educationists are greatly concerned over this crucial issue. As biodeterioration is one of the major causes of deterioration of cultural property so is mind-degradation. While extensive studies have been done in the area of biodeterioration, no study has begun on mind-degradation. Conservation and preservation of cultural property is important for the future generation but mind-degradation study is as important as that of biodeterioration study. The latter has gained a greater momentum all over the world with the establishment of research institutes and laboratories. An in-depth study needs to be done on the development of human brain and human behaviour at different stages with the influence of major disciplines in general and moral values drawn from different religious faiths in particular.

After synthesizing major disciplines and moral values, a proper mechanism should be devised which can be applied to control the mind.

The entire system of Buddhist education must be rooted in faith (*saddhā*), faith in the Triple Gem, and above all, in the Buddha as the fully Enlightened One, the peerless teacher and supreme guide to right living and right understanding. Based on this faith students must be inspired to become accomplished in virtue (*sīla*) by following the moral guidelines of the five precepts. These precepts represent kindness, honesty, purity, truthfulness, and sobriety. They must also acquire the spirit of generosity and self-sacrifice, so essential for overcoming selfishness, greed, and the narrow focus on self-advancement that dominates our present-day society. Our true welfare is to be achieved through harmony and good will.

The Buddhist system of education is formulation of the Buddhist Saṅgha. The rules that we find in Buddhist education 'are not the invention of the Buddha but modelled upon those of numerous monastic orders professing other faiths, Brāhmaṇism itself'. In spite of this Buddhist system exhibited distinctiveness. For instance, the Brāhmaṇical education was based on individual teacher. It was imparted in the preceptor's residence, and was confined to Brāhmaṇas and people of upper castes. The consideration of caste was thus the main criterion for admission of students.

BUDDHIST CONTRIBUTION TO EDUCATION

The education imparted in Buddhist universities of this period was broadly divided into four types.

1. Spiritual Education
2. Moral Education
3. Literacy Education
4. Technical Education

Spiritual Education

Instruction on Buddha's teachings, Buddhist philosophical doctrines, and the essentials of spiritual progress were imparted under this category of spiritual education. Besides this theoretical aspect of spiritualism, practical ways and means of truth-realization, yogic practices (*yoga-caryā*), mystical trances (*dhyāna* and *samādhi*), mastery over the body and the mind and attainment of gnostic powers, must have occupied much time of the Buddhist masters and sages in their daily life. Scriptural study became an aid in spiritual education and self-cultivation.

Moral Education

Moral lessons were of primary importance. The notices of foreign accounts and inscriptions of the time reveal that the monks and scholars maintained high moral conduct and ethical excellence. It was in the monastic colleges that Buddhist and non-Buddhist students learnt rules of purity, cleanliness, proper food, etiquette of salutation, respect for all forms of life and obedience to elders and so forth. Practice of five moral precepts may be taken to have been the first moral lesson taught to the students.

Literacy Education

Monastic education and general literacy had progressed considerably during this age. Reading and writing, study of the *Vinaya* books, especially of the *prātimokṣa* and general knowledge of the *Tripiṭaka* and Sanskrit grammar seem to have been the compulsory subjects of a monk's preliminary education.

Technical Education

Technical education with special reference to Buddhist art – architecture, sculpture and painting – seems to have been a part of education for inscriptions of the time refer to local artists of Nalanda. The inclusion of *Śilpasthāna vidyā* in the list of studies also points to this fact. An inscription found from Nalanda describes monks of that *Mahāvihāra* as versed in the scriptures and arts (*āgama-koṭi-vikhyāta-vidvadjanāḥ*).

All monastic universities taught five *vidyās* namely,

1. *Adhyātma vidyā*, which included inner science or spiritual science, metaphysics and psychology.
2. *Hetu vidyā* or *Tarkaśāstra*, which included logic, epistemology and the arts and rules of debate.
3. *Śabda vidyā* or *Vyākaraṇa*, which included the linguistics, grammatical and literary studies of Sanskrit language. *Cikitsā vidyā* or medicine and pathology. *Śilpasthāna vidyā* or arts and crafts.

The Buddhist monasteries were organized on the ideal of a residential university. Members of the monastery were full-time residents while those coming from outside were taught in the day time. Monks who were highly educated and experienced were selected as teachers.

R.K. Mukherjee says:

> The idea of organization in education, and the application to it of the methods of collectivism were emphasized very much by Buddhism in the special conditions in which it worked. Buddhism was built up on the basis of monastic brotherhood which its *Bhikshus* or monks organized. It has thus to deal with a large number of monks for whose education the method of individual treatment and of the personal contact between the teacher and the pupil in small homes of learning was not applicable. The orthodox brāhmaṇical *gurukula* system of education did not lend itself to formalism, scale, collective responsibility and specialization. In this system the pupil desiring to learn more and specialize more had to go from one *gurukula* to another with the guru's permission and if the guru found himself deficient in a branch of learning, either he himself went to another *gurukula*, or sent the pupils elsewhere.

Thus, the three aspects of practical training of monks consisted of: 1) *Pariyatti*; 2) *Paṭipatti*; and 3) *Pativāda*. *Pariyatti* has been defined as what may be called scriptural learning. *Paṭipatti* denoted the actual spiritual practices for realisation of the highest truth and culmination of all these were the *Pativāda* or insight into the truth. In the *Mahāvagga* of the *Vinaya piṭaka*, we get detailed descriptions of the life led by monks and novitiates. The daily life of the monk-pupils, their duties and obligation, the duties of the preceptors (*ācārya* and *upajjhāya*) and the relations between the preceptor and disciples are dealt with a beginning as resort during the rains a Buddhist monsteries at a stage turned into great centre of learning. The account of such a transition from residence to seats of learning is remarkable in the history of Buddhism in India. The growth of the *vihāra* as an educational centre may also be noticed in the following passage from the *Manoratha pūraṇī*:

> Even if there be a hundred or a thousand *Bhikkhus* practising *upāsanā* (meditation) there will be no realization of the noble path if there is no learning (doctrine, *pariyatti*).

We are here concerned specifically with the transformation of *vihāras* into temples of learning. As H.D. Sankalia remarks:

> The purpose of the *vihāra* and other dwelling places in the words of Buddha was this: To give *vihāra* to the *Saṅgha* where in safety and in peace to meditate and think at ease, the Buddha calls the best of gifts; let then the able man, regarding his own weal, have pleasant monasteries built and lodge there learned men.

From the above it is clear that *vihāra* gradually became the abodes of learned men and academic studies. The connotation of learning was widened to include secular subjects like grammar, logic, medicine, arts and crafts. Moreover, the Buddhist monks had to contend with the leaders of other sects, who were mostly erudite scholars in different subjects. So in order to defeat them in polemical disputes monks had to study the doctrines of other faiths as well as some secular subjects. This naturally widened the scope of monastic learning and brought it *on a par* with the secular educational programme.

The study of students in monasteries included, besides the *piṭaka*s, the other *śaśtra*s and *vidyā*s which comprised the four Vedas, six *Aṅga*s, ten *Grantha*s, fourteen *Vidyā*s, eighteen *Śilpa*s and sixty-four *Kalā*s.

Chinese and Tibetan sources give us a lot of information about the ancient Nalanda University, its scholars, its curriculum of studies, its international status and the different kings who successively patronised this centre of learning.

The accounts of the Chinese pilgrims, Fa-xien, Xuanzang and Yi'jing are the most important sources, in addition to archaeological and epigraphic materials that help us to construct a fairly clear picture of the University of Nalanda, its buildings, its staff, its curriculum of studies during the days of its zenith.

Yi'jing mentions that the University of Nalanda was granted 200 villages by successive generations of kings. S. Dutt says,

> The motive for all this liberality and generous assistance is perhaps to be found in the fact that, by the time of Śakrāditya, Buddhist monasteries had developed as seats and centres of learning. To build monasteries and provide for their upkeep was regarded more as a service rendered to the cause of learning and culture than to the cause of Buddhism.

The Nalanda University came to the Pālas as a cultural legacy of the past, which they being Mahāyāna Buddhists were bound to cherish and foster and also they were keenly interested in the promotion of Buddhist learning within their territories.

THE ADMISSION PROCEDURE

The entrance examination was conducted by a scholar who generally guarded the portals of the university and those candidates for admission who could not withstand the trial had to go back.

THE CURRICULUM FOLLOWED AT NALANDA

The curriculum of Nalanda as it existed during the days when Xuanzang was a student included: The Great Vehicle (Mahāyāna), works belonging to 18 (Hīnayāna) sects, the Vedas, the *Hetu vidyā* (logic), *Śabdavidyā* (grammar and philosophy), *Cikitsā vidyā* (medicine), esoteric science (of *Atharva-veda*) and the *Sāṅkhya* system of philosophy. For the purpose of gaining proficiency in the part of disputation, great stress was laid on the study of logic (*Hetu vidyā*) and the Nalanda University was centre of the Medieval School of Indian Logic.

Yi'jing described at great length how daily life in the great university was regulated by means of the water-clock (*Vari yantra*). The day commenced early in the morning with the stroke of a drum. The entire day was divided into periods of study and worship, each period being announced by the beating of a drum and the blowing of a conch-shell.

The night was also divided into watches and it was the duty of a special officer Karmadāna to regulate the entire routine of the university by rigidly fixing the hours of study and worship. The amenities of life provided for the staff and students of the university seem to have been superior to those in ordinary monasteries, providing more spacious cells, broader stone-beds and an extra cell added for storage of books and personal belongings.

A time was fixed in the forenoon for all the residents to go out for bath. There were ten great ponds on the campus in which the inmates took their bath.

About intellectual accomplishments and erudition of the *ācārya*s of Nalanda we read,

> There are 1000 men (at Nalanda) who can explain twenty collections of *sūtra*s and *śāstra*s, 500 who can explain thirty collections and perhaps ten men including the master of the law who can explain fifty collections. Śīlabhadra alone has studied and understood the whole number.
>
> The Nalanda University developed efficient schools of Tibetan, Nepalese and Chinese studies in addition to the indigenous schools of Sanskrit so as to be able to turn out scholars who would be linguistically equipped for carrying on their work in the aforesaid foreign languages like Chinese and Tibetan (Mukherjee).

The study of *Dhamma* (doctrine) and *Vinaya* and monastic rules were much emphasized in monasteries. Apart from it, there were other subjects taught therein. The *Dīghanikāya* and the *Mahāvagga* record various branches of knowledge concerning worldly matters, talk of kings, robbers, ministers, wars, battles, food-drink and clothses, talk of relations and acquaintances, talk of villages and towns, talk of women, heroes, talk of creation of the land or sea, talk on becoming and not becoming, and the like.

The *Milindapañho* enumerates nineteen branches of learning. These were: the revealed tradition, secular lore, the *Sānkhya-yoga*, *Nyāya* and *Vaiśeṣika darśanas*, accountancy, music, medicine, the four Vedas, the *Pūraṇa*s, the oral traditions, astronomy, logic, spells, fighting, poetry and reckoning figures, and the *Navakamma* (knowledge of making repairs to the building) engineering is also referred to in later work. The *Cullavagga* mentions that experienced and competent monks used to prescribe the course of studies for the learners. It further gives us the names of subjects that were taught in a monastery. The *Aṅguttara Nikāya* further provides us with a list of monks and nuns who occupied the topmost places in certain subjects. The Chinese pilgrim accounts that admission to both laymen and monks was thrown open. Education was imparted to all learners with great care. Pupils were divided into two classes, i.e., *Māṇava*s (commoners) and *Brahmacārin*s (students). "But they had, of course to bring their own boarding expenses, for they could not under rules be fed from the property of the *Saṅgha* unless they had done some labourious work for the *Saṅgha*, who might then pay for it in the shape of funding them according to their merit. The Suttantas were those who propounded the *Dharma* or *Sutta*. The Vinayadharas were those who discussed and shaped the *Vinaya*. Thus, gradually the *Dharma* was developed and systematized in the *vihāra*s, by specialists and professors. It was not a sudden development, but a gradual process spreading over decades or even centuries. There is a scope for philosophical speculations in the teachings of the Buddha which were embodied in the *piṭaka*s. In the texts and in the inscriptions we come across terms like *Vinayadhara*, *Suttantika*, *Dharmakathika*,

Mahādharma-Kathika, and *Āgatagama Dhammadhara*. The university attracted students from distant places. Xuanzang, the Chinese pilgrim, states learned men from different cities who desired to acquire renown in discussion, came here in multitudes to settle their doubts.

The pillared *maṇḍapa*s which were generally found in the middle of the *vihāra* complexes are believed to have been the places where inmates met and discussed canonical matters. M. Winternitz quotes Tārānāth that by the time of the Pāla dynasty, "that is to say from the 9th to 11th century yoga and magic were paramount in Buddhism". This perhaps is not far from truth considering the already long period of evolution and development of Buddhism extending to international communities.

37

XUANZANG LEGACY AS INSPIRATION TO HIGHER EDUCATION

Cheng, Wei-Yi

At the dawn of the 21st century, interests in the 7th century Chinese Buddhist pilgrim monk, Xuanzang, seems to have gone from academic specialists such as art history, silk road archaeology and Buddhist philosophy, to a much wider audience of mass media, as Sally Wriggins notes towards the end of her popular book, *The Silk Road Journey with Xuanzang*:

> Xuanzang is featured in *Murder on the Silk Road,* a mystery by Stefanie Matteson. He is also the subject of *Ultimate Journey* by Richard Berstein. Both *Time* magazine and the *BBC News* mention Xuanzang's seventh century eyewitness description of the Bamiyan statues of Buddha. A university in Taiwan as part of its Digital Library has an interactive website on 'The World of Xuanzang'. And so it goes.[1]

Yet, she fails to mention Hsṳan-chṳang[2] University, a university that was inspired by and founded on the basis of Xuanzang legacy. It reveals that, as much as Xuanzangology has expanded to various areas related to the study of Xuanzang, Xuanzang legacy as inspiration to higher education has been seldom noted.

XUANZANGOLOGY

The term 'Xuanzangology' (*xuanzang xue*) might be new, or even unheard of, in the Western academia, but it has been used within the Chinese academia for some time and is increasingly popular.

Although I don't know when exactly this term was first used, by 1981 there was already a book called *Introduction to Xuanzangology*[3] published in Taiwan. According to the author of the book, Xuanzangology refers to the study of the Buddhist philosophy that Xuanzang propagated,[4] mainly the Wei-shih philosophy.[5] We know that the Wei-shih philosophy lost its popularity in China shortly after Xuanzang's death.[6] It was not until the turn of the 20th century that we see a revival of interests in the Wei-shih philosophy. The revival of the Wei-shih philosophy in China bears many similarities to features of what Heinz Bechert calls "Buddhistic Modernism" that occurs elsewhere in Asia such as moving away from traditional understanding of Buddhism to rely on the new interpretation of the recently-rediscovered lost or forgotten texts and a tendency to demythologize Buddhism and to emphasize the rational/scientific elements in Buddhism.[7]

It has been pointed out that the revival of the Chinese interest in the Wei-shih philosophy was induced by the combination of the reintroduction of the Wei-shih texts, which had been long lost in China from Japan, and the nationalist desire to find a traditional Chinese thought contestable to the Western rationalistic philosophy.[8] As the main translator and codifier of Chinese Wei-shih texts, interest in the study of Xuanzang grew as well.

Unlike decades ago when Xuanzangology concerned primarily with Xuanzang's teachings and contribution to Buddhist philosophy, Xuanzangology at the turn of the 21st century has expanded to almost all areas related with Xuanzang. For example, the Xuanzangology Center at Hsụan-chụang University, which holds conference on Xuanzangology periodically, does not limit its research interests to the area of Buddhist philosophy but also includes the study of Chinese Buddhist history, art and literature.

XUANZANG LEGACY

Xuanzang legacy exemplifies individual achievement in academic study and, therefore, a role model and inspiration for the Chinese. It is not unusual to find Chinese Buddhists praise Xuanzang for having attained the level of academic achievement 'unmatchable' by anyone.[9] As an individual, Xuanzang was a highly accomplished scholar. We know that he spent years studying at the ancient Nalanda University, and while in India, he studied not only Buddhism (of different schools), but also logic, Sanskrit, astronomy and many other subjects.[10] The profound Wei-shih philosophy that he propagated after his return to China testifies to his personal academic achievement.[11] Moreover, according to Xuanzang's biographers, the very reason for Xuanzang's journey to India was the inadequacy that he found in the existing Buddhist teachings available in China at the time. Although by that time, Buddhism had been in China for centuries, Buddhist scriptures were still relatively inconsistent in terms of philosophic discourse. Xuanzang, therefore, vowed to take the long journey to India in order to bring back Buddhist scriptures for the Chinese.[12] Hence, we have this image of someone who was not only a highly accomplished scholar but also thirsted for *Dharma* and was willing to sacrifice his own comfort in order to travel to India for the good of *Dharma* and the whole Chinese nation. Regardless of the historicity in his biographies,[13] there is little doubt that legacy as such has made Xuanzang a symbol and role model of academic achievement in the minds of Chinese Buddhists. This is of little surprise then that when Taiwanese Buddhists of the 20th century wanted to found a Buddhist university, the name 'Xuanzang' was the choice. The goal of Hsụan-chụang University is said to be "Promoting the spirit of Xuanzang through education; cultivating the talents for the world through academic study."[14] The influence of Xuanzang legacy is obvious here.

Secondly, Xuanzang legacy symbolizes the efforts and devotion to the collective welfare of Buddhist education, a point usually argued through the influence of Xuazang's translation works.[15] Xuanzang's contribution to the translation of Buddhist scriptures has been widely studied. It is basically about how Xuanzang, through his translation works, elevated the standard of Buddhist learning in China, for he made available large volumes of scriptures and through translation aids and preaching, he educated many who later turned out to be great Buddhist scholars themselves (e.g., Kuiji). In other words, Xuanzang legacy not only serves as an inspiration to individual academic achievement but also represents the efforts and devotion to the collective welfare of Buddhist education.

Admittedly, Xuanzang was not the first Chinese to travel to India in search of Buddhist scriptures (the other known ones included Faxian).[16] But it has been pointed out, by both

Buddhists and academicians, that whether by quantity or by quality, Xuanzang's translation of Buddhist scriptures surpasses anyone before or after him.[17] Undoubtedly, this success is due to Xuanzang's own academic strength, but it also reflects the advantage of imperial patronage that Xuanzang was able to solicit. Even though long before the time of Xuanzang, institutional education in the form of both state and private schools had become common in China, the Chinese state's tendency to emphasize Confucianism marginalized, if not excluded, Buddhist study.[18] Xuanzang's friendly association with the Chinese emperors not only guaranteed financial resources for his translation but also a politically-secured environment for Buddhists to study and translate Buddhist scriptures. It indeed has been shown that Xuanzang's friendship with two Chinese emperors was an important factor for Buddhist study of Tang dynasty to excel.[19]

The struggle between the Chinese state's attitude and Buddhist interests toward education continued centuries after Xuanzang and was one of the factors for the founding of Hsụan-chụang University. According to Ven. Liao Chung, the founder of Hsụan-chụang University, it was out of the concern of the Chinese state's unfavourable attitude towards Buddhism that the idea of Buddhists founding their own university emerged. It is hoped that through such a university, the interests of Buddhism might be respected and Buddhist learning be undisturbed.[20] The founding of Hsụan-chụang University was not easy and it took many decades to realize the idea. The idea of founding Hsụan-chụang University might be traced back to the late 19th century. In face of Western imperialist threat, there emerged a trend in China to convert temples, including Buddhist monasteries, into secular schools for the ideal of spreading 'secular and scientific' education to the masses. Buddhist interest was severely damaged. It naturally caused Buddhist reform movement of which the reformers sought to preserve the well-being of Buddhism through education. The Republican government that moved to Taiwan in 1949 continued the indifferent attitude towards religious education for sometime and it was not until 1984 that religious study as a secular subject was permitted in private universities in Taiwan.[21] Even though the environment may not be sympathetic to Buddhist education, the call to found a university based on the ideals of Xuanzang legacy had emerged pretty early, probably as early as 1965. After decades of hard efforts, Hsụan-chụang University was eventually opened in 1997.[22] This is another example of how Xuanzang legacy has become a symbol of devotion to the collective welfare of Buddhist education.

The third point is about Xuanzang's unique legacy in the internationalization of education. If anything, the uniqueness of Xuanzang legacy in education lies in its degree of internationalization. It is not uncommon for Chinese Buddhists to emphasize the international elements in Xuanzang legacy. For example, Dongchu Mahathera (1908-1977) hails Xuanzang as a great hero to the Chinese culture because of his contribution to the translation of Sanskrit texts, development of the Wei-shih philosophy, cross-cultural communication and foreign diplomacy.[23] Three of the four reasons cited are related with the internationalization in Xuanzang legacy. Xuanzang lived at the time when the interactions between China and other countries were frequent. We know that flow of trade, Buddhist pilgrims and Buddhist missionaries travelling between China, Central Asia and India had existed before Xuanzang's journey in CE 627.[24] Zhangan, the capital of Tang empire, was a cultural and political centre where merchants and scholars of different nationalities converged. Buddhist study excelled here.[25] Xuanzang's introduction of Indian Buddhist philosophy to China, translation of Chinese texts into Sanskrit and the foreign students who came to study under him deepened the internationalization of Buddhist study in Tang China. It is clear from the website of Hsụan-chụang University that

Xuanzang's legacy in the internationalization of Buddhist study was one of the main reasons of naming the university after him. Therefore, in the area of education, Xuanzang legacy represents innovation and openness to different cultures.

NOTES AND REFERENCES

1. Sally Hovery Wriggins, *The Silk Road Journey with Xuanzang*, Oxford, Westview Press (2004), 9. 223.
2. 'Hsụan-chụang' 玄奘 is spelt as 'Xuanzang' in the Pinyin system.
3. Chu Bosi, *Xuanzang Xue Gailun*, Taipei, Xin Wenfeng (1981)《玄奘學概論》, 褚伯思著。.
4. *Ibid*, pp. 131-33.
5. For more detail, see Dan Lusthaus, *Buddhist Phenomenology: A Philosophical Investigation of Yogācāra Buddhism and the Ch'eng Wei-shih Lun*, London and New York, Routledge Curzon (2002).
6. Xuanzang is often said to be the founder of the Chinese Buddhist school, Faxian Zong. But this notion has been much disputed in modern time.
7. Heinz Bechert, 'Buddhistic Modernism: Present Situation and Trends', paper presented at the 7th International Conference on Buddhist Education, Taipei: Institute for Sino-Indian Buddhist Studies (1990).
8. Zheng Dezong, 'Xuanzang Zhexue Sixiang De Fazhan Ji Qi Lishi YingXiang' in Ma Pe and Zheng Dezong (eds), *Xuanzang Yanjiu*, Kaifeng, China, University of Henan Press (1997), pp. 271-368. 『玄奘 哲學思想的發展及其歷史影響』, 張德宗著, 摘自《玄奘研究》, 馬佩主編, 張德宗副主編, 開封市：河南大學出版社。.
9. For example, Daoan, 'Xuanzang Dashi Da Jingshen – qiankun wangu yi wanren' in Zhang Mantao (ed.), *Xuanzang Dashi Yanjiu Xia*, Taipei, Dasheng Wenhua (1977), p. 34. 『玄奘大師的精神—乾坤萬古-完人』, 道安著, 摘自《玄奘大師研究（下）》, 張曼濤主編。.
10. See Wriggins (2004), pp. 120-35.
11. See Zheng (1997)..
12. *Datang Da Cien Si Sanzang Fashi Zhuan* T50(2053).【大唐大慈恩寺三藏法師傳】。.
13. Since Xuanzang did not write any memoir himself, it is possible that some of the accounts in his biographies, written by his disciples, might have been exaggerated.
14. See the website of Hsụan-chụang University, http://www.hcu.edu.tw, accessible on 31/1/2006.
15. For example, see Hean, 'Xuanzang Xixing Yu Fojiao Fazhan', *Faguang Zazhi*, No. 143 (August 2001) 『玄奘西行與佛教發展』, 荷安著,《法光雜誌》。.
16. See *Xiyu Ji* T(2085-91).【西域記】。.
17. Cheng Suiguan, 'Xuanzang Zhuan Lu' in Ma Pe and Zheng Dezong (eds), *Xuanzang Yanjiu*, Kaifeng, China, University of Henan Press (1997) 程遂营著,『玄奘傳略』。.
18. For details, see Yu Benfa and Xiong Xianjun, Zhongguo Fazhan Si, Taipei: Shida Shuyuan (1995) 喻本伐, 熊賢君著,《中國教育發展史》。.
19. Cheng (1997), pp. 141-55.
20. Liao Chung, 'Yi Chuangban Fojiao Hsụan-chụang University Lai Jinian Xuanzang Dashi Danchen', *Hai Chao Yin*, Vol. 70 No. 2 (Feburary 1989) 『以創辦佛教玄奘大 學來紀念玄奘大師誕辰』,《海潮音》。.
21. Li Menghan, 'Xiandai Fojiao Jiaoyu Yu Ṙenwen Jingshen', Proceedings of the 8th International Conference on Buddhist Education, Taipei, Institute for Sino-Indian Buddhist Studies (1994) 『現代佛教教育與人文精神』, 李夢翰著。.
22. See the website of Hsụan-chụang University (http://www.hcu.edu.tw), accessible on 31 January 2006.

23. Shi Dongchu, 'Xuanzang Sanzang Dui Zhongguo Wenhua Zhi Gongxian', in Zhang Mantao (ed.), *Xuanzang Dashi Yanjiu Xia*, Taipei, Dasheng Wenhua (1977), pp. 92-101. 釋東初著，『玄奘三藏對中國文化之貢獻』。
24. Tansen San, *Buddhism, Diplomacy and Trade: The Realignment of Sino-Indian Relation, 600-1400*, Honolulu, University of Hawai'i Press, 2003.
25. Wang Yarong, 'Wengu zhixin: gudai Changan Fojiao da xueshuxing tedain dui lianan Foxue Yanjiu yu jiaoyu da qishi', in *Jianwang Zhilai: lianan Foxue jiaoyu yanjiu xiankuang yu fazhan yantaohuilu lunwenji,* Taipei, Chung Hwa Institute of Buddhist Studies (2002), 『溫古知新：古代長安佛教的學術性特點對兩岸佛學研究與教育的啟示』，王亞榮著，摘自《鑒往知來：兩岸佛學教育研究現況與發展研討會論文專集》。

38

NALANDA AS A CENTRE OF WORLD LEARNING

Satya Dev Kaushik

Nalanda University was one of the famous universities of the world. It was famous due to its education system, discipline and talented scholars who used to teach there various subjects. Nalanda was famous even before the establishment of the university. It was a prosperous town called Nāla or Nālaka. Śāriputra was born here. Maudgalyāyana was also born in the same place near Rājgṛha. It could not be separated from Nalanda. Both of them were fast friends and they were ordained as monk by Sañjaya Parivrājaka. They got *parinirvāṇa* in the same place. Buddha built a *chaitya* for his favourite disciples in Rājgṛha. Buddha also got *Mahāparinirvāṇa* after his disciples in Kuśinārā on *Vaiśākha Pūrṇimā*. Nalanda was advanced in the age of Kumaragupta. The contributions of Harṣa and Pāla emperors further made it famous. It was such an institution where students, after completing their primary education, joined this academy for higher knowledge. According to Xuanzang, getting admission in Nalanda was not easy. The students who were eager to join this academy had to pass an examination taken by subject experts. The ratio of candidates who passed the examination was only 2% or 3%. Foreign students also joined this academy to remove their doubts and for acquiring reputation. According to Yi'jing, before and after him 56 scholars came to India from China, Japan and Korea during 40 years. Most of them came here to study. Yi'jing has described some students as (1) Prakāśamati (Śramaṇa Hiuen-Tchao), (2) Śrī Deva (Tao-hi), (3) Buddha Dharma (Fo-tovo-ta-movo) who was the native of Tukharistan, (4) Chandra Deva (Tao-cheng), (5) Mahāyāna Pradīpa (Ta-cheng-Teng), (6) Śīlabhadra (Tao-lin), and (7) Prājña Deva (Ling-yun).

Xuanzang has described some of the most important teachers of Nalanda as Śīlabhadra, Gunṇamati, Sthiramati, Prabhāmitra, Jinamitra and Jñānachandra. Śīlabhadra was the most talented and reputed among them all. He was the Vice-Chancellor of Nalanda Mahāvihāra. According to Xuanzang, Śīlabhadra belonged to a Brāhmaṇa family. He was the prince of Samtaṭa before becoming a monk. Xuanzang is counted among the ten most talented scholars. He was the disciple of Śīlabhadra. Dharmapāla, the teacher of Śīlabhadra who used to live in Kāñcī, is described with great admiration and devotion by Xuanzang. Xuanzang and Yi'jing taught in Nalanda for seven years. Through the description of Xuanzang, it is evident that the most talented scholars, students and teachers belonged to Nalanda. According to Tārānātha the most talented scholars of their time were Nāgārjuna, Suviṣṇu, Āryadeva, Asaṅga, Vasubandhu, and Diṅgnāga who were the teachers of Nalanda.

According to Xuanzang, students not only studied tenets of Mahāyāna but also the eighteen sects of Buddhism. They studied Veda, *Hetu vidyā* (logic), *Śabda vidyā* (grammar), *Atharvaveda* and *Saṁkhya*. According to Yi'jing, courtesy was not only followed in Nalanda Vihāra but also in other monasteries. Sanskrit grammar *Aṣṭādhāyāyī* was also studied there. According to *Aṣṭādhāyāyī*, grammar was known as *Śabda vidyā* which was one of the five *vidyās*. There are five types of *vidyā*, viz., *Śabda vidyā*, *Śilpasthāna vidyā*, *Cikitsā vidyā*, *Hetu vidyā*, and *Adhāyatma vidyā*. There are five kinds of *Śabda Vidyā* – *Siddha*, *Śāstra*, *Dhātu*, *Khila*, and *Vṛttasūtra*. The knowledge of grammar was necessary for higher education. Students had to study grammar at the age of fourteen years.[1] From the biography of Dharmaswāmin,[2] we learn about the teachings of Buddha in Nalanda Vihāra.

> In the early part of the 13th century Dharmaswāmin began his journey from Tibet to Vajrāsana.[3]

He had a keen desire to travel to Bodhgaya and other sacred places. He visited the renowned seat of learning, Nalanda. It was the time of Muslim invasion.

> The resident monks had been alerted of the imminent danger and had fled before the Muslim soldiers arrived.[4]

Dharmaswāmin began to live with his guru Ācārya Rāhula Śrībhadra.

> It is said that the Muslim soldiers who came in search of Dharmaswāmin and Rāhula Śrībhadra had even reached the very place where they were hiding but could not find them.[5]

Dharmaswāmin described an image of Jñānanātha as "slightly bigger than life size and painted in green".

> At Nalanda, Dharmaswāmin had also noticed the worship of several other Mahāyāna gods like Khasarpaṇa Lokeśvara, Mañjuśrī, Tārā and the practice of extremist Tantric cults like Guhyasāmaja.[6]

Thirty Buddhist books were also written by him. He died at the age of sixty.

> Tibetans honoured Dharmaswāmin by making him the chief incumbent of many a Tibetan monastic establishment. The Tibetan scholar passed away in the year CE 1264.[7]

Through the description of Nalanda University, we collect information about the education system, teachers and students who were eligible and disciplined. Now it is desirable to discuss such scholars who followed the tradition and knowledge of Nalanda in the foreign countries, especially in Asian countries, to promote the light of knowledge. The scholars Xuanzang and Dharmaswāmin who studied there and propagated Indian culture in foreign countries acquired the first rank. In the second rank there were Indian scholars who belonged to Nalanda, and conveyed the message of Indian culture in Asian countries. The writings of Śīlabhadra, Dharmapāla and Candragomin played an important role for improving and maintaining the Tibetan culture. Ācārya Śāntarakṣita, Ācārya Padmasambhava and Ācārya Kamalaśīla settled there. In China, Kumārajīva, Paramārtha, Śubhaṅkarasiṁha and Dharmadeva propagated the Indian culture.

It is necessary to mention here that at that time in Tibet there was an earlier form of Buddhism influenced by *Bon Dharma*. This *Dharma* had its own beliefs, rituals, gods and *tantra-mantras*. On getting the invitation of the king, Ācārya Padmasambhava arrived in Tibet. Travelling through many parts of Tibet, he expounded the Buddhist teachings to strengthen Buddhism. He established there a *Saṅgha*. He also included some essential tantrik of *Bon Dharma*.

> Padmasambhava advised the king to send a body of monks from Tibet to India to study the Buddhist texts. At the request of the king he selected a site for a monastery and Ācārya Śāntarakṣita consecrated it. The king built the Sam-yas monastery a few miles away from Lhasa on the model of the famous Odantapurī Mahāvihāra of Magadha. Ācārya Śāntarakṣita was appointed the head of the new monastery. It is the greatest monastery ever built in Tibet. It contains a number of fine shrines and has a good collection of Sanskrit and Tibetan books. With the construction of the monastery, Buddhism made steady progress in Tibet. But a fierce controversy arose over the interpretation of the Buddhist teachings among the followers of Śāntarakṣita and the pupils of the Chinese Buddhist Ho-Shang.[8]

In order to defend Śāntarakṣita, the king invited Kamalaśīla from India.

> A philosophical debate was organized and Kamalaśīla won. His victory was indeed, 'an important landmark in the religious history of Tibet'.[9]

Ācārya Kamalaśīla, the disciple of Śāntarakṣita, was the Ācārya of Nalanda. Padmasambhava went to Tibet from Nalanda at the invitation of King Khri-Sron-ide-btsan in CE 743. According to *Chronology of Ladakh,* he is also known as the *ācārya* of Nalanda. According to Franke's description, the king invited Padmasambhava from Odantapurī and not from Nalanda.

> Towards the close of the 8th century Padmasambhava procured a number of manuscripts of the Buddhist texts from Kashmir. Many learned monks were appointed to render them into Tibetan. Of them a monk named Vairocana of Kashmir was the best. The Sam-yas monastery thus became a great centre of literary activity in Tibet. Both Śāntarakṣita and Padmasambhava collaborated with each other in expounding the teachings of Buddhism. At their request many monks of the Sarvāstivāda school of Buddhism came to Tibet from Magadha for translating the Buddhist texts into Tibetan. Many young men were also ordained by them.[10]

The monks who went to China from Nalanda played an important role in propagating Buddhism. Some of them are described here. Dharmadeva (Fatiyan) was a monk from Nalanda. He translated many scriptures from 972 to 1001. In 982 the king gave him the title Chuan Cha-O Ta Shih or a very onerous teacher of Buddhism. He died in 1001.

According to Chinese *Tripiṭaka* collection, he was known as the writer of 118 scriptures, out of which 46 were written by him under the name of Fa-Tian and the remaining scriptures were written under the name of Fa-Zien.

Śubhaṅkarasiṁha was also the native of middle country and belonged to the dynasty of Śākyamuni's uncle, Amṛtodana. He carried with him many Buddhist texts and died in 735 at the age of ninety-nine at Nalanda.[11]

The contribution of Paramārtha cannot be ignored. He was related with Nalanda and Ujjain. The king of Bu-ti sent a talented group to Nalanda for the collection and translation of Mahāyāna scriptures in 539. He requested the emperor of Magadha to help him.[12] Accepting the request of the king, Kumāragupta sent Paramārtha to China with the collection of scriptures. There he translated into Chinese from Sanskrit dividing seventy original texts into three hundred parts. Living in China he translated till his death.[13]

Nalanda became the centre of world learning due to its rare method of teaching and the higher quality of various subjects. This tradition of translation remained as a fort protecting knowledge. Although many scriptures were destroyed or ruined, even then they have been preserved in Chinese, Tibetan, and other Asian languages due to translation.

NOTES AND REFERENCES

1. Memoirs of the Archaeological Survey of India, No. 66, *Nalanda and its Epigraphical Material*, Hiranand Shastri, p. 17, Swati Publications, Delhi, Reprint, 1991.
2. *Encyclopaedia of Buddhism*, Vol. IV, Fascicle 4: Published by the Government of Sri Lanka. Printed at: Tisara Packaging Industries, Dehiwala, Sri Lanka, 1989, p. 561.
3. *Ibid.*, p. 563.
4. *Ibid.*, p. 563.
5. *Ibid.*, p. 563.
6. *Ibid.*, p. 563.
7. *Ibid.*, p. 563.
8. *Ibid.*, p. 229.
9. *Ibid.*, p. 229.
10. Anukul Chandra Banerjee, *Buddhism in India and Abroad*, Calcutta, The World Press Pvt. Ltd. First Published February 1973, p. 227.
11. Chau-Siyanga-Kumang, *History of Chinese Buddhism*, Hindi Translation by Atman, Leader Press, Allahabad, *Samvat* 2013: *Vikram* (1956), p. 135.
12. V. Smith, *Early History of India*, p. 533, Third Edition; Memoirs of the Archaeological Survey of India, No. 66, Hiranand Shastri, *Nalanda and its Epigraphical Material*, p. 8, Swati Publications, Delhi, Reprint, 1991.
13. Chau-Siyanga-Kumang, *History of Chinese Buddhism*, Hindi Translation by Atman, Leader Press, Allahabad, *Samvat* 2013: *Vikram* (1956), p. 95.

Part VI

NALANDA EXPERIENCE

39

THE SPIRIT OF NALANDA

Ven. Dhammadīpa

Nalanda has emerged in history as the most important seat of Buddhist learning in the world. The place is inseparably linked to the *Prajñāpāramitā* movement of which it has become a symbol.

Even though the available historical documents speak of Nalanda obtaining an official status of university during the late Gupta period, nevertheless both Chinese and Tibetan sources speak of Nalanda emerging as an important centre of learning as early as the first century BCE, or even at the time of King Aśoka.

No matter whether as a monastery or as university, Nalanda seems to have been from the very early times a meeting place of monks of different schools and interests, who gathered around particular teachers, laying emphasis on particular aspects of learning.

Gradually, the scale of learning extended to all the important branches of learning known at that time and laymen were allowed to study side by side with monks.

It seems from the available documents, that treatises of all the eighteen Buddhist sects were studied in Nalanda, together with *Āgama*s, Mahāyāna *sūtra*s and different revisions of *Vinaya piṭaka*.

Nalanda, however, became especially famous as the place of study and composition of most valued treatises.

We further learn from the documents and from the excavations themselves that meditation and personal cultivation were inseparable parts of students' training; a strict adherence to *Vinaya* rules was a must for all without exception.

These high standards of Nalanda University mentioned by Xuanzang remained for long linked with the incomparably high standards of learning and moral cultivation attained by the two most prominent exponents of the *Mahāyāna Prajñāpāramitā* philosophy, Nāgārjuna and Asaṅga.

According to Tibetan sources (Buston, *History of Buddhism*), Nāgārjuna was ordained and received his education at Nalanda, and according to Tārānātha (*History of Buddhism in India*), Asaṅga spent twelve years in Nalanda, became a teacher there and expounded to students three *piṭaka*s of *Śrāvaka*s and five hundred Mahāyāna *sūtra*s.

From the writings of the early exponents of Buddhism in China, especially Dharmarakṣa and Kumārajīva, and from the study of inscriptions (Schopen, *Mathura Inscriptions*), it seems that Mahāyāna and Hīnayāna schools of as late as 5th or even 6th centuries generally not regarded

as two different trends opposing each other, but rather two interpretations of the same tradition complementary with each other. This can also be concluded from a careful study of *Mahāvibhāṣā śāstra*, dating to the historical beginnings of Mahāyāna.

The spirit of tolerance and deep understanding of the whole Buddhist tradition together with high standard of moral and spiritual cultivation was at the background of growth of Nalanda into the most important centre of intellectual and spiritual learning in India, from which Buddhism was transferred to other Asian countries, especially China and Tibet.

The benevolent rulers of India who sponsored Nalanda were fond of organizing intellectual debate due to which the high standards of Nalanda could be maintained, and different traditions came to a full bloom.

The formation and blooming of the two most important *Prajñāpāramitā* or Mahāyāna traditions, that is *Śūnyavāda* and *Yogācāra*, was a process stretching over a long period of many centuries.

Even though there is no historical evidence available to link the formation of these two great traditions with Nalanda, it is not surprising that the process of their formation and the life, work and lineages of their early exponents came to be lined with Nalanda.

To understand the true spirit of Nalanda as the centre in which the whole Buddhist heritage came to be revaluated in the sense of *Prājñāpāramitā* interpretation, and in which this tradition attained its full bloom, nothing is in my view as rewarding as the study of two works summarizing the whole of tradition of Buddhism in the light of *Prajñāpāramitā*.

The first is *Mahāprajñāpāramitā śāstra*, available in Chinese only, attributed to Nāgārjuna and the second is *Yogācārabhūmi śāstra*, extant in both Tibetan and Chinese and partially in original Sanskrit.

The second work is attributed to Asaṅga in the Tibetan tradition and to his legendary teacher, Maitreyanātha in Chinese tradition.

From the textual studies of both works it seems that their composition was a matter of collective effort of different teachers, possibly done during a long period of time.

What do these two works have in common?

No matter whether we attribute their authorship to two founders of the most important traditions studied at Nalanda or not, they both give expression to a pioneering spirit of inquiry on the base of a deep-rooted tradition, which must have been existing before their compilation.

Both these works reveal that Mahāyāna arose as a trend not opposing the Śrāvaka heritage but merely interpreting it in the light of *Prajñāpāramitā* literature and yoga practice related to it.

Both works aim at liberating the tradition from the narrowly fixed confines of the *Abhidhārmic* interpretations. They reveal clearly that the *Prajñāpāramitā* movement's overwhelmingly negative tone in denying the existence of the conventional was in no way linked with a denial of the categories, as often understood, but was only meant to interpret them in the light of non-dualistic thinking.

In these works the emphasis is on interpreting the common heritage from the point of view of *Prajñāpāramitā* rather than creating a new form of Buddhism.

Both works take it for granted, just as *Mahāvibhāṣā śāstra* does, that the question of meaning of Buddhahood, path to it and its implications are considered legitimate by all Buddhist schools.

Hence they both summarize the vehicle of Śrāvakas first and add to it the *Prajñāpāramitā* knowledge and practice as additional wisdom, necessary for all aspiring for the highest.

Both works understand the *Śravakyāna* as the path of correct discrimination, but understand this discrimination as inconclusive, therefore, in need of *Prajñāpāramitā* interpretation to become complete.

Both works start interpreting the *Bodhisattva* vehicle, that is *Prajñāpāramitā* vehicle or Mahāyāna by explaining the meaning of Buddha's universal knowledge, that is a complete and correct knowledge of both absolute and relative. Though the *Bodhisattva* does not possess the second knowledge, he uses the first to attain the second and thus completes the path to Buddhahood.

He can indeed do so, from the point of view of *Prajñāpārāmitā*, because the two are ultimately one.

Both works resort to many genuine devices of dividing knowledge of reality and knowledge of the path to a comprehensive understanding of it into different categories of perception, all contained within the Buddha's enlightened knowledge.

PRAJÑĀPĀRAMITĀŚĀSTRA (P.P.S., TAISHO, VOL. 25)

P.P.S. at its beginning (p. 59b) attempts to synthesize Buddha's teachings of two truths, containing the whole of undivided reality by explaining four systems of doctrines (*siddhāntas*).

This allows all teachings of Buddha to be true within the framework of different perspectives of understanding.

The first system of teaching is mundane, explaining the worldly nature of all phenomena, where mundane is understood as created in dependence (*pratītyasamutpanna*).

The second system of teaching is based on understanding of individual inclinations (*xin xing*) of beings. This system allows the teaching about the existence of individual *karma* and individual retribution, taught to those inclining to annihilation view, and teaching about the non-existence of one receiving retribution of *karma*, taught to those inclining to eternity view, to exist side by side. Both teachings are equally true within the framework of mundane truth.

The third system of teaching, also belonging to the mundane level of truth, is remedial teaching (*dui zhi jiao*). It is teaching of friendliness to check anger, impurity, to check lust, etc. In the *P.P.S.* however even the teaching of impermanent, sorrowful and selfless nature of all phenomena belongs to this system. They are taught to counter the misapprehension of permanence, happiness and self in the worldly realities.

To the question why impermanence is true in relative sense only, the *P.P.S.* replies (p. 60c):

> Because all the dharmas belonging to saints are fruits of retribution, and everybody of wisdom accepts it as truth.

Hence all the teachings based on the notion of an existing nature of entities are not comprehensive; they only belong to the mundane level of truth. They are dependable on discourse, and as such can be objected to refutation.

The true *Dharma*, realized by Arahats, Pratyekabuddhas and Buddhas is comprehensive, because it is unchanged, it is free from the faults of language, and cannot become object of clinging or dispute.

This reality is the base for the fourth ultimate teaching, denying a true independent existence of all *dharmas*, without exception, by showing their relativity.

Just as milk exists relative to its smell, taste and touch, that is when these causes exist milk also exists as a relative phenomenon, not as a faulty imputation like a third hand. Similarly, individuals and their aggregates exist as mundane relative entities.

In this context the *P.P.S.* (scroll 12 = chap. 12) distinguishes three kinds of existence, relative (*xiang dai*), like cars or persons, nominal (*jia ming*), like the third hand, and one born from *Dharma* (*fa you*), like the five aggregates. All of them are unreal from the ultimate point of view. The nature of these three realities must be distinguished clearly, as ultimate (*pubbe dhammā thiti ñañaṁ, pacchā nibbānañānaṁ*).

Relating existence born from *Dharma* into the sphere of mundane existence is the particular emphasis of the *Prajñāparamitā* method.

In relation to this, the *P.P.S.* (ch. 18) distinguishes three methods of teaching *Dharma*, that is, *Prajñāpāramitā*, namely, the *sūtra* method accepting the relative existence of entities such as beings, the *Abhidharma* method based on existence of phenomena born from *Dharma*, and lastly the Emptiness method denying a true, self-existence of all entities.

The three methods are to be seen as complementary, one not excluding the other; this is the spirit of *Prajñāpāṛamitā* at its best. On the base of a deeper understanding of these teachings, which enable one to deny the notion of existence of all *dharma*s without denying them altogether, the Boddhisattva is said to excel Śrāvakas by two kinds of wisdom (ch. 35).

First he sees all *dharma*s as empty without seeing emptiness, and due to this practice of non-differentiation frees himself of all clinging to them. Secondly, on the base of this insight and due to his great compassion he sees the relative existence of everything, making no difference between *saṁsāra* and *nirvāṇa*.

In this way the *Bodhisattva* sees all *Dharma*s as suchness (*tathatā*), free from duality, yet does not ignore the dual nature of all phenomena, including suchness, that is, their being both mundane and absolute. In this sense the *P.P.S.* (ch. 51, p. 369a) speaks of two suchnesses, one relative, characterized by particular characteristics like hardness of earth, and the other, which is identical with *nirvāṇa*, the true way of things (*dharmatā*) or final reality (*bhūta koṭi*). One is not different from the other in absolute sense.

Practising the *Prajñāpāramitā* in this way, the *Bodhisattva* does not see all names, remains in the true nature of things, and learns gradually to master all *dharma*s to help oneself and all beings without clinging to anything.

According to the *P.P.S.* (ch. 28) wisdom of *nirvāṇa*, wisdom of the ultimate purity is the same for *Śrāvaka*s and the Buddha, but the first lacks skilful means connected with wisdom, while the second has a perfect knowledge of them. The knowledge of realized *Srāvakas* is called omniscience (*sarvajñatā*, yi qie zhi), while the knowledge of Buddha is called omniscience in regard to all forms of knowledge (*sarvākārajñāna*, yi qie zhong zhi).

As the *Bodhisattva* is one who strives for the same knowledge as the Buddha, but has not acquired it yet, the *Prajñāpārāmitā*, as the method of liberation, strictly speaking, does not belong to the realized of the three vehicles, but to *Bodhisattva*s.

In this sense, the practice of emptiness common to all disciples of Buddha is according to the *P.P.S.* also of dual nature, practice of emptiness without skilful means and practice of emptiness with skilful means. The second is said to be the essence of *Bodhisattva*, of Mahāyāna and of the *Prajñāpāramitā* itself.

This emptiness with skilful means is said to contain the wholesome *dharma*s of all three vehicles (ch. 27, p. 374a), because the *Prajñāpāramitā* identifies wholesome as skilful with *nirvāṇa*. Thus, *nirvāṇa* understood as unborn mind is said to be the *Prajñāpāramitā* itself and the true characteristic of all *dharma*s (p. 323c).

In this way within the framework of synthesis of the mundane and supramundane in the empty mind, the *Bodhisattva* is said to have two objects, which stand for two inseparable aspects of his practice. He takes beings as object, while practising the great compassion and *Dharma* as object, and also practising the *Prajñāpāramitā* (p. 267b). Though not being in *Nirvāṇa*, he practises the cause of *nirvāṇa*, that is, the *samādhi* of emptiness, desirelessness (*apraṇihita*) and signlessness (*animitta*). He progresses gradually in the three entries (*mukha*) to *nirvāṇa* till his attainment of

Buddhahood, when the concept of beings disappears altogether, after his realization of skilful means is complete.

The path to Buddhahood as portrayed in the *P.P.S.* is gradual, and many types of gradation are mentioned in regard to the practice of thirty-seven limbs of enlightenment, six perfections and all the *dharma*s of *Bodhisattva*. Of particular interest is the scheme of five realizations (p. 382a):

1. Realization of the *Bodhicitta*.
2. Realization of the correct method of taming the mind by seeing effects in causes.
3. Realization of purity, being the character of all *dharma*s, that means the realization of the *dharmakāya* (at the first stage of *Bodhisattva's* enlightenment).
4. Realization of a complete tolerance of the unborn (*anutpattikadharmakṣānti*) and thus freedom from all defilements (at the seventh stage).
5. Realization of the supreme enlightenment.

In the *P.P.S.*, the traditional Buddhist practices, especially the thirty-seven limbs of enlightenment are coordinated with the practice of perfections, so that the attainment of the eightfold noble path, which is the consummation of the enlightened practice, coincides with a complete understanding of suchness. Suchness thus remains at the background of all practices, which are understood in the framework of a double perspective, with differentiation (*savikalpa*) and without differentiation (*nirvikalpa*), or mundane and supramundane.

As the *Prajñāpāramitā* itself is understood as mundane and supramundane (p. 369a), all practices such as the four bases of mindfulness or the perfection of giving, etc. are also understood as mundane and supramundane.

They belong to a purely supramundane level only after a complete realization of the tolerance of unborn, when the *Bodhisattva* becomes freed from all objects of differentiation.

THE *YOGĀCARABHŪMI ŚĀSTRA* (Y.B.S., TAISHO, 30)

The same picture of the *Prajñāpāramitā* encompassing the whole wide range of all known Buddhist learning and practices we get in Asaṅga's *Y.B.S.*

The main difference is that the *Y.B.S.* as the title itself reveals is principally concerned with yoga, understood in the Buddhist sense as *Śamatha* and *Vipaśyanā* practice and their objects. Accordingly, all classifications of knowledge with objects and means of knowledge are directly or indirectly linked with this main theme.

In order to contain all the Buddhist practices within the scheme of *Bodhisattva*'s striving for Buddhahood, the *Y.B.S.* explains four levels of knowledge for explaining reality (*siddhānta*s) (*Bodhisattvabhūmi*, ch. 4, p. 25).

The first level is reality as accepted by worldly people (*lokaprasiddhasiddhānta*) and the second level is reality established by reason (*yuktiprasiddha*). These two realities must be thoroughly understood in order to understand the conventional.

The third level is reality as understood by saints free from *āsavas* (*anāśravadṛṣṭilabdhagocara*).

The fourth level is reality as understood by a fully enlightened Buddha, free from all obstacles to knowledge (*jñeyāvāraṇaviśuddhajñānagocara*). These two realities must be understood in order to comprehend the ultimate.

Hence the *Y.B.S.* in contrast to *P.P.S.* understands the ultimate reality of *Śrāvaka*s and Buddhas to be different not only in quality, but also in nature. It is so because the knowledge or mind is for *Yogācāra* a truly existing reality.

Accordingly, the *Y.B.S.* speaks of four types of *nirvāṇa* instead of the traditionally accepted two. It adds to *nirvāṇa* with remains (*sopādhiśeṣa*) and to *nirvāṇa* without remains (*nirupadhiśeṣa*) other two kinds of *nirvāṇa*. It is *nirvāṇa* as a natural state of all beings (*prakṛtinirvāṇa*) and *nirvāṇa* of one who has realized this state of suchness, *nirvāṇa* without base (*apratiṣṭhitanirvāṇa*), attained by the Tathāgata.

He does so by four investigations (*paryeṣaṇa*) in regard to all differentiated perceptions (*vikalpas*) that appear to his mind. That is, he investigates their names (*ming*), he investigates them as given reality (*shi, vastu*) arisen in dependence on causes and conditions, he investigates their common nature (*Zong xing*), that is emptiness and particular nature like breaking into parts, being the nature of *rūpa*, differentiating being, the nature of *vijñāna*.

Contemplating the mind in this way, using the same aids to meditation as *Śrāvaka*, but enlarging his understanding by practice of *Bodhicitta*, great compassion and perfections, *Bodhisattva* attains to objectless meditation, revealing to him the true nature of mind as being identical with emptiness.

In the perspective of *Y.B.S.* the path of *Śrāvaka*s and the path of *Bodhisattva*s both lead to realization of emptiness, being the true nature of mind, free from affirmation (*samāropaṇa*) or negation (*apavāda*). However the emptiness of *Śrāvaka*s is said to be non-comprehensive as it cannot comprehend the original *nirvāṇic* nature of all realities.

The key to understanding the mind, its bondage in *saṁsāra* and its liberation by correct practices is explained in the *Y.B.S.* especially in reference to understanding of attention. (*manasikāra* which means literally making in the mind).

Two kinds of attention, attention founded in reality (*yoniso manasikāra*) and the first is the source of all liberations and the second of all the bondages.

Both *Śrāvaka*s and *Bodhisattva*s train their minds by mastering attention through the practice of *Śīla* with *Śamatha, Vipaśyanā* in reference to a limited and not limited spheres of knowledge respectively. Thus, for example a *Śrāvaka*, while practising mindfulness of body (*kāyānupaśyanā*) uses his attention to a limited image of body (*pratibimba*) conceived as truly existing, while *Bodhisattva* uses his attention to a body as being neither existent nor non-existent, thus avoiding all notions of it. Therefore, his understanding of body becomes free from limitations.

In the *Śrāvakabhūmi* of the *Y.B.S.* (p. 193) the supporting objects of meditation are analyzed in detail in terms of what is pervaded (*vyāpyālaṁbanaṁ*), objects for purification of conduct (*caritaviśuddhanālambanaṁ*), objects for skilfulness (*kauśalyālambanaṁ*) and objects for purification of defilements (*kleśaviśodhanālambanaṁ*).

As in the *Y.B.S.* the inseparability of *Śamatha* and *Vipaśyanā* is particularly emphasized; the sphere of objects for both overlaps and so does also attention to them.

In the *Y.B.S.* the mastery of attention is explained as the most important component of yoga, therefore all aspects of the *Śamatha-Vipaśyanā* practice are included in it.

The training starts by cultivating the one-pointedness of mind, that is *Śamatha*, explained by nine dwellings of mind with four kinds of attention in the sense of application of mind to object (*āvāhana*) connected with it. (That is forceful, with interruption, without interruption and effortless [*anābhogāvāhana*]) (S.B. 363-66).

When effortless application to objects is achieved in *samādhi*, yogi's practice of analyzing mind it is *Vipaśyanā*, it ripens parallel to his ripening of worldly and supramundane *samādhi*. This is explained by four levels of *Vipaśyanā* (p. 367) with three methods of their application (That is *Vipaśyanā* with signs, with investigation and with observation).

In this context six objects are to be investigated in order to leave all attachment to sensual perception and its object; this is a requisite for both *Śamatha* and *Vipaśyanā* practice (p. 368).

The six objects are meaning (*artha*), given object (*vastu*), characteristics (*lakṣaṇa*), moral quality (*pakṣa*), time (*kāla*), and way of constructing the object (*yukti*).

These six objects are understood by attention comprehending characteristics of objects (*lakṣanapratisaṁvedīmanasikāra*), the first in the seven kinds of attention, the mastery of which leads to a complete knowledge of both *Śamatha* and *Vipaśyanā*, hence to liberation.

The liberation is here understood as two kinds of liberation, that is, liberation from *āsavas* achieved by successful practitioners on all three vehicles, and liberation from obstructions to objects of knowledge (*jñeyāvaraṇa*), achieved by *Bodhisattvas* by extending their sphere of knowledge.

Having known the disadvantages of a not liberated mind in both *Śamatha* and *Vipaśyanā* practice by the first kind of attention, the yogi practises the second attention, namely, the determined attention (*adhimokṣamanasikāra*), which enables him to stay in the sphere of knowledge.

Having attuned himself to this sphere, the yogi practises next three attentions with the view to abandon rough, middle and subtle forms of defilements respectively (to both *Śamatha* and *Vipaśyana*). These are attention for remaining aloof (*pravivekya*), for gathering meditative joy (*ratisaṁvāhaka*), and investigative attention (*mīmāṁsāmanasikāra*).

Having succeded in keeping the mind free from defilements, the yogi practises attention of successful effort (*prayoganiṣṭha*) in virtue of which he can enter any kind of absorption (*dhyāna*).

The effortless attention which allows him to dwell in it is called the fruit of successful effort (*prayoganiṣṭhaphala*), necessary for practitioners in all three vehicles. The higher the vehicle of realization, the higher mastery of it must be achieved in order to get liberation.

Equipped with a mastery of many different kinds of skilful attention towards appropriate objects, all objects become gradually objects of *Śamatha* and *Vipaśyanā* (p. 193-97).

If attention is paid to a differentiated image (*savikalpapratibimba*), the pervaded object becomes a *Vipaśyanā* object, if to an undifferentiated image (*avikalpapratibimba*), the object is a *Śamatha* object.

In a limited sphere of knowledge of *Śrāvakas*, when both *Śamatha* and *Vipaśyanā* are practised side by side (*yugalanaddha*) with a knowledge of the supramundane, one attains the third pervaded object belonging to the liberated *Śrāvakas*, called the limit of all given objects (*vastūparyanta*).

If the sphere of knowledge is extended infinitely by knowledge of perception free from differentiation (*nirvikalpajñāna*) practised by *Bodhisattvas*, the sphere of knowledge of the Buddha can be attained.

This sphere of knowledge, free from limitations of knowledge and objects known, is called the pervaded sphere of successful activities (*kāryapariniṣpatti*).

In this sphere the knowledge of characteristics of what is perceived (*grāhya*), of who perceives (*grāhaka*), of names perceived (*parikalpita*), of realities subjected to clinging (*paratantra*), and of what is not subjected to clinging (*pariniṣpanna*) is comprehended fully. With the realization of this sphere, just as explained in the *Āgamas* (*Dīgha Nikāya* 28, *Sampasādanīya Sutta*), the *dharmas* attained by *Śrāvakas* are only deepened by a superior practice and knowledge. This knowledge is, however, understood in the *Y.B.S.* just as in the *P.P.S.* to be in regard to the same components of reality as realized by the *Śrāvakas*.

Thus, both the *Śrāvakas* and the Buddha attain to the same limits of realities (*vastu*) in terms of their phenomenal appearance that is summarizing them as five aggregates, elements of perception, four noble truths, etc., as well as to a true understanding of their nature (*yathabhavikata*) in totality as being suchness or *nirvāṇa*.

BIBLIOGRAPHY

M.P.P.S., Taisho, no. 1509.

Y.B.S., Taisho, vol. 30.

Dutt, N. (ed.), *Bodhisattvabhūmi*, Jayaswal Research Institute, Patna.

Ramanan, V., *Nāgārjuna's Philosophy*, New Delhi: Motilal Banarsidass, 1975.

Willis, J.P., *On Knowing Reality*, New Delhi: Motilal Banarsidass, 1983.

Buston, *History of Buddhism*, tr. by E. Obermiller.

Tārānātha, *History of Buddhism in India*, tr. by Alaka Chattopadhyaya and Lama Chimpa.

Julien, S., *Histoire de la vie de Hiouen Thsang*, Paris, 1853.

Julien, S., *Memoires de Hiouen thsang* (Xi you ji).

Legge, James, *The Travels of Fa-hisan*.

40

REVITALIZING THE SPIRIT OF NALANDA

Ven. Fa Qing and Ven. Wei Wu

1. THE NALANDA UNIVERSITY

1.1 A Short History

Nalanda, the full name is Nalanda-saṅghārāma, has been a renowned Indian centre of Buddhist learning, as both Xuanzang[1] and Yi'jing studied there.

In his *The Biographies of Tang Monks Seeking Dharma in India*, Yi'jing stated: "Nalanda Monastery was constructed by the ancient King Śakrāditya."[2] Xuanzang mentioned that there were six kings who subsequently built the monastery. They were Śakrāditya, Budhagupta, Tathāgatagupta, Bālāditya, Vajra, and Śīlāditya.[3]

The initial founder, Śakrāditya probably was Kumāragupta (414-455 鸠摩罗笈多).[4] It was during the time of the movement of the renaissance of Sanskrit, that Asaṅga and Vasubandhu had been preaching Mahāyāna *Yogācāra*. Their methodology on treatise studies and the oratory style of teaching rapidly spread out and became a trend. The building of Nalanda expanded widely, as well as their stress on treatise studies.[5]

In CE 455, after King Kumāragupta passed away, the Gupta dynasty declined. Ephthalites (厌哒) from the North invaded India and soon they controlled West and North India. The invasion by Ephthalites badly destroyed Buddhism in North India. In CE 519-521, Chinese envoys Song-yun (宋云) and Hui-sheng (惠生) from North Wei (Bei-wei 北魏) dynasty went to India and at that time, Gandhāra (乾陀罗) was under the control of Ephthalites for the second generation.[6]

In the year CE 630, Xuanzang passed through North India. The declining condition of Buddhism was somehow related to the invasion of the Ephthalites, though it was also connected with the destruction of the *Dharma* by Mihirakula (摩醯逻矩罗).[7] The Gupta dynasty not only suffered from external invasion, but also faced internal conflicts. East Magadha and South West Mālavā were separated.

1.2 The Spirit of Nalanda

The fame of Nalanda and other Buddhist universities spread over the greater part of Asia through the works and achievements of their eminent scholars. Nalanda University remained a source of attraction to foreign Buddhists. It was the greatest centre for the study of Buddhist logic and Mahāyāna philosophy and the doctrines of the 'Eighteen Schools'. Sanskrit was the medium of instruction there. It had a wide academic repertoire: grammar (*vyākaraṇa*), logic (*Hetu vidyā*), *Abhidharma*, *Vijñānavāda*, and other branches of humanities and sciences were taught. The scholars produced by Nalanda were well treated and its professors were respected throughout Asia. Under the Pālas who were devout Buddhists, the glory of Nalanda as a centre of learning was maintained for several centuries at a high level.[8]

Nalanda was a centre of higher education and advanced studies; only students who possessed the necessary qualifications were admitted to its courses. Admissions were restricted and preceded by a pre-admission test. A monk-scholar would act as pre-admission examiner. He would pose a few difficult questions to the candidates. Many were unable to answer and were denied entry.[9] Only twenty to thirty per cent of those seeking admission succeeded at the 'entrance examination'. Xuanzang wrote:

> Scholars from different places and foreign countries desired to enter the hall of debate and discussion. Most of them encountered difficulties, thus went back feeling dejected. Those who were well versed in olden and modern learning were admitted. Thus, having visited [Nalanda] as a guest, one further debated in detail to show his talents. Failures were seven or eight out of ten, only two or three succeeded.[10]

The students and teachers of Nalanda led a very academic and moral life.

> They were looked upon as role models by all in India; learning and discussing they found the days too short; day and night they admonished each other, juniors and seniors mutually strove for perfection. If any of them were found unable to discuss the profound meaning of the *Tripiṭaka*, such persons, being ashamed, left withdrawn. Hence learned men from foreign countries, who desired to acquire knowledge quickly to become renowned in discussion, came here to settle their doubts, and then became famous. Because of this, those who stole the name [of the Nalanda] were highly respected wherever they went.[11]

The Tibetan sources tell us that there were three large buildings for housing books. They were located in an area known as the 'Treasure of Religion' (*Dharma-gañja*). These three library buildings were poetically named Ratnasāgara, Ratnodadhi and Ratnarañjaka. Of these, Ratnasāgara housed the collection of *Prajñāpāramitā Sūtra*s and the *Tāntrika* texts.[12]

The construction of Nalanda was of great significance to Buddhism. In fact, many famous Buddhist scholars came from Nalanda. Nalanda University produced a large number of eminent scholars, debaters and authors who flourished during the 7th and the 8th centuries CE. Mention may be made of Dharmapāla, Candrakīrti, Dharmakīrti, Śīlabhadra, Buddhabhadra, Jayasena, Guṇamati, Sthiramati, Jñānacandra Ratnasiṁha, Jinamitra, Prabhāmitra, Sāgaramati, Siṁharaśmi, Prajñāraśmi, Candradāsa, and Śāntideva, all of whom lived in the seventh century CE, and were mentioned either by Xuanzang or by Yi'jing.[13]

In the 8th century CE, the university had many distinguished scholars as its teachers and students. Sarvajñamitra of Kashmir studied Tantras there. Śāntarakṣita who was probably the most learned philosopher was the Chancellor of Nalanda in the middle of the century, and Kamalaśīla was the professor of Tantras there; Dharmottara of Kashmir, Padmasambhava of Uḍḍiyāna and Prajñākaramati, and Śubhākarasiṁha were also associated with the academic activities of Nalanda.[14]

Nalanda had a truly universal character, free from religious, political or national barriers; it threw open its door to all irrespective of caste, colour, creed or country. This universal spirit of Buddhist culture earned India an international reputation and attracted scholars from far-off countries.[15]

2. INTERNATIONAL BUDDHIST COLLEGE IN THAILAND

There are many conflicts in the world today, and these conflicts are mostly created in the name of religion. Different schools should respect each other's teachings. People with different backgrounds and cultures, may tend to favour certain schools more than others. Thus, we need to inculcate respect and appreciation for the different traditions, rather than be in conflict with each other.

The International Buddhist College (IBC) is built to provide a suitable place for the various Buddhist traditions to come together so as to promote better understanding among themselves.

This institute of higher learning seeks to combine the rigours of academic scholarship with appreciation of the richness and diversity of Buddhist traditions.

The IBC began its first intake in July 2000 offering courses in Pāli Buddhist studies. Its temporary campus is strategically located in Hatyai, the largest city in Southern Thailand.

It environs a fully residential college, with appropriate living quarters for *bhikṣus*, *bhikṣuṇīs*, male and female lay students. To provide an environment of good spiritual community, three monasteries will be constructed to house the teachers and students. The teachers and students can choose to stay in any of the three monasteries. The Theravāda monastery will be named Aśoka College, the Chinese monastery as Yi'jing College and the Tibetan College as .Atīśa College. Our aim is to provide a conducive environment where scholars and students of different Buddhist traditions can gather under one roof so as to promote mutual understanding and learning and thereafter to promote Buddhism in a modern context to different parts of the world with an open mind.

NOTES

1. A Ping-Yin system will be used for all Chinese characters.
2. T51, No. 2066, 5b (Taisho *Tripiṭaka*, Volume 51, number 2066, page 5 and column b): 那烂陀寺，乃是，为 为北天苾刍曷罗社盘所造。.
3. T51, No. 2087, 923b-c. See also, T51, No. 2066, 237b.
4. S. Dutt, identified Śakrāditya with Kumāragupta. See, Sukumar Dutt, *Buddhist Monks and Monasteries of India*, Delhi, Motilal Banarsidass, 1988, p. 329. According to *The Biography of Vasubandhu* (T50, No. 2049 婆藪槃豆法師傳), the Nalanda Monastery was built by Vasubandhu.
5. Yin Shun, *The History of Indian Buddhist Thought* 印度佛教思想史. Taiwan: Zhen Wen Publication, 1993, pp. 321-31.
6. T51, No. 2092, 1020c: *The Records of Buddhist Monasteries in Long Yang* 洛阳伽蓝记.
7. Yin Shun, "北印度之教难"『妙云集』下编九『佛教史地考论』, pp. 311-21.
8. S.R. Goyal, *A History of Indian Buddhism*, Jodhpur, Kusumanjali Prakashan, 1994, p. 358.
9. Lal Mani Joshi, *Studies in the Buddhistic Culture of India*, Delhi, Motilal Banarsidass, 1977, pp. 134-35.
10. T51, No. 2087, 923c: 殊方異域欲入談議門者。詰難多屈而還。學深今古乃得入焉。於是客遊後進詳論藝能。其退飛者固十七八矣。二三博物眾中。.
11. T51, No. 2087, 923c: 請益談玄竭日不足。夙夜警誡少長相成。其有不談三藏幽旨者。則形影自愧矣。故異域學人欲馳聲問。咸來稽疑方流雅譽。是以竊名而遊咸得禮重。. Cf. Thomas Waters, *On Yuan Chwang's Travels in India*, New Delhi, Munshiram Manoharlal, 1996, II. 165.
12. Joshi, p. 136.
13. *Ibid.*, pp. 136-37.
14. *Ibid.*, p. 137.
15. *Ibid.*, p. 133.

BIBLIOGRAPHY

T50, No. 2053 (*The Taisho Chinese Tripiṭaka*, Vol. 50, No. 2053): *The Biography of Great Tang Tripiṭaka Master* 大唐大慈恩寺三藏法師傳, by Hui-li.

T50, No. 2049: *The Biography of Vasubandhu* 婆藪槃豆法師傳. Trans. Paramārtha.

T51, No.2066: *The Biography of Tang Eminent Monks Seeking Dharma in India* 大唐西域求法高僧传, by Yi'jing.

T51, No. 2087: *A Record of Western World in Tang Dynasty* 大唐西域記, by Xuanzang.

T51, No. 2092, 1020c: *The Records of Buddhist Monasteries in Long Yang* 洛阳伽蓝记.

Thus Have I Heard: The Long Discourses of the Buddha. Translated by Maurice Walshe, London, Wisdom Publications, 1987.

Dutt, Sukumar, *Buddhist Monks and Monasteries of India*, Delhi: Motilal Banarsidass, 1988.

Goyal, S.R., *A History of Indian Buddhism*, Jodhpur, Kusumanjali Prakashan, 1994.

Joshi, Lal Mani, *Studies in the Buddhistic Culture of India*, Delhi: Motilal Banarsidass, 1977.

Legge, James (Trans.), *A Record of Buddhistic Kingdoms* (reprint), Delhi: Munshiram Manoharlal, 1991.

Obermiller, E., *The History of Buddhism in India and Tibet* (reprint), Delhi: Sri Satguru, 1986.

Takakusu, J. (Trans.), *A Record of the Buddhist Religion as Practised in India and the Malay Archipelago* (reprint), Delhi, Munshiram Manoharlal, 1966.

Waters, Thomas, *On Yuan Chwang's Travels in India* (reprint), New Delhi: Munshiram Manoharlal, 1996.

Yin Shun, *The History of Indian Buddhist Thought* 印度佛教思想史. Taiwan: Zhen Wen Publication, 1993.

——. '北印度之教难" 『妙云集』下编九『佛教史地考论』', pp. 311-21.

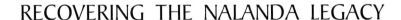

41

RECOVERING THE NALANDA LEGACY

Joseph Loizzo

INTRODUCTION: NALANDA AND THE INDO-TIBETAN BUDDHIST SCIENCES

A half century ago when Tibet's leading minds fled to India with His Holiness the Dalai Lama, they came onto the world stage as a living legacy of the great monastic university of Nalanda. As the twenty-first century dawns, that living legacy has once again taken root in its native soil and spreads from India around the world. In the West, growing interest in Tibetan civilization has focused on the meeting of the Indo-Tibetan Buddhist mind-sciences and healing arts with Western psychotherapy. My own interest in Nalanda and its legacy grew out of contacts with Tibetan emigrees and their first Western students. Over time, I focused on interdisciplinary study of the similarities and differences between Western empirical science and Indo-Tibetan meditative science.

Comparisons between the ancient Buddhist and modern Western scientific traditions have generally employed one of three methodologies. Translator-scholars working within the Western academy have used the methods of philology, sometimes enhanced by hermeneutics, comparative philosophy, anthropology or sociology. Research scientists working within the biomedical community have relied on disciplines like philosophy, phenomenology, psychology, linguistics or artificial intelligence. Health practitioners working in various clinical settings have preferred the methods of the case study or clinical trial, sometimes refering the works of Buddhist scholars.

As one would expect, the findings of comparative studies of these two traditions have diverged as widely as these three methods. Scholarly comparisons between Buddhist and Western science typically cite a shared methodological preference for reason and evidence over authority and revelation, as well as a shared conceptual preference for causal explanation and impersonal description. Research comparisons typically cite physiologic or mechanistic findings that support traditional claims about the effects and mechanisms of meditation. Clinical comparisons typically cite a congruence in psychological theories along with demonstrable health benefits of techniques like meditation. The main limits of these three main approaches stem from their narrow scope and ethnocentric choice of method.

Comparing Buddhist and Western views of reason and revelation obscures some key distinctions between these two scientific traditions. While Śākyamuni and his heirs criticized Vedic notions of divine authority and scriptural revelation, they also developed their own critical concepts of valid authority (*pramāṇa*) and traditional teaching (*āgamadharma*). Although these concepts were restricted in principle to hypothetical matters beyond the scope of ordinary perception and inference, the requirement that empirical and/or rational demonstrations must also be consistent with all scriptural statements without exception places the Buddhist tradition somewhere between the empirical method of modern science and the analogical method of systematic theology in the West. Assuming an ethnocentric bias in Western science and scientific scholarship, such content-based comparisons obscure the major discontinuity between the Indian and Western scientific traditions.

In my view, the major discontinuity facing comparisons of Western and Buddhist science is between a science in which mathematics is the privileged language and mechanics the privileged method and one in which those roles are played by linguistics and mind/body self-regulation instead. Although both types of science were developed in the West, the former has so defined our view of science since Galileo that the latter, found in the modern social sciences and prior contemplative sciences, is either dismissed as pseudo-science or relegated to the role of a proto- or para-scientific discipline. While the conventional wisdom has it that only Galilean science can yield knowledge that is objective or exact and effects that are reproducible, even the most vocal defenders of modern science have had to admit in recent years that objectivity, precision and efficacy in science are inexorably relative and conventional concepts.

In their efforts to apologize for the therapeutic logic and qualitative methods of Buddhist science, researchers and clinicians unversed in the latest critical thinking have been caught in this methodological mismatch. Wanting to show the validity of Buddhist sciences and techniques in practical terms, they remain bound to the conventional methodology of their respective disciplines. Contrary to their intentions, their attempt to validate the Buddhist sciences using the mechanistic theories and quantitative measures of the Western physical sciences is at best heuristic and at worst self-defeating. However clearly we show that Buddhist meditation has an effect on the brain or on stress, the theories and methods by which this is shown are decidedly not those by which the effect itself is achieved. Therefore, while such demonstrations may be welcome to all as proof that meditation is not simply a culture-bound ritual, they add nothing to the qualitative principles and inter-subjective practices by which Buddhist science formulates, replicates and validates its desired effects. At the same time, they run the risk of reinforcing serious cross-cultural misunderstanding. While trying to open Western science to Buddhist influence, they confirm the ethnocentric bias that modern 'empirical methods' offer humanity the only clear and reliable route to objective, precise, reproducible knowledge. However inclined we are to cling to quantifiable measures as more objective, exact or reliable, in researching sciences of the qualitative type these are at best insufficient, and at worst confusing or off the mark. Insisting on them as the gold standards of evaluation or translation of Buddhist science in spite of these risks betrays both an ethnocentric bias and a fatal methodological misunderstanding. One is reminded of a remark from philosopher Ludwig Wittgenstein's *Investigations*:

> If I tell someone, 'Stand roughly here' – may not this explanation work perfectly? And cannot every other one fail too? But isn't it an inexact explanation? – Yes; why shouldn't we call it 'inexact'? Only let us understand what 'inexact' means. For it does not mean 'unusable' .... Thus the point here is what we call 'the goal.' Am I inexact if I do not give our distance from the sun to the nearest foot, or tell the joiner the width of a table to the nearest thousandth of an inch? No *single* ideal of exactness has been laid down; we do not know what we should be supposed to imagine under this head (p. 88).

From the perspective of our post-modern consensus on science, the modern Western dichotomy of exact versus inexact, objective versus subjective science does not do justice to the discontinuity between modern Western and traditional Buddhist science. In order to say which type of science is more useful, one would first need to specify a human interest or aim relative to which the question can be answered. Today we are in a position to understand what Śākyamuni meant when he was asked in an exchange recorded in one of the Pāli scriptures to explain why one should follow a human teacher like him rather than a religious tradition supposedly revealed by an omniscient God. Picking up some leaves with one hand and pointing to the nearby woods with the other, the Buddha asked, "Which contains more leaves, my hand or that wood?" When his interlocutor affirmed that the handful contained fewer leaves, Śākyamuni replied, "The leaves in my hand represent the number of things one needs to know to reach freedom." While fully unpacking the difference in aims assumed by these two traditions would need another paper, let me mention here that the interests which have defined Buddhist science from the outset more closely resembles the therapeutic and liberative aims of the 'human sciences' defined by Paul Ricouer than those of our physical sciences. In terms of comparative intellectual history, both traditions transgress the artificial limits imposed on human beings by authoritarian religious traditions. The difference is that while modern Western science does so with an aim to perfect human knowledge and technical mastery, Buddhist science aims to perfect humanity itself. In terms of regulative ideals, Western science has preserved theological concepts of omniscient and omnipotent agency but distributed these across human communities over time, conceding to monotheism that individual humans are not perfectible. Buddhist science rejected theological concepts of omniscient and omnipotent agency and replaced them with appropriate concepts of relatively omniscient, omni-compassionate agency, insisting that the only sure route to human freedom and happiness is for humans to realize and master our god-like genius. Hence Diṅgnāga and Dharmakīrti argued that Buddhist science is impossible without a regulative ideal of a perfected human agent, one who embodies or personifies science. Anticipating Hans Gadamer, science is progressive not because it discards authority and tradition, but because it insists, one might say democratically, that each and every individual can and should personally reproduce and advance what is best in humanity and human cultural traditions. For that, among other things, is entailed in the Mahāyāna aim of reproducing the Buddha's social agency. The discontinuity in methods used by the Western physical sciences and Buddhist mind-sciences stems from this distinction in aims. Qualitative, intersubjective methods are preferred because they are appropriate to the goals of such human sciences, not to mention the mind/body systems in which our self-limitation exists and must be corrected.

Understanding this discontinuity in aims and methods helps expose the limits of recent approaches to comparing Western and Buddhist science. Those limits stem from an ethnocentric assumption that one can 'translate Buddhism' without a serious attempt to translate the experience and practice of Buddhism in one's own mind and life; that one can 'validate' meditative techniques by some measure other than valid personal experience and self-transformation; and that one can 'study' Buddhist therapies in some way short of learning to heal oneself well enough to help others reproduce the results.

METHODOLOGY: CONTEXTUAL COMPARISON AND TRANSLATION

Assuming that language is embedded in the context of cultural behaviour, I began by hypothesizing that the partiality of recent comparative efforts reflected a mapping of Buddhist theories and methods into Western contexts that would not support a full rendering of their intended meaning and use. For reasons which I shall return to shortly, let me draw an example from the scholarly study of Mahāyāna Buddhism. Until recently, Nāgārjuna's thought was almost exclusively linked by Western scholars to his *Fundamental Central Way Verses* (*Mūlamadhyamakakārikā*), and translated as a work of academic philosophy. As a result, he was misread as a skeptic or nihilist until he was translated by Western scholars familiar with the living context of the Tibetan monastic curriculum, where his thought was put to its intended contemplative-ethical use as indicated by Candrakīrti's *Central Way Introduction* (*Madhyamakāvatāra*).

THE CONTEXT OF MULTIDISCIPLINARY HUMAN SCIENCE IN THE BUDDHIST TRADITION

The first finding that emerged from my comparative survey of scientific learning in Buddhism and the West was that the cultural distance between these two traditions for most of history was far less than it is today. The prime reason for this is that the major discontinuity between Western and Buddhist science took place in and around the European Renaissance. In Western history, both types of science were known to the Greeks, with mathematics and physics privileged in the quantitative Pythagorean-Aristotelian tradition and linguistics and meditation in the qualitative Empedoclean-Platonic. Since qualitative science was preferred by the Graeco-Roman academy of Christian monasticism, Renaissance figures like Galileo chose the quantitative paradigm as an alternative to Church-controlled science. Since that time, the relationship between these two paradigms has been inverted to the point where the word 'science' is increasingly reserved for the quantitative, physical science of Galileo and his heirs.

When it comes to the Indo-Tibetan tradition, the history of science is markedly different. Among the many reasons for this, two in particular stand out in my mind. First, while the Indians were certainly not behind the Greeks in mathematics or physics, they were far ahead in linguistics and self-regulation. Like Euclid's geometry and Archimedes' physics, Pāṇini's grammar and Patañjali's yoga provided Indians with linked conceptual and practical systems so elegant and powerful that they quickly became and remained definitive in the analytic description and technical control of nature. This paradigm was associated with the syncretic Buddhist-Vedic tradition of linguistic philosophy (*Vyākaraṇa*). Although an alternative conceptual-practical system associated with the refinement of formal logic and physics gained some momentum in classical India, linked with Buddhist and Vedic logical traditions (*Pramāṇa-Naiyyāyika*), it never replaced the qualitative methods of linguistics and self-regulation but was retained for elementary studies. Second, comparing the fate of Socrates and his peripatetic academy with that of Śākyamuni and his mendicant community, it is obvious that Indian social and religious institutions could marshal far greater tolerance and support of liberal, scientific education than their Western counterparts.

These two factors represent a complex of conditions that put education on a different trajectory in India than in the West. I characterize this difference by distinguishing the way the institution of monasticism interfaced with learning in the two civilizations. In the West, monasticism served as a tool of religious-political authority, helping Rome coopt the progressive academic traditions of Hellenism. In India, Śākyamuni crafted it into a liberative institutional vehicle that helped the Buddhist academy play a progressive role in the evolution of Indian science, society and religion. Although monasticism gave birth to universal education in both civilizations, Mahāyāna universities arose roughly a thousand years earlier than their Christian counterparts. Nāgārjuna and Asaṅga based their liberal, scientific curricula on critical, universalized versions of the qualitative methods of Pāṇini and Patañjali, without the spectre of repression by Indian political or religious authority. Although alternate versions of the curriculum based on Diṅgnāga's logic were developed by Bhāvaviveka and Dharmapāla, they never displaced the qualitative curriculum of Nāgārjuna and Asaṅga, as defined by Candrakīrti and his heirs. I believe this reflects the degree to which the Buddhist scientific tradition was free to develop critical versions of both linguistic and formal logical methods and felt no need to concede on either front to Vedic orthodoxy. So it was that when Tibetans set out to forge a Central Asian renaissance of Indian Buddhist science and civilization, they revived the Nalanda curriculum much as it was, with its integrated use of formal logical methods for the basic arts and sciences and qualitative methods for advanced disciplines, cognitive self-correction (*cittaviśodhana*), and esotericism (*tantra*). As a result, the most perspicuous historical point of reference from which to survey the entire Buddhist scientific tradition lies midway between the eras of Śākyamuni and Tsong Khapa, in the seventh century when formal and qualitative method were refined by Candrakīrti and Dharmakīrti, respectively.

This thumbnail history of East-West science leads me to the second finding of my basic research: that comparisons must reflect the way science or refined knowledge is actually viewed and used in the Buddhist tradition. If we are to arrive at a comparison of the Western and Buddhist scientific traditions that permits a general and working translation, that comparison must reflect truth and method evolved to support the most advanced levels of the Buddhist curriculum. Most comparisons of Buddhist and Western science are based on one of two textual reference frames: the basic scientific canons (*abhidharma*) of Buddhagoṣa and/or Vasubandhu; and the logical canon (*pramāṇa*) of Diṅgnāga.

I have already alluded to the cultural bias Western scholars and scientists have against qualitative methods. A survey of 'Buddhology' since its inception shows one glaring consequence of that bias that sets the stage for an objection to my choice of Centrism as a focus of comparison. Given the commitment modern science has made to realistic theories and formal methods, Western scholars of Buddhism have consistently aligned Theravāda traditions with empirical science and Mahāyāna traditions with mystical or skeptical religion. This has fostered an alignment of Protestant Buddhology with the reformation rhetoric of some Theravādins, casting Pāli Buddhism in the role of pure or early Greek Christianity and Mahāyāna Buddhism in that of Roman Catholic tradition. So the conventional wisdom against my choice of Nāgārjuna and his heirs as representative of Buddhist science has two prongs: first, Centrism is too skeptical, mystical or nihilistic to be compatible with science in any form; second, Centrism is a revisionist form of Buddhism that mistakes and displaces Śākyamuni's intention.

As for the first prong, the objection stands or falls with mystical-skeptical readings of Centrism dispelled by recent Indo-Tibetan Buddhist scholarship, such as Robert Thurman's work on reason and enlightenment in Tsong Khapa's hermeneutics. As I discussed in my dissertation, the objection is equally incoherent from a Western standpoint given the recent turn towards relativistic and constructivist views of science. As for the second prong, privileging the realistic theories and methods of Buddhaghoṣa, Vasubandhu and Diṅgnāga based on claims to the purity and priority of Theravāda Buddhism is anachronistic since critical traditions and Nāgārjuna himself preceded their writings by centuries, it ignores evidence that a *Mahāsanghika-Mahāyāna* version of the Buddhist canon in Sanskrit co-evolved more or less contemporaneously with the Theravāda version in Pāli.

The third finding of my comparative study – the compatibility of Theravāda and Mahāyāna versions of Buddhist science – further counters this objection. In contrast to the sectarian rhetoric exemplified in the Śrī-Lankan reformation, the institutional structure and curriculum of Mahāyāna universities like Nalanda presupposed an inclusive framework more in line with Buddhist hermeneutics and the cumulative logic of science than with sectarianism. For instance, Xuan-zang and Yi'jing both indicate that mastery of the Theravāda canon was assumed along with language proficiency as a requirement tested by Nalanda's entrance examination. This report alone would suggest that institutions like Nalanda saw themselves as providing higher education meant to build on elementary learning offered by local schools of various Buddhist and non-Buddhist denominations. It is also consistent with the fact that students who entered Nalanda as novices would eventually be ordained as *Mūlasarvāstivāda* monks, effectively becoming Theravādins who may or may not also uphold a complementary Mahāyāna philosophy or practice. A final consideration here is the pedagogic inclusiveness that characterizes Buddhist teaching – Theravāda and Mahāyāna. Expressed in the doctrine of liberative art (*upāyakauśalya*) and the prohibition against rejecting any Buddhist precept or faction, this inclusiveness was reflected in the Mahāyāna strategies of gradualism. The fourfold pedagogic gradualism expressed in Nāgārjuna's *Jewel Garland* (*Ratnāvalī*), for instance, includes three levels of teaching consistent with Theravāda practice and only one with Mahāyāna. His other works support this by aligning his critical theory of two realities of the four noble truths: voidness is the ultimate pedagogic convention meant like a cathartic to free us from reifying all conventions, just as *nirvāṇa* is the ultimate liberative truth meant to heal us of all self-defeating cognition and action. By insisting that all scientific theories and logico-empirical methods are mere conventions whose truth is relative to the ultimate aim of freeing beings from self-limiting habits of mind and action, Nāgārjuna is reiterating a critique of knowledge and expertise that is fundamental to all Buddhist arts and sciences – Theravāda and Mahāyāna. And by insisting that the only ultimately coherent Centrist methodology is a consensual or dialogical language that empathically assumes others' view-points, Candrakīrti is able to bring the Mahāyāna academy back down to its Theravāda foundations. In sum, the choice of Nāgārjuna and Candrakīrti's methodology as definitive for the Nalanda curriculum defines the Mahāyāna academy by its decision to subject the production of scientific knowledge and technical expertise to the human quality control of a self-corrective art and science of enlightened social agency.

This brings us to the fourth major finding of my comparative study: the contextual definition of Buddhist science as a multidisciplinary human science. Once we understand that the institutional strategy of the Mahāyāna academy is to extend the progressive social role of Theravāda learning into the mainstream of Indian science and civilization, it is a fairly simple matter to map the Centrist canon and its use into the context of Nalanda's universal curriculum and mission.

Far from the disarticulated, disembodied knowledge sought in the modern West, the modern Buddhist academy continues to integrate humanly relevant knowledge with meditation and ethics based on the aims and methods spelled out in the four noble truths.

Thus, Nāgārjuna's *Wisdom* and Candrakīrti's *Lucid Exposition* elaborate a relativistic theory of knowledge to apply to the discipline of wisdom, while the *Jewel Garland* and *Introduction* define an altruistic style of social agency to align technical expertise with the discipline of ethics. In an effort to bridge the gap between Buddhist and Western traditions of Centrist studies, I chose to base my comparative study on texts that help contextualize Centrism by providing a missing link between its self-corrective approach to knowledge and its altruistic approach to social agency. Aligned with the core discipline of meditation, Nāgārjuna's *Reason Sixty* (*Yuktiṣaṣṭikā*) and Candrakīrti's *Reason Sixty Commentary* (*Yuktiṣaṣṭikāvṛtti*) describe how the de-reifying language of Centrist philosophy is put into practice as a self-corrective method of contemplation that in turn serves to foster the Mahāyāna ethos of enlightened altruism and universal social agency. Taken together these meta-disciplines govern the universalization of the Buddhist arts and sciences in the Mahāyāna academy, with linguistics (*śabdavidyā*) and logic (*hetuvidyā*); self-corrective contemplation universalizing psychology (*adhyātmavidyā*); and altruistic agency universalizing physical science and technology (*śilpasthāna*), medicine (*cikitsāvidyā*) and political-economy (*arthaśāstra*).

As a final note I must say a few words about the interpersonal context of scientific education in Buddhism. Another key way in which the Mahāyāna academy extended the structure of Theravāda learning to further its universal mission was to integrate its vast, content-driven curriculum of text-based classes with an equally intricate process-driven system of human self-correction basic to all Buddhist monastic education. This process included traditions of scholarly tutelage, ethical contemplative self-development and collective self-correction through group confession or debate. This compound strategy helps flesh out the unique context of the Mahāyāna academy and shows how its integral curricular content and pedagogic process worked together to foster an institutional culture of self-corrective ideals and procedures. Far from the context of Western scientific academy in which a professor typically teaches her own textbook to a lecture-hall full of students the context of the Buddhist scientific academy is explicitly self-corrective and profoundly dialogical. The typically Buddhist classroom is at the centre of a network of dialogical relationships stretching through a complex community over time, arraying ten or more people, actual and virtual, around one text: the Buddha and his student in an original source context; a textual commentator and his student in a secondary source context; an oral commentator and his student in a tertiary source context; the second generation oral commentator and student of the text and commentary; the current student's extra-curricular personal tutor (*ācārya*); his extra-curricular practical guardian (*upādhyāya*); and his peer(s) in a debate, retreat and/or confessional group. While this complexity has been observed by Robert Thurman in the context of the esoteric Mahāyāna refined in the *Extremely Brilliant Lamp* (*Pradīpodyota*) attributed to Candrakīrti, it is rarely observed as basic to all Buddhist education. In any event, such extended dialogical networks constitute a deep procedure of self-correction that complements the logic and method of self-correction central to all Buddhist learning. Together the self-corrective procedures of linguistic self-analysis, contemplative validation of experience and inter-subjective replication of results take the place in the Buddhist scientific tradition filled in the West by the de-personalizing procedures of statistical formulation, experimental validation and inter-laboratory replication.

THE CONTEXT OF MULTIDISCIPLINARY HUMAN SCIENCE IN MODERN WEST

The fifth and final finding of my comparative study is perhaps the most difficult: that is, to select the closest contextual match or matches for Buddhist science in the West. We have already dealt with many of the problems that arise when translators assume a match between the institutional mission and context of the Western and Buddhist academy. My own experience searching for a context at one major American university is a case in point. Relegated to a secular department of religion, the Buddhist studies programme is surely the most hospitable place in which to teach Buddhist literature. Yet the disciplinary requirement that such teaching remain abstract and theoretical becomes obvious once one takes the next step in Buddhist learning, to teach classes in the practice of meditation or ethics. As a religion professor at Columbia, my course on religious experience and contemplative states was extremely well received by all, with the clear understanding that I stop at teaching students *about* meditation.

TOWARDS A GLOBAL RENAISSANCE OF THE NALANDA LEGACY

By way of introduction to my recent efforts at creating a context for translating the Buddhist mind and health-sciences in the West as Freud founded his psychoanalytic institute to get around the limitations of the European academy, I have recently set about founding the first Buddhist psychotherapy institute I know of in the West to circumvent the limits of the American academy. Based in midtown New York, I designed the Nalanda Institute for Meditation and Healing to create a suitable context for a working translation of those aspects of the Indo-Tibetan sciences that readily apply to New York life. Although free-standing, the institute is affiliated with the Center for Buddhist Studies at Columbia University and the Center for Complementary and Integrative Medicine at the nearby Cornell Medical College. These affiliations link the work of the institute with the scholarly translation system and clinical research behind it.

While drawing on its links with the Western academy, the aim of the Nalanda Institute for Meditation and Healing is to create a unique learning environment where people can study all three disciplines of Buddhist science simultaneously and with the benefit of individual practice of cognitive, attitudinal and behavioural self-correction.

Observing the Nalanda tradition of serving the secular and lay Buddhist community as well as monastic professionals, the institute offers classes and counselling to the public as well as training and supervision for physicians and psychotherapists. Classes in meditation and yoga cover the full spectrum of principles and practices within the Nalanda curriculum, while the inter-personal structure of Nalanda pedagogy is recreated by complementing classes with individualized programmes in professional development, meditation-based psychotherapy, stress-reduction and mind/body health, abstinence and recovery.

While modern philosophers of science have had to adapt themselves to this way of thinking in recent years, it is all so new and obscured by debates that few individuals and fewer communities in the West have had time to evaluate or respond to the view. One voice in the Anglo-American academy that may be a harbinger of the kind of shift needed for a genuine recognition of the pre-science and timeliness of the Buddhist sciences is legal philosopher Thomas Nagel. I leave you with some quotes from Nāgārjuna and Candrakīrti, followed by excerpts from Nagel's classic *The View from Nowhere*. First, from Nāgārjuna's *Reason Sixty*:

> Alienated beings who hold the self real
> Misperceive being and nothingness;
> Confused and under the influence of addictions,
> Their own minds deceive them (*YS*, 24).
>
> Just as the Victors say "I" and "mine"
> For a heuristic purpose,
> So they speak of "life systems," "media" and "elements,"
> For a heuristic purpose (*YS*, 33).
>
> Explanations of things such as material elements
> In reality reduce to consciousness;
> And since insight can dispense with them,
> Are they not artificial constructions? (*YS*, 34)

Alas! Those who insist
On a non-relative self or world
Are impoverished by worldviews
Like idealism and materialism (*YS*, 44).

Once one comes to reify being,
One holds intolerable, malignant views,
Which foster attachment and aversion,
And give rise to conflict (*YS*, 46).

The magnanimous are free
From [self-centered] conflict or bias;
For they who have no [egocentric] position,
How can there be opposition? (*YS*, 50)

Like a child attached to his reflection
Because he perceives it as real,
The world is caught in a trap of [false] objectivity
Because of [consensual] delusion (*YS*, 53).

Seeing with their wisdom eye
That things resemble reflections,
The magnanimous do not get caught
In the mire of so-called "objectivity" (*YS*, 54).

Those who contemplate the void
And do not waver with the wavering mind,
Cross the intractable sea of existence,
Seething with snakes of addiction (*YS*, 59).

Given below are remarks from Candrakīrti's *Commentary*:

Once the practitioner sees that what the "God" of his consciousness reifies as being existent or non-existent is deceptive and fictive in nature, he sees it as uncreated with respect to intrinsic reality and hence definitively understands it. Since the mind thus poised knows [things as] uncreated with intrinsic reality, it is purged of endless [constructs of] things like material elements that are created with such [apparent reality], and hence becomes free of them as a reflected image ceases when the form reflected is removed (*YSV*, ad.k.34, 752-753).

The activity [of mind] which interferes with the vitality of the faculty for exalted wisdom is referred to by Nāgārjuna as its 'demon'... it is evident in their [reified] construction of things that the misbegotten have not escaped the realm of misknowledge and hence are 'in the range of their demon.' Once one no longer creates such [reified constructions], one does not fall under the demon's dominion, as it cannot invade one's subjectivity (*YSV*, ad.k.36, 756).

Once one makes the presumption of being, one will succumb to derivative views which objectify such [being] by constructing its beginning, middle and end; hence that reifying habit is the root from which all worldviews spring. Once one has arrived at a worldview, the addictions which arise from that [view] as cause develops. One develops attachment to one's own view and takes pride in that; and one develops aversion to opposing views, and therefore gets completely confused (*YSV*, ad.k.45, 775).

When freed from egocentric position and opposition by their freedom from [reifying] being as such, those [magnanimous individuals] with such [purged] intuition will definitely terminate their addictions (*YSV*, ad.k.50,780).

> In the empathic objectivity of the noble, [egocentrically biased minds] seem like children, ignorant of the nature of existence, caught in the trap of the [addictive] lifeworld, whatever they do. With an intellectual eye purified by wisdom [however], the noble see objective reality precisely as it is, "the [magnanimous] do not get stuck in the mire of so-called 'objectivity'" (*YSV*, ad.k.53, 784).

Finally, compare these excerpts by Nagel:

> I shall offer a defense and also a critique of objectivity. Both are necessary in the present climate, for objectivity is both underrated and overrated, sometimes by the same persons ... These errors are connected: they both stem from an insufficiently robust sense of reality and of its independence of any particular form of human understanding (5).
>
> What really happens in the pursuit of objectivity is that a certain element of oneself, the impersonal or objective self, which can escape from one's creaturely point of view, is allowed to predominate is actually a special form of idealism, for it puts one type of human understanding in charge of the universe (9-10).
>
> I want to do something else and that is to describe a kind of reconciliation between the objective standpoint and the inner perspective of agency, one which reduces the radical detachment produced by initial contemplation of ourselves as creatures in the world (126).
>
> This involves the idea of an unlimited hypothetical development on the path to self-knowledge and self-criticism, only a small part of which we may actually traverse. We assume that our own advances in objectivity are steps along a path that extends beyond them and beyond all our capacities (128).
>
> We cannot act on the world from outside but we can in a sense act from both inside and outside our particular position in it (135).
>
> Our objectivity is simply a development of our humanity, and doesn't allow us to break free of it; it must serve our humanity and to the extent that it does not we can forget about it. The objective self is a vital part of us, and to ignore its quasi-independent operation is to be cut off from oneself as much as if one were to abandon one's subjective individuality (221).

Of course, the art and science of self-correction, Buddhist or Western, are in no way meant to exclude or substitute for any other science and technology. They are meant to complement and enhance conventional science, much as alternative science is meant to guide the ordinary physical and social sciences in the *Kālacakra* tradition or extraordinary science improves normal science in Kuhn's vision. Philosophically aligned with the Centrism of Nāgārjuna and Candrakīrti, Nagel sees the true path of science as a middle way between reified extremes like scientism and anti-scientism. As the cradle and time-capsule of that extraordinary tradition of scientific learning, Nalanda and its living legacy stand among the most precious gems of human civilization. We have every reason to expect that their recognition and refurbishing in the present climate of global crisis and opportunity will spark a second renaissance of the classical world's liberating wisdom and healing arts.

REFERENCES

Gadamer, Hans, *Truth and Method,* New York: Seabury Press, 1975.

Kitcher, Phillip, *Science, Truth and Democracy,* Oxford: Oxford, 2001.

Kuhn, Thomas, *The Essential Tension,* Chicago: Chicago, 1977.

Loizzo, Joseph, *Candrakīrti and the Moon-Flower of Nalanda: Objectivity and Self-Correction in India's Central Therapeutic Philosophy of Language,* University of Michigan: University Microfilm Services, 2001.

——, 'Intersubjectivity in Wittgenstein and Freud: Other Minds and the Foundations of Psychiatry', *Journal of Theoretical Medicine*, Vol. 18, No. 4, 1997.

——, 'Commentary on Insight, Delusion and Belief', *Philosophy, Psychiatry and Psychology*, 1995, Vol. 1, No. 4.

——, *Nāgārjuna's Reason Sixty with Candrakīrti's Commentary*, Translated from the Tibetan with Introduction and Critical Editions, American Institute of Buddhist Studies, Columbia University Press (in Press).

——, Charlson, M., Altemis, M., Peterson, J., Briggs, M., Wolfe, M., *The Effect of Meditation on Quality of Life in Women with Breast and other Gynedigic Cancer: A Preliminary Report*, 2005, University of Michigan, Microfilm Services, 2005.

Nagel, Thomas, *The View from Nowhere*, Oxford: OUP, 1986.

Ricoeur, Paul, *Hermeneutics and the Human Sciences*, Translated by J. Thompson, Cambridge: Cambridge University Press, 1982.

Thurman, Robert, 'Tsong Khapa's Speech of Gold: Reason and Enlightenment in the Central Philosophy of Buddhism', Princeton: Princeton, 1984, Vajra Hermeneutics, in D. Lopez (ed.), *Buddhist Hermeneutics*. Hawaii, 1992.

Wallace, Vesna, *The Inner Kālacakratantra*, Oxford: OUP, 2001.

Wedemeyer, Christain, *Vajrayāna and its Doubles: The Tāntric Works of Āryadeva*, Michigan: University of Michigan, Microfilm Services, 2000.

Wittgenstein, Ludwig, *Philosophical Investigations*, New York: Macmillan, 1953.

42

NALANDA UNIVERSITY: ITS INFLUENCES ON THE DEVELOPMENT OF BUDDHIST LEARNING

(BUDDHIST STUDIES IN TAIWAN AND THE FO GUANG SHAN BUDDHIST ORDER)

Ven. Bhiksuni Chuehmen

Nalanda University was a famous centre of Buddhist learning beginning in the 5th century and a flourishing town with over ten thousand scholars and an extensive library. Scholars including foreigners from China and Tibet were at one time among the thousands of scholars at Nalanda, especially the famous Chinese Xuanzang[1] (601-664). In his 18-year journey, he set out to understand the many different Buddhist sects throughout China, Afghanistan and India and he provided vivid accounts of the richly sculptured towns in his *Great Tang Records of the Western Journey* (大唐西域).

The courses offered at Nalanda included the study of scriptures of Mahāyāna and Theravāda schools, Brāhmaṇical Vedic texts, philosophy, logic, theology, grammar, astronomy, mathematics, medicine and others. The university helped to spread Indian culture in China and Central Asia and also in South-East Asian countries. After Buddhism was brought into China, it flourished into eight schools,[2] and was later spread into Korea, Japan and Tibet around CE 372, CE 552 and CE 641. After the World War two eminent masters from China immigrated to Taiwan. Though encountering years of difficulties and obstructions, now Buddhism in Taiwan is considered one of the most prosperous of Buddhist learning in close connection with society.

Today, Buddhist learning has become popular with people regardless of nationality or cultural background. It is no longer just taught by monks and nuns in monasteries, but it has also become part of academic studies in many universities regardless of whether it is a Buddhist-based educational institution or not. When we look into the history of Buddhist institutions of higher learning, we cannot deny that Nalanda University, founded in the 5th century CE, was an ancient seat of educational learning having thousands of lecturers and students from all over India as well as monks from China and Tibet. It certainly was one of the first Residential International Universities in the world.

The Buddha was one of the greatest educators in the world, and Buddhism is what he taught. Buddhism is a spiritual tradition that puts high emphasis on education, and through education we can perfect our lives. To ascertain our life goal and to fulfil a meaningful livelihood is the basis of life taught by Buddha.

The world's first well-established Buddhist University followed Buddha's concepts, the excellence of education and purity of monastic life. A long succession of kings extended their royal patronage to ensure the progress and prosperity of the university from the 5th through the 12th century CE, when the invasion of the Turko-Afghan Muslims, having no tolerance and respect for other cultures and belief systems, destroyed this ancient heritage. Its material form may be gone, but the heritage of wisdom and spiritual practice received by internationally renowned, eminent monks and scholars who once studied in Nalanda, took their learning to their respective countries and thereafter continued to spread it far and wide.

THE EARLIEST BUDDHIST UNIVERSITY

The Buddha was a great educator. In the *Aṅguttara Nikāya*, it is mentioned:

> A unique being, an extraordinary man arises in this world for the benefit of the many, for the happiness of the many, out of compassion for the world, for the good, benefit, and happiness of gods and men. Who is this unique being? It's the Tathāgata, the Exalted, and the fully Enlightened One (AN I, 1, 13, p. 22).

The Buddha was the first chancellor at the Kuṭāgāraśālā, Jetavana, Bamboo, Markaṭahṛada Lecture Halls and others. His great leading disciples including Śāriputra, Mahā Moggallāna, and lay disciples Vimalakīrti[3] and Śrīmāla were distinguished lecturers, and the one thousand two hundred fifty monastic disciples were graduates as well as thousands of other students. Though Buddha had left no written records of his teachings, his disciples preserved them by committing to memory and transmitting them orally from generation to generation into the *Tipiṭaka* – the basket of discipline (*Vinaya Piṭaka*), the basket of discourses (*Sutta Piṭaka*) and the basket of ultimate learning.

The Buddha's teaching emphasizing the cultivation of speech and action is the 'law of rule' (morality); embracing body and mind is 'life study' (concentration); and the elevation to develop one's true nature is 'logic' (wisdom). To deduce the three trainings, the Buddha had set up many programmes of study. For example, for ethics and rules he established the by-laws, rules and regulations, and precepts. In organizational management, he gave a good example of the *Saṅgha* six points of reverent harmony[4] (六和敬). Regarding the subject of astronomy, the *Jingluyixiang*[5] *Sūtra* (經律異相) is the Buddhist encyclopedia which describes every detail of the universe. The Buddhist concept of conditional causation and natural emptiness clearly explain the ties of the universe and gives a very satisfactory answer on matters. The phrase 'form is emptiness; emptiness is form' is perhaps the most celebrated paradox associated with contemporary physics theory.

In his teachings on time and space, he taught about the past, the present and the future. In this future, another planet or other dimension is Futurology, a new subject in academic institutions. The Buddhist concepts of 'Mind-Only' and 'Consciousness-Only' analyzing human metal functions are a clear explanation of today's psychology. The 'Twelve Links of Dependent Arising', explain the cycle of human relationships.[6] The connection of the universe and human life mentioned in the *Four Noble Truths* is a subject of Life Philosophy. There are also many writings on medical matters including *fo-yi-jing* (*Sūtra of Healing* 佛醫經), *liao-bing-zhi-jing*[7] (*Sūtra on Curing Piles* 療痔病經) and *zhi-jing*[8] (*Sūtra on Dental Hygiene* 齒經). Furthermore, Buddha had already seen that "a bowl of water contains limitless bacteria" even before science discovered them. The Buddha skilfully taught according to the needs of respective individuals, for instance when teaching merchants he would talk about business management; to farmers he taught agriculture; to politicians he taught the ruling of a country; to *Kṣudrapanthaka*, the slow thinker,

Buddha taught 'Rajoharaṇaṁ' (I am sweeping away impurity). For the human world, he had drawn up many teaching materials similar to the different faculties, colleges, or departments in a university. After his *parinirvāṇa*, his disciples convened six councils to compile scrolls of writings into complete teaching materials. He was a good example of a great educator, and his abundance of teaching materials has been carried from generation to generation to benefit the masses.

NALANDA UNIVERSITY AND ITS ACCOMPLISHMENT

In order to continue the teachings of the Buddha, Buddhism had its first well established university, which was the well known Nalanda, built between 414 and 455 CE[9] (now a ruin in the eastern Indian state of Bihar, about 72 km off the present capital Patna). It was a great, leading and outstanding centre of Buddhist learning and intellectual activities in ancient India and an impressive place with majestic buildings including shrine halls, temples, hostels, lecture halls, meditation halls, libraries, lakes and so forth.

A. Symbolic of a Prestigious Buddhist University

According to Xuanzang in *Great Tang Records of Western Journey*,

> Not long after the *parinirvāṇa* of the Buddha, the Gupta (笈王朝) King Śakrāditya[10] (414-455) in his respect and esteem for the one Vehicle and his high honor for the Triple Gem, selected the auspicious spot and built saṅghārāma to commemorate the Buddha.

As mentioned by Xuanzang, King Śakrāditya (帝日) or Kumāragupta was the founder of the Nalanda University. After King Śakrāditya, his son King Budhagupta[11] (覺護) continued the excellent undertaking of his father and built another *saṅghārāma* to the south. When his grandson King Tathāgatagupta (如來) was ruling the country and following the practice of his ancestors, he built another *saṅghārāma* in the east.

When Śakrāditya's great grandson Bālāditya (幻日) took over the country, he built another *saṅghārāma* on the north-east side of the one built by his father, King Tathāgatagupta. This *saṅghārāma* was still called the College of Bālādityarāja during the time of Xuanzang's visit. Moreover, he constructed a great *vihāra* 300 feet high with dimensions and a statue of Buddha resembling the great *vihāra* built under the *Bodhi* tree. During the inauguration ceremony, a grand celebration was held with ten thousand people, including two monks from China. King Bālāditya was 'filled with gladness' on seeing the determination of these two foreign monks from such a distant country coming to the great celebrations at Nalanda. He gave up his throne to enter the monastic order.

His son King Vajra (金剛) continued to patronize the work and built a Brahmā Palace in the north of the monastery. This Brahmā Palace had a special regulation that it was for resident monks according to their rank related to their seniority and age. The reason was when King Bālāditya was ordained, due to his period of monkhood, he was placed on the last line of the monks. His heart was always uneasy and restless because when he was a king, he was above all people. The poor ex-king consequently told his grievance to the superiors of the *Saṅgha*, and a meeting was convened to resolve that those monks who had not yet received the *bhikṣu* vow should be classed not according to the number of years of monkhood, but according to years of seniority in age until the time of receiving full ordination. This was a change in the monastic custom at Nalanda so that the ex-king Bālāditya did not have to stand in the last position of the whole community, but he had all the young novice monks behind him as he was then an old man and his ambition was satisfied.

After King Vajra, another king known as Harṣavardhana of Kanauj continued to build to the north a great *saṅghārāma*. The six kings who patronized in making these buildings created the institution into the most significant Buddhist monastery complex. According to Xuanzang, Nalanda was a six-storey building, a residential university where the staff and students had free board and lodging and for admission had to go through a tough entrance test. The university offered a choice of many subjects of study, including Hīnayāna, though it specialized in Mahāyāna Buddhism. Instructions were offered in Brāhmaṇical Vedic texts, logic, grammar, philosophy, astronomy, theology, literature, mathematics and medicine. The method of discussion was used as a teaching method in the classrooms. During this prosperous period, within the university complex, it had a large library widely renowned with over nine million volumes of literature.

Many eminent Buddhist *ācārya*s were associated with Nalanda including Nāgārjuna, Āryadeva, Asaṅga, Vasubandhu, Diṅgnāga, Dharmakīrti, Śāntarakṣita, Dharmapāla, Śīlabhadra and others. All these scholars of Nalanda produced a vast literature in all branches of knowledge, and their contribution to logic was unchallenged.

B. Receiving the Lineage of *Dharma* in Nalanda

Two of the famous Chinese monks, namely, Xuanzang (601-664)[12] and Yi'jing (635-713) who had learned profoundly at Nalanda, brought home extensive number of Buddhist scriptures and pilgrims' records which were translated into Chinese and later transmitted all over the world. When Xuanzang was there more than 1300 years ago, the famous Śīlabhadra (戒賢), known as the 'Treasure of Right Law', was head of the university, with whom Xuanzang developed a close connection. Xuanzang stayed and studied under his leadership and gave a detailed description of the situations prevailing during that period in his record, *Great Tang Records of the Western Journey*. When Xuanzang toured Bodhgaya and was to set out for Kukkuṭapādagiri (雞足山) to pay his respect to Mahā Kassapa, who was holding the Buddha's robe and alms bowl awaiting to hand them over to Buddha Maitreya, four monks from Nalanda came to receive him at the university. The next morning, they arrived at the village, and he was led to rest at a *stūpa*. But, a little while later over 200 monks leading thousands of people each holding a flower, walked in line to receive him. This was an official reception to welcome him to Nalanda. When they reached the mountain gate of Nalanda, residents of the university were already waiting eagerly. Xuanzang, though pleased and grateful that such a reception was arranged to receive him, felt shameful that due to the few merits he had troubled all the people to come there to meet him. A seat was arranged in the hall, and twenty monks accompanied him to meet the 'Treasure of Right Law' (正法藏). Śīlabhadra, the Head of Nalanda who was already over 100 years old, was well known for his great knowledge. Xuanzang was excited to meet him and showed his great respect by walking on his knees to kiss the teacher's feet. When Śīlabhadra heard that Xuanzang was from China and had come to learn *Yogācara*, he started to weep.

Śīlabhadra then told his disciple Bodhibhadra (覺賢), who was already over seventy years old, to tell about an incident concerning a sickness three years before. Śīlabhadra had been suffering from rheumatism for over twenty years, and when it attacked, his whole body would cramp, and the pain was unbearable as if he was burning and his flesh being cut. Three years before, the attack worsened, and he could never tolerate such pain so Śīlabhadra decided to starve to death. But that night he had a dream. Three persons – one golden in colour, one crystal and one silver – appeared in his room. The golden one said,

> So, you think you want to get rid of your physical body. It is taught in the *sūtra* that having a physical body is suffering, but it does not teach one to commit suicide. In past lives, you were once a king and were happy to make people suffer. So you are now being given retribution for your past negative actions. You should show remorse and sincerely repent your past deeds, willingly accept such retribution and devote yourself to give more *Dharma* teaching.

The golden person then introduced himself as Mañjuśrī, the crystal one as Avalokiteśvara, and the silver one as Maitreya, and said,

> To destroy your body will do you more harm, so I am here to advise you. You should follow my words to spread the true *Dharma* of *Yogācara* and others widely so that many will benefit. In this way, your sickness will be cured. Three years later, a monk from the Tang Dynasty in his great love for the *Dharma* will be here to learn from you, you should wait for him and teach him with all your effort.

Śīlabhadra bowed to show his respect to the three persons, but when he got up, they were gone. When he awoke, he realized that it was a dream. Later, his rheumatoid suffering gradually decreased and was finally cured.

Though Xuanzang was a new member in the university, the treatment he received was extraordinary, including the food. It was recorded that among over 10,000 resident monks and guests at Nalanda, only ten persons received such a privilege, and Xuanzang was one of the ten. This showed how Śīlabhadra treasured such a talented person to continue the lineage. Xuanzang arrived at Nalanda in 630 CE and listened to Śīlabhadra's teaching of *Yogācārabhūmi* (瑜伽師地論) the following year. For the next five years, he studied the *Nyāyānusāra* (順正理論), *Prakaraṇāryavācā-śāstra* (顯揚聖教論), *Pramāṇa-samuccaya* (集量論) and others.[13] Upon instruction from Śīlabhadra, he also taught at the university the *Mahāyāna-saṁparigraha-śāstra* (攝大乘論).

During the flourishing years of Nalanda, after Xuanzang many more Chinese monks continued to study there including Xuanzhao from Taizhou (太州玄照), Yi'jing (義淨) in CE 676 (who stayed until the autumn of CE 685), Daolin from Jingzhou (荊州道琳), Daosheng from Jinzhou (并州道生), and Zhihong from Luoyang (洛陽智弘). All studied extensively the many texts. In the beginning, Nalanda was an important city for the Buddhist Mind-Only School but gradually became a centre for the Esoteric School. In the eighth century, the Gupta Empire started to decline and Hinduism began to flourish.

In the twelfth century due to the Muslim invasion, Nalanda University was destroyed, but one record mentions that during the early years of the emperor Yuanting of the Yuan Dynasty (CE 1324-1327), a monk named Vinayabhadra from Nalanda came to China. So, part of the university might have still remained. Some Buddhist learning colleges and institutions today have taken the name 'Nalanda' as a connection to the great Buddhist university, for example the New Nalanda University in Bihar inaugurated in July 1920; the Sri Lanka Nalanda College, Colombo inaugurated in November 1925; the Karma Shri Nalanda Institute inaugurated on November 18, 1981 and officially recognized in 1984 by the government of Sikkim and its Department of Ecclesiastical Affairs in India; and the Nalanda College of Buddhist Studies founded by Suwanda H.J. Sugunasiri in 2000 at 47 Queen's Park, Crescent East, Toronto, Ontario, Canada M5S 2C (near the University of Toronto).

A thousand years ago, Nalanda University was famous for its knowledge and discipline, having fostered thousands of talented people. Contemporary, careful excavation of the site has revealed many *stūpas*, *chaityas*, temples, hostels, staircases, meditation halls and lecture halls which speak of the splendour Nalanda once enjoyed as the prestigious centre of high academic standards and strict discipline. The ruins are a reminder of the past influence, and the knowledge that was transmitted continues to prevail and is now known from east to west.

C. Buddhism Moved into China

Buddhism made its way to China in CE 67 at the invitation of Emperor Ming Ti (CE 57-75) of the Eastern Han Dynasty by way of Indian monks with sacred books, pictures and relics. Conversions multiplied, and during the next few centuries, the communications between the two countries were very close. The supplanting of the earlier form of Buddhism in the northern areas of India in the second century led to a corresponding change in the Buddhism of China. The later missionaries, being mostly from the north of India, brought with them the new teachings, and in a short time the Mahāyāna, or Northern School Buddhism, prevailed. Many Buddhist missionaries from India came to China, and Chinese monks made pilgrimages to the sacred places in India. Of these pilgrims, the most noted are Faxian[14] who journeyed to India and Ceylon (CE 399-414) and two centuries later Xuanzang and Yi'jing made extensive travels in India. Xuanzang was inspired to obtain the true teachings of the Buddha. His journey was extremely difficult, having to cross high mountains and deserts, and he was also confronted by bandits, but he never lost his determination and vowed:

> I would rather die proceeding to the West (India), than to retreat alive to the East (return back to China).

After eighteen years of studying at Nalanda and pilgrimage to Central Asia, Xuanzang returned to China in CE 644 with a large collection of Buddhist texts, which he translated during the remaining years of his life. With his profound understanding of Buddhism and excellent skill in languages, his translations marked a new period in Buddhist literature. His travel record *Great Tang Records of Western Journey* gives detailed descriptions of Central Asia and India and provides an eye-witness account of these regions during his time.

At the beginning of the seventh century CE, during the early Tang Dynasty, Buddhism reached out to more and more people and soon became an important part of Chinese culture and had great influence on Chinese art, literature, architecture, sculpture and philosophy. Moreover, Chinese translations of Buddhist texts had increased tremendously, and the Buddhists were faced with the problem of how to study the voluminous number of Buddhist texts and how to put their teachings into practice. Gradually, eight schools of Buddhism arose, with each school concentrating on certain texts for their study and practice. However, the two most prominent schools were the Chan[15] and the Pure Land[16] schools which became two of the most important Chinese schools of Buddhist practice.

Following a hundred years of development, Buddhism during the Tang Dynasty had a breakthrough when Baizhang[17] (CE 720-814), a Chan Master established a set of 'Pure Rules' (*Qing-guei*) for the monastic community. Chan Master Mazu Daoyi's establishment of the *conglin,* which literally means 'forest' and refers to a gathering of monastics practising in unity, has the connotation of a university. So, it could be said that the first Buddhist university in China started with the founding of the *conglin,* and Master Baizhang could be said to be the first chancellor.

Buddhism in China also had its ups and downs or degeneration into superstitions and only practice in seclusion. Therefore, in the early part of the twentieth century, there was an attempt to modernize and reform the tradition in order to attract wider support from the masses. One of the most well known reformists was Master Tai-xu[18] (CE 1889-1947), a monk noted for his Buddhist scholarship. Besides introducing many reforms in the monastic community, he also introduced Western-style education, which included the study of secular subjects and foreign languages for Buddhists. Venerable Master Hsing Yun, the founder of the Fo Guang Shan Buddhist Order in Taiwan, as a young monk took enthusiastic interest in Tai-xu's reform which brought together the revival of Buddhism when he settled in Taiwan in the early 1950s. In the 1960s, during the Chinese Cultural Revolution, Buddhism in China was suppressed, many monasteries were either destroyed or closed and monks and nuns were forced to disrobe. Fortunately, many eminent monks who had earlier immigrated to Taiwan after the Second World War had preserved the true teachings.

DEVELOPMENT OF BUDDHIST STUDY IN TAIWAN

The flourishing of the growth of Buddhism in Taiwan perhaps is more extensive than anywhere else in the world. Since restrictions on the formation of religious organizations were lifted in 1987, the number of Buddhist organizations rose rapidly, reflecting the popularity and strength gained from their decades of diligent missionary work. Of the numerous organizations, four[19] are particularly influential, namely, the Buddhist Compassion Relief Tzu Chi Foundation Taiwan (臺灣佛教慈濟慈善事業基金會) led by Master Cheng Yen (證嚴上人), Dharma Drum Mountain (法鼓山) led by Master Sheng Yen (聖嚴法師), Chung Tai Mountain (中台山) led by Master Wei Chueh (惟覺和尚), and Fo Guang Shan (佛光山) led by Master Hsing Yun (星雲大師). Also, the Buddhist women of Taiwan are among the most progressive and active in the world, contributing their energies to spiritual and social growth. Many Buddhist nuns and lay-women are taking leadership roles. Another example is the increase in attendance in the Buddhist summer camps for school children, teenagers, college students, and teachers. More than 100 Buddhist camps are sponsored by local temples and education authorities throughout Taiwan each summer, attracting thousands of participants in all. There are currently more than sixty societies for Buddhist research in Taiwan's colleges and universities. There are also a number of periodicals and other media efforts devoted to encourage people to follow Buddhism.[20]

The Buddha's Light International Association (BLIA), ROC formed on February 3, 1991 in Taipei was another pioneering feat in the history of Buddhism in Taiwan. In essence, the BLIA is a manifestation of Hsing Yun's long-standing concern for the continuation of social involvement and a society lacking in order, values, and faith. He is optimistic that the *Saṅgha* and the laity joining forces,[21] people will be assisted in their study of the Buddhist *Tripiṭaka* and in upholding of the 'Five Precepts'. As a result, society will be able to achieve a state of purity and serenity.[22]

In 2002, the world-acclaimed Buddha Finger Relic coming to Taiwan saw the unity of the Taiwan Buddhist communities: the Four Mountain Heads (四大山頭), Nine Great Groups[23] (九大門派), and the Five Large Organizations[24] (五大團體) all participated in this historic event. It was on January 30, 2002, when venerable Master Hsing Yun, representing Buddhist groups in Taiwan, signed an agreement with the Mainland Chinese Buddhist Association in Hong Kong to bring the sacred relic enshrined at Famen temple (法門寺), Xian for display in various places in Taiwan for about 37 days. Having the Buddha's Finger Relic coming to Taiwan was not only an historic event in Buddhist history, it also marked as one of the most important cross-Straits spiritual exchanges. Moreover, Buddhists were encouraged to explore a different reflection on life and the creation of peace and harmony. This event was indeed a significant reflection of the Buddha's appearance in this human world. It was estimated that about five million people paid their respect when the sacred relic was displayed at the various temples and stadiums in North, Central and South Taiwan. Since the sacred relic came to Taiwan on February 23rd until its departure to Famen temple on March 31st, a large number of people in Hong Kong and China also watched the ceremonies in special television broadcasts.

A. Early Buddhism in Taiwan

Near the end of Ming Dynasty (明朝), immigrants from Fujian (福建) and Guangdong (廣東) Province carried the Buddhist faith with them as they set sail for Taiwan. As Taiwan was then under the Dutch rule, practice was prohibited. After the arrival of Admiral Zheng Ho (鄭和) in December 1661, he chased away the Dutch; Buddhism then began to gain attention. His son Zheng Jing (鄭經), a devout Buddhist, erected the Mituo temple (彌陀寺) and his mother invited the *Saṅgha* to take care of the Kaiyuan temple (開元寺). During the Ming-Zheng (明鄭) period (CE 1662-1683), many temples enshrined the Amitābha statue, but the practice of 'Pure Land' was not clear. During the Qinglin (清領) period (CE 1683-1895), many temples enshrined a Guanyin *Bodhisattva* (Avalokitesvara) statue, and Buddhist beliefs were mixed with local traditions. Only a minority of the orthodox temples practiced Chan of the Linchi (臨濟) and Huangpo (黃檗) schools.

Japanese Buddhism was introduced into Taiwan during the Japanese colonization from CE 1896-1945. By 1925, a large number of Japanese monks from different Pure Land School including Jodo Shu (淨土宗), Jodo Shinshu Honganji (淨土真宗本願寺派), (淨土真宗大谷派) arrived and were in a leading position in many established temples. Buddhism in Taiwan gradually took on a Japanese cast, particularly in disciplinary code less strict, resulting in many Taiwanese monastics abandoning celibacy and vegetarianism. Some monastics altered their practice by wearing their robes only within the temple walls. Together with practitioners from sects such as Longhua (龍華派) and Xiantian (先天派) who were not required to take monastic vows, it was often difficult to distinguish between monastics and those who were not. The irregularity and non-uniformity of the monastic lifestyle and appearance caused many misconceptions about Buddhism.[25] Moreover, monks and nuns did not have facilities for disciplinary training in Taiwan, and they had to go to Fujian, China in order to have higher ordination. The Japanese Jodo Shu and Jodo Shinshu sects established many educational institutions and training schools, but these were basically secular.

After the Japanese left, Taiwan witnessed the re-establishment of the Chinese Mahāyāna tradition and renewed the requirement of moral and disciplinary codes and monastic ordination ceremony. The three local leading Buddhist sects in the North, Central and South of Taiwan began to organize ordination ceremony for monks and nuns: Ling-quan temple (靈泉寺) of the Yue-mei Mountain (月眉山) led by Master Shan-hui (善慧) in Northern Taiwan; Fayun temple (法雲寺) led by Master Jueli (覺力) in Miaoli, Central Taiwan; the Kai-yuan temple (開元寺) in the South. Most Buddhist temples during this period belonged to one of these three sects. The Buddhist Association of the ROC (中國佛教會) established in 1947 in Nanjing, China by Master Zhang-chia (章嘉) followed the Chinese Nationalist Government and shifted to Taiwan to establish the Taiwan provincial chapter of the Buddhist Association of the ROC. Since the 1950s, the Buddhist Association of the ROC has held ordination ceremonies[26] for Buddhist monks and nuns, and only temples which were recognized by the Association could organize a higher ordination ceremony on rotation.[27] But now no such restrictions are required as long as the organizing temples have the facilities and capabilities, and most important of all is requirement of the Ten Ordination Masters to conduct and witness the ordination procedures.

B. Beginning of *Saṅgha* Education

During the early years there weren't any *Saṅgha* institutes. Though life was difficult, Master Zhen-chang (1900-1946) was determined to promote the establishment of a Taiwan Buddhist Association. So when the Japanese surrendered and left Taiwan in August 1945, in December the same year, a first meeting to convene a Taiwanese Buddhist organization was held at the Lungshan temple (龍山寺) in Taipei. Zhen-chang wanted to establish a Buddhist institution at the parent Fayun temple (法雲寺) in Miaoli and named it 'Central Buddhist Institute' (中央佛學院). Master Zhen-chang (真常法師) passed away on January 30th the following year, and this plan did not materialize. On February 25th the same year, another meeting was again held at Lungshan temple with the first board of directors being elected and echoed to promote *Saṅgha* education as proposed by Master Zhen-chang. Nevertheless, the plan was not put to action either. In January 1947, at the fourth board of directors' meeting held at Shandao temple (善導寺) in Taipei, an education committee was formed and resolved to establish a Buddhist research institution, named Taiwan Buddhist Institute (台灣佛學院) at Yuanguang temple (圓光寺) in Chungli (中壢). In April 1948, a Female Training School (女眾學園) was established at the Shenzai Tang (慎齋堂) in Taichung, followed by the Yuanping Buddhist Institute (延平佛學院) at Kaiyuan temple (開元寸) in Tainan. The Taiwan Buddhist Institute inaugurated in December 1948 was closed down six months later in June 1949 due to financial problems. On May 25, 1949, Master Ci-hang (慈航法師) upon invitation by Master Dazhen (達真法師) and Rujing (如淨法師) to take charge of the Lion Mountain Buddhist Institute (獅山佛學院) had the inauguration of the institute on May 28th at Kaishan temple (開善寺). But not long after the closing down of the Taiwan Buddhist Institute, the Lion Mountain Buddhist Institute was also terminated. Lifespan of the Buddhist institutions were short due to financial difficulties. Moreover, many refugee monks from Mainland had also taken shelter in those temples, adding heavier financial difficulties to the temples.

Saṅgha education stands an essential position to endure the *Dharma*, besides generating spiritual practice. It is the responsibility of the *Saṅgha* members to educate and purify human minds in society. A few of the eminent masters who deserve praise for their enthusiasm in establishing *Saṅgha* education include Master Ci-hang (1895-1954), Master Zhi-xing (1884-1964), Master Wu-shang (1918-1966), Master Bai-sheng (1904-1989), Master Xin-shu (1906-2004), Master Hsing Yun (1927-) and Master Sheng-yin (1930-). Master Hsing Yun has in fact contributed greatly to actualizing *Saṅgha* education, secular education and lay Buddhist education.

In 1965, the Buddhist Association of the ROC produced a 'Work Report' that said that there are over twenty[28] residential Buddhist institutions established within Buddhist temples from after World War II to1965, but quite a number had either discontinued or were interrupted only to restart later. As usual, the reason for discontinuation or temporary termination was financial. The Shou-shan Buddhist College, later renamed as Eastern Buddhist College,[29] was established in 1965 and now is affiliated with the Fo Guang Shan Tsung-lin University. It is one of the few which has not been interrupted, and in the 1990s developed other institutions in many countries, namely, Hong Kong,[30] South Africa,[31] India,[32] Australia,[33] Malaysia,[34] Brazil,[35] and San Diego.[36]

A statistic from 2002 shows the number of Buddhist institutes established since 1949 was over ninety including those which had been closed, or their name being changed. The breakdown of the data showed that four institutes were established in the 1940s (1947-1949); approximately fourteen in the 50s (1950-1959); nineteen in the 60s (1960 -1969); twenty-two in the 70s (1970-1979); twenty-five in the 80s (1980-1989); and from 1990 to 2002, about seven more residential Buddhist institutes were also established.

C. Rapid Development in Buddhist Learning

Early Buddhism in Taiwan was criticized for being superstitious and backward. It was also considered a belief system for old people or for someone who had passed away and the family needed a monastic to conduct religious rituals. At that time, the Buddha's teachings were rarely heard, making it difficult for many to have a correct understanding of Buddhism. Life was difficult, and many people had very little formal education or none at all. What made it more problematic was the disorganization of the monastic communities. Most temples were either in the forest or remote countryside or in the backstreets of small towns, and many monastics preferred practicing in seclusion. Half a century under the Japanese rule, Taiwanese people were socially repressed and deprived of education, also lacking a correct view on religion.

The rapid development of Buddhist learning in Taiwan has much in connection with living Buddhism. Master Xin-shu (1906-2004), a scholarly monk has written a great number of books in promoting the concept of 'human world Buddhism' in the 1960s, but the sower of *Bodhi* seeds had already started in Ilan by Master Hsing Yun in the early 1950s. As a young monk in China, Master Hsing Yun was already very much influenced by Master Tai-xu, the Buddhist reformist's idea to advocate living Buddhism. After arriving to Taiwan in 1949 at a young age of 23, and having gone through much difficulties, Master Hsing Yun finally settled down at Leiyin temple (雷音寺), North Taiwan in 1953. Though the conditions were not very conducive to spreading the *Dharma*, he was prepared to help Ilan become the first site to practice Humanistic Buddhism,[37] and it was here that 'his career as an influential leader and teacher began to take shape.'[38] Due to the prevalent illiteracy of the 1950s, Master Hsing Yun first employed the most accessible method of reciting the Buddha's name for attracting the people. The chanting services paved way into the arena of regular *Dharma* lectures.

Over the years, due to the diligent efforts of nuns and leading monks sympathetic to their development, the first formal ordination of nuns occurred in 1953. Nuns now enjoy a high social position in Taiwan[39] and play not only active but leadership roles in monastic affairs and society including education, charity, publishing and the mass media. One most ardent promoter has been venerable Master Hsing Yun, founder of the Fo Guang Shan Buddhist Order in 1967 who currently has over 1200 ordained disciples,[40] of which 78% are nuns. Many of the young ladies who had helped him during his work in Ilan are the senior nuns who have contributed in the building of the FGS Monastery.

The Tzu Chi Foundation with over 5 million supporters and over 30,000 certified commissioners across the globe has been contributing to better social and community services, medical care, education and humanism. Master Cheng Yen firmly believes that suffering in this world is caused by material deprivation and spiritual poverty. She felt that "lack of love for others" has been the root of many problems in this world, and "to save the world, we must begin by transforming human hearts". A volunteer-based, spiritual as well as welfare organization, Tzu Chi's mission focuses on giving material aid and inspiring love and humanity in both the givers and receivers. Emergency aid to typhoon-stricken Bangladesh in 1991 marked the beginning of the foundation's international relief efforts. Firmly believing that, "Nothing is more valuable than life", Tzu Chi demonstrates first hand that "All beings are equal". They overcome obstacles of time, distance, and politics, to provide relief and hope to victims of war, flood, and drought. As of August 2005, over fifty-seven countries in five continents have received Tzu Chi's aid. Tzu Chi also has its own TV station to serve achieve their goal of purity in the heart, a harmonious society and a world without disasters. Tzu Chi Da-Ai TV is available in various countries either through cable or satellite dish. It also streams live online at **http://www.newdaai.tv.**

The Dharma Drum Mountain which houses the Chung-Hwa Institute of Buddhist Studies, Dharma University, Dharma Drum Zen Monastery, the Museum of Buddhist History and Culture, a meditation centre, and an international conference hall, offers academic studies and academic seminars and conferences. Meditation courses are offered for locals and foreigners. The three-hour retreat includes 15 minutes of warm-up exercise and two half-hour sessions of sitting meditation, broken up by yoga exercises and walking meditation, concluding with a discussion.

Chung Tai Chan Monastery has a large main shrine, a striking piece of architecture perched on a hill near Puli, opened in 2001, appeals to educate city dwellers, and has gained popularity by organizing meditation courses and retreats for white-collar workers. This is Buddhism in the 21st century, as the grounds feature not only Buddhist icons, vegetable gardens, dormitories, and study halls, but also a gigantic television screen of the kind normally found in sports arenas.

The Nine Great Groups have much longer history than the four influential groups; the Five Large Organizations, publishing house, societies and clubs have also contributed in one way or another to the growth of Buddhism today. Several Buddhist TV stations, namely, Da-ai Television (大愛), Universal Culture Television (法界衛星), and Buddha Compassion TV Station (佛衛電視慈悲台) have also served extensively through satellite and programmes being viewed in Taiwan and overseas.

Dramatic societal transformations in the 1970s and 1980s included a remarkable and rapid economic take-off in Taiwan where people gained more freedom to travel overseas either for touring or study, and the end of martial law allowed the development of a civil society including free religious practice. So with the improvement of Taiwan economy and the commitment of both *Saṅgha* and laity, the Taiwan Buddhist communities have managed to have their own path to elevate the potential of the *Saṅgha*. A statistics done by the Taiwan Ministry of the Interior on religions for the *Taiwan Yearbook 2004* shows, Buddhism has high population.

Statistics on Religions in Taiwan

Items	*Temples and Churches*	*Believers*	*Universities and Colleges*	*Hospitals*	*Publishing Houses*
Religions					
Taoism	8,604	4,546,000	1	2	9
Buddhism	4,037	5,486,000	8	3	28
Yi Guan Dao	3,218	887,000	—	21	30
Protestantism	3,609	605,000	7	14	—
Catholicism	1,135	298,000	3	11	9
Lord of the Universe Church	53	260,000	—	—	2
Tian De Jiao	5	200,000	—	—	1
Li-ism	131	187,000	—	—	1
Syuan Yuan Jiao	21	150,000	—	—	1
Islam	6	53,000	—	—	1
Tenrikyo	150	30,000	—	—	—
Baha'i	7	16,000	—	—	1
Mahikarikyo	9	1,000	—	—	—
Others	2,161	241,300	—	—	4
Total	23,146	12,960,300	19	51	87
Source: Civil Affairs Department, Ministry of the Interior					

FO GUANG SHAN BUDDHIST ORDER

The headquarters of the Fo Guang Shan Buddhist Order (website: **www.fgs.org.tw**) is situated in Kaohsiung County, South Taiwan. FGS inherited its spirit of antiquity of a traditional monastery of the Tang Dynasty[41] and combined this with the ideals of modern management. It functions as a well-organized entity energized by human and financial resources. Venerable Master Hsing Yun founded Fo Guang Shan (Buddha's Light Mountain) in May 1967. Master Hsing Yun was born in 1927 in Jiangdu, in Jiangsu Province, China and came to Taiwan in 1949, where he was involved mostly in education, writing and editing in order to realize his great vow to promote Humanistic Buddhism. In 1953, he was invited to Lei Yin temple, Ilan in Northern Taiwan where he started his journey of spreading the *Dharma*. In May 1967, he established Fo Guang Shan with his four main objectives, namely, (1) to promote Buddhism through cultural activities, (2) to foster talents through education, (3) to benefit society through charitable activities, and (4) to purify human minds through Buddhist practice. He has transformed a mountain-top bamboo forest, an area of about 100 acres, in the township of Dashu, Kaohsiung County into an internationally recognized Buddhist organization. Under his guidance, FGS has achieved much in all areas since it was established 39 years ago, abiding by the guidelines for the propagation of Humanistic Buddhism.[42] FGS now has more than 200 branch temples[43] around the world and has established over 100 overseas Chinese schools, three universities (University of the West,[44] Nanhua[45] and Fo Guang[46]) and various Buddhist colleges in five continents. *The Merit Times Daily News*,[47] Fo Guang Publishing, the Devotees Open University, Humanistic Buddhism Reading Association and many libraries and art galleries have been created with the aim of purifying human minds.

A. Torch of Wisdom – Promoting Buddhism Through Culture

In order that the teaching of the Buddha may endure, FGS emphasizes the promotion of Buddhist culture, thus started with the Sanchung Cultural Services Center in 1959 in Northern Taiwan. Master Hsing Yun said, "Without the Sanchung Buddhist Cultural Services Center, there would be no Fo Guang Shan." During that time, Buddhist cultural services were not common, and it was difficult to get Buddhist books or related materials. Venerable Master and his elder disciples travelled widely to promote Buddhist books and also helped to find the source for various publications and products including wooden-fish[48] from Hanzhao, chanting beads, wearing monastic shoes, and so forth, thus nurturing the seeds of Buddhist *sūtra*s and books which can now be found everywhere in Taiwan.

Starting from Sanchung Cultural Services Center, FGS later established the Fo Guang Publishing House (Taiwan) and Buddha's Light Publishing (U.S.A.). In respect of publication, starting from *Awakening the World Periodicals*, FGS has also published the *Universal Gate Magazine*,[49] *Merit Times Daily News, Universal Gate Buddhist Journal*[50] and others. The Master created a historic event in Buddhist history by giving *Dharma* teaching on television. And now FGS has her own Life Television Station,[51] Gandha Samudra Culture Company and Voices of the Ganges. In the past, though undergoing economic restrictions and hardships, Master Hsing Yun's determination to promote Buddhist culture and education has never been deterred as these are done with the purpose of making Buddhism more easily accessible, better understood, and be spread to every corner of the world. Going through the history of Fo Guang Shan, one will notice that Fo Guang Shan did not initially build temples merely for rites and ceremonies that have traditionally been the main source of financial income in many temples.

Now Fo Guang Shan has published voluminous collection of publications. The *Fo Guang Buddhist Dictionary* (8 volumes) won a Golden Cauldron Prize after its publication in 1988. It is now on CD-ROM making it more accessible for spreading Buddhism further in the world, so is the *Fo Guang Tripiṭaka – Āgama Canon* (16 volumes publication) and *Chan Canon* (53 volumes), *A Collection of Contemporary Buddhist Works*, totaling 100 volumes which offer MA theses and PhD. dissertations done by scholars from China and Taiwan. The 132 volumes of the *Selected Chinese Buddhist Texts in Modern Writing*, the 44 volumes of *Diary of Master Hsing Yun* recording each day's experience and thoughts of the Master from the period 1989 to 1996 are also published. The 20 volumes of *Illustrated World Buddhist Arts* is in progress of editing.

In order to spread Buddhism effectively in the contemporary era so that people from all over the world will have the opportunity to be exposed to the teaching, the FGS International Translation Center, officially inaugurated in Los Angeles, is also the successor that continuously expands this mission. Several translation centres have also been set up to coordinate translation and publication including in San Diego, U.S.A., Argentina, Brazil, Canada, Germany, Holland, India, Indonesia, Japan, Korea, Thailand and Russia, South Africa, Sri Lanka and U.K., whereby making the *Dharma* propagation more essential.

B. Fostering Talents Through Education

At present, FGS educational enterprises can be grouped into three main categories, namely, *Saṅgha* education, social education and devotee education.

(1) Saṅgha Education

In 1967, when FGS began its construction, it did not start by building a temple for ritual purposes. It was the Eastern Buddhist College[52] that was the first building constructed in the mountain. Master Hsing Yun said, "It is people that promote the Way, not the Way that promotes people" (人能弘道，非道弘人). Abiding by Master Hsing Yun's principle, this Buddhist institution, which was later renamed Fo Guang Shan Tsung-lin University, currently divided into the Institute of Chinese Buddhist Studies, Men's Buddhist College, Women's Buddhist College, Foreign Students Department, Japanese Buddhist College, English Buddhist College, Srimala Buddhist Institute[53] (勝鬘書院), and Buddhist Distance Learning on TV, and other Buddhist Colleges outside Taiwan including in Hong Kong, Malaysia, Australia, India, Brazil, South Africa and U.S.A.

(2) Social Education

Education is to help students build up a character of integrity and pursue a life of satisfaction. Besides *Saṅgha* education, FGS has also established many secular institutions ranging from kindergartens,[54] elementary,[55] junior and senior high schools,[56] vocational institute[57] and university level. To nurture the offspring of *Bodhi* wisdom, FGS established the first kindergarten – Jen-ai Kindergarten – at the Ilan Lei-yin temple, Ilan, Northern Taiwan in July 1956. This kindergarten is to combine the unique teaching of the Buddha with pre-school education. The kindergarten has thus fostered many outstanding students who are now holding high positions in society. The University of the West (formerly known as Hsi Lai University)[58] in U.S.A. is not a Buddhist university; its main purpose is to cater to the trend and needs of American multi-cultural society. It is a bridge that links the Eastern and Western cultures. The Fo Guang[59] University situated at Lin-mei Mountain in Chiaoshi, is the first university ever established in Ilan County. It involves countless human, material and monetary resources during the seven-year period of environmental impact assessments and miscellaneous works on Campus. The Nanhua University[60] adopts small-class teaching style and focuses on healthy personal developments in students. Overseas Chinese schools were established in most overseas branches to provide the young generation with an opportunity to get in touch with traditional cultures and living Buddhism to benefit all sentient beings.

(3) Devotees' Education

As early as 1950s, Master Hsing Yun had already implemented various methods to generate the general public interest on Buddhist learning and participation in Buddhist works. In March 1951, the Buddhist Choir was established to generate the young adults' interest to learn Buddhism. Master Hsing Yun personally wrote the verses and requested Yang Yung-pu to compose the lyrics. In 1953, he initiated the use of a slide projector during his *Dharma* lecture so that the audience could comprehend his teachings. To highlight the interest and increase the punctuality of the audience, the Master included a story of the *Imperial Master Yu Lin* and when the story came to an interesting point, he would say, "To be continued tomorrow."

On July 27, 1969, after the completion of the Eastern Buddhist College Building, a Buddhist Summer Camp for college students was inaugurated at FGS. Thereafter, other Buddhist activities for young adults were also created. In order to take Buddhist teachings out of the temple and to the public, on October 20, 1975, Master Hsing Yun gave a three-day *Dharma* talk at the Taipei National Arts Hall; it was the first time that a Buddhist function was held at a public venue. Appreciating the vast experience of senior citizens, FGS inaugurated a Senior Citizens' Summer Camp on May 17, 1976 to utilize the elders' wisdom, their confidence and their dedication through the *Dharma*. From August 8-15, 1979, FGS first organized an eight-day Children's Summer Camp. Its aim was to generate benevolence and to cultivate good moral character. On September 4, 1979, FGS's first TV production, *Sweet Dew* was aired on the Chung Hua TV Station and continued for three years. In the subsequent years, other productions were broadcast in Taiwan and overseas. FGS established its own TV station[61] in 1998 to prevail and realize the concepts of truth and virtue, to instill the spirit of Humanistic Buddhism into peoples' lives and thus bring blessing, peace, joyfulness and happiness to the society and the world.

In 1980, FGS initiated the Chinese New Year Festival of Light and Peace. Besides serving to expound the *Dharma*, it was also to pray for the prosperity of the country, and this festival has since been celebrated every year. In 1980 FGS started a Summer Camp for Mothers to let the working mothers who had always been busy doing housework to have an opportunity to learn Buddhism and to elevate self-image. On July 11, 1984 FGS organized the first Four-day Teenager Buddhist Summer Camp; thereafter, such camps were held yearly. In celebration of the 20th anniversary of FGS Monastery, a one-month alms procession from the north to the south of the island, covering 600 kilometre, was held on April 5, 1987. In order to give the lay people an opportunity to experience a monastic life, FGS initiated a short-term novitiate programme on August 1, 1988; thereafter two programmes are held yearly in winter and summer school vacations. From September 17 to October 1, 1988, a *Dharma* function – *Return to the Epoch of the Buddha* – was held in northern, central and southern Taiwan attended by over 120,000 devotees. From February 10, 1994, a 49-day Vegetarian Chan Talk was organized to bring Buddhism to people from all levels of life so that they could put aside their busy schedules and enjoy a vegetarian meal and simultaneously listen to the *Dharma* talks.

All the above programmes were established to benefit FGS supporters and devotees. When Master Hsing Yun stepped down as Head Abbot of FGS in 1985, he started to travel internationally and upon the request by the many Taiwanese devotees who have immigrated overseas, in their pursuit for Buddhist learning and spiritual practice, the Buddha's Light International Association (website: **www.blia.org**) was inaugurated in Taiwan in February 1991, and the World Headquarters inaugurated the following year in Los Angeles. The inauguration of the BLIA World HQ was in response to the rapid growth of FGS overseas. It also illustrated the strength of the BLIA as an international organization. Currently BLIA, has more then one million members with 132 chapters over the five continents. In Taiwan, Chunghwa HQ has five regional chapters and over 400 sub-chapters. The establishments of the BLIA Young Adult Division, Buddha's Light Scouts Division, FGS Buddhist College, Buddha's Light Open University are all meant for educating the devotees. The Humanistic Buddhism Reading Association (人間佛教讀書會) inaugurated on January 1, 2002 with the aim to create a literate society, currently has about two thousand study groups.

C. Love in Human World – Benefiting Society through Charitable Programmes

FGS has always adhered to the Buddha's teaching of:

> Give the education to the poor, give medicine to the ill, protect those without protection, be a refuge for those without refuge, and save those without a saviour.

Due to this powerful feeling of relief and charity work with loving kindness and compassion, the Charity Hall was founded in 1963 to organize charitable acts and programmes. Later, with expansion in the range of charitable activities, the Hall was upgraded to become the Charity Trust. The main work of the Charity Trust is in medical clinics, relief work, check-ups, as well as social work with children, youth, the elderly, and the physically challenged, in addition to activities for the public good. The Compassion Foundation, Da Ci Children's Home,[62] the Renai Senior Citizens Home[63] for the elderly in Ilan, the Fo Guang Elders Home,[64] Evergreen Senior Citizens Home[65] in Fengshan, *Dharma* teachings in prisons, drug rehabilitation, hospice work, the Fo Guang Medical Clinic[66] situated down the mountain gate, the Yunshui (Cloud and Water) Mobile Clinic,[67] Dai Ci Learning Centre[68] and others. Most important emphasis of FGS charitable programmes is lending a helping hand during natural disasters and in time of emergency relief tasks around the world. In this way, the light of the Buddha's love can shine everywhere, letting more and more people bathe in its grace.

D. Spiritual Pursuits – Purifying Human Minds through Buddhist Practice

For both lay and monastic disciples and devotees at FGS and its many branch temples, after arising on hearing the sound of the morning bell, the day's cultivation begins by going to the shrine for morning service, be it meditation in the Chan Hall, reciting the Buddha's name in the Buddha Hall, or chanting *sūtras* and *mantras*, and then taking meal in the main Dining Hall. There are many large and small Dharma Services that are held yearly. For example, The Festival of Light and Peace (Chinese New Year), Bathing the Buddha Dharma Service (commemoration of Buddha's birth), Medicine Buddha Dharma Service, Amitābha Dharma Service, Ullambana Dharma Service, the Great Compassion Repentance for allaying misfortune, the Emperor Liang Jeweled Repentance, the Water and Land Dharma Service, and many others. Within these *Dharma* services there are also *Dharma* talks by monks and nuns, as well as worship and chanting of the *sūtras*.

E. FGS – The Revival of Chinese Buddhism

When looking around FGS Monastery today, one sees the verdant trees, the golden tiled rooftops and the Great Buddha receiving all atop the mountain. Over these years, FGS has progressed from an unknown forest-covered mountain, into a real model of a monastery and a place of spiritual cultivation. Here, spirituality, culture, education and charity, all become one. Apart from the glorious shrines and halls and the modern facilities, FGS has also brought forth many new innovations in the arena of teaching and spreading the *Dharma*, for example, the Buddhist Choir, Buddhist College City Campuses, structure and systematization of the monastic and lay communities, short-term novitiate programmes, the Buddha Light International Association and an organization of Buddhist speakers. Under the united efforts of all involved, FGS has not only become a stronghold of Buddhist spirit in Taiwan, but also embraces the entire world as its sphere of activity and cultivation.

On August 11, 2003, during a press conference presided over by Wu Po-hsiung (BLIA World HQ Deputy President) to commemorate Venerable Master Hsing Yun's 50 years of teaching the *Dharma*,[69] Mayor Ma Ying-jiu of Taipei, Taiwan praised Venerable Master's 50 years of conscientious effort. He said that Venerable Master Hsing Yun's contribution is equivalent to 500 years of previous teachers, and his foremost contribution has been in humanizing and popularizing Buddhism, especially in the area of literary works, which have brought Buddhism and daily life together. In this way, the promotion of Humanistic Buddhism has spread to every part of the world. Professor Charles Kao, an economist, commented that Venerable Master Hsing Yun's achievements are one of the great contributions to the history of Taiwan. Hong Tong-kuei, Deputy Minister of the Overseas Chinese Affairs Commission in Taiwan, frankly stated that the education system established by Master Hsing Yun exceeds the educational system of most countries. Wu Po-hisung said that Venerable Master Hsing Yun started teaching and spreading Buddhism step by step in Ilan County and now the Buddha's light shines over the whole globe, and the *Dharma* stream flows through the five continents.

Darui Long in his paper "Humanistic Buddhism from Venerable Tai Xu to Grand Master Hsing Yun"[70] said:

> If we say that Venerable Tai Xu made the first effort to re-connect us with the essential Buddhist spirit in the first half of the 20th century, then Grand Master Hsing Yun has continued this endeavor and made it realized throughout the world. In this sense, Grand Master Hsing Yun is both a practitioner and theoretician. His integration with the tradition and modernity make him unique in the history of Buddhism, unique in a way that he is truly reviving Chinese Buddhism.

CONCLUSION

Buddhism is the teaching of the Buddha. It is natural for temples to organize different kinds of seminars and establish educational institutions. Buddhism is a spiritual tradition that puts emphasis on the practice of wisdom to elevate our spiritual attainment and to promote the teachings to benefit the masses. The vast teachings of the Buddha are the universal truth for human life, directing one to walk towards the correct path. Nalanda, the first ever well-established Buddhist university, has set a model for the lineage to be transmitted. The contribution of this past world seat of learning, after being destroyed by the Muslims and been buried for centuries, was identified by Alexander Cunningham in 1860s and excavations of the ruins started. Moreover, the detailed record of Master Xuanzang also brought back alive the Buddhist philosophy and educational activities at Nalanda over 1500 years.

Generally speaking, the rapid development of Taiwan Buddhism has its features and different factors. For example, the Tzu Chi Foundation (website: **www.tzuchi.org/global**) emphasis on charitable works to benefit society has promoted medical services and education to help the poor and educate the rich. The Dharma Drum Mountain (website: **www.dharmadrum.org**) has grounded in protecting the spiritual environment and pillared on actualizing the Three Types of Education,[71] the spiritual enlightenment campaign aiming to build a pure land on earth. Chung Tai Chan Monastery (website: **www.ctworld.org**) with her mission to create right understanding of the *Dharma* has developed human world Buddhism, academic Buddhism and art Buddhism and living Buddhism. Fo Guang Shan (website: **www.fgs.org.tw**) with the four main objectives to promote Buddhism through cultural activities, to foster talents through education, to benefit society through charitable activities and to purify human minds through Buddhist practice has produced significant results on localization, systemization, modernization, humanization and internationalization to benefit the masses. Other smaller temples and organizations also have their own features in developing energetic activities and programmes, creating their own ways and levels and somehow actualize the concept of human world Buddhism.

After Buddhism was introduced to China, eminent monastics, emperors and ministers had patronized and contributed to its growth and popularity. Temples had always served as an educational institution providing people from all walks of life to learn Buddhism, and when eminent monks were to give teachings, gatherings of a few hundred people were assembled to listen to the *Dharma*. Many monasteries usually have a building, called Zang-jing-lou (藏經樓), especially for storage of the canons and scriptures, which is similar to a modern library, and this could be considered similar to present academic centres of Buddhism. Buddhism, suppressed in China during the Cultural Revolution, did not hinder its growth in other parts of the world. In the past, Buddhist learning might have put an emphasis on research and study, but in the last decades, we see changes from theory and idealist learning to living and practice.

The teachings of the Buddha are about the truth of all matters and things within the universe. Though the interpretation and dissemination may vary in accordance with changing times and regional circumstances, the doctrine and spirit are inextricable; and Taiwan has recognized that the prosperity of Buddhism lies through spirituality and hard work of both the *Saṅgha* and lay members.

The Buddha has shown us a very good example: a person is to put into practice and follow the path in order to achieve a moral, healthy and wholesome character. A wise person not only concentrates on learning, but knows that practice is equally important. Nalanda University has fostered so many eminent masters, and we can follow its example to foster others.

NOTES

1. A great master of the Tang Dynasty and one of the four great translators in Chinese Buddhist History; he brought back from India many collections of works, images, pictures, as well as 150 relics to China. Of his most famous works is the *Great Tang Records of the Western Journey* (大唐西域).
2. Vinaya School (律宗), Tṛi-Śāstra School or Sanlun School (三論宗), Pure Land School (淨土宗), Chan School (禪宗), The Lotus School or T'ien-t'ai School (天台宗), The Garland School or Hua-yen School or Avataṁsāka School (華嚴宗), Dharmalakṣaṇa School or Fa-xiang School (法相), Esoteric School (密宗).

3. A famous lay disciple of the Buddha and an elder of Vaisali, although he was a layperson, was an expert on the Mahāyāna doctrines and already achieved high cultivation. An associated *sūtra* known as the *Vimalakīrti Sūtra*, discoursed by Vimalakīrti, emphasizes the practices of the *Bodhisattva* path.
4. (1) Harmony of precepts: the equality of rules that everyone observes, (2) Harmony of view: everyone shares the same understanding and there is unity of thought, (3) Harmony of benefit: everyone sharing equally, (4) Harmony of association: this is the way to live together focusing on the spirit of teamwork, (5) Harmony of speech: the harmony of language using praise, encouragement and loving words to inspire each other's practice can reduce conflict and argument, (6) Harmony of mind: makes everyone feel joyful.
5. Taisho, Vol. 53, No. 2121, consists of 50 scrolls.
6. The first graduate department in Life-and-Death Studies in Taiwan was established in Nanhua University. Ven. Huei Kai, a monk from the Fo Guang Shan Buddhist Order with a doctoral degree from Temple University, U.S.A. is chairman of the department.
7. *Taisho Sutra*, No. 1325.
8. *Taisho Sutra*, No. 1327.
9. *The Historic Data of World Buddhism,* 2nd edition, Fo Guang Publishing.
10. Śakrāditya has been identified with Mahendrāditya, i.e., Kumāragupta I (c. 413-455).
11. Budhagupta (c. 476-96).
12. Another record says that Xuanzang was born in CE 600, the 20th year of founding year of Sui Dynasty.
13. *The Historic Data of World Buddhism*, p. 77.
14. Travelled to India in the 4th century.
15. Founded by Bodhidharma, it emphasizes the cultivation of intrinsic wisdom, and teaches that enlightenment is clarifying the mind and seeing one's own true nature. Another major statement of the Chan School is that *Dharma* is wordlessly transmitted from mind to mind.
16. Its main aim is to be reborn into the Pure Land by the practice or reciting Buddha's name. Its founder was Master Huiyuan in Eastern Jin Dynasty, who spent his lifetime promulgating the belief in Amitābha.
17. Chan Master Baizhang Huaihai studied with Chan Master Mazu Daoyi and established the system in which the *Saṅgha* provides for its own daily necessities by cultivating vegetables.
18. Usually known as Tai-hsu, was a reformer of Chinese Buddhism in the late 19th and early 20th century. He was also the pioneer to propagate Humanistic Buddhism. His works are included in the set of the *Complete Works of Taixu.*
19. The National Policy Foundation has addressed this 'four' as the Four Mountain Heads (四大山頭).
20. 'As Buddhism Grows, So Grows Its Impact,' by Diana Lin in *Free China Review*, 9.
21. Lay members of FGS and BLIA who met the qualifications and requirements would be recognized as 'Lay Dharma Lecturers' or 'Lay Dharma Teachers' and join the forces to spread the Buddha's teachings and make Buddhism more accessible and available to the public.
22. *Handing Down the Light*, Fu Chi-ying, p. 232.
23. Yuen-mei Sect (月眉派), Guangyin Shan Sect (觀音山派), Fayun Yuanguang Sect (法雲圓光派), Dawu Fayun Sect (大湖法雲派), Dagang Shan Sect (大崗山派), Kaiyuan Shi Sect (開元寺派), Daxian Shan Sect (大仙山派), Wan Fo Shan Sect (萬佛山派), Qing-liang Shan Sect (清涼山派), and Tunghe Shi Sect (東和寺派).
24. Chinese Buddhist Temple Association (中華佛寺協會) inaugurated on May 1992 with membership of 31 temples islandwide; Chinese Buddhist Lay Association (中華佛居士會) founded in 1969 by Lee Sai; Chinese Sangha Supporting (中華護僧協會); Chinese Young Buddhist Association (中華青年會); and Buddha's Light International Association (國際佛光會) inaugurated in 1992 by venerable Master Hsing Yun.
25. *Handing Down the Light*, p. 45.
26. The first monastic ordination in Taiwan was held in 1953 at the Daxian temple (大仙寺).
27. Fo Guang Shan held the first higher ordination for monks and nuns in 1977. In 1988, Fo Guang Shan held an international ordination at Hsi Lai temple in Los Angeles whereby for the first time, Theravāda nuns from Nepal and Sri Lanka had the opportunity to take the '*bhikhunī* ordination'.

Many Western nuns both from the Theravāda and Vajrayāna Schools also participated. FGS organized few more ordinations in 1991, 1992 (Hsi Lai temple), 1993, 1996, 1998 (Bodhgaya), 2000 and 2004 (Nan Tien temple, Australia).

28. Ling-wen Buddhist Institute in Xin-zhu (新竹靈隱佛學院), Zhuxi Buddhist Institute in Tainan (台南竹溪寺佛學院), Chinese Tipiṭaka Buddhist temple in Taipei (台北中國佛教三藏學院), Chinese Buddhist Research Institute in Taipei (台北中國佛教研究院), Maitreya Buddhist Institute in Xizhi (汐止彌勒內院佛學院), Ci-ming Buddhist Institute in Taichung (台中慈明佛學院), Lingshan Buddhist Institute in Taichung (台中靈山寺佛學院), Kaiyuan Buddhist Institute in Tainan (台南開元寺佛學院), Tienlung Buddhist Institute in Chiayi (嘉義天龍寺佛學院), Tungshan Buddhist Institute in Pingtung (屏東東山寺佛學院), Puto Buddhist Institute in Taichung (台中南普陀佛學院), Lungyun Buddhist Institute in Taipei City (台北市龍雲寺佛學院), Keelung Buddhist Institute (基隆佛學院), Linji Deguang Buddhist Institute in Taipei (台北臨濟寺戒光佛學院), Lungwuyuan Buddhist Institute in Tainan (台南龍湖岩佛學院), Shoushan Buddhist Institute, later renamed Eastern Buddhist College (高雄壽山佛學院).
29. Shou Shan Buddhist College in Kaohsiung was established in 1965. Later, to meet the overwhelming response for enrolment, land was purchased to construct the Eastern Buddhist College in 1967 at its current venue at Fo Guang Shan.
30. FGS Buddhist College, Hong Kong.
31. The African Buddhist Seminary was established at the Nan Hua temple in South Africa, in October 1994. The main objective is to foster talent through Buddhist study within the local cultures.
32. FGS Buddhist College, Bodhgaya, India.
33. FGS Buddhist College, Nan Tien, Australia.
34. FGS Buddhist College, Dong Zen, Malaysia.
35. FGS Buddhist College, Zulai, Brazil.
36. FGS Buddhist College, San Diego, U.S.A.
37. Prof. Lai Yung-hai, Dean of Chinese Cultural Research Institute of Nanjing University, in his paper said, 'Humanistic Buddhism is the Mainstream of Contemporary Buddhism,' and, 'The reform for today's Buddhism could basically be based on two aspects, firstly the emphasis on 'human world', and secondly the stress on 'human life".'
38. Fu Chi-yang's *Handing Down the Light*, 2004, English edition, p. 54.
39. Unlike the case historically in China and nuns in the Theravāda School.
40. Current figure of nuns 1085 and monks 132 from different parts of the world includes Australia, Brazil, Canada, China, Congo, Germany, Hong Kong, India, Indonesia, Malaysia, Nepal, New Zealand, Singapore, Switzerland, Taiwan, Thailand, U.S.A.
41. The traditional monastery is called *conglin* which literally means forest, and refers to the community of monastics just like a thick forest. This system was first established by Chan Master Mazu Daoyi in the Tang Dynasty, and later made complete by Chan Master Baizhang Huihai and he established the Pure Rules.
42. 'The True Meaning of Humanistic Buddhism' – everything spoken by the Buddha, anything that is needed by human beings, and anything that is pure and good.
43. All FGS branch temples, local and overseas, serve as a centre of Buddhist learning. Besides Buddhist studies, worldly skills are organized for young and old devotees, supporters and BLIA members.
44. Hsi Lai University in Los Angeles, later renamed University of the West – The Local Educational Board gave its approval in 1991 to take in students. In September 2002 approval was also granted to issue graduate degrees and organize continuing education. In September 2001, the university became eligible to offer undergraduate degrees. The university has been granted Candidacy Status in the accreditation process by WASC (the Western Association of Schools and Colleges) by Los Angeles County, California, effective from July 1, 2002.
45. Nanhua University – The Ministry of Education gave approval on March 21, 1996 for the Nanhua University to accept applications and a new semester began on 29th the same year (website: www.nhu.edu.tw).

46. Fo Guang University – This campus is situated at the Chiao-hsi Township in the Ilan County. The foundation stone-laying ceremony was conducted on October 17, 1993 and in September 2000 and 2001, approval was given to accept graduate and undergraduate students respectively.
47. *Merit Times Daily* – Launched on April 1, 2000, it is the first daily newspaper ever established by a Buddhist organization in Taiwan. This paper emphasizes the bright side of human nature, moral ethics and warmth with an enriching content of culture, art, education and new information for readers.
48. A type of ritual instrument commonly used in Chinese Buddhist ceremonies usually to guide the speed of the chanting. It is made of wood and shaped like a fish, symbolic of diligence and always awakened, like a fish not closing its eyes while sleeping.
49. A monthly publication launched in October 1979. This magazine hopes to follow *Avalokiteśvara* (Great Compassion), *Bodhisattva's* vow to provide spiritual shelters for all sentient beings, to bring Buddhism in daily life and to build a humanistic pure land.
50. A bi-monthly publication of academic review in Chinese, Japanese and English, also including book review, Buddhist academic activities and new book digest. Besides providing rich contents in academic field, it is also a pioneering work in the Buddhist community.
51. Inaugurated on December 14, 1996, it is an unpolluted and pure television channel on social-educational programmes without commercials to promote a moral society and to increase public potential.
52. Eastern Buddhist College was constructed in 1967 at the current venue at Fo Guang Shan, to meet the overwhelming response for enrolment of the Shou Shan Buddhist College in Kaoshiung, which was established in 1965.
53. The objective of this institute is for working women between the ages of 25 to 45 to have an opportunity for spiritual practice and exposure to insight and multi-cultural aspects while on study tours.
54. Other kindergartens include Hui-tzu in Shanhua township, Tzuhang in Tainan and Little Star in Hsin-ying, Fo Guang Shan Mañjuśrī in Papua, New Guinea.
55. Ren Wen Elementary School in Ilan County.
56. Pu Men High School in 1977, Jiun Tou Elementary and Junior Secondary School inaugurated in August 2004.
57. Chih Kuang Vocational Institute (智光高級職業學) established in 1964 in Yung He City, Taipei County by Masters Hsing Yun, Nan Chang and Wu Yi in memorial of Master Chih Kuang.
58. The local Educational Board gave its approval in 1991 to take in students. In September 2002 approval was also granted to issue graduate degrees and organize continuing education. In September 2001, the university became eligible to offer undergraduate degrees. The university has been granted Candidacy Status in the accreditation process by WASC (the Western Association of Schools and Colleges) by Los Angeles County, California effective from July 1, 2002 (website: www.uwest.edu).
59. This campus is situated at the Chiao-hsi township in the Ilan County. The foundation-laying ceremony was conducted on October 17, 1993 and in September 2000 and 2001, approval was given to accept graduate and undergraduate students, respectively (website: www.fgu.edu.tw).
60. The Ministry of Education gave approval on March 21, 1996 for the Nanhua University to accept applications and new semester began on 29 of the same year.
61. Buddha's Light Television.
62. Approval for the establishment was issued by the Kaohsiung County Government on December 15th, 1970 and the Home was completed on January 6th, 1975. Besides Taiwanese children, children from Africa, Indonesia and Thailand have also stayed here; it is the first international children's home to be established by a Buddhist organization.
63. The Ren-ai Senior Citizens Home's former name was Ren-ai Relief Centre established in May of 1964 by a Christian named Dong Honglie. Due to a financial crisis, pre-head county Lin Caitian passed the centre to Venerable Master Hsing Yun in July of 1969. In 1973, Venerable Yi Rong and Venerable

Sao Jue after graduation from the Eastern Buddhist College were assigned to manage the Home. Since then the dining hall, hostel, Buddha Hall and lounge have been built. In 1998, Senior Citizens Care Centre and Evergreen College were also opened.

64. Fo Guang Senior Citizens Home is situated in the western part of Fo Guang Shan. It consists of three-storey buildings. Every building contains four large suites and 24 single and double small suites. Among the public facilities is a dining hall, kitchen, Chanting Hall and park.
65. The Evergreen Senior Citizens Home was constructed in 1994 by the government of Kaohsiung Country and in 1997 requested Fo Guang Shan Compassion Foundation to administer the running of the Home. The aim was to provide a comfortable living environment for the senior citizens. Among the facilities were a KTV lounge, sports room and recreational room.
66. Situated opposite the temple main entrance.
67. The Cloud and Water Mobile Clinic inaugurated in 1983, tours the remote region on a weekly basis. The clinic trucks drive medical supplies into remote areas moving like clouds and water, carrying the loving kindness that sees all beings as one.
68. Da Ci Learning Centre was established in August 2001. The aim was to extend service to the community by organizing lectures based on life education and Fo Guang Shan's cultural art. The centre accommodates students from primary school to senior high school.
69. Fo Guang Shan has created a series of presentations titled *Cloud and Water* which include a photo-biography exhibition and a Buddhist music performance to illustrate Venerable Master's efforts and contributions. A 50-year Anniversary Photobiography consisting of 2000 pictures selected from over 50,000 photos has been published.
70. Hsi Lai, *Journal of Humanistic Buddhist*, Vol. 1, 2000, pp. 53-84.
71. Education through academics, education through public outreach and education through caring service.
72. The Chinese edition was published in 1995 after two years of many personal interviews with the Master, various visits to FGS and other branch temples including related organizations and having travelled to Jiangdu-China, Nanjang-China, Hongkong, Germany and the U.S. for gathering of materials.

REFERENCES

One Hundred Years of Taiwan Buddhism (台灣佛教一百年) by Guang Zheng-zhung, 1999 first edition, Tungda Library Publishing Limited Company.

Treasures of China Buddhism – Biography of Master Xuanzang (中國佛教之-寶-玄奘大師傳) by Upasaka Yuanxiang, 1996 second edition, Fo Guang Publishing House.

The Year Book of Buddhist Colleges and Buddhist Institutes in Taiwan (台灣佛學院所教育年鑑第一輯), October 2001, the first issue by Chung Hwa Institute of Buddhist Studies.

The Historic Data of World Buddhism (世界佛教史年表), June 2005 second edition, Fo Guang Publishing House.

Taiwan Buddhism and Modern Society (台灣佛教與現代社會) by Chiang Chan-deng, 1992, Tung Ta Publishing.

Cloud and Water – A 50-Year Anniversary Photo-biography of Master Hsing Yun, 2003, by FGS Religious Affairs Committee.

Handing Down the Light – The Biography of Venerable Master Hsing Yun, by Fu Chi-ying,[72] 2004, English edition, Buddha's Light Publishing.

Universal Gate Buddhist Journal, Vol. 11, by FGS Religious Affairs Board.

43

DHARMA IN BRAZIL:
A NALANDA-INSPIRED EXPERIENCE

Ricardo Sasaki

Though on the opposite sides of the globe, India and Brazil have a lot in common – the size of their geographical boundaries, the hot weather, the joy and colourful nature of their culture, their appreciation of chilli, mango and rice, the religious inclination of their common people. While India is one of the most ancient cultures in the world and birthplace of the Buddha's *Dharma*, Brazil, however, is a very new country when it comes to the teachings of the Buddha.

In Brazil, all Eastern things are still seen as exotic and mysterious.

To spread the *Dharma* in Brazil is not an easy work. To spread the Theravāda version of the *Dharma* is even harder. There are no communities of Lao, Thai, Burmese or Sinhalese immigrants, people usually associated to Theravāda. It means no initial support, financial or motivational, no *bhikkhu Saṅgha*, no specialized literature in Portuguese language, no support whatsoever from associations or groups from outside.

The present paper deals with the spread of the Theravāda *Dharma* in Brazil as experienced by the work of Nalanda Theravāda Buddhist Community.

BEGINNINGS

The first time I came to Nalanda was in 1987 close to the eve of the New Year. Not many people used to visit here at that time; not like today. I came to Nalanda in my pilgrimage to the Buddhist places of India. I was lucky enough to meet two young Bhutanese students at Nalanda. Their brother was away and they offered me his room to stay a few days. This simple gesture of delicate kindness, so common to find when living in India and so rare more and more in the West certainly helped to make a strong impression in my mind. Here I was, with those two Bhutanese students, talking about the Buddha's teachings and Bhutanese culture, next to those amazing ruins of Nalanda.

Brazil is so tiny a place when it comes to Buddhism and Asian studies. Though Chinese are reported landing in Brazil as far as 1810 for temporary work, Buddhism effectively came to Brazil through the Japanese immigrants aboard the first ship that ever arrived in Brazilian lands to bring Japanese workers eager to check its promising fertility. The ship 'Kasato-maru' arrived in 1908. Buddhism grew in the following decades mainly within the community of Japanese immigrants that kept arriving in Brazil. My own father came in one of those first ships. Later, Chinese and Korean immigrants, also looking for better job opportunities, added their own kind of Buddhism. Brazil has today the largest Japanese colony in the world.

The first decades after the arrival of 'Kasato-maru' saw an unsystematic growth of Japanese Buddhism, restricted to Japanese families that lived mostly on farms in the countryside. It was only in 1952 that the Honpa Honganji, a Pure Land Japanese school, established itself officially in Brazil, followed in the subsequent years by the Higashi Honganji, Zen, Nichiren and Shingon. In 1962 the Chinese Mo Ti temple was founded, mainly to assist the Chinese community.

Theravāda Buddhism came only in 1967, establishing a Sri Lankan Theravāda temple in the city of Rio de Janeiro. The temple was founded by Theosophists that invited a Sri Lankan monk to visit. In this way, the first decades saw a strong Theosophical influence on the temple, with many of its associates and speakers belonging in one way or another to the numerous branches of Theosophy or other Occultist/Esoteric tendencies. In the beginning it was a place for talks and practices of many Buddhist schools and other denominations, only later becoming more limited to Theravāda Buddhism. It was first run by Venerable Anurudha and later by Venerable Puhuwelle Vipassi, both monks from Sri Lanka.

BRAZILIAN NALANDA IS ESTABLISHED

Until recently, Buddhism was something basically practised within ethnic communities. The fact is that in spite of first established so long ago, and the huge number of Japanese and Chinese immigrants, Buddhism in Brazil, as a cultural and religious phenomenon, is still very young there. During a long time Buddhism was mainly an ethnic issue, a religious and social gathering of Asian immigrants that made their temple a second home, a haven protecting from the difficulties of a foreign land. Regarding Theravāda, the situation was and still is even more critical. Contrary to Europe and the United States, we have not had waves of immigrants from Laos, Cambodia, Thailand, Burma or Sri Lanka, the countries traditionally associated with Theravāda.

So, in 1989, Nalanda Buddhist Center of Brazil was created. The name, of course, was a tribute to the great Nalanda, the most famous University in the Buddhist world, birthplace of Śāriputra and a city so associated to the Buddha's own life. Nalanda was then the second Theravāda centre to be created in Brazil, 22 years after the Sri Lankan temple was first established. Through the inspiration and encouragement of my gracious teachers Phra Maha Ghosananda, the Supreme Patriarch of Cambodian Buddhism, who first introduced me to Theravāda; Ajahn Buddhadasa, the eminent Thai monk and scholar; and the generous Rewata Dhamma Sayadaw, the master of *Abhidhamma* who made India his home for so many years, Nalanda in Brazil from the beginning tried to follow humbly in the footsteps of the great and original Nalanda.

MEDITATIONAL – RITUALISTIC ORIENTATION

We started with regular courses on Buddhism and meditation, soon followed by short meditation retreats. Following the trend in Western Buddhism we noticed that Brazilians were mostly interested in the yogic or meditational aspects of Buddhism, contrary to the preference for ritualistic and devotion-oriented practices of Asian temples. While in Asia Buddhism is largely supported by a strong community of lay devotees, in Brazil the main interest is for the practical means of mind cultivation.

In Buddhist countries, people are born Buddhists, learn basic chants and rituals from childhood and grow with an inner sense of belonging to the cultural and religious Buddhist framework. In Brazil, on the contrary, people are born within a strong Christian background, often mixed with African influenced religious practices and spiritual doctrines. While for Asians to enter into a Buddhist temple is to reconnect to a familiar and ancestral heritage, for Brazilians its ambience evoked first of all their complete distance to the aimed ideal. Ceremonies in foreign language; priests and monks hardly able to speak Portuguese; poorly written materials; everything was set up to scare but the most tenacious or to attract the most passionate for the new and different.

The aim of the courses was then to introduce the essence of the Buddha's message, beyond time and geography, following the often recited verse that says that the *Dharma* is *akāliko*, 'not bound to time'. If we are to significantly introduce the *Sāsana* in new lands, we ought to adapt, be creative, be sensible to the cultural and psychological trends of the new audience.

Our missionary work did not stop in theoretical courses and short retreats. For the past 17 years we have invited world known teachers to come to Brazil, for teaching and leadership of longer ten days retreats that started to happen for the first time in Brazil regarding Theravāda Buddhism. We have organized the first S.N. Goenka course in Brazil. Ven. Rewata Dhamma Sayadaw and Ven. Uttaranyana Sayadaw from Burma (Myanmar); Ven. Henepola Gunaratana from Sri Lanka; Ajahn Santikaro, Matthew Flickstein, Ven. Yogavacara Rahula from the U.S.; and Venerable Aruno from Malaysia, are some of the names who already came regularly through our sponsorship.

The contact of experienced Asian teachers with Brazilians eager to know the *Dharma* was most satisfactory for both sides. The warm weather, the plants and fruits, as well as the warm and affectionate interpersonal dealings of Brazilian people were some of the factors that our Asian teachers always were keen to point out and something that helped them to feel immediately at ease. Those were factors that certainly helped to create a bond between Brazil and India, as well as the countries in its borders.

PORTUGUESE LANGUAGE BOOKS

Paṭipatti should always be accompanied by a strong *Pariyatti*. *There is no wisdom without meditation*, the Buddha used to say. Nalanda in India was a major centre of knowledge production. The work produced there fed generations of scholars and saints in their search for enlightenment. Until twenty years ago Buddhist books published in Brazil were almost zero. No path of practice is possible without knowledge.

To the almost inexistent Theravāda literature in Portuguese language, or for that matter to the Buddhist literature as a whole, we started to add writings and translations. Through *Nalanda Editions*, names like Maha Ghosananda, Ajahn Buddhadasa, Rewata Dhamma Sayadaw, Ajahn Chah, Upasika Kee Nanayon, Bhikkhu Bodhi, Ajahn Sumedho and many others are now available for Portuguese speaking people. Presently I am preparing a critical edition of the *Dhammapada* to be published in Pāli and Portuguese together with explanations and stories of the *Aṭṭhakathā*, the traditional commentary; a translation of major *sutta*s in a gradual presentation; and a translation of the classical *Milinda-pañho*.

We have also produced a Pāli 'Chanting Book' that incorporates both classical Pāli chantings with line by line Portuguese translations. Based in Ajahn Buddhadasa's Suan Mokkh Monastery, chanting occurs with Pāli and Portuguese together. Its line by line translation, a model also used for the *Dhammapada* translation, helps the listener/reciter to incorporate the traditional Pāli language while understanding its meaning. *A Life of the Buddha based on the Pāli canon* is soon to come as well as a history of the first 500 years of Buddhism in India.

NALANDA IN THE TECHNOLOGICAL AGE

Communication is essential in our age. IT and web-based services are an integral part of the lives of many people and Buddhism must also integrate those aspects in its spread of *Dharma* knowledge. The rocky and desert routes of old times, travelled by the eminent Chinese pilgrims Fa-xien, Xuanzang and Yi'jing, are now the fast routes of cyberspace.

The Nalanda's webpage was one of the first multiservice sites to appear in Brazilian virtual space. It does not only give information about the centre and its activities, but provides a number of services to the visiting public. Key articles of many authors are offered in Portuguese at our 'Study Room'. A php-based Forum is offered for questions and discussions; a chat room is opened occasionally for interaction with visiting teachers; an Album and FAQ (Frequently Asked Questions) complement the sharing of information.

In the beginning of 1998 we created Buddhismo-L, the first mailing list through the internet for the discussion of Buddhism in Portuguese language, which has become the major open email-based forum for discussion about Buddhism in Brazil, where beginners and experienced practitioners coming from all Buddhist schools can get together to exchange ideas and have their questions asked and answered. Through the mailing list many friendships were established among members living in far-away places in Brazil, away from Buddhist centres. Interested Buddhists from Portugal, Argentina, Columbia, Mexico and other countries of Spanish or Portuguese language also are counted among its members. A specific Theravāda mailing list was soon also established as well as service of updated Theravāda news and short comments was established.

For 2006, besides all those regular activities, plans are that Nalanda in Brazil will start Courses at Distance in Portuguese language using the internet resources. Their main aim will be the people living away from Buddhist learning places. This is an innovative initiative that is much needed in Brazil. Due to its large geographical size, most of the present Buddhist centres concentrate in five or six large cities while a significant percentage of the interested population live in areas far away of any Buddhist centre or group. We hope that distance learning can fill a gap for those people unable to be physically present due to distance or other reasons.

NALANDA AT FOREST

We never forget that the main events of Buddha's life happened near or within forests. His birth, enlightenment, first sermon and *Parinirvāṇa* occurred among trees and we feel that contact with Nature is a key aspect of *Dharmic* life.

In 1999 we began the establishment of Nalandarama Retreat Center, the first Theravāda centre in South America exclusively dedicated to intensive meditation retreats in the forest tradition. Since then we have hosted a number of retreats, courses and community-oriented events, with local and international teachers, lay and monks alike. For the first time Brazilians were able to experience longer retreats and receive guidance and teachings from renowned Theravāda teachers. All international Theravāda activity happening in Brazil in the last seventeen years began from Nalanda's initiative.

Establishing Nalandarama was not an easy task. It was and still is a 100% Brazilian funded project. Due to the absence of traditionally Theravāda immigrants in Brazil (like Burmese, Sinhalese or Thai) and the lack of funding of any institution abroad we had to rely entirely on our own means to build and maintain the centre. The results are humble but spiritually most satisfactory and rewarding. We now count with a meditation room, a kitchen and lodging for over thirty people in a forest environment quite similar to the forest tradition monasteries of Burma and Thailand. Future plans are to be able to host Buddhist monks for longer periods.

DHARMA BROTHERHOOD

In the true Nalanda spirit of being a place of friendship and understanding among the various traditions, Nalanda in Brazil is one of the rare Buddhist centres that actively opened her doors to other Buddhist traditions besides its own. In Brazil, rarely a teacher of a different lineage is seen or heard in a centre of a different school. The original Nalanda in India, as R.K. Mookerji says, was an experiment in liberty of teaching, where *sectarian differences were merged in a common life and service, in the service to a common ideal* (*Ancient Indian Education*, Delhi: Motilal Banarsidass, 1989, p. 572). Admission to Nalanda was based on the question, *Have you the right disposition?* rather than, *Have you the true belief?* In this way, we have actively supported the coming of teachers from other Buddhist traditions to speak at Nalanda in the spirit of friendship in *Dharma*. Through *Nalanda Editions* we have published classics from Japanese and Chinese traditions (like the "Life and Works of Shinran" and the teachings of Hsu Yun), books on Korean Buddhism and about the interfaith dialogue with Christianity.

In 2005, Nalanda in Brazil was one of the key coordinators to establish, for the first time in Brazilian history, a Buddhist Union that gathers the major Buddhist traditions present in Brazil, giving a public and political face that might be able to deal with the misunderstandings of the media as well as to foster the true sharing of Buddhist values to society at large.

Nalanda now is the major Theravāda community in Brazil, with associated groups in three cities; people who study and meditate on the *Dharma* through the inspiration of Nalanda in India. An ongoing work of translation by different members, reception of newly arrived people, regular courses and workshops happen in all associated groups. We receive and go to schools by invitation to present Buddhist ideals to teenagers and university students. Recently, we have published a *Dharma* book authored by a member and specifically targeted to the children and pre-adolescent public.

To bridge the gap of traditionally Buddhist teaching and the Brazilian outlook of life is not a work of one generation but many. Talks, seminars, retreats, books, web presence, incentive to the formation of small groups for practice and study, adaptation to modern conditions without altering the essence of the teaching are some of the areas we have been concerned with.

44

BUDDHIST INTERRELATIONSHIP BETWEEN KOREA AND INDIA

Lee Ki Woon

KOREAN PRIESTS WHO CAME TO INDIA

Korean priests had an admiration for the countries of Buddhism so they went abroad to study Buddhism. Several Korean priests went to India with a concentrated mind. Gyeomik of Baekje, Euisin (義信), Hyecho (慧超), Muru (無漏), Wonpyo (元表), Jino (眞悟), Hyuntae (玄太) of Silla, and Hyunyu of Korea from (『大唐西域求法高僧傳』) of Hiuen Tsang (玄奘), are among the many unknown priests.

(1) The high priest of Baekje went to Sanganadaeyulsa in India CE when King Seong (聖王 CE 526) ruled and studied for five years Buddhist precepts. When he came back home, he brought the famous book of *Fifth Vinayapiṭaka* (五部律) from India and translated it.

Following the record of Mireukbulgwansa (彌勒佛光寺), Gyeomik came to Sanganadaeyulsa of India through sea route to seek for Buddhist precepts at the time of King Seong of Baekje. After he learned Sanskrit for five years, he brought *Abhidharma-piṭaka* and *Fifth Vinayapiṭaka* written in Sanskrit with Baedalda (倍達多). At that time, the king welcomed and wanted them to stay in Heungryunsa (興輪寺). And he ordered 28 reputed high priests to translate seventy-two books of Uparkṣa. This is the beginning of Yuljong (律宗) in Baekje. Following this, two Buddhist priests of Damuk (曇旭) and Hyein (惠仁) wrote thirty-six books of the interpretation of *Vinayapiṭaka* and gave them to the king. Although the king wrote prologue and dedicated a shrine, Taeyojeon (台曜展) to a deity, the king passed away.

When Gyeomik came back from India, he translated the writing of *Vinaya*. Damuk and Heyin wrote 36 books of comments about this and also the king wrote an introduction of these translated books. Gyeomik went to India at the time of King Seong (CE 526) and came back home after five years (531). Since that time, he introduced a lot of material about Buddhism he brought from India to the country of Baekje. The fact that Baekje was not affected by China but the priests of Baekje had the precious *Fifth Vinayapiṭaka* as they went to India and took the *Vinayapiṭaka* by themselves meant that Baekje had the *Vinayapiṭaka* of *Tripiṭaka* earlier than China did. China had not had all of *Fifth Vinayapiṭaka* at that time. Nevertheless, Baekje introduced the *Vinayapiṭaka* having comments on it. It means the country had great development to know Buddhism.

When it comes to *Fifth Vinayapiṭaka*, it is in five domineering parts of *Vinayapiṭaka*, that is, *Sarvāstivāda*, *Dharmaguptaka*, *Mahāsaṅghika*, *Mahisāsaka*, and *Kāśyapīya*. The year and the number of volumes translated in Korean are as follows:

India Fifth Vinayapiṭaka	Translated in China
薩婆多部 (*Sarvāsti* 說一切有部) 律	十誦律 61 卷, 弗若多羅 羅什共譯 (404-409)
曇無德部 (*Dharmaguptaka* 法藏部) 律	四分律 60 卷, 佛陀耶舍 竺佛念公譯 (410-412)
摩訶僧祇部 (*Māhasaṅghika* 大衆部) 律	摩訶僧祇律 40 卷, 佛駄跋陀羅 法顯共譯 (416-418)
彌沙塞部 (*Mahisāsaka* 化地部) 律	五分律 30 卷, 佛陀什 竺道生共逆 (422-423)
迦葉遺部 (*Kāśyapīya* 飮光部) 律	解脫戒經 1 卷 (五分律 同), 瞿曇般若流支 (543)

As seen above, the volume of *Vinayapiṭaka* in Baekje is less than the one in China. It seems that there had been some part of *Fifth Vinayapiṭaka* which was summarized. After that, Baekje had more developed *Vinaya*. And a *bhikṣuṇī* in Japan came to learn *Śīla* (律) at the 55th year of the King Wideok (588) and took a complete *Śīla* to be a perfect *bhikṣuṇī* and then came back home when she was 23.

(2) The honoured priest in Silla, Euisin (義信) is the one among such as came at Beobjusa (法住寺). The exact time is not known but the priests went to India to learn the religious precepts and they stayed at the first temple on their way to home with Buddhist scriptures on horses. So some people guess the name of temple. Beobjusa was built in the 14th year of the rule of King Jinheung. So had this been predicated (李能和,『朝鮮佛敎通史』下 大法住寺本末寺法,).

(3) Hyecho (慧超) went to India through sea route in the country of Dang (唐) at the time of King Seondeok (702-732). After he visited East, Central, South, West and North India, he came back to Jangan through Silk Road of Central Asia. The record of his trip is written in 『往五天竺國傳』. This book is regarded as a precious material to study India (8-9 cent. CE) because there are detailed information about not only the location, size, natural source, kings of 51 countries but also the servants and people. Although Hyecho (慧超) came home through Patna, Rajgir, Bodhgaya, it is questionable there is no record about Nalanda.

(4) Muru (無漏) was a prince of Silla but there is no data to prove when he became a priest. In『宋高僧傳』, it is said that he went to India after he was in Dang. After he learned Buddhism in China, he made a pilgrimage to five areas of India to worship at the eight-storeyed *Śarira stūpa*. He passed through Taklamakan Desert, the Pamirs and stayed at a temple but he had to come back with an illness. There is a record that when he was in India, he educated a wild dragon and was in *dhyāna* in front of Avalokiteśvara at the temple『宋高僧傳』卷21(大正藏!50, p. 846上～下).

(5) Wonpyo (元表) was one of them who went to India after staying in China to pay reverence to the relics of the Buddha. There is no specific record about him except that he was taught by a *Bodhisattva* Simwang (心王菩薩) in India.

(6) There is a record about the works of Jino (眞悟) in "大唐靑龍寺三朝供奉大德 行狀". He went to Dang in 781 and stayed at Cheongryongsa (靑龍寺) to be initiated in the secrets of Hyegwa (慧果) Esoteric Buddhism. After he finished the study, he left Jangan and went to Central India through Bhoṭa (西藏). He found the book of *Mahā-vairocanābhisadharmaparyāya* (大日經) written in Sanskrit. He died near Bhoṭa while bringing the Buddhist scriptures written in Sanskrit in 789. He went to India to seek for *sūtra* as a priest of Esoteric Buddhism.

(7) Hyeonyu (玄遊) of Korea went to China to study but did not come back as he became a priest staying in the country of Simhala (師子國) with his teacher, Seungcheol (僧哲). 『大唐西域求法高僧傳』卷下 僧哲禪師傳(大正藏5.

(8) The Buddhist priest of Hyuntae (玄太) was from Silla and his name in Sanskrit was Salpasinyajeba (薩婆頋若提婆). He went to the country of Dang (650-655) and India to study Buddhism. He arrived at Central India through Bhoṭa and Nepal. He came back after worshipping a Bodhidruma, translating and censoring *sūtra* and *Vinaya*. On his way home, he met the Buddhist priest of Doheui (道希法師) at Togokhon (土谷渾) and went to Daegaksa (大覺寺) together. There is no record proving where he had been after he went to Dang.

There are two more priests who are unknown. They went to South Sea from Jangan (長安) by ship. But they died with an illness at Parosaguk (婆魯師國), the west part of Sillibulseoguk (室利佛逝國). Although most Korean priests tried to study in India passing through China, many of them couldn't come back from China. Nonetheless, it is quite valuable that Gyeomik brought texts of Buddhism to Korea and contributed to the development of Buddhism.

KOREAN PRIESTS WHO STUDIED AT NALANDA

In『大唐西域求法高僧傳』written by Xuanzang, there are mentioned eight Korean priests; one Hyeonyu was from Koguryo and the others were from Silla. It seems they had studied at Nalanda, passing through China but actually only Ariyabalma (阿離那耶跋摩), Hyeeop (惠業), Hyeryun (惠輪) and Hyungak (玄恪) had studied at Nalanda. And there is no special record about the other two unknown priests including Hyuntae, Hyunyu. Here I summarize the work of Korean priests who studied at Nalanda.

(1) The priest of Silla, Ariyabalma studied in China at the reign period of the King Jinpyung (579-632) and went to India leaving Jangan at the reign period of Jeonggwanyeonjung (627-649). He sought for the teaching of Buddha and stayed at Nalanda to pay reverence to the relics of Buddha. He learned *Vinaya* and theories and tried to bring the Buddhist scriptures. But he passed away at the age of 70 at Musangsa (無常寺) in Yongcheon (龍泉) area (大正藏 51, p. 2 中.).

(2) Hyeeop was from Silla and he went and worshipped the relics of Buddha staying at Borisa (菩提寺), when he was in the western part of Jeonggwanyeon. After that, he went to Nalanda and took lectures for a long time. When Euijeong (義淨), the high priest of China censored the classical books written in Chinese he found a sentence in Yangron (梁論) saying that the priest of Silla, Hyeeop records and copies this under the tree where the Buddha's teeth were buried.

(3) Hyeryun was from Silla and his name in Sanskrit was Banyabalma (般若跋摩). Becoming a Buddhist priest in Silla, he went to study abroad adoring the relics of Buddha. He was in attendance on Hyunjo (玄照) who left Jangan and went to India together. They went and worshipped the remains of Buddha and had stayed at Sinjasa (信者寺) in Amaparaguk (菴摩跛羅國) for 10 years. Moving to places, Hyeryun stayed in Geondarasandasa (健陀羅山茶寺). He was really good at Sanskrit and *Abhidharmakośaśāstra*.

Taking a look at the life of Hyunjo, he went to North India with the help of the princess, Munseong of Bhoṭa through Sarantaguk (闍蘭陀國) for four years and stayed at Maggabori (莫訶菩提) to worship the remains of Buddha. Finally, he stayed at Nalanda for three years. He learned *Madyāmakaśāstra* and *Ṣaṭśāstra* from the Buddhist priest of Seunggwang (莫訶菩提) where he was initiated in yoga from the Buddhist priest of Bosaja (寶師子). After he stayed at Sinjasa, he came back to Jangan with his companion in 664. Since there is no special record that he came back to China or Silla, we could guess he died in that place.

(4) Hyeongak from Silla also went to China with Hyeonjo. This fact gives us the possibility of his being with Hyeryun. If they were together, probably he studied at Nalanda too. But it is said that he worshipped at Daegaksa in Magadha and died at the age of around 30.

Dhyānabhadra (指空 1289-1363) arrived in Korea. Dhyānabhadra was the prince of Magadha and became a Buddhist monk at the age of 8. He came to the priest of Yulhyeon at Nalanda to learn Buddhism. When he was 19, he entered Nalanda and got the five Buddhist commandments (against murder, theft, adultery, falsehood and intemperance); for 11 years he also studied *The Great Wisdom Sūtra, Mahā Prajñā*. He took lessons of *Tripiṭaka*.

After that, he left Magadha and was taught by Sāmanta Prandhāsa (普明) and took over the spirit of his teacher's work and made it his own at Gilsangsan (吉祥山) in Neunggaguk (楞伽國) of South India to be the 108th founder of a religious sect. He arrived at Yeongyung (燕京), the country of Won (元), through Tibet and India. After studying he came back to Korea. He educated people in Korea for two years and seven months. When he was staying at Gamrosa (甘露寺), Gaegyung (開京), the people of Korea thought that he might be Śākyamuni who was born again and welcomed him like they met Bodhidharma (『指要錄』序). He meditated at Yujeomsa (楡岾寺) of Geumgang mountain. After he came back to Gaegyung, he stayed at Sungsusa (崇壽寺) at the request from Sunbi (順妃), and set a Buddhist seminary to learn *Śīla*. He gave *Śīla* equally to the king, servants of the palace and people. And then he visited Tongdosa (通道寺) in February 1328. There were bone relics of the Buddha. He worshipped these and held a Buddhist mass. It seemed like Dhyānabhadra who had those kinds of works and had left Korea after September in 1328. In Yeongsanhyun (靈山縣), Geumryun (金倫) who was rich at that time built a palace at Borimsa (寶林寺) to have priests teach *Prajñā sūtra* to people. Especially when he made a field investigation to Hoiamsa (檜巖寺) one day, he said to Naong (懶翁) that the physical aspect of this place was same as the one of Nalanda, India. That's why Hoiamsa was established (『牧隱文藁』 卷2 天寶山檜巖寺修造記).

After he came back to Won, he stayed at Beobwonsa (法源寺). At this time he taught Naong from 1348 to 1358. There were high priests of Korea such as Gyunghan (景閑), Jacho (自超) and Jicheon (智泉) and they were of great help to develop Buddhism at Josun Dynastic court. He died at Gwihwabangjang (歸化方丈), the country of Won on 29th, Nov. 1361. Considering his body was cremated in 1368, some part of his body was buried at Pagoda in Hoiamsa in the reign of King Gongmin (恭愍王 1372).

Relating his work, there is 『禪要錄』, 『文殊舍利無生戒經』 which Zen priests brought and which he copied. His religious transmission gave a great deal of inspiration to the people of Korea. There are temples such as Hoiamsa, Sinreuksa (神勒寺), Bulamsa (佛巖寺), Tongdosa and Seonamsa (善嚴寺) where there is a scroll of his portrait.

We might call Hoiamsa (檜巖寺)–Dhyānabhadra (Jigong 指空) thought – "Nalanda of Korea". The temple was built by Jigong. He envisaged Nalanda having 266 rooms of a big temple. Naong had studied Buddhism for ten years at Beobwonsa, Yeongyung and got a note from Jigong when they had to say good bye. The note said to Naong that "if he came back to Korea and stayed among the stream of three mountains, there would be a Buddhist canon". Naong rebuilt the temple in 1378 following the words of his teacher and stayed there. So there is a three-storeyed pagoda at the back of the temple for Jigong (指空), Naong and Jacho (自超), a student of Naong. If we say Nalanda in India is the school for 10,000 students to learn Buddhism, Hoiamsa in Korea is the place where 300 priests had lived and learned Buddhism.

As the education from Jigong was a great effect to Korea, Nalanda is an important factor connecting the Buddhism of Korea and India.

XUANZANG AND PRIESTS OF KOREA

Xuanzang learned Buddhism in Nalanda, India and came back to China to educate people. Lots of Korean students who were in China could be educated by the new study of *Vijñānamātratā*.

When Xuanzang came back to China and educated people after he finished studying Buddhism, Gyugi (窺基 632-682) from China and Woncheuk (圓測 613-696) from Silla were the important priests who had an important role to play. Besides Woncheuk, there were Sinbang (神昉) and Sungyung (順璟) who were Korean priests under Xuanzang. Sinbang (神昉) is regarded as his best student.

One of two works from Woncheuk (『宋高僧傳』) has somewhat lowered his work by a fine piece of writing of the monument. The front part of writing Woncheuk is as follows:

Woncheuk (圓測) was good at various studies from *Abhidharma*, *Satyasiddhśāstra*, *Abhidharma-kośāśāstra* to old books. When Xuanzang met Woncheuk for the first time, he wanted to translate books such as *Yogācārabhūmi, Satyasiddhiśāstra, Vijñānamatratā* and *Tripiṭaka* with Woncheuk. Asking priests of Seomyeangsa (西明寺) to come back to the temple, he taught *Vijñāptimātratāsiddhi-śāstra* (成唯識論). At that time Samjang Jibagara of Central India came to Seoul and took an order to let five priests translate the Buddhist scriptures such as Mileom (蜜嚴).

Woncheuk contributed the new study of *Vijñānamātratā*. Śilabhadra had said that Diṅgnāga (陳那菩薩) was the only one who could know this theory. After Xuanzang heard this and told his students, Sungyung from Silla learned and conveyed the knowledge to Wonhyo (元曉). As Wonhyo heard this, he translated it right-away. And Sungyung educated in China called Wonhyo Diṅgnāga's reincarnation and bowed three times toward Headong (Korea).

45

BUDDHISM IN ASIA

Sulak Sivaraksa

HISTORICAL BACKGROUND

Buddhism in Asia can be discussed geographically and traditionally or rather in the different schools (*Yānas*). The two main schools are Theravāda (also known as Hīnayāna and Sāvakayāna) and Mahāyāna.

The East Asian countries of China, Korea, Japan and Vietnam are all Mahāyāna; only in South Vietnam is there a small group of Theravāda. Tibet, Mongolia and part of the former Soviet Union espouse the Vajrayāna tradition that grew out of Mahāyāna and influences China, Korea and Japan. The South and South-East Asian countries of Sri Lanka, Burma, Laos, Cambodia and Siam (now officially called Thailand) all follow the Theravāda tradition.

Some modern scholars, especially Malalasekera of Sri Lanka, who founded the World Fellowship of Buddhists (WFB) in 1950, felt the term Hīnayāna (small vehicle) pejorative. He proposed the name of Theravāda that was historically one of the 18 schools within Hīnayāna. The term Theravāda is now officially accepted in Buddhist countries in South and South-East Asia.

Some years ago, I was invited to give lectures in Taiwan and Japan on Thai Buddhism. Most members of the audience were surprised that we also believed in serving all sentient beings, for the benefit of others rather than ourselves. The prevailing belief among Mahayanists is that the Hinayanists only care for their personal liberation. We need to understand each other more appropriately.

This reminds me of my late teacher, the renowned Bhikkhu Buddhadasa who said that we must know the essence of our tradition, which is to overcome selfishness – to transform greed into generosity, hatred into loving kindness, and ignorance or delusion into wisdom or right understanding. He also warned that many negative elements appear in Buddhism, especially when it coexists with nationalism, Hinduism, feudalism, occultism, capitalism and the like.

We should not boast that our Buddhist tradition is the best. We must not only tolerate but also study and respect our friends' traditions and religions, including Christianity, Islam, Hinduism, Sikhism and Judaism although their customs and languages may be different from ours. With an open heart and sincerity, we can really learn from different religions and traditions, if we use skilful means in applying *dharmic* language beyond worldly language.

Bhikkhu Buddhadasa urged all of us to collaborate with friends from different traditions and religions – even agnostics and atheists – since all humans are spiritual beings, who can really go beyond being an economic or political animal, trapped by intellectual pursuits. He felt that if human beings unite together spiritually, we could be a strong moral force to overcome the modern worldly evils of greed – economism and consumerism; hatred – militarism and imperialism; and delusion – mainstream education without contemplation and mainstream mass media.

Buddhism in Asia became part and parcel of nationalism or the *Saṅgha* was too close to the powers-that-be.

This is especially true in East Asia starting with China of the Tang dynasty (618-906) when Buddhism was very vigorous and powerful, politically, socially and spiritually. Once the rulers who supported Buddhism were got rid of, the Confucians made it clear that Buddhism could remain in the Middle Kingdom provided that it only cared for the welfare of those in the next world and for those who sought inner peace without any social or political commitment. This is true of Korea, Japan and Vietnam, too.

In Japan, it was as late as the Meji period that Buddhism lost its role entirely – not only politically but socially, too. Monks who resisted state powers were killed, put in prison and demonized. The book *Zen at War* by Brian Victoria shows us clearly that Japanese people used meditation practice to serve the emperor and the nation violently. Monks were encouraged to marry and now there are very few unmarried priests who perform religious rituals.

In Korea, especially after the Japanese occupation in the 19th century, monks were encouraged to marry in the Japanese fashion. Most of the abbots who had been meditating without social or political awareness, urged their followers to pray for the Japanese emperor. Young patriots and intellectuals became Christians to fight for Korean independence. Being Christian, one was protected politically by Western imperialism that used Christian missionaries for political purposes. The results are that of all Asian Buddhist countries, only in Korea are there more Christians than Buddhists and the Christians hold all the important political positions.

Since 1860 Vietnam was a French protectorate. French missionaries were backed by the French government to educate Vietnamese Catholics to serve the new rulers and to advance socially, economically and politically in a limited degree. The Buddhists were left behind to pursue personal well-being in the so-called backward Vietnamese culture, where even language had to adopt the Romanized form.

As for the Theravāda tradition in South and South-East Asia, every country, except Siam, became part of the British or French empires. However, the monks remained the core of the lay people at village level. The patriarchs who used to influence the kings lost their role, except in Siam. The Siamese were more fortunate as one of the princes, Mongkut, joined the *Saṅgha* for 27 years. He not only studied Pāli, the sacred language of Theravāda Buddhism, and Buddhist tradition, but also English and Latin. So he was more advanced than his contemporaries in Asia vis-à-vis Western imperialism. He also studied Western science and technology. This put him in a position to challenge Christian missionaries in their teaching of the gospels that were being questioned by Westerners of the 19th century. His skilful means also encouraged him to be gentle and flexible with Western expansion. After the demise of his brother, he became King Rāma IV in 1851 and opened the country for Western capitalism. Siam remained independent despite some disadvantages and Siamese Buddhism could be proved as not inferior to Western science.

One of his lay disciples, Chao Phya Dīpankaravamsa, who later became Foreign Minister and a great historian, wrote a book against Christian accusation that Buddhism was antiquated and full of superstition and magic. The author argued that the essential teaching of the Buddha was scientific and could be proved logically by modern western approaches. The book was summarized in English by Henry Albaster and published in London in 1871 with the title of *The Wheel of the Law*.

This must be the first sign of modern Buddhism in the West. Likewise, in Sri Lanka, Buddhist monks had a big debate against the Christian missionaries in 1873 with a strong impact that Buddhism is more relevant to the modern world than Christianity. The news of this debate reached the U.S.A. Hence Colonel Olcott and Madame Blavatsky travelled from the New World to Sri Lanka. Colonel Olcott was the first Westerner who declared himself to be a Buddhist and wrote a number of books on Buddhist catechism. He and Madame Blavatsky influenced Dharmapāla who became a champion of modern Buddhism, with the establishment of the Maha Bodhi Society in India to propagate the teaching of the Buddha in the land of its Founder. The Society was also established in England to spread Buddhism in the West.

The Pāli Text Society was founded in England in 1881, followed by the teaching of Buddhism in one or two English universities, which led to the foundation of the Buddhist Society in London in 1925 – the first landmark of Buddhism beyond Asia.

In China, the modern attempt to revive the *Saṅgha* from its state of intellectual and moral decline was part of a general movement towards national growth which arose around the beginning of the 20th century as a response to two oppressive forces: the general backwardness of China's feudal society, and impact of the West. It took place in an international context. The Buddhist revivalists established contacts with Japan, India and the Buddhist countries of southern and South-East Asia, and even with Buddhist societies in the West. Some of them studied Chinese history for the first time, the Theravāda tradition of the Pāli canon, and occasionally, after many centuries, Chinese Buddhist scholars even took up the study of Sanskrit. Moreover, the attempt to revive Buddhism must be regarded as a reaction against one aspect of Western dominance: the impact of Christianity. The movement was deeply influenced by the presence of well-organized Catholic and Protestant missions in China, which stimulated the reformers to get organized and develop institutions and missionary methods similar to those of their Christian rivals.

The first Buddhist revivalits were – characteristically – culture laymen who around the beginning of the last century launched a movement to produce Buddhist scriptures and treatises using modern printing techniques and founding Buddhist seminaries. The political situation was unfavourable, for both the late Ch'ing and early Republican governments regarded the clergy as an easy target, and did not hesitate to confiscate Buddhist institutions to be made into schools, and to appropriate monastic landed property in order to finance their modernization programmes. Various attempts to organize the *Saṅgha* on a national scale in order to resist the combined pressure of government policy and Christian missions finally led to the founding, in 1929, of the nationwide Chinese Buddhist Association by the two leaders of the revival movement: the venerable abbot T'ai-hsu (1899-1947), who represented the more progressive wing, and the more conservative Yuan-ying (1878-1953).

In the following decades the Association undertook a number of activities that led to a revival of Buddhist studies and a heightened awareness of the values of Buddhism. But a large-scale renaissance did not take place. The general intellectual and political climate in China, dominated by the force of scholar ideologies such as Nationalism, 'Wholesale modernization', and Marxism-Leninism, left little room for religious activism. And, most important, the revival remained restricted to a small modernizing elite of monks and cultured laymen. The overwhelming majority of the *Saṅgha* was not touched at all. Moreover, the new Buddhist organizations generally suffered from inexperienced leadership, personal controversies and lack of funds, and the close relations between Chinese and Japanese Buddhist institutions.

After the establishment of the Chinese People's Republic in 1949, tensions were aggravated. In general, the new regime abstained from direct and forceful repression; however, violent action against the clergy and widespread vandalism were committed during political mass campaigns, particularly in the hectic years of the Cultural Revolution (1965-69), and the Tibetan Revolt in 1959. This was followed by harsh repressive measures against Tibetan Buddhism. In so far as Buddhism is tolerated, it clearly is a truncated Buddhism reduced to religious worship, and divested of all the social and economic functions that monasteries used to have. The *Saṅgha* itself, for which there is no reliable quantitative data, has no doubt been decimated by laicization and lack of new ordinations. To some extent, the updated Chinese Buddhist Association set up after 1949 has been politically useful as a channel for implementing religious policy, and as a representative people's organization in entertaining formal contacts with Buddhist groups abroad.

In general, the prospects for the Buddhist clergy in China are rather gloomy. It may be argued that the Chinese *Saṅgha* has for many centuries been exposed to the pressure of hostile ideologies and still managed to survive. But the monasteries, large and small, always remained in the possession of the material means to do so. Since the early 1950s, their economic base has been destroyed. Temple lands have been confiscated and redistributed, and, apart from a few ancient temples that are at least physically preserved as historical monuments, Buddhist institutions are wholly dependent on the believers' contributions. Even if in the most recent years (since 1976) there are signs of a somewhat more liberal policy, yet the ideological pressure and the lack of means of subsistence, this time coupled with an excessive emphasis on wholesale modernization, are not conducive to the existence, let alone the flowering, of Chinese Buddhism as an organized religion.

Buddhism in Taiwan fared no better than the mainland as long as the Kaomintang ruled the Republic of China dictatorially. When the country became democratic, Buddhism was free of State control and began to have a role in social welfare and as Taiwan became prosperous economically Chinese Buddhism from the Republic of China expanded worldwide. Yet its role is yet to involve social change using Buddhist skilful means.

Vietnamese Buddhists awakened after the American occupation of the country; it was too late to gain any significant ground. Buddhist leader Thich Nhat Hanh was in exile for over three decades before being allowed to return to the country briefly in 2004-5 and the *Saṅgha* in Vietnam was oppressed by the Communist regime, no better than China until the visit of Thich Nhat Hanh. It seems the Vietnamese government began to realize that the *Saṅgha* could play a vital role in restoring traditional Vietnamese culture to stop the influx of Western monoculture of consumerism.

However, the awakening of the Buddhists in South Korea after the Korean War and the eclipse of Korean dictatorship gave hope for the revival of Buddhism there, despite the mainstream *Saṅgha* that is connected too closely with materialism and consumerism. Indeed, Buddhism in any capitalist country of Asia faces this new danger to such a degree that most leaders, in the *Saṅgha* as well as in the laity, are not fully aware of.

After Mongolia has gained its independence, Buddhism plays a major role in developing democracy and alternative education. The kingdom of Bhutan has also developed the notion of Gross National Happiness instead of Gross National Product. This has attracted attention of many movements in the world which seek alternative to mainstream on economism.

India, despite the slumber of Buddhism for many centuries, once Ambedkar declared himself to be Buddhist in 1956, millions of the untouchables have embraced the path of the Buddha and since the Dalai Lama and Tibetan teachers came to live in India after the Chinese invasion of Tibet in 1959, quite a number of Indian leaders have embraced Buddhism.

BUDDHISM IN A NEW ERA

I believe that the challenges and prospects for contemporary Asian Buddhists is to convey the teachings of the Buddha appropriately for the 21st century. Many good Buddhist teachers are excellent in providing techniques for inner peace, which is the core for world peace. However, contemporary Buddhists need to understand the complexity of the modern world.

A major problem that the post-colonial world has long faced is how to be modern yet non-Western. The discourse of modernity (in the context of development) often smacks of imperialism. Developmental modernity is deeply rooted in old-fashioned, racially defined Europeanization, implying racial hierarchies. As such, the threat of alienation looms over those who unequivocally adopt such modernism. For the bulk of humanity, which is non-Western (and non-White), this is a major problem they have long been confronting.

The capitalist promise of emancipation through continuous economic growth and technological advancement has also been a vain hope. This is because without a proper perspective, the economy can never grow large enough; technological advancement can never be advanced enough; we never have enough wealth and so on.

Economic growth brings with it great danger such as ecological disaster and increasing income disparity. In New York City, Noam Chomsky reports that nearly 60% of black youth lack economic and educational opportunity, have no access to even the most basic social services and little sense of security. Their plight is not significantly different from the inhabitants of Bangladesh. Similar situations are present in Europe.

With this understanding, my vision of the future is not rooted in the capitalist myth of emancipation. For me, the future must be built on traditional wisdom and culture. As Helena Norberg-Hodge has argued in her book *Ancient Futures*, the future of the world cannot be found in New York, London or other Western metropolis. Rather, it is found in communities we find in the Indian states of Ladakh and Kerala and grassroot movements like the Assembly of the Poor in Siam. Indeed, when Tibet becomes autonomous that would set example of a modern state of stressing on with Buddhist democracy, peace, non-violence, ecological balance with respect to indegineous cultures and spirituality.

The future of the world must not neglect the spiritual perspective. There is a wealth of wisdom that can be garnered from religious traditions. The counter-modernity spirit advocated and practised by Gandhi is helpful.

As a Buddhist, I feel that the teachings of the Buddha have much to offer to mitigate suffering in the world. There are differences between the East and West although I do not see them as opposites or hierarchical relationships where one side is privileged. Seeing the world in terms of opposites is a source of intolerance, bigotry, fundamentalism and racism. Once you say "I am", the terms "you are" and "we and they" naturally follow, leading to conflict and fragmentation, threatening the cultivation of the whole unit at the individual and collective levels.

In the current phase of transnationalism there may be similarities between the fate of Easterners and Westerners. There seems to be an emerging powerful capitalist class of elites in nations across the globe engaging in similar patterns of capital accumulation, consuming, and thinking. We live in a world characterized by the intensification, radicalization, and universal spread of an extreme form of modernity that now relies simply on its own justification and devours all other forms of actualization of human beings.

Consumerism and unlimited growth directly contradict the concept of environmental sustainability and technological advancements and can only delay the impending ecological disaster. This leads to the question of whether the whole international capitalist system – from its agents, institutions, and structures to its basic culture and ideology – is inherently defective. From a Buddhist perspective, it definitely is.

The real meaning of the word *Buddha* is 'to be awake'. When we are awakened to simplicity and humility and aware of the suffering engendered by greed, hatred, and delusion, our consciousness is restructured. We become mindful about ourselves and others and are naturally led to restructure human society. The restructuring of the individual human consciousness and the society is complementary to each other and both are desperately needed. The global economy is fueled by insatiability and makes a virtue of greed and consumerism. The Buddha taught that the wheel of righteousness (*dhammacakka*) must control the wheel of power (*anacakka*). In the modern world, the quest for greater profit ultimately determines the actions of the rich and powerful. Thus any top-down attempt to redress class and ecological problems is likely to fail. The teachings of the Buddha, however, state that the rich and powerful, especially the rulers, must have only one overriding concern – the upholding of the law of *Dhamma*.

The Buddha was a simple and humble monk. I would like everyone captivated by the culture and ideology of consumerism and indoctrinated into a belief in the linearity of history to see this simple truth. Then consider the truth that the Buddha's simple and humble teachings provide a different way of seeing the world and if properly understood and practiced, leading a way to a noble life.

BIBLIOGRAPHY

Acharya, P.K., *Encyclopedia of Hindu Architecture*, Bhopal: J.K. Publishing House, 1998.

Aldrich, V., *Philosophy of Art*, Englewood Cliffs: Prentice Hall, 1963.

Alfonsa Ferrari, *Mk'yen brste's Guide to the Holy Places of Central Tibet*, Rome (IsMEO).

Alice Getty, *The Gods of Northern Buddhism* (Reprint), Tokyo: Charles E. Tuttle Co., 1962.

Altekar, A.S., *Education in Ancient India*, Varanasi: Nandkishore & Bros., 1965.

Amritananda, *Dharma-Koṣa-sangraha*, MS. No. 8055 in the library of the Asiatic Society, Calcutta, 1826, Ed. Lokesh Chandra, New Delhi, 1973.

Annual Report, Archaeological Survey of India, Eastern Circle, 1915-16 to 1920-21.

Annual Report, Archaeological Survey of India, Eastern Circle, 1915-16 and onwards.

Antoinette K. Gordon, *The Iconography of Tibetan Lamaism*, New York: Columbia University Press, 1959.

Anton Schiefner, *Taranatha's Geschichte des Buddhismus in Indien*, St. Petersburg, 1869.

Asher, F.M., *The Art of Eastern India (300-800)*, Minnesota, 1980.

Asher, F.M., and G.S. Gai, *Indian Epigraphy*, New Delhi: Oxford and IBH Pub. Co., 1985.

Bagchi, P.C., *India and China*, Bombay, 1944.

Banerjea, J.N., *Development of Hindu Iconography*, Calcutta, 1941.

Bapat, P.V. (ed.), *2500 years of Buddhism*, New Delhi: Govt. of India, Publication Division, 1987.

Barua, D.K., *Viharas in Ancient India: A Survey of Buddhist Monasteries*, Calcutta: Indian Publications Monograph Series No. 10, 1969.

Beal, S., *Buddhist Records of the Western World* (by Hiuen Tsang), 2 vols., London, 1906.

——, (trans.), *The Life of Hiuen-Tsiang by the Shaman Hwui Li, with an Introduction Containing an Account of the Works of I-Tsing*, London, 1911. Reprint: New Delhi, Munshiram Manoharlal, 1973.

——, *St-Yu-Ki: Buddhist Record of the Western World*, Part III, 1906, trans. From the Chinese of Hiuen-Tsang (AD 629), London Trubner – 1984: reprint ed., Delhi, 1969.

Bendall, Cecil, *Catalogue of Buddhist Sanskrit Manuscripts*, Cambridge University Library (Bodlian), 1983.

Bentor, Y., *Consecration of Images and Stūpas in Indo-Tibetan Tantric Buddhism*, Leiden, 1996.

Bernard, Elizabeth Anne, *Chinnamastā: The Aweful Buddhist and Hindu Trantric Goddess*, Delhi: Motilal Banarsidass, 1994.

Bernet, A.J. Kempers, *The Bronzes of Nalanda and Hindu-Javanese Art*, Leiden, 1933.

Beyer, Stephen, *Magic and Ritual in Tibet: The Cult of Tara*, New Jersey: Univ. of California Press, 1978.

Bhandarkar, D.R., *A List of Inscriptions of Northern India in Brāhmi and its Derivative Scripts from about 200 A.D.* Appendix to E.I. and Record of the Archaeological Survey of India, 1927-36, Vols. XIX, XXIII, Delhi, 1983.

Bhattacharyya, Benoytosh, *The Indian Buddhist Iconography*, Calcutta: K.L. Mukhopadhyay, 1958.

——, *Niṣpannayogāvalī of Mahapandita Abhayakaragupta*, Baroda: Oriental Institute.

Bhattacharya, B. (ed.), *Sādhanamālā*, Baroda: Oriental Institute, 1925.

—— (ed.), *Sādhanamālā*, Vol. I (1925), Vol. II (1928), G.O.S., Nos. XXVI and XLI, Baroda (SM) (I, II).

—— (ed.), *Guhyasamājatantra*; G.O.S., Vol. LIII, Baroda, 1931.

—— (ed.), *Nishpanna Yogāvalī of Mahapandita Abhayakaragupta*, Baroda, 1944.

Bhattacharya, B.T., *The Indian Buddhist Iconography, Mainly based on the Sādhanamālā and other Cognate Tantric Texts of Rituals*, Calcutta: K.L. Mukhopadhyay, 1961.

Bhattacharya, D.C., *Iconology of Composite Images*, Delhi, 1980.

——, *Studies in Buddhist Iconography*, Delhi: Manohar Publishers, 1978.

——, *Tāntric Buddhist Iconography Sources*, New Delhi: Munshiram Manoharlal, 1974.

Bhattacharya, K.L., *Saraswatī: A Study of her Concept and Iconology*. Calcutta, 1983.

Bhattasali, N.K., *Iconography of Buddhist and Brāhmaṇical Sculptures in the Dacca Museum*, Dacca Museum Committee, 1929.

Blakiston, J.F. (ed.), *Archaeological Survey of India – Annual Report 1925-26* (Reprint), New Delhi, 2002.

Bloch, T., *Supplementary Catalogue of the Archaeological Collection of the Indian Museum*. Calcutta, 1911.

Bosch, F.D.K., A Hypothesis as to the Origin of Indo-Japanese Art, *Rupam*, No. 17, 1924.

Bose, P.N., *Indian Teachers of Buddhist Universities*, Madras, 1923.

Boucher, D., 'The Pratītyasamutpādagāthā and its Role in the Medieval Cult of Relics', *Journal of the International Association of Buddhist Studies* 14, 1-27, 1991.

Brian Houghton Hodgson, *Essays on the Language, Literatures and Religion of Nepal and Tibet* (Reprint), New Delhi: Manjusri Publishing House, 1972.

Broadley, A.M., *Ruins of the Nalanda Monasteries of Badgaon, Subdivision of Bihar, Zilla Patna*, Calcutta, 1872.

——, 'The Buddhist Remains of Bihar', *JASB*. XLI, 3 (1872): ASB. Proc. 1872 (reprinted edn.), Varanasi: Bharati Prakashan, 1979.

Burgess, James, *Indian Antiquary*, Vol. I, Delhi, 1971.

Buston, *History of Buddhism*, trans. from Tibetan by E. Obermiller.

Chakravarti, N., 'Pāla Inscriptions in the Indian Museum', *JPASB* IV, 1908.

Chattopadhyay, D.P. (ed.), *History of Science, Philosophy and Culture in Indian Civilization*, New Delhi: Centre for Studies in Civilizations (This project has brought out several volumes on different topics in different years).

Chaudhari, S.N. (trans.), *Jatakamala*, Delhi: Motilal Banarsidass, 1991.

Chau Siyanga-Kumang, *History of Chinese Buddhism*, Allahabad: Leader Press.

Chi, R.S.Y., *Buddhist Formal Logic: A Study of Dignaga's Hetucakra and K'eui-Chi's Great Commentary on the Nyayapravesa* (Reprint), Delhi: Motilal Banarsidass, 1990.

Conze, Edward, *Buddhism*, Oxford, 1953.

——, *Buddhist Meditation*, London: George Allen & Unwin, 1956.

——, *Buddhist Thought in India*, London: George Allen & Unwin, 1983.

Coomaraswamy, A.K., *History of Indian and Indonesian Art*, London: Edward Goodston, 1927; reprinted, New York: Dover, 1965 and New Delhi, 1972.

Cunningham, A., *Ancient Geograpy of India* (eds.) S.N. Majumdar and M.N. Sastri, Calcutta, 1924.

——, *Report for the Year 1871-72*, ASR, III, Calcutta, 1873, reprinted: Delhi and Varanasi: Indological Book House, 1966.

——, *Archaeological Survey of India: Four Reports Made during the Years 1862-63-64-65* (Reprint), New Delhi, 2000.

Dalai Lama, *The Buddhism of Tibet*, trans. and ed. by Jeffrey Hopkins, Ithaca, New York: Snow Lion Publications.

——, *The Path to Enlightenment*, ed. and trans. by Glenn H. Mullin, 1997, Ithaca, New York: Snow Lion Publications, 1994.

——, *Kindness Clarity and Insight*, ed. by Jeffrey Hopkins, Ithaca, New York: Snow Lion Publications, 2006.

Dallapiccoal, A. (ed.), *The Stūpa: Its Religious and Historical Significance*, Weisbaden, 1980.

Das, S.C., *Indian Pandits in the Land of Snow*, Calcutta, 1893.

Davidson, Ronald M., *Indian Esoteric Buddhism: A Social History of the Tantric Movement*, Delhi: Motilal Banarsidass, 2004.
Dayal, H., *Bodhisattva Doctrine in Buddhist Sanskrit Literature*, Delhi: Motilal Banarsidass, 1999.
Dhargyey, Geshe Ngawang, *Kālacakra Tantra*, trans. by Alan Wallace, Dharmasala: Library of Tibetan Works and Archives, 1985.
Dragpa, Panchen Sonam, *Overview of Buddhist Tantra*, trans. by Martin J. Boord and Losang Norbu Tsonawa, Dharmasala: Library of Tibetan Works and Archives, 1996.
Dravid, R.R., *The Problem of Universal in Indian Philosophy*, New Delhi: Motilal Banarsidas, 1972.
Dreyfus, G., 'Would the True Prasangika Please Stand? The Case and View of "Ju.Mi.pham"', in G. Dreyfus and S. McClintock, *The Svatantrika-Prasangika Distinction*, Somerville, MA: Wisdom, 2003.
Dutt, N., *Bodhisattvabhumi*, Patna: Jayaswal Research Institute.
Dutt, Nalinaksha *Buddhist Sects in India* (Reprint), Delhi: Motilal Banarsidass, 1998.
Dutt, N.N., and K.D. Vajpayee, *Uttar Pradesh Main Bauddha Dharma ka Vikas*, Lucknow, 1950.
Dutt, S., *Early Buddhist Monachism (600 B.C. to 100 A.D.)*, London, 1924.
Dutt, Sukumar, *Buddhist Monks and Monasteries of India: Their History and their Contribution to Indian Culture.* London: George Allen & Unwin Ltd., (first edn.), 1962.
Encyclopaedia of Buddhism, Published by the Govt. of Sri Lanka, Tisara Packaging Industries, Dehiwala, Srilanka, 1989.
Fausball, V. (ed.), *Jātakas* (5 vols.), London, 1979-91.
Ferdinand Diederich Lessing, *Yung-ko-kung*, Stockholm, 1942.
Francis, H.T., and E.J. Thomas (trans.), *Jataka Tales*, Bombay, 1967.
Franklin Edgerton, *Buddhist Hybrid Sanskrit: Grammar and Dictionary*, Vol. 2 Dictionary, New Haven: Yale Univ. Press, 1953.
Gadamer, Hans., *Truth and Method*, New York: Seabury Press, 1975.
Geiger, W. (ed.), *Mahāvaṁsa*, London, 1908, 1912.
Ghosh, A., 'A Bronze Image Inscription from Nalanda', *EI* XXV, 1939-40.
——, *Indian Archaeology: A Review* (Report of the Director General of Archaeology in India), Delhi, 1953-54, 1955-56.
——, *Nalanda* (6th edn.), New Delhi, 1986.
—— (ed.), *An Encyclopaedia of Indian Archaeology*, 2 vols., New Delhi, 1989.
Giles, Herbert Allen (trans.), *The Travels of Fa-hien (399-414) or Record of the Buddhist Kingdoms*, Cambridge University Press, 1923.
Giuseppe Tucci, *Indo-Tibetica*, Rome: Reale Academia d'ltalia, 1932.
——, 'A Propos the Legend of Naropa', *JRAS*, 1935.
——, *Tibetan Painted Scrolls*, Rome, 1949.
Gomez, Louis O., *Buddhism in Practice* (ed. by Donald S. Lopez), Princeton University Press, 1995.
Gomez, L., and Barabudur Woodword, *History and Significance of a Buddhist Movement*, California, 1981.
Goswami, A., *Indian Temple Architecture*, Calcutta, 1959.
Grunwedel, A., *Mythologie des Buddhismusin Tibet und der Mongolei*, Leipzig: F.A. Brockhaus, 1900.
Gudumunsen, Chris, *Wittgenstein and Buddhism*, London: Macmillan, 1977.
Gupta, H.C. (trans.), *Tibetan Historical Literature* by A.I. Vostrikove, trans. from Russian, Calcutta, 1970
Gupta, P.L., *Patna Museum Catalogue of Antiquities*, Patna, 1965.
Gyatso, Geshe Kelsang, *Clear Light of Bliss: The Practice of Mahamudra in Vajrayana Buddhism* (2nd edn.), Tharpa Publications, 1992.
Hakaju Ui *et al.*, *A Complete Catalogue of the Tibetan Buddhist Canons* (Bkah-hgyur and Bstan-hgyur), Sendai: Tohoku Imperial University, 1934.
Hare, E.M., *Gradual Sayings – Aṅguttara Nikaya*, London: Pali Text Society, 1995.
Heissig, W., *Die Pekinge lamaistischen Blockdrucke in Mongolischer Sprache*, Wiesbaden (Otto Harrassowitz), 1954.
Heluth von Glasenapp, *Buddhistische Mysterien, die geheimen Lehren und Riten des Diamant-Fahrzeugs*, Stuttgart (W. Spemann Verlag).

Heras, M., 'The Royal Patrons of the University of Nalanda', *JBORS* XIV, 1928.

Holt, Clair, *Art in Indonesia: Continuities and Change*, Ithaca, New York: Cornell University Press, 1976.

Horner, I.B. (trans.), *The Book of the Discipline (Vinaya Piṭaka)*, London: P.T.S. Luzac and Co. Ltd.

——, *Milinda's Questions*. 2 vols., London, 1963.

Huntington, S.L., *The 'Pāla-Sena' Schools of Sculpture*, Leiden, 1984.

Isshi, Yamada, *Karunāpuṇḍarīka* (Vols. 1 and 2), London: School of Oriental and African Studies, 1968.

Jackson, V.H. (ed.), *Journal of the Patna and Gaya Districts* by Buchanan Hamilton, Patna, 1925.

Jameson, R.C., *Nāgārjuna's Versus on the Great and the Heart of Dependent Origination*, Delhi, 2000.

Jean Fillozat, *Catalogue du Fonds Sanscrit*, Paris Adrien-Maisonneuve, 1941.

Jha, Ganganath (trans.), *The Tattva Sangraha of Śāntarakṣita* (2 vols., with comm. of Kamalasīla), Delhi: Motilal Banarsidass, 1986.

Johnston, E.J., *Buddhacarita or Acts of the Buddha* (original work by Aśvaghoṣa), Blue Dove Pr., 1998.

Joshi, N.P., *Iconography of Balarāma*, Delhi, 1979,

Jowett, B., *The Dialogues of Plato*, New York: Random House, 1977.

Julien, S., *Histoire de la vie de Hiouen Thsang*, Memoires de Hiouen thsang (Xi you ji), Paris, 1853.

Kalupahana, David, *Mūlamadhyama Kārikā of Nāgārjuna* (Reprint), Delhi: Motilal Banarsidass Publishers, 1999.

——, *Buddhist Thought and Ritual*, Delhi: Motilal Banarsidass, 2001.

Kern, H., *Manual of Indian Buddhism: New Impression*, ed. by C. Mani, Delhi: Bharatiya Kala Prakashan, 1995.

——, (trans.), *Saddharmapuṇḍarika-sūtra* (The Lotus Sūtra of the True Law), Kessinger, 2003.

Kitcher, Patricia, *Freud's Dream: A Complete Multidisciplinary Science of Mind*, Cambridge: MIT Press, 1998.

Kitcher, Phillip, *Science, Truth and Democracy*, Oxford: Oxford Univ. Press, 2001.

Kempers, A.J.B., *The Bronzes of Nalanda and Hindu-Javanese Art*, Leiden, 1933.

Kempers, Bernett, *Hindu Javanese Bronzes: Lecture Delivered in Indian Society*, Jan. 24, 1934.

Kramrisch, Stella, 'Pāla and Sena Sculptures', *Rupam* XL (40), ed. O.C. Gangoly, Oct. 1929.

——, *The Hindu Temple*, Vol. II, Delhi, 1976.

Krishnamachary, E. (ed.), *Tattva-Sangraha of Śāntarakṣita with Commentary*, Vol. I-II, Baroda, 1926.

Kuhn, Thomas, *The Essential Tension*, Chicago: Chicago Univ. Press, 1977.

Kuraishi, M.H., *Excavations of Nalanda*, ASI, A.R. 1929-30, Delhi, 1935.

——, *A Short Guide to the Buddhist Remains Excavated at Nalanda*, Calcutta: Govt. of India, 1970.

Kuraishi, M.H. and G.C. Chandra, *Excavations at Nalanda*, ASI, A.R. Pt. II, 1930-34.

Lama Chimpa and Alaka Chattopadhyaya (trans.), *Tārānātha's History of Buddism in India*, Shimla, 1970.

Law, B.C., *Geography of Early Buddhism*, London, 1927.

——, *Historical Geography of Ancient India* (2nd edn.), France, 1968.

Legge, J., *Travels of Fa-hien*, Oxford, 1816.

Legge, James (trans.), *A Record of Buddhist Kingdom: Being an Account by the Chinese Monk Fa-hein of His Travels in India and Ceylon (AD 399-414) in Search of the Buddhist Books of Discipline*, Oxford: Clarendon Press, 1986.

Levi, S. (ed.), *Mahāyāna Sūtrālankāra of Asaṅga*, Vol. I, Paris, 1907.

Lodoe, Yangchen Gawai, *Paths and Grounds of Guhyasamaja According to Arya Nāgārjuna*, trans. by Tenzin Dorjee and Jeremy Russell, Dharmasala: Library of Tibetan Works and Archives, 1995.

Chandra, Lokesh, *Eminent Tibetan Polymaths of Mongolia*, New Delhi: International Academy of Indian Culture, 1961.

——, 'Les Imprimeries tibataines de Drepung, Derge et Drepung', *Journal Asiatique*, 1961.

——, 'The Rin-Ihan and Rin-hbyun', *Oreins Extremus*, 1962.

——, *Hymn to Tārā*, Aginsky Xylograph entitled *Rje-btsun Sgrol-mahi phyag-htshal nt-su-rtsa-gcig-ma*, with Sanskrit transliteration, Mongolian and Tibetan translations, New Delhi: International Academy of Indian Culture, 1967.

——, *Materials for a History of Tibetan Literature* (Reprint), Kyoto: Rinsen Book Co., 1981.

——, *Tibetan Sanskrit Dictionary*, Kyoto: Rinsen Book Co., 1982.

——, *Buddhist Iconography*, New Delhi: Aditya Prakashan, 1987.

Majumdar, N.G., 'Nalanda Inscription of Vipulasrīmitra', *EI* XXI, 3 July 1931.
——, *A Guide to Sculptures in Indian Museum* (2 parts), Calcutta, 1937.
——, *The Classical Age, Vol. III: History and Culture of the Indian People*, Bombay: Bharatiya Vidya Bhawan, 1955.
Majumdar, R.C. and A.D. Pusalkar (eds.), *The Classical Age*, 1954.
Malalasekera, G.P., *The Pali Literature of Ceylon*, London, 1928.
Mäll, Linnart, *Studies in the Aṣṭasāhasṙikā Prajñāpāramitā and Other Essays*, Delhi: Motilal Banarsidass, 2005.
Mani, B.R., *The Kushan Civilization*, New Delhi: D.K. Printers, 1985.
Mani, C. (ed.), *The Social Philsophy of Buddhism*, Sarnath: Central Institute of Higher Tibetan Studies, 1972.
——, *Arya Asaṅga and Vijñavāda* (Tibetan part ed. by Ngawang Samten), Leh, Ladakh: Institute of Buddhist Philosophy, 1995.
Marcelle Lalou, *Repertoire du Tanjur d'aprs le Catalogue de P. Cordier*, Paris (Bibliotheque Nationale), 1933.
Marie-Therese de Mallmann, *Introduction a l'iconographie du Tantrisme Bouddhique*. Paris (Adrien-Maisonneuve).
Marshall, John, H. (ed.), *AR of the ASI 1923-24*, Calcutta, 1926.
——, *The Buddhist Art of Gandhara*, Cambridge University Press, 1960.
——, (ed.), *Archaeological Survey of India Annual Report 1916-17*, Part I (Reprint), New Delhi, 2002.
Martin, M., *The History, Antiquities, Topography and Statistics of Eastern India*, Allen and Co., Vols. I and II.
Memoirs of Asiatic Society of Bengal, Vol. V, No. 3, Pls. XXV-XXVI.
Memoirs of the Archaeological Survey of India, No. 55.
Michaelson, *Gilded Dragons*, London, 1999.
Miller, R.J., *Monasteries and Culture Change in Inner Mongolia*, Wiesbaden, Otto Harrassowitz, 1959.
Mishra, B.N., *Nalanda* (3 vols.), Delhi: B.R. Publishing Corporation, 1989.
Mitra, Debala, *Buddhist Monuments*, Calcutta: Sahitya Samsad, 1971.
Mitra, R.L., *Buddha-Gaya: The Hermitage of Sakyamuni*, Calcutta: The Bengal Secretariat Press, 1878, reprinted Delhi, Varanasi: Indological Book House, 1972.
——, *The Sanskrit Buddhist Literature of Nepal*, Calcutta, 1882.
Mitra, Sisir, K. (ed.), *East Indian Bronzes*, Calcutta: Centre of Advanced Study in Ancient Indian History and Culture. Calcutta University, 1979.
Mookerjee, S., *Buddhist Philosophy of Universal Flux*, New Delhi: Motilal Banarsidass, 1975.
Mukherjee, Radha Kumud, *Ancient Indian Education (Brāhmanical and Buddhist)*, London, 1947.
Mulin, Glenn H., *Readings on the Six Yogas of Naropa*, New York: Snow Lion, 1977.
Muses, C.A. (ed.), *Esoteric Teachings of the Tibetan Tantra*, York Beach, Maine: Weiser Publications, 1982.
Nagel, Thomas, *The View from Nowhere*, Oxford: Oxford Univ. Press, 1986.
Namgyal, Takpo Tashi, *Mahamudra: The Quintessence of Mind and Meditation* (Tr. by Lobsang P. Lhalungpa), Delhi: Motilal Banarsidass, 2000.
Narendradeva, Acharya, *Bauddhadharma aur Darshan*, Delhi, 1994.
——, *Abhidharma Kosha of Vasubandhu* (Hindi translation of *valley de la poussant*).
Nehru, Jawaharlal, *Glimpses of World History* (Reprint), USA: Oxford University Press, 1990.
——, *The Discovery of India* (Reprint), Penguin Books India, Reprint, 2004.
Newman, Richard, *The Stone Sculpture of India: A Study of the Materials used by Indian Sculpture from circa 2nd Century B.C. to 16th Century A.D.*, Cambridge, USA: Harward University Art Museum, 1984.
Pal, P., *Light of Asia, Buddha Sakyamuni in Asian Art*, Los Angeles Country Museum of Art, 1984.
Pandey, D.P., *Surya: Iconographical Study of the Indian Sun-God*, New Delhi: Parimal Publishers, 2005.
Pandey, G.C., *Foundations of Indian Culture*, 2 vols., Delhi: Sundeep Prakashan, 2004.
——, *Studies in the Origins of Buddhism*, Delhi: Motilal Banarsidass, 1999.
Pandey, R.B. (ed.), *Historical and Literary Inscriptions*, Varanasi, 1962.
Panth, Dr. R., *Nalanda and Buddhism*, Nalanda: Nava Nalanda Mahavihara, 2002.
Pott, P.H., *An Introduction to the Tibetan Collection of the National Museum of Ethnology*, Leiden, 1951.
Radhakrishnan, S., *Indian Philosophy*, 2 vols., London: George Allen & Unwin, 1941.

Ramanan, V., *Nāgārjuna's Philosophy*, Delhi: Banarsidass, 1975.
Randle, H.N., *Fragments from Dinnaga*, Delhi: Sundeep Prakashan, 1981.
Rao, T.A., G., *Elements of Hindu Iconography*, Madras: Law Printing House, 1914-16; reprint edn., 2 vols., New York.
Rapson, E.J., *Cambridge History of India* (2nd edn.), Vol. I, Delhi, 1962.
Rawson, P., *The Art of South East Asia*, London, 1967.
Ray, Chaudhuri, Hemachandra, *Political History of Ancient India* (6th edn.). Calcutta, 1953.
Ray, N., *Idea and Images in Indian Art*, Delhi, 1973.
Ray, Nihar Ranjan, Karl Khandalavala and Gorakshkar, *Eastern Indian Bronzes*, New Delhi: Lalit Kala Academy, 1986.
Rene de Nebesky-Wojkowitz, *Oracles and Demons of Tibet*, S-Gravenhage (Mouton & Co.).
Ricoeur, Paul, *Hermeneutics and the Human Sciences*, trans. by J. Thompson. Cambridge: Cambridge Univ. Press, 1982.
Rinpoche, L. Samdong, and C. Mani, *Madhyamika Dialectic and Philosophy of Nagarjuna*, Sarnath: Central Institute of Higher Tibetan Studies, 1985.
Rizzi, Ceasre, *Candrakirti*, Delhi: Motilal Banarsidass, 1988.
Robinson, Richard, H., *Early Madhyamika in India and China*, Madison: University of Wisconsin Press, 1967.
Rowland, Benjamin, *Art and Architecture of India*, Pelican History of Art (3rd edn). Harmondsworth: Penguin Books, 1970.
Russell, B., *History of Western Philosophy* (2nd edn.), Routledge, 2004.
Ryle, G., *The Concept of Mind*, New York: Barnes and Noble, 1949.
Ryujun Tajima, *Les deux grands mandalas et la doctrine de l'esoterisme Shingon*, Tokyo (Maison Franco-Japonaise).
Saletore, B.A., *India's Diplomatic Relations with the East*, Bombay, 1960.
Samaddar, J.N., *Glories of Magadha* (2nd edn.), Patna, 1927.
Sankalia, H.D., *The University of Nalanda*, Madras: B.G. Paul & Co., 1934; 2nd edition, Delhi, 1972.
Sankaracharya, *Brhamasūtra-Bhāṣya*, trans. by Swami Ghambirananda, Advaita Ashrama, 1996.
Sankrityayana, R. (ed.), *Siddha Sarahapāda Kṛita Dohākoṣa*, Patna: Bihar Rashtra-bhasha Parishad, 1957.
——, (ed.), *Buddhacharyā*, Varanasi, 1980; *Vinaya-Piṭaka*, Varanasi, 1994.
Saraswati, S.K., *Survey of Indian Sculpture* (2nd edn.), Delhi, 1975.
——, (ed.), *Tantrayāna Art: An Album*, Calcutta: Asiatic Society, 1977.
Sarkar, D.C., *Select Inscriptions Bearing on Indian History and Civilization* (2 vols.), Calcutta and Delhi, 1965-83.
Sasaki, *Mahāvyutpatti*, Tokyo, 1926.
Sastri, N. Aiyaswami (ed.), *Ālambanaparīkṣā and Vritti by Dinnāga with the Commentary of Dharmapāla*, Madras: The Adyar Library, 1942.
Sastri, H., *Nalanda in Ancient Literature*, Proceedings of the Fifth Oriental Conference, I, 1933. Poona, 1920.
——, *Excavations of Nalanda*, in Annual Report of the Director-General of Archaeologoy in India for 1919-20, Calcutta, 1922.
——, 'The Nalanda Copper-plate of Devapāladeva', *EI* XVII, 1923-24.
——, *Advayavajra-Sangraha*. G.O.S., XL, Baroda, 1927.
——, 'Nalanda Stone Inscription of the Reign of Yasovarmadeva', *EI* XX, 1 Jan. 1929.
——, 'The Clay Seals of Nalanda', *EI* XXI, 2 Oct., 1931.
——, *Nalanda and its Epigraphical Material*, MASI, LXVI, Delhi: Manager of Publications, 1942.
Sastri, H., and N.G. Majumdar, *Nalanda Copper-plate of Devapaladeva*, Monograph of the Varendra Research Society, I. Rajshahi, 1926.
Schiefner, F.A., *Tārānātha's Geschichte des Buddismus in Indien*, St. Petersburg: Commissionare der Kaiserlichen Akademie der Wissenschaften, 1869.
Schopen, G., *Bones, Stones and Buddhist Monks*, Honolulu, 1997.
Schroder, Ulrich Vön., *Indo-Tibetan Bronzes*. Hong Kong: Visual Dharma Publication, 1981.

Schulemann, G., *Geschichte der Dalai Lamas*, Leipzig.

Sen, A.C., *Rajagriha and Nalanda* (2nd edn.), Calcutta: Indian Publicity Society, 1964.

Shastri, D.N., *The Philosophy of Nyāya-Vaiṣeṣika and its Conflict with Buddhist Dignāga School*, Bharatiya Vidya Bhavan, 1976.

Shastri, T.G. (ed.), *Ārya-Mañjuśri-Mūlakalpa*, Pt. I (1920), Pt. II (1922), Pt. III (1925).

Shahśnara, Hussain, *Everyday Life in the Pāla Empire*, Dacca, 1968.

Shereman, E., Lee, *A History of Far Eastern Art* (Revised), London, 1975.

Singh, Jaideva (ed.), *Conception of Buddhist Nirvāṇa of Stcherbatsky*, Delhi: Motilal Banarsidass, 1977.

——, *Introduction to Madhyamaka Philosophy*, Varanasi, India: Bharatiya Vidya Prakashan, 1968.

Sivaramamurti, C., *Indian Bronzes*, Bombay: Marg Publications, 1962.

——, 'An Interesting Gupta Chaturmukha of Sūrya', *Bulletin of the National Museum*, New Delhi, No. 3, 1972.

Smith, Vincent A., *Early History of India: from 600 B.C. to the Mohammadan Conquest*, Oxford: 1906, ASIAR, 1924-25.

Snodgrass, Adrian, *The Symbolism of the Stūpa*, Delhi: Motilal Banarsidass, 1985.

Soper, Alexander C., *Literary Evidence for Early Buddhist Art in China*, Ascona, 1959.

Spooner, D.B., *The Royal Asiatic Society's Excavations at Nalanda*. ASI E, EC, 1915-16, pp. 33-38; 1916-17.

——, *Excavations at Nalanda*, ASIR, EC, 1917-18.

——, *Excavations and Explorations*, EC, ASIAR, 1921-22.

——, *The Nalanda Goddess Who Tramples Ganesa*, ASIAR, 1922-23.

Stcherbatsky, Theodore, *Buddhist Logic*, Dover Publications Inc., 1962.

——, *The Central Conception of Buddhism and the Meaning of the Word 'Dharma'* (Reprint), South Asia Books, 2001.

Steinkellner Ernst, and Helmut Tauscher, *Contribution of Tibetan Language, History and Culture*, 2 vols. Delhi: Sundeeep Prakashan, 1995.

Strong, J., *Legend of King Asoka*. Princeton, 1983.

Suzuki, D.T. (trans.), *The Lankāvatāra Sūtra: A Mahayāna Text* (Reprint), London, 1956.

——, *Studies in the Lankāvatāra Sūtra*, Delhi: Munshiram Manoharlal Publishers, 1998.

Takakusu, J. (trans.), *A Record of the Buddhist Religion as Practiced in India and the Malay Archipelago* (AD 671-695); by I-tsing, Oxford: The Clarendon Press, 1896.

Thaplyal, K.K., *Studies in Ancient India Seals: A Study of North Indian Seals and Sealings from 3rd Century B.C. to mid-7th Century A.D*, Lucknow: Akhil Bharatiya Sanskrit Parishad, 1972.

Thera, Mahānāma-Sthavira, *Mahāvaṁsa: The Great Chronicle of Sri Lanka*, Asian Humanities Press, 1998.

Thurman, Robert, *Tsong Khapa's Speech of Gold: Reason and Enlightenment in the Central Philosophy of Buddhism*. Princeton: Princeton Univ. Press, 1984.

——, 'Vajra Hermeneutics', in D. Lopez (ed.), *Buddhist Hermeneutics*, Hawai, 1982.

Tillemans, Tom J.F., *Materials for the Study of Āryadeva, Dharmapāla and Candrakīrti*, Delhi: Motilal Banarsidass, 2006.

Tiwari, M. (ed.), *Nidānakathā, the Chaukhamba Sanskrit Series*, Varanasi, 1970.

Toni Schmid, *Saviour of Mankind II, Panchen Lamas and Former Incarnations of Amitāyus*, Stockholm, 1964.

Trainer, Kevin, *Relics, Ritual and Representation in Buddhism*, Cambridge, 1997.

Trenckner, V. (ed.), *Milindapañho*, London, 1928.

Trenckner, V. and R. Chalmers (eds.), *Majjhima Nikāya*, London (Vol. I), 1888-99.

Upasak, C.S. (ed.), *Nalanda: Past and Present*, Nalanda: Nava Nalanda Mahavihara, 1977.

Vadekar, R.W. (ed.), *Milindapañho*, Bombay University Publication, 1960.

Vaidya, P.L. (ed.), *Lalitavistara*, Darbhanga: The Mithila Research Institute, 1958.

——, *Divyāvadāna*, Darbhanga: The Mithila Research Institute, 1959.

——, *Avadanaśatakam*, Darbhanga: The Mithila Research Institute, 1958.

——, *Śikshā-samuchchaya of Śāntideva, Divyāvadāna*, Darbhanga: The Mithila Research Institute, 1961.

——, *Mahāyāna-sūtra Sangraha*, Buddhist-Sanskrit Text, No. 17, Pt. I, Darbhanga: The Mithila Research Institute, 1961.

Varela, Francisco, Evan Thompson and Roach Katherine, *The Embodied Mind*, Cambridge: MIT Press, 1990.

Venkata Ramanan, K., *Nāgārjuna's Philosophy*, Delhi: Motilal Banarsidass, 1978.

Vidyabhushan, S.C., *History of Indian Logic*, New Delhi: Motilal Banarsidass, 1978.

Vogel, J. Ph., *Indian Serpent Lore or the Naga in Hindu Legend and Art*, London, 1926.

Waddell, L.A., *The Buddhism of Tibet or Lamaism*, London, 1985.

Wallace, Vesna, *The Inner Kalacakratantra*, Oxford: Oxford Univ. Press, 2001.

Warren, Henry Clarke, *Buddhism in Translations*, Harvard University Press, 1896.

Wayman, Alex, 'Analysis of the Tantric Section of the Kanjur Related to Tanjur Exegesis', *Indo-Asian Studies*, Vol. I, ed. Raghuvira, New Delhi: International Academy of Indian Culture, 1962.

——, *The Buddhist Tantras: Light on Indo-Tibetan Esotericism*, Delhi: Motilal Banarsidass, 1973.

Wedemeyer, Christain, *Vajrayāna and its Doubles: The Tāntric Works of Āryadeva*, University of Michigan: Microfilm Services, 2000.

Wentz, W.Y. Evans (ed.), *The Tibetan Book of the Great Liberation or the Method of Realisation: Nirvāṇa through Knowing the Mind* (trans. from Tibetan), New York, 1954.

Williams, Joanna, G. (ed.), *The Art of Gupta India Empire and Province*, New Delhi: Heritage Publications, 1983.

Willis, J.P., *On Knowing Reality*, Delhi: Motilal Banarsidass, 1983.

Wittgenstein, Ludwig, *Philosophical Investigations*, New York: Macmillan, 1953.

Wood, Thomas E., *Mind Only: A Philosophical and Doctrinal Analysis of the Vijñànavāda*, University of Hawaii Press, 1991.

Zimmer, H., *The Art of Indian Asia: Its Mythology and Transformation*, Vol. I, New York, 1955, Completed and edited by J. Campbell, Canada, 1955, Bolingen Series, Pantheon Books.

JOURNALS AND MEMOIRS

Ancient India, No. 6. Bulletin of the Archaeological Survey of India – 'Geographical and Chronological Factors in Indian Iconography' by C. Sivaramamurti.

Annual Bibliography of Indian Archaeology, Kern Institute, Leinden, 1928, 1954-57.

Annual Report of the Central Circle (ASI), Patna, 1925-26, 1926-27, 1928-29.

Annual Reports of the Archaeological Survey of India: 1903-04, 1916-17, 1919-20, 1920-21, 1921-22, 1923-24, 1925-26, 1926-27, 1927-28, 1929-30, 1930-34 (Part II), 1935-36.

Archaeological Survey of India Reports by A. Cunningham and others. Vol. I (1871), Vol. III (1873), Vol. III (1878), Vol. XI (1880) and Vol. XVI.

Artibus Asiae, XXXII – 'The Broadley Collection' by F.M. Asher, V. No. XXV – 'From Gupta to Pāla Sculpture' by Shiela L. Weiner.

Buddha Jayanti Exhibition, 1956 – Tibet Collection, Sikkim Durbar Press, Gangtok.

Epigraphica Indica: XXIII, XXIV, XXV.

Indian Historical Quarterly: XV-3, XV-4, XIX-1, XXX-4, XXI-4, XXXII-2 and 3.

Journal of the Asiatic Society of Bengal, Calcutta, Nos. I-1, III-1, XII-2. Vol. XLI, Pt. 1.

Journal of the Bihar and Orissa Research Society, Patna, Nos. IX, IX-1 to 4, XXVIII, XXXVII-3 and 4.

Journal of the Bihar Research Society, Nos. XIV-1 to 4, XLVI-1 to 4.

Journal of the Department of Letters, University of Calcutta, Nos. XI, XXX, XXXII.

Journals of the Mahabodhi Society of India: 1. *The Mahabodhi*. 2. *The Dharmadoot*.

Journal of the Numismatic Society of India, Varanasi, No. XII-II.

Journal of the Royal Asiatic Society, 1928.

Journal of the Uttar Pradesh Historical Society, Lucknow, Nos. New Series I-II, XXIII.

Lalit Kala, Nos. 1-2, New Delhi, 1955-56.

Memoirs of the Archaeological Survey of India, No. 20: The Origin and Cult of Tara by Hiranand Sastri, 1925. No. 66: Epigraphical Material from Nalanda by Hiranand Sastri. No. 73: *Sanskrit Literature and Art: Mirrors of Indian Culture* by S. Sivaramamurti, Calcutta, 1955.

Proceedings of the Indian History Congress: 1938, 1958.

Rupam, an Illustrated Quarterly of Oriental Art, Chiefly Indian, Nos. 30, 40.

INDEX